Income, Employment, and Economic Growth

Eighth Edition

Supplementary to this text: *Study Guide to Accompany Wallace C. Peterson and Paul S. Estenson's* INCOME, EMPLOYMENT, AND ECONOMIC GROWTH, Eighth Edition, by Harold R. Williams

EIGHTH
EDITION

Income, Employment, and Economic Growth

Wallace C. Peterson
University of Nebraska

Paul S. Estenson
Gustavus Adolphus College

W. W. Norton & Company
New York   London

Copyright © 1996, 1992, 1988, 1984, 1978, 1974, 1967, 1962 by
W. W. Norton & Company, Inc.
Copyright renewed 1990 by W. W. Norton & Company, Inc.
All rights reserved.

Printed in the United States of America.

The text of this book is composed in Times Roman
with the display set in Helvetica Bold
Composition by University Graphics, Inc.
Manufacturing by Maple Vail
Book design by Andrew Zutis

Library of Congress Cataloging-in-Publication Data
Peterson, Wallace C.
    Income, employment, and economic growth / Wallace C. Peterson.
Paul S. Estenson.—8th ed.
       p.   cm.
    Includes index.
    1. Macroeconomics.   I. Estenson, Paul S.   II. Title
HB172.5.P453   1995
339—dc20   95-13314

ISBN 0-393-96854-5

W. W. Norton & Company, Inc., 500 Fifth Avenue, New York, N.Y. 10110
W. W. Norton & Company Ltd., 10 Coptic Street, London WC1A 1PU

2 3 4 5 6 7 8 9 0

For Andrew, Bonnie, Cary, Laura, Lisa, Rebecca,
and Shelley

WCP

For Julie, Graham, and Leif
Virgil and Elizabeth

PSE

Contents

5 Money and Interest in the Keynesian System   142

PART III
Exploring the Foundations of Aggregate Demand and Aggregate Supply   **209**

8 Investment and Finance   260

11 Money and Output   400

12 Output, Employment, and Inflation   455

PART IV
Growth, Fluctuations, and Public Policy   503

13 Productivity and Growth   505

14 Business Cycles and Forecasting   545

15 Sixty-five Years of Macroeconomic Policy   576

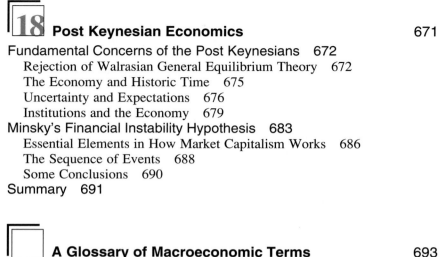

Preface

When the First Edition of this text appeared, challenging questions about the economy's macroeconomic performance occupied center stage in the U.S. politics. Now, three decades later this is still true, especially with a presidential election in the offing. The question "How is the economy doing?" has always been of great concern to Americans, although macroeconomics—the subject of this text and the theory to which we turn for answers—has been a formal part of economic study for just sixty years. It was in early 1936 that John Maynard Keynes published his monumental work, *The General Theory of Employment, Interest and Money*, a book that transformed completely the way in which economists, politicians, policymakers, and most ordinary people think about the economy and its performance.

Revising this text again has been a labor of love, particularly because of the loyal support given it over so many years by teachers and students alike. What has made the task both challenging and interesting is that change and growth are intrinsic to macroeconomics, as is true of the economy it seeks to explain and analyze.

In doing this revision, we have tried to maintain the clarity of exposition, consistency, and integrity that users say have been characteristics of this text since the First Edition. Our primary aim is to set forth a clear and complete exposition of the forces that drive the aggregate economy. This is what macroeconomics is about. An economics textbook should enable students to understand and apply economic principles to the world about them with a minimum of outside help. This frees the instructor to use valuable classroom time to explore more fully special facets of the subject and to discuss important policy issues.

A major emphasis throughout the text is on understanding the aggregate economy and the economic principles that apply to it. As in all prior editions, formal mathematics is used sparingly—economics is about people, not numbers—although every effort is made to help the student become familiar with the most important kinds of data used in macroeconomic analysis and policy. To help in doing this, the text stresses the major macroeconomic problems of our era, places them in historical context, and links them to policy issues whenever appropriate. This allows the student to become familiar with and feel comfortable in seeking out and analyzing real-world problems.

For about three decades the theoretical house of macroeconomics has been divided, with several diverse perspectives competing for dominance. This competition, covered in detail in Chapters 16, 17, and 18, reflects the turbulence and change that are continually present in the real-world economy. Overall, there is more agreement than disagreement among macroeconomists. Nevertheless, divisions do exist. Therefore, it is important to make clear to users the approach to macroeconomics found in this text.

The Perspective of This Text

In an article that appeared in the U.S. journal of opinion the *New Republic* about a year before *The General Theory* was published, John Maynard Keynes explained the basic difference between his emerging thought and the ideas of the classical school of economics in which he was trained at Cambridge University.

"On the one side," Keynes said, "are those economists who believe . . . that the existing economic system is in the long run self-adjusting, though with creaks and groans and jerks, interrupted by time lags, outside interference, and mistakes." These economists, he continued, ". . . do not believe that the system is automatically or immediately self-adjusting, but . . . it has an inherent tendency towards self-adjustment."

On the other side of the gulf, Keynes said, are economists who have ". . . rejected the idea that the existing economic system is, in any significant sense, self-adjusting." They believe that ". . . the failure of effective demand to reach the full potentialities of supply, in spite of human psychological demand being immensely far from satisfied for the vast majority of individuals is due to much more fundamental causes."

The gulf between these two perspectives, Keynes said, ". . . is deeper than most on either side of it realize. . . . I range myself with the heretics. . . . The system is not self-adjusting, and, without purposive direction, it is incapable of translating our actual poverty into potential plenty."[1]

Keynes's words, written sixty-one years ago, accurately describe a basic,

---

[1] John Maynard Keynes, "Is the Economic System Self-Adjusting?" *New Republic*, February 20, 1935.

philosophical fault line in contemporary macroeconomics. It is a division between those who believe the economic system, if left alone, will move toward a full-employment level of output and those who do not believe this. In a practical sense, this basic schism in macroeconomic theory raises a fundamental question about government's role in the economy. If the economy is truly self-adjusting, then the economic role of the government should be minimal—the stance of most conservatives. If the economy is not self-adjusting, as Keynes maintained, then government becomes the entity that can give the economic system the purposive direction it requires. The latter, which is the Keynesian perspective, is the view of this text.

The explosive revival of interest in Keynes and his work over the last decade validates this perspective in gratifying ways. A number of biographies, many scholarly papers, and the completion of the thirty volumes of Keynes's *Collected Writings* are evidence of this. As one scholar has noted, current interest in Keynes's work and ideas has been exceeded only by the attention given them in the decade following the publication of *The General Theory*.[2] Some of the reasons for this revival are discussed in detail in Chapters 17 ("The New Keynesian Economics") and 18 ("Post Keynesian Economics"), while others are found at different points throughout the text. Of particular interest today is Keynes's treatment of uncertainty and expectations, which offers a simpler and more realistic view of human behavior than that found in rational expectations theory. Keynes's theory of inflation, drawn from the neglected Chapter 21 of *The General Theory*, in our view, provides the best explanation of the strong surge of inflation that beset the economy in the 1970s.

Text Plan and Innovations

Part I, which includes the first two chapters, explains in detail the major measures used by economists to take the pulse of the economy. Measurement is the starting point for all scientific endeavor, so it is essential at the outset that the student become familiar with the important ways in which economists measure economic activity at the macroeconomic level. In these chapters, as well as others to follow, boxes are used to underscore particular concepts, historical points of significance, or other ideas that have an important and special relationship to the analysis being developed in the text. This section also contains an explanation of the conceptual foundations of the national income and accounting system through which we measure the economy's performance.

Part II, Chapters 3 through 6, develops in detail the theoretical ideas that form the core material for contemporary macroeconomics. This part has a strong historical orientation. The student is first introduced to classical macroeconomic ideas. This sets the stage for developing the basic Keynesian

[2] John B. Davis, "Introduction: The Interpretation of Keynes's Work," in John B. Davis, ed., *The State of Interpretation of Keynes* (Boston: Kluwer Academic Press, 1994).

model of output and employment determination, usually described as the Keynesian income-expenditure approach. This approach is the most satisfactory way to analyze macroeconomic behavior, irrespective of an observer's philosophical orientation. It is our conviction that mastery of the core ideas in these chapters prepares the student not only to cope with the theoretical refinements that come later, but also to assess intelligently the contributions made by the different perspectives on macroeconomics now found in the profession.

An extremely important point stressed in this part, as well as throughout the text, is that the Keynesian income-expenditure model involves *both* aggregate demand and aggregate supply. Too many contemporary intermediate-level texts neglect Keynes's fundamental theoretical point that levels of output and employment in the modern economy depend on an interaction between aggregate demand and aggregate supply. Thus, Chapter 4 carefully develops the aggregate supply curve as originally envisaged in *The General Theory*, as well as in the form used more recently by many macroeconomic theorists. Keynes's concept of aggregate supply is also important because it provides a microeconomic foundation for his theory of inflation (Chapter 12).

Part III, "Exploring the Foundations of Aggregate Demand and Aggregate Supply," examines closely the theoretical ideas and empirical foundations that undergird the basic concepts of aggregate demand and aggregate supply. The latter are, of course, the strategic determinants of the economy's overall performance. Here the student becomes familiar with economic theory that explains consumption and investment spending, government economic activity, international transactions and their relation to output and employment, the behavior of money, and how output and prices are linked. Although this part stresses the basic theory that lies behind the aggregates, theory is always tied closely to the real economic world and important public policy issues. Here we put flesh on the bare bones of the income-expenditure model developed in Part II.

All the theoretical and empirical material of Part III has been fully updated, but a special effort has been made to underscore the growing importance of international economic transactions to both macroeconomic theory and domestic economic policy in Chapter 10, "The International Economy." It cannot be stressed too strongly that the United States is increasingly a part of a fast-growing, fiercely competitive global economic system, one over which individual nation-states have little control. On the theoretical level, the development in this chapter of the balance-of-payments curve (*BP*) in the context of the *IS-LM* model provides an extremely important theoretical tool to analyze this trend.

One major innovation in this edition is to shift the material on the modern quantity theory, which formerly had its own chapter, to Chapter 11, "The Theory of Money." Since Professor Milton Friedman's approach to money constitutes a fundamental challenge to Keynes's belief that he had succeeded in developing a monetary theory of production in *The General Theory*, it is appropriate to include this material in the basic theoretical chapter on money.

Furthermore, empirical data on money, output, and prices from the 1980s raise significant doubts about the validity of the modern quantity theory.

In Chapter 12, "Output, Employment, and the Price Level," new and challenging material on the Phillips curve by British economist Paul Ormerod is introduced. By developing empirical support for the view that the standard downward-sloping Phillips curve shifts its position over time, he shows how a revised Phillips curve concept can be a useful policy tool, as well as offer a challenge to the argument that the Phillips curve is vertical at the natural rate of unemployment.

Part IV stresses the major public policy issues relevant to macroeconomics, including economic growth and productivity (Chapter 13), problems of business cycles and economic forecasting (Chapter 14), and the story of policy decisions and actions from the Great Depression through the Clinton administration (Chapter 15).

Three major innovations are found in this part. First, there is a much more extensive treatment of the nation's productivity crisis in Chapter 13 than in earlier editions. This crisis can be traced back to the early 1970s, when the long-term growth rates for key economic variables (productivity, real wages, real family income, and real GDP) decreased sharply or even turned negative. The probable causes of this deterioration include military spending, insufficient public investment in the nation's infrastructure, and changes in the composition of private investment.

Second, an entirely new section on endogenous growth theory has been added to Chapter 13 as a complement to the theories of economic growth developed by Evsey Domar, Roy Harrod, and Robert Solow. This approach treats key factors such as technological change, population growth, and institutions as inherent—or endogenous to—the growth process, whereas earlier theories (Harrod-Domar and neoclassical growth theory) had treated them as exogenous.

Finally, Chapter 15 has been almost completely rewritten to provide a succinct but accurate history of macroeconomic policy actions from the onset of the Great Depression in 1929 to the administration of Bill Clinton. In this chapter the threads of theory and policy are drawn together to review critically all major macroeconomic policies over this sixty-seven-year period. The possible effects of the Republican "revolution" at the ballot box in 1994 on the future of macroeconomic policy are analyzed.

Finally, Chapters 16 through 18 in Part V review and analyze three perspectives on macroeconomics that either challenge or bolster the dominant Keynesian income-expenditure approach. The new classical economics, which is essentially Walrasian in its approach, largely succeeded modern monetarism as the major challenge to Keynesian economics. It is our conviction that the force of this challenge is about spent. The other perspectives, the new Keynesian economics and Post Keynesian economics, represent an expansion and enrichment of the core ideas found in *The General Theory*. These divergent perspectives are grouped together in this last section because of the conviction expressed earlier that it is essential that students master a consistent, coherent theoretical model before being introduced to challenges and major theoretical refinements in that model. We believe that this text is unique in devoting a whole chapter to each of three macroeconomic perspectives that have an identity separate from mainstream income-expenditure analysis.

ACKNOWLEDGMENTS

It is impossible to acknowledge fully the many colleagues, students, and friends who have contributed to the substance and success of this text through the years and successive editions. Their help and encouragement is sincerely appreciated. As always, though, there are a few who have been especially helpful with their comments and suggestions for the current revision. These include Michael Moohr, Bucknell University; Tracy Mott, Denver University; F. Gregory Hayden and Jerry Petr, University of Nebraska—Lincoln; Warren Samuels, Michigan State University; Hyman Minsky, Jerome Levy Institute; Paul Bush, University of California—Fresno; Ronnie J. Phillips, Colorado State University; Elba Brown-Collier, Eastern New Mexico University; and Robert Baskins, Lincoln, Nebraska.

At Norton, a special thanks is due to W. Drake McFeely, Ashley Deeks, Carol Loomis, Ed Parsons, and Richard Rivellese for their expertise and skill in editing the manuscript. From the time of the First Edition, Donald S. Lamm, presently chairman of the board at Norton, has been a major source of encouragement and support in the writing and revision of this text.

Authors are always indebted to their spouses for patience and understanding. Thus, we thank Julie Estenson and Bonnie Peterson for their help.

As with earlier editions, Harold Williams of Kent State University has developed the *Study Guide* for this text. Many instructors will find this workbook a valuable adjunct that enables students to review and apply material in the text in a practical way. Paul Estenson has revised the *Instructor's Manual*, which includes chapter summaries to be used in discussions and a wide range of questions.

Finally, for kind permission to quote from *The General Theory of Interest, Employment and Money*, we wish to thank Harcourt, Brace & World, Inc.; Macmillan & Co., Ltd; and the trustees of the estate of the late Lord Keynes.

As senior author, I want again to express my debt to my late spouse, Eunice Vivian Peterson. Through years of illness and pain, she was unflagging in her encouragement and support in the initial writing and subsequent revisions of this text. It will always belong to her as well as to me.

Wallace C. Peterson
Lincoln, Nebraska

Paul Estenson
St. Peter, Minnesota

Introduction and Measurement

An Overview of Macroeconomics

THE LAST QUARTER CENTURY has been a time of turbulence and change for the U.S. economy. In the 1970s, there was too much inflation, too much unemployment, sluggish growth, and lagging productivity. As the 1980s began, the nation plunged into the most severe economic downturn since the Great Depression of the 1930s. The recovery that began in late 1982 became the longest sustained peacetime expansion in the nation's history; it lasted 92 months before the nation slid into its ninth post-World War II recession in July 1990. In addition to recession and expansion, the 1980s saw soaring federal deficits, an adverse trade balance, and continued problems of inadequate productivity growth. These developments took place against the backdrop of the nation's increasing vulnerability to global economic conditions. The lesson to be drawn from this is that fluctuation, change, and uncertainty are the usual condition of the dynamic, ever-restless U.S. economy. It is an economy always in motion; usually it moves upward, but sometimes it goes down. One thing is certain: it never stands still!

Macroeconomics, the subject of this book, is the study of the economy in motion, of changing levels and rates of economic activity. "Macro," which comes from a Greek word meaning large, suggests that macroeconomics is concerned with the problems and behavior of the entire economy. Specifically, the focus of macroeconomics is on how the economy performs in four major ways: (1) the total production of goods and services, including the growth over time in that production; (2) the overall behavior of prices; (3) the provision of employment for the nation's work force; and (4) the conduct of economic relations with the rest of the world.

No person, no family, no business firm, nor any governmental body is untouched by the performance of the economy. The new graduate seeking a job, the worker nearing retirement, the business firm contemplating building a new plant, the school district planning a bond issue for a new school, and the federal government looking for revenue to finance military spending have in common the basic fact that the success or failure of ambitions and plans depends heavily on the state of the economy's health. Understanding the forces that determine this health is the fundamental task of macroeconomic analysis.

It is not just the ordinary citizen who has a stake in how the economy performs. The economy's performance is of critical concern for the national government as well, not simply because the government's economic fortune, like those of the family and the business concern, is tied to the performance of the economic system. The federal government also has a special responsibility to ''promote the general welfare,'' as specified in the Constitution. The Employment Act, which Congress passed in 1946, stated more specifically that the federal government has a responsibility to ''promote maximum

---

How Keynes Viewed the Economy's Behavior

In *The General Theory of Employment, Interest and Money*, the 1936 book that created modern macroeconomics, John Maynard Keynes wrote,

> . . . it is an outstanding characteristic of the economic system in which we live that, whilst it is subject to severe fluctuations in respect of output and employment, it is not violently unstable. Indeed it seems capable of remaining in a chronic condition of sub-normal activity for a considerable period without any marked tendency either towards recovery or towards complete collapse. Moreover, the evidence indicates that full, or even approximately full, employment is of rare and short-lived occurrence.

These words, written by Keynes 60 years ago, remain uncannily accurate in describing the actual economic situation in the Unites States since 1973. During this period, the performance of the U.S. economy has been subnormal with respect to overall growth and the level of unemployment, a condition that might best be described as a "silent depression."* It has been a "depression" because the effects have been widespread and because it has lasted twice as long as the Great Depression of the 1930s. It has been "silent" because, unlike the 1929 crash and the events that followed, its impact, like a dangerous cancer, has been slow and insidious, little noticed by the media or policymakers.

*See Wallace C. Peterson, *Silent Depression: The Fate of the American Dream* (New York: Norton, 1994).

employment, production, and purchasing power."[1] More recently another act, the Full Employment and Balanced Growth Act of 1978, was even more explicit in prescribing the responsibilities of the federal government in the pursuit of such national goals as full employment, economic growth, and stable prices. Although the economy's performance in recent years has fallen far short of most of the goals embodied in these legislative acts, they represent commitments that cannot be neglected indefinitely. Their existence also means that the study of government policy, of the actions taken by the federal government in relation to production, employment, the price level, and the nation's international economic situation, is a legitimate part of macroeconomic analysis. Understanding the successes and failures of economic policy is one of the purposes of this text.

Macroeconomics is but one of the two large divisions into which economists divide their subject. The other is microeconomics. "Micro" also is derived from the Greek, meaning small. What microeconomics does is focus on the behavior of the individual units of the economy, particularly that of households, wage and salary earners, and business firms. Microeconomics seeks to understand how markets work in establishing individual and relative prices for the goods and services produced, how economic resources get allocated among different uses, and how payments are made to the owners of resources (land, labor, and capital) for the services the resources render. Although micro and macro are different and distinct branches of economic science, they are closely interrelated. Since macroeconomics reflects the aggregate behavior of the many millions of primary economic units—households, firms, and government bodies—there is no essential conflict between these two fundamental branches of economics; in fact, they complement one another. Traditionally, the macro branch of economics is referred to as income and employment theory, in the sense of *national* income and *national* levels of employment. The micro branch is described as value and distribution theory, because of its emphasis on the ways that markets set prices and allocate the goods produced in the economy. Until the late 1960s there was not much effort made to link macro- and microeconomic theories, but now there is a significant amount of research being devoted to the discovery of the microeconomic foundations of macroeconomics.

Measuring the Economy's Performance

One useful way to appreciate the essential nature of macroeconomics is to look at several key aggregates to which economists turn for measurement and evaluation of the economy's performance. "Aggregate" is a term used to describe a variable that pertains to the entire economy. There are many such

---

[1] Employment Act of 1946, Public Law 304, 79th Congress.

aggregates, but measures of total output, prices, unemployment, and foreign trade are of special significance. In Chapter 2 these measures are analyzed in greater depth; here a brief sketch of the well-known and widely used measures will help us understand the nature and scope of macroeconomics.

The National Output

Undoubtedly, the best-known measure of economic performance is the *gross domestic product,* or GDP as it is often called. Hardly a day passes without some reference to this figure in the nation's press or on the radio or TV. What is the gross domestic product? Simply put, it is the monetary value of all goods and services produced in the economy in a specified time period. Normally, the latter is the calendar year, although GDP data are prepared and made available quarterly. GDP also measures the total income created through the production of goods and services. In the United States, the responsibility for the preparation and publication of gross domestic product data rests with the Bureau of Economic Analysis of the U.S. Department of Commerce.[2]

Nominal versus Real GDP

Essentially, the GDP is obtained by adding up the expenditures made for the vast variety of goods and services produced and sold in the economy in a given period of time. In Chapter 2 we shall examine the major types of spending, which, when added up, give us an output total. At this point, however, let us note that an expenditure for a good or service involves two things: the *quantity* of the good or service purchased and the *price* at which it is purchased. Thus, when the appropriate purchases of goods and services during a year are summed up to get the gross domestic product figure, the result is what economists call the *nominal* GDP.[3] Nominal GDP data measure output in current prices.

Nominal GDP figures are important and useful, but we cannot use them if we want to compare one year with another. The reason is that from year to year the nominal figures reflect changes in prices as well as changes in pro-

---

[2] The U.S. Department of Commerce publishes a monthly magazine, the *Survey of Current Business,* which contains extensive data on the GDP and related income and product measures. Another monthly publication, *Economic Indicators,* published by the Joint Economic Committee of the Congress, contains a wealth of current statistical information about the economy, including the latest GDP figures.

[3] ''Appropriate'' in this sentence refers to what economists define as final goods and services. This means that in the adding up to get GDP figures, intermediate products purchased by business firms are not counted since their value is included in the price of the goods and services destined for sale to the ultimate user. For example, bread is a final product, and its price covers the cost of wheat and flour, which if added up separately, would result in double counting, and an overstatement of the amount of actual production taking place.

duction. Thus, we might find that the nominal GDP for a particular year was greater than that of the previous year only because prices had risen, with no change in production. For comparisons over time we need a measure of GDP that has removed from it any changes in the prices of the goods and services that enter into the output total. This is called the *real* gross domestic product. It is a measure of production that is not distorted by any change in prices. Each year expenditures are calculated in prices for a particular year, known as the *base year*. When this is done we have a GDP figure in constant prices, or a measure of real GDP.

To illustrate the difference between nominal and real GDP, consider the figures for 1990 and 1991. In 1991 nominal GDP was $5,722.9 billion, a figure $176.8 billion higher than the nominal GDP of $5,546.1 billion in 1990. This looks like a sizable gain, but it was due entirely to the fact that prices in 1991 were 3.9 percent higher than in 1990. Actually, real GDP in 1991 was $35.9 billion *lower* than real GDP in 1990, as the economy was in a recession from July 1990 until March 1991. Because of the sluggish recovery throughout most of 1991, real output for the entire year was below the 1990 output.[4]

Until 1991, the primary measure of the country's output was the *gross national product*, or GNP. The primary difference between GDP and GNP is that GNP includes income earned (or output produced) by U.S. corporations overseas and U.S. citizens working and living abroad, whereas GDP does not. GDP measures the value of the goods and services produced within the United States, including output produced by foreign firms and citizens located in or residing in the United States. Most countries use GDP as the basic measure of economic activity, so the switch from GNP to GDP put the United States more in line with current international practices for measuring economic activity. For some purposes GNP is more useful. Published GDP figures, both nominal and real, extend back only to 1959, whereas estimated values for GNP go back to colonial times. Practically, however, the numerical differences between the two measures are small. At times in the text we will use GNP rather than GDP because for particular statistical series more data are available or because GNP was used in particular research.

Figure 1–1 traces real and nominal GDP as measured in constant 1972 prices from 1900 through 1994. This figure shows that growth is not smooth for either nominal or real output. Output fluctuations are greater from year to year for nominal as compared to real GDP, something to be expected since the nominal figure includes price changes as well as actual output changes. Note that prior to 1972 the nominal GDP curve lies *below* the real GDP line. This is because before 1972 the prices used to measure nominal GDP were lower than prices in 1972; after 1972 prices in each year were higher than prices in 1972.

In Figure 1–2 we look at the path of real GDP over the course of this

---

[4] *Economic Report of the President*, 1994, pp. 268, 270.

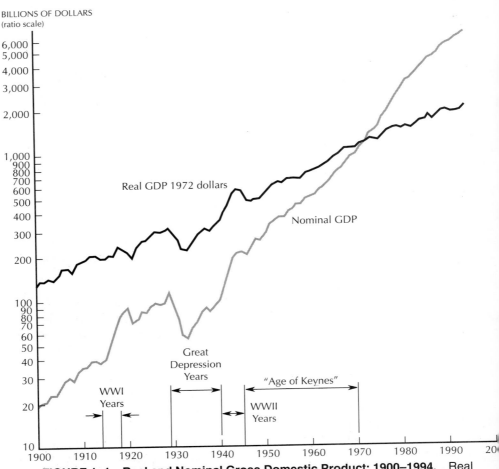

FIGURE 1–1   Real and Nominal Gross Domestic Product: 1900–1994.   Real
GDP measures output in constant prices (1972), and nominal GDP measures output in current prices, or the prices of each year.

Note: The GDP series from *Historical Statistics* have not been updated to reflect 1987 as the base year.

Sources: Historical Statistics of the United States and *Economic Report of the President,* 1995.

century from a different perspective. In this figure, annual rates of change in real GDP are plotted for every year since 1900. The figure is instructive in two respects. First, it shows more dramatically than Figure 1–1 the extremes of year-to-year fluctuations in output that have been characteristic of the U.S. economy's long-term performance. In some years output jumped by more than 15 percent, whereas in other years it dropped by almost as large a percentage. Second, it is clear from this figure that there has been a noticeable dampening down in the cyclical behavior of the economy in the post-World War II period. Whether or not this is the result of the active use of policy

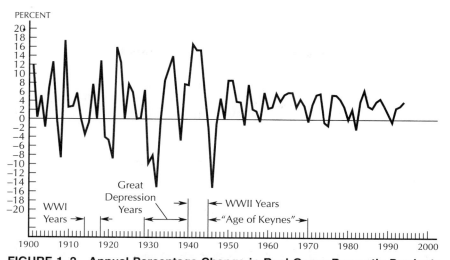

FIGURE 1–2   Annual Percentage Change in Real Gross Domestic Product: 1900–1994. Fluctuations in real output (GDP) are the norm, although they have diminished in scope in the post-World War II era.

Sources: Historical Statistics of the United States and Economic Report of the President, 1995.

measures based on the kind of macroeconomic knowledge and principles that are the subject of this text is disputed by some economists. Nevertheless, there is now more stability in the economy than before World War II. It is also worth noting that in the post-World War II period negative changes in real GDP were much less frequent and much less severe than in the prewar era. This reflects the long post-World War II boom, a time when recessions were relatively mild and when prices, though moving up, did so at a relatively slow pace, at least until the 1970s. These years have been called the *Age of Keynes* by the distinguished British economist and Nobel laureate Sir John Hicks.[5]

While the ups and downs of the business cycle have been tamed over the last half century, other serious problems not revealed directly by Figures 1–1 and 1–2 have emerged in the U.S. economy. One is the almost continuous growth in the federal deficit, even during periods of prosperity and low un-employment. To illustrate, the federal deficit (the difference between the government's current revenues and expenditures) rose from $40.2 billion (1.6 percent of the GDP) in 1979 to $254.7 billion (4.0 percent of the GDP) in 1993.[6] The federal deficit and the nation's trade deficit are sometimes called the *twin* deficits of the U.S. economy. The reasons for and economic effects of the federal deficit are examined fully in Chapters 9 and 15.

The other serious macroeconomic problem is the nation's lagging rate of

---

[5] Sir John Hicks, *The Crisis in Keynesian Economics* (New York: Basic Books, 1974), p. 1.

[6] *Economic Report of the President*, 1994, pp. 268, 359.

productivity growth. There is no single economic measure of greater importance to the overall material well-being of the nation than productivity—the amount of output produced on the average by a worker. Productivity growth plays a major role in determining the rate at which the economy grows and our *real* standard of living advances. Since 1973, output per worker has grown at an annual average rate of 1.0 percent, compared to the economy's long-term historic average of 2.5 percent. Unless productivity growth returns to its pre-1973 average, the generation of Americans now in their twenties—the "Generation X" cohort—will be distinguished as the first generation of Americans to live less well than the previous one. The productivity problem is analyzed in detail in Chapter 13.

Potential GDP

There is yet another way to calculate national output that is of interest and value. This is *potential* GDP. It is a measure (in *real* terms) of the goods and services that the economy would be capable of producing if the labor force were fully employed. There is no absolute or precise definition of "full employment," although it is generally interpreted as a situation in which people able and wanting to work can find jobs. In recent years labor has been regarded as fully employed if not more than 6 percent of the labor force is out of work. Thus the measure of potential GDP will depend on how full employment is defined. The question of the appropriate rate of unemployment in a fully employed economy is complex and controversial, as is the problem of computing an appropriate measure of potential output. Problems involved in defining and measuring both employment and unemployment are discussed more fully in Chapter 2. In Chapter 13 two different ways to measure potential GDP are explained and illustrated with actual data.

The Price Level

A second major area of concern in macroeconomics involves price. This is a matter of prices in general, not the prices for particular goods or services. The latter are the province of microeconomics. In recent years, interest in pricing behavior has focused on the inflation rate because a rising price level has existed in the U.S. economy since the end of World War II. It has not always been this way; historically, there have been periods in American life, such as the second half of the nineteenth century and the 1920s, when the general trend for prices was downward. However, for much of the nation's history, the trend has been inflationary, and certainly for the immediate future it is not likely that the economy will experience a stable or declining price level. Inflation is likely to be the rule rather than the exception in the future. Therefore, it is important not only that economists measure what is happening to prices, but also that they be able to explain what they observe about prices. The study of the price level is, thus, an important part of contemporary macroeconomics.

Index Numbers

Measurement of the price level—in contrast to the measurement of prices for particular goods or services—has always presented difficulties. It is possible, of course, to collect reasonably precise data for the prices of particular goods or services. But it is not possible to measure directly the prices of all goods and services. To do this, economists resort to using the statistical device known as an *index number*. Basically, an index number is a statistical device for comparing the amount by which one or more prices have changed over some specific period of time. As in the case of real GDP, a particular year is selected as the *base year*. Prices in all other years are measured as a percentage of the price in the base year. For example, suppose that in 1987— our assumed base year—the price of a bushel of wheat was $3.00, but we found that by 1996 this price had risen to $4.75 per bushel. To construct an index for the price of wheat, using 1987 as a base year, we divide the current year price ($4.75) by the price in the base year ($3.00) and multiply the result by 100. Thus, ($4.75 ÷ $3.00) × 100 = 158.3. The reason we multiply by 100 is to represent the price in the base year—1987 in this instance—as 100 (or 100 percent). The index tells us the relative change in a price (or prices) since the base year. To read an index number as a percentage change, simply drop 100 from the index for the year in question. In our example the 1996 index of 158.3 for a bushel of wheat means that wheat has gone up in price by 58.3 percent since 1987, the base year.

Construction of index numbers when a large number of prices are involved is a much more complex statistical problem, although the fundamental technique is essentially the same as that just described. To construct an index for prices generally—the general price level—it is necessary to *weight* the various individual prices that enter into the index in accordance with their *relative* importance. Unless this is done, the resulting price index will not accurately reflect relative (or percentage) changes in the general level of all prices.

Consumer Price Index. Three major price indexes are used in the United States. They are reported regularly by the press, radio, and television and watched carefully by officials in government, key figures in business and industry, and ordinary citizens. The best known of these indexes is the *consumer price index,* or CPI. The CPI measures relative (or percentage) changes in the prices of a representative marketbasket of goods and services presumed to be typical of spending by approximately 80 percent of the population. This particular index traces back to a pioneer survey of expenditures by wage earners and clerical workers made in 1917–19. Periodically, the index undergoes a major revision to update both the groups included in the index and the marketbasket of goods and services purchased. The CPI now uses the average of consumer spending in 1982–84 as its base.

In 1994 the consumer price index was 148.2. This means that prices for the representative marketbasket of goods and services purchased by a consumer in 1994 were 48.2 percent higher than in the period 1982–84. To put it another way, this index tells us that it took, on the average, $148.20 to purchase the same marketbasket of goods and services that $100 purchased in 1982–84.

Producer Price Index. A second index, not quite so well known as the CPI, but also important, is the *producer price index.* It measures changes in prices for a vast array of commodities purchased, not by consumers or households, but by business firms. Typically, the commodities represented in the producer price index are raw materials entering into the manufacturing of other goods, capital equipment such as machinery and tools, or finished consumer goods acquired by business firms for ultimate resale to consumers and households. The producer price index covers prices for nearly 3,000 commodities, but unlike the CPI it does not include services. Since prices for the commodities included in this index are reflected eventually in the prices of goods and services sold at retail, many economists view changes in producer prices as forerunners of later changes in the general level of consumer prices. This, though, is not a hard and fast rule. The base year for this index is 1982.

Implicit GDP Deflator. The third important price index is called the *implicit GDP deflator.* This measure of price changes tells us how much the prices of *all* the goods and services entering into the gross domestic product have changed as compared to prices in the base year used in the determination of real GDP. For example, nominal GDP in 1994 was $6,738.4 billion; its value in 1987 prices was $5,344.0 billion. The ratio of *nominal* to *real* value is 1.261, which means that prices for all the goods and services that make up the GDP figure rose by 26.1 percent between 1987 and 1994. Put another way, the implicit GDP deflator stood at 126.1 in 1994, using 1987 as 100. Because the gross domestic product is the most comprehensive measure of production we have, many economists regard the implicit GDP deflator as the best single measure of price changes available. However, it is neither as well known nor as widely used as the consumer price index. It is the latter, for example, that is most often used in the process of *indexing* wage contracts, Social Security payments, and other transactions. "Indexing" refers to the process of adjusting the monetary value of a contractual obligation to reflect changes in the general price level. In many labor-union contracts it is common practice to provide for annual or semiannual adjustments in wage rates to reflect an increase in the cost of living as measured by changes in the consumer price index. These are called COLAs, an acronym for *cost-of-living adjustments.*

Responsibility for compiling the consumer and producer price indexes rests with the Bureau of Labor Statistics in the U.S. Department of Labor. These indexes are issued monthly. When the Bureau of Labor Statistics issues its monthly report on consumer and producer prices, it not only reports on the most recent value for the index, it also reports the percentage change in the index over the preceding month. This figure is also reported on an annual rate and thereby gives the public some idea of how rapidly consumer and producer prices are changing at the time the figures are released. The GDP deflator is compiled by the Bureau of Economic Analysis of the U.S. Department of Commerce. It is issued quarterly.

Patterns of Price Changes

What happened to prices in the United States during this century? Like real output, they have been subject to turbulence and change, but the pattern of price changes differs significantly from that of the gross national product. Figures 1–3 and 1–4 tell the story of the price level over the past 94 years, using the *implicit GDP deflator* for this purpose. Long-term trends are shown

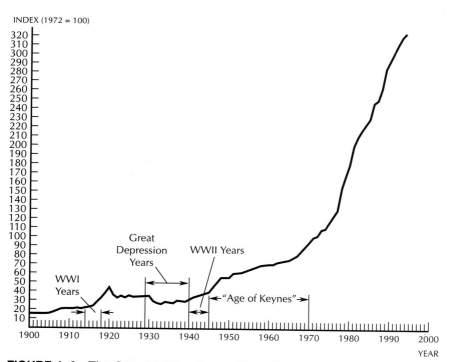

FIGURE 1–3 The General Price Level: 1900–1994. The period since World War II has been one of almost continuous inflation, although this was not the case before the Great Depression.

Note: The price level is measured by the implicit GDP deflator. 1972 = 100.

Sources: *Historical Statistics of the United States* and *Economic Report of the President*, 1995.

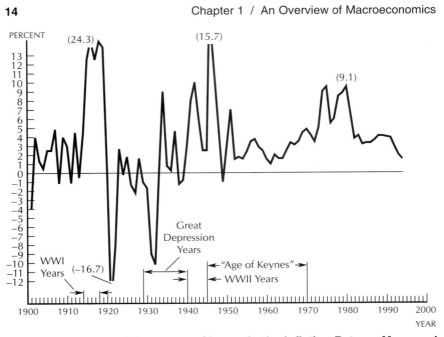

FIGURE 1–4   Annual Percentage Change in the Inflation Rate as Measured by the Implicit GDP Deflator: 1900–1994. The inflation rate, like the rate of change in real GDP, also fluctuates, often more violently than the growth rate.

Note: The price level is measured by the implicit GDP deflator.

Sources: Historical Statistics of the United States and Economic Report of the President, 1995.

in Figure 1–3, which plots the index of the implicit GDP deflator from 1900 through 1994; in this series, 1972 equals 100. As in Figure 1–1, 1972 is being used as the base year to measure the change in the price level because this gives a continuous series back to 1900. Now the GDP deflator uses 1987 as the base year, but the data have not been revised back to 1900 to reflect this change. Unlike the pre-1940 period for real GDP, prices were relatively stable during most of the 40 years from 1900 to 1940. World War I brought a sharp burst in the inflation rate, as have all previous wars in U.S. history. This was followed by a collapse in prices after the war, although they did not fall entirely back to their prewar level. The war, in other words, had a ratcheting effect on the price level.

The relative stability of pre-1940 prices ended with World War II. As Figure 1–3 shows in dramatic fashion, prices began rising in 1940 and they have continued to rise ever since. As a matter of fact, there was only one year (1949) in this 54-year span that the GDP deflator showed a decline—and this was less than 1 percent. If the 1930s can be characterized as the years of the Great Depression, it is possible to characterize the years after World War II, especially the 1970s, as the years of the "Great Inflation." Between 1940 and 1994 prices in the United States (as measured by the GDP deflator) increased 11.2 times. According to British economic historian E. H. Phelps Brown, there was only one other period in the last thousand years of economic history in Western nations when a comparable price explosion occurred. This was in the sixteenth century, an age characterized by the disintegration of feudalism, by the beginnings of capitalism and a commercial economy, and, above all, by a vast influx of gold and silver into Europe from the newly discovered lands of the Western hemisphere.[7]

If we look at the inflation rate on an annual basis, however, we find similarities to the behavior of real GDP as shown in Figure 1–2. Annual percentage changes in the inflation rate (measured by the GDP deflator) are shown in Figure 1–4. These data, which tell much the same story as told by Figure 1–3 but from a different perspective, suggest several things. First, it is apparent there has been little year-to-year stability in prices, as is the case with real output. Second, before World War II there were enough downward movements offsetting upward movements in the price level so that—except for the experience of World War I—there was a rough overall stability in prices. Finally, Figure 1–4 shows that, since World War II, instability in pricing behavior still exists in the economy, but the instability is primarily upward. There was a sharp acceleration in the inflation rate in the 1970s, followed by a slowing of inflation in the 1980s and 1990s.

Employment and Unemployment

The third major area of measurement for the economy's performance is employment and unemployment. As with output and pricing figures, economists use a variety of measures to determine how effectively the economy is performing in the realm of jobs. Ever since the catastrophic experience of the 1930s—the decade of the Great Depression more than half a century ago—the U.S. public has worried about unemployment. Consequently, the federal government's Bureau of Labor Statistics produces an abundance of data on who is working and who is not working.

The best-known measure of performance in the jobs area is the *unemployment rate*. This is the percentage of the labor force actually unemployed at a particular time. Like the indexes for consumer and producer prices, this figure is computed by the Bureau of Labor Statistics and published on both a monthly and an annual basis. To illustrate, in 1994 the unemployment rate was 6.1 percent; this meant that on the average during the year approximately 8.0 million Americans were without jobs. There were also 4.4 million people working part time who wanted to work full time, but could not find full-time jobs.

---

[7] E. H. Phelps Brown and Sheila V. Hopkins, "Seven Centuries of the Price of Consumables Compared with Builders' Wage-Rates," *Economica,* November 1956, p. 305.

Labor Force Participation Rate

Unemployment depends not only on the number of people who are not working and want jobs, but also on the size of the labor force. To be in the labor force means to be working or actively seeking work. The size of the labor force is not a fixed figure but depends ultimately on the size and age structure of the nation's population. Economists regard the noninstitutionalized population 16 years of age and older as the pool from which the labor force comes. The proportion of this population making up the actual labor force varies with time, circumstance, and custom. For example, women of all ages, including married women with children, are much more a part of the labor force now than was the case even a quarter of a century ago. Economic conditions also determine this proportion; in good times it may rise, and in bad times it may fall. The latter happens because the lack of jobs causes some people to drop out of the labor force. The Bureau of Labor Statistics calls such people *discouraged workers.* Persons not in the labor force are not considered as officially unemployed. They are people who for a variety of reasons choose not to seek work.

The proportion of the noninstitutionalized population aged 16 and over that is actually in the labor force at any particular time is called the *labor force participation rate.* In the post-World War II period there has been a persistent rise in this figure, from 55.8 percent in 1946 to 66.6 percent in 1994. Primarily this has come about because of the increased participation of women in the labor force. In 1948, their labor force participation rate was 32.7 percent, but by 1994 it had reached 58.8 percent. In the same time span the rate for men declined from 86.6 to 75.1 percent. The percentages are for both men and women 16 years of age and older. More details on the changing composition of the labor force are found in Chapter 2.

Fluctuations in Unemployment

Figure 1–5 shows the unemployment rate for the civilian labor force from 1900 to 1994. Like all the other statistical series we have reviewed that relate to the economy's overall performance, this rate has fluctuated widely from year to year. Beyond this, however, these data underscore dramatically the impact of the Great Depression and war on jobs in the United States. At the depth of the depression in 1933, unemployment reached the staggering level of 24.9 percent of the nation's work force, a level of joblessness experienced neither before nor since in U.S. history. Even in the worst post-World War II recession—the 1981–82 slump—unemployment never got over 11 percent. The other development noted by these data is that it has been primarily during wartime that unemployment has fallen below the band in the figure labeled "Full-Employment Zone." For most peacetime years, both before and after World War II, the unemployment rate has been higher than the 4 to 5 percent range designated by this band. These data also show a slow, upward drift in

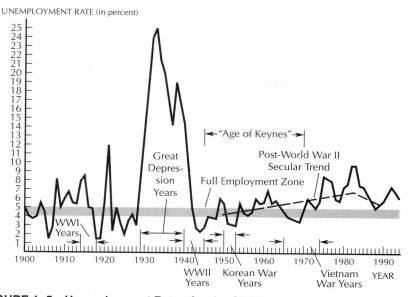

FIGURE 1–5   Unemployment Rates for the Civilian Labor Force: 1900–1994 Unemployment Rates (in percent).   Unemployment since World War II has at no time approached the levels of the Great Depression, although in recent years it was on an upward trend until 1983. Then it turned downward, but rose again after 1990.

Sources: Historical Statistics of the United States and *Economic Report of the President,* 1981, 1985, 1995.

the unemployment rate from 1950 through 1982, followed by a trend back toward the Full-Employment Zone since then. This is shown by the dashed line in the figure labeled ''Post-World War II Secular Trend.''

Designating unemployment in the range of 4 to 5 percent as the Full-Employment Zone raises a fundamental conceptual and policy question. Is there any agreed-on measure among economists for full employment? A tentative answer is no, but this is a matter that we shall explore further in Chapter 2. If we accept for the moment the notion that full employment lies between 4 and 5 percent as shown in Figure 1–5, another fact emerges from data on unemployment. This is that certain segments of our society have never experienced anything remotely resembling full employment, by whatever standard it is measured. Many economists, except the most conservative, hesitate to call unemployment rates persistently in excess of 6 percent full employment. Yet for blacks and other minorities, not to mention teenagers, this has been the reality throughout the post-World War II period. Figure 1–6 compares unemployment rates since 1948 for whites, nonwhites, and teenagers.

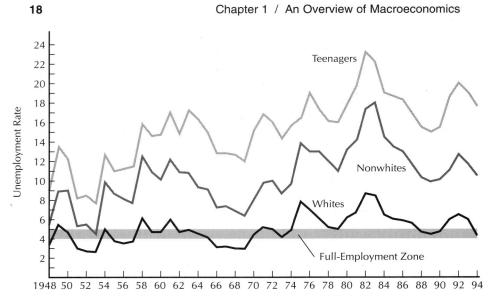

FIGURE 1–6   Unemployment Rates for Whites, Nonwhites, and Teenagers: 1948–1994.   Unemployment rates for both teenagers and nonwhites have almost always been higher than the rates for whites and have rarely been close to a full-employment level.

Source: Economic Report of the President, 1981, 1985, 1995.

The Trade Balance

A fourth area of measurement centers on the linkages between the domestic economy and the rest of the world. There are several key ways in which such linkages are measured, including fluctuations in the rate of exchange and flows of money and credit between nations, but the best known and most highly publicized is the *trade balance.*

The *trade balance* is the difference between the value of all the goods and services a nation exports and the value of all the goods and services it imports. *Exports* are goods and services a nation sells to foreigners, whereas *imports* are goods and services produced abroad that are purchased by individuals or organizations within the nation. Because exports and imports figure importantly in the gross domestic product, the nation's economic relations with foreign countries can have a large impact on domestic economic activity.

If exports exceed imports, the trade balance is said to be positive and the nation to have a *trade surplus.* If the opposite is the case, imports exceed exports, the trade balance is said to be negative and the nation to have a *trade deficit.* Throughout most of the post-World War II era, the U.S. economy consistently exported more goods and services than it imported and thus experienced a *favorable balance of trade.* In the 1950s, for example, the excess of exports over imports, when measured in current (nominal) dollars, averaged $4.7 billion per year. In the 1960s, this surplus fell to an average of $2.2

billion per year, and in the 1970s it averaged a negative $7.5 billion per year. For the whole of the 1980 to 1994 period, the trade deficit averaged a negative $71.5 billion per year, a figure many times larger than the average surpluses in the earlier decades.[8] What this means is that during the 1980s the nation's international status shifted from being a net creditor to being a net debtor. The assets (or claims) that foreign residents hold in the nation now exceed those that U.S. residents hold abroad. Where the experience of the 1950s and 1960s had allowed macroeconomists and other observers largely to ignore U.S. links to the global economy, the trade deficits since then made clear the significance of those links.

The Trade Balance in Merchandise

Figure 1–7 traces the merchandise trade deficit over the twentieth century. It shows merchandise imports as a percent of merchandise exports from 1900 through 1994. A percentage figure less than 100 indicates a positive trade balance—exports exceed imports—whereas a percentage figure greater than 100 shows the opposite, a negative trade balance. Throughout most of the twentieth century the nation has had a positive balance in its merchandise trade, although since the early 1970s the balance has turned negative.

One thing that shows up clearly and dramatically in the figure is the impact of global events—economic and noneconomic—on the nation's economic ties with the rest of the world. In both World Wars I and II—especially in World War II—the merchandise trade balance shifted dramatically to a widening surplus. This reflected the crucial role the United States played in both wars as a supplier of food and civilian goods (exports of military hardware are excluded from these figures) to the Allied nations, as well as the inability of England, France, and lesser Allied powers to continue with peacetime patterns of exports.

During the Great Depression of the 1930s there was an equally dramatic swing in the nation's trade balance. It went from a positive balance through the early years of the depression to a negative balance that peaked in 1939 when merchandise imports reached 187 percent of merchandise exports. How did this happen? The early years of the depression—from 1929 through 1933—saw a collapse of world trade, as nations scrambled to protect their domestic economies by trying to shift unemployment and falling production to foreigners whenever possible. What the depression brought, together with idle men and idle factories, was a wave of intense economic nationalism, which in the case of Nazi Germany degenerated into out-and-out economic warfare. In the United States, exports and imports fell by almost identical amounts between 1929 and 1933: exports dropped 62 percent in this period, and imports fell by 65 percent. Thus, the merchandise trade balance stayed positive during the years when the downturn was at its worst.

It was only after 1933 that the trade balance turned negative, when imports

---

[8] *Economic Report of the President,* 1995, p. 275.

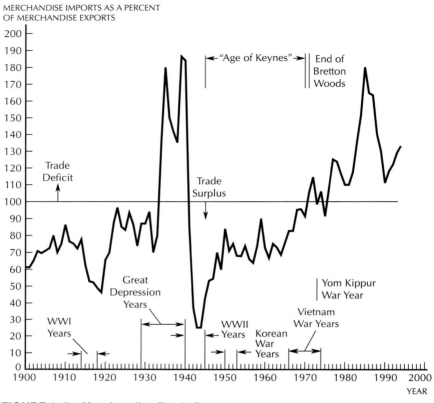

MERCHANDISE IMPORTS AS A PERCENT
OF MERCHANDISE EXPORTS

FIGURE 1–7 Merchandise Trade Balance: 1900–1994. Merchandise imports are shown as a percent of merchandise exports to reflect the nation's changing trade balance and the effect of global events on that balance.

Sources: Historical Statistics of the United States and Economic Report of the President, 1995.

bounced back much more rapidly than exports. Why? One major reason was that the Roosevelt administration under the leadership of Cordell Hull, Roosevelt's Secretary of State, launched a program of Reciprocal Trade Agreements, the aim of which was to reduce tariffs and other barriers to trade between nations. This was a 180-degree turnabout from the extreme economic nationalism embodied in the Smoot-Hawley tariff of 1929, an act which raised U.S. tariffs to the highest level on record. A second reason was the rapid recovery that began after the economy hit bottom in 1933. Even though the Great Depression did not end until World War II came along, there was a strong recovery between 1933 and 1937, when a second slump occurred. Imports grow with expansion, and given the fact that the United States under Hull's leadership moved toward a restoration of freer trade more rapidly than other nations did, imports boomed. Between 1933 and 1939, U.S. merchandise imports soared by 251 percent, while exports grew by only 54 percent.

In the 1950s and 1960s the merchandise trade balance returned to the pattern that prevailed in the early years of the century, with imports averaging between 70 and 80 percent of exports. From the early 1970s onward, however, the trade balance moved back toward the negative range, a pattern that continued in the 1980s and 1990s. A number of dramatic developments played a role in this most recent change. They include the Yom Kippur War of 1973, an event which ushered in enormous increases in the international price of oil; the ending of the Bretton Woods system in the same year, an action that created a regime of freely fluctuating exchange rates; and the Reagan administration federal deficits of the 1980s, a development that indirectly pushed up the foreign exchange value of the U.S. dollar.

A rise in the foreign exchange value of the dollar made U.S. goods more expensive for foreigners, and foreign-produced goods cheaper for Americans; this increased the United States' imports and reduced its exports. The situation improved somewhat after 1985, although sizable trade deficits have continued into the 1990s. Chapter 10 examines fully the linkages between the United States' international economic transactions and its domestic economy. It is important to realize that increasingly the setting for the nation's macroeconomic activity and problems has shifted from a national to a global basis. This is a profound transformation, one which is still continuing and one which is so subtle that many people do not realize it is happening. Roughly from the Great Depression through the Age of Keynes it was quite appropriate, especially in the United States because of the sheer size of our continental economy, to approach and analyze most macroeconomic problems within the context of the national economy. A *closed economy* is the way economists describe such a system. Now the appropriate frame of reference is the global economy. U.S. policymakers must deal with macroeconomic problems in the context of an *open economy.*

This brings us back to the nature of our subject—what macroeconomics is all about. Macroeconomists seek answers to the kind of problems reflected in the data and trends shown in the foregoing figures. Why is it that the economy behaves in such irregular fashion? Why did we have simultaneous inflation and high unemployment in the 1970s? Is it likely that we will experience a return of these conditions? What caused the enormous federal budget deficits of the 1980s, and how have they affected the economy? What is the source of the nation's large trade deficit, and how does this affect our economic well-being? Does this situation—the trade deficit—have to be turned around, and, if so, how can it be done? What about productivity? Is the downtrend in productivity reversible? What will happen if productivity does not improve? What *are* the policy measures that can be used to improve the economy's performance?

We look to macroeconomic theory to provide us with answers to these and other questions and to offer us insight into policies that will work. Macroeconomic theory is an organized body of scientific knowledge directed to these ends. Like all scientific knowledge, it is less than perfect, but its objective is the discovery of broad and enduring principles that explain the facts that are observed.

Origins of Contemporary Macroeconomics

Economists are in much less agreement today than they were 30 years ago on the nature of the theoretical relationships that explain the aggregate behavior of the economy. Economic turbulence in recent years plus the absence of a consensus on the kind of policies necessary to cope with inflation, unemployment, the federal deficit, and sagging productivity have led to a search for new explanations, new insights into the workings of the economy.

Although modern macroeconomics dates to Keynes and the Great Depression, its antecedents stretch well back into the nineteenth century—and even earlier. It is not correct to say that a formal body of macroeconomic analysis existed prior to the mid-1930s, but it is correct to say that important ideas existed before then about how the economy in the aggregate worked. Two such ideas are of special significance, particularly because they have reappeared in recent years in modern dress as important challenges to what was until relatively recently the dominant theoretical approach in macroeconomics. These ideas are Say's law of markets and the classical quantity theory of money. A brief explanation of each is in order. They will be discussed more fully in Chapter 3 as part of the explanation of what economists now call the classical theory of employment.

Say's Law of Markets

Say's law of markets is named after Jean Baptiste Say, a French economist of the early nineteenth century who disseminated and popularized the ideas of Adam Smith in France and elsewhere on the European continent. His law is the formal expression of the idea that widespread and involuntary unemployment because of general overproduction is impossible. To put the matter differently, there cannot be any involuntary unemployment because of a deficiency of total demand. The simplest possible statement of this doctrine is that "supply creates its own demand." The meaning of this statement is that in some sense the whole of the costs of production must necessarily be spent in the aggregate, directly or indirectly, on purchasing the product. Every producer who brings goods to the market (that is, creates supply) does so in order to exchange them for other goods (that is, creates demand). Consequently, every act of production necessarily represents the demand for something.

The conclusion that follows from the assertion that all supply is potentially the demand for something is that there cannot be any general overproduction

Economics as a Science

The idea that economics is a science is not clearly understood by some people. There seem to be two reasons for this. One is that the public knows that there is much disagreement among economists. This is true, although more often than not the disagreement is over policy—over what is to be done—rather than over basic theory. More important, perhaps, is the belief that economics, unlike such "hard" sciences as physics and chemistry, lacks precision, especially when it comes to prediction and forecasting.

What is lacking in such perceptions is an understanding of the essential nature of *all* science. Science is fundamentally a method, a way of gaining certain kinds of knowledge. The word itself comes from the Latin word *scire,* meaning to know, to gain understanding, to be able to explain. What all science does is, first, observe and, second, discover systematic and dependable relationships among the things observed. The discovery of relationships, always a creative and imaginative act, lies at the heart of science. Such relationships are what is meant when we speak of the "laws" of science.

And what use are scientific laws or relationships? They tell us what will happen under specific, prescribed conditions. This is the practical side of science. Without the scientific "laws" of motion developed by Sir Isaac Newton, for example, we could not build airplanes that fly or put men on the moon. How do we know if a scientific "law" is true? Always the test of "truth" in science is reality. Does the real, observed world behave the way in which it is described as behaving by the "law"? That is the ultimate test. What some, but by no means all, of the sciences can do is test scientific "laws" by the artificial creation of reality—doing controlled experiments in a laboratory. Economics cannot do this.

To sum up: the essence of all science is observation, generalization, prediction, and verification. This is the scientific method, a way of gaining knowledge and understanding of the world around us. It is a method that can be and is applied to the physical world, to the biological world, or to the social world. It is the application of this method to gaining understanding of the economic side of the social world that justifies the claim of economics to scientific status.

---

or deficiency of total demand for the economy as a whole. True, there may be some misdirection of production and therefore an oversupply of some commodities, but the pricing mechanism will correct this and cause some entrepreneurs to shift their output to other and more profitable lines. But such oversupply cannot be the case for the whole economy because the act of production always creates sufficient value or purchasing power to take off the market all goods and services produced. If there cannot be deficiency of total demand in the economy, it also follows that involuntary unemployment because of overproduction is impossible.

Quantity Theory of Money

The second idea of importance is the quantity theory of money, whose lineage can be traced back to Jean Bodin (also French) in the sixteenth century and whose influence runs almost straight down to the contemporary monetary views of Milton Friedman. Simply put, the quantity theory of money (nineteenth-century version) holds that the prime determinant of the price level is the supply of money. In equation form, the quantity theory says that $p = f(M)$, where p is the general level of prices and M is the money supply. This relationship, known as the classical quantity theory of money, is a natural corollary to Say's law of markets, because if the economy works so that full utilization of resources is the normal state of affairs, the only economic variable that the money supply can affect is the price level. There is more to the quantity theory than this, as we shall see in Chapter 3, but the link between money and the price level is its essential message. As suggested earlier, these two ideas do not represent a fully developed explanation of macroeconomic performance, but their widespread, and often tacit, acceptance by economists in the nineteenth century and early part of the twentieth century largely had the effect of removing macroeconomic problems from the theoretical agenda of economists. If the economy performed well most of the time in terms of output and employment, there was little need for macroeconomic theory.

All this changed drastically with the crash of 1929 and the deep depression that engulfed Western economies during the 1930s. The collapse of output and prolonged underemployment swept away faith in the validity of Say's law of markets. Furthermore, at a time when prices (including money wages) plunged to historic lows, the classical quantity theory, with its traditional stress on the inflationary dangers inherent in too much money in circulation, was equally irrelevant to the problems of the moment. What was clear to most economists and the general public was that these ideas no longer sufficed to explain what was happening to the economy. New ideas and a new theory were needed.

Keynesian Theory

The new ideas and the new theory were supplied by the British economist John Maynard Keynes, one of the most influential economic thinkers in the twentieth century. Keynes is the "father" of modern macroeconomics. In 1936 he published *The General Theory of Employment, Interest and Money*,[9] a work destined to change the manner in which people thought about the working of the economic system in advanced Western nations. The impact of Keynes on theory has been so great that few would disagree with John Kenneth Galbraith in calling *The General Theory* "the most influential book

---

[9] John Maynard Keynes, The General Theory of Employment, Interest and Money, First Harbinger ed. (New York: Harcourt, Brace & World, 1964).

on economic and social policy in this century. . . . By common, if not yet quite universal agreement, the Keynesian revolution was one of the great modern accomplishments of social design.''[10] As another observer has said, ''finance ministers around the world approach the problems of economic management through an analytical framework which, perhaps for want of a better word, commentators rightly called Keynesian.''[11]

What kind of a book is *The General Theory?* Basically, Keynes set out to explain the forces that shape and determine the level and rate of growth of national production and employment, a subject not well understood by either economists or lay people prior to the catastrophic depression of the 1930s. In this he succeeded exceedingly well. *The General Theory* laid the foundation for what has become a highly developed body of economic theory and policy directed toward the most pressing problems of the economy as a whole— output, employment and unemployment, economic growth, and inflation.

Keynesian ideas continue to occupy a central place in the body of modern macroeconomic theory. In this connection, three points are crucial. First, Keynes established the basic conceptual framework within which contemporary economists of every persuasion approach and analyze the problems of the macroeconomy. This is the framework of aggregate demand and aggregate supply, the essentials of which are developed in Chapter 4. Second, the primary stress of Keynesian economics—at least as his ideas were largely interpreted in the quarter century after World War II—has been on understanding what determines the level of total demand for the economy's output over relatively short periods of time. For this reason, the Keynesian analysis is often described as an *income-expenditure approach* to macroeconomic theory, because total spending is the key to output and total income determines total spending. The policy counterpart of this approach is the concept of ''demand management,'' that is, the belief that through fiscal and monetary action the central government can manage the level of aggregate demand and bring about a high level of production and employment without excessive pressure on the price level. To an important degree, an income-expenditure perspective is the natural consequence of the fact that Keynes wrote *The General Theory* during the depths of the worst economic collapse in the history of Western market economies. Because not all of today's macroeconomic problems—such as the persistence of inflation during the 1970s when there was serious slack in the economy—are readily explained by either an excess or a deficiency of total demand, economists are seeking new theoretical insights into the economy's overall behavior. Nevertheless—and this is the third point—the aggregate demand and supply framework and the relationships that Keynes and succeeding economists developed within that framework remain the essential core of modern macroeconomics. As a body of theory,

---

[10] John Kenneth Galbraith, ''Came the Revolution,'' *New York Times Review,* May 16, 1965.

[11] D. E. Moggridge, *Keynes* (London: Macmillan & Co., 1967), p. 9.

it has been subjected to more testing and rigorous analytical scrutiny than any competing approach.

Monetarism: The Modern Quantity Theory

Clearly the most influential challenge to Keynesian ideas in the post-World War II era has come from Professor Milton Friedman, Nobel laureate and for many years member of the economics department at the University of Chicago. In a monumental work published in 1964,[12] Professor Friedman, in collaboration with Anna Jacobson Schwartz, developed the basic thesis that the money supply is the single most important, strategic variable that determines in the short term the level of nominal gross domestic product and the level of employment. Friedman's theories, which are cast in a Keynesian framework even though they stress different variables, are described either as monetarism or the modern quantity theory. Both terms reflect Professor Friedman's intellectual indebtedness to the quantity theory of money mentioned earlier. Among the important ideas that have emerged from the monetarist school is, first, the belief that since it is primarily the money supply that affects current spending, there is neither need nor justification for trying to influence output and employment through changes in government spending and taxes. Contemporary monetarism, in other words, rejects the idea that fiscal policy (the use of taxes and government expenditures to influence the economy) is an appropriate tool for economic stabilization. Second, the monetarists see variations in the stock of money as being chiefly responsible for the upheavals and fluctuations that have characterized U.S. economic life throughout our history. A market system, they believe, is inherently stable and may be subject to shocks brought about by monetary mismanagement. Consequently, their primary policy recommendation is that the money-creating authority—in the U.S. case, the Federal Reserve System—be required to keep the money supply growing at a constant rate. The latter should be determined by the growth in the economy's underlying real factors, such as the rate of technological change and growth in the labor force, plus a margin that allows people to hold a fraction of their wealth as money balances in a growing economy. Basically, the monetarists seek to limit the government's discretionary power to manage the economy.

New Classical Economics

More recently there has emerged a more radical, far-reaching challenge to Keynesian theory. Known as the *new classical economics,* this movement embraces two diverse but related sets of ideas. Although both have deep roots in classical economics, they differ in important ways. From the standpoint of

---

[12] Milton Friedman and Anna Jacobson Schwartz, *A Monetary History of the United States* (Princeton, N.J.: Princeton University Press, 1964).

analytical elegance, the most important development is the *theory of rational expectations.* In a nutshell, this theory argues that because people are rational, they anticipate the results of actions and behave accordingly. When combined with a Walrasian[13] general equilibrium model, which shows that markets always clear, rational expectations theory holds that a market system, *if free from government intervention,* will quickly and efficiently achieve an equilibrium at full employment. Staunch new classical macroeconomists maintain that *no* macroeconomic policy whatsoever can significantly alter the real course of the economy. In this respect, they go well beyond monetarists in arguing against any positive policy acts whatsoever; the monetarists believe at least that the path of the economy can be influenced by following a monetary rule for a fixed rate of growth in the money supply. An important subset of the new classical economics is the *real* business cycle theory, a development explored in detail in Chapter 17.

New Keynesian Economics

A third perspective is a hybrid of new classical and Keynesian ideas. The new Keynesian approach seeks to build a macroeconomics on well-established microeconomic foundations. It uses rational expectations in explaining how expectations are formed, but it does not use the assumption of new classical economics that markets *always* clear. Rather, it develops a microeconomic foundation based on imperfectly competitive firms, labor markets that systematically do not clear because of long-term contracts and other considerations, and financial institutions that ration funds rather than allocate them through the market by means of the rate of interest.

Like the new classical economists, the new Keynesians believe that people act rationally, but they also believe that the strategies people adopt within the economy's institutional structure can and do generate less than full-employment conditions. Because of this—and in sharp contrast to the new classical economics—the new Keynesians find justification for government intervention in the economy. Even though people are assumed to behave rationally in accordance with rational expectations theory, the economy may not *by itself* adjust to a full-employment equilibrium.

In a sense, the new Keynesians have brought the debate full circle. In the 1950s and 1960s, debate was focused on the question of how best to use the basic tools of macroeconomics for policy purposes. It was a foregone conclusion that policy action was needed. By the 1970s and 1980s, however, the monetarist and new classical challenges called into question the possibility that any discretionary monetary or fiscal policy would be successful. The new

---

[13] Leon Walras was a nineteenth-century French economist who developed mathematically a model of a multimarket economy in which he demonstrated how markets could clear and there could be a simultaneous equilibrium in all markets. Walras' analysis is usually described as a theory of general equilibrium, where ''general'' in this case means the entire economy.

Keynesians have not only reopened the debate, but also demonstrated the necessity and usefulness of macroeconomic policy.

Post Keynesian Economics

The approach of this perspective on macroeconomic behavior takes a sharply different tack. Operating under the label *Post Keynesian economics,* adherents of this viewpoint argue, first, that the interpretation of Keynesian theory that became standardized after World War II[14] was seriously deficient because it had the practical effect of pushing Keynes's contributions back into a classical mold. Second, the Post Keynesians, who have their own scholarly journal *(Journal of Post Keynesian Economics),* maintain that contemporary macroeconomic theory is deficient because it fails to integrate into the theory key insights about aggregate behavior that are either explicit in *The General Theory* or strongly suggested by its tone and temper. The most significant omitted insights center on uncertainty and its impact on economic decisions; the fact that the economic process takes place in real, historic time; and, finally, the crucial role that economic and political institutions play in determining outcomes in the real economic world. In connection with the latter point, the Post Keynesians are especially critical of economic theory that neglects the impact that market power has on economic behavior, particularly in the explanation of inflation. Although there is agreement among the Post Keynesians on the foregoing points, they have not yet developed an agreed-on macroeconomic model of the economy.

Summary

1. Macroeconomics is concerned primarily with the analysis and measurement of the overall performance of the economy. It concentrates on such key variables as total production, employment and unemployment, and the general level of prices.

2. Gross domestic product, measured in both current prices (*nominal* GDP) and constant prices (*real* GDP), is the most widely used single measure of economic performance.

3. Prices in general are measured through indexes. The three basic indexes used in macroeconomics are the consumer price index, the producer price index, and the GDP deflator.

---

[14] Professor Paul Samuelson of MIT coined the term "the neoclassical synthesis" to describe this view of Keynesian economics, because it combined Keynesian principles relating to aggregate demand with traditional—or "classical"—ideas about how demand and supply forces operating in competitive markets allocate resources and distribute income. See Paul Samuelson, *Economics, An Introductory Analysis,* 6th ed. (New York: McGraw-Hill, 1955), p. 337.

4. Employment and unemployment are strategic measures of the economy's performance. They are closely tied to the general level of production. Unemployment is the proportion of the labor force without jobs.

5. In the 1980s the balance of trade emerged as another important measure of macroeconomic performance. During recent years the U.S. trade balance turned negative.

6. Analyses of statistics of output, employment, and prices over the long term show that the economy grows, but that growth is never smooth. Volatility and change are basic characteristics of the U.S. economy.

7. Economics, like other sciences, observes, establishes relationships among things observed, and predicts what will happen under specific circumstances. Tests of predictions are the ultimate tests of the validity of all science, including economics. Unlike many of the natural sciences, economic hypotheses cannot be tested in laboratories.

8. Modern macroeconomics is no longer a unified body of theory. Several interpretations of the way the economy works are contending with one another for dominance. These include the income-expenditure approach, monetarism, new classical economics, new Keynesian economics, and Post Keynesian economics.

Measuring the
Economy's Performance

ONE OF THE GREAT accomplishments of macroeconomics in the last two-thirds of a century has been the development of sophisticated statistical techniques for measuring important macroeconomic variables like the national output (income), employment, and unemployment. In this chapter we shall examine the basic concepts that underlie the measurement of the economy's performance, including a discussion of specific measurements widely used for this purpose.

The Nature and Uses of National Income Accounting

The techniques of national income accounting developed in the United States and other nations are like the accounting systems developed for and utilized by business firms. Balance sheets and profit and loss accounts provide a numerical record of the activities of the business firm. To conduct successfully the affairs of a firm, a business executive must have accurate and current information concerning sales receipts, expenditures, and the profit of the firm. From information provided by the firm's accounting system, the state of economic health of the enterprise is judged.

National income accounting is designed to do for the economy as a whole what traditional forms of accounting do for the business firm. The basic objective of a system of national income accounting is to provide a systematic and factual record of the performance of the economy during a specified period of time.[1] The Bureau of Economic Analysis (BEA) of the U.S. Department of Commerce compiles the statistical data that go into the nation's national income accounting system. Statistics of national income are published at periodic intervals in the *Survey of Current Business,* a monthly publication of the Department of Commerce.

The most important use of national income accounting is in the formulation of economic policy, primarily by governments, but also by business firms and labor organizations.[2] Since the great stock market crash of 1929 there has been a vast expansion in the role played by government (federal, state, and local) in the economy; between 1929 and 1994, for example, the purchase of goods and services by all levels of government rose from 8.6 percent of national output to 17.4 percent.[3] As a consequence, public policies relating to taxes and expenditures have become one of the most strategically important determinants of the overall performance of the economic system. Given the growing complexity of the modern economy, detailed statistical information on its performance as provided by systems of national income accounting is indispensable in developing intelligent and workable public policies.

Another important application of national income accounting is to trace fluctuations and growth in total activity, as described in Chapter 1. Aggregate data of this nature provide us with helpful information about the use and availability of resources in the economy. When national income data are broken down into different sectors and industries, we are able to gain important insights into the structure and anatomy of the economic system. Such information is invaluable in analyzing the effect of specific policies on prices, production, and employment in different parts of the economy. Furthermore, interrelationships between different parts of the economy are clarified. Business firms, too, make use of national income data, especially as a background for important business decisions pertaining to production, purchasing, bor-

---

[1] In the United States, national income accounting got a major start in 1920, when the National Bureau of Economic Research, a private research organization, began extensive work on the measurement of national income. After the onset of the Great Depression and as a result of a 1932 Senate resolution, the U.S. Department of Commerce began to compile national income statistics for the U.S. economy. Professor Simon Kuznets, the fourth economist awarded a Nobel Prize in this field, directed the early work of the National Bureau on national income measurement and worked closely with the Department of Commerce in preparing its first estimates. These later were published in 1934 as a report, *National Income 1929–32.* For a more detailed review of the history of national income accounting, see John W. Kendrick, *Economic Accounts and Their Uses* (New York: McGraw-Hill, 1972), Chap. 2.

[2] "National income accounting" is a broad and descriptive term covering a wide variety of economic accounts that apply to the economic system. The best known of these include national income and product accounts, flow of funds accounts, input-output analysis, balance of international payments accounts, and statements of national wealth. For a detailed discussion of various forms of national income accounting see Kendrick, *Economic Accounts and Their Uses.*

[3] *Economic Report of the President,* 1991, p. 287; 1995, p. 274.

rowing, and capital spending. For these purposes, the July issue of the *Survey of Current Business* each year is especially valuable because it contains highly detailed tables on the key areas of the economy.

The usefulness of national income data reaches beyond the domestic economy. Important comparisons between nations can be made on the basis of their respective national income accounting systems, especially because the terminology and conceptual framework for such systems are becoming increasingly standardized. National income accounting as explained in this chapter is the most widely used frame of reference for making forecasts and projections of economic activity.

Income and Wealth

Having sketched out the nature of national income accounting, we shall analyze, first, the concept of income and, second, the meaning of income in reference to the whole society. A similar discussion on wealth will follow; then we shall discuss the relationship between income and wealth.

The Concept of Income

There are a number of different ways in which income can be defined, but the one thing common to all definitions is the idea that income is a *flow* phenomenon. By a *flow* is meant something that is *measured over time.* For the individual, the income flow is usually thought of in terms of money received between two points of time, although one might just as readily—and correctly—conceive of it as a flow of satisfactions during a period of time. The business firm, too, usually thinks of income as money received over time. But no matter how we choose to define income, the crucial element in our definition is flow.

This last statement brings us to the question of what we mean when we talk in terms of the income of the whole society—what, in short, is the meaning of *national income?* Since economic activity aims at satisfaction of human wants and since satisfaction of wants results from consumption of goods and services, the performance of the economy must be measured in terms of the amount of productive activity taking place in a period of time. Productive activity culminates in the output of valuable goods and services. Thus, income from the standpoint of the whole society is a *flow of output over a period of time.* This is an extremely important point. When we speak of income for the nation, we are speaking about output. When we speak of income for the individual or the business firm, we are speaking about money. It is important to keep this distinction in mind.

The basic definition of income in a social sense as a flow of output presents a difficult problem in measurement. Output consists of a vast and heterogeneous quantity of goods and services that cannot be added together unless they can be reduced to a common unit of measurement. As a practical matter, the only way in which we can add together all the different kinds of goods and services produced by the economy during a period of time is by reducing them to their money value. Money value is the common denominator that enables us to sum up and reduce to a single figure the complex aggregation of goods and services contained in the economy's flow of output during some definite period.

It is possible to reduce the economy's flow of output to its monetary valuation because in a market economy practically all productive activity will be reflected in money transactions. Most activities that are productive—that lead to the creation of goods and services—are carried on through the mechanism of the market and will thus carry a price tag. If a way can be found to summarize all the monetary transactions that reflect productive activity, it is possible to measure in money terms the total income, or flow of output, of the society.

Although, in principle, the summing of money transactions describes the technique by which the output of the whole society is measured, several qualifications to the above statement should be noted. For one thing, all monetary transactions do not necessarily reflect current productive activity; this is the case with sales of secondhand goods or the purchase and sale of various financial instruments, such as stocks and bonds. Second, some productive activity does not pass through the mechanism of the market and thus is not reflected in a monetary transaction. The labor of the homemaker is a case in point. Finally, money itself is not a stable unit of measure since the value of money fluctuates as the general level of prices changes. This problem, as we saw in Chapter 1, is corrected by measuring output in constant prices.

The Circular Nature of Economic Activity

Income, as we have stressed, is a flow phenomenon. But it is important to note the *circular* character of this flow. This basic concept is illustrated in Figure 2–1, a highly simplified model of the economy. Output originates in the producing units of the economy—including the government as a producing entity—and moves from there to the economy's households, which are not only the ultimate users of the economy's output, but also the owners and suppliers of the economic resources that enter into the creation of output. The existence of a flow of output means there must be a corresponding flow of inputs, for, as shown in Figure 2–1, the essence of the productive process is the transformation of the services rendered by the economic resources of land, labor, and capital into economically useful goods and services.

Figure 2–1 presents a simplified view of the matter because it lumps all goods and services together and assumes that all the output is directed toward the households or the consumer of the economy. Actually some of the output consists of capital or investment goods, of which firms rather than households are the ultimate users. Moreover, households do not spend all their income, as some is saved and some is taxed. These exceptions, though, should not

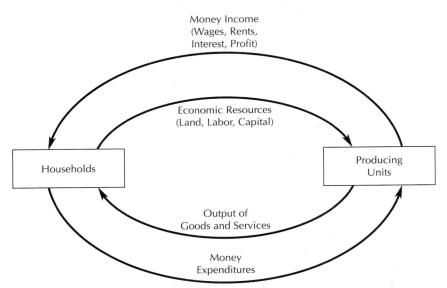

FIGURE 2–1   The Circular Flow of Economic Activity.   In the circular flow of economic activity, the flow of output and the services of the resources needed to produce that output is matched by money flows equaling the value of the output and input flows.

cloud our understanding of the basically circular character of the economic process.

The input and output flows that constitute the essence of the economic process are matched by two flows of money—one of income and one of expenditure. As shown in Figure 2–1, resource owners exchange the service of their resources for money incomes, while the producing firms in the economy exchange their output of goods and services for the flow of expenditures originating in the households of the economy. The flow of income and expenditure matching the real flows of the economy is seen to be circular in the same sense that the underlying flows of product and services of economic resources are circular.

The circular flow diagram, though oversimplified, illustrates a number of important propositions relating to the economic process and the flow of income. First, the diagram shows that income (or output) creation involves an interaction between the two basic kinds of markets that exist in the economy. Exchanging the services of economic resources for money incomes, depicted in the top half of the diagram, reflects transactions taking place in the resource (factor) market, whereas the expenditure of money income for the economy's output, depicted in the lower half of the diagram, represents the total of transactions taking place in markets for goods and services. Second, the circular flow diagram aids in understanding why the flow of income, the flow of output, and the flow of expenditures for output are necessarily equal *once*

Using Models in Economics

Figure 2–1 reflects a practice that has become common in economic analysis—the use of *models*. Most of us are familiar with the idea of a model as a physical representation, a replica in miniature of something that exists or can be observed. In a planetarium we see models of the solar system, and, of course, everyone is familiar with model airplanes or cars.

What, though, is an economic model? Essentially—and as the term "model" suggests—it is a representation of all or parts of the economic system. The diagram shown in Figure 2–1 is an economic model in graphic form. Graphic models are common, as in the case of supply and demand diagrams found in elementary textbooks. Such diagrams are models of how markets work. Increasingly, however, economic models are constructed in equation form, involving both algebra and calculus. Econometric models, involving a marriage of mathematics and statistics, have grown rapidly in number and complexity in recent years. Some of these models include three hundred or more equations!

Unlike a model car or airplane, which is an exact replica in miniature of the real thing, economic models, no matter how many equations they embrace, are *simplifications* of the real world, not exact replicas. Figure 2–1 illustrates this point well. It represents how the real world economy behaves, but in an abstract, highly simplified way. Models in economics play a highly useful role, but we must be on guard not to confuse them with the reality they are used to illustrate and explain.

they have taken place. The reason for this equality is that all these flows are different measures of the same thing—the volume of productive activity in the economy. Since the circular flow analysis reveals that the total flow of current income is always equal to the value of current output, this means that the productive process will always generate sufficient total money income to purchase the current output of the economy. This does not mean, however, that all the income so generated will be spent by those who first receive it, as some may be saved and some may be taxed. There may be spending by business that offsets saving and by government that offsets taxes, but this does not necessarily have to happen.

The Concept of Wealth

Wealth and income are concepts so closely related that it is easy to confuse them and not see that they are distinct entities. As a starting point, let us define *wealth* as all material things, including natural resources, that possess economic value. Wealth consists of *physical* things that can command other goods and services in exchange. This definition of wealth varies from more casual usage, in which individuals and families typically regard as wealth the money, bank accounts, stocks, bonds, and other financial assets they possess.

Several important aspects of our definition of wealth should be noted. One of the most important is that wealth is a *stock* concept in contrast to income, a *flow* phenomenon. Wealth relates to the total of material things that exist at a moment in time, whereas income has to do with the flow of output or money over a period of time. This basic difference between income and wealth is reflected in the way in which the two are measured. Income can be measured only by reference to some distinct period of time, a day, a week, a month, or a year. Wealth, however, can be measured by reference to some specific moment in time, such as the final day of the week, the month, or the year. The difference may be illustrated by reference to the profit-and-loss statements and the balance sheet for the business firm. The profit-and-loss statement is analogous to the income concept; it depicts the receipts and expenditures flowing into and out of the firm over a specific period of time, usually one year. The balance sheet is analogous to the wealth concept; it reveals the position of the firm at a given moment in time, usually at the close of business on the last day of the year.

It is also important to note that wealth, because it involves a stock of material things, is exhaustible: it can be wholly used up. Income, because it is a flow, is capable of being continuously renewed. Some forms of wealth, such as natural resources, cannot be replaced. Oil in the ground is an example; when it is gone, it is gone forever. Manufactured forms of wealth, such as buildings and machines, are different. They do wear out, but they can be replaced. To do this requires, however, that some part of society's current production—its national income—be used for this purpose. This is what economists generally mean by *investment*—using a part of current output to replace goods worn out in production or to add to the stock of manufactured forms of wealth.

The Capital Goods Component of Wealth

This brings us to the form of tangible wealth that is most critical with respect to the general level of economic activity—capital goods. Economists use the term ''capital goods'' to describe all the manufactured things—tools, machines, buildings, all productive equipment—used to produce the goods and services that make up the national output and to get these goods and services to their ultimate users. The latter are the consumers, business executives, government, and residents of other nations. Capital goods are unique because they do not satisfy human wants directly. Rather, they are manufactured resources that, in conjunction with other resources such as human labor, natural resources, and entrepreneurial skills, are combined to produce the goods and services that directly satisfy human wants. As indicated earlier, capital goods, like all forms of wealth, do wear out, but unlike natural resources, they can be replenished. This, as we also noted, involves investment, using a portion of the economy's current income (output) to produce new capital goods, either for replacing or augmenting the nation's stock of real capital. In national income accounting, investment is measured by business spending for new plant and equipment and for inventories and by the purchase of new homes by individuals and families.

Items of tangible wealth, other than houses, held by individuals and families—automobiles, refrigerators, washing machines, radio and televison sets, and other household appliances—do not fit neatly into the foregoing description. These are capital goods because they are manufactured and do not satisfy wants directly, but do provide their owners with services that satisfy wants. This form of wealth may properly be designated as *consumer capital,* although in national income accounts, the purchase of any of these items is lumped together with all other purchases of goods and services by consumers.

The Concept of Human Capital

In recent years some economists have applied the wealth concept to the investment by human beings in skills and knowledge. The skills, education, and knowledge that human beings acquire in a broad sense is a form of capital that contributes in a significant way to the process of production. Professor Theodore W. Schultz, a Nobel laureate and an early advocate of the idea that economic analysis should take into account human as well as material capital, points out that not only does wealth in the form of human skill and knowledge require investment for its creation, but this form of wealth has grown in Western societies at a much faster rate than other, nonhuman types of capital. Furthermore, Professor Schultz says, the growth of human capital may be the most distinctive feature of the modern economy, contributing more to the growth of output over the long run than conventional forms of wealth.[4]

Measurement of the economic value of human capital presents formidable statistical difficulties, although, roughly speaking, the net worth of an individual's human capital depends on the income that person expects to earn over his or her working life. (Chapter 8 discusses the problem of how the current economic value of any item of wealth, or capital, that produces an income is determined.)

Aside from statistical difficulties in measuring human capital, there is a reluctance—and perhaps even a repugnance—among economists and others to suggest even remotely that human beings might be looked on as capital goods. As Professor Schultz points out, to regard human beings as capital that can be augmented by investment runs counter to deeply held values, primarily because of the long struggle of Western people to rid society of any form of slavery or indentured service.[5] Nevertheless, economists have continued to refine the concept of human capital and to measure its value.

---

[4] Theodore W. Schultz, "Investment in Human Capital," *American Economic Review,* March 1961.
[5] Ibid.

Investment in human capital is linked to our growing involvement in the global economy, an economy that is driven by a dynamic and rapidly changing technology. Knowledge is the key to the ability of the nation to remain productive and able to compete in today's fast-moving international economy. Work and production require ever-higher levels of knowledge and information. Knowledge and information have become a new kind of economic resource, one that is fundamentally different from the traditional resources identified by economists—land, labor, and capital. Knowledge and information are not bound by time and place. In this age of the microchip and the computer, they can and do move instantaneously across national borders, anywhere, anytime. Everything we produce, how we produce, what and how we trade, and how we communicate is profoundly influenced by the explosion of knowledge and information surging across the globe. Investment in human capital through education is the means—the only means—by which the nation can hold its own in an increasingly competitive world.

Interactions between Income and Wealth

We have outlined some of the basic differences between income and wealth; it is important also to have a clear understanding of the way in which they are linked together.

Our fundamental definition of income from the point of view of the whole society is that of a flow of goods and services. Given this definition, a key question is: What use or disposition is made of the economy's income? The simplest answer is that whatever the economy produces in any particular period of time must be either consumed or not consumed. To consume output means, of course, to use up goods and services in the satisfaction of human wants. If a good or service can satisfy a human want, it is said to have utility. Consumption, therefore, involves using up utilities as wants are satisfied. Production, on the other hand, involves the creation of utilities so that wants can be satisfied.

But what happens to the output that is not consumed during the income period in which it is produced? This output becomes an addition to the existing stock of wealth of the economy. Here is the essential relationship between income and wealth; whenever current income exceeds current consumption, the stock of wealth automatically is increased, and whenever current consumption is in excess of current income, the stock of wealth will automatically be reduced. We need to inject a word of caution here. The relationship just described between output (a flow) and wealth (a stock) involves an after-the-fact change, what economists call an *ex post* change (see the box on *ex ante* and *ex post* values). It does not necessarily follow that the increase (or decrease) in the economy's stock of wealth was desired. This is a matter we shall deal with fully in Chapter 8. Another way to look at the relationship between the flow of income, consumption, and the stock of wealth is to liken it to a reservoir of water. In the reservoir, the water level (that is, the stock of water) depends on the rate at which water flows into the reservoir as compared with the rate at which water flows out of the reservoir. If the rate of inflow is greater than the rate of outflow, the water level within the reservoir will rise, whereas if the rate of outflow is greater than the rate of inflow, the water level will drop.

If some part of the current output of an economy is not consumed during the period in which is is produced, *saving* has taken place. Three things about saving should be noted. First, saving, like income, is a flow phenomenon. The assets (real and monetary) of both a nation and an individual may increase because of saving. Second, saving is a negative act, since basically it represents the *nonconsumption* of current output. Third, saving should be distinguished from *liquidity*, an important concept developed by Keynes in *The General Theory*. Liquidity is the immediate command over valuable goods and services that any asset may possess. Saving when held in money form provides immediate liquidity, but when converted to another form, such as a share of stock or a bond, may have less liquidity. Saving is an act—a negative act, to be sure—whereas liquidity is a characteristic of an asset.

There is, however, another facet to the nonconsumption of current output. The addition to the economy's existing stock of wealth that is the inevitable consequence of the act of saving was defined earlier as *investment*. In this economic sense, investment means a net addition to the stock of wealth of the economy. The important underlying idea is that the act of investment always involves something *real,* in the sense that it has to do with changes in the economy's stock of wealth. In everyday speech, the term investment is used in a "portfolio" sense, which refers to the total of income-producing claims owned by an individual. Thus, a person's "investment portfolio" consists of all the income-producing claims owned by the person.

The relationship between output and wealth should be viewed in another way. Not only is it true that the stock of wealth is augmented when the economy does not consume all current output, but it is also true that output is a flow that has its origins in the size, quality, and use made of the economy's stock of both material and human wealth. The act of investment (discussed later) is essential if a society is to maintain intact—or increase—its stock of wealth. Unless the society makes provision for investment, the income flow will be imperiled.

Whenever we discuss or measure saving and investment in an *ex post,* or after-the-fact, sense, they are necessarily equal. This follows from the way in which we have defined these phenomena. If some part of the economy's current output is not consumed, we say that saving has taken place, but by the same token we say that this represents investment because an act of nonconsumption will add to the economy's stock of wealth. The notion that investment and saving are identical when defined in this manner is highly important in economic analysis, and will be encountered frequently in subsequent chapters.

Output and Income Measures

Now that we have analyzed some fundamental principles that underlie most systems of national income accounting, we turn, first, to a discussion of some of the specific measures for output and income now in use in the United States, concentrating on five well-known aggregate measures: (1) gross domestic product, (2) net domestic product, (3) national income, (4) personal income, and (5) disposable income. We shall follow this with an examination of concepts and problems involved in measuring employment and unemployment; we shall be especially concerned with concepts such as the natural rate of employment, full employment, and the labor force participation rate.

Gross Domestic Product

Gross domestic product, also called gross domestic income or gross domestic expenditure, is the best known and most widely used of the various statistical measures developed to gauge the economy's performance. Formally, it is defined as *the current market value of all final goods and services produced by the economy during an income period.* The normal income period for most national income accounting systems, including that of the United States, is the calendar year. As an expenditure total, gross domestic product (or GDP as it is usually called) represents the total purchases of goods and services by consumers and governments, gross private domestic investment, and net for-

---

Ex Ante and *Ex Post* Values

Economists look at variables in basically two ways—*ex ante* and *ex post.* Literally, *ex ante* means from before and *ex post,* from behind. Thus, a variable measured in an *ex ante* sense involves looking forward to what is intended, expected, or planned to happen. When economists construct schedules involving functional relationships, as with the Keynesian consumption function, the values imparted to the variables in the schedule are *ex ante* (or intended) values. They are descriptive of what will happen under certain circumstances, not what has actually happened. *Ex post* refers to variables that are measured by looking back to an event that has happened. GDP for 1995, for example, is an *ex post* measurement; it gives us that value of the national output after the fact, what GDP was in a year that is now past.

eign investment. As an income total, GDP shows both the total income created as a result of current productive activity and the allocation of this income. The output total included in the GDP figure is described as gross because it does not take into account capital goods that have been consumed or worn out during the process of production. It is termed "domestic" because it refers to the productive activities of the residents of a particular nation, including the contribution to current output of property resources owned by these residents. Table 2–1 shows GDP data for selected years for the United States during the period 1960 to 1994.

The numbers in Table 2–1 are of astronomical proportions. The nation's GDP in 1994 was *six trillion, seven hundred thirty-six billion, nine hundred million* dollars! A sum that large is nearly incomprehensible. The most realistic way to reduce such a staggering sum to a manageable size is to divide the GDP (and its component parts) for any one year by the population of that year. This reduces the numbers to a more human scale. To illustrate, the nation's population in 1994 was 260.7 million. If the GDP in 1994 of $6,736.9 trillion is divided by population, we get $25,842 in 1994 dollars. This is the amount of goods and services on a per person (or per capita) basis produced in the nation in 1994. If we do the same thing for the other components of GDP, we find that on the average, consumption output was $17,748 per person, government spending on goods and services per person was $4,507, output per person for investment goods sold to business firms was $3,980, and net exports were minus $392 per capita. The latter, negative figure means that on the average, each U.S. resident bought $392 more foreign-made goods than U.S.-made goods were sold abroad.

Now we shall examine carefully the individual components of GDP—consumption, investment, government purchases, and net exports. These also

TABLE 2–1   Gross Domestic Product or Expenditure; Selected Years, 1960–1994 (in billions of current dollars)

Year	Gross Domestic Product	Personal Consumption Expenditure	Gross Private Domestic Investment	Government Purchases of Goods and Services	Net Exports of Goods and Services
1960	$ 513.3	$ 332.4	$ 78.7	$ 99.8	$ 2.4
1965	702.7	444.6	118.0	136.3	3.9
1970	1,010.7	646.5	150.3	212.7	1.2
1975	1,585.9	1,024.9	226.0	321.4	13.6
1980	2,708.0	1,748.1	467.6	507.1	−14.7
1985	4,038.7	2,667.4	714.5	772.3	−115.6
1990	5,546.1	3,761.2	808.9	1,047.4	−71.4
1993	6,343.3	4,378.2	882.0	1,148.4	−65.3
1994	6,736.9	4,627.0	1,037.5	1,174.9	−102.1

Source: Economic Report of the President, 1995, pp. 274, 275.

Simon Kuznets: Father of the GDP

If the great British economist John Maynard Keynes can be regarded as the inventor of modern macroeconomic theory, Russian-born Simon Kuznets is rightfully regarded as the father of the system by which the bare bones of Keynesian theory were clothed in numbers. Professor Kuznets, who was born in 1901 and who came to this country not long after the 1917 Revolution in Russia, was the third American to receive the Nobel Prize in Economic Science. It was awarded to him on October 15, 1971.

Professor Kuznets has had a long and varied career in economics, but it was primarily for his massive two volume study, *National Income and Its Composition: 1919–38,* published by the National Bureau of Economic Research in 1941, that he received the Nobel award. This far-reaching study established the basic concepts and framework for the system of national accounts used in the United States and every other modern nation. His 1941 work was the culmination of study and research on national income and measurement that dates back to the 1920s.

When the Great Depression devastated the U.S. economy in the early 1930s, there was little factual knowledge about the economic structure of the nation, including the scope of unemployment and the magnitude of the collapse in income. As Kuznets recalls, "No one knew what was happening." Faced with the need to act and the need for information on which to base action, the U.S. Senate authorized the collection of data on national income. Working in cooperation with the U.S. Department of Commerce, Kuznets and the National Bureau went to work on the problem and published their first findings on January 4, 1934 in a report entitled *National Income, 1929–32.* This report revealed just how devastating the crash was; it showed that the nation's income dropped from $89 billion in 1929 to $49 billion in 1932. This represented a 45 percent fall!

National income analysis and measurement have been only one facet of Professor Kuznets' long and productive career. After 1945 he increasingly directed his energies to the question of economic growth, not only to its statistical measurement, but also to the discovery of the secrets of successful long-term economic growth. A monumental study of growth and economic structure appeared in 1971, and this followed earlier studies on patterns of income distribution in the United States. Throughout his academic career, which included positions at Harvard, Johns Hopkins, and the University of Pennsylvania, Kuznets never lost his zest and enthusiasm for economics. "What drives me?" he once asked. "A great curiosity and a great delight in discovering something I didn't know before."

are the key variables that enter into aggregate demand in the basic Keynesian income-expenditure model developed in detail in this text. After that we shall look at other key measures of output and income.

Consumption Goods and Services (C)

In most societies the largest proportion of current output consists of consumer goods and services. These are goods and services designed to satisfy human wants. The usual method for measuring the economy's output of consumer goods and services is to add up the expenditures made by all households and private nonprofit institutions. Beyond this it is customary in national income accounting to break this category down into three subcategories: expenditures for consumer durables (automobiles, household appliances, household furnishings, etc.), nondurables (mostly food and clothing), and services. (In all subsequent discussion and analysis we shall designate this particular component of the national output by the capital letter C.)

Investment Goods (I)

In a broad sense the investment goods category of the national output should consist of all additions to the economy's stock of wealth; this is the basic meaning usually given to the term "investment." From the standpoint of national income accounting, however, it has been necessary to modify this because it is impractical and statistically impossible to include all additions to the economy's stock of wealth in the investment goods category. (The capital letter I will be used in this and later chapters to designate the investment component of output.)

The practice in national income accounting is to measure the economy's output of investment goods by the expenditures made during the income period by the end-users (generally business firms) for goods of the type listed below. These are what the Department of Commerce classifies as domestic investment expenditure:

1. All purchases by business firms of new construction and durable equipment
2. All purchases of new houses, that is, all residential construction
3. All changes (increases or decreases) in inventories held by business firms

Gross and Net Investment. In the investment goods category of the economy's output it is important to distinguish between investment that is gross and investment that is net. Once the reader understands the difference between gross and net investment, there will be no difficulty in understanding the difference between gross and net output, a distinction that is useful in economic analysis. Gross investment is the output of *all* goods in the investment goods category during an income period. This total is gross because it includes capital goods for replacement and for additions to the economy's stock of physical wealth. It is logical that some part of the economy's current total output of investment goods should constitute replacement for the portion of the economy's existing stock of productive wealth that is used up in the course of producing the current output. Thus, in any income period some part of the total stock of capital equipment or productive wealth is exhausted and must be replaced. The share of the total investment goods output that serves to replace worn-out capital instruments is termed *replacement investment.*

If we subtract from the total output of investment goods in any income period the amount representing replacement investment, we are left *net investment.* This total is net because, if our figure for replacement purposes is accurate, the difference between this figure and the total must represent the amount by which the economy's stock of productive wealth has increased during the current income period. Net investment involves a society's increasing its stock of productive capital instruments. If, during an income period, net investment is positive, the economy will have experienced an absolute increase in its physical stock of productive wealth, which means that its ability to produce goods and services has been enlarged. On the other hand, if net investment is negative, there has been a reduction in the economy's total stock of productive wealth, a development that normally implies an impairment of productive capacity.

Government Purchases of Goods and Services (*G*)

Up to this point we have discussed two major categories of output: consumption goods and services, and investment goods. In general, it is the practice in national income accounting to measure the amount of output in each of these categories by the expenditures made during the income period by the end-users of each kind of output, namely, households and other nonprofit institutions (for consumption goods and services) and business firms (for investment goods). This is possible because the bulk of the goods and services that fit into these categories are produced and sold on a private basis through the mechanism of the market; consequently, expenditure totals are a good indicator of output.

The prior classification, however, is incomplete, because it leaves out a third important category—the output of the public (or government sector) of the economy. The public sector produces a vast array of economically valuable goods and services, ranging from material things like highways, parks, dams, and schools to intangibles like police and fire protection, the services of judicial systems, and the activities of regulatory bodies, such as the Federal Communications Commission. Output originating in the public sector differs from output originating in the private sector primarily because it has a collective character. Public sector goods and services also differ from privately produced goods and services because the decision to produce the former is a political one, made through government, whereas the latter is private, made by individual producers in response to the quest for profit.

In general, the output of the public sector consists of goods and services that normally would not be produced by private firms or, if they were produced, would not be produced in sufficient quantities. Such goods and services are collective in the sense that they are indivisible; that is, their benefits accrue to society as a whole. The individual, to be sure, benefits from their production, but only by virtue of the fact that she or he is a member of the society in which such goods are being produced. The nation's judicial system is a case in point. All members of a nation receive some benefit, intangible though it may be, from the existence of a system of courts, yet there is no practical way to measure the amount of this benefit that accrues to each citizen. And if the benefit cannot be measured individually, then it is impractical to attempt to produce the good or service privately.

Of course, not all the goods and services produced by the public sector are clearly of a collective and indivisible character. Education, for example, can be and is produced and sold on an individual basis. In spite of this, the greater portion of education is produced collectively. If our system of public education were entrusted to private enterprise for production at a profit, there would not be an adequate supply of educational services. The well-being of the whole society would be endangered. The same is true with respect to other goods and services produced by the public sector, such as highways, parks and recreational areas, dams, and many different types of services. The private production and sale of such goods and services is not impossible, but in most instances the private plus the social benefit would be small as compared to the benefit that results when such goods are produced on a collective basis.

In addition to their social character, goods and services produced in the public sector differ from privately produced goods and services in another important way. In the private sector of the economy, output is normally disposed of by sale to the end-user of the output, but in the public sector the usual procedure is to distribute this output without charge to the society as a whole. Governments, in other words, normally do not sell on an individual basis the collective goods and services that it is their responsibility to provide. This means that we cannot measure the value of the output of the public sector in the same way that we measure the value of the private sector, namely, by the total of expenditures made by those who purchase the different categories of output. Since the output of the government sector is distributed free to all or most members of the community, the only practical measure of the value of this output is in terms of what it costs to supply it to the community at large. For the public sector to carry out its function of providing the economy with an array of collective goods and services, it must obtain economic resources; generally, it does this either directly through the hire of labor or indirectly through purchase of part of the output of the private sector. Therefore, the public sector's purchases of goods and services constitute the input of resources necessary to produce collective goods and services. In national income accounting, government purchases of goods and services are used as a measure of the portion of the total output that originates in the public sector. (It is the usual practice to designate this category of output by the capital letter G.)

Transfer Expenditures (*TR*) and Taxes (*TX*)

It is necessary to distinguish another, and important, type of government expenditure that *does not enter directly into the computation of output totals.* These expenditures, which occur at all levels of government, are called *transfer payments*, primarily because they involve transfers of income by the government from group to group rather than the acquisition of resources necessary to the production of governmental output. Transfer expenditures, in other words, provide income (real or monetary) to the recipients of such expenditures, but the government unit does not receive either goods or services in return. Old-age pensions, unemployment compensation, aid to dependent children, and assistance to war veterans are common forms of transfer payments. Insofar as the national economy is concerned, interest on the public debt and subsidies to business firms are considered to be transfers. Transfer expenditures may be viewed in another way, too, for they are, in a sense, negative taxes. Just as the recipient of a transfer payment does not directly provide the government unit making the payment with an equivalent value of either goods or services in exchange, neither does the government, in collecting taxes, provide each citizen individually with an immediate and equivalent value of goods or services in exchange. Transfer expenditures, in other words, are a one-way flow of income from the government to the individual or business firm; taxes, on the other hand, are a one-way flow of income from the individual or the business firm to the government. It is in this sense that we can also speak of taxes as being negative transfers. (In subsequent discussion in this text we shall designate transfer expenditures by *TR* and taxes by *TX*.)

Net Exports (*X* − *M*) or (I_f)

The category of GDP known as net exports is equal to the difference between a nation's exports of goods and services and its imports of goods and services. If there are no *transfers* of income to or from foreign residents, net exports may also be identified as *net foreign investment,* designated as I_f. The latter is subject to a number of qualifications, but for the moment it will serve as a working definition of foreign investment. A nation's exports represent expenditures for its output that originate outside the nation's borders, whereas a nation's imports represent spending by its residents for output that originates in foreign countries. If a nation's exports of goods and services exceed its imports of goods and services, net foreign investment is positive. On the other hand, if imports of goods and services are in excess of exports of goods and services, net foreign investment is negative. Positive net foreign investment increases the claims of the residents of a country against residents of other countries; negative net foreign investment does the reverse. (In our discussion we shall designate exports of goods and services as *X* and imports as *M*.)

Since we seek to link the various categories of the national output to expenditures made by end-users for each of these categories, it is important to understand the sense in which net exports constitute an expenditure category. If exports of goods and services exceed imports, the difference should be counted as an addition to the other categories of expenditure, the total of which is a measure of the national output. On the other hand, if imports of goods and services exceed exports, the difference should be subtracted from the sum of the other categories of expenditure. Expenditures by the nation and its residents for imported goods and services are normally included in the other categories of expenditure, since there is no practical way to distinguish the exact portion of expenditures for imports in each category. Consequently, total expenditures by residents for imported goods and services should be deducted in order to avoid counting them as output. This will be done automatically by making the net foreign investment category negative whenever imports of goods and services exceed exports of goods and services.

Net foreign investment, when positive, is similar in its economic effects to expenditure for investment goods. Expenditure leading to production of capital goods has the effect of creating money income within the economy equal to the amount of the expenditure. But there is not created in the same income period an offsetting volume of consumer goods and services, owing to the durable character of capital goods that produce value equal to their cost in the form of consumer goods only over their entire life, which usually encompasses several income periods. An excess of exports over imports (positive net foreign investment) will have the same economic effect, because the production of goods and services for export creates money income in the national economy, but no offsetting volume of goods and services for domestic purchase is immediately available. If imports fall short of exports, an excess of money income over the total of goods and services available for purchase during the income period exists. This excess is equal to the difference between exports and imports. On the other hand, an excess of imports over exports means that the physical volume of goods and services available for purchase by the nation and its residents is in excess of the amount of money income created by the process of producing the national output. It also means that there are more goods and services available to satisfy wants than are being produced by the domestic economy. Expenditures on imported goods and services, it may also be noted, are similar in their economic effects to saving, because use of any part of current income to finance the purchase of imported goods means that a part of current income is not being spent on domestically produced output. This is the same thing that takes place when some part of current income is saved. Thus, in an economic and conceptual sense, imports of goods and services are a counterpart of saving, whereas exports of goods and services are a counterpart of domestic investment.

Final and Intermediate Goods and Services

In defining GDP, we stated that it is a measure of the economy's output of final goods and services during an income period. In national income accounting, it is necessary to distinguish between *final goods and services,* which are the end products of the economy, and *intermediate goods and services,* which normally are goods and services purchased for resale. We must make this distinction to avoid double counting. Intermediate goods and services enter into the production of final goods and services. Therefore, if we added up expenditures for final goods and services as well as expenditures for intermediate goods and services, we would count the same goods and services twice. This would give us an exaggerated total for GDP. For example, the production of bread involves several stages and several transactions. Wheat is produced by the farmer and sold to the miller, who in turn processes the wheat and produces flour, which is sold to the baker, who uses it to produce bread. In this simple example wheat and flour are intermediate products, whose values will be reflected in the value of the final product, bread. Therefore, it would be an error to add separately the value of the wheat produced by the farmer, the value of the flour produced by the miller, and the value of the bread produced by the baker.

There is no exact rule by which we can clearly determine whether a good or a service is an intermediate or final product. In our example, flour is an intermediate product because it is sold to the baker for further processing. But if flour were sold directly to a homemaker, it would be classified as a final product, since the homemaker is the ultimate user of the product (as contrasted to the baker, who clearly is not the ultimate user). To distinguish between intermediate and final products in national income measurement, the Department of Commerce has adopted the working definition that a final product is one that will not be resold, whereas an intermediate product is one that is purchased with the normal intention that it be resold. Thus, in the example cited, wheat sold to the miller and flour sold to the baker constitute intermediate products, because in both instances the products will be resold, although in altered form. Bread purchased by the homemaker normally will not be resold and therefore can be considered a final product.

Monetary Transactions and Productive Activity

Since GDP is a measure of productive activity, the basic technique for its measurement is through the summation of all monetary transactions that reflect productive activity. There is a problem here because some monetary transactions do not represent current productive activity, while certain types of productive activity, on the other hand, will not show up in any monetary transaction. The most common monetary transactions that are not measures of current output are (1) those involving the purchase and sale of used or secondhand goods, because such goods constitute part of the output of a previous income period; (2) those involving purchase and sale of various financial instruments, such as bonds and equities; and (3) transfer payments, both public and private. All these transactions should be excluded from any monetary measure of current productive activity.

For productive activity not reflected in a monetary transaction, the homemaker's activities can again serve as an example. If a homemaker bakes the family's own bread, no monetary transaction reflecting the sale of a final product is involved, although there will be such a transaction if the family's bread is purchased in the bakery or grocery shop. Yet in both instances productive activity has taken place. The same sort of thing takes place if a homeowner chooses to paint the house rather than hire a professional painter to do the job. When the homeowner does the painting, productive activity occurs that is not reflected in the current GDP. But if a painter is hired, the resulting productive activity involves a monetary transaction and hence appears in the current output figures.

Ideally, GDP should be a measure of all current productive activity in the economy, whether or not the activity is reflected in a market transaction. But as a practical matter it is quite impossible to measure with any degree of statistical accuracy the total value of all the do-it-yourself types of productive activities and other nonmarket transactions that occur in the economy. The U.S. Department of Commerce limits its data to economic production. The basic criterion used for classifying an activity as economic production is whether it is reflected in the sales and purchase transactions of the market economy. The only exception to this is that the Department of Commerce makes estimates of certain income and product flows that are not reflected in transactions in the market. The most important of these *imputations*, or estimates of nonmarket production, are wages and salaries paid in kind rather than money, food produced and consumed on the farm, and the rental value of owner-occupied homes. Aside from these imputations, the Department of Commerce does not attempt to measure and record productive activity that is of a nonmarket character. The decision as to what nonmarket production ought to be included in national income and product measures is necessarily an arbitrary one.

Other Measures of Product and Income

We have devoted a relatively large amount of space to the discussion of GDP not only because it is the most widely used national income aggregate, but also because it is the best point of departure for the consideration and understanding of the other aggregates that make up the Department of Commerce's five-family series of national income and product measures.

Net National Product

Net national product (NNP) is defined by the Department of Commerce as the market value of the *net* output of final goods and services produced by the economy during the relevant income period. In a theoretical sense it is a measure of the nation's output after allowance has been made for the consumption of capital in the current process of production. NNP is derived by subtracting capital consumption allowances from the GDP and then making another adjustment that reflects receipts of factor incomes (wages, interest, rents, and profits) from the rest of the world less the payments of factor incomes made from the nation to the rest of the world. NNP, in other words, is the net value of the goods and services produced within the nation's borders. If business reserves for depreciation and the other items that enter into capital consumption allowances accurately reflected the real depreciation of the nation's stock of physical capital, net national product would measure exactly the amount of output that the nation could use for consumption, for the public sector, or for adding to the existing stock of capital without any impairment of productive capacity because of a failure to provide for the replacement of consumed items of real capital. Unfortunately, existing measurement techniques do not permit an accurate measurement of real capital consumption, so the net national product figure is not widely used.

National Income

National income is the sum of the factor costs incurred during production of the economy's current output. More specifically, the Department of Commerce defines national income as the aggregate earnings of labor and property that arise from the production of goods and services by the nation's economy. This measure is also described as the *net national product at factor cost* because it is a measure of the amount of income earned by the owners of the factors of production (land, labor, and capital) in return for supplying the services of these factors to the productive units of the economy. As such, it is the major source of money income or spending power for the purchase of most of the national output. The national income figure is usually derived by deducting indirect business taxes and the other minor charges from the net national product. It should be noted that the national income is both a measure of product (in the sense that it represents the factor cost of the current output) and a measure of money income earned by the factors of production.

Personal Income

Although national income is a measure of income earned by the owners of economic resources through participation in the productive process, it does not measure money actually received by persons and households during the current income period. The reason is that some parts of earned (or factor) income are not actually received as money income by persons or households, whereas some households and persons receive money income that is not earned through supplying the services of economic resources to the productive process. The latter consists of transfer payments and interest income from consumers and government. Although the Department of Commerce defines personal income as the current income "received" by persons from all sources, this is not strictly correct. The Department of Commerce normally measures personal income on a before-tax basis, but since some income taxes are withheld from wage and salary income, such income is not actually received. The intent, though, is to show the money income that persons are entitled to from all sources.

The usual procedure for obtaining the personal income measure is to deduct from national income the major categories of earned (or factor) income that are not actually received as money income by persons or households and then add to this figure the total of transfer incomes received from both government and business. The major deductions are (1) contributions to social insurance, (2) corporate profits tax liability, and (3) undistributed corporate profit. The chief forms of government transfer payments that must be added in are (1) interest on the public debt, (2) pensions paid to retired persons, (3) unemployment compensation, (4) various forms of relief payments, and (5) benefits extended to war veterans.

Disposable Income

The final widely used measure of income is that of disposable income, which the Department of Commerce defines simply as the income remaining to individuals after deduction of all taxes levied against their income and their property by all governmental entities in the economy. It is obtained by deducting such taxes from the personal income total, and it represents a measure of the after-tax purchasing power at the disposal of persons or households. Disposable income less personal consumption expenditures gives the total of personal saving in the economy. Gross private saving consists of this figure plus corporate saving (undistributed corporate profits) and capital consumption allowances.

The manner in which the five aggregates of both output and income are linked together is shown in Figure 2–2. Not only does this schema show the interrelationships existing among these product measures, it also underscores the *flow* character of the gross domestic product and its various components and serves to demonstrate this flow of product (income) and expenditures through the major sectors of the economy—households, businesses, and governments, as well as to the rest of the world. Figure 2–2 is an expanded and complex view of the circular flow of money in the economy depicted in Figure 2–1.

Price Indexes and Comparisons Over Time

The practice of the Department of Commerce is to report the money value of national income and product statistics in terms of the prices prevailing during the reporting period. Thus, GDP data for 1994 are reported in prices of 1994. If we are interested only in the statistics of income or output for a particular year, this does not create a special problem; but if we want to make comparisons between a number of years, then it is necessary to correct for changes in the general level of prices.

Let us assume that we want to convert GDP data for 1994 to 1987 prices so we can compare the actual physical change in GDP between these two

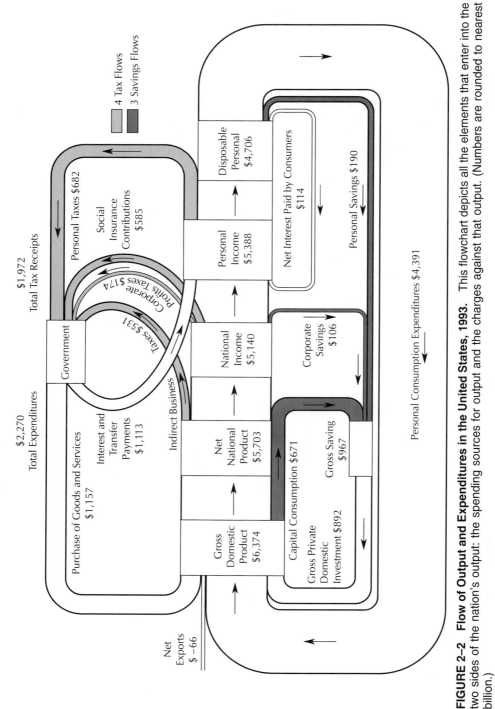

FIGURE 2-2 Flow of Output and Expenditures in the United States, 1993. This flowchart depicts all the elements that enter into the two sides of the nation's output: the spending sources for output and the charges against that output. (Numbers are rounded to nearest billion.)

Source: *Economic Report of the President*, 1994.

dates.[6] Since, by definition, GDP is a measure of the monetary value of the current output,

$$\text{GDP}_{1994} = O_{1994} \times P_{1994}. \tag{2-1}$$

This equation means that the value of current 1994 output is equal to the actual output (O) times the price (P) at which the output is sold in that year. From our prior discussion of price indexes, it also follows that the index of prices for 1994, using 1987 as the base year, is equal to the ratio of 1994 prices to 1987 prices. Thus,

$$\text{Price index for 1994} = \frac{P_{1994}}{P_{1987}}. \tag{2-2}$$

If we divide the GDP data for 1994 by the above price index, the result will be a measure of the physical output of 1994 valued in the prices of 1987. The following equations show algebraically why this is true.

$$\frac{\text{GDP}_{1994}}{P_{1994}/P_{1987}} = \frac{P_{1994} \times O_{1994}}{P_{1994}/P_{1987}}. \tag{2-3}$$

From Equation (2–3) it follows that

$$\frac{\text{GDP}_{1994}}{P_{1994}/P_{1987}} = P_{1994} \times O_{1994} \times \frac{P_{1987}}{P_{1994}}. \tag{2-4}$$

In Equation (2–4) the two expressions for 1994 prices, P_{1994}, on the right-hand side cancel out, and thus we have

$$\frac{\text{GDP}_{1994}}{P_{1994}/P_{1987}} = O_{1994} \times P_{1987}. \tag{2-5}$$

By dividing GDP measured in current (1994) prices by the current (1994) price index, the GDP data are converted to a figure which values the current output in prices for a selected base year. Table 2–2 shows the United States GDP in both current and constant dollars (or prices) for selected years since 1950. The table also includes in column 3 the price indexes used to deflate the current dollar amount.

---

[6] The Department of Commerce uses 1987 as its base year for constructing GDP price *deflators*, i.e., indexes used to convert GDP data to constant dollars.

TABLE 2–2 Gross Domestic Product in Constant Dollars; Selected Years, 1960–1994 (in billions of current and constant dollars)*

(1)	(2)	(3) Price Index† 1987 = 100	(4) = (2) ÷ (3) GDP in Constant Dollars
Year	GDP in Current Dollars		
1960	$ 515.3	26.0	$1,970.8
1965	702.7	28.4	2,470.5
1970	1,010.7	35.2	2,873.9
1975	1,585.9	49.2	3,221.7
1980	2,708.0	71.7	3,776.3
1985	4,038.7	94.4	4,278.3
1990	5,546.1	113.3	4,897.3
1994	6,736.9	126.1	5,342.3

*Data in all columns are rounded. The U.S. Department of Commerce in computing both the GDP deflator and GDP in constant dollars carries the calculations to more than one decimal point.

†Implicit GDP deflator.

Source: Economic Report of the President, 1995, pp. 274, 276, 278.

Limitations Inherent in Aggregate Measures of Income and Product

Although GDP and the other aggregates are used extensively to measure the material performance of the economy, they are subject to a number of limitations, particularly with respect to economic welfare (material performance and welfare are not always identical). The most important of these limitations can be briefly summarized.

Economic versus Social Values

National income and product figures measure the economic rather than the social value of current productive activity. These data are largely limited to measuring economic value in terms of the market prices that different types of goods and services may command. But the market price of a good or a service may not accurately reflect the value to the society of the good or service in a more fundamental, philosophical sense. A society, for example, might spend identical sums on education and tobacco, and yet one would hesitate to assert that the social, as distinct from the economic, values of these two types of expenditures are the same. As the late Professor Robert Lekachman forcefully put it, "The national income expert totals not only the value of oil pumped up from the Santa Barbara channel [from oil spills] or the Gulf coast but also the expenses of cleaning up beaches and salvaging fishing grounds in the wake of oil-well blowouts. . . .[7] A closely related criticism of

[7] Robert Lekachman, *National Income and the Public Welfare* (New York: Random House, 1972), p. 7.

the GDP is that it does not "net out" the value of natural resources used in production. Since such resources are not replenishable, their exhaustion through production should be taken into account. The basic problem is that the social value of the national output is necessarily a subjective matter, dependent on individual judgments concerning what ought to be. There are no simple, direct, or objective criteria for measuring the social value of the national output. It is essential, nevertheless, that the distinction between economic and social value be clear; the former is not always representative of the latter.

Economic versus Social Costs

Much of what we have said about economic and social values applies equally to economic and social costs. There is no necessary identity between the economic costs of producing the current national output and the social costs of the output. Economic costs include items such as factor costs, capital consumption allowances, and indirect business taxes, for which a monetary valuation is available. Social costs, on the other hand, relate to subjective and intangible phenomena such as the general deterioration of the physical and social environments as a result of productive activity. For example, the beauty of the countryside may be irreparably marred, as has often happened in mining and industrial areas; rivers and the atmosphere may be contaminated through the disposal of industrial wastes; and disease and crime-infested slums may result as a by-product of industrial growth and urbanization. These costs are not measured directly by gross domestic product figures. Nevertheless, social costs are as much a part of the real cost of the national output as the more readily measurable economic costs, but because of their subjective nature there are no obviously certain criteria for judging their magnitude. Their existence, though, should be recognized by the serious student of economics.[8]

There are indirect ways in which social costs will be reflected in gross domestic product and other output measures. First, the money spent for workers and other resources needed to repair environmental damage from the past will be reflected in the output figures for the period in which such expenditures are made. Existing techniques for national income accounting and measurement do not distinguish between expenditures of this type and other expenditures that reflect newly created goods and services. Second, the expenditures that are made to prevent further environmental deterioration or pollution also enter into gross domestic product accounting, although these expenditures do not directly increase either the quantity of goods and services we consume or our stock of capital instruments. Expenditures of this nature will grow rather than decrease in the future. Finally, and in a more subtle way, the social cost of environmental deterioration may show up in the higher wages needed

---

[8] A leading proponent of this viewpoint is the British economist E. J. Mishan. See his *The Cost of Economic Growth* (New York: Praeger, 1967).

to attract workers to deteriorating areas and in the growing congestion and higher taxes in areas to which people flee to escape depressing surroundings.

The Value of Leisure

In any analysis of the economic welfare or well-being of a nation, the amount of leisure time at people's disposal should rank high in importance; yet the national income and product statistics do not measure directly the value of leisure to society. Over the last half-century the length of the standard work-week has fallen from 60 or 70 hours to fewer than 40 hours—a development that represents a drastic improvement in welfare. This means, in part, that people have been willing to exchange relatively fewer goods and services for more leisure. One needs to be careful on this point, for no simple trade-off is involved. The reason, of course, is that the productivity of the work force—what an average worker can produce in a unit of time—has gone up, so it is possible to work less and yet enjoy the same or even a larger bundle of goods and services as compared with an earlier time. In this sense, GDP figures do not—they cannot—measure directly the value of leisure to a society. None-theless, a society that produces a larger volume of material goods and services with an equal or even smaller expenditure of human effort is better off.

Qualitative Changes in the National Output

The discussion of price indexes in Chapter 1 pointed out the need to eliminate the distortion produced by changes in the prices of goods and services entering into the national income product statistics if comparisons are to be made between the national outputs at different points in time. Unfortunately, it is not possible to make the same adjustments for changes in the quality of goods and services. It is possible, for example, that the economy might spend (in terms of constant dollars) about the same amount today as it did ten years ago for television sets, but today's set in a qualitative sense is a vastly different product from one produced ten years ago. In some instances, qualitative changes may be so great that for all practical purposes no basis exists for comparing the value of a product now being produced with the value of the same or a similar product in an earlier period. Currently, no satisfactory technique exists for taking into account qualitative changes in the income and product totals.

The Composition of Output

The various aggregates just discussed are limited as measures of economic welfare because they do not tell us much about the composition of the national output, except in the broad terms of consumption, investment, and govern-ment expenditure. The welfare implications of an increase in the national

Does GDP Measure Happiness?

National income and product statistics provide us with a comprehensive body of data for measuring material production and income. But do they measure happiness? Material well-being is no doubt essential for happiness, but it is no guarantee of happiness.

The quest for a "happiness" index is the quest for some indicator that will provide a better measure of social well-being and the quality of life than do current income and product measures. More than a century ago John Stuart Mill looked forward to a time when there would be no more "trampling, crushing, elbowing, and treading on each other's heels," characteristics, he thought, of a life of unbridled competition. So the search for a better quality of life and ways to measure it is not new.

Not long ago two well-known American economists—James Tobin and William Nordhaus, both of Yale University—developed an experimental measure of economic welfare, one designed to convert the conventional GDP figure into a better measure of economic welfare. They designated their measure MEW, an acronym for *measure of economic welfare.* Since consumption is presumably the main purpose of economic activity, Professors Tobin and Nordhaus believed that any statistic designed to measure economic welfare ought to be oriented toward consumption rather than production. Conventional national income data emphasize production more than consumption.

As the Johnson administration was leaving office at the end of the 1960s, the then Department of Health, Education, and Welfare (HEW) published *Toward a Social Report,* a document which urged that the government develop a set of social indicators and publish an annual *Social Report* modeled after the annual *Economic Report of the President.* Legislation to this effect was introduced into the Congress, but nothing came of it.

In a related vein, but at the opposite end of the spectrum, Jimmy Carter as a candidate for President in 1976 came up with the notion of a "Misery Index." This was the sum of the inflation and unemployment rates. Carter used this issue effectively in the 1976 campaign, but then it was used against him with devastating effect four years later when Ronald Reagan won the presidency.

No consensus has yet emerged among economists on either the desirability or form for some measure of social well-being. But existing measures of income and product are not the last word on how the economy is doing, and the quest for a "happiness" index will go on.

output (in constant dollars) cannot be assessed without some knowledge of the composition of that output. For example, real GDP in the United States rose sharply during World War II, yet it would be ridiculous to say that the whole of this increase represented an increase in our well-being. In addition, over long periods of time the composition of the national output may change drastically. Today, transportation by air is commonplace; sixty to seventy years ago, this kind of service did not exist. Thus, to evaluate fully the welfare implications of an increase in a society's real domestic product, it is necessary to know the composition of the product total and changes that may have taken place in this composition over relatively long periods of time.

The Distribution of the National Output

Although national income and product data serve as highly useful measures of the economy's overall productive performance, they do not tell us how the output total is distributed among the members of society. It is impossible, though, to ignore the distribution of output (and income) in any analysis of the welfare implications of a given level of economic activity. There are no wholly objective or purely scientific criteria for proper distribution of output and income in a society. Economists have largely taken themselves out of the "theoretical-philosophical question of how income ought to be distributed."[9] Nevertheless some economists argue, for example, that society's welfare will be increased if a thousand dollars is taken from a rich man and given to a poor sharecropper with four or five children. The difficulty in such arguments is that there are no objective criteria to tell how far to push such a proposition.[10] In any event, some knowledge of the actual distribution of income in society, and some ideas about how income ought to be distributed is necessary for an evaluation of the economy's performance in terms of economic welfare.

Income and Output per Capita

Finally, we must take into account changes in population as well as changes in real output totals if meaningful comparisons of economic welfare are to be made over time. A rise in real income will not bring an improvement in the material level of well-being if population grows at a faster rate than the output total. For many purposes it is desirable that the aggregate data of national output and income be reduced to a per capita basis before comparisons are made. For example, between 1959 and 1994 real GDP grew by 176 percent, whereas per capita GDP grew by only 89 percent.

Employment and Unemployment

Let us now turn to the matter of defining and measuring employment and unemployment in the economy. Historically, it was the enormous scarcity of jobs during the Great Depression of the 1930s that led Keynes and others to develop theories to explain aggregate economic behavior. For many people,

---

[9] Alice M. Rivlin, "Income Distribution—Can Economists Help?" *American Economic Review,* May 1975, p. 5.

[10] Ibid., p. 6.

the primary criterion of whether or not the economy is performing well is the availability of jobs for all persons seeking work. Consequently, the meaning of *employment* and *unemployment* needs to be examined carefully and fully.

The idea that employment is a proper and desirable objective of public policy gained widespread acceptance in the United States and most of the nations of Western Europe during and immediately following World War II. In the United States, the Employment Act of 1946 gave legislative sanction to the view that the federal government has a direct responsibility for the level of employment and income prevailing in the economy. The act specifically stated:

> The Congress hereby declares that it is the continuing policy and responsibility of the Federal Government to use all practicable means consistent with its needs and obligations and other essential considerations of national policy, with the assistance and cooperation of industry, agriculture, labor, and State and local governments, to coordinate and utilize all its plans, functions, and resources for the purpose of creating and maintaining, in a manner calculated to foster and promote free competitive enterprise and the general welfare, conditions under which there will be afforded useful employment opportunities, including self employment, for those able, willing, and seeking work, and *to promote maximum employment, production, and purchasing power.*[11]

The Meaning of Maximum Employment

Although the Employment Act made maximum employment an objective of public policy, it did not define precisely what constitutes a labor force employed to the maximum. Yet without some idea of the meaning of maximum employment, administration of the act in any practical sense is impossible. A good working definition is the absence of *involuntary unemployment.* This situation exists when all persons willing and able to work can find jobs at prevailing wages in their desired trade or occupation. If we let N' represent the labor force and N the actual level of employment, a condition of maximum employment exists whenever $N' - N$ approaches zero.

Note that the phrase "approaches zero" is used rather than "equals zero." This is because a condition in which *every* member of the labor force is at work never is attained in reality. In any society there will always be some *frictional unemployment,* which results whenever some people are temporarily out of work because of imperfections in the labor market. At any given time some workers will be in the process of changing jobs or occupations; others will be experiencing temporary layoffs because of the seasonal nature of their work, shortages of materials in some industries, or shifts in demand that reduce the need for some types of workers and increase the need for others.

---

[11] Employment Act of 1946, Public Law 304, 79th Congress (italics added). The act also established the three-person Council of Economic Advisers, directly under the President, and requires the President to make an annual economic report to the Congress. The council also makes an annual report to the President.

Through the 1960s the term "full employment" was generally used by economists and policymakers to describe a condition in which *frictional* unemployment was at a minimum. More recently, however, the phrases the "natural rate of unemployment" and "high employment" have come into use. This change in terminology resulted in part from the unprecedented inflation that plagued the economy in the 1970s and in part from the influence of Professor Milton Friedman on macroeconomic theory and policy. Professor Friedman and his followers believe that policy can influence nominal output and employment only over a short period of time. In the longer run, they argue, output and employment are determined by the economy's underlying "natural" forces embodied in the growth rates of technology, population, and the labor force.

What, then, is the natural rate of unemployment? The usual definition is that it is the minimal rate of unemployment attainable *without* an acceleration in the rate of inflation. This is also called the "nonaccelerating inflation rate of unemployment," or NAIRU for short. Note carefully that these definitions do not require a zero rate of inflation; they require only that the inflation rate not be increasing. If unemployment falls below the natural rate, job markets will be tight, labor will be scarce, and employers will bid up wages in order to get more labor. This, in turn, will cause prices to rise. On the other hand, when the unemployment rate rises above the natural rate, labor will be plentiful and there will be little or no pressure on wage rates and thus no upward pressure on the price level.

There is no agreed-on definition among economists of either the full or natural unemployment rate. The precise meaning attached to these concepts has evolved since the Employment Act made maximum employment an objective of public policy. Prior to the Kennedy presidency (1961–63), no administration attached a specific figure to the concept. In 1962, however, the Kennedy administration set a 4 percent unemployment rate as its interim maximum unemployment target. The Johnson administration (1963–68) continued to use this figure, but in the 1970s under Presidents Nixon and Ford the figure was gradually revised upward to 5.5 percent. This rate also appeared in the *Economic Reports* of the Carter administration, but during the Reagan presidency there was no commitment to any specific level of unemployment as representing full employment. In its 1990 economic report, the Bush administration suggested a value of 5.3 percent for NAIRU, but in subsequent economic reports avoided any reference to a desired unemployment rate. President Clinton's economists in their first economic report (1994) discussed the possibility that the natural rate of unemployment was rising, but did not specify what this rate was or ought to be.[12] It seems reasonably certain that the debate will continue among economists and policymakers over the precise numerical value that ought to be given to the concept of the full or natural unemployment rate.

---

[12] *Economic Report of the President,* 1990, p. 184; 1994, pp. 109–113.

Problems in Measuring Unemployment

So what are we to conclude from the foregoing? It is clear that there is no agreement among economists on a precise measure for the full or natural unemployment rate, irrespective of which term is used to describe a desirable job situation for the economy. It should also be clear that over the past quarter of a century or more, economists have been revising upward their estimates of the full or natural rate of unemployment. Noneconomists may suspect that political considerations enter to some extent into the matter, a point for which there is some justification because the *Economic Reports* are political as well as economic documents. Nevertheless—and granted that *every* Council will present the administration it serves in the best economic light possible—these *Reports* have been remarkably honest and accurate, especially in their statistical underpinnings.

If we look at the whole post-World War II period—the years from 1948 through 1994—we find that civilian unemployment averaged 5.7 percent of the labor force. Is this a good record? Certainly in contrast to the devastating experience of the 1930s, the record after World War II looks exceptionally good. In 1933, the low point of the Great Depression, unemployment stood at 24.9 percent of the civilian labor force: one worker out of every four was jobless. Even as late as 1939, 10 years after the crash of 1929, 17.2 percent of U.S. workers were without jobs.[13] If, however, we use a 4 to 5 percent unemployment rate as a benchmark for a full or natural job situation, the post-World War II record is less rosy. It was only during the Korean War (1950–53) and the Vietnam War (1966–69) that the unemployment rate fell below the 4 percent target set by the Kennedy administration. In 35 out of the 47 years since 1948 (74 percent of the time), unemployment was above 5 percent, and during 17 years in this period (36 percent of the time), the rate went above 6 percent.

The problem with averages such as the overall unemployment rate is that they often exclude as much as they reveal. Some segments of our society have never experienced anything that remotely resembles full employment, by whatever standard it is measured. Blacks and other nonwhite minorities as well as teenagers are in this category. The overall situation for women is less clear-cut, although from the mid-1950s through the 1970s, women, both white and nonwhite, had higher unemployment rates than white males. In these years, the unemployment rate for white males averaged 3.8 percent, white females 5.0 percent, and nonwhite females 8.8 percent. From 1980 through 1994, the unemployment situation took a turn for the better for white females, averaging 5.3 percent as compared with 5.5 percent for white males. For nonwhite females, however, the situation worsened, as their average unemployment rate jumped to 12.0 percent during these years.[14] The other bleak

---

[13] *Historical Statistics of the United States,* bicentennial ed., Vol. 1 (Washington, D.C.: U.S. Government Printing Office, 1975), p. 135.

[14] *Economic Report of the President,* 1995, p. 321.

fact is that nearly all the time in the years of prosperity that followed World War II, nonwhite minorities and teenagers confronted depression-like conditions in the nation's job markets.

Why this condition persists in good times and bad for these two groups (there is obviously some overlap) is by no means readily apparent. It has been suggested that somehow teenagers and minorities are less attached to the labor force and the idea of working, because many of the jobs available to both groups are not only low paying, but dead-end.[15] In a formal sense this view is embodied in the *dual labor market hypothesis,* which holds that the nation's labor market really consists of two basic markets—a *primary* sector and a *secondary* sector.[16] In the primary sector are the better-paying, preferred jobs, characterized by good working conditions, reasonable employment stability, and opportunities for advancement. Unemployment in this sector, when it occurs, is usually described as *cyclical* or Keynesian, in that it comes about when the economy falls into a recession or depression. In the secondary sector, the situation is quite different; there we find low pay, poor working conditions, frequent layoffs, high turnovers, and little opportunity for advancement. Workers in this sector frequently drift from one low-paying job to another. The kind of unemployment found in the secondary sector is called *structural,* a broad term which has come to mean unemployment that is not frictional and that persists even when times are good. Economists are by no means in agreement on the extent of such unemployment—obviously not all minority and teenage unemployment is of this nature—but there is considerable consensus that such unemployment is much more difficult to cure than the Keynesian variety. The fact that there have been such high rates of joblessness for minorities and teenagers in good times and bad ever since World War II attests to this.

More recently another type of structural unemployment has made an appearance in the economy. This has to do with a greater-than-normal displacement of workers in the goods-producing sector of the economy following the 1981–82 and 1990–91 recessions. The long-term trend in employment has been away from the goods-producing sectors (mining, construction, and manufacturing) to the services. In 1948, for example, 42 percent of the nonagricultural work force was employed in the goods-producing sectors. By 1994 this percentage had dropped to 20.7 percent.[17] The concern is with the fact that many of the workers displaced from higher-paying jobs in manufacturing during these recessions never regained those jobs during the following recoveries and expansions. Typically in almost every business downturn in the post-World War II period, there has been a sharp decline in jobs in manufacturing during the recession. The normal pattern has been for this job loss to

[15] Martin Feldstein, "The Economics of the New Unemployment," *The Public Interest,* Fall 1973, p. 14.

[16] Peter B. Doeringer and Michael J. Piore, "Unemployment and the 'Dual Labor Market,'" *The Public Interest,* Winter 1975, p. 70.

[17] *Economic Report of the President,* 1995, p. 324.

be regained by the time a new cyclical peak is reached, even though the long-term trend for goods-producing employment is down. But this did not happen in either the 1981–82 or 1990–91 recessions and subsequent recoveries. These displaced workers are among the new structurally unemployed. Some, of course, did find jobs in the service sectors, but since wages and weekly earnings are significantly lower in services, displacement meant a lowering of living standards for the workers involved.

Finally, comment is in order with respect to the fact that the official unemployment statistics, particularly the unemployment rate, may seriously underestimate the amount of actual unemployment. (See Table 2-3.) Primarily this is because the government does not count among the unemployed the so-called discouraged workers. These are people who want work but have, in effect, dropped out of the labor force because they do not believe that they can find work. It is only since the late 1960s that the Bureau of Labor Statistics of the U.S. Department of Labor began to count discouraged workers; reliable

TABLE 2–3 Official and Adjusted Unemployment for Civilian Workers: 1970–1994

Year	(1) Civilian Labor Force*	(2) Unem-ployment*	(3) Unem-ployment Rate	(4) Discouraged Workers*	(5) Adjusted Unem-ployment*	(6) Adjusted Unemployment Rate
1970	82,771	4,093	4.9%	639	4,732	5.7%
1971	84,340	5,016	5.9	778	5,794	6.9
1972	87,034	4,882	5.6	771	5,653	6.5
1973	89,429	4,365	4.9	689	5,054	5.7
1974	91,949	5,156	5.6	695	5,851	6.4
1975	93,775	7,929	8.5	1,093	9,022	9.6
1976	96,158	7,409	7.7	925	8,334	8.7
1977	99,009	6,991	7.1	1,026	8,017	8.1
1978	102,251	6,202	6.1	863	7,065	6.9
1979	104,962	6,137	5.8	771	6,908	6.6
1980	106,940	7,637	7.1	993	8,630	8.1
1981	108,670	8,273	7.6	1,103	9,376	8.6
1982	110,204	10,678	9.7	1,568	12,246	11.1
1983	111,550	10,717	9.6	1,641	12,358	11.1
1984	113,544	8,539	7.5	1,283	9,822	8.7
1985	115,461	8,312	7.2	1,204	9,516	8.2
1986	117,834	8,237	7.0	1,121	9,358	7.9
1987	119,865	7,425	6.2	1,026	8,451	7.1
1988	121,669	6,701	5.5	954	7,655	6.3
1989	123,869	6,528	5.3	859	7,387	6.0
1990	124,787	6,874	5.5	890	7,764	6.2
1991	125,303	8,426	6.7	941	9,367	7.5
1992	126,982	9,384	7.4	1,063	10,447	8.2
1993	128,040	8,734	6.8	974	9,708	7.6
1994	131,056	7,996	6.1	447	8,443	6.4

*Thousands of persons.

Sources: Economic Report of the President, 1995; U.S. Department of Labor, Bureau of Labor Statistics, Employment and Earnings, January issues.

data on their numbers exists only since 1970. If they are counted among the unemployed, as many economists think they should be, it makes an important difference in measuring unemployment.

Table 2–3 shows this difference. In the table, column 2 shows (in thousands of persons) the number unemployed as reported officially by the Bureau of Labor Statistics. Column 3 gives the official unemployment rate, which is obtained by dividing the number of unemployed persons by the civilian work force (column 1). Column 4 shows the number of discouraged workers for each year between 1970 and 1994. If we add this figure to the official number of unemployed persons for each year, we get an adjusted unemployment number (column 5), which now takes into account the phenomenon of discouraged workers. The final, adjusted unemployment rate is then obtained by dividing the adjusted unemployment figure by the figures for the civilian labor force. This is shown in column 6.

If we look at the whole period (1970 to 1994), we find that including discouraged workers in the data changes the unemployment picture significantly. On the basis of official statistics, unemployment averaged 6.6 percent for the period. When discouraged workers are figured into the calculation, the unemployment rate jumps by nearly a full percentage point to 7.6 percent. In terms of people this means that, on the average, more were unemployed during these two decades than reported in the official statistics.

There is yet another way in which the official statistics may understate actual unemployment. This comes from the Bureau of Labor Statistics' practice of counting as employed persons who work only part time but who would work full time if the opportunity were available. These numbers are not small. In the 1980s they averaged 5.3 million persons per year.[18] If the official unemployment rate were adjusted to reflect part-time workers seeking full-time employment, it would be even higher. To date, however, no formula has been devised to do this.

Employment and Output: The Production Function

The foregoing sections stressed that full or maximum employment for the nation's labor force has become a public policy objective of major significance in contemporary U.S. society. It is equally important to understand that a close link exists between the employment level and the output level. In other words, we can expect the amount of employment to vary more or less directly with the volume of production. Since the latter constitutes the real income of society, it follows that the employment level serves as an indicator of the economy's overall performance. Conversely, the output level is a good indicator of the prevailing employment situation in the economy. This, of

---

[18] *Current Economic Indicators,* April 1990, p. 11.

course, applies to the overall average, not the specific employment situation for any particular segment of the labor force at any given time.

The formal relationship between employment and ouput is expressed in the concept of the *production function*. This shows that the economy's output level (Y) depends on the use (or inputs) of labor (N), capital (K), and the existing level of technology (T). "Technology" is a catch-all term that represents everything that contributes to the effectiveness with which labor and capital are combined to produce useful goods and services. In a formal sense, the production function embodies the functional relationship between the quantity of input and the quantity of output. In the short run, it can be expressed symbolically as

$$Y = f(N,\ K,\ T). \qquad (2\text{--}6)$$

The concept of the production function is depicted graphically in Figure 2–3, which shows output on the vertical axis and labor input (people at work) on the horizontal axis. The output curve will eventually level off because of diminishing productivity. On the curve labeled Y_a, an increase in the income level from Y_1 to Y_2 results when employment increases from N_1 to N_2. The same increase in income may be obtained with no change in employment if the entire production function shifts upward to the level depicted by the curve Y_b. This would result from a change in the stock of capital and natural resources, a change in technology, or a combination of the two.

The foregoing discussion provides a basis for understanding the close theoretical relationship that exists between employment and output over short periods of time, during which it is assumed that the quantity of capital and

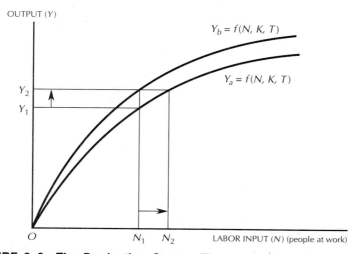

OUTPUT (Y)

$Y_b = f(N,\ K,\ T)$

$Y_a = f(N,\ K,\ T)$

Y_2
Y_1

O N_1 N_2 LABOR INPUT (N) (people at work)

FIGURE 2–3   The Production Curve. The curve shows that output (Y) increases but at a decreasing rate as more workers (N) are employed.

the level of technology remain relatively fixed. By implication, then, productive capacity is also relatively fixed.

There is no way to define precisely the length of real time involved in the short run, although a satisfactory working definition is that it is long enough to permit some cyclical fluctuations in income and employment, but not sufficiently long to show a definite trend. The significant factor for our analysis is that the short run is not a long enough period of time to permit any really significant changes in the economy's productive capacity. Consequently, we may assume that the underlying determinants of capacity in Equation (2–6) have relatively fixed magnitudes, although the extent to which they are actually utilized in production is variable. This is particularly true with respect to the labor force, because the level of employment N can quite obviously depart rather widely at times from the size of the labor force. For the economy as a whole, the output level Y will tend to vary in the short run directly with the employment level N. Thus, a good workable hypothesis is

$$Y = f(N). \tag{2–7}$$

In this formulation the level of employment N has meaning not only in relation to the overall supply of labor (N'), but also as a barometer of the extent to which the economy's productive capacity is actually being utilized. In the chapters that follow we will make frequent use of this simple but important notion that over relatively short periods of time employment and real income move together.

Summary

1. The comprehensive system of national income and product statistics developed over the last two-thirds of a century has been a major achievement of macroeconomics.

2. Income and wealth are distinct concepts: income is a *flow* phenomenon, measuring what happens over time, and wealth is a *stock* phenomenon, measuring the amount of material things in existence at a point in time. For economic analysis, capital goods are the most important form of wealth.

3. The concept of wealth as applied to human beings involves seeing the education, knowledge, and skills possessed by people as a form of human capital.

4. The basic relationship between wealth and income is that, to add to the stock of wealth, a part of income must be saved and invested. This is true for all societies.

5. Gross domestic product (GDP) is defined as the current market value of all final goods and services produced by the economy during an income period.

6. Net national product (NNP) is obtained by subtracting capital consumption allowances from the GDP.

7. The national income (NI) is defined as the factor cost of the net national product. It can be obtained by summing up all factor costs—wages, interest, rents, and profits—or by deducting indirect business taxes from the NNP.

8. Personal income (PI) is the sum of money income from all sources that goes to persons or households. It is obtained by subtracting from the national income, income earned by the factors of production but not actually paid out, and adding in transfer payments.

9. Disposable income (DI) is equal to personal income less all taxes paid by persons and households. It measures income available for consumption or saving.

10. All income measures are subject to important limitations, including the fact that they measure only economic gains and costs. They do not adequately measure the value of leisure, the quality of output, or the distribution of the national output.

11. The Employment Act of 1946 was a watershed measure that explicitly made the federal government responsible for attaining satisfactory levels of employment and minimizing unemployment.

12. Full employment and the natural rate of unemployment are important concepts, usually defined in terms of a percentage of the labor force not working. There is no agreement among economists on the precise percentage of the labor force unemployed that represents the maximum level of employment specified in the 1946 Employment Act.

13. There is a close correlation between output (Y) and the level of employment (N); the two rise and fall together. The production function is the formal, theoretical expression of this relationship.

Appendix

The various component parts of the national output can be linked together in a series of *identity equations.* An identity equation defines one variable in terms of other variables; it is an equation asserting an equality that is true by definition. Such equations are normally derived by taking a total (or aggregate) and expressing it as the sum of its parts. Identity equations are to be contrasted with *behavior equations,* which express a relationship between variables. Behavior equations are not necessarily true in the same sense as identity equations. They are a mathematical statement of a hypothesis concerning economic behavior, and consequently, the relationships involved in such equations are causal in nature.

For a series of identity equations that describe how the component parts of the national output fit together, the following symbols are used:

Y = the national output, or national income

I = investment expenditures (output of investment goods)

I_f = net foreign investment (net exports, or $X - M$)

C = consumption expenditures (output of consumer goods and services)

S = saving

G = government expenditures for goods and services (output of community or collective goods)

X = export expenditures (domestic output that is exported)

M = import expenditures (foreign output that is imported)

TR = transfer expenditures

TX = taxes

Start with a highly simplified economic system with no government and no economic ties with any other nation. In this hypothetical system, the origin and disposition of income can be expressed symbolically as

$$Y \equiv C + I, \qquad (A2-1)$$

$$Y \equiv C + S. \qquad (A2-2)$$

Equation (A2–1) states that output (income) originates from expenditures for consumption goods and services and investment goods. Equation (A2–2) expresses the idea that income created in the productive process must be either consumed or not consumed (that is, saved).

From these equations we can derive a third equation showing the identity between saving and investment. Since income and consumption are common terms in both of the above equations, it follows that investment and saving must be equal to one another. Thus,

$$I \equiv S. \qquad (A2-3)$$

The above identities are *ex post* equations because they are descriptive of that which exists or is actual; they do not in any way describe economic behavior in what is called an intended, planned, or *ex ante* sense. This is what *behavior* equations do. It should be recognized that these two magnitudes must be identical in an *ex post* sense because of the way in which they are defined, but this does not mean that the amounts saved and the amounts invested in the economy in any specific income period always coincide with the amounts that firms or persons *intended* to save and invest.

We can proceed closer to reality in the development of our identity equations by adding government. We will retain for the moment, however, the assumption that our economy has no relationships with other economies; in other words, it is a *closed* economy. Assume, too, that the only function of our government is to provide for collective goods and services; it does not engage in transfer expenditures. On the basis of this set of assumptions, we have the following identities:

$$Y \equiv C + I + G, \tag{A2-4}$$

$$Y \equiv C + S + TX, \tag{A2-5}$$

$$S + TX \equiv I + G, \tag{A2-6}$$

$$S \equiv I + (G - TX). \tag{A2-7}$$

Equation (A2–4) means that output consists of consumption goods and services, investment goods, and collective goods. Equation (A2–5) relates to the disposition of income and shows that with the introduction of government a third alternative is now available for the disposition of current income, namely, taxes. The economic effect of taxes is similar to saving because taxes also represent a nonexpenditure of current income for consumption goods and services.

Equation (A2–6) is a modification of the saving-investment identity. Saving plus taxes, both of which are leakages from the current income stream, are equal to investment plus government expenditures for goods and services. Reversing the identity, investment and government expenditures are offsets to leakages in the form of saving and taxes. Equation (A2–7) transfers taxes to the right-hand side of the equation and shows that saving is equal to investment *plus* the government deficit or *minus* the government surplus. The terms "deficit" and "surplus" as used here refer to the current income and product transactions of *all* governmental units (federal, state, and local) in the economy.

Now we drop the assumptions of a closed economy and of no transfer expenditures. When we drop these assumptions, the structure of the identity equations becomes realistic and describes accurately how the component parts of the national output fit together. This gives us the following identity equations:

$$Y \equiv C + I + G + X - M, \tag{A2-8}$$

$$I_f \equiv X - M, \tag{A2-9}$$

$$Y \equiv C + I + G + I_f, \tag{A2-10}$$

$$Y \equiv C + S + TX - TR, \tag{A2-11}$$

$$S + TX - TR \equiv I + G + I_f, \tag{A2-12}$$

$$S \equiv I + G + I_f - (TX - TR). \tag{A2-13}$$

Equation (A2–8) is essentially the same as Equation (A2–4), except that we have now added expenditures for exports and subtracted expenditures for imports. Since the difference between exports and imports is equal to net foreign investment, as in Equation (A2–9), the basic identity equation describing the origin of output and income takes the form shown in Equation (A2–10).

The existence of transfer expenditures means that we must modify the equation describing the disposition of income to take such transfers into account. This is done in Equation (A2–11), in which transfer expenditures are subtracted from taxes. Since transfers are, in effect, negative taxes, they offset taxes as a leakage from the current income stream. Moreover, once we have introduced transfers into the system, they must be deducted from the components on the right-hand side of the disposition of income equation, or else they would be counted twice. This is the case because transfer expenditures are income to the recipients of such expenditures, and as such can be a source of consumption expenditures, saving, or tax payments just as much as income derived from the process of production. Thus, transfer expenditures will be reflected in consumption, saving, and taxes, in Equation (A2–11), showing the disposition of current income.

Finally, the basic saving-investment identity is modified to take into account net foreign investment, which offsets not only saving and taxes in the same manner as investment and government expenditures, but also the effect of transfer expenditures on the deficit or surplus of the public sector with respect to income and product transactions. Thus, saving plus net taxes ($TX - TR$) is equal to investment plus net foreign investment and government expenditures for goods and services in Equation (A2–12). If net taxes are shifted to the right-hand side of this equation, the basic identity equation relating saving and investment takes the form shown in Equation (A2–13).

The Basic Theory of Income and Employment

The Classical System

H AVING DISCUSSED THE main measures of economic performance—output, employment, price level, and trade balance—in Chapters 1 and 2, we now turn to the task of developing a basic theory about what determines these measures and how they interact with one another. We shall proceed in historical sequence and look in this chapter at how the classical economists of the nineteenth century explained output and other macroeconomic variables and in Chapters 4 to 6 at the twentieth-century Keynesian framework. The classical system discussed in this chapter is still alive in the monetarist, new classical economics, and real business cycle challenges to the Keynesian view.

Functional Relationships in Economics

Before discussion of the classical model, it is important to stress three ideas that provide a common thread for economic analysis at *all* levels, whether micro or macro. The first idea is that important economic relationships are normally expressed in functional form. The idea of a functional relationship between economic quantities is essential to an understanding of economic analysis. In fact, this is perhaps the most important single concept the reader can grasp. If one understands clearly the nature of the functional idea, the way to a thorough comprehension of economic analysis is open.

A functional relationship exists between two variables when they are related in such a way that the value of one depends uniquely on the value of the other. Such a relationship can be expressed in equation form as

$$y = f(x). \tag{3--1}$$

This equation reads ''*y* is a function of *x*.'' It means, simply, that the variable expressed by the letter *y* is related in a systematic and dependable way to the value represented by the letter *x*. In this relationship, *y* is the dependent variable and *x* is the independent variable. The concept of a functional relationship enables us to express symbolically (that is, in mathematical form) the essence of a particular economic theory.

Functional relationships are also depicted as schedules. Technically, a schedule is an array showing all the possible values for the variables involved in a functional relationship. One of the earliest ideas that many students encounter in the principles of economics course is that of a demand schedule. The term ''schedule'' is used to describe the data of a functional relationship arrayed in tabular form, whereas the term ''curve'' refers to the graphic representation of a schedule. This is the usage followed in this text.

An important point about the fact that functional relationships are shown as schedules or curves pertains to change and how it is treated in economics. Whenever we confront functional relationships in the form of curves, two kinds of changes can be analyzed. There can be *movement* along a given curve, which means that the dependent variable is changing because the independent variable has changed. There can also be a *shift* in the entire curve; this involves a different set of values for both the dependent and the independent variables in the functional relationship.

The second idea concerns the sense in which the variables found in functional relations in economics are measured. In Chapter 2 (page 40) it was explained that economists define and measure economic variables in either an *ex ante* or an *ex post* sense. An economic schedule or curve is an *ex ante* construct; this means that the values for the economic variables shown in the schedule or curve are intended or expected, not actual, values. They represent values that become actual—or realized—only *if* certain things happen.

For example, the typical supply schedule for a commodity as depicted in microeconomic analysis shows how much of the commodity will be supplied at various possible prices. Price is the condition that determines how much of the commodity will be supplied in a particular market. Such a schedule is *ex ante* in the sense that it depicts the intended responses of suppliers to different possible prices for the commodity. A price that brings a particular quantity of the commodity to the market is called the *supply price* for that quantity of the commodity. A supply schedule, therefore, is a series of supply prices for varying amounts of a commodity. This concept of a supply price is especially important for the construction of the aggregate supply schedule used in the Keynesian aggregate supply and aggregate demand model.

The third idea is that the curves used most widely in economic analysis involve demand and supply. This is elementary but fundamental. Demand and supply curves are the analytical tools used by economists at all levels of analysis. Values for the important economic magnitudes that are of prime interest to economists—individual prices, the level of employment, the size of output, to name but a few—are determined by an interaction between demand and supply curves. This is true for both micro- and macroeconomics. Supply and demand analysis is thus the thread that ties all economics together.

Classical Economics before Keynes

"Classical economics" is the term used to describe the system of economic analysis developed in England in the late eighteenth and early nineteenth centuries, a system which stood largely intact until the 1930s as the main body of economic principles accepted by economists.[1] As indicated in footnote 1, there is a technical distinction between classical and neoclassical economics. But this is not important for the purposes of this text. We shall use the term "classical" essentially as Keynes used it, namely to describe pre-1930s theorizing about the determinants of output, employment, and the price level. Before Keynes, an explicit classical macroeconomic theory did not exist. It was implicit, however, in the writings of the classical economists, but until *The General Theory* described the assumptions and relationships that the classical economists believed determined the overall output and employment level, economics did not have a clear, classical, macroeconomic model.[2] The overall tenor of pre-Keynesian, classical economic thought is best exemplified in Alfred Marshall's *Principles of Economics*. By the time of Marshall, the dominant thrust of the theories and concepts that made up classical economics was to explain how an economy organized on the basis of free, competitive markets and the private ownership of land and manufactured capital is supposed to work. The prime objective of classical analysis was to show how through markets an economic system so organized establishes prices for everything that is produced and prices for the resources re-

[1] This is how John Maynard Keynes in *The General Theory of Employment, Interest and Money* used the term "classical economics." The term itself, according to Keynes, was invented by Karl Marx to describe the ideas of David Ricardo and his predecessors. Strictly speaking, economic theory before Keynes can be divided into ideas developed by the classical economists as just described, and the theory developed by the neoclassical economists, those economists who came after Ricardo and before Keynes.

[2] In Chapter 2 of *The General Theory*, Keynes set forth what he regarded as the essential postulates of the classical economist. By doing this, Keynes, in effect, "invented" classical macroeconomics; ever since, the models of classical economics found in textbooks have built on his analysis.

quired so that production can take place, how efficiency in the use of resources is obtained, and how the material welfare or well-being of all participants in the system is maximized.

Classical economics rested on two major assumptions, both of which are important for an understanding of the recent resurgence of classical views. The first was that the economy is dominated by the kind of rigorous competition that denies any control over prices to either the sellers of goods and services or the sellers of the services of economic resources. This is what modern textbooks describe as pure competition. The social function of competition is to ensure that the free play of self-interest in the commodity and resource markets will lead to results that are desirable for the whole economy. Adam Smith, the father of modern economic analysis, was the first economist to develop the concept of a self-adjusting market economy. In such an economy *all* wages and prices are flexible. In the *Wealth of Nations* he made his famous statement to the effect that every producer, in seeking to promote his own gain, is led by "an invisible hand to promote an end that was no part of his intention."[3] Smith's "invisible hand" working through markets harnessed personal greed (the pursuit of self-interest) to the social good (the maximum production of the things people want). This was a magnificent, intellectual *tour de force.*

The second underlying assumption of the classical economists was that people are rational. Rationality to the classical economists meant essentially the pleasure-pain calculus. In all activities, including those pertaining to economics, people would rationally attempt to order their affairs so as to maximize pleasure and minimize pain. The balancing of pleasure against pain, or gain against cost, is, according to the classical view, the strategic, motivating force in the economic system. As consumers, people attempted to maximize the satisfaction derived from the expenditure of income, whereas as resource owners or entrepreneurs, people sought to maximize the return obtained from the sale of the goods and resources at their disposition. On the basis of this sweeping assumption concerning human nature, the classical economists constructed through deductive logic an elegant and complex structure of economic analysis, much of which remains in use. The rationality postulate is the key to an understanding of the theory of *rational expectations,* a foundation stone to the new classical economics.

Three Propositions

Embodied in the classical analysis of how markets organize economic activity through competition and the pursuit of self-interest is a theory of employment (and output) and a theory of resource allocation and income distribution. Classical employment theory consists of three basic propositions. First, the

---

[3] Adam Smith, *An Inquiry into the Nature and Causes of the Wealth of Nations,* Cannan ed. (New York: Modern Library, 1937), p. 423.

level of employment is determined by the total demand for and supply of labor. A corollary to this is that, once employment is determined, output is also determined because how much is produced depends on the number of people at work. The production function as shown in Chapter 2 explains this: as labor inputs go up, so does output. In classical macroeconomic theory the labor market is really the labor market for the individual business firm writ large and applied to the whole economy. Practically speaking, the classical school regarded the full employment of labor as a normal state for the economy—a proposition mocked by the mass unemployment confronting the economy in the 1930s.

The second classical proposition involves Say's law of markets, which we sketched out in Chapter 1. Even though the level of employment is determined by the total demand for and supply of labor, and this level utilizes all workers seeking work, the possibility exists that the output produced with this labor might not be sold. In its simplest form, Say's law asserts that "supply creates its own demand," which means that every act of production creates income and therefore demand equal to the value of that production. No general overproduction is possible. In a crude form, Say's law is valid in a barter economy, since no person would bring goods to market except to exchange them for other goods. In an economy that uses money, matters are not so simple. Production generates money income for the producers, but one of the virtues of money is that one does not have to spend it immediately. Thus, in a money-using economy, the possibility exists that some income arising from production may not be spent immediately; it might, in other words, be saved. Classical economics got around this problem by adding a corollary to Say's law, namely, a theory that links the supply of savings to the rate of interest and the latter to borrowing by the business executive to purchase new capital goods, that is, structures and equipment. Therefore, if more is saved, interest rates will fall, and more borrowing and spending for real capital will take place. If less is saved, the reverse will happen. The essential point is that, in the classical theory, *saving cannot cause a decline in spending and thus be responsible for more being produced than can be sold.* Assuming that all savings are supplied to businesses for investment, Say's law works in a money-using economy as well as in a barter economy. This was the classical view, echoes of which are heard today in the argument that the economy is suffering from a shortage of saving.

This brings us to the third classical proposition, which is about the role of money in the theory. Basically, money's purpose is to make the economy more efficient by avoiding the clumsiness of barter. Money serves, primarily, as a medium of exchange; that is to say it is generalized purchasing power readily convertible into almost anything. Therefore, any change in the amount of money will lead to more or less spending, but since resources are normally fully employed, more or less spending affects the price level primarily. The idea that prices are linked directly to the money supply is the quantity theory of money, discussed in Chapter 1.

Jean Baptiste Say

A French economist, Jean Baptiste Say (1767–1832) gained fame for two reasons. During his lifetime he was widely regarded, especially in Europe, as a popularizer of the ideas of Adam Smith. Joseph Schumpeter in his masterful *History of Economic Analysis* says that Say also made many original contributions. One of them is Say's law of markets. In his 1803 work, *A Treatise on Political Economy,* he said:

> . . . that a product is no sooner created, than it, that instant, affords a market for other products to the full extent of its own value. When a producer has put the finishing hand to the product, he is most anxious to sell it immediately, lest its value should vanish in his hands. Nor is he less anxious to dispose of the money he may get for it; for the value of money is also perishable. But the only way of getting rid of money is in the purchase of some product or other. Thus, the mere circumstances of the creation of one product immediately opens a vent for other products. . . . *

Say's law is usually given simply as: *Supply creates its own demand.* The meaning is that every act of production necessarily creates sufficient purchasing power to buy back that production. Hence, a general overproduction, or glut of goods, is impossible.

In spite of the Keynesian attack on Say's law (Chapter 4), the "law" is by no means defunct. Say's law played a central role in George Gilder's 1981 work, *Wealth and Poverty,* which argued that "The essential thesis of Say's Law remains true: supply creates demand. There can be no such thing as a general glut of goods. . . . Private savings . . . *are* invested."[†] Gilder's book, in the eyes of many observers, provided much of the theoretical rationale for the Reagan economic program; this shows that, for good or for evil, Say's law is by no means a relic of history.

*Treatise on Political Economy, 6th ed., Book I, Chap. 15, p. 1836.
[†] *Wealth and Poverty* (New York: Basic Books, 1981), p. 39.

Combining the foregoing propositions with competitive markets and the free play of self-interest by business executives, workers, and consumers gives us *all* the necessary ingredients for a self-regulating economic system, one which employs resources fully and in the most efficient way possible. The logical, or "natural," policy conclusion derived from this view is that of *laissez faire,* or noninterference by government in the running of the economy. Classical economics thus did what good economic theory should do: It explained (how employment, output, and prices were determined), it predicted (full employment would be the norm), and it prescribed (governments should keep their hands off the economy).

The Formal Classical Model

The key propositions of classical employment theory discussed above come together in a formal model. We shall construct this model first as a series of simple algebraic equations that sum up the key elements in classical theory and second as a diagram that draws these elements together. The formal classical model embodies the labor market, a theory linking both saving and investment to the rate of interest, and a theory of the price level. The theory that links saving and investment is essential to preserve the working of Say's law in a money-using economy. Before examining each of these theoretical building blocks for classical macroeconomics, we need to look at some of the microeconomic roots for classical theorizing about employment.

Some Microeconomic Foundations for Classical Analysis

To grasp how the classical economists developed an explanation of the overall employment level using schedules for the *aggregate* demand for and supply of labor, we must examine some basic propositions drawn from traditional economic analysis pertaining to the business firm and its behavior. There are two such key propositions: the concept of the individual firm's production function (including the notion of diminishing productivity) and the principle of profit maximization.

Let us begin with the individual firm's production function. If we assume, as classical analysis does, that the quantity and quality of capital and natural resources as well as the level of technology are fixed,[4] then the output of the individual firm will depend on the quantity of labor it employs. At this point the profit maximization principle enters the picture. Classical economics assumes that entrepreneurs always attempt to maximize profits; consequently, entrepreneurs will be guided by the profit maximization principle in the use of labor. Essential to the most profitable use of labor is the principle of *diminishing returns* or *diminishing productivity.*

According to the principle of diminishing productivity, the additional product resulting from the employment by the firm of additional units of labor will become smaller and smaller as the total labor used increases. In more technical language this principle means that in response to increased employment, the *marginal physical product* of additional units of labor will decline. What interests a firm is the yield that results from the employment of additional amounts of labor. This depends not only on the additional output it gets from additional labor, that is, the marginal physical product, but also on the price at which the additional units of output are sold. For the sake of sim-

---

[4] This is a standard assumption made in microeconomic analysis for the short run, that is, a period in which plant size is fixed and output varies only within the confines of the existing plant size.

plicity, let us assume a firm operates in a purely competitive market. Insofar as the firm is concerned, this means that all output can be sold at a constant price. Because of diminishing marginal productivity, though, the *value* of the firm's marginal physical product will inevitably decline as more labor is employed.

Profit maximization requires that each firm adjust its level of operations to the point at which the value of additional output is just equal to the cost of that output. When this principle is applied to employment, it means that a firm should adjust its employment to that point at which the cost for the last units of labor hired is just equal to the value of the marginal physical product of that labor. If this is done, the firm will be in a position of equilibrium in employing labor. The cost to a firm of the additional (or marginal) amounts of employment depends on the number of additional workers hired and the prevailing money wage. Thus, a firm's equilibrium position with respect to the employment it is willing to offer in a purely competitive situation is one in which the marginal physical product of the last workers hired multiplied by the price at which the product sells is equal to the number of workers in the last group hired multiplied by the money wage at which they are hired. With these microeconomic ideas as a backdrop, let us now turn the discussion to the three key theoretical propositions in classical employment theory.

The Labor Market

The classical theory of the labor market consists of the demand for and supply of labor and the production function. Employment is determined by the interaction of the demand for and supply of labor, and output through the production function is determined by the employment level. As will be explained shortly, the latter is normally a full-employment level. In equation form we have the following:

$$N_d = f(w/p) \qquad \text{The demand for labor} \qquad (3–2)$$

$$N_s = g(w/p) \qquad \text{The supply of labor} \qquad (3–3)$$

$$N_d = N_s \qquad \text{Equilibrium in the labor market} \qquad (3–4)$$

$$Y = f(N, K, T) \qquad \text{The production function} \qquad (3–5)$$

In the above equations, w is the money wage, p is the price level, N is the level of employment, K is the stock of capital, and T is technology. In Equation (3–5) the stock of capital and technology are given; therefore, output (Y) depends on the level of employment.

In the classical analysis both the demand for and the supply of labor are a function of the *real wage* (w/p). The real wage represents the purchasing power of the money wage and in a competitive economy is the value of the marginal product of labor. Classical economics also rests on the maximizing postulate, namely, that individuals in their economic behavior seek to maximize their satisfaction or gain. For the business executive this means maximizing profit, and for the worker (or consumer) it means maximizing the satisfaction to be obtained through consumption.[5] The real wage (w/p) enters into both the demand for and supply of labor curves through the maximization postulate. The real wage is also designated W.

When business executives hire labor (or use more of any resource), they will employ more labor up to the point at which the marginal product of the last unit of labor hired is just equal to the real wage. This is how the gain from the use of labor is maximized. Because of the economic law of diminishing marginal productivity,[6] when more labor is employed, the added product from additional units of labor will decline. Normally, too, the price at which additional units of output can be sold will decline. Thus, the real wage (w/p) must decline if the business firm is to use more labor. By applying this relationship to the whole economy, the classical economists derived an aggregate demand curve for labor that slopes downward to the right. The demand for labor N_d is, in other words, an inverse function of the real wage (w).

By application of the maximization postulate to the supply of labor, the classical economists derived their aggregate supply curve for labor. Just as the business executive seeks to maximize gain from the employment of labor, workers in offering their labor services seek to maximize their incomes. Since the real wage reflects the purchasing power of the money wage, maximizing their incomes will also maximize the satisfactions derived from consumption. In the classical view, furthermore, work is irksome, involving "disutility." Therefore, the utility (satisfaction) of the real wage must overcome the disutility (irksomeness) of work if more people are to be employed. Consequently, the classical aggregate supply curve for labor slopes upward to the right; this shows that the supply of labor (N_s) is a direct function of the real wage (w).

The functional relationship between the supply of labor and the real wage is also based on the classical assumption that workers and other resource owners do not suffer from the *money illusion*. The term "money illusion" was coined by the American economist Irving Fisher and refers to "a failure to perceive that the dollar or any other unit of money expands and shrinks in value."[7] In other words, the monetary unit is believed to be stable in value, and thus a rise in money income is considered, *ipso facto,* a rise in real income. In an economy suffering from the money illusion, the supply of labor

---

[5] For the economy as a whole, if we assume the short run and labor as the only variable input, the marginal product of labor is equal to $\Delta Y/\Delta N$ (the Greek letter Δ stands for "a change in"). The monetary value of the last unit of output (ΔY) produced by the last unit of labor hired (ΔN) is equal to ΔYp. The cost to the employer of the last unit of labor hired is equal to ΔNw. Therefore, the profit maximization principle requires that $\Delta Yp = \Delta Nw$. By rearranging this equation, we get $\Delta Y/\Delta N = w/p$. This is essentially how Keynes in *The General Theory* described the classical demand for labor.

[6] For a more detailed discussion of the concept of diminishing marginal productivity, see Edwin Mansfield, *Microeconomics*, 8th ed. (New York: Norton, 1994), pp. 186ff.

[7] Irving Fisher, *The Money Illusion* (New York: Adelphi, 1928), p. 4.

could just as easily be a function of the money wage as the real wage. But this is not the classical view of the matter. Money, to the classical economist, is fundamentally a medium of exchange, a means to an end; classical economists thought the use of money should not obscure the fact that basically the economic process is concerned with an exchange of goods for goods. Money is significant only because it is more convenient to have a generally accepted medium of exchange than it is to resort to barter. The implication of such a view is that resource owners, including workers, will value the services of their resources in terms of the real returns they can command. Further, money does not affect actual output, so money in the classical view is said to be neutral.

Figure 3–1 shows both the classical demand and supply curves for labor and how the interaction between these two curves determines the level of employment in the economy. The equilibrium employment level depicted in Figure 3–1 must be one of full employment. If any unemployment (aside from frictional unemployment) exists after equilibrium is obtained, it has to be voluntary. This is true for two reasons. First, the classical analysis implies that if nonfrictional unemployment persists after the equilibrium situation, it is because some workers are demanding wages too high in relation to the marginal productivity of labor. These workers are unemployed because of

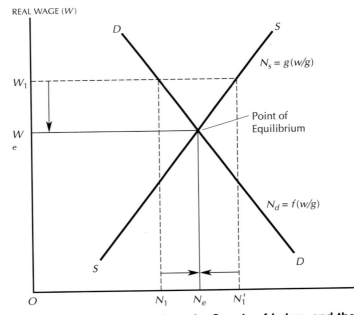

FIGURE 3–1   The Demand for Labor, the Supply of Labor, and the Equilibrium Level of Employment.   If the real wage (W) is at the level W_1, then the quantity of labor demanded (ON_1) will fall short of the quantity supplied ON_1'. Thus, the real wage will fall and labor demanded and labor supplied will shift to an equilibrium.

their refusal to accept lower money wages; their unemployment must be regarded as voluntary. If they would accept a reduction in money wages, the real wage would decline, other things being equal, and more employment would be forthcoming.

The second reason why the employment level is one of full employment is simply that the classical theory maintains that *money* wage bargains between workers and entrepreneurs determine the *real* wage; consequently, the workers in general are in a position to determine their real wage (through money wage bargains), and therefore, the level of employment. If this is true, it necessarily follows that any unemployment that exists at a given level of real wages has to be voluntary unemployment, frictional unemployment aside.

The Concept of Equilibrium

Figure 3–1 illustrates one of the oldest and most important ideas used in economic analysis—the concept of an equilibrium. It is an idea borrowed from the physical sciences, where it describes a situation in which there is a balance between opposing forces. When this happens, the system of which the opposing forces are a part achieves a state in which any action taking place will repeat itself continuously. For example, the motion of the earth around the sun or the moon around the earth represents a system in a state of balance, so that the earth stays in its orbit around the sun or the moon in its orbit around the earth.

Equilibrium in a market situation treats economic phenomena as analogous to physical forces; they interact with one another in such a way that they tend toward a state of balance. It is not a situation without motion, for an equilibrium price means that the inflow into the market (quantity supplied) is just equal to the outflow (quantity demanded). As long as there is no change in the balance between these two forces, price will not change. In Figure 3–1 the inflow is the supply of labor services and the outflow is the demand for the services of labor. Economists call such a situation *static equilibrium,* one in which there is no change over time in the underlying balance of forces in the system.

Equilibrium is a useful device in analyzing the many different types of situations encountered in the real-world economy. But it should not be confused with reality. It is rare, if ever, that we find a situation in the real world in which the economic forces are so precisely balanced that observed variables such as price, wages, income, production, and others remain fixed in their magnitude for a long period of time. Rather, equilibrium is an intellectual tool which can help us to understand how changes take place whenever any of the economic forces responsible for the outcome of economic events are disturbed. For example, we draw on the equilibrium concept to show how and in what direction a price may change because the demand for the good or service being priced has changed. The reader will be saved much misunderstanding if he or she remembers that fundamentally equilibrium is a helpful concept but it is not reality.

Say's Law and the Classical Theory of Interest

Output (Y) in classical theory is determined via the production function and depends on what happens in the labor market. As we have seen, involuntary unemployment is impossible in this situation, given the nature of the classical demand and supply schedules for labor. But there remains the possibility that some of the output produced by the fully employed labor force will not be sold, that there may be a glut of goods. This means that total demand may not be sufficient to clear the market of all goods produced. Say's law, however, makes this impossible; it asserts that every act of production in effect constitutes a demand for something. There is no problem with Say's law in a barter economy. But once money is introduced into the picture, difficulties may ensue. In a money-using economy, production normally generates sufficient income in the aggregate to buy back what is produced. To this extent Say's law holds when money enters the picture. But when we resort to the use of money rather than barter, a loophole opens. This is because a part of money income can be saved rather than spent; if this happens, demand for what is produced (spending) may turn out to be less than the money income generated by production (supply). At this point the classical theory of interest enters the picture to save the situation.

Saving, Investment, and the Rate of Interest

By making both saving (S) and investment (I) functions of the rate of interest, the integrity of Say's law in a money-using society is preserved. Saving via changes in the rate of interest will always translate into more or less investment spending. Thus, there cannot be any interruption to the flow of spending (demand) because of saving. The rate of interest in classical thought is the nexus that unites decisions to abstain from consumption, that is, to save, with decisions to provide for future consumption, that is, to invest.[8] As long as this is the case, Say's law is intact. In equation form we may summarize these ideas as follows:

$$S = g'(i) \qquad \text{The supply of saving} \qquad (3\text{--}6)$$

$$I = f'(i) \qquad \text{The demand for saving for investment} \qquad (3\text{--}7)$$

$$I = S \qquad \text{Equilibrium of saving and investment} \qquad (3\text{--}8)$$

Figure 3–2 presents geometrically classical thinking with respect to the rate of interest. In the figure, DD is the demand for investible resources, while SS is saving, or the supply of investible resources. Since saving is nonconsumption, the act of saving releases resources from the production of consumer goods and services. The demand for these resources is similar to the

---

[8] Keynes, *The General Theory,* p. 21.

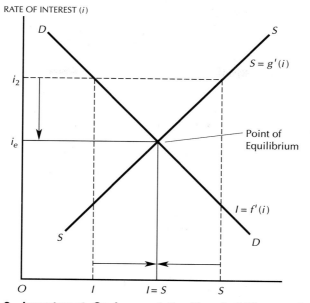

RATE OF INTEREST (i)

FIGURE 3–2   **Investment, Saving, and the Classical Theory of Interest.**   If the supply of saving exceeds demand, which happens at an interest rate of i_2, interest will fall; this will reduce the supply of savings and increase the demand for saving. Eventually, the market will reach equilibrium.

demand for any economic resource; that is to say it depends basically on the productivity of the resource. Thus, the *DD* schedule in Figure 3–2 has its origins in the productivity of capital.

The productivity of capital is one of the key ideas in the entire fabric of classical economic thinking. Capital is not important only as a form of spending that must, in a money-using economy, offset saving if Say's law is to hold. It is also important because it is the chief means by which the economy progresses, the instrument for ensuring economic growth and the enhancement of the material standard of life. Capital is wanted because it is productive, which is to say that the investment of resources in equipment and structures will yield an enlarged flow of output in the future. These aspects of the classical view of capital and its importance are analyzed in Chapter 8, which focuses on investment, productivity, and economic growth.

According to Figure 3–2, if individuals, households, and business firms attempt to save more out of current income than business firms want to spend for new capital equipment at the prevailing market rate of interest, forces will be set in motion that will reduce saving and increase investment until they are brought into equality with one another. For example, if the market rate of interest is at i_2 in the figure, this means that saving groups in the economy are attempting to save more than is wanted for the purchase of new capital equipment. But this disequilibrium will cause the rate of interest to fall, and as it falls, the incentive to save will be lessened, while the incentive to invest (i.e., to purchase capital goods) will increase. Market adjustment will continue until the market rate of interest has reached the level at which the demand for and the supply of savings are equated. In Figure 3–2 this condition prevails at the indicated interest rate of i_e.

The Theory of the Price Level

Classical economic thinking about the role of money in the economy and the determination of the price level is summed up in the quantity theory of money. The quantity theory of money is rooted in the equation of exchange, a truism that says that the monetary value of output (Y_p) is equal to the quantity of money in circulation times its average rate of turnover (Mv). In this expression v equals the income velocity of money, which is obtained by dividing Y by M. If we assume that Y is a given because the normal state of the economy is one of full employment—hence Y is fixed by the amount of employment—and that turnover (the velocity of circulation v) is stable because it is rooted in payment habits, which are slow to change, the price level will vary directly with the amount of money. This follows from the classical view that the *primary* function of money is to serve as a medium of exchange. Hence, more money means more spending and less money means less spending. In equation form we have

$$Mv = Yp \qquad \text{The equation of exchange} \qquad (3–9)$$

$$p = f(M) \qquad \text{The quantity theory} \qquad (3–10)$$

The classical theory of the price level can be depicted geometrically, as is done in Figure 3–3. Real income is shown on the vertical axis, whereas the general price level is charted on the horizontal axis. The Mv curve provides the necessary link between real income (output) and the price level. In mathematical terms this curve is known as a *rectangular hyperbola,* which is one in which the product of coordinate values on the two axes is a constant. This means that with fixed values for the money supply and the velocity of circulation, real income can rise only if the price level falls and the price level can rise only if real income declines. As long as the money supply and velocity are fixed, real income and the general price level must move inversely to one another.

The way in which an increase in the money supply will affect the general price level can be shown in the figure. Assume that Y_1 is the full-employment level of output and that M_1 represents the initial supply of money in the economy. Velocity is also a constant and given by v. Under these circumstances the general price level will be p_1. What will happen if the money supply is increased from M_1 to M_2? Since we have assumed that the economy

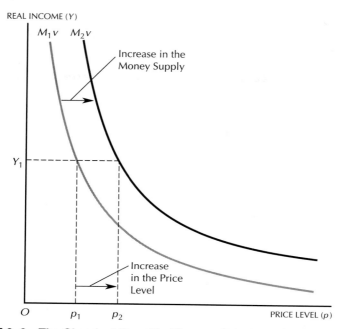

REAL INCOME (Y)

$M_1 v$ $M_2 v$

Increase in the
Money Supply

Y_1

Increase
in the Price
Level

O p_1 p_2 PRICE LEVEL (p)

FIGURE 3–3   The Classical Quantity Theory of Money.   Because the level of employment is a constant in classical theory, an increase in the money supply, depicted by a shift to the right in the Mv curve, will always raise the price level.

is at full employment, real income Y cannot change. The only thing that can change is the general price level; it will rise to the level indicated by p_2 in the figure. The curve of constant expenditure shifts to the M_2v level; this tells us that total spending for a given output (Y_1) is now larger because of higher prices.

The Complete Classical Model

Now that we have discussed separately the three major propositions that enter into the pre-Keynesian classical theory of employment, it is useful to draw these propositions together in a single diagram and show how they interact to provide a formal model for the classical theory. This is done in Figure 3–4, which may be summarized as follows:

1. Part A in the diagram has two parts. The upper diagram depicts the classical production function. Its purpose is to show that with a *given* technology and a *fixed* quantity of resources other than labor, output depends uniquely on the level of employment. To explain what determines the employment level, we must turn to the bottom portion of part A, where are found

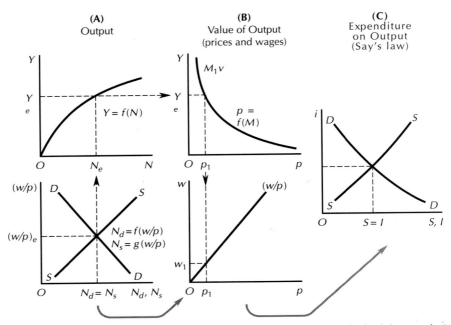

FIGURE 3–4   The Complete Classical System.   Equilibrium in the labor market determines output, given the classical production function, whereas the money supply determines the equilibrium price level, and the rate of interest in the investment-savings market ensures the workings of Say's law.

the classical demand and supply curves for labor. Interaction between demand and supply as shown here determines both the level of employment and the real wage. The classical equilibrium shown in part A is a unique one involving output, employment, and the real wage.

2. Turn now to part B. In the lower portion of part B we introduce a new curve, one labeled w/p. This shows the price level on the horizontal axis and the money wage on the vertical axis. The slope of the line (w/p) measures the real wage as determined by the demand for and supply of labor given in the lower portion of part A. The steeper the slope of this line (w/p), the higher is the real wage. The upper portion of part B shows how the monetary value of the real output level, determined from the production function in part A, depends on the money supply and velocity. If the latter is given, then the money supply becomes the prime determinant of the price level and hence the monetary value of any real output level. An increase in the money supply is depicted by a shift to the right in the $M_1 v$ curve. The additional money will simply increase the price level. By changing any of the variables in the classical system or shifting a relevant function, it is possible to trace through the impact of any such change on output, real wages, employment, the price level, or money wages. To gain familiarity with the workings of the classical model, the reader should work out such changes on her or his own.

3. Finally, part C shows how Say's law fits into the analysis by assuring

the necessary equality between savings and investment so that there is no interruption in spending flows because of any deficiency in total demand. Note that in the classical model the rate of interest cannot have any impact on the output level; its role is to determine the division of output between investment and consumption, as well as to ensure that all savings flow into investment spending.

In summary, there are two important things to be said about the classical model just discussed. In the first place, the system is constructed so that it tends *automatically* toward a level of full employment. The demand for and the supply of labor curves have the role of determining the actual employment level, but they are conceived so that this employment level is by definition one of full employment. Moreover, Say's law of markets, in conjunction with the classical theory of interest, makes certain that there is no possibility of involuntary unemployment in the system because of any deficiency of aggregate demand. Second, if there is within the system any temporary deviation away from the full-employment equilibrium, the appropriate remedy is clearly indicated. This is a reduction in the real wage, which can be brought about either by an increase in the money supply, with its consequent effects on the general price level, or by a cut in money wages. The essential condition for the system to work in this fashion is *flexibility* for *all* wages and prices. These two ideas are important because they remain very much alive in the challenges to the Keynesian orthodoxy mounted since the 1970s.

A Classical Aggregate Supply and Aggregate Demand Model

The classical economists focused on issues of supply. It was not until Keynes that demand questions entered prominently into the analysis of the macroeconomy. Since Keynes's work, members of the new classical and other perspectives descended from the classical tradition have developed a view of both supply and demand in the classical framework. In this section our purpose is to examine how the classical model of aggregate supply and demand works. We should note that the pre-Keynesian classical model developed in the preceding sections does not contain any *explicit* aggregate supply and demand schedules (functions). Thus, the emergence of an aggregate supply and demand model in a classical context is a *post-Keynesian* development. Chapter 4 develops the full Keynesian aggregate supply and demand model.

The fundamental characteristic of the classical aggregate supply and demand model is that it relates the level of real output (income) in the economy to the price level. The usefulness of such a model stems from the fact it can be used to analyze the impact of changes in consumption and investment spending, monetary and fiscal policies, and even the capital stock, technology, and the labor force on *both* output (including employment) and the price level. An aggregate demand and aggregate supply model is similar to the microeconomic model of supply and demand, in which the price and production of an individual good is determined. The analogy should not be overemphasized, however, because at the level of the individual market, the microeconomic level, a supply or demand schedule links output (or amount purchased or sold) to a single price—the price of the good or service being supplied or demanded. But when it comes to aggregate supply and demand, the relationship is between output and prices in general, the price level, in other words. This is both a vital distinction and a more complex relationship.

The Classical Aggregate Supply Curve

Let us begin by asking the question: what effect would an increase in the general price level have on real output in the classical world? The answer is none. To see why this is true, examine Figure 3–5, which shows the classical labor market. At the real wage W_e there is equilibrium between the supply and demand for labor, an equilibrium which leaves us with the level of employment at N_e. We know from the previous analysis that this is full employment and that it is related to the full-employment level of output in the classical model through the production function. What happens if we increase the price level, assuming money wages (w) remain unchanged?

A higher price level will reduce the real wage and thereby create a disequilibrium in the labor market. Why? As noted earlier workers in the classical world do not suffer from the money illusion. Thus, in the labor market

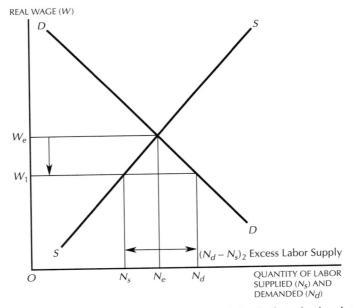

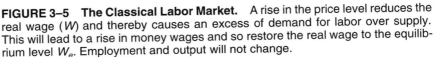

FIGURE 3–5   The Classical Labor Market.   A rise in the price level reduces the real wage (W) and thereby causes an excess of demand for labor over supply. This will lead to a rise in money wages and so restore the real wage to the equilibrium level W_e. Employment and output will not change.

workers focus on real rather than nominal (or money) wages. When prices rise, workers recognize that this means their real wage has fallen, so they move down their supply schedule: less labor is offered in the market. In Figure 3–5 as the real wage falls from W_e to W_1, the quantity of labor supplied falls from N_e to N_s.

Employers, too, recognize that the real wage has fallen; this prompts them to move down along their demand curve for labor from N_e to N_d. What results is an excess of demand for labor at the real wage W_1. What happens then is that nominal (money) wages will be bid up by employers until the equilibrium real wage is restored at W_e. From this we can conclude that in the classical model, if there is no money illusion and if nominal (money) wages are flexible, a change in the price level will lead to a change in money wages, but *no* change in the level of employment. Since the level of employment is the variable which in the classical world determines how much output the economy produces in the short run, we can also conclude that a change in the price level will have no effect on actual output.

From the foregoing we must conclude that the classical aggregate supply curve should be drawn as a vertical line at the full-employment output level. Such a schedule is shown in Figure 3–6, which shows the price level (p) on

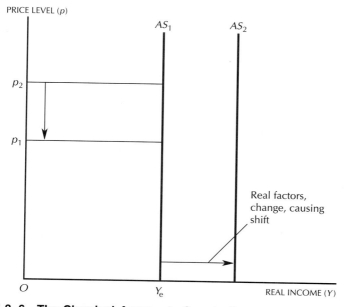

FIGURE 3–6 The Classical Aggregate Supply Curve. In the short run, the classical aggregate supply curve appears as a vertical line at the full-employment output level. It is unaffected by changes in the price level. In the long run, the supply curve shifts to the right as a result of changes in such real factors of the stock of capital, labor supply, or technology.

the vertical axis and output (Y) on the horizontal axis. The curve in the figure reflects the classical belief that nominal values such as the price level, money wages, and the money supply *do not* affect the level of real output.

The factors that do affect the level of output are important. In the short run, real output is fixed at full employment as determined by the supply and demand for labor. But the long run is a different story. Here real factors such as an increase in the stock of capital, growth in the labor force, or a change in technology come into play. Basically, what classical economics argues is that any increase in the quantity of capital or labor or improvement in technology shifts the entire production function upward (*part A* of Figure 3–4) and thereby increases the marginal product of labor. When this happens, the demand for labor will increase along with a higher real wage and a higher full-employment level. What this means is that the classical aggregate supply curve shifts to the right. In Figure 3–6, aggregate supply shifts from AS_1 to AS_2.

The Classical Aggregate Demand Curve

The classical aggregate demand curve begins with the equation of exchange introduced earlier, $Mv = pY$. On the left side of this equation are the money supply (M) and velocity (v), the rate at which money turns over or changes hands in a year. These are nominal variables, which represent total spending or aggregate *money* demand in the economy. On the right-hand side of the equation we find real output (Y) times the price level (p), which represents the nominal, that is money, value of output.

To construct the classical aggregate demand curve, we must make the following assumptions:

1. The velocity of money (v) is fixed.
2. The supply of money (M) is fixed.
3. Real output (Y) is a variable.
4. The price level (p) is a variable.

If we rearrange the variables in the equation of exchange, we get an equation which shows there is an inverse relationship between the price level (p) and real output (Y):

$$Y = Mv/p. \qquad (3\text{--}11)$$

Figure 3–7 graphs this relationship. In the figure, the price level (p) is shown on the vertical axis and the real output (Y) on the horizontal axis. When the price level falls from p_2 to p_1, assuming velocity and the money supply remain constant, the level of real output that can be purchased increases from Y_1 to Y_2. In effect, a lower price level frees up purchasing power so that more output can be bought. If we reverse the process, assuming that the price level

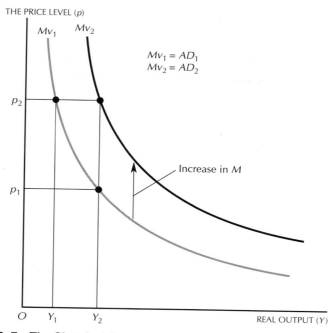

THE PRICE LEVEL (p)

Mv_1 Mv_2

$Mv_1 = AD_1$
$Mv_2 = AD_2$

Increase in M

p_2

p_1

O Y_1 Y_2 REAL OUTPUT (Y)

FIGURE 3–7   The Classical Aggregate Demand Curve. As long as the money supply (M) and velocity (v) are fixed, real output (Y) will vary inversely with the price level (p). This is the nature of the classical aggregate demand curve.

rises, then the existing money supply and velocity support less output. What we have shown here is that, given the assumptions set forth above, the classical *aggregate* demand curve embodies an *inverse* relationship between output and the general level of prices. To put this in the familiar context of standard demand theory, the higher the price level, the less demand there is for output, other things being equal, and the lower the price level, the greater the demand for output.

As conceived and shown in Figure 3–7, the money supply (M) and the velocity of circulation of money (v) are the prime determinants of the classical aggregate demand curve. So what happens if either the money supply or the velocity of circulation or both change? If there is more money, people can purchase more goods and services without a change in the price level. If the velocity increases, the same thing is possible because the faster circulation of money allows people to purchase more output. Either change is shown by a shift to the right of the Mv curve. This kind of a shift was shown earlier in Figure 3–3 and is shown again in Figure 3–7.

Let us examine carefully what happens when the Mv curve shifts. If the economy is initially in equilibrium at a full-employment output level of Y_2 and p_1, and the Mv_1 curve shifts to the level of the Mv_2 curve because of an increase in the money supply, the result will be an increase in prices to the level p_2. The price level will have increased in direct proportion to the increase in the money supply. Since Y_2 is a full-employment output level, the increase in spending that goes with the increase in the money supply only serves to drive up prices. This chain of events also reflects the classical belief that money is neutral, that is, that money cannot affect real economic phenomena such as output or employment.

The Complete Classical Model of Aggregate Supply and Demand

Figure 3–8 brings together the classical aggregate supply and aggregate demand curves to give us a modified and slightly different classical macroeconomic model as compared to the one discussed earlier (Figure 3–4). The model shown in Figure 3–8 rests implicitly on all the assumptions embodied in the pre-Keynesian version of classical economics, but is developed on the basis of aggregate schedules that relate total output and total demand to the price level.

In Figure 3–8 the economy reaches an equilibrium of both output and prices at the point of intersection between the aggregate demand curve (Mv_1) and the aggregate supply curve (AS_1). At the equilibrium price level (p_e) enough income is generated to support the level of output the economy can

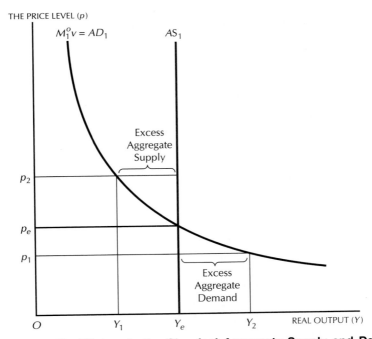

FIGURE 3–8   Equilibrium in the Classical Aggregate Supply and Demand Model.   In this version of the classical model equilibrium results from the interaction of aggregate supply and demand. The price level (p) is the adjusting factor and brings total demand into line with total supply. The latter is fixed in the short run at the full-employment output level (Y_e).

produce with a fully employed labor force. This output is Y_e. What happens when the price level deviates from p_e? Market forces in the labor and product markets bring the price level back to the equilibrium. Consider, for example, the price level of p_2. At this price level, given the money supply and the velocity of money, only a level of aggregate demand sufficient to buy output Y_1 can be sustained. The real money supply is smaller, and people now have correspondingly smaller real money balances. This means that there is an excess aggregate supply equal to the difference $Y_e - Y_1$. In short, nominal wages and prices are too high to allow all the output that is being produced to be purchased. Workers and business firms respond by bidding down nominal wages and prices. As the price level falls, the existing money supply can support a higher level of aggregate demand. This continues until the price level returns to p_e.

This chain of events is reversed in the case of a price level below its equilibrium value, such as p_1. Here the real money supply is increased because of lower nominal wages and prices. Hence, people have larger real money balances, which they can use to purchase goods and services. But the level of output that can be produced is still fixed at Y_e. Therefore, there is excess demand equal to the amount $Y_2 - Y_e$. In this case, nominal wages and prices are bid upward; this results in smaller real money balances and decreases in aggregate demand. This will continue until the economy is once again in equilibrium at the price level p_e.

Real and Nominal Shocks in the Classical Model

Now that we have seen how the economy reaches a full-employment equilibrium in the classical model, how does this equilibrium change? In the classical world equilibrium changes only when there is a disturbance to the system, a *shock* from outside, so to speak. Such shocks are described as being either *real* or *nominal*. *Real* shocks consist of developments such as technological improvements, basic changes in the labor force, or increases in the stock of capital—all of which work their way into the economic system through the production function. They raise the economy's potential output. *Nominal* shocks are different; they reflect changes in the monetary valuation of things, such as a change in money wages, changes in the general level of prices, or a change in the money supply itself. As seen in our discussion of the classical aggregate supply curve, nominal changes, or shocks, cannot affect employment and real output.

The story is different, however, when it comes to real shocks. To show why this is the case, let us trace the effect of an external shock in the form of a major technological change on the equilibrium of the classical system. This is done in Figure 3–9, wherein key elements in the classical model are shown as follows:

1. Part A shows the classical production function.
2. Part B contains the classical labor market.

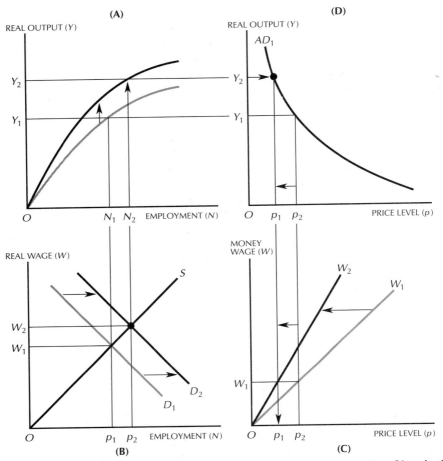

FIGURE 3–9 The Impact of Technological Improvement in the Classical Model. (A) A technological change shifts the production function upward. (B) The production function shift, in turn, causes a shift to the right in the demand for labor. (C) Output Y rises. (D) Because the money supply M and velocity v are fixed, the price level p falls. This increases the real wage W.

3. Part C contains the curve that links the price level and the money (nominal) wage. As noted on page 88, the slope of the curve measures the real wage W. The steeper the slope, the higher the level of the real wage.

4. Part D contains the classical aggregate demand curve, with the axes transposed from their depiction in Figure 3–7. As noted earlier, the classical aggregate demand curve is constructed by holding both the money supply (M) and velocity (v) constant.

The initial impact of the technological change is depicted in part A by an upward shift in the production function. Since, however, a rise in the production function *raises* the marginal product of labor, this translates into an increase in the demand for labor. Thus, the demand curve for labor as shown in part B shifts to the right. The increase in the demand for labor combined with no change in the supply curve for labor results in a higher equilibrium level of employment in the labor market. This is N_2 in the figure. Given the higher production function, this higher level of employment is associated with an increase in the output level (Y) from Y_1 to Y_2, as shown in part A.

Move now to part D, where the classical aggregate demand curve (AD_1) is shown. Since the money supply and velocity are fixed, a higher level of real output (Y_2) can be sustained only if the price level falls. That is what must happen, as the price level shown in part D drops from p_2 to p_1. The fall in the price level with the money wage unchanged results in a higher real wage—a result depicted in part C by the shift of the W curve upward, that is, W_2 is steeper than W_1.

Policy Implications of the Classical Theory

As already noted, the classical theory of employment implies a *laissez faire* policy that minimizes the extent to which government intervenes in the operation of the economy. In a broad sense there are two major reasons why government might intervene in the economy. The first is that imperfections in the market economy may lead to an undue concentration of economic power in private hands. The second is that the private or market sector of the economy may not function sufficiently well to provide jobs for all members of the labor force actively seeking employment.

Both of the above possibilities are denied by the classical system. Classical economists assumed that competition is a normal characteristic of the economy. The kind of competition they envisioned as being dominant in the economy was the *atomistic* variety, in which the number of firms in every industry is so great in relation to the demand for the output of the industry that no single firm can exercise any control over the price at which its product is sold. If no firm is in a position to exercise any control whatsoever over price, no firm (or person) can possess any real economic power over other firms (or persons). All firms and persons are at the mercy of the impersonal market forces of supply and demand. If this is a correct evaluation of the situation in the economy, then there is no basis for intervention by the state for the sake of redressing any abuse of private economic power. The latter does not exist in the classical scheme.

The second reason for state intervention is the continued existence of a significant amount of *involuntary* unemployment. As we have seen, classical employment theory leads to the conclusion that involuntary unemployment on a large scale for anything more than brief periods is an impossibility. If the economy has an inherent and automatic tendency toward equilibrium at full employment, then there is no real need for public intervention on the ground that employment is inadequate. Under such circumstances *laissez faire* is the appropriate policy.

Competition plays a vital role in this respect because its presence within the economic system ensures the flexibility of wages and prices, including the rate of interest. The system will move toward an equilibrium at full employment only if wages respond instantly to the least discrepancy between the demand for and supply of labor in the market. The same holds true for the rate of interest, for, unless interest responds to any discrepancy between the demand for and supply of saving, the system will not attain the equality between saving and investment necessary to ensure the working of Say's law in a monetary economy. Price and wage flexibilities stem from competition, and the more highly competitive the system, the more responsive wages and prices will be to market forces.

Classical Economics and the Great Depression

The Great Depression (1929 to 1939) provided a severe, though unplanned, "experiment" of the kind that John Stuart Mill described as being cast up by history. Money wages and prices proved to be extremely flexible downward during the collapse (1929 to 1933), but this flexibility did not prevent output and employment from dropping sharply. Classical economics taught the opposite; yet during the opening years of the Great Depression, prices, wages, output, and employment *all* dropped by large percentages. Table 3–1 shows what happened to some of the key economic variables from 1929 to 1933. The data in the table pertain to the manufacturing sector, which was hardest hit by the collapse but was also representative of what happened to the economy generally. The economy simply did not behave the way it was supposed

TABLE 3–1   Changes in Key Economic Variables: 1929–1933 (in percent)

Variable	Percent Change, 1929–1933
1. Average hourly earnings*	−21.5%
2. Average weekly earnings*	−32.8
3. Employment*	−46.0
4. Real gross national product†	−31.5
5. Consumer price index‡	−24.4
6. Total labor force	6.5

*For manufacturing.
†In 1958 prices.
‡1958 = 100.
Source: *Historical Statistics of the United States*, pp. 118, 137, 170, 197, 210.

to on the basis of classical economic theory.[9] Between 1929 and 1933, the Federal Reserve discount rate (the key rate for determining the general level of interest rates) declined by 50.4 percent, but gross private domestic investment spending collapsed almost totally. The percentage decline for the latter between 1929 and 1933 was 83.7! The fact that the classical analysis could neither account for the magnitude of the 1929 collapse nor provide a viable remedy for the Depression set the stage for the appearance of the Keynesian model in 1936.

Summary

1. Three basic propositions make up the essence of classical economics. They are the total demand for and supply of labor, the quantity theory of money, and Say's law of markets. A corollary of the latter is the classical theory linking the supply of savings and the demand for savings for investment to the rate of interest.

2. The classical theory assumes flexibility in all money wages and prices. As a result, the employment level determined by the interaction between the classical demand for and supply of labor is necessarily a full-employment level. *Laissez faire* is, therefore, the major policy implication of the classical theory.

3. The first two points largely summarize the classical system as it existed up to the time of Keynes. In the 1970s and 1980s refinements were made to the classical system, primarily in the form of aggregate supply and aggregate demand schedules that relate output (Y) to the price level.

4. The failure of the classical model to either account for or provide a remedy for the Great Depression led to its theoretical overthrow. The Keynesian system that replaced it was not permanent, however, for modernized versions of classical economics endure and provide a springboard for contemporary challenges to the Keynesian orthodoxy.

[9] Since the consumer price index and average hourly earnings fell by approximately the same amounts, *real* hourly earnings did not change drastically between 1929 and 1933. At best, this means according to the classical theory, the demand for labor should have remained about the same. But employment in manufacturing dropped 46 percent. In real terms average weekly earnings actually declined, because their nominal drop (32.8 percent) was greater than the decline in consumer prices (24.4 percent). This should have increased the demand for labor.

4. The Keynesian System

Modern macroeconomic theory and policy grew out of the traumatic experience of the Great Depression of the 1930s, which showed the inability of classical economics either to explain or to generate effective policies for coping with the economic crash. John Maynard Keynes wrote his masterwork, *The General Theory of Employment, Interest and Money,* not only to explain how the Great Depression could happen—how there could be poverty in the midst of potential plenty—but also to provide a theoretical alternative to the classical explanation of how employment and output are determined in the modern economy.

In this chapter we shall develop two general models for explaining output and employment, models that draw on the concepts of aggregate supply and demand developed by Keynes. The first model developed in this chapter is the *income-expenditure model,* as it is built around Keynes's fundamental belief that the key to the level of output and employment in the economy is the volume of total expenditures, which are in turn determined by income. In constructing this model, we take an essentially historical approach and draw on the way Keynes developed his analysis in *The General Theory.*

The second model developed in this chapter employs an aggregate supply and aggregate demand framework. It blends together key ideas found in the Keynesian income-expenditure approach and classical concepts embodied in the formal classical aggregate supply and aggregate demand model discussed

John Maynard Keynes: Architect of a Revolution

John Maynard Keynes was one of the most extraordinary economists who ever lived. In a profession not noted for colorful personalities, he was an economist, a speculator, a civil servant, a writer, and a patron of the arts. No economist in this century had a greater impact on formal economic theory, the policy of governments, or contemporary systems of market capitalism. Born in 1883, Keynes grew to maturity in the atmosphere of Edwardian England; he attended Eton and Cambridge University, where he graduated from Kings College, one of the most prestigious of the Cambridge colleges. After a brief stint as a civil servant in the India office, he returned to Cambridge and Kings as a fellow (professor), the only academic post he ever held. Keynes was 63 when he died on Easter Sunday in 1946.

Keynes ranks as one of the three greatest economists, along with Adam Smith and Karl Marx, because his 1936 book, *The General Theory of Employment, Interest and Money,* coming as it did during the worst economic depression in history, showed modern governments how to use their formidable economic power to offset fluctuations in the private market sectors of the economy. In this way stability would come to the economic system. Keynes's *The General Theory* wrought revolutionary changes in economic theory, but it was a "revolution" that aimed to preserve the essentials of market capitalism. Keynes became the architect for the modern mixed market economy, one lying somewhere between the extremes of the pure capitalism of Adam Smith and the pure communism of Karl Marx.

The General Theory appeared toward the end of Keynes's extraordinary and varied career. In 1919 he was a member of the British delegation to Versailles, but resigned in anger over the terms of the treaty; he returned to London to write *The Economic Consequences of the Peace* in protest. The harsh terms of the peace, he predicted, would lead ultimately to economic collapse and possibly another war. He was tragically right. During the 1920s he taught at Cambridge; edited *The Economic Journal,* the leading economic journal in Western society; and made a fortune for himself and Kings College by speculation in the foreign exchange and commodity markets. In the mid-1920s he decried Winston Churchill's wrong-headed decision as Chancellor of the Exchequer to restore Britain to the gold standard at the pre-World War I rate of exchange. Events proved him right again. In the early 1930s he published his *Treatise on Money,* now seen as a prelude to *The General Theory.* During World War II he served in the Treasury, where he played a major role in shaping wartime finance. As the war was ending, he became the chief British delegate to the Bretton Woods Conference, where he played a leading role in the construction of the international monetary system that lasted from 1946 until 1973. On a personal level, Keynes was married to Lydia Lopokova, a Russian ballerina; was active in the Bloomsbury Group, a noted artistic and literary circle in London; and generously gave his time, talents, and money in support of the arts in London and Cambridge. He was a twentieth-century Renaissance man.

in the concluding section of Chapter 3. This approach is described as a Keynesian-classical model because of the marriage in it of Keynesian and classical ideas. These three models—the classical, the Keynesian, and the Keynesian-classical—give us appropriate theoretical tools to discuss and analyze practically every problem and policy question of a macroeconomic nature the economy is likely to confront.

The Essence of the Income-Employment Problem

In classical analysis the main economic problem is to maintain the flexibility of money wages and prices. This would ensure full employment at all times. But with the collapse of classical employment theory as a result of the Great Depression, the focus of the economic problem necessarily shifted. Mass unemployment and idle factories became the problem to be explained. The place to begin was not with the labor market, as the classical economists did, but with the idea of *capacity*. Capacity is the economy's potential for the production of goods and services. If we begin with the concept of capacity, certain consequences logically follow. First, output will depend on the extent to which this capacity is being utilized. This will be true up to the limits of capacity. Second, output will depend upon the level of employment as long as all resources other than labor are fixed. This brings us to the key question of modern employment theory: *What is it that determines the extent to which the economy's productive capacity is being utilized?*

In a sense the answer to this question is deceptively simple, for it is the *expectations* of the business executives that they will be able to sell what they produce that lead them to make use of the productive capacity at their disposal. The presumption here is that the output will be sold at prices that cover costs of production. Stated in more formal terms, productive capacity will be brought into use (or production will take place) whenever there exists the expectation that demand for the output will be sufficient to clear the market of what is being produced. Note carefully two points. First, this statement describes the conditions under which productive capacity will be utilized in a market economy, that is to say, an economy in which the basic decisions about what is to be produced and in what quantities are made by private individuals rather than public authorities. Second, the key word in the statement is "expectation," which is a way of stressing the fact that production in a market economy is carried on, for the most part, in anticipation of demand.

If we assume that the expectation of demand is the essential condition required to bring productive capacity into use, it follows that *the theory of income determination in the modern economy is basically a theory of aggregate demand.* In other words, if we are to understand how the levels of output and employment are actually determined, it is necessary to understand how demand for the output of the whole economy is determined. In sum, aggregate demand is the crucial determinant of the level of income and employment during short periods when productive capacity is assumed to be relatively fixed. This is the central theme of Keynes's *The General Theory*. It is not quite the full story, however. The Keynesian income-expenditure model involves *both* aggregate demand and aggregate supply. Thus, to construct such a model, we must have two schedules, one representing aggregate supply and one representing aggregate demand.

Keynesian Aggregate Supply

Early in *The General Theory*, Keynes defined the aggregate supply price of the output resulting from a given amount of employment as ''the expectation of proceeds which will just make it worth the while of the entrepreneur to give that employment.''[1] What Keynes meant was a schedule that would show for any and all possible levels of employment the volume of receipts from the sale of output that would justify the varying quantities of employment. The receipts would have to be sufficient to cover all costs incurred by the entrepreneur plus a profit. Keynes believed that entrepreneurs sought at all times to maximize their profits. The receipts—or expected proceeds—must cover costs plus profits for the economy's total employment in the same way that price must cover costs and a unit profit for the supply of a particular good or service. Such a schedule shows the amount of employment that entrepreneurs in the aggregate can be expected to offer on the basis of any and all possible volumes of proceeds from the sale of the output resulting from the different amounts of employment. Keynes linked output (Y) through employment *not* to the price level as the classical economists did, but to the income (or proceeds) expected from the sale of output. He used employment as the dependent variable because at the time he was writing (1936), statistical techniques for the accurate measurement of aggregates such as GDP were not highly developed. Keynes believed employment was the best single measure of total (aggregate) economic activity.

A highly simplified version of a Keynesian aggregate supply schedule is illustrated by the hypothetical data in Table 4–1, which relate employment and expected proceeds. For the sake of simplicity we assume that labor is the only resource, and thus the only cost of production to be covered in the aggregate by the sales proceeds are labor costs.[2] It is further assumed that the normal workweek is 40 hours, and that workers are employed for 52

---

[1] Keynes, *The General Theory*, p. 24.

[2] Profit, too, is ignored in order to focus on the essential costs which are embodied in the aggregate supply function and which must be covered by expected proceeds. The aggregate supply function developed in this chapter is highly simplified.

TABLE 4–1   The Aggregate Supply Schedule

Employment N (in millions of workers)	Schedule A		Schedule B	
	Money Wages w (per hour)	Aggregate Supply Price Z (in billions of dollars)	Money Wages w (per hour)	Aggregate Supply Price Z' (in billions of dollars)
104	$8.00	$1,731	$8.40	$1,817
106	8.00	1,764	8.60	1,896
108	8.00	1,797	8.80	1,976
110	8.00	1,830	9.00	2,059
112	8.00	1,864	9.20	2,143
114	8.00	1,897	9.40	2,229
116	8.00	1,930	9.60	2,316
118	8.00	1,964	9.80	2,405

Note: A 40-hour workweek and a 52-week workyear are assumed. Thus, each employee works 2,080 hours per year. To get the aggregate supply price for any level of employment, this figure is multiplied by the average hourly wage and then by the total number of workers employed (N). If H equals annual hours worked, then $Z = H \times (w) \times N$.

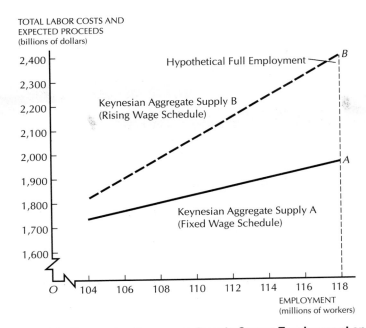

FIGURE 4–1   The Keynesian Aggregate Supply Curve: Employment and Proceeds. The aggregate supply curve slopes upward to the right because total labor costs rise as more workers are employed and therefore require higher proceeds (sales receipts) to justify higher employment.

weeks each year. In the table there are two schedules: Schedule A and Schedule B. Schedule A is based on the assumption that the money wages of workers remain constant at $8.00 per hour, regardless of the actual level of employment or demand for labor. Schedule B is based on the assumption that the money wage will rise as more employment is offered. This implies that, as the demand for labor increases, its price—the money wage—will rise. Note, too, that money wages rise in Schedule B at different rates as the employment level increases.

Let us examine each of these schedules in a little more detail. Schedule *A* shows what the minimum expected sales proceeds must be for entrepreneurs to offer employment to specified numbers of workers. Recall, again, that profit is ignored in this example. For example, if employers in the aggregate are to offer employment to 104 million workers, the expected proceeds from the sale of the output produced by these 104 million workers must at a minimum equal $1,731 billion. Why is this? The $1,731 billion represents the total money costs of this amount of production that must be covered by sales proceeds if entrepreneurs in the aggregate are to continue to offer this amount of employment. Thus, the $1,731 billion is the aggregate supply price of this amount of employment if we assume a money wage of $8.00 per hour. In Schedule B the aggregate supply price for each level of employment subsequent to 104 million is higher because of the assumption that the money wage will rise from $8.40 per hour to $9.80 per hour as the total volume of employment climbs from 104 to 118 million workers.

Figure 4–1 illustrates graphically the Keynesian aggregate supply schedule.[3] In the figure, employment is plotted on the horizontal axis, and expected sales proceeds on the vertical axis. Plotting the data of Table 4–1 gives the two curves shown in the figure. The one labeled *A* is the aggregate supply schedule based on a fixed money wage of $8.00 per hour, whereas the schedule labeled *B* reflects the fact that the money wage may rise as the level of employment rises. The more rapidly the money wage rises (in percent) with actual changes in the level of employment, the less responsive is the employment level to any given change in expected proceeds. Technically, this means that, as the elasticity of the employment level decreases, the money wage becomes more sensitive to any increase in the demand for labor. The aggregate supply relationship will become perfectly inelastic with respect to expected proceeds at the level of employment that represents full employment of the existing labor force. If, for example, the employment level of 118 million workers is the upper limit to the labor supply in our hypothetical economy, then the two curves A and B will terminate at this point. Since no more workers are available once employment has reached the 118 million level, actual employment cannot exceed this amount, irrespective of what

---

[3] The student should not confuse these curves with those of the production function, which normally shows the relationship between employment and output. The supply schedule as depicted could be made more realistic by the addition of a markup factor to total labor costs, which would represent the entrepreneur's profit. This does not change the basic principle involved, however. The aggregate supply price still must cover all the necessary costs associated with a given amount of employment.

happens to expected proceeds. This is shown in Figure 4–1 by the dashed line extending vertically upward at the 118 million mark on the horizontal axis.

Aggregate Supply: A Real-World Example

The simplified and hypothetical aggregate supply schedule and curve shown in Table 4–1 and Figure 4–1 illustrate not only Keynes's view that expected proceeds must cover the costs associated with a given level of employment, but also his view that the aggregate supply curve, like the supply curve for a commodity or service, normally slopes upward to the right. From this perspective, the curve labeled *B* in Figure 4–1 is the more realistic, since it shows the money wage rising as more workers are employed. This is the way the economy actually behaves. Table 4–2 shows the behavior of output (real GDP), total employment, and money wages over the period 1970–94. As

TABLE 4–2   Output, Employment, and Money Wages: 1970–1994

Year	Real Output*	Percent Change	Civilian Employment†	Percent Change	Money Wages‡	Percent Change
1970	2,874	0.0	78.7	1.0	$ 3.23	6.3
1971	2,956	2.9	79.4	0.9	3.45	6.8
1972	3,107	5.1	82.2	3.5	3.70	7.2
1973	3,269	5.2	85.1	3.5	3.94	6.5
1974	3,248	−0.6	86.8	2.0	4.24	7.6
1975	3,222	−0.8	85.8	−1.2	4.53	6.8
1976	3,381	4.9	88.8	3.5	4.86	7.3
1977	3,533	4.5	92.0	3.6	5.25	8.1
1978	3,704	4.8	96.0	4.4	5.69	8.4
1979	3,797	2.5	98.8	2.9	6.16	8.3
1980	3,776	−0.5	99.3	0.5	6.66	8.1
1981	3,843	1.8	100.4	1.1	7.25	8.9
1982	3,760	−2.2	99.5	−0.9	7.68	5.9
1983	3,907	3.9	100.8	1.3	8.02	4.4
1984	4,149	6.2	105.0	4.2	8.32	3.7
1985	4,280	3.2	107.2	2.1	8.57	3.0
1986	4,405	2.9	109.6	2.2	8.76	2.2
1987	4,540	3.1	112.4	2.6	8.98	2.3
1988	4,719	3.9	115.0	2.3	9.28	3.7
1989	4,838	2.5	117.3	2.0	9.66	4.0
1990	4,897	1.2	117.9	0.5	10.01	3.8
1991	4,868	−0.6	116.9	−0.8	10.32	3.1
1992	4,979	2.3	117.6	0.6	10.58	2.5
1993	5,135	3.1	119.3	1.4	10.83	2.4
1994	5,342	4.8	123.1	3.2	11.12	2.7

*Billions of 1987 dollars, rounded to the nearest billion.

†Civilian employment (in thousands of persons).

‡Average gross hourly earnings, private nonagricultural industries.

Source: Economic Report of the President, 1995, pp. 276, 277, 312, 326.

output and employment rose during these years, the money wage also rose, even during recession years (1974–75, 1980, 1982, and 1991), when output and employment fell.

A factor *not* reflected in the hypothetical data in Table 4–1 and Figure 4–1 is diminishing productivity. Not only do money wages rise as output expands, but as more workers are employed, the marginal product of labor declines. This raises the cost per unit produced, and even if money wages remained constant, the aggregate supply curve would rise faster than curve *A* in Figure 4–1, the supply curve based on an assumed fixed value for the money wage. What this means is that a real-world aggregate supply curve, which reflects not only rising money wages, but diminishing returns and other costs, rises even more rapidly than Schedule B in Figure 4–1. Such a schedule is shown in Figure 4–2. In this figure output, as measured by GDP in constant 1987 prices, is shown on the horizontal axis, and the nominal value of that output (GDP in current prices) is measured on the vertical axis. Thus, the schedule (*ZZ*) shown in Figure 4–2 embodies price as well as output changes. It should be noted carefully that curve *ZZ* was constructed from actual GDP data in constant (1987) and current prices for the period 1970 through 1994; it is, therefore, an *ex post* formulation. The *ZZ* curve is fitted to the dots representing the values of GDP in constant and current prices in order to illustrate with actual data the concepts we have been discussing. For analytical purposes the aggregate supply curve must be formulated in an *ex ante* sense; that is to say it must reflect intended or planned values. When Keynes spoke of the "expectation of proceeds" necessary to hire a particular amount of labor, he was thinking in *ex ante* terms. It is to the development of an aggregate supply curve in this sense that we now turn.

The *Ex Ante* Aggregate Supply Curve

The simple aggregate supply function that we developed using money wages only linked employment to expected proceeds (income) primarily because Keynes thought employment to be the most satisfactory measure of changes in the economy's output. This is no longer true. The extensive development of national income accounting provides the economist with techniques by which the heterogeneous complex of goods and services produced by the economy can be reduced to a single aggregate. Procedures exist for the measurement of *real* changes in an aggregate supply function in terms of total output (or real income) rather than level of employment; this has become the standard practice in modern employment theory.

Before we proceed to construct an aggregate supply curve framed in terms of real output (GDP valued in constant prices), another problem has to be resolved. In developing aggregate supply and aggregate demand functions, we must not lose sight of the fact that we are dealing with behavioral relationships, that is, the responses of producers and users of the national output to the variables that determine their responses. It is important, therefore, that we specify correctly the functional relationship in terms that are relevant to

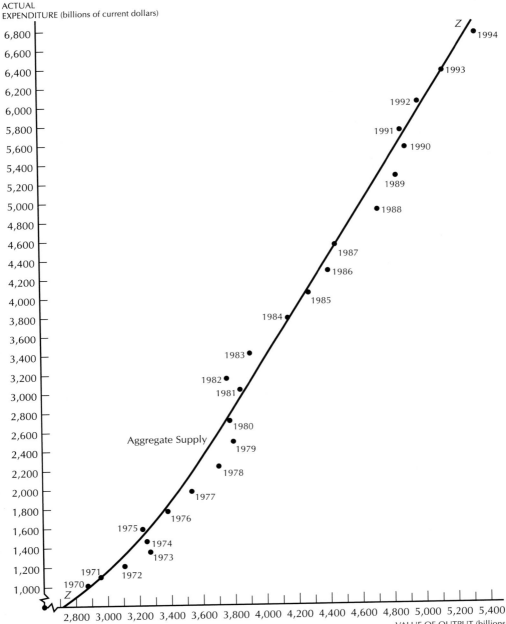

FIGURE 4–2 The Aggregate Supply Curve: Expected Proceeds in Current Prices and Value of Output in Constant Prices. Real output rises with higher expenditures, but not as rapidly as expenditure; this reflects diminishing returns and rising money costs (labor, materials, etc.) as a result of higher output.

Source: Economic Report of the President, 1995.

it.[4] Keynes formulated the aggregate supply relationship for labor in terms of the "expectation of proceeds." This is the money income that firms expect to get from the sale of output. The relationship is specified, therefore, in money (or nominal) terms; this is appropriate because, after all, it is money profit that the business firm is seeking. "Profit maximization" is how economists have explained business behavior all the way back to Adam Smith.

When we turn to the users of the national output—consumers, business firms buying capital goods, and governments—the situation is different. Users and their behavior enter into the aggregate demand relationship, the construction of which will be developed in the next section. But here is where we encounter the problem mentioned above. Normally, in macroeconomic analsysis the aggregate demand curve and all its component parts are specified in real terms. This, too, is appropriate because the users of the national output are interested in the real satisfaction they get from the goods and services purchased.[5] This is true for consumers, business firms buying capital goods, and governments purchasing the goods and services needed to provide public output. What concerns users is the utility of the goods and services they get by spending money. Consequently, their spending decisions as reflected in the aggregate demand curve are formulated in real output.

Here we have the gist of the problem. Aggregate supply, as developed originally by Keynes and depicted in Figures 4–1 and 4–2, is specified in *nominal* or money terms, but aggregate demand is specified in *real* or constant dollar terms. To have a workable model, it is essential that both the aggregate supply and aggregate demand relationships be specified in the same terms. The solution to this problem is to construct an aggregate supply curve that is formulated in terms of output rather than employment and to measure the expected proceeds that motivate business behavior in constant rather than current prices. This preserves Keynes's critical idea that it is profit expectations (as reflected in expected proceeds) that lead business firms to hire labor, and also formulates aggregate supply in the same terms as aggregate demand. Conceptually, this is done by deflating expected proceeds by the appropriate price index.

Such a formulation of the aggregate supply curve is shown in Figure 4–3. The aggregate supply curve is represented by the line OZ, which, it should be noted, bisects the origin at an angle of 45°. To understand the significance of the 45° line, remember that the aggregate supply curve consists of a series of points, each of which represents the supply price for the output associated with different amounts of employment. The quantity of employment related to any given output depends on the production function. The aggregate supply curve must show the conditions under which entrepreneurs in the aggregate will produce a particular volume of goods and services and, more important, will continue to produce that volume. This is what the 45° line in Figure 4–3 attempts to do.

---

[4] Victoria Chick, *Macroeconomics After Keynes* (Cambridge, Mass.: MIT Press, 1984), p. 67.
[5] Ibid.

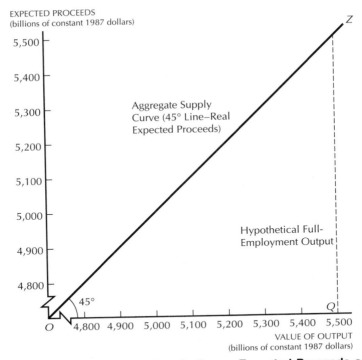

FIGURE 4–3   The Aggregate Supply Curve: Expected Proceeds and Value of Output in Constant Prices.   The vertical axis shows the proceeds (expected) that entrepreneurs must receive to cover the costs of producing the output shown on the horizontal axis; both are measured in constant dollars.

It is essential at this point to recognize that the 45° line in the figure is an aggregate supply *behavioral* relationship in the sense that we have been discussing the concept up to this point. A simpler translation in some texts describes the 45° line as a line along which output and expenditures are equal. But this lets slip away one of the most essential points of contemporary macroeconomic analysis, that output (and employment) levels result from an interaction between aggregate supply and aggregate demand. If there is no aggregate supply curve in the true, behavioral sense of the term, then it is not possible to talk about equilibrium in any meaningful way. At this point, it is important to recall that important magnitudes in economic analysis are determined by the interaction between supply *and* demand curves. If, for example, expenditures, measured in current prices on the vertical axis in Figure 4–2, were converted to constant 1987 dollars, then the schedule connecting the vertical and horizontal axes would be a 45° line. Let us now return to the main theme and examine more fully the 45° line *as an aggregate supply schedule*.

In Figure 4–3, real income is measured on both the vertical and horizontal axes of the figure, but the sense in which we are measuring real income differs for each of the two axes. The horizontal axis measures the money value in constant prices of the economy's current output of goods and services; this is also equivalent to the total cost, including a normal profit, incurred by entrepreneurs in the aggregate in producing any given output. Statistically and in the aggregate, the value of any given quantity of physical output must be equal to the costs of producing that output. Thus, we can interpret the horizontal axis of the figure as a measure of current output seen from the viewpoint of the costs that entrepreneurs incur when they decide to produce a particular volume of goods and services. Specifically, the costs involved are wages, rents, interest, profits, capital consumption allowances, and indirect business taxes.

Since the aggregate supply curve must show the conditions under which any particular level of production will continue, it follows that entrepreneurs in the aggregate must receive a return flow of expenditures (proceeds) equal to the costs they incur if they produce any given aggregate of goods and services. Because Figure 4–3 measures real income (output values in constant prices) on both the horizontal and vertical axes, the *only* possible line that will conform to the conditions described above is the 45° line that bisects the point of origin. In other words, if the vertical axis is viewed as measuring the *flow of expected proceeds in constant prices,* then the 45° line must of necessity be the aggregate supply curve, for each point on such a schedule represents the amounts that entrepreneurs must receive back as receipts (as measured on the vertical axis) if they are to continue to produce varying amounts of output (as measured on the horizontal axis).

As was the case with the simple wage-based aggregate supply curve (Figure 4–1), there will be some level of output that represents full employment for the 45° aggregate supply schedule. This may be represented by a point on the horizontal axis, for once the economy has achieved full employment (capacity production), no further increases in output are possible. In Figure 4–3 this point is represented by the vertical line ZQ. It is possible, though not customary, in modern income analysis to measure employment as well as output on the horizontal axis. This can be done because each possible level of output will correlate with a specific amount of employment. Because of the law of diminishing returns, however, employment will not necessarily vary in the same proportion as output—a fact that makes it difficult to compute the exact amount of employment that might be associated with each and every possible level of real output (see footnote 3). As a consequence, most modern income theorists have been content to measure real income only on the horizontal axis and simply assume—correctly—that employment will vary more or less directly with changes in the level of real income. A statistical relationship known as *Okun's law* after the late Arthur Okun, former chairperson of the Council of Economic Advisers, says that for every 2.5 to 3.0 percentage point increase in real GDP, the unemployment rate will drop by 1 percentage point. This rule is approximate, but does reflect the tie between output changes and employment changes.

Keynesian Aggregate Demand

The second major analytical tool in modern income and employment theory is aggregate demand. Just as aggregate supply is conceived of as a schedule showing the expected proceeds necessary to induce a given quantity of employment or amount of output in the economy, aggregate demand is also conceived of as a curve showing the amounts the major spending units in the economy are prepared to spend at each and every possible level of real income. It is a curve that links real income and spending decisions for the economy as a whole. The idea that the aggregate demand curve involves a relationship between decisions to purchase the different categories of output and the level of output itself is an oversimplification of a concept that is quite complex. But such a definition of the aggregate demand curve is, nevertheless, a good point of departure for our analysis.

Figure 4–4 depicts the relationship described above. The line *DD* is the aggregate demand curve. As in Figure 4–3, the vertical axis measures income as a flow of expenditure, and the horizontal axis depicts income as a flow of output. Thus, the curve *DD* can be said to represent the spending decisions associated with any and all possible levels of output, or real income.

Since the aggregate demand curve seeks to show how much the economy is disposed to spend for the various categories of output at different levels of real income, it is therefore an *ex ante* phenomenon. The aggregate demand curve does not represent any particular level of statistical demand, but rather the demand that will prevail if certain conditions are satisfied. The notion of an aggregate demand curve is important for our analysis because it underscores the fact that those who make the decisions to spend are not necessarily the same individuals or groups who make the decisions for production and employment. This will become fully apparent when we examine the process by which the income and employment levels are actually determined.

The Origin of Spending Decisions

Where do the spending decisions of the economy originate? Or, stated in different terms, who or what are the spending units in the economy? This question concerns the component parts of the aggregate demand curve, and a complete answer depends on detailed discussion in later chapters. But a brief answer can be given here that will serve to outline the basic problem involved in the analysis of demand for the output of the whole economy.

If we ignore for the moment any economic ties the economy may have with other nations,[6] decisions to purchase a portion of the current output of the economy must originate in one of three major economic sectors: (1) the

---

[6] For the balance of this chapter, we shall assume a *closed* economy. In Chapter 5 we shall shift the analysis to an *open* economy, one that has important economic ties to other nations.

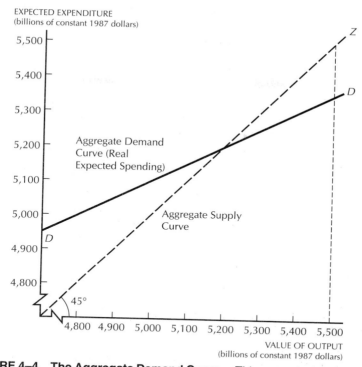

EXPECTED EXPENDITURE
(billions of constant 1987 dollars)

FIGURE 4–4   The Aggregate Demand Curve.   This curve depicts the spending decisions associated with any and all levels of real output in the economy.

household, or consumer, sector, which is the purchaser of consumer goods and services; (2) the business, or firm, sector, which is the purchaser of capital, or investment, goods; and (3) the public, or government, sector, which is the point of origin for decisions relating to the economy's output of government, or collective, goods and services. In a symbolic sense, then, aggregate demand will be equal to the sum of consumption C, investment I, and government expenditure G, for goods and services. In other words,

$$DD = C + I + G. \qquad (4\text{--}1)$$

Since the aggregate demand curve represents the spending intentions of the major spending units in the economy, a corollary question concerns the source of spending power at the disposal of these spending units. In a monetary economy, spending power requires access to a quantity of money, and thus the question pertains to the source of supply of money for the economy's spending units. Fundamentally, there are three possible sources of spending power for an individual spending unit in the economy. First, a spending unit may finance its current expenditures by drawing on assets accumulated during past income periods. These may be in the form of holdings of money or in the form of other assets that can be converted into money. A household, for example, might finance some of its current expenditures by drawing down a savings account, or perhaps by the sale of some of its holdings of stocks or bonds. Second, current expenditures may be financed out of current income. For the household, or consumer, sector of the economy and for the bulk of government purchases of goods and services, this is the typical pattern. Most individuals have to depend on current money income to finance the major portion of their current expenditures.

In the past, the more usual practice in the business sector of the economy was to finance capital expenditures by borrowing, rather than by using current and internal resources. Increasingly, however, business firms are resorting to internal financing for major items of capital expenditure; moreover, the firm can, like the consumer, draw on assets accumulated in past income periods to finance current outlays. But borrowing remains important as the third and final source of spending power for current expenditures. Consumers usually resort to loans for financing large items of expenditures, such as houses, automobiles, and other durable goods, whereas it is quite commonplace for government units in the economy to borrow to meet a portion of their current expenditures. National governments, we may note in passing, possess the unique distinction of having the power to create money.

These remarks about the source of the money that provides the basis for spending power in a monetary economy apply to the whole economy in much the same way as they apply to individual spending units within the economy. For the aggregate of all spending units, in other words, spending, or purchasing, power can be derived from current income, borrowing, or drawing down previously accumulated cash balances. If all spending units resort to the latter two sources for some portion of their purchasing power, new or additional quantities of funds are injected into the economic system. With these general observations about the origins of spending decisions in mind, let us turn to some more specific *theoretical* relationships that exist concerning such decisions. We shall explore much more fully all these relationships in Chapters 7 to 10, but an overview is useful at this point. Table 4–3 shows for selected years since 1929 the relative importance of these three major components of aggregate demand. Each spending component—consumption, investment, and government—is shown as a percent of the GDP for the year indicated.

Consumption Spending

As Table 4–3 shows, consumption spending is by far the largest spending component of the GDP; it makes up, in other words, the largest element in aggregate demand. One of the imaginative and important contributions made by Keynes was his theory of how the aggregate level of consumption is determined in the modern economy. This theory is explored in detail in Chapter 7. Here it will suffice to say that Keynes believed that the primary determinant

TABLE 4–3 Consumption, Gross Investment, and Government Purchases of Goods and Services as a Percent of GDP, Selected Years, 1929–1994

Year	Consumption Spending	Gross Investment	Government Purchase of Goods and Services*
1929	74.4%	16.1%	8.6%
1933†	81.2	2.9	14.8
1939	73.4	10.4	14.9
1944‡	51.2	3.6	45.9
1950	66.6	19.1	13.5
1955	63.5	17.2	18.6
1960	64.7	15.3	19.4
1965	63.6	16.8	19.4
1970	64.0	14.9	21.0
1975	64.6	14.3	20.3
1980	64.6	17.3	18.7
1985	65.3	17.7	18.9
1990	67.8	15.0	18.9
1994	68.7	15.4	17.4

*Federal, state, and local governments.

†Depth of the Great Depression.

‡Peak of the war effort, World War II.

Note: Net exports $(X - M)$ are excluded so the percentages for any single year will not ordinarily add to 100 percent.

Source: Economic Report of the President, 1995, pp. 274, 275.

of total consumption was income itself, that is, the total of income created through the act of production. The relationship between income and consumption Keynes called the *consumption function*. Total consumption (C) was held to be primarily determined by the level of income (Y).

Specifically, Keynes believed the relationship is depicted by a curve of the equation

$$C = a + bY. \tag{4–2}$$

In this equation a is the level of consumption when income is zero, and b is the slope of the curve, which measures the amount (in percent) by which consumption increases with each dollar increase in income. Keynes called the latter the *marginal* propensity to consume. He said there exists a "fundamental psychological law" relating changes in consumption to changes in income; ". . . men," he said, "are disposed, as a rule and on the average, to increase their consumption as their income increases, but by not as much as the increase in their income."[7] What this means is that if your income increases by one dollar, you will not spend the entire dollar increase—a part

[7] Keynes, *The General Theory*, p. 96.

of the increase will be saved. In algebraic form, Keynes's fundamental psychological law, the marginal propensity to consume, is expressed as $\Delta C/\Delta Y$. (The Greek letter Δ means a change in the variable it precedes.) The normal value of this ratio is less than 1. Figure 4–5 depicts Keynes's consumption-income relationship. Keynes's concept of the *consumption function* is the fundamental building block for the Keynesian aggregate demand curve.

Investment and Government Spending

What of the other two components of aggregate demand in a closed economy—investment spending (I) and government purchases of goods and services (G)? As Table 4–3 shows, investment spending is a highly volatile component of the GDP: it fell to a low of 2.9 percent of GDP in the depth of the Great Depression (1933) and rose to a high of 19.1 percent in 1950. Government spending is far less volatile, but it has grown steadily in relative importance since 1929, the eve of the Great Crash. During World War II, government purchases reached a peak of 45.9 percent of the GDP (in 1944). Most of this, of course, was for war materials and pay to the armed forces; it overwhelmingly represented federal spending. Since 1960, the total buying of goods and services by government has averaged about 19 percent of the GDP. One-fifth of the output pie, in other words, goes to the purchase of

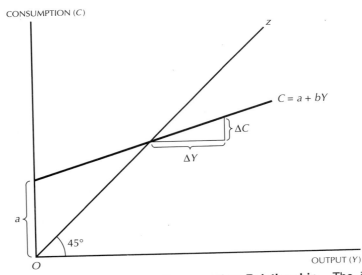

FIGURE 4–5 Keynes's Income-Consumption Relationship. The income-consumption curve depicts the relationship between consumption spending (C) and income (Y). The slope of the curve ($\Delta C/\Delta Y$) is called the marginal propensity to consume (MPC). The distance a represents consumption at a zero income level, which is consumption independent of income.

goods and services by the various levels of government. The public, or government, sector has become a stable and significant element in the overall aggregate demand picture. A word of caution is in order here. The total we are discussing, including the percentages shown in Table 4–3, *does not* include transfer payments. They do not enter directly into aggregate demand—a point we shall explore much more fully in Chapter 9.

Keynes had much to say about investment spending, but actually very little about government spending. Most of macroeconomic theory concerning government spending and aggregate demand developed after World War II. Essentially, what Keynes did was to accept the basic classical view that investment spending was related inversely to the rate of interest (as depicted in Figure 3–2), but to add to this argument a new element—uncertainty. Investment spending is geared to future expectations about what demand will be for the goods and services produced with the help of newly created capital goods. Capital is, of course, the end result of investment spending. But since the future is *always* an unknown, the decision by business executives to undertake investment spending is a shot in the dark. This accounts for the volatility and instability of investment spending. Keynes believed that the volatility of investment spending was the single most important source of instability in a system of market capitalism. We shall analyze how Keynes developed his theory and the current status of macroeconomic thinking about investment spending in Chapter 8. At this point, the minimal theoretical relationship necessary for the development of the basic Keynesian model is the idea that, other things being equal, investment spending is a function of the rate of interest.

What both consumption spending and investment spending have in common is that they are determined by other *economic* variables—income in the case of consumption and interest in the case of investment. Government spending for goods and services is different. It is an economic variable, but the *magnitude* of the government component of the GDP is a consequence of political rather than economic factors. It is the action of the Congress, the state legislatures, and the many thousands of units of county and city governments, not to mention school boards, that accounts for the size of the *G* element in the structure of aggregate demand. This is not to say that economic factors do not play an important role in determining the size of government spending for goods and services. They do, as we shall see in Chapter 9, but it is not possible at this point to suggest any basic functional relationship between *G* and other economic variables, such as income or the rate of interest.

Constructing the Keynesian Aggregate Demand Curve

Does the fact that investment and government spending are not related directly to income mean we are stymied in our task of building an aggregate demand curve that can be juxtaposed to the aggregate supply curve and

thereby show how output and employment are determined in a pure Keynesian model? By no means. The key to doing this lies in another idea frequently
used in economic analysis—the idea that a particular variable is *autonomous*
with respect to another specific variable. *Autonomous* in this context simply
means that the value of an economic variable is independent from the value
of the other economic variable; it does not, as in a functional relationship,
depend on the value of the second variable.

Let us apply this idea to both investment and government spending. Although investment spending may be linked functionally to the rate of interest,
and government spending may depend on other, as yet unnamed economic
variables, we can say that both types of spending are *autonomous* with respect
to income. To put it another way, we can assume for the purposes of our
analysis at this point that investment (I) and government spending (G) are
independent of the income level. Unlike consumption spending (C) they do
not change as income changes. This is, of course, an oversimplification, but
a useful and necessary one at this stage of our analysis.

By using the consumption function (Figure 4–5) as our basic building
block and combining it with the idea that *both* investment (I) and government
spending (G) are autonomous with respect to the level of income (Y), we can
now construct the basic Keynesian aggregate demand curve for a closed economy. This is done in Figure 4–6. All we need to do is to add to the consumption curve for each possible level of output or income (shown on the

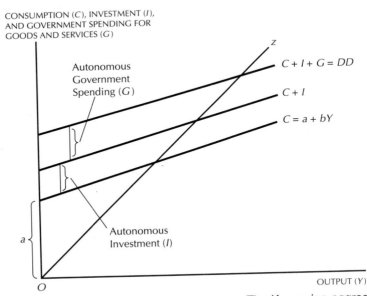

FIGURE 4–6 The Aggregate Demand Curve. The Keynesian aggregate demand curve is constructed by adding an autonomous volume of investment (I) and
government spending on goods and services (G) to the Keynesian consumption
function ($C = a + bY$).

horizontal axis), an *autonomous* quantity of both investment and government spending. The fact that we are assuming for the moment that investment and government spending are autonomous with respect to income does not mean they do not have an economic value. We are simply assuming for the moment that this value is a *given*.

What this procedure gives us is an upward-sloping aggregate demand curve, which includes all three components of aggregate demand—consumption, investment, and government spending—and whose basic slope is determined by the underlying slope of the consumption curve. Thus, as investment and government spending are added to consumption in Figure 4–6, the line shifts up but remains parallel to the consumption line. Further, the overall level of the aggregate demand curve depends on not only the autonomous values assumed for investment and government spending, but the value given to a in the consumption function ($C = a + bY$). Recall that a was defined as the level of consumption when income is zero; this means a is the autonomous element in consumption spending.

The Equilibrium Level of Income and Employment

The aggregate supply and aggregate demand curves take us directly to the heart of modern income and employment theory. The basic, and in many respects simple, idea that Keynes put forth in *The General Theory* is that the *aggregate supply and demand curves* of the economy between them determine the level of income and employment. According to Keynes, "the volume of employment is given by the point of intersection between the aggregate demand function and the aggregate supply function. . . . This is the substance of the General Theory of Employment."[8] This statement from Keynes also underscores why it is so important to develop *fully* the concept of an aggregate supply curve. Models that ignore this simply miss what is the most fundamental point in *The General Theory*.

The way in which aggregate supply and aggregate demand, considered together, determine the income and employment level is shown in Figure 4–7. As in Figures 4–3 through 4–6, real income is shown on both the vertical and horizontal axes. Again, the 45° line OZ is the aggregate supply curve, whereas the line DD is the aggregate demand curve. Given these two curves, the volume of income and employment will inevitably adjust to the level found at the point they intersect. This is represented by the income level Y_e, which is both the equilibrium income level and the equilibrium employment level.

The reason income and employment must of necessity adjust to the level represented by Y_e and why this particular level represents income and employment equilibrium can best be understood if we analyze what will happen assuming for the moment that some other income level exists in the economy.

[8] Ibid., p. 25.

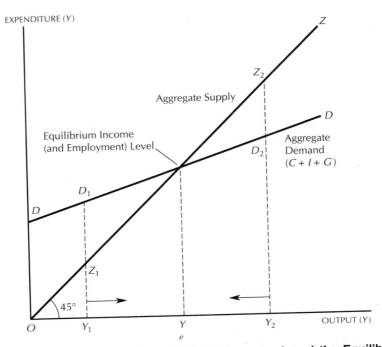

FIGURE 4–7 Aggregate Supply, Aggregate Demand, and the Equilibrium Level of Income. When aggregate demand exceeds aggregate supply, output and employment will rise, but when aggregate supply exceeds aggregate demand, output and employment will fall.

Let us assume that business firms (in the aggregate) anticipate or expect sales equal to Y_1Z_1; therefore, they will produce that amount of goods and services and pay out income to owners of economic resources equal to OY_1 in the process. What is the situation with respect to aggregate demand? The current income level Y_1 is not an equilibrium income level, because at this particular level aggregate demand DD exceeds aggregate supply OZ. Total *ex ante* spending is equal to Y_1D_1. This is an unstable, or *disequilibrium*, condition that cannot be sustained; instead it will drive the economy toward higher levels of income and employment.

Let us look more closely at what is taking place in the current income period. In the first place, additional purchasing power over and above the amounts generated by current income is being injected into the economy's income stream. Diagrammatically, this is represented by the distance Z_1D_1, since the excess of aggregate demand over aggregate supply is a measure of the amount of purchasing power required beyond that being generated by the process of production. For our immediate purposes the exact source of this purchasing power does not matter; what does matter is that new spending power is being injected into the income system. If the distance Z_1D_1 is a measure of the excess of current spending intentions over current (actual) output, how will the spending plans of the economy's spending units be satisfied? Since our analysis is in real terms, we have precluded any increase in the general level of prices as a result of the excess of aggregate demand. But if we rule out price changes and if current supply falls short of demand, there remains only one other alternative: the excess of aggregate demand must be satisfied by sales out of existing stocks *(inventories)* of goods. The distance Z_1D_1 represents not only the excess of aggregate demand over aggregate supply in the current income period, but also the amount by which current inventories of goods must be drawn down to satisfy this demand. From the standpoint of the whole economy, the distance represents *unintended (unplanned) disinvestment* in stocks. Such disinvestment is unintended because it results solely from the failure of production or output plans to coincide with spending plans in the current income period.

How does the situation that we have been describing appear from the point of view of the business firms of the economy? Typically, in this situation business firms will find their sales running ahead of current production; consequently they will revise their production plans upward for the next income period in the belief that the existing demand is a reliable indicator of demand in subsequent income periods. If most firms in the economy act accordingly, then output and employment will rise throughout the whole economy. This process of adjustment will necessarily continue until a situation is achieved in which output and spending decisions coincide. In Figure 4–7 this is the situation depicted by the intersection of the aggregate supply and aggregate demand curves.

The foregoing analysis serves not only to show the essentials of the process by which income and employment adjust toward equilibrium values, but also to underscore the fact that disequilibrium, which always implies change, occurs whenever expected, or *ex ante,* values diverge from actual, or *ex post,* values. In the analysis we have been pursuing, entrepreneurs expected demand to be at the level Y_1Z_1; this led them to produce output at the rate Y_1. But aggregate demand turned out to be at the level Y_1D_1, reflecting the spending intentions of consumers, business firms (for investment), and governments. Changes in the income and employment levels in subsequent income periods stem from this initial divergence between expected and actual values. There is no inherent reason why expected and actual values should always coincide. Modern income and employment theory stresses that spending and output decisions are made by different groups or persons, so there is no reason to expect the two values always to be equal. The reader should note this carefully, for it is basic to the explanation of the *why* of changes in income and employment levels in the modern economy.

To round out our present discussion of the equilibrium income level, let us postulate a situation just the opposite of the one we have considered. Let us assume that in the current income period the supply of output is in excess of the demand for that output. In Figure 4–7 this is depicted at the income level Y_2, as measured on the horizontal axis. At this income level the aggregate supply curve OZ lies above the aggregate demand curve DD. Output in the current income period equals Y_2Z_2, but *ex ante* spending decisions or current demand for that output only add up to the distance D_2Y_2, with the consequence that, for the income period in question, *there is unintended (unplanned) investment* in stocks or inventories. More money income or purchasing power is being generated by current output than is being spent on that output; once more, a disequilibrium situation exists.

The typical business firm sees this as an unhappy situation in which sales fall short of current production and the firm suffers losses. Unless an immediate change to a better sales position is anticipated, the firm will have no choice but to revise downward its production plans for subsequent income periods. As most firms in the economy do this, output and employment levels for the whole economy will decline. Such a downward adjustment of income and employment must continue until a point is reached at which the supply of output is no longer in excess of current demand for the output. This, again, is the situation shown in Figure 4–7 by the intersection of the aggregate supply and aggregate demand curves.

Let us enter here an important *caveat*. Do not forget, as was stressed in the box on page 83, equilibrium is an intellectual tool we use to try and understand the workings of the real-world economy. It is an extremely valuable tool, but it should not be mistaken for a description of economic reality. The real-world economy is always in motion, continually adjusting to constantly changing forces.

A Numerical Example

The process of adjustment of income and employment to an equilibrium level can be illustrated by means of a simple arithmetic example that employs a set of hypothetical data pertaining to employment, aggregate demand, and aggregate supply. Table 4–4 provides these data. In column 1 are shown the varying amounts of employment associated with different levels of aggregate

TABLE 4–4   The Equilibrium of Income and Employment

(1) Employment N (in millions of workers)	(2) Aggregate Supply or National Income OZ (in billions of dollars)	(3) Aggregate Demand DD (in billions of dollars)	(4) Direction of Change in Income and Employment	(5) Unplanned Inventory Change (in billions of dollars)
100	$4,700	4,900	Rise	$-200
102	4,800	4,950	Rise	-150
104	4,900	5,000	Rise	-100
106	5,000	5,050	Rise	- 50
108	5,100	5,100	**Equilibrium**	—
110	5,200	5,150	Fall	+ 50
112	5,300	5,200	Fall	+100
114	5,400	5,250	Fall	+150
116	5,500	5,300	Fall	+200

output (or national income) for our imaginary economy. The various possible levels of national output are given in column 2, which is the aggregate supply schedule. For each of these various output levels, producers will incur costs exactly equal to the value of the output produced. Column 3 is the aggregate demand schedule and shows the amounts that spending units are prepared to spend at each possible income or output level shown in column 2. Column 4 tells us in which direction income and employment can be expected to change in response to the various levels of aggregate supply and aggregate demand. Column 5 shows the unplanned inventory changes that result when DD and OZ are unequal. All figures are in constant dollars.

In Table 4–4 there is only one possible income level at which total spending in the economy is just equal to the value of current output. This condition occurs at an output level of $5,100 billion and an employment level of 108 million. At all other possible values for income and output, disequilibrium is present. Suppose, for example, that current output is equal to $4,800 billion. At this level the aggregate demand schedule, column 3, shows that spending units in the aggregate intend to spend at a rate of $4,950 billion. Total spending, in other words, will run ahead of total output by an amount equal to $150 billion. Under these circumstances, and in view of our explicit assumption that prices remain constant, there can be only one possible outcome: employment and production must rise. Under these circumstances, the $150 billion of excess demand represents the amount by which stocks of goods will be drawn down during the income period so that the spending intentions of the spending units can be satisfied.

Just the reverse will hold true if output in any income period rises above the equilibrium level of $5,100 billion. If production proceeds, say, at an annual rate of $5,300 billion, producers are doomed to disappointment because at this particular income level the total of spending decisions in the economy amount to only $5,200 billion. Producers will find that inventories of unsold goods are accumulating at an unwanted rate of $100 billion per year. The economy has not failed through its current productive activity to generate enough purchasing power to clear the market of all goods and services produced, but rather it has failed to spend this purchasing power at the same rate at which it is being created.

Characteristics of the Income Equilibrium

The analysis so far attempts to explain how, in a most fundamental sense, aggregate demand and aggregate supply are the key determinants of income and employment levels. *This is the crux of Keynesian employment theory.* If the aggregate supply and aggregate demand schedules (and curves) are known, it is possible to determine both the income and employment level for the economy.

But—and this is a point of critical importance—the equilibrium level of income and employment brought about by the interaction of aggregate demand and aggregate supply will not automatically be one of *full employment.*

Since decisions to produce and decisions to spend are made independently, it is largely a matter of chance whether or not they happen to coincide at a level of output that represents full employment of the economy's labor force. The economic forces embodied in the analytical concepts of aggregate supply and aggregate demand must of necessity drive the economy toward an equilibrium position, but there is nothing special in these forces that will in any way make full employment the normal state of affairs in the economy.

In fact, one basic lesson of modern income and employment analysis is that *any* level of employment may be normal in the sense that it may be sustained over a considerable period of time. For example, during the whole decade of the 1930s, large-scale unemployment was the normal situation in the U.S. economy. More recently, from the 1970s into the 1990s, unemployment averaged more than 2 percentage points higher than it did in the first quarter century after World War II. If there is a deficiency of aggregate demand relative to a full-employment output, the economy will experience a *deflationary gap* and may reach equilibrium at less than full employment. On the other hand, if aggregate demand persistently runs ahead of full-employment aggregate supply, there will be an *inflationary gap*. The latter situation is characterized by strong upward pressure on the price level and the percentage of the labor force unemployed will fall below the level normally thought of as full. The essential point to remember is that, in the short run, the economy can achieve equilibrium of income and employment at levels that represent full employment, less than full employment, or even "overly" full employment. This last is made possible through inventory adjustments, that is, drawing down inventories. No one level is in any sense inherently more normal than any other level. The economy does not automatically move through market processes toward such a full-employment equilibrium. It all depends on the relationship existing in any given time interval between aggregate supply and aggregate demand.

But one should not assume that use of the equilibrium concept as a technique for analyzing change means that the economy necessarily settles down into a steady situation with respect to income and employment. The main thrust of Keynes's great work is instability—not just the failure of the economy to attain full employment much of the time, but the inherently unstable nature of a market economy. The basic reason is that the economic forces that lie behind aggregate demand, especially investment spending, are unstable—a subject which we shall develop in greater depth subsequently. Thus, the economy may be tending toward an equilibrium as depicted in Figure 4–6 and Table 4–4, but before it reaches a stable situation, the aggregate demand schedule may change. How this type of change affects the system is discussed in the next section.

Changes in Income and Employment

Besides explaining how the level of employment is determined, the foregoing analytical framework serves to explain the how and the why of change within the economic system. The vital principle running through our analysis is that change is the inevitable outcome of a situation in which expected and actual events do not agree; that is to say change will occur whenever *ex ante* and *ex post* values do not coincide. Insofar as income and employment are concerned, this means that these magnitudes will be changing whenever aggregate supply and aggregate demand are not in balance.

Recall the comments made at the beginning of Chapter 3 about movements along a curve versus shifts in a curve. Within the broad Keynesian framework just described, these two distinct kinds of change can take place. In the first instance, change may come about because, with given curves of aggregate supply and aggregate demand, actual output or income fails to correspond to the demand for that output. This is the kind of situation depicted in Figure 4–7. The resultant change is the adjustment of the income and employment levels toward equilibrium values that are based on a given position for the curves of aggregate supply and aggregate demand. Changes of this type originate with the producing units of the economy because they come about as a result of the failure of entrepreneurs to judge accurately the level of demand for the output of the whole economy.

Change is also involved in the movement of the economic system from one equilibrium level to another. In the short run, such change results from a shift in the position of the aggregate demand curve that occurs when the spending units of the economy are predisposed to spend more (or less) of current output at any and all levels of income. This shift in the position of the aggregate demand curve will disturb a previously existing equilibrium between spending and output decisions and thereby set in motion all the forces involved in the adjustment of the economy toward equilibrium values for income and employment.

The latter type of change is illustrated in Figure 4–8. Schedule DD represents the original position of the aggregate demand curve; output will adjust to the level Y_e, which is the intersection of the aggregate supply curve OZ and the aggregate demand curve DD. If, however, aggregate demand shifts to the level represented by curve $D'D'$, then the existing equilibrium income level Y_e is disturbed. The immediate consequence of this shift is to create a new situation in which aggregate demand at Y_e exceeds aggregate supply or output. This will set in motion forces making for change; income and employment will rise until a new equilibrium results at the level Y'_e. The important thing to note is that the original impetus for this type of change came from the spending rather than the producing units in the economy.

The Keynesian Multiplier

This brings us to another of Keynes's major conceptual inventions. This is the *multiplier*. Careful examination of Figure 4–8 reveals that, geometrically, the change in income (Y) that brought the economy to the new equilibrium income level of Y'_e is greater than the amount by which the aggregate demand curve (DD) has shifted upward. This is the *multiplier effect*. Algebraically,

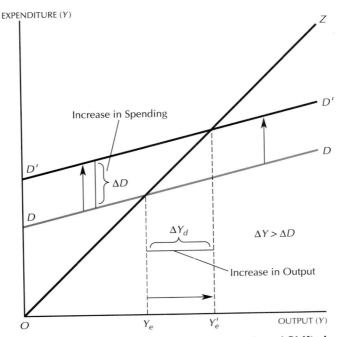

FIGURE 4–8   Aggregate Supply, Aggregate Demand, and Shifts in the Equilibrium Level of Income.   An upward shift in the aggregate demand curve will upset an existing equilibrium and cause output and employment to rise until the economy reaches a new equilibrium. Note that the increase in output (ΔY) is greater than the increase in spending (ΔD). This is the multiplier effect.

ΔY is greater than ΔD. The multiplier idea also can be illustrated with a simple, numerical example. This is done in Table 4–5. The original aggregate demand schedule is shifted upward by $50 billion—an *autonomous* shift because at all possible income levels aggregate demand (DD) is $50 billion higher than it was originally (Table 4–4). According to the figures in Table 4–5, the new equilibrium level is $5,200 billion, an amount $100 billion greater than the prior equilibrium of $5,100 billion. Thus, a $50 billion autonomous increase in aggregate demand leads ultimately to a $100 billion increase in output (Y). This is the multiplier at work.

How is this to be explained? The secret lies in Keynes's theory of the consumption function. More precisely, the multiplier effect arises out of Keynes's fundamental psychological law, the idea that when our income goes up, we spend a portion but *not all* of the increase. As we saw earlier, the percentage of the increase in income spent is called the "marginal propensity to consume." When aggregate demand shifted upward as in Figure 4–8 and Table 4–5, the economy experienced an *autonomous* increase in spending, irrespective of why the shift took place or how it was financed. But an increase in spending means that someone's income somewhere in the economy has risen. So what happened?

TABLE 4–5   A Shift in the Equilibrium Level of Income and Employment

(1) Employment (N) (in millions of workers)	(2) Aggregate Supply or National Income (OZ) (in billions of dollars)	(3) Aggregate Demand (DD) before Shift (in billions of dollars)	(4) Aggregate Demand (D'D') after Shift (in billions of dollars)	(5) Direction of Change in Income and Employment after DD Shift
100	$4,700	$4,900	$4,950	Rise
102	4,800	4,950	5,000	Rise
104	4,900	5,000	5,050	Rise
106	5,000 Original	5,050	5,100	Rise
108	5,100 ←equilibrium→ 5,100 New		5,150	Rise
110	5,200	5,150←equilibrium→5,200		—
112	5,300	5,200	5,250	Fall
114	5,400	5,250	5,300	Fall
116	5,500	5,300	5,350	Fall

Change in aggregate demand (DD) = $50 billion.
Change in income (Y) = $100 billion.

According to Keynes's psychological law, persons experiencing an increase in income will spend a portion of that increase on consumption goods and services. Those who supply the consumption goods and services to meet this increase in spending will find that their incomes go up. So they, too, will respond by spending more for consumer goods and services. Here we have the nub of the multiplier process. *Any* autonomous increase in spending stemming from one or more of the aggregate demand components will set off a chain reaction of spending and respending, the ultimate size of which will be greater than the original increase in spending that started the process. Every chamber of commerce in the country has an instinctive grasp of the multiplier process. If a new business with a sizable payroll is brought to town, the chamber knows that the payroll dollars spent each month will circulate and recirculate and thereby give an overall stimulus to the local economy much greater than just the size of the payroll for the new business.

Why does the process run down? Why does not the chain of spendings and respendings go on indefinitely? Here is where the marginal propensity to consume again comes on stage. It runs down eventually because people spend *only* a portion of the increase in income, not the whole of the increase. Thus, in each successive round of spending, the increase in consumption spending gets smaller. Eventually, the increases in consumption spending are so small they are negligible. The process has run its course.

All this was given a formal, theoretical explanation by Keynes in *The General Theory;* we shall do the same in Chapter 7. For our purpose at this point in the analysis, we shall simply define the multiplier, which Keynes designated k, as being equal to the reciprocal of 1 minus the marginal propensity to consume (b in Equation 4–2). Algebraically, we have

$$k = 1/(1 - b). \tag{4–3}$$

Statics and Dynamics

Figure 4–8 describes a particular kind of economic change, namely, the shift from one equilibrium position to another. Technically, this is described as an exercise in *comparative statics*. In economic analysis the term "statics" applies to a situation in which the motion of the system is toward an equilibrium position, as in the examples discussed of the movement toward an income equilibrium. Such a situation is deemed static because all the underlying determinants of the schedules involved—the aggregate demand and supply schedules—are "givens" (or parameters). The motion takes place in response to the economic forces embodied in these schedules—schedules whose positions are presumed known. When one of the schedules changes, as is shown in Figure 4–8, the system will shift to a new equilibrium position, but it still represents an essentially static situation because no further change can take place until there is a new disturbance. Hence, we have the term "comparative statics."

"Dynamics" on the other hand, is a term that connotes continuous change and movement. Equilibrium diagrams of the kind discussed earlier in this chapter are not suitable for the discussion of constant change. One reason is that if change is continuous, then time must become a part of the analysis. But the usual supply and demand types of diagrams so widely used in economic analysis do not embody time. A dynamic approach will view the behavior of the economy as essentially a process taking place through time, whereas a static approach will look at the economy's behavior as a system that tends toward a state of balance. Neither is the only correct approach; both have their uses in helping us to understand the real-world economy.

The means that Keynes came up with to measure how much income would change was to multiply the autonomous change in spending—the shift upward in DD in Figure 4–8 and Table 4–5—by the multiplier. Again, algebraically, we have

$$\Delta Y = k \times \Delta DD. \qquad (4\text{–}4)$$

Now if we assume a value of 0.5 for the marginal propensity to consume of the consumption function that undergirds aggregate demand in Figures 4–7 and 4–8, then the value of the multiplier is 2 $[1/(1 - 0.5) = 2]$. When the autonomous change in spending ($50 billion) brought about by the upward shift in aggregate demand (DD) is multiplied by the multiplier (2), we have the ultimate increase in total income, namely $100 billion.[9]

[9] There are, of course, formal algebraic proofs showing why the multiplier in its simplest form must be equal to the reciprocal of 1 minus the marginal propensity to consume. These proofs are developed in Chapter 7.

The Keynesian Income-Expenditure Model Summarized

The essential elements of the income-expenditure model developed to this point may be summarized as follows:

1. In the short run, defined as a period of time in which productive capacity is fixed, the employment level will vary directly with the extent to which productive capacity is being utilized.

2. In the private sector of the economy, the extent to which productive capacity is actually utilized depends on the entrepreneur's expectation that the sales proceeds will be sufficient to cover the costs incurred in the production of any given volume of output. The aggregate supply schedule represents the formal, analytical expression of this idea, because it is a schedule (or curve) showing the expected proceeds necessary to induce entrepreneurs in the aggregate to offer a given amount of employment or produce a given output of goods and services on a continuing basis.

3. The aggregate demand schedule associates spending decisions with differing levels of real income. It shows, in other words, the amounts that will be spent for output at each and every possible income level.

4. With aggregate supply and aggregate demand shown as curves, the equilibrium level of income and employment for the economy will be determined by their intersection. There is nothing inherent in these forces of aggregate supply and aggregate demand to assure that this equilibrium will be one of full employment.

5. Change in the economy's level of income and employment results from the failure of the output and spending plans embodied in the curves of aggregate supply and demand to coincide. In the short run, such changes may take the form of a movement toward an equilibrium position, given an initial imbalance between output and spending, or a movement from one equilibrium position to another. This latter type of change is contingent on a shift in the aggregate demand curve.

Bringing Economic Policy into the Analysis

We are at a point where it is appropriate to introduce some general comments about *economic policy* into our discussion. The word ''policy'' refers to some course of action that is designed to realize or bring about some specific objective or end. Policy is concerned with what we want and how we get it. *Economic* policy thus has to do with the means that individuals, groups, or the whole society may utilize to achieve ends or objectives that are primarily of an economic nature. Economic policy was not discussed in Chapter 3 because it lies outside the classical system, unnecessary and unwanted.

In the Keynesian system, economic policy is necessary and desirable. The ends or objectives of economic policy include, among others, full employment, a stable price level, maximum output, and a desirable rate of economic growth. More specifically, we can define economic policy as using theoretical economic knowledge to achieve objectives broadly agreed on by society. Policy, in other words, involves the application of what we know about how the economy works (our theoretical knowledge) to attain socially desirable ends, such as full employment or an adequate rate of growth. Policy may be likened to engineering, an applied activity that draws on basic theoretical knowledge in physics and chemistry to build bridges, make airplanes, construct gasoline engines, and do a host of other things that are commonplace to the modern world.

As far as the overall macroeconomic performance of the economy is concerned, there are two fundamental policy instruments available in modern systems of market capitalism. These instruments are normally used by the national government to attain the kind of objects sought by the 1946 Employment Act (discussed in Chapter 2). They are *fiscal* and *monetary* policy.

Fiscal policy involves using the spending and taxing power of the national government to influence such things as output (Y) and employment (N), the price level (p), or the rate of economic growth. Fiscal policy normally works through the budget of the central government, the federal government in the United States. For example, if taxes were cut for the *primary* purpose of putting more spending power into the hands of consumers so that the economy would be stimulated, this would be a fiscal policy action. In the United States, the administration in control of the White House in cooperation with the Congress is responsible for initiating and carrying out fiscal policies. This is because all matters involving federal taxing and spending normally come about through the combined action of the White House and the Congress.

Monetary policy is different. It involves using the money supply (M) and the price of money (the rate of interest) to influence the level of economic activity. Money and its cost (i.e., the rate of interest) are key variables which enter into many private and public decisions about production and the buying of output. Hence, control over money and interest is an important means to influence economic activity. Unlike fiscal policy, whose design and execution is divided between the executive and legislative branch of the federal government, the design and execution of monetary policy is centered in the nation's central bank, known as the Federal Reserve System. We shall examine more fully in Chapters 5 and 11 money and its influence on the economy, as well as the workings of the Federal Reserve System.

What is crucial to grasp, especially in connection with the analysis that we are pursuing in this chapter, is that *both* fiscal and monetary policy work *primarily* through the impact they have on the aggregate demand. From the perspective of the Keynesian income-expenditure model, the object of policy is to modify the economy's performance by influencing one or more of the spending components that enter into the aggregate demand function, namely, consumption (C), investment (I), government spending for goods and services (G), and, in an open economy, the net export-import balance ($X - M$). To bring policy into the discussion, we must show how policy actions affect either aggregate demand, aggregate supply, or both. This generalization applies not only to the Keynesian income-expenditure model just discussed, but also to the Keynesian-classical model we shall discuss in the remaining pages of this chapter, as well as the classical model discussed earlier in Chapter 3. One of our main purposes is to have a theoretical mechanism by which we can show how a variety of policy measures will affect the economy's performance.

A Keynesian-Classical Model

In the concluding section of Chapter 3 we developed a formal classical model in an aggregate demand and aggregate supply framework. This model, as we noted, was a post-Keynesian development. It drew heavily on the fundamentals of classical thinking as Keynes explained them in *The General Theory,* but put classical ideas into the framework of aggregate demand and supply—something Keynes did not do in his masterwork. In this section we turn to the second objective of this chapter, namely to develop an aggregate demand and aggregate supply model that incorporates classical ideas about the relationship between output and the price level, and Keynesian ideas about the relationship between output and total spending. As noted at the beginning of this chapter, this model is characterized as Keynesian-classical because of the way it blends together Keynesian and classical ideas. It gives us a useful theoretical mechanism to explain the effect of policy decisions on prices as well as on output and employment. It also helps in comparing the policy implications inherent in the various perspectives in macroeconomic thought.

The Keynesian-Classical Aggregate Demand Curve

The Keynesian-classical aggregate demand curve is an extension of the classical demand curve developed in Chapter 3. To be precise, the aggregate demand curve in a Keynesian-classical context shows the *inverse* relationship between the price level (p) and spending for output (Y), holding *constant* expected profits from investment, the nominal (actual) money supply ($M°$), and *real* government spending and taxation. Holding the latter variables constant means, in effect, that the Keynesian aggregate demand curve is a given at any particular price level.

The reason given in Chapter 3 for a downward-sloping aggregate demand curve is that at higher prices, a given money supply and velocity of money can only support spending on a smaller quantity of real output. And at a lower price level, once again given the quantity of money and a constant velocity of circulation, a larger quantity of real output could be purchased. The relationship between the price level and real output is also known as the *real balance effect*. This is because with a lower price level, the *real* purchasing power of a given quantity of money (*M*) is greater. With a higher price level, the result is, of course, the opposite. There are two other important reasons that the aggregate demand curve slopes downward. These are the *interest rate effect* and the *trade balance effect*.

The interest rate effect depends on the real balance effect. If there is a given demand for money, an increase in the price level will lead to a smaller *real* money supply—the real balance effect. But this will drive the interest rate higher and thereby cause less spending for investment and durable consumer goods. Aggregate demand in the Keynesian sense declines. When the price level falls, the opposite will happen. A lower price level means a *larger real* money supply, which leads to lower interest rates and thereby increases aggregate demand because of more investment and consumer spending for durable goods.

The trade balance effect reflects the impact of higher domestic prices on exports and imports. When the domestic price level increases relative to foreign prices, domestic goods become more expensive on world markets. As a result, the trade balance moves toward a deficit as the demand for exports shrinks and the demand for imports increases. The net result is a lower level of aggregate demand at the higher price level. If domestic prices fall relative to world prices, exports increase and imports fall. This leads to a surplus in the trade balance and an increase in aggregate demand at the lower domestic price level.

We can use the Keynesian income-expenditure model developed earlier in this chapter to derive the Keynesian-classical aggregate demand curve. Figure 4–9 shows an income-expenditure model with two aggregate demand curves, each of which is related to a different price level. When the price level rises from p_1 to p_2, the real balance, the interest rate, and the trade balance effects lead to a lower level of aggregate spending, as reflected in the downward shift of the aggregate demand curve from $D(p_1)$ to $D(p_2)$. As a result, equilibrium output falls from Y_2 to Y_1. The lower half of the diagram traces out this change and shows how an increased demand for output is associated with a lower price level. In principle, there is a unique level of aggregate spending associated with every possible level of prices. Thus, the Keynesian-classical aggregate demand curve (*AD*) is constructed by linking all possible levels of spending (aggregate demand) to all possible price levels.

The Keynesian-Classical Aggregate Supply Curve

Among the assumptions embodied in the classical model are those of wage and price flexibility and the absence of a money illusion. Given these assumptions, the classical model shows that *any* disequilibrium in the labor

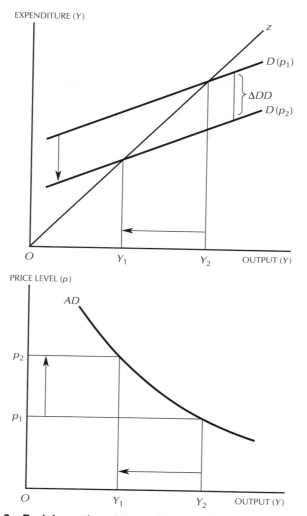

FIGURE 4–9 Deriving the Keynesian-Classical Aggregate Demand Curve. When the price level increases, the real balance, interest rate, and trade balance effects cause a reduction in aggregate demand, which in turn leads to a reduction in output from Y_2 to Y_1.

market involving involuntary unemployment is self-correcting: it will be eliminated quickly by competitive wage bidding among workers. If the *real* wage is above its equilibrium value, the absence of a money illusion means that workers and employers will recognize this fact. Therefore, money wages will be bid downward (the classical economists assumed that wages and prices were flexible) until the equilibrium real wage is restored. This argument leaves us with the classical conclusion that both monetary and fiscal polices are unnecessary and unworkable. The short-term classical aggregate supply curve appears as a vertical line at the level of output (and employment) determined by the aggregate demand for and aggregate supply of labor (Figure 3–6).

Now, however, we need to ask a different question. What would be the theoretical shape of a price-output-related aggregate supply curve if the assumption of *no* money illusion were relaxed? We shall explore this question here, and examine, too, some empirical (actual) data on output and the price level to see which theoretical construct best fits reality. Later, in Chapter 12, we shall look critically at the assumption of wage and price flexibility, a key pillar for all classical analysis.

The Money Illusion and Aggregate Supply

The classical policy implications stem from the assumptions that underlie a competitive labor market and the classical belief that people do not suffer from a money illusion, even in the short run. At all times, in other words, it is assumed that people make their employment and production decisions on the basis of real wages and relative prices. But to really do this, people would have to make correct forecasts of prices at all times. For the worker this is correct because the real wage is the ratio of the money wage to the prices that a worker must pay for goods and services over the period during which a money wage is received. The workers know the money wage, but prices must be forecast. The foregoing idea is summarized in Equation 4–5:

$$W = w/p^e \tag{4–5}$$

where W = the real wage,

      w = the money wage,

      p^e = the expected price level.

The real wage that the worker "knows" is only a perception based on a forecast of the future price level. Here is the key: any mistaken forecast will result in an error in the perceived real wage and consequently workers will make errors in their decisions to supply labor.

To see this, assume that prices and money wages rise by more than workers expect. As mentioned above, workers know the money wage, but because they do not have perfect information about prices, they must make a forecast of future prices. If, as assumed, money wages and prices both rise by more than workers expected, they will perceive that the real wage is now higher. This leads them to increase their quantity of labor supplied. Workers suffer from the money illusion because they respond to a higher money wage as though it were a higher real wage. If, on the other hand, money wages and prices fall by more than workers expected, they would react to a lower money wage as if their real wage had fallen and would reduce the quantity of labor supplied.

There are two rules to remember in analyzing the behavior of workers when the money illusion is present:

1. If money wages and prices rise by more than workers expect, they will increase the quantity of labor supplied.
2. If money wages and prices rise by less than workers expect, they will react by decreasing the quantity of labor supplied.

The presence of a money illusion also has implications for producers. Microeconomics teaches that production decisions in market economies depend on *relative* price signals and not on general price level changes. However, individual producers often cannot distinguish between general and relative price changes. For example, imagine that Rebecca, a computer chip manufacturer, sees the prices of her chips rise. How does she know whether the increase is because of an increase in the demand for computer chips (a relative price change) or because of a general increase in all prices? The answer is that she doesn't; she can only judge the price increase relative to her forecast, that is, her expectation, of the future price level. When the price of chips rises by more than she had expected the general price level to rise, she interprets it as a relative price increase for her chips. Since she may not recognize that prices and money wages in general are increasing, she believes that her costs will remain stable. Therefore, Rebecca expects higher profits from additional chip sales, so she responds by producing more chips. Conversely, if the price of her chips rises by less than she had expected the general price level to rise, she interprets this as the result of a decrease in the demand for her chips, and since she believes her costs will remain stable, she reduces production.

From this discussion we can derive two rules for producer behavior with respect to general price increases when the money illusion is present:

1. When prices rise by more than expected, the difference is interpreted as a relative price increase and producers increase their output.
2. When prices rise by less than expected, the difference is interpreted as a relative price decrease and producers reduce their output.

What would a price-level–output–structured aggregate supply curve look like if we relax the assumption of *no* money illusion? Logic tells us that the aggregate supply curve would not be vertical; rather, it would slope upward and to the right. When other factors such as the expected price level, technology, and the stock of capital are held constant, a higher price level (p) will lead to higher levels of output (Y). Figure 4–10 shows such an aggregate supply curve (AS). Assume that initially the price level is p_1 and that people don't expect the price level to change in the future; that is, $p^e = p_1$. Output is at Y_1, and since actual and expected price are equal, there is, momentarily, no money illusion.

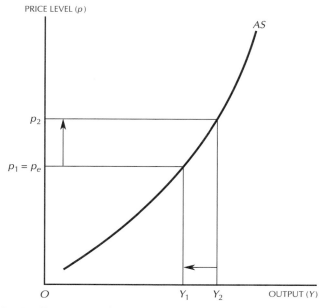

FIGURE 4–10 The Keynesian-Classical Aggregate Supply Curve with a Money Illusion.   When the actual price level is equal to the price level that workers and producers expect, output and employment are at Y_1. When prices and nominal wages rise unexpectedly, labor supply and output increase due to the money illusion. Output moves to Y_2.

Suppose, however, that the price level rises unexpectedly from p_1 to p_2. What will happen? Recall the rules just discussed. Producers, seeing the price for their product rise more than they expected—remember all prices are rising—may believe there has been a *relative* price increase. Hence, they will produce more. As they proceed to increase production, they demand more labor. This will result in a rise in money wages. Workers, seeing the money wage rise more than expected, mistake this in turn for an increase in the real wage and, therefore, supply more hours of labor. Because both workers and business firms suffer from a money illusion, they respond to an increase in the general price level (p) by increasing both output (Y) and employment (N).

If the price level and nominal wages fall below those which workers and businesses expect, the above result is reversed. Businesses see the prices they require for their products fall by more than they expect. Instead of taking the price reduction for what it is, a general reduction in all prices, businesses see it as a fall in the relative prices of their products. Hence, businesses cut production and so reduce their demand for labor and with it the money wage. Workers interpret the reduction in the money wage as a lower real wage,

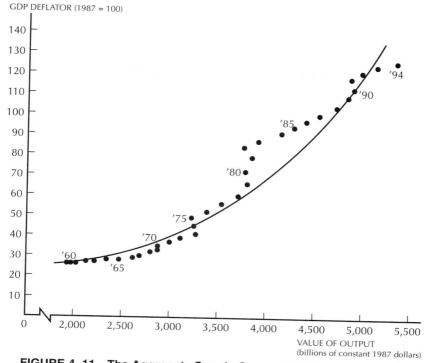

GDP DEFLATOR (1987 = 100)

FIGURE 4–11   The Aggregate Supply Curve: GDP Deflator and the Value of Output in Constant Prices.   The price level as measured by the GDP deflator rises as GDP measured in constant dollars increases; this reflects the Keynesian-classical output–price-level relationship.

Source: Economic Report of the President, 1995.

since they do not recognize that prices are also falling, and reduce their supply of labor.

Does this Keynesian-classical conception of the aggregate supply schedule correspond with reality? The answer is yes, surprisingly well. This is shown in Figure 4–11, in which a curve has been fitted in rough fashion to a scatter diagram linking the price level as measured by the GDP deflator to output as measured by the GDP in constant prices. The data go back to 1959 (35 years), so they cover much of the post-World War II period. The figure shows clearly that a rising level of output (Y) is associated with a rising price level (p). At this point the reader should compare Figure 4–11 with Figure 4–2, discussed earlier in this chapter. Figure 4–2 also is a scatter diagram, which linked output, GDP measured in constant prices, to expenditures for that output, GDP measured in current or nominal prices. Both these figures tell the same story: in the *real* world higher output is associated with higher prices. A word of caution is in order here. The statistical curves shown in both Figures 4–2 and 4–11 *do not* tell us anything about causation. For that we need the insights

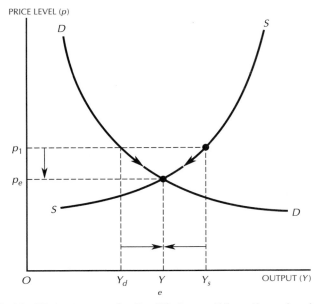

FIGURE 4–12 Macroeconomic Equilibrium. When the price level (p_1) is above the equilibrium price level (p_e), there is a greater aggregate quantity of output supplied than is demanded ($Y_s > Y_d$). With flexible wages and prices, the price level is bid downward until p_e is reached. This is a point at which the aggregate quantities supplied and demanded are equal.

and judgments of economic theory. What the curves do accomplish, however, is help us see if we are on the right track with our theory.

Macroeconomic Equilibrium in a Keynesian-Classical Context

Now that we have developed both the aggregate supply and demand curves in their Keynesian-classical form, we can bring them together to show a macroeconomic equilibrium. Figure 4–12 shows our Keynesian-classical aggregate supply (AS) and aggregate demand (AD) curves. At price level p_1 the price level is too high to sustain output at Y_s, the aggregate quantity of output supplied. This is because the real balance, interest rate, and trade balance effects will only generate an aggregate quantity of output demanded equal to Y_d. Therefore, we have an excess aggregate quantity supplied at price level p_1. Since we are still working under the assumption of wage and price flexibility, the problem will be corrected by competitive bidding of money wages and prices downward. As the price level falls, the real balance, interest rate, and trade balance effects will lead to increases in the quantity of aggregate output demanded. The falling price level will also generate a smaller quantity of aggregate output supplied. When the price level reaches p_e, it will be low enough to sustain an equilibrium level of real output.

Comparing the Keynesian-Classical and Classical Views of Aggregate Demand and Aggregate Supply

In this chapter we constructed within the Keynesian framework two basic models of aggregate demand and aggregate supply. The first model, which is derived directly from *The General Theory,* links the supply of output and the use of output to expected spending decisions by consumers, businesses, and governments. Aggregate supply and aggregate demand are both related in a functional way to spending decisions in the economy. The suppliers of output—the business firms in the economy—make their decisions to produce and hire labor on the basis of their expectations about the levels of demand that will prevail when the output is ready for sale. The users (or buyers) of output—consumers, business firms, and governments—make their decisions to purchase output *independently* of the decisions made by suppliers. For some users, like consumers, decisions to spend are related directly to the income generated by output itself (the consumption function), but for others, like business firms and governments, different factors are involved.

A key point in this analysis is that these two sets of decisions about output are *independent* of each other. Thus, there is no automatic adjustment of the economy to a point where decisions to produce output and decisions to use that output always coincide. There is no guarantee, in other words, that aggregate demand will always adjust to the level of aggregate supply. In the Keynesian framework there is no assurance that Say's law works. As noted at the beginning of this chapter, the Keynesian approach is known as the income-expenditure model. This is the core approach employed in this text; the bulk of our discussion of both theory and policy is developed within this framework. The income-expenditure framework offers the best way for the intermediate student to grasp the complexities of contemporary macroeconomic analysis.

The second aggregate demand and aggregate supply model developed in this chapter has its roots in classical economics, standard microeconomic analysis, and Keynes's income-expenditure theory. This model puts output and buying decisions in the context of the general level of prices, rather than expenditure totals as is done with the income-expenditure model. On the supply side, as we have seen, output is a positive function of the general price level, whereas on the demand side, the decisions to purchase output vary inversely with the general price level. This approach is the analog of the supply and demand schedules used extensively in microeconomic analysis to explain how output and prices in *individual* markets are determined. These price-level–output–related schedules should not be viewed as an alternative and competing approach to the income-expenditures model; rather, they serve to complement and enrich the core income-expenditure approach and provide us with means to analyze some situations not always amenable to the income-expenditure technique.

At this point it is appropriate to underscore the close similarity of the aggregate supply and demand schedules developed in the latter part of this chapter with the Post Keynesian classical aggregate supply and demand schedules worked out in the latter part of Chapter 3. As we have seen, there is no essential theoretical difference between the classical and the Keynesian-classical aggregate demand schedules. For all practical purposes they are identical. This is not the case, however, with aggregate supply. As we saw in Chapter 3, the classical aggregate supply schedule is depicted by a vertical line, the location of which is determined by what happens in the classical labor market. Output in the classical scheme is unaffected by the price level, at least in the short run. The Keynesian-classical aggregate supply schedule has, however, a positive slope; this shows that output (Y) increases as the price level (p) itself increases.

What we have done in this chapter and in Chapter 3 is to develop the fundamental frame of reference through which *all* perspectives in contemporary macroeconomic theory analyze problems and policies pertaining to the whole economy. The unifying thread in this frame of reference is the use of the concepts of supply and demand, two of the most basic analytical tools used by economists of every persuasion. This provides an important bridge between micro and macro analysis, besides offering a coherent means to analyze problems of the economy as a whole.

Summary

1. The central question that macroeconomics must answer is: What determines the extent to which the economy's productive capacity is being utilized?

2. Aggregate demand is the key determinant of the extent to which the economy's productive capacity is used in the short run.

3. An aggregate supply schedule shows levels of output associated with proceeds (income) that entrepreneurs require in order to produce any particular level of output.

4. Aggregate supply schedules and curves can be shown in various ways, depending on whether required proceeds are measured in current or constant prices.

5. An aggregate demand schedule is the counterpart of an aggregate supply schedule; it shows the amount of spending by major spending units—households, firms, governments, and the rest of the world—associated with different income levels.

6. Consumption spending makes up the largest portion of aggregate demand.

7. Investment and government spending are the other two components of aggregate demand in a closed economy. Investment spending, though a small proportion of aggregate demand, has an impact on the economy that is more than proportional to its size.

8. The equilibrium level of income (output) and employment is determined by the intersection of the aggregate demand and aggregate supply curves.

9. Changes in output (and the employment level) come either because the economy is not yet at the level of equilibrium, as determined by the intersection of the aggregate demand and aggregate supply curves, or because of shifts in the aggregate demand curve.

10. The multiplier shows the change in income that is due to an autonomous shift in the aggregate demand curve.

11. The principal macroeconomic policy tools that are available to governments are fiscal and monetary in nature.

12. The Keynesian-classical aggregate supply and aggregate demand model is a Post Keynesian development that combines classical ideas about the relationship between output and prices and Keynesian ideas about the relationship between output and spending.

13. The Keynesian-classical aggregate demand schedule shows the inverse relationship between spending for output and the price level.

14. The real balance, interest rate, and trade balance effects lie behind the downward slope of the Keynesian-classical aggregate demand curve.

15. The Keynesian-classical aggregate supply curve slopes upward to the right because workers and producers are assumed to suffer from the money illusion.

16. The empirical evidence shows that in the real world output and prices are positively related, as is suggested by the Keynesian-classical aggregate supply curve.

17. Macroeconomic equilibrium occurs in the Keynesian-classical model when a price level is achieved that equates the aggregate quantity supplied with the aggregate quantity demanded.

5 Money and Interest in the Keynesian System

THE MAIN TASK of this chapter is to introduce both money and the rate of interest into the Keynesian system. In our development of the Keynesian income-expenditure model in Chapter 4, money and interest were mentioned only briefly. The primary object there was to explain aggregate demand and its key role in the determination of output (Y) and employment (N). Yet this is only part of the story, for in the Keynesian analysis, not only are the rate of interest and money intimately related, they also have strategically important roles in market capitalism. These roles are fundamentally different from those played by money and interest in the classical world, where money had no "real" effect. From the classical perspective, if the money supply increased or decreased, the price level went up or down but nothing else happened.

To introduce money and interest into the basic income-expenditure framework developed in Chapter 4, we need to do the following. First, we need to make some broad observations about money, its nature and its supply. Money is not only a fascinating subject, but one of extreme complexity. Among other things, these observations will stress how the Keynesian conception of money differs from the classical view. Second, we need to examine the two major theories that economists have developed to explain how interest rates are determined in market-based economies. These are the *loanable funds theory of interest,* whose antecedents are found in classical thinking on interest rates as discussed in Chapter 3, and the *liquidity preference theory of interest,* whose explanation of interest Keynes developed in *The General Theory*. Finally, we need to show how the interest rate can be related to the level of aggregate demand. Specifically, we shall explain why much investment spending (I), some government buying of goods and services (G), and the balance between exports and imports ($X - M$) are influenced by the rate of interest. By bringing money and the rate of interest into the analysis in the ways just described, we shall have taken another major step toward the development of a complete general model (or theory) for explaining macroeconomic behavior, not only at the national level, but on a global basis.

The Nature of Money

There is one fact about money on which there is nearly universal agreement: It is neither easily nor simply defined. Nearly a century ago an economist made the following observation:

> It is a singular and, indeed, a significant fact that, although money was the first economic subject to attract men's thoughtful attention, and has been the focal center of economic investigation ever since, there is at the present day not even an approximate agreement as to what ought to be designated by the word. The business world makes use of the term in several senses, while among economists there are almost as many different conceptions as there are writers upon the subject.[1]

The situation is not quite that bad today, although the Federal Reserve System regularly publishes data for four major measures of the nation's money stock, because of a lack of agreement on a single, all-inclusive definition of money (see the box on page 150). Probably the best place to start is with the fundamental characteristic of money; it is a generalized *claim* that can be exercised against all other goods, services, and claims of whatever kind and irrespective of their origin. Thus, the essential nature of money does not lie in the physical properties of whatever material substance may happen to fulfill the role of monetary exchange in a society at any particular time; it springs from the fact that the material substance in question is universally accepted as a generalized claim against all other things that possess economic value. The modern demand deposit, a major form of money in many highly developed economic systems, can hardly be said to possess physical properties of value. It consists of nothing more than notations in the ledger of the bank; yet it is something that is almost universally accepted in the payment for goods and services or in the settlement of claims.

Given the nature of money as a generalized claim against all things or

---

[1] A. P. Andrew, "What Ought to be Called Money," *Quarterly Journal of Economics,* January 1899, p. 219.

┌───┐
│   │
└───┘

From Gold to Electronic Blips: A Capsule History of Money

The origins of money are obscure, lost somewhere in antiquity. But money in Western civilization and, more important, the technique by which money is created are not so ancient. Money really began with the goldsmiths of Medieval Europe.

Why the goldsmiths? Gold is, has been, and probably always will be valuable. Goldsmiths, therefore, had strongboxes, safe places to keep gold. Gold is not only valuable, but also bulky. Sometime, somehow, people, especially people engaged in business, began taking their excess gold to the goldsmiths for safekeeping. In exchange they got a receipt stating that so much gold had been left with the goldsmith for safety.

Gold left for safety with the goldsmith became the first bank deposits, and goldsmiths eventually became the first bankers. How? Rather than go back to the goldsmith for some of their gold every time they had to make a payment, people began simply to transfer their receipts. The receipts became, in effect, a form of money. They were the first bank notes.

It was not long before the goldsmiths discovered an interesting fact. They had gold "on deposit," but people did not come in very often and turn in their receipts for gold. The receipts circulated as money, and the gold remained safely in the strongboxes of the goldsmith. Perhaps, on average, only 10 percent of the receipts were presented in any one month or year for redemption.

Once this discovery was made, it was not long until the goldsmiths became true bankers. They realized that they could "loan out" some of the gold they had on hand. Why not? It was just sitting idle in the strong box, and the chances were good that very few people would come in and want their gold. So a loan could be made by issuing the borrower a new "receipt." In this way the modern day bank note based on credit was born.

When this practice began, the principle that underlies modern banking and money creation was also born. This is the *principle of fractional reserves.* Banks keep some form of real money on reserve against their deposit liabilities, equal to only a fraction of the value of their deposits, to meet the routine demands of depositors to convert their deposits into real money.

Here in a nutshell we have both the secret of how banks create money and the stuff out of which the history of banks and money has been made. Banks create money by lending out some portion of whatever form of real money they hold as a reserve against the claims of depositors. When there is a run on a bank, depositors claim more than the bank holds in reserve, and the bank fails. Clearly, this would be disastrous for depositors, which is why a federal agency, the Federal Deposit Insurance Corporation, guarantees the safety of all deposits up to $100,000.

Now we return to the history of money. In the beginning the reserve of real money that the bank held against the claims of depositors was gold (or silver)— metal in other words. Then it became gold and the legal tender paper money issued by a government—money we now call currency. After central banks like the Federal Reserve System were created, the reserves became deposits of the bank with the Federal Reserve.

These deposits are the real money which backs up the money created by the bank making loans. Before the computer and the marvel of instantaneous electronic transfers, such real money was a bookkeeping entry in the ledgers of the Federal Reserve System. Now real money is no more than a blip on a computer screen and instantly transferable anywhere in the world.

---

entities that possess economic value, it follows that money is the most *liquid* of all assets. *Liquidity* relates to the ease or convenience with which an asset can be converted from one form to another *without loss of value* and with a *minimum* of transactions costs. Money meets this requirement better than any other type of good or claim. Furthermore, the costs of holding money are negligible as compared with the carrying costs that may be involved if one's assets are held in some other form. Understanding the notion of liquidity is a key to understanding a major way in which money can affect the general level of economic activity.

Although money is the asset with the highest degree of liquidity, it suffers from the disadvantage that it does not yield its holder any return, as normally is the case with other kinds of assets. This, too, is a matter of basic importance for understanding how money enters in a causal way into the scheme of things.

The Functions of Money

Economic analysis traditionally states that money performs four major functions. First, money serves as a *standard for the measurement of value*. Without some such standard it would be impossible to reduce the vast and heterogeneous activity of the modern economy to anything meaningful and comprehensible. Unfortunately, money is not a perfect measuring rod because its value will fluctuate as the general price level changes, although this defect can be compensated for (to some extent) by statistical techniques for eliminating the effect of price changes on our measurements. Second, money acts as a *medium of exchange*. In this sense, money is extremely important to the efficient functioning of the economy, because without some medium that everyone is willing to accept in exchange for any good, service, or asset, the economy would have to operate on a barter basis; this would be clumsy and inefficient. Third, money serves as a *store of value*. Since money is essentially a generalized claim to all forms of economic value, this means that economic value can be kept intact over time in the form of money. Of course, any claim or form of wealth that is not highly perishable can serve to store value over time, but money is best suited for performing this function. Finally, money can function as a *standard of deferred payments*. It is customary to measure a debt or promise for future payment in terms of money, rather than some commodity or service.

Of the four functions of money we have outlined, the second and third—money as a medium of exchange and as a store of value—are most germane to the analysis in this chapter.

Neutral versus Nonneutral Money

The foregoing discussion on the function of money conceals a fundamental distinction between Keynesian and classical thought with respect to money. This is the issue of the neutrality of money. Just as Keynes and the classicals are poles apart on the matter of the self-correcting nature of the economic system, they are also poles apart on whether or not money is neutral. Let us see what this means.

In the classical view, money is neutral. It can only affect nominal, not real values. A *monetary economy,* on the other hand, is one in which money plays a role of its own. It is *not* neutral. Money, as Keynes said, ". . . affects motives and decisions and is, in short, one of the operative factors in the situation, so that the course of events cannot be predicted, either in the long period or in the short, without a knowledge of the behavior of money between the first state and the last. And this is what we ought to mean when we speak of a *Monetary Economy.*"[2]

In discussing the basic functions of money, it was observed that the medium-of-exchange and store-of-value functions were most germane to some of the ideas discussed in this chapter. The medium-of-exchange function corresponds to the classical idea that money is neutral. The classical economists believed that the only practical use of money was to spend it—an attitude of mind reflected in the quantity theory of money. In our discussion of the quantity theory in Chapter 3, it was shown that the only effect of a change in the money supply is on the price level. If there is an increase in the quantity of money, the price level will rise. This implies two things. First, whenever people get more money, they will spend it; the function of money that really counts is the medium of exchange. Second, since the price level is the only thing affected by a change in the money supply, money is neutral. Real values such as output (Y) and employment (N) remain unaffected by a change in the money supply.

Keynes took a different perspective; he stressed not only the medium-of-exchange function of money but also its role as a store of wealth. In a famous article written in 1937 he posed the following:

> Money, it is well known, serves two principal purposes. By acting as a money of account it facilitates exchanges without its being necessary that it should ever itself come into the picture as a substantive object. In this respect it is a convenience devoid of significance or real influence. In the second place, it is a store of wealth. So we are

---

[2] John Maynard Keynes, "On The Theory of A Monetary Economy," in *Festschrift fur Arthur Spiethoff* (Munich: Duncker & Humblot, 1933); reprinted in *Nebraska Journal of Economics and Business* Vol. 2 No. 2 (Autumn 1963).

told without a smile on the face. But in the world of the classical economy, what an insane use to which to put it! For it is a recognized characteristic of money as a store of wealth that it is barren; whereas practically every other form of storing wealth yields some interest or profit. Why should anyone outside a lunatic asylum wish to use money as a store of wealth?[3]

Keynes went on to answer his own query by introducing uncertainty into the picture. People want to hold money as a store of wealth because they distrust their own calculations about what the future holds; they are uncertain. People are uncertain of the future value of other forms of holding wealth— debt and equity instruments. The possession of money, Keynes said, "lulls our disquietude" when our beliefs about what the future holds are shaken. Money becomes a safe haven whenever we become nervous and worried, fearful that other forms of holding wealth may lose their value.

Keynes, as we shall see shortly, used the store of wealth function as the basis for developing his own *liquidity preference theory* of the rate of interest. His theory of interest is the vehicle through which money loses its neutrality. An important consequence of Keynes's argument for the nonneutrality of money is the realization that there exists in the economy a *monetary sphere of activity* which is distinct from the real or *goods sphere of activity*. This distinction plays a crucial role in the full development of our macroeconomic model, the topic we pursue in Chapter 6.

The Supply of Money

There must be an adequate supply of money in an economy to perform the four functions discussed earlier. Money, we have seen, means essentially all things which are generally acceptable in payment of debt and payment for goods and services and which also serve to measure and store value over time. The supply of money refers to the quantity of things in existence that accord with the foregoing definition. Throughout history the question of not only what constitutes money; where it comes from has been both important and controversial (see the box "From Gold to Electronic Blips: A Capsule History of Money"). It is important and controversial because money plays a vital role in how the economy performs; hence, whoever or whatever controls the money supply is in a powerful position to influence economic events. Money today consists of assets or claims created by the financial and banking system. In this system the Federal Reserve, the United States' central bank, plays an important and powerful role, although its power is by no means absolute. The following section discusses in general how the actions of the Federal Reserve, also known as the Fed, enter into the determination of the

---

[3] John Maynard Keynes, "The General Theory," *The Quarterly Journal of Economics,* Vol. 51, February 1937.

money supply. The fundamental theoretical problems associated with the money supply (M^o) are analyzed in Chapter 11.

Before turning to this discussion, some other preliminary comments on money and its nature are in order. Since money is *something,* it must be measured at a particular point in time. This means that, in contrast to income, which is measured over time, money is a *stock,* not a *flow,* phenomenon. Since it is a stock, this also means that the amount of money in existence at any point in time must be held by some entity in the economy. This is a point of significance because economists, in their analyses of the role played by money, make a distinction between the amount of money in existence at any point in time (and which must be held simply because the amount is something that exists) and the amount that people and institutions may want to hold for various reasons. Most people, of course, would like to have more money than they actually have, but this is not the point. In an analytical sense, such a distinction is a useful one, because it enables us to employ the concepts of equilibrium and disequilibrium in conjunction with money, just as we have employed these concepts earlier in conjunction with the income level.

When the amount of money actually being held coincides with the amount that individuals, businesses, and governments actually want to hold, a condition of *monetary equilibrium* exists. This, too, is an important concept, one that is essential for understanding how money as a phenomenon in its own right may significantly influence the level of employment, income, and prices. The counterpart to monetary equilibrium is, of course, *monetary disequilibrium,* a situation in which actual and desired holdings of money are not in balance.

Money and Its Creation

Although the definition of money and its supply as discussed above is relatively straightforward, the actual measurement of money in the modern economy has become an extremely complex matter. The reason is that there is in practice and in actual circulation in the economy a fairly large variety of financial assets that serve as money in one way or another. The Federal Reserve System employs four measures for money that actually circulates among the public. (See box, page 150.) The best definition of money, according to the Federal Reserve, is one which is capable of reasonably accurate measurement and which is related in a predictable way to the performance of the economy. It is just because no single monetary measure meets these criteria that the nation's central bank (the Federal Reserve System) must use several different measures of money for its purposes.

The best way to approach the problem of what constitutes money in the modern economy and where it comes from is to start with two fundamental categories. These are, first, the *monetary base* (or reserve money, as it has been called) and, second, *circulating media.* Technically, the Federal Reserve System defines the *monetary base* as the required reserves for *all* financial institutions plus *all* currency in circulation and in the vaults of the commercial banks. It is through the monetary base that the Federal Reserve System maintains its control over the money supply. Before the growth in recent years of the many different forms of financial instruments that serve as media of exchange—these instruments are sometimes described as "near monies"—*circulating media* could have been described accurately by the term "deposit money." Until the late 1970s most of the money other than currency that circulated through the economy consisted of demand deposits in the nation's commercial banks. Now that view is too restrictive because of the recent growth of so many new types of financial assets against which people may write checks, and thus which serve as money in the economy. For example, in 1980, checkbook-type money originating outside the commercial banks represented only 9.6 percent of all deposits against which people could write checks. By 1994, however, noncommercial bank checkable deposits were actually greater than the demand deposits of the commercial banks, $402.3 billion for the former as against $383.3 billion for the latter.[4]

From the standpoint of monetary control, the most strategic monetary variable is the monetary base, or as it is also called, central bank money. It consists, as just noted, of all the reserves of financial institutions on deposit with the Federal Reserve banks and all the currency in actual circulation or in the vaults of the commercial banks.[5] Currency in the United States now consists entirely of notes issued by the Federal Reserve System. Central bank money, not all of which actually circulates, is also known as *high-powered money*, because it is the primary instrument through which the Federal Reserve can influence the total money supply in the economy. It is called high-powered because every dollar of central bank money provides a support base for several dollars of money in actual circulation. Put somewhat differently, the monetary base is strategically important because changes in it have the power to produce multiple changes in circulating money. The size of the monetary base fluctuates with changes in the assets and liabilities of the central bank. It is primarily through central bank open market purchases, changes in reserve requirements, and variations in the discount rate that the monetary base changes; as this happens, the circulating money supply may also change. What the Federal Reserve has under its direct control is the size of the monetary base. Whether or not changes in the monetary base actually lead to changes in the money in circulation depends on how the public (including banks and other financial institutions) reacts to such a change. In the final analysis, it is up to the public to decide whether or not to change its holdings

---

[4] *Economic Report of the President,* 1995, p. 354.

[5] Another way to define the monetary base is all the monetary liabilities of the central bank (the Federal Reserve) to the public, including private financial institutions. This would include the deposits of financial institutions with the Federal Reserve banks since a deposit is a liability of the institution in which the deposit is located, as well as currency (bank notes) in circulation. The standard Federal Reserve note is a liability of the Federal Reserve System.

Measuring the Nation's Money Supply

The Federal Reserve System defines the money supply (M^o) in four ways. These are:

M1—This is the most widely used measure of money in circulation and corresponds most closely to the common notion of what money is. It is made up of currency, all deposits that can be transferred by check, and traveler's checks. In December 1994 it totaled $1,147.8 billion.

M2—This consists of M1 *plus* savings deposits and small time deposits (under $100,000) at all deposit institutions and two types of "overnight" assets, which means assets redeemable the next day. These are "repurchase" agreements by U.S. commercial banks, a form of lending between banks, and "Eurodollar" deposits by U.S. residents in Caribbean branches of member banks. Eurodollar deposits are dollar deposits in banks outside the United States. M2 was $3,614.5 billion in December 1994.

M3—M2 *plus* large time deposits (more than $100,000) at all deposit institutions and longer than overnight repurchase agreements (loans between banks). M3 in December 1994 was $4,304.3 billion.

L—M3 *plus* other liquid assets such as short-term obligations of the U.S. Treasury (Treasury bills), bankers' acceptances and commercial paper (short-term IOUs of business firms), U.S. savings bonds, and Eurodollar deposits held by U.S. citizens. The Federal Reserve regards L as a very broad measure of all liquid assets. In November 1994 it totaled $5,287.4 billion.

of currency, demand deposits, and other financial assets that serve as money in response to any significant change in the monetary base. Thus, the link between the monetary base and the total of money in circulation is a real one, but it is not an exact and mechanical one.

The Federal Reserve definitions of money in circulation begin with the measure of money that is most closely linked to the monetary base and then proceeds to enlarge this definition by adding specialized types of financial assets that have an important monetary role, although they are not necessarily of the kind that are used by the general public. Milton Friedman has said that money ought to be thought of as any asset that serves as a "temporary abode for purchasing power"—a definition that fits well with the Federal Reserve's most basic definition of money in actual circulation. The latter is what the Federal Reserve now calls M1, and it consists of currency outside the Treasury, demand deposits at all commercial banks, checkable deposits at other financial institutions (NOW and POW accounts), and traveler's checks of nonbank origin. The four major money measures now used by the Federal Reserve System are described in the box above.

How Interest Rates Are Determined

We now turn to the second major task of this chapter, namely to examine the processes by which interest rates are determined in a market-based capitalistic system. Two basic theories are involved, the loanable funds and the liquidity preference approaches to explaining interest. Before turning specifically to analyzing these theories, a few general observations about interest are in order.

As most of us know, interest is a price, even though it is always measured as a *rate,* not as an absolute sum, such as $4.50 for a movie, $29.95 for a book, or any other dollar amount for a specific good or service. We also know that as a price it involves money—what we have to pay for the use of money borrowed. It is more complicated than this, but the commonsense idea that the rate of interest is the price we must pay for the use of borrowed funds is a good place to start.

A second point is that the locale for interest, its domain if you will, is in the world of finance. In the world of finance there are, broadly speaking, two basic markets. One is the *capital market,* which includes all markets involving the borrowing and supplying of funds for the investment component (I) of the aggregate demand function. As in all markets, buyers and sellers are brought together in an exchange process. The usual financial instruments exchanged in the capital market are stocks (equities) and bonds. The other market is the *money market,* which includes all markets for the exchange, the buying and selling, of financial assets (securities) with a maturity date of one year or less. What is important about both the capital and the money markets is that the link between the buyers and sellers on each side of the market is the rate of interest.

Our third observation about interest is that it is the strategic variable through which real variables like output (Y) and employment (N) are shown to be affected by money and activity related to money. It is through the interest rate that Keynes introduces the idea of the nonneutrality of money into the analysis of how output and employment are determined. Since interest is the key link between the goods and monetary spheres of the economy, it is important to see how it is determined.

The Loanable Funds Theory of Interest

This is a supply and demand explanation for the interest rate, one which is a direct descendent from the classical theory of interest. In Chapter 3, it will be recalled, the interest rate was determined by the interaction between the supply of savings and the demand for savings (Figure 3–2). The demand for savings comes from businesses that want savings for investment (I), whereas

Bond Prices and Interest Rates

Suppose in 1985 you bought a $5,000 high-grade, 25-year corporate bond that yielded 9.5 percent interest per year ($475). The interest paid on the face value of the bond—the amount that must be repaid to the bond holder when the bond comes due—is called the *coupon* rate. Now suppose you decided to sell the bond in 1994, when interest rates on high-grade corporate bonds had fallen to 7.25 percent. How much would you have received for your bond? Whoever bought your bond would continue to receive $475 per year until its maturity date. At a lower rate of interest—7.25 versus 9.5 percent—it takes more money to purchase a financial investment that will yield $475 per year. Thus, you were able to sell your bond for more than its purchase price of $5,000. How much more? To get the answer, divide the current income from the bond ($475) by the rate of interest at the time of the sale (7.25 percent)—a process commonly referred to as the *capitalization of income.* According to this formula, you would have received $6,552 for your bond in 1994, and so had a *capital gain* of $1,552. The principle illustrated by this example is that in the marketplace, interest rates and bond prices move inversely to one another; bond prices fall when interest rates rise, and rise when interest rates fall.

the supply of savings (S) comes from decisions by persons to abstain from consumption. It is a capital market model in which the rate of interest equalizes decisions to invest with decisions to save.

The best vehicle for understanding the loanable funds framework for interest rate determination is the bond market. The bond market is the point at which individuals, business firms, financial institutions, and even some branches of governments with funds to lend meet other business firms, financial institutions, and branches of government that want to borrow those funds. Bonds, it will be recalled, are promises to pay, debt obligations, given by borrowers. It should be noted parenthetically that individuals as borrowers do not issue bonds. Only institutions (or collective entities) issue bonds. What happens in the bond market (or markets) is that transfers of cash take place between borrowers and lenders. The borrower gets cash in exchange for a promise to repay cash in the future, an amount equal to the principal value of the bond plus interest payments. Interest is the compensation made to the lenders for parting temporarily with cash—giving up the liquidity inherent in money, as Keynes phrased it—and for the risk the lender assumes that the sum loaned might never be repaid. It is relatively easy to construct a model of the bond market built around the concept of *loanable funds.* Such a model draws on the time-tested concepts of supply and demand, with which all students of economics are familiar.

The Supply Curve for Loanable Funds

Figure 5–1 depicts two curves. In the left-hand part of the figure we have a supply curve for loanable funds. The curve shows that the quantity of funds available for lending that flows into the bond market is a direct function of the rate of interest. The right-hand part of the figure shows a downward-sloping curve. This is the demand curve for bonds. This curve shows an inverse relationship between the price of bonds and the quantity of bonds demanded. Buyers in the bond market are the suppliers of funds; thus, the obverse of the supply curve for loanable funds is the demand curve for bonds. These two curves also illustrate the principle that the price of bonds and the rate of interest vary inversely with each other.

There are two questions we need to answer with respect to the supply curve for loanable funds. The first is: what is the source of loanable funds? The second question is: what determines the position of the supply curve for loanable funds shown in Figure 5–1? The pioneer theoretical work for the loanable funds approach to interest rate determination was done by Knut Wicksell, a Swedish economist, and D. H. Robertson, an English economist. Essentially, they expanded the classical view by including not just savings, but also additions to the money supply and *dishoarding* in the pool of money available for lending. "Dishoarding" means drawing down accumulated cash balances, making these balances available to lenders. Dishoarding is not a major source of loanable funds, but we need to include it not only for the sake of theoretical completeness, but also because the notion of hoarding and dishoarding plays an important role in the theory of interest developed by Keynes.

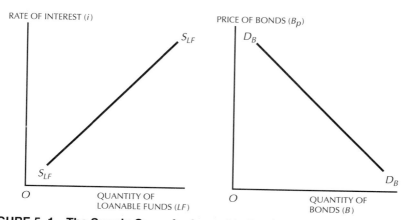

FIGURE 5–1   The Supply Curve for Loanable Funds and the Demand Curve for Bonds.   The supply curve for loanable funds slopes upward to the right and thus shows more funds for lending will flow into the market as interest rates rise. The demand curve for bonds is the counterpart to this supply curve; people who demand bonds are simultaneously the suppliers of loanable funds.

On a practical level in the modern, open economy there are three main sources for the money that flows into the market for loanable funds. The first is saving by people, by business firms, and by governments within the economy. In 1992 personal saving accounted for 24.2 percent of gross saving, private business saving 75.8 percent, and government saving at all levels a minus 27.3 percent. The second source of loanable funds for the domestic economy is money that flows into the economy from abroad. This source, which economists describe as *capital inflows,* involves the purchase of bonds and other securities by foreigners. In recent years it has grown significantly in importance as a source of loanable funds in the U.S. economy. In 1992, for example, the net capital flow into the United States was 24.8 percent of net private saving.[6] Finally, there is the increase in the money supply. During the 1980s and through 1994, the M1 measure of the money supply rose at an annual average rate of 7.7 percent, a figure that gives us a rough measure of the contribution of increases in the money supply to the flow of money into the market for loanable funds.[7]

The second question, the position of the supply schedule for loanable funds, depends on several factors. These include the policies of the Federal Reserve System, the growth in the economy's *real* wealth, expectations about future returns on bonds (interest rates), and attitudes toward risk on the part of the public. These are factors which must necessarily be held constant— the *ceteris paribus* assumption—in order to draw the curve in the first place. When they change, the position of the schedule will necessarily shift. A shift in *any* supply schedule means that there is more (or less) of the good or service being supplied, in this case loanable funds, without any change in price (the rate of interest).

For example, suppose the Federal Reserve System decides to engage in an expansionary open market operation. It will do this by going into the bond market and buying bonds. This will drive up the price of bonds and lead to an increase in funds flowing into the market for loanable funds. This results in a rightward shift in the supply curve for loanable funds. If the Federal Reserve pursues a contractionary monetary policy, the supply schedule shifts to the left (downward).

What about an increase in the economy's stock of *real* wealth? The public would undoubtedly want to hold a part of this increase in the form of bonds. So we can depict this wealth effect as a rightward shift in the demand curve for bonds, which is also the same as an increase (shift to the right) for the supply schedule for loanable funds. Now suppose the public changes its expectations about future rates of interest and decides that they are going to go up. This is tantamount to expecting that the *future* price of bonds will fall. Under these circumstances, the supply curve for loanable funds would shift

---

[6] *Economic Report of the President,* 1995, pp. 308, 395.

[7] Ibid., p. 353.

to the left because of anticipated lower yields. On the other hand, if the rate of interest is expected to fall, it means that the public anticipates bond prices will rise—a change which will shift the loanable funds supply schedule to the right.

Finally, let us note that *risk* plays an important role in determining the position of the supply schedule for loanable funds. A bond represents a promise to pay geared to the future, but it is valuable only so long as the issuer of the bond can make interest payments, not to mention repay the principal. The buyer of a bond always assumes some risk of default. Purchasers of U.S. government bonds, for example, acquire a very safe financial instrument because the federal government has the power to tax and use tax income to make interest payments to bondholders. On the other hand, people who in the "go-go" 1980s bought junk bonds issued by Donald Trump to finance his Taj Mahal gambling casino have had much to worry about. If we assume that people seek to minimize the risks inherent in owning bonds, the supply schedule for loanable funds will shift when there is a change in their appraisal of risk. If, for example, people decide holding bonds has become riskier than before, the loanable funds curve will shift to the left. At each interest rate fewer bonds will be purchased and thus the inflow of cash into the loanable funds market will be reduced. If their perception of the risk in bond ownership goes down, then the supply curve for loanable funds will shift to the right.

The Demand Curve for Loanable Funds

The demand for loanable funds arises from the uses that businesses and branches of government have for funds. A business might issue bonds to finance a promising investment project. A local government may use the proceeds of a bond issue to fund new parks, roads, or other city projects. The Treasury Department needs to issue billions of dollars in new bonds each year to finance the federal deficit. Each new issue of bonds represents an additional demand for loanable funds. Particularly in the case of business and state and local government it is likely that the cost of funds (the interest rate) enters significantly into the question of whether or not to issue bonds, or in other words, whether or not to borrow. This is the idea that lies behind the demand curve for loanable funds.

Figure 5–2 also contains two curves. In the left-hand part of the figure we have the demand curve for loanable funds, drawn with a negative slope. In the right-hand part of the figure we have an upward-sloping curve. This is the supply curve for bonds, the counterpart of the demand curve for loanable funds. These figures, too, illustrate the principle of the inverse relationship between bond prices and the rate of interest. When bond prices are low, interest rates are high; this results in a weak demand for loanable funds. The suppliers of bonds are the demanders of loanable funds. For example, in Figure 5–2, if the interest rate is at i_2, bond prices will be correspondingly low at a level of B_{P_1}. Few bonds are being offered in the bond market; this

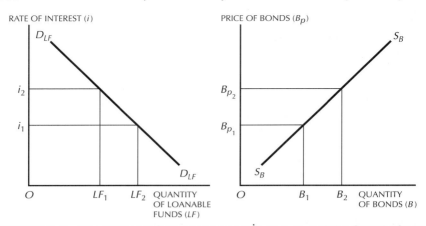

FIGURE 5–2   The Demand Curve for Loanable Funds and the Supply Curve for Bonds. The demand curve for loanable funds slopes downward to the right and thus shows that as the rate of interest falls, the quantity of loanable funds demanded increases. The counterpart to this curve is the supply curve for bonds, which shows that the supply of bonds increases as their price rises. People who supply bonds are the demanders of loanable funds.

means a low demand for loanable funds. On the other hand, if the interest rate drops to the level i_1, bond prices will be high at B_{P_2}, and the demand for loanable funds will be brisk.

As with the supply curve for loanable funds, the position of the demand curve for such funds is influenced by factors besides the rate of interest and the quantity of loanable funds being demanded. When a loanable funds demand curve is drawn, these factors are assumed to be constant: *ceteris paribus* prevails. But a change in any of them will cause the curve to shift. What are these factors? The three most important are the federal government's fiscal policy, business profit expectations from investment projects, and the expected inflation rate.

Federal fiscal activity affects the demand for loanable funds because it involves changes in the quantity of bonds issued by the U.S. Treasury. If, for example, there is an increase in the federal deficit, the Treasury must sell more bonds to finance the higher deficit. This will lead to an increase—a shift to the right—in the demand curve for loanable funds. In the bond market, the corresponding action is a rightward shift in the supply curve for bonds. On the other hand, if the federal deficit is reduced, fewer bonds will be issued; this will lead to a shift to the left in the demand curve for loanable funds. In the unlikely event that the federal government had a budget surplus, these effects would be even more pronounced.

Business expectations of the profitability of planned investment projects also affect the position of the demand curve for loanable funds. If profit expectations are good, firms will sell more bonds, because of a high demand for borrowed money. Any favorable increase in profit expectations will, in other words, lead to a rightward shift in the demand curve for loanable funds. If, however, profit expectations change significantly for the worse, as happens frequently in the world of business, the demand curve will shift to the left. Fewer bonds will be offered in the bond market as business borrowing falls off.

What about *expected* inflation? How does it affect the demand for loanable funds? When a business firm issues (sells) a bond, it is making a commitment to pay interest over the future life of the bond on the amount borrowed, the principal value of the bond. The *real* cost to the firm of these commitments is uncertain because it depends on what happens to the inflation rate over the life of the bond. For example, assume that Big Red, Inc., borrows $1 million for a five-year period at the current market rate of interest of 10 percent. It must pay $100,000 to the bondholder each year for five years. If there is no inflation, Big Red, Inc.'s real cost remains at $100,000. But what if the rate of inflation is 5 percent per year over the life of the bond? Then the *real* rate of interest is just 5 percent, the nominal rate of 10 percent minus the inflation rate of 5 percent. This cuts the firm's *real* interest outlays in half, from $100,000 to $50,000.

How does this affect the demand curve for loanable funds? If firms expect the inflation rate to *rise* in the future, this would tend to shift the demand curve to the right. The reason is that it then makes sense to borrow more money at the prevailing nominal (actual) rate of interest than it would if no change were expected in the inflation rate. Thus, the moral of this story is that it makes good economic sense for both borrowers (business firms) and lenders (buyers of bonds) to try to anticipate the inflation rate. To illustrate, if inflation increases and both borrowers and lenders foresee this, borrowers will have a better idea of the *real* cost of getting funds and lenders will have a better idea of the *real* gains from lending.

All that remains to bring this discussion of the loanable funds theory of interest to a conclusion is to put together in one diagram the supply and demand curves for loanable funds, as in Figure 5–3. This is a standard supply and demand model in which the rate of interest is the "price" that balances the demand for loanable funds against the available supply. If the rate of interest is at i_2, the quantity of loanable funds supplied is Q_s and the quantity demanded is Q_d. This represents an excess supply of loanable funds (the quantity of bonds demanded in the bond market exceeds the supply). At the interest rate i_2, the public is willing to lend a larger quantity of funds (OQ_s) than businesses are willing to borrow (OQ_d). Consequently, the interest rate will fall, bond prices will rise, and eventually an equilibrium will be reached at which the demand for and the supply of loanable funds are in balance.

One final note before turning to the alternative theory of interest developed by Keynes. The loanable funds theory of interest is a *flow* theory of interest rates. What the figures developed in this section purport to measure is the flow of money to loan *into* the market, a flow which originates with lenders, and the flow of money *out* of the market, a flow which originates with borrowers. The market is in balance when these two flows are equal. This point

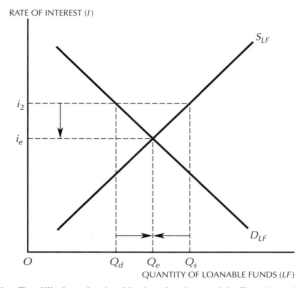

FIGURE 5–3   Equilibrium in the Market for Loanable Funds.   At interest rate i_2 there is an excess supply of loanable funds $(Q_s - Q_d)$. The interest rate is bid downward until equilibrium is restored at i_e and Q_e.

about the flow character of loanable funds is important because Keynes's theory, which we shall now consider, involves money *stocks* rather than *flows*.

☐ The Liquidity Preference Theory of Interest

In *The General Theory* Keynes devised an alternative to the classical theory of interest. In part he was motivated by the desire to refute the classical idea that it was through the rate of interest that the flow of savings was absorbed into investment. This is because it was through their interest theory that the classical economists preserved the working of Say's law in a monetary economy. But Keynes also needed an alternative theory of interest to demonstrate why money is not neutral, to make it clear that we cannot understand how the economy *really* works without a knowledge of the behavior of money.

Keynesian interest theory is derived from the idea that money may be wanted as a store of value just as much as it may be wanted as a medium of exchange. In Keynes's liquidity preference theory of interest, the primary consideration is the demand for money as an asset, as a means for holding wealth. Later in Chapter 11 we shall explore fully all the theoretical issues involved in the demand for money for all its uses, but for now we need only be concerned with the role of money as a store of value.

Fundamental to an understanding of the liquidity preference approach is the concept of interest that is embodied in the analysis. In the classical theory, interest is regarded as the price that equates the supply of and demand for saving; it is considered a phenomenon related to flows rather than stocks. Moreover, interest is seen primarily as the price that is paid for abstinence— the necessary price that must be paid to persuade people not to consume some portion of their current income. The essence of the classical view is that interest is a reward for waiting.

But it is precisely this concept of interest as a reward for saving that Keynes challenges in *The General Theory*. Interest, he argues, cannot be a reward for saving as such because, if a person hoards his savings in cash, he will receive no interest, although he has, nevertheless, refrained from consuming all his current income. Instead of a reward for saving, interest in the Keynesian analysis is *a reward for parting with liquidity*. Interest is the price that must be paid to persuade those who hold idle money balances to part with the liquidity inherent in such balances. This particular view of the nature of interest takes us back to the question Keynes raised in his 1937 *Quarterly Journal of Economics* article: Why should anyone wish to hold money as an asset in preference to some other form of asset that will yield an income? As indicated, the answer is fear and uncertainty with respect to the future value of assets held in forms other than cash. It is necessary to pay people a premium in the form of interest to compensate for the insecurity and diminished liquidity involved in holding assets in other than monetary form at a time of uncertainty. The greater the degree of uncertainty with respect to future economic values, the higher will be the rate of interest. It is important to note, however, that in today's economy the distinction between money in the form of cash and other types of assets with respect to liquidity is less clear-cut than it was when Keynes wrote in the 1930s. Insured bank deposits with attached credit cards often earn interest and are nearly as liquid as money. Nonetheless, and as demonstrated by growing fears in the early 1990s about the safety of even insured bank deposits, legal tender, cash money, remains the most liquid of all assets.

In *The General Theory* Keynes defined interest as "... the 'price' which equilibrates the desire to hold wealth in the form of cash with the available quantity of cash."[8] This implies, he went on to say, that if the rate of interest—the reward for parting with cash—were lower, the aggregate amount of cash the public would wish to hold would exceed the supply, and if the rate of interest were higher, there would be a surplus of cash that no one would wish to hold.[9] What actually determines the rate of interest, according to Keynes, is the demand for cash as an asset—a demand for liquidity because of fear and uncertainty about the future—in conjunction with whatever amount of money is available to satisfy that demand. The latter would consist

[8] John Maynard Keynes, *The General Theory*, p. 167.
[9] Ibid.

of whatever part of the total money supply were not immediately needed to sustain current transactions.

We can put these ideas in more formal theoretical terms by designating the demand for money as an asset as L_a, and the portion of the total money supply available to hold as an asset as M_a^o. Keynes postulated that the demand for money as an asset, the demand for liquidity, would take the form of a "smooth curve which shows the rate of interest falling as the quantity of money is increased."[10] Such a curve represents a demand schedule for money to hold as an asset, a demand schedule for liquidity. This approach to the theory of the interest rate embodies demand and supply concepts, but it is oriented toward *stocks* rather than *flows* as in the classical and the loanable funds approach to interest rate determination.

The mechanism through which the rate of interest is determined in the liquidity preference theory is demonstrated in Figure 5–4. Interest is on the vertical axis, whereas the demand for money for asset purposes L_a and the supply of money for asset purposes M_a^o are shown on the horizontal axis. The asset demand function, $L_a = f(i)$, is shown as a curve that slopes downward to the right, as suggested previously, and the money supply is shown as a straight line drawn parallel to the vertical axis. This signifies that the supply of money for asset purposes is autonomous with respect to the rate of interest. The reason for this is that the liquidity preference analysis assumes that the supply of money available to hold as an asset M_a^o is a *residual* which is determined by subtracting the quantity of money required for current trans-

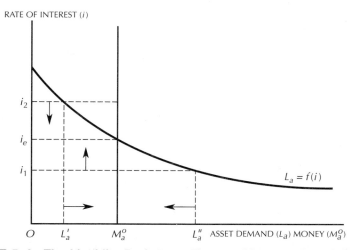

FIGURE 5–4 The Liquidity Preference Theory of Interest Rate Determination.   Keynes's theory of interest holds that it is the interaction between the demand for money as an asset (liquidity preference) and the money available to hold as an asset that determines the rate of interest, not the demand for and supply of savings as in the classical theory.

[10] Ibid, p. 171.

actions from the total money supply M_a^o. Given this assumption, the rate of interest is determined by the intersection of the M_a^o and L_a schedules, for only at this point will the demand for money as an asset be in balance with the quantity of money available to satisfy the speculative motive. This rate is the equilibrium rate and it is designated in the figure as i_e.

In order to understand more fully why the demand for L_a and the supply of M_a^o must be in balance at this particular level of interest rates, let us analyze what will transpire if, momentarily, some other level of the interest rate prevails. For example, what will happen if the interest rate is at the level of i_2, which is higher than the equilibrium rate i_e? At this particular level the asset demand for money L_a' is smaller than the available supply M_a^o, and, consequently, the rate of interest must fall. Why must it fall? Because at the rate i_2 there exists a situation in which the current price for the surrender of liquidity is so high that people do not want to hold all the asset money that is available. There is, in other words, a surplus of money to hold as an asset, and under such circumstances it is to be expected that the price necessary to persuade people to part with liquidity will come down. This price will continue to fall until a level is reached at which the surplus of asset money is no longer available. This is the equilibrium rate i_e.

The reverse will be true if the rate of interest is below the equilibrium level. Thus, at the rate i_1, the demand of money for asset purposes L_a'' is in excess of the available supply M_a^o. The rate of interest i_1 is therefore a disequilibrium rate and must rise, because as long as people want to hold more money as an asset than is currently available for this purpose, they will bid up the price for the surrender of liquidity in an effort to persuade some holders to part with their asset money.

The Significance of Keynesian Interest Theory

The significance of Keynes's liquidity preference theory of interest does not lie in the fact that it is simply an alternative to the classical theory, an alternative which casts the analysis in terms of stocks rather than flows. The Keynesian theory of interest is important for two major reasons. First, it spells out precisely the nature of the monetary sphere of the economic system. Keynesian interest theory makes it clear that monetary equilibrium is the product of forces different from those that produce equilibrium in income and employment. The demand for money as an asset is a major economic force in its own right, but the principles that govern this demand are significantly different from those that govern the demand for goods and services.

Second, and as noted earlier, Keynes's interest theory provides the necessary theoretical framework to demonstrate that money is not neutral. In classical theory, money is unimportant precisely because it is neutral, which is to say that money has no role to play in the determination of output and employment. It functions simply as a medium of exchange; it in no way affects the underlying real process of production, exchange, and consumption. Keynes called an economy that uses money merely as "a neutral link between transactions in real things and real assets and does not allow it to enter into motives or decisions . . . a *Real-Exchange Economy*.'' But in the Keynesian analysis money, operating through the liquidity preference function, is capable, under the right set of circumstances, of exerting a powerful influence on the level of both output and employment.

Which Theory?

At this point the reader may be somewhat concerned, if not perplexed. Which of these two theories—loanable funds or liquidity preference—best explains how interest rates are determined? The answer is that *neither* by itself is sufficient to explain interest rates. Interest is a price, a complex price, influenced by different factors in different circumstances. As with most other phenomena it studies, economics does not have a single, all-inclusive theory to explain how interest rates are determined in all conceivable circumstances. What these two theories do, in a sense, is look at interest from two distinctly different perspectives—the perspective of a *flow* in the case of loanable funds and the perspective of a *stock* in the case of liquidity preference.

Refer back for a moment to Figure 5–4. Let us consider within the context of the bond market what happens if the rate of interest is momentarily above its equilibrium rate, i_e in Figure 5–4. This situation can be interpreted not only as one in which the supply of cash exceeds the demand for cash ($M_a^o > L_a$), but also as one in which people prefer to hold bonds rather than money. In terms of a *stock* rather than a *flow* analysis, there is an excess stock of money and a shortage of bonds. Money (cash), therefore, will gravitate toward the bond market, push up the price of bonds, and drive down the rate of interest until equilibrium with respect to the holding of both bonds and money is restored. This will happen at the rate of interest i_e (and an equivalent equilibrium price for bonds) in Figure 5–4.

The two approaches to interest rate determination just discussed are supply and demand models that show how the rate of interest is determined through transactions in the market place. This, however, is not the whole story, because the Federal Reserve System has formidable power to influence the rate of interest. Through the discount rate—the rate of interest charged banks when they borrow from the Fed—and through open market operations, the Federal Reserve not only sets a floor below which interest rates rarely fall, but it also strongly influences the general level of *all* interest rates.

In the very short run—on a monthly or even weekly basis—the Federal Reserve plays a powerful role through its ability to affect the *federal funds rate*. The federal funds rate is the interest rate banks charge each other for borrowing. When one bank borrows from another, its deposits in the Federal Reserve System are transferred to the borrowing bank from the lending bank. This gives the Fed leverage to influence the federal funds rate. If, for example, the Fed wanted to lower the federal funds rate, it would purchase securities in the open market, and thereby pump more reserve money into the banking system. With increased bank reserves, there would be less borrowing between banks, the federal funds rate would fall, and a general reduction in interest rates would occur. Interest rates that banks charge businesses and consumers are strongly influenced by the federal funds rate.

Over the years the Federal Reserve System has wavered back and forth between a policy of using its powers to influence interest rates directly, primarily through the federal funds rate and a policy of using its control over bank reserves to affect the size of the money supply. In 1979, shortly after Paul Volcker became chairperson of the Board of Governors of the Federal Reserve System, the Fed switched from controlling interest rates to controlling the money supply. Volcker's acceptance of Milton Friedman's modernized version of the quantity theory—prices are determined primarily by the money supply—was the reason for this shift. When Volcker took over as chairperson of the Fed, inflation was the major economic problem confronting the Carter administration.

During the 1980s and into the 1990s, the close correlation between growth in the money supply and in the inflation rate presumed by Friedman's quantity theory broke down; this led the Fed largely to abandon a strict policy of controlling the money supply. Federal fund targeting regained importance on the central bank's policy agenda. In general, though, monetary policy as practiced by the Fed in recent years has been much more eclectic, at times directed toward interest rates, at times focused on the money supply, and at times even aimed at the foreign exchange rates for the U.S. dollar.

The important lesson is that interest rates in the real-world economy are determined by a combination of market forces as reflected in *both* the loanable funds and liquidity preference approaches, plus the formidable institutional powers exercised by the Federal Reserve System. Interest rates in the real world, in other words, are both market driven and administered.

Interest Rates and Aggregate Demand

We now come to the third major task of this chapter, which is to examine the impact that interest rates and, more specifically, *changes* in interest rates have on aggregate demand. This is the appropriate approach because in the income-expenditure model we are developing, the aggregate demand function is the strategic determinant of output (Y) and employment (N). In the global context that has become the appropriate setting for contemporary macroeconomic analysis, aggregate demand (DD) equals the sum of consumption (C), investment (I), and government spending (G) *plus* the nation's international trade balance, exports minus imports ($X - M$). In equation form and as we saw in Chapter 2,

$$DD = C + I + G + (X - M). \qquad (5\text{--}1)$$

Interest rates affect to some degree every component of the aggregate demand function. Investment spending, as both the classical economists and Keynes realized, is linked in an inverse fashion to the rate of interest. The higher the rate of interest, *ceteria paribus,* the lower will be the volume of spending for capital equipment, and the lower the rate of interest, the higher the volume of spending for capital equipment. Consumer spending, too, is affected by interest rates, especially consumer purchases of big-ticket durable goods. When interest rates are high, consumers buy fewer automobiles, boats, recreational vehicles, and home appliances, such as refrigerators, stoves, washing machines, and television and stereo sets. Since many if not most consumer big-ticket items are purchased with borrowed money, the higher the interest rate, the greater is the total cost to the consumer. When interest rates go down, the opposite effects prevail and consumers will increase their durable goods purchases.

The government component (G) of aggregate demand is also affected by interest rates. This is especially true at the state and local level, where bond funding is common for school construction, water and sewage development, parks, swimming pools and other recreational projects, and even some road construction. The willingness of communities to vote to issue bonds to finance desired projects is influenced in part by the interest that must be paid on the bonds. Finally, there is the nation's trade balance ($X - M$), a component of aggregate demand that is increasingly infuenced by international differences in interest rates and the flow of money and finance between countries.

Investment spending (I) and the trade balance ($X - M$) are the two components of aggregate demand for which macroeconomics has developed the most complete theoretical understanding of how they are affected by interest rates. Solid empirical data are available, too, to underscore the relationships involved. So in bringing our analysis of the impact of interest rates on the aggregate demand function to a conclusion, we shall concentrate on investment and the trade balance.

The Rate of Interest and Investment Spending

Investment spending in Keynes's *The General Theory* emerges as not only the most strategically important determinant of the level of aggregate demand, but also the most volatile component entering into the aggregate demand function. This makes the determination of the actual level of investment spending at any one time one of the most complex theoretical problems encountered in macroeconomics. These are matters we shall explore in depth in Chapter 8. However, the frame of reference that Keynes used to analyze investment behavior is neither complex nor difficult to understand. This frame of reference descends directly from the classical analysis (Figure 3–2), but with some modifications in language and terminology.

Whereas the classical economists spoke of a negatively sloped "demand for savings for investment curve," Keynes postulates an investment demand curve, which also is negatively sloped.[11] Keynes's investment demand curve is based on what he calls the *marginal efficiency of capital*. This is the special terminology he used to describe the *expected* profitability (the rate of return) from investment in *new* capital assets. This is also how Keynes introduces *uncertainty* into the investment decision. *All* investment decisions rest on uncertain knowledge about the future profitability of capital goods. Keynes's thinking about investment spending is forward-looking and dynamic. Whenever a firm continues to buy new capital goods—machinery, structures, or additions to its inventories—the *marginal efficiency* of the particular type of capital acquired will decline. This is because the expected profitability or prospective yield for *any* kind of capital will fall as its supply is increased— diminishing returns at work—and also because the cost of each added unit of capital can be expected to rise. The reason for the latter is that the industries producing capital goods, like most industries, have upward-sloping supply curves. Because of the interaction beween diminishing returns and the supply price for new capital goods, Keynes concluded that the general slope for *all* investment demand schedules is negative.

How do we relate the foregoing to the rate of interest? It is easily done as long as we keep sight of the fact that Keynes's investment demand curve rests on his *marginal efficiency of capital* concept, which is a measure of the expected profitability of new capital, in terms not of dollars and cents but of a *rate,* a percentage return per dollar of investment in new capital. Figure 5–5

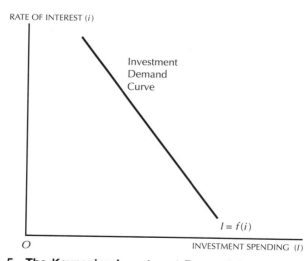

FIGURE 5–5   The Keynesian Investment Demand Curve. Keynes's investment demand curve slopes downward to the right; this shows that as the rate of interest falls, investment spending will increase. A lower rate of interest reduces the cost of borrowing, so more investment will take place.

---

[11] Ibid., p. 136.

shows a Keynesian investment demand curve. The rate of interest (i) appears on the vertical axis, and the level of investment spending (I) is found on the horizontal axis. Since the rate of interest represents the cost of borrowing funds (or the opportunity cost of using internal funds if no borrowing takes place), business firms will push investment spending (I) to the point at which the interest rate equals the expected profitability (the marginal efficiency of capital) from the added capital. If interest rates fall, *ceteris paribus,* investment spending will increase, and if interest rates rise, investment spending will drop.

As we saw in Chapter 2, the investment component (I) of the GDP consists of all purchases of equipment and buildings by business firms, all residential construction (new homes purchased), and all changes (increases or decreases) in inventories of goods held by business firms, finished and unfinished. Obviously, not *all* these components of investment spending are equally sensitive to the interest rate and interest rate changes. In general, the longer-lived the item of capital in question is, the more sensitive spending on that type of capital is to fluctuations in the interest rate. Housing is a clear case in point. Figure 5–6 shows for the period 1963 through 1994 how housing starts rise when interest rates for homes (mortgage rates) fall and drop when interest rates rise. The swings in housing starts in response to changes in mortgage rates are quite dramatic.

What Keynes did by developing his version of the investment demand

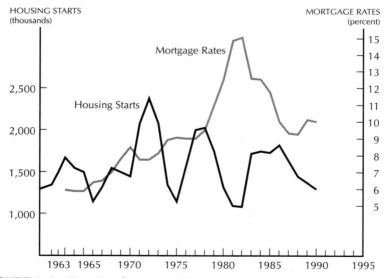

FIGURE 5–6 Housing Starts and Mortgage Rates: 1963–1994. Residential construction is one of the major components in investment spending. There is a close correlation between housing starts and mortgage rates. When mortgage rates rise, housing starts decline, and when mortgage rates fall, housing starts increase.

Source: Economic Report of the President, 1995.

schedule is move away from the assumption made temporarily in Chapter 4 that investment is autonomous. We have made investment a function of the rate of interest $[I = f(i)]$; investment (I) and consumption (C) are now linked to other variables—the rate of interest (i) and income (Y)—in the general income-expenditure macroeconomic model of the economy we are constructing.

Before we turn to the analysis of the rate of interest and the balance of trade, another comment is in order on differences between the classical and the Keynesian treatments of investment spending and the rate of interest. In concept (and diagrammatically) they are almost identical, but in a more fundamental philosophic sense, they are poles apart. The classical curve (Figure 3–2) is stable, appropriate to a world in which there is no uncertainty. Not so with Keynes. The Keynesian investment demand curve is highly volatile—a point we shall explore fully in Chapter 8. Here it will suffice to say that the reason for the curve's volatility is the uncertainty that surrounds *all* estimates of the future yield of a newly purchased capital good. In *The General Theory* Keynes aptly described this matter:

> The outstanding fact is the extreme precariousness of the basis of knowledge upon which our estimates of prospective yield have to be made. Our knowledge of the factors which will govern the yield of an investment some years hence is usually very slight and often negligible. . . .[12]

Interest Rates and the Trade Balance

The route by which interest rates affect the nation's trade balance is more circuitous than that by which interest rates affect investment. It involves differences between interest rates at home and abroad plus linkages with the foreign exchange market. To trace out this route, we first need to understand some of the essentials of the foreign exchange market and how that market works. Again we find ourselves in territory where we can apply the familiar economic tools of supply and demand.

Before we analyze the mechanics of this market, it is necessary to define the following terms: "foreign exchange," the "foreign exchange rate," and the "foreign exchange market." *Foreign exchange* refers to purchasing power in a foreign currency. For an American, foreign exchange consists of British pounds, German marks, French francs, or any other foreign currency that may be wanted. The *foreign exchange rate* is the price at which units of a foreign currency exchange for units of domestic currency. For example, the dollar–French-franc rate might be 4.25, which means one unit of U.S. currency ($1.00) will purchase 4.25 units of French currency. To put it slightly differently, $100 would buy 425 French francs. Like many other prices in today's world, foreign exchange rates are continually changing. There is not,

[12] Ibid., p. 149.

or course, a single foreign exchange rate, but as many rates as there are currencies to exchange. The *foreign exchange market* is not a place, like a stock exchange, where buyers and sellers meet to trade and establish prices. It is a huge, decentralized system of traders spread across the globe, a vast network of banks and other places (currency exchanges) where the currencies of the world's nations (foreign exchange) are bought and sold. Modern tele-communications provide for near-instantaneous worldwide communication 24 hours a day between every part of this network. Daily, billions of dollars worth of national currencies change hands.

The Foreign Exchange Market. When individuals and businesses buy im-ported goods and services, finance travel abroad, pay interest and dividends to foreigners, or buy foreign assets or when governments make foreign aid grants, they must buy foreign currency to carry out these transactions. To simplify our analysis at this point, we shall concentrate on only those inter-national transactions that involve goods and services, although the general principles involved apply to *all* international transactions.

In an international transaction a point of fundamental importance is that the price paid—what we may call the *effective price*—is a combination of the actual price of the good or service in the country of origin and the price that must be paid to obtain the foreign currency (foreign exchange) needed to undertake the transaction. For example, let us assume that a bushel of Canadian wheat sells for $3.00 *in* Canada ($3.00 in Canadian dollars) and that the exchange rate between the U.S. and the Canadian dollar is $1.00 U.S. to $0.85 Canadian; that is to say Americans will receive $1.176 Canadian for each U.S. dollar they spend buying Canadian money. Conversely the effective price in the United States for Canadian wheat is $2.55 ($3.00 divided by 1.176).

What will happen if the Canadian dollar appreciates, that is, if its value in U.S. dollars increases? Suppose the exchange rate goes to $1.00 U.S. equals $0.90 Canadian. Now the effective price in the United States for Canadian wheat is $2.70 ($3.00 divided by 1.11, the ratio of the U.S. to the Canadian dollar in the foreign exchange market). What this example shows is that changes in the exchange rate will lead to changes in the effective prices for goods and services traded internationally.

Figure 5–7 contains a model of the foreign exchange market. On the ver-tical axis we show the foreign exchange rate, which is the price of a foreign currency measured in dollars. If our model pertained to a particular foreign exchange market, say, for example, the British pound, the vertical axis would show the price of British pounds measured in dollars. Since Figure 5–7 is a general model of the foreign exchange market, we will view the vertical axis as representing the dollar price for a generalized quantity of foreign exchange. This is not unrealistic, as the Federal Reserve System compiles an index showing the foreign exchange value of the U.S. dollar relative to a combined and weighted measure of a number of foreign currencies (see Figure 5–8).

Let us examine this model more closely. The demand curve for foreign

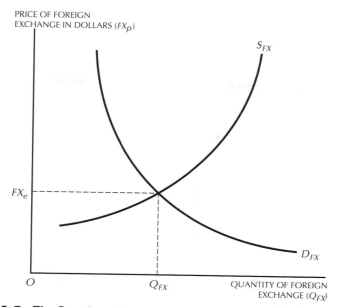

FIGURE 5–7 The Supply and Demand for Foreign Exchange. The demand curve for foreign exchange slopes downward. When the price of foreign exchange is high, less will be demanded because there will be a high effective price for imported goods. The supply curve for foreign exchange slopes upward. When the dollar price of foreign exchange is high, more will be supplied because foreign currency will buy more U.S. goods. Interaction between the quantity demanded and quantity supplied of foreign exchange will lead to equilibrium in the foreign exchange market.

exchange, like the demand curve for *any* good or service, slopes downward to the right. If the price of foreign exchange rises, there will be less demanded by Americans. Why? An increase in the dollar price of foreign exchange is the same thing as a decrease in the foreign exchange value of the dollar: it costs more in dollars to obtain a unit of foreign currency. The dollar is *depreciated;* this means it has lost value in terms of foreign currencies. Therefore, foreign-made goods and services cost more in dollars (in the United States), so the quantity demanded will be less. To put it differently, when the price of foreign exchange rises, a dollar will buy less abroad. Conversely, when the price of foreign exchange falls—a downward movement on the vertical axis—the purchasing power of the dollar in terms of foreign currencies has increased, and thus there will be a greater quantity of foreign exchange demanded.

Turning now to the supply curve for foreign exchange, we see that this curve, like supply curves generally, slopes upward to the right. Where does this supply curve come from, and why does it have a positive slope? For Americans the source of foreign exchange is foreigners wanting dollars. When the price of foreign exchange is high (the dollar is depreciated), foreigners get more dollars for each unit of their currency; this means U.S.-made

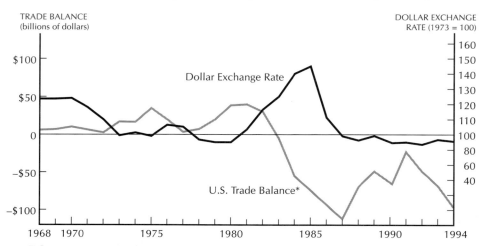

FIGURE 5–8   The U.S. Dollar Exchange Rate and the U.S. Trade Balance: 1968–1994.   The foreign exchange value of the U.S. dollar and the trade balance of the United States generally move in an inverse relationship to one another. This tendency was especially evident in the early 1980s, when the foreign exchange value of the dollar rose sharply and the trade balance worsened significantly.

*Balance on goods, services, and income.

Source: Economic Report of the President, 1995.

goods and services are cheap for foreigners. Consequently, the quantity of foreign exchange supplied to the market will be high. Conversely, when the foreign exchange rate is low, the value of the dollar will have appreciated; this means that each unit of foreign currency buys fewer dollars. Hence, U.S.-made goods and services will have become more expensive for foreigners, and less foreign exchange will be offered on the market.

When the demand for and supply of foreign exchange schedules are brought together as in Figure 5–7, we see that market forces lead to an equilibrium exchange rate, where there is a balance between the quantity of foreign exchange demanded and supplied. Any exchange rate above this equilibrium rate (FX_e in Figure 5–7) will create temporarily an excess supply of foreign exchange. Market forces will, therefore, drive the exchange rate down to the equilibrium level. On the other hand, an exchange rate below the equilibrium level results in an excess demand for foreign exchange, a situation that market forces will also correct by driving the price for foreign exchange back to the equilibrium level.

Under normal circumstances, the trade balance ($X - M$) is related negatively to the rate of interest and to the foreign exchange value of the U.S. dollar. Figure 5–8 traces out for a 26 year period (1968 through 1994) the U.S. trade balance and the foreign exchange value of the U.S. dollar in terms of a weighted basket for foreign currencies. Most of the time, as the figure shows, the trade balance worsened when the foreign exchange value of the dollar rose and improved when the dollar weakened.

What about shifts in the demand and supply curves for foreign exchange? As in any market situation, prices may change because of a temporary disequilibrium between demand and supply or because the demand and supply curves shift. As far as the foreign exchange market is concerned, economists are in general agreement that two factors largely account for shifts in the curves. One factor involves price differences between countries for the goods and services entering into trade. For example, if the price of wheat *in* Canada rose from $3.00 to $3.50 a bushel, this is the kind of a price differential that could cause a *shift* in the demand schedule for foreign exchange. Economists regard changes in exchange rates that result from price differentials between countries as a long-run matter, a topic that we shall consider in Chapter 10.

The other factor that accounts for shifts in the curves is interest rate differentials between nations. Economists believe that these differentials play a major role in foreign exchange systems where the rates are left free to find their own levels on the basis of market forces. Interest rate differentials are also viewed as primarily a short-term phenomenon, a point of that is reflected in our following discussion of how interest rates affect aggregate demand through the trade balance.

Interest Rate Differentials and the Trade Balance

The key to understanding how interest rates affect aggregate demand through the trade balance is the idea just introduced of the *interest rate differential.* Simply stated, this is the difference between an average of interest rates in the United States and an average of interest rates abroad. If we designate the average of interest rates in the United States as i_{US} and the average of the rest of the world (ROW) as i_{ROW}, symbolically the interest rate differential is $(i_{US} - i_{ROW})$.

Why does such a differential matter? It matters a great deal, as events of the early and mid-1980s demonstrated. When U.S. interest rates rise significantly above world levels, large amounts of money and credit flow into the country. We live in a restless economic world with billions of dollars and similarly huge quantities of other currencies moving continuously around the globe in search of profit. Foreigners wanting to profit from higher average interest rates in the United States than in their own countries buy U.S. securities—bonds, short-term notes, and even stocks. But to buy U.S. securities, they must have dollars. To get dollars, foreigners enter the foreign exchange markets. If they do so in sufficiently large numbers, the foreign exchange value of the dollar will rise; in the jargon of the financial world a *strong dollar* will be the result.

Unfortunately, a strong dollar is not necessarily a good thing for the economy overall. This is because it tends to stimulate import demand and depress export sales; the trade balance will worsen, in other words. Since exports are part of the overall demand for the nation's output (the GDP), a worsening of the trade balance (a drop in exports or a rise in imports) is tantamount to a

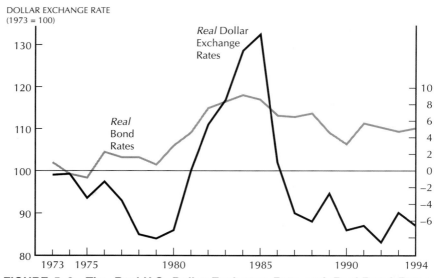

FIGURE 5–9 The *Real* U.S. Dollar Exchange Rate and *Real* Bond Rates: 1973–1994. Interest rates as measured by the rate for long-term bonds and the foreign exchange rate for the U.S. dollar generally move together. In the figure both interest rates and exchange rates are corrected for the effects of inflation.
Source: Economic Report of the President, 1995.

drop in aggregate demand. Output (Y) and employment (N) will, thereby, be affected adversely.

Figure 5–8 does not reveal the relationship between interest rates and foreign exchange rates. Figure 5–9 does show this for the period 1973 through 1994. Both the interest rate (for AAA-rated bonds) and the exchange rate are adjusted for inflation. Thus we are measuring *real* interest and exchange rates. It is clear from Figure 5–9 that the two rates roughly move together—an outcome our prior discussion would lead us to expect. We need answer one final question. What caused the sharp rise in U.S. interest rates beginning in the late 1970s? There were two developments. First, the Federal Reserve began to slow down the rate of growth in the money supply after 1978, and, second, massive federal deficits emerged in 1982. Both actions pushed nominal interest rates to unprecedented levels in the early 1980s. As both Figures 5–8 and 5–9 show, the sharpest rise in the dollar exchange rate came in the early 1980s.

Summary

1. In the classical model money exists independently of the rate of interest and only influences the price level.

2. Money is a key strategic variable in the Keynesian model. The effects of money work through the rate of interest to effect the demand for investment goods and the trade balance.

3. Money is the most liquid of all assets. It is a generalized claim against all goods, services, and other assets that have economic value.

4. Money functions as a standard for the measurement of value, a medium of exchange, and a store of value.

5. Bond prices and interest rates are inversely related.

6. The supply of money is crucial for understanding the macroeconomy. This entails knowledge of how the Federal Reserve System can affect the money supply through its central role in the system of fractional reserve banking.

7. The loanable funds theory of interest is drawn directly from the classical theory of the interest rate. It shows how the interest rate is determined in the bond market via the supply and demand for loanable funds.

8. The liquidity preference theory of the interest rate shows that interest is determined by the demand for money as an asset, relative to the supply of money that is available to use as an asset.

9. The trade balance $(X - M)$ and investment (I) are the two components of aggregate demand that are affected significantly by the rate of interest.

10. The market for foreign exchange operates much like any other market. When the price of foreign exchange (the exchange rate) rises, more of it is supplied and less of it is demanded. When the price of foreign exchange falls, a smaller quantity is supplied and a greater quantity is demanded.

6 The *IS-LM* Model

O UR ANALYSIS IN THIS chapter brings together the two basic strands in the income-expenditure approach to macroeconomics developed in the preceding chapters. These involve the demand for output as developed in Chapter 4 and the role played by money as set forth in Chapter 5. The primary object is to develop a general macroeconomic model that shows how equilibrium is obtained simultaneously in both the goods and monetary spheres of the economy. In the goods sphere, the focus is on output (Y) and employment (N), whereas in the monetary sphere the focus is on money (M^o) and the rate of interest (i). It is the *interdependence* of the rate of interest and the level of income that makes the model truly general; the functional relationships that underlie the system operate in such a manner that it is not possible to determine the equilibrium level of income without simultaneously determining the rate of interest.

This model, one of the best-known theoretical techniques used in macroeconomics, is called the IS-LM *model*. It is so named because it is built around two basic curves that constitute the essence of the model—the *IS* curve showing the goods side of the economy and the *LM* curve showing the money side.[1] It is constructed to show how equilibrium comes about simultaneously

---

[1] This model was developed originally by British Nobel laureate John R. Hicks. See his "Mr. Keynes and the 'Classics'; A Suggested Interpretation," *Econometrica,* April 1937, pp. 147–159. The reason

in the goods and the monetary spheres. This also is why it is often described as the IS-LM *model*.

The approach that we will use in the development of the *IS-LM* general model is to demonstrate the necessary conditions under which equilibrium may result in the goods and monetary spheres of activity taken separately. Then we shall explain the conditions under which equilibrium will exist in both spheres simultaneously. It is the latter analysis that enables the model to demonstrate the nature of equilibrium in the economic system as a whole. This involves analyzing separately the parts that make up a whole and then, as Keynes suggested, allowing for the interaction of all the factors that enter into the situation. This enables us to begin with some basic theoretical relationships and then bring additional, complicating variables into the analysis. By means of this process we get a relatively simple but powerful model for understanding the complexities of the real-world macroeconomy. This is what good theory in *any* area always does—reduce the complexities of reality to a relatively few basic relationships. It is for this reason that the *IS-LM* model represents a highly significant theoretical achievement in the area of macroeconomics.

Aside from explaining how interactions between the income level (Y) and the rate of interest (i) lead to equilibrium simultaneously in the goods and monetary spheres, the *IS-LM* model has other significant uses. In addition to its utility as a means to integrate all the important variables that enter into the theory of income and employment determination, the model emphasizes the essential differences between the goods and monetary spheres in the economic system. The distinction between these two sides of the economy is one of the most fundamental contributions to emerge from the Keynesian income-expenditure analysis. The model also provides a direct and useful way to introduce the price level into a general theory that explains how income and employment are determined in the modern economy. Further, the *IS-LM* framework gives us a simple but highly effective means to demonstrate and contrast the nature and effects of fiscal and monetary policy actions.

Constructing the *IS-LM* Model

To construct the *IS-LM* model, we begin with the essentials of the Keynesian system. These are the consumption-income relationship (the consumption

---

for using the symbols *IS* and *LM* to represent the goods and monetary sides of the economy respectively is that this model was developed originally from the basic Keynesian model in which there are neither government purchases nor economic ties with the rest of the world. In this basic model, equilibrium with respect to output requires equality between intended saving and investment; hence the use of *IS* to designate the output or goods side of the economy. In this same basic model, *M* represents the money supply and *L* the demand for money (liquidity demand); here equilibrium requires equality between these two variables. Thus, *LM* came to represent the monetary side of the economy.

Sir John Hicks and the *IS-LM* Curves

Economists gain enduring fame in a variety of ways. Some, like Adam Smith, Karl Marx, and John Maynard Keynes, build impressive systems of thought that move nations and change the world. Others work at a different level; they develop concepts and tools of analysis that find their way into the body of economic theory and become a part of the training of every economist.

John R. Hicks, an English economist, belongs in the latter category. Professor Hicks's famous invention is the *IS-LM* curves by which economists can bring together in a single diagram the key elements in Keynesian theory to show how output (and employment) is determined by the intersection of forces at work in two basic sectors of the economy: the goods sector and the monetary sector.

Professor Hicks—Sir John Hicks, as he was knighted in 1966—first developed his ideas in a now famous article published in 1937, just a little more than a year after Keynes published *The General Theory.* Professor Hicks's article, which was entitled "Mr. Keynes and the 'Classics'; A Suggested Interpretation" and which appeared in the statistical journal *Econometrica,* was intended to show explicitly in equation form the nature of classical economics, the nature of Keynesian economics, and the relationship between the two. In order to do this, Professor Hicks said in the article, "we have invented a little apparatus."

The little apparatus that Professor Hicks invented turned out to be the *IS-LM* curves, which subsequently have found their way into practically every macroeconomics textbook ever written and still provide the most esthetically pleasing geometrical model of the Keynesian system yet devised. In Professor Hicks's original formulation, the money equilibrium curve was described as an *LL* schedule, but this later got transformed into the *LM* curve, which is now the standard term in all texts.

As is often the case with an invention, the inventor is not always happy with the uses made of his invention. Many years later (1976), Professor Hicks said that although he believed that Keynes approved of his interpretation of *The General Theory,* he (Hicks) was not too happy with the subsequent use to which his model has been put. He feared that it helped to push the Keynesian analysis too much back into a static, equilibrium mold. Time gets abstracted from the analysis—a fact that Professor Hicks feels is an error (as we will see in Chapter 19).

Although inventing one of the most widely used analytical techniques of modern economics was a major reason for Professor Hicks's fame, it was only a small facet of a long and distinguished career. He was a professor at Oxford until 1965 and has continued to write and lecture extensively since his retirement. Besides his many contributions to macroeconomics, he has done research and written in the fields of wage theory, capital theory, taxation, the business cycle, and economic history. He received the Nobel Prize for Economics in 1972.

function), the investment demand schedule, the demand for money as an asset schedule that is part of the liquidity preference theory of interest, and the part of the money supply available to hold as an asset. We can put these "bare bones" ingredients of the Keynesian system together in a simple algebraic model as follows:

$$Y = C + I \tag{6-1}$$
$$Y = C + S \tag{6-2}$$
$$I = S \tag{6-3}$$
$$C = f(Y) \tag{6-4}$$
$$I = f(i) \tag{6-5}$$
$$L_a = f(i) \tag{6-6}$$
$$M^o = M^o \tag{6-7}$$

The first three equations are identity equations for an economy *without* a government sector or any ties with the rest of the world. As will be recalled from the discussion in the Appendix to Chapter 2, an identity equation defines one variable in terms of other variables. The values found in identity equations are *ex post* as compared with *ex ante* values in behavioral equations (functional relationships). Thus, in Equation (6–3) investment and saving are equal in an identity or *ex post* sense. They are *always* equal in this sense. This is an important point to which we shall return shortly.

The last four equations are behavioral equations, which express relationships between variables. The values to be found in behavioral equations are *ex ante* in nature, which is to say they represent intended or planned values. The variables contained in the schedules that are at the heart of economic theory and analysis are always *ex ante*. Equation (6–4) is the Keynesian consumption function as developed in Chapter 4, whereas Equation (6–5) is the Keynesian investment demand function. Equation (6–6) is the demand for money as an asset function explained in Chapter 5. Equation (6–7) means that the total money supply is treated as an autonomous variable; that is to say its quantity is not determined by any of the other variables that enter into the above model. These seven equations give us the necessary elements to build our *IS-LM* general equilibrium model.

Equilibrium in the Goods Sphere

The *goods sphere* refers essentially to those economic activities involving the production and use of goods and services. Our concern is with the forces that center in aggregate demand and supply and with the conditions under which an equilibrium exists with respect to the demand for and the supply of goods and services for the economy as whole.

In Chapter 4, the equilibrium level of income was defined by the intersection of aggregate demand (*DD*) and aggregate supply (*OZ*). As shown in Figure 4–7, the intersection of these two schedules represents a level of activity at which planned or *ex ante* spending for output (*DD*) is just equal to planned or *ex ante* production. There is a balance between aggregate demand and aggregate supply. We should note again at this point that the equilibrium output (*Y*) level resulting from the interaction between the Keynesian aggregate demand and supply schedules is not necessarily one of full or high employment. It was one of the key points developed by Keynes in *The General Theory* that a market system could find its equilibrium at *any* level of employment.

Now there exists another way to define an equilibrium level of income, a way that is particularly germane to our present task—building the *IS-LM* model. Refer back to the three identity equations in the basic algebraic model sketched out in the prior section. In an identity sense, as noted, investment (*I*) and saving *(S)* are *always* equal. But in an *ex ante* or planned sense they are equal only when the economy is in equilibrium. This is easy to understand. Saving in the Keynesian sense—and in our "bare bones" model outlined above—is the difference between output (*Y*) and consumption (*C*). For the economy to be in equilibrium, therefore, whatever is saved at any level of income must be absorbed by *ex ante* or planned investment spending. If this is not the case, then the income level will move up or down until an equilibrium is established.

For example, suppose at the current level of output (*Y*), planned saving (*Y − C*) exceeds planned investment (*I*). If this happens, there will be unsold goods, inventories will mount, and business firms will cut back on production. This will lead to a fall in both output (*Y*) and employment (*N*), which will continue until a balance is reached between spending (*DD*) and output (*Y*) or until investment (*I*) and saving (*S*) *ex ante* are once again in balance. If planned investment exceeds planned saving, the opposite will happen. Sales will run ahead of production; inventories will be drawn down; and business firms, seeing good times ahead, will expand output and employment. Thus, in a simple economy without government or foreign transactions, a second rule for equilibrium is that *ex ante* investment and saving must be equal. Later in this chapter we shall show how this rule can be broadened to take into account government spending and taxes and the foreign trade balance. For the moment, however, we shall assume a simple closed economy, without government or foreign transactions.

The *IS* Curve

The interaction of schedule values for investment (*I*) and consumption (*C*) in the determination of an equilibrium value for income is shown in Figure 6–1. Part A of the figure shows an investment demand curve relating investment outlays inversely to the rate of interest. In formal theoretical terms the algebraic expression for this schedule is $I = I_0 - gi$. I_0 is the amount of

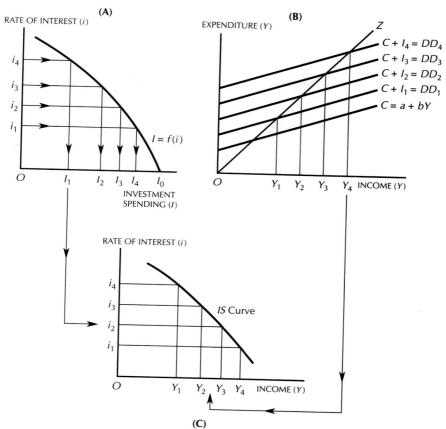

FIGURE 6–1 Equilibrium in the Goods Sphere. The *IS* curve is a series of points representing equilibrium values for income (*Y*) at alternative rates of interest (*i*). The interest rate determines investment (*I*), and given the consumption function, investment determines the equilibrium income level.

investment that is independent of the rate of interest, whereas *g* is the coefficient that relates investment spending negatively to the rate of interest. In part A of Figure 6–1, I_0 is determined by the point at which the investment demand curve intersects the horizontal axis. As the rate of interest rises above zero, investment spending (*I*) will necessarily fall below the I_0 value. In part B of the figure, the different levels of investment spending associated with varying rates of interest are added to a Keynesian consumption function. The result is a series of aggregate demand curves and different equilibrium income levels. Each *higher* income level is linked to a *lower* interest rate.

To illustrate, let us assume that initially the rate of interest is at the level i_4. This rate will yield a level of investment expenditure equal to I_1. The latter is measured on the horizontal axis of the diagram in part A.

In part B of Figure 6–1, the aggregate demand curve associated with I_1 expenditure yields the equilibrium income level Y_1. If the rate of interest declines to i_3, the investment spending level will rise to I_2 and produce an upward shift of the aggregate demand curve to the $C + I_2$ level, which will move the equilibrium income level to Y_2. As the rate of interest (i) continues to fall, this process will continue and lead to ever higher equilibrium income levels. At each equilibrium income level, equality will also exist between the *ex ante* values for investment (I) and saving (S).

Part C in the figure brings together in a new curve the relationship between the rate of interest, the level of income, and successive equilibrium positions in the goods sphere. In part C income *(Y)* is measured on the horizontal axis, and the rate of interest *(i)* on the vertical axis. Since an equality between investment and saving at successively higher income levels results only as the rate of interest declines, the curve that links income and the rate of interest in terms of the investment-saving equilibrium will slope downward to the right. This is the *IS* curve because each point on it relates equilibrium in the goods sphere to income and the rate of interest. We will show shortly how this curve can be readily expanded to reflect government spending and the export-import balance.

The shape of the *IS* curve depends on the essential character of the consumption function and the investment demand function. If, for example, the investment demand curve is assumed to be relatively *interest inelastic,* then it logically follows that the *IS* curve, too, will be relatively interest inelastic because any given changes in the rate of interest will have only a modest effect on the volume of investment spending. As a consequence, the income level will also be little affected by changes in the rate of interest. The effect of changes in the interest elasticity of the investment demand function on the slope of the *IS* curve is explored in more detail in Chapter 8. A change in the position of either the consumption curve or the investment demand curve shifts the overall position of the *IS* curve. For example, an upward movement in the investment demand curve will shift the *IS* curve to the right and make equilibrium possible at a higher level of income than heretofore. A shift of this type is depicted by the dashed IS_2 curve in Figure 6–2.

Equilibrium in the Monetary Sphere

The *monetary sphere* refers to economic activities that center around the demand for and the supply of money available to be held as an asset. A large and important body of theoretical literature has grown up around the concept of the demand for money—literature we shall explore fully in Chapter 11. For our purposes here it is sufficient to note again, as stressed in Chapter 5, the idea of a distinct monetary realm where the rules of the game differ from the realm of production and employment is strictly a Keynesian invention. Further, without such a realm (or sphere), the *IS-LM* model we are now exploring could not exist.

To understand better the idea of equilibrium in the monetary sphere, review

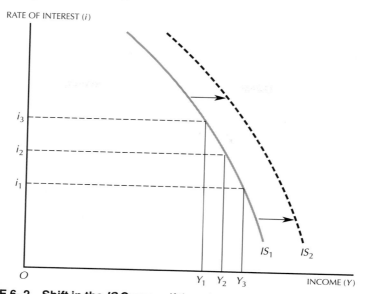

RATE OF INTEREST (*i*)

i_3

i_2

i_1

O

IS_1 IS_2

Y_1 Y_2 Y_3

INCOME (*Y*)

FIGURE 6–2   Shift in the *IS* Curve.   If there is an upward shift in the investment demand curve, the *IS* curve will shift to the right; this will indicate that there will be a higher level of equilibrium income (*Y*) associated with each level of interest (*i*).

the discussion of Figure 5–4 (page 160). The demand for money as an asset curve—of the schedule that Keynes described as the demand for liquidity—slopes downward to the right and thus indicates an inverse relationship between the amount of money people want to hold as an asset (L_a) and the rate of interest (*i*). This makes sense, for the higher the rate of interest the less attractive it is to forgo earning interest by holding financial wealth in money form. Since it is unlikely that every dollar of money in active circulation—mostly currency and demand deposits—is needed to sustain transactions in goods and services, some amount of money will be available to satisfy the liquidity demand for money. This, it will be recalled, is the meaning of the vertical money supply curve labeled M_a^o. What we are saying is that whatever quantity of money may be available to meet the demand to hold money as an asset, that quantity is *autonomous* with respect to the rate of interest. Thus, as we saw in Chapter 5, Keynes argued that the rate of interest is strictly a monetary phenomenon, determined by the demand for liquidity and the amount of money available to satisfy that demand. Monetary equilibrium exists when the demand for money for liquidity (L_a) is equal to the supply of money available to meet this demand (M_a^o).

The *LM* Curve

All well and good. But Keynes's liquidity preference theory of the interest rate taken by itself is not sufficient to permit us to construct the other half of the general equilibrium model, the *LM* curve. For this something more is needed. That something more is what happens to the asset demand curve for money—the $L_a = f(i)$ schedule—when the level of real output (Y) increases. If we think of the demand for money as an asset as being *in concept* like the demand for any good, we can draw on a well-established principle of microeconomic analysis to explain what will happen. Given the demand curve for any particular commodity, one of the other variables held constant by the *ceteris paribus* assumption is the level of income. But if income changes, then the position of the demand curve will shift: it will move to the right with an increase in income and to the left with a decrease in income. And so it is for the demand curve for money as an asset. If the level of real income (Y) increases, we can expect that the demand for money as an asset curve will shift to the right. What we have, therefore, is not a single liquidity preference curve, but a series of such curves, each of which is uniquely related to a particular level of income. Figure 6–3 depicts this.

Now we are in a position to move ahead and derive a second curve that is conceptually similar to the *IS* curve, but shows equilibrium values in the monetary sphere in relation to the rate of interest and the level of income. This is what we mean by the *LM* curve. Figure 6–4 shows how, on the basis of the relationships presented in Figure 6–3, the *LM* schedule can be constructed.

In the figure we begin with part A. This shows the demand for money as an asset as a series of smooth curves sloping downward to the right. As in Figure 6–3, each demand curve for money is associated with a different in-

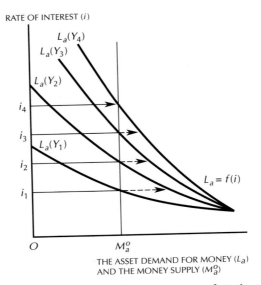

FIGURE 6–3 The Demand for Money as an Asset and the Income Level. The demand for money as an asset curve, like any demand curve for a good or service, shifts to the right when the income level rises. Thus, there exists a series of demand for money as an asset curves, each of which is associated with a different income level.

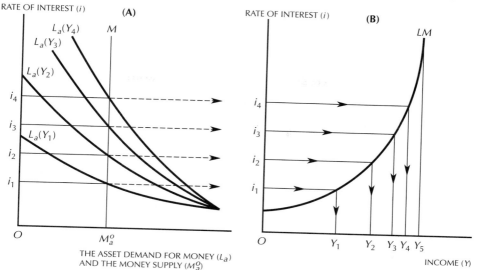

RATE OF INTEREST (*i*) (A)

$L_a(Y_4)$ M

$L_a(Y_3)$

$L_a(Y_2)$

i_4

i_3 $L_a(Y_1)$

i_2

i_1

O M_a^o

THE ASSET DEMAND FOR MONEY (L_a)
AND THE MONEY SUPPLY (M_a^o)

RATE OF INTEREST (*i*) (B)

LM

i_4

i_3

i_2

i_1

O Y_1 Y_2 Y_3 Y_4 Y_5

INCOME (*Y*)

FIGURE 6–4 Equilibrium in the Monetary Sphere. The *LM* curve is a series of points also representing equilibrium values for income (*Y*) at alternative rates of interest (*i*). For a given quantity of money available to be held as an asset (M_a^o), higher (or lower) levels of income will be associated with higher (or lower) levels of the rate of interest for equilibrium between the demand for and the supply of money to hold as an asset. The *LM* curve is predicated on a fixed amount of money being available to hold as an asset.

come level. M_a^o represents the supply of money available to be held as an asset. Let us begin the analysis with the rate of interest given at the level i_4. At this rate of interest, the demand for money (L_a) is equal to the available money supply (M_a^o). This equilibrium level in the monetary sphere corresponds to the income level Y_4. The point to underscore in this figure is that with a fixed money supply curve (M_a^o), higher equilibrium values for income (*Y*) will be associated with higher rates of interest.

Having established this initial equilibrium point, we need to trace through the consequences of a change in income. If the level of income falls to Y_3, the asset demand for money will also decline to the curve labeled $L_a(Y_3)$. A new equilibrium in the monetary sphere will be established for the interest rate i_3 and the demand for money L_a and the supply of money M_a^o. As the income level falls, in other words, the demand for money as an asset shifts downward and allows equilibrium at a lower rate of interest.

We can, in effect, follow the above procedures for all possible values for income and the rate of interest. This will give us a series of equilibria in the monetary sphere, equilibria defined in terms of the rate of interest and the level of income. This yields the *LM* curve found in part B of the figure. More precisely, the *LM* curve, given the underlying asset demand for money, and given, too, the money supply curve, describes all possible equilibrium values in the monetary sphere. It is constructed by showing on the horizontal axis the level of income (Y) associated with monetary equilibrium ($L_a = M_a^o$) for all possible values of the rate of interest (i). Equilibrium in the monetary sphere means the demand for and the supply of money available to be held as an asset are in balance in terms of a relationship between the income level and the rate of interest.

In Figure 6–4 it will be noted that at relatively low income levels the *LM* schedule lies flat, or in technical terms, is elastic with respect to the rate of interest. On the other hand, at relatively high income levels the *LM* schedule becomes vertical, or inelastic, with respect to the rate of interest. What are the reasons for this? The *LM* curve is constructed, it will be recalled, on the assumption that the total supply of money is relatively fixed. This being the case, at low levels of income the need for money for income (product) and other transactions will be relatively low. Therefore, a large portion of the money supply will become available for holding as an asset, for holding as idle balances, in other words. As the supply of money available to hold as an asset (M_e^o) increases, the rate of interest will fall. However, there is thought to be a limit to which the rate of interest can fall; at very low levels of the rate of interest the demand for money as an asset function (Figure 5–4) may become perfectly elastic. This has been called the *liquidity trap,* because once interest rates fall to this critical level, a further increase in the amount of money available to be held in idle balances won't affect the rate of interest.

In *The General Theory,* Keynes said "There is the possibility . . . that, after the rate of interest has fallen to a certain level, liquidity preference may become virtually absolute in the sense that almost everyone prefers cash to holding a debt which yields so low a rate of interest. In this event the monetary authority would have lost effective control over the rate of interest. But *whilst this limiting case might become practically important in the future, I know of no example of it hitherto.*"[2] Even though the liquidity trap may be a rarity in the real economic world, it is useful to discuss it for the sake of theoretical completeness. Moreover, it is useful, as we shall see subsequently, in pointing up some of the differences *at the extreme* between the policy implications that stem from a Keynesian as compared with those that stem from a classical analysis. In the classical world there is no demand for money as an asset. There is one other point to be noted in connection with the interest elastic portion of the demand for money as an asset curve. When interest rates are low, either absolutely or relative to past experience, bond prices (as well as the price of other fixed income assets) will be high. This means there is an increased risk in owning bonds because the higher the price of *anything* is relative to experience, the greater the risk is that this price will fall in the future. Therefore, at low interest rates the desire to hold cash will be strong and the desire to own bonds will be weak.

The vertical character of the upper reaches of the *LM* curve is explained by the fact that, without action by the monetary authorities to increase bank reserves, the money supply can become a bottleneck that will choke off an

---

[2] Keynes, *The General Theory,* p. 207 (italics added).

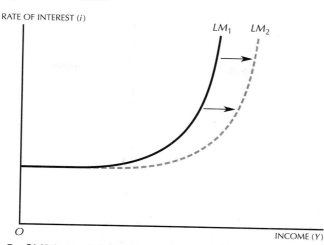

RATE OF INTEREST (*i*)

INCOME (*Y*)

FIGURE 6–5   Shift in the *LM* Curve.   If there is an increase in the money supply, the effect will be to shift the *LM* curve to the right and thereby make possible a higher level of equilibrium income (*Y*) at each level of the rate of interest.

expansion of income beyond some given level. As the income level rises, the need for more money to carry on more economic activity will increase. A higher level of income means more transactions, and more money will be needed to sustain the larger volume. But if the *total* money supply does not grow as transactions increase, additional quantities of money for transaction purposes can be obtained only by drawing them out of idle balances.[3] The cost of doing this is a higher rate of interest, and, as the income level rises, interest rates must rise higher and higher. Eventually the economy will reach a critical level at which any further expansion in the income level becomes impossible because the entire money supply is now needed to sustain output transactions. There are no longer any idle balances to be drawn into active circulation. In Figure 6–4, part B, Y_5 is assumed to be the maximum income that the money supply can sustain.

The effect of an increase in the money supply function on the position of the *LM* curve is shown in Figure 6–5. The initial position of the *LM* curve is shown by the solid line LM_1. The dashed line LM_2 represents a shift in the position of the curve. This type of shift would reflect action by the central bank to increase the money supply, presumably by putting more reserves into the commercial banks. The reason an increase in the money supply will shift the curve to the right can be easily understood by referring once again to Figure 6–4, part A. The existence of a fixed money supply schedule meant that monetary equilibrium at each and every possible income level was

[3] This assumes, of course, that the income velocity of money is unchanged. An increase in velocity can have the same effect as an increase in the money supply. Our purpose, though, is to analyze the effect on the monetary sphere, particularly interest rates, of a rise in the output level if we assume velocity is relatively constant and the supply is not perfectly elastic. Income velocity is equal to the level of output (*Y*) divided by the total money supply (M^o). In 1993 the income velocity for M1 was 5.6.

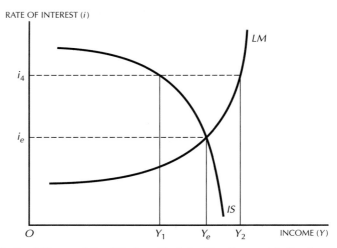

FIGURE 6–6 A General Equilibrium Model of the Economic System. Putting together the *IS* and *LM* curves in a single diagram shows the simultaneous determination of equilibrium values for income (*Y*) and the rate of interest (*i*).

uniquely associated with a particular rate of interest. An increase in the money supply shifts this curve to the right and makes possible monetary equilibrium at any particular income level at a lower rate of interest than heretofore. To show this situation in terms of the *LM* curve, it is necessary to shift the curve to the right as is done in Figure 6–5. Each point on the LM_2 curve represents a particular income level that is uniquely correlated with a rate of interest that is lower than the rate correlated with the point representing the same income level on curve LM_1. The effects of a decrease in the money supply would be just the reverse; that is, the *LM* curve would shift to the left.

General Equilibrium

By combining the *LM* and *IS* curves in a single diagram, we are able to construct in graphic form a general model of the economic system that shows, particularly, the manner in which the monetary sphere and the goods sphere are linked together through the rate of interest. Such a graphic model is shown in Figure 6–6. This model can be employed to demonstrate how the rate of interest and the income level are mutually determined in the income-expenditure system and to show a number of different and important situations that may be characteristic of the economic system.

In Figure 6–6 the *IS* and *LM* curves intersect at a point where net national product is at Y_e and the rate of interest is at i_e. These are equilibrium levels with respect to income and the rate of interest, both of which are mutually determined by the intersection of the *IS* and *LM* curves. At the point of intersection of these curves, the output level (*Y*) and the rate of interest (*i*) are such that saving (*S*) and investment (*I*) are in equilibrium, and the demand for money as an asset (L_a) and the supply of money available as an asset (M_a^o) are also in equilibrium. There are any number of levels of both the rate of interest and income that are compatible with equilibrium of either saving and investment alone or the demand for and supply of money alone, but there is only *one* rate of interest and *one* level of income that are consistent with equilibrium in both the monetary and the goods sphere. The actual level of both income and interest that is consistent with equilibrium in the two spheres depends on the shape and level assumed for the *LM* and *IS* curves, and this, in turn, depends on the characteristics of the functions that lie back of these curves.

The reasons why the point of intersection of the *IS* and *LM* curves depicts a condition of general equilibrium for the whole economy can best be seen if we imagine that income and the rate of interest are, momentarily, at a level different from Y_e and i_e.

Let us assume for a moment that the rate of interest and income are actually at levels represented by i_4 and Y_2 as shown in Figure 6–6. This represents a disequilibrium condition in the system as a whole, for although these values for both income and the rate of interest are compatible with equilibrium in the monetary sphere, they are not compatible with income in the goods sphere. At the interest rate i_4, for instance, income would have to be at the level Y_1 to bring equilbrium in the goods sphere, as determined by the *IS* curve. The system will of necessity move toward an equilibrium point; at the interest rate i_4 investment expenditure will not be sufficient to maintain an income level of Y_2, and hence the latter will decline. But as the income level declines, a portion of the money supply is released from use in response to the transactions motive, and as this happens, the rate of interest declines and thereby makes possible equilibrium in the monetary sphere at successively lower rates of both interest and income. This adjustment process will continue until a level of interest rates and income is reached that is compatible with equilibrium in both spheres of economic activity. Then, and only then, will a general equilibrium condition for the whole economy prevail.

Expanding the *IS-LM* Model

Before we turn to the theoretical question of shifts in either the *IS* or the *LM* curve, we need to examine how the model can be expanded to accommodate the government sector (G) and transactions with the rest of the world through the export-import balance ($X - M$). This can be done quite easily. What we must keep in mind is that government spending for goods and services (G) and the export-import balance ($X - M$) are components of aggregate demand. This means that the effect of adding government and international economic transactions to the basic model shows up in the goods sphere of the economy. What we need to do, in other words, is incorporate government spending for goods and services and the export-import balance into the *IS* curve.

Let us proceed by analyzing first what happens when the government sector is introduced into the model. At this point we need concentrate on only
two basic economic functions of government. These are, first, the purchase
of goods and services (G) to carry out whatever activities are appropriate to
the public sector and, second, the levy of taxes (T) to finance such purchases.
When we bring government into the picture, the algebra of our basic Keynesian model is modified as follows:

$$Y = C + I + G \tag{6–8}$$
$$Y = C + S + T \tag{6–9}$$
$$I + G = S + T \tag{6–10}$$
$$C = f(Y) \tag{6–11}$$
$$I = f(i) \tag{6–12}$$
$$G = G_0 \tag{6–13}$$
$$L_a = f(i) \tag{6–14}$$
$$M^o = M^o \tag{6–15}$$

What we have done is enlarge the first three identity equations in the
algebraic model to include the public sector. We now find that *ex post* ($I +
G$) must be equal to ($S + T$). Equation (6–13) tells us that G is now a part
of the behavioral side of the model, but its value is deemed autonomous with
respect to income. The other equations in the algebraic model are unchanged.

Two things follow from these changes in our algebraic model. First, the
aggregate demand curve as shown in part B of Figure 6–1 is shifted upward
by the amount of autonomous government spending (G). This means, *ceteris
paribus,* a higher value for the equilibrium income level (Y_e), given the
amount of investment spending (I) determined by the rate of interest (i). Thus,
the *IS* curve is shifted to the right. For every level of investment spending
associated with a particular rate of interest, the equilibrium income level will
be greater than it was prior to the introduction of a given amount of autonomous government spending into the analysis.

Our second point concerns equilibrium and how it is defined. As always
in the Keynesian-based income-expenditure model, the equilibrium level of
income is determined by the intersection of aggregate demand (DD) and
aggregate supply (OZ). We have not changed this principle, only modified it
by expanding aggregate demand to include government spending for goods
and services. We do need to modify, however, the second rule discussed
earlier for defining income equilibrium in terms of equality between *ex ante*
saving (S) and investment (I). By adding in government spending (G) and
taxes (T), the *ex ante* equality necessary for income equilibrium becomes $I +
G = S + T$. As just noted, we have added in government spending. But what
we have also done, in effect, is to factor in a second kind of leakage from the
income stream, a leakage that must necessarily be offset by spending if the
income equilibrium is to be maintained. In the simple model without government, savings are a leakage because they represent income received that is
not spent on currently produced goods and services. Taxes, too, are a leakage

because they represent income that is, momentarily at least, taken out of the income stream. The government normally spends its tax revenue, but until it does we have an income leakage. The point is a simple but fundamental one: unless such leakages as savings and taxes are offset precisely by an equal amount of spending, income equilibrium cannot be maintained.

Figure 6–7 shows the foregoing analysis in diagrammatic form. The reader will note the similarity with Figure 6–1. Essentially, what has been done is to add a fixed (autonomous) amount of government spending (G) to the original investment demand curve $[I = f(i)]$. As the interest rate falls, investment increases and shifts the aggregate demand curve upward by the change in investment spending *plus* autonomous government spending (G). This leads

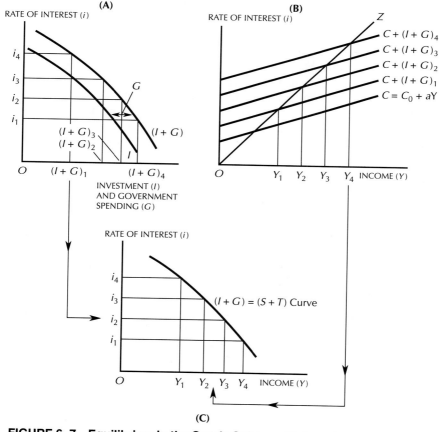

FIGURE 6–7 Equilibrium in the Goods Sphere with Investment and Government Spending. The $I + G = S + T$ curve consists of a series of points that represent equilibrium values for income (Y) at various rates of interest (i). The aggregate demand curve includes investment (I) plus an autonomous amount of government spending for goods and services (G). The interest rate determines investment, and given both the consumption function and a value for government spending, investment then determines the equilibrium income level.

to higher levels of income associated with lower rates of interest, a relationship which gives us the expanded *IS*, or $I + G = S + T$, curve shown in part C of Figure 6–7.

To bring the export-import balance $(X - M)$ or net exports (X_n) into the model, we need only follow the same procedures as we followed for government expenditures. The first three identity equations in our basic algebraic model now become:

$$Y = C + I + G + X - M \qquad (6\text{–}16)$$

$$Y = C + S + T + M \qquad (6\text{–}17)$$

$$I + G + X = S + T + M \qquad (6\text{–}18)$$

What this modification means is that now we have added net exports $(X - M)$ to the aggregate demand curve; this has raised it further and also shifted the basic *IS* curve further to the right. Net exports are that part of the national output (Y) that is sold abroad. Note carefully at this point that net exports may be negative, as has been the case for the U.S. economy since 1983. When they are negative, it means that Americans, on balance, are buying more goods and services from foreign countries than foreign residents are buying from the United States. Note, too, that momentarily we are treating the export-import balance as being autonomous with respect to the income level (Y). This is a useful assumption for the full development at this point of the *IS-LM* model, but as we shall see in Chapter 10, the actual situation is much more complicated. In that chapter we shall analyze fully all the variables that enter into the determination of the value of both exports (X) and imports (M).

As we did earlier in connection with government spending, the introduction of the export-import balance into the model means another modification of the second rule for defining income equilibrium. Now the *ex ante* condition for income equilibrium becomes $I + G + X = S + T + M$. Since imports reflect goods and services that are produced abroad but purchased by domestic residents, they represent another type of leakage out of the economy's current income stream. The same logic discussed earlier applies here: for an income equilibrium to be maintained, all leakages out of the current income stream— savings, taxes, and now imports—must be offset by an equal amount of spending. Since consumption always appears in the identity equations that define both output and its disposition (or use), the logical offsets to the three types of leakages we have identified are investment (I), government purchases of goods and services (G), and exports (X).

Figure 6–8 depicts a modified general equilibrium model of the economic system that incorporates both the public sector and the links between the domestic economy and the rest of the world (ROW), insofar as the latter are reflected in the nation's export-import balance $(X - M)$. In this model the *IS* curve as it was originally depicted in Figure 6–6 has been transformed into an $I + G + X = S + T + M$ curve. What we have in Figure 6–8 is basically an open economy, general equilibrium model, which we shall find increasingly useful as we probe more deeply into both the theoretical and policy

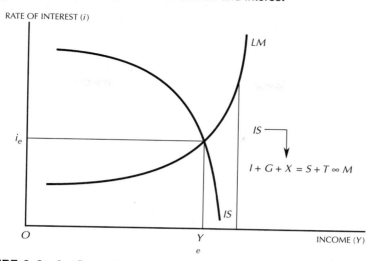

FIGURE 6–8   An Open Economy, General Equilibrium Model. By bringing government spending (G) and the export-import balance (X − M) into the IS-LM general equilibrium model, the IS side of the model becomes an expanded curve representing equilibrium values for the level of income (Y) and the rate of interest (i). The necessary condition for income equilibrium in an open economy is that I + G + X = S + T + M.

aspects of contemporary macroeconomics. For the sake of both clarity and simplicity in our subsequent analysis, we use the terminology IS-LM (both in the text and in diagrams) as a shorthand expression for the full-fledged open economy, general equilibrium model we have just developed. Both the text and the diagrams would become unnecessarily cumbersome if in every instance we had to point out that, in reality, the IS curve embodies government spending and net exports as well as investment spending. This should be understood.

Changes in the Equilibrium Values of Income and Interest

A change in the equilibrium level of the net national product and the rate of interest comes about within the framework of our graphic model of the economic system as the consequence of a shift in the position of either the IS or the LM curve. It should be noted carefully that all shifts in equilibrium values for income embody the multiplier process, which is to say that every equilibrium value for income shown in the model is arrived at after the multiplier process has worked itself out.

For convenience in our analysis, we can describe changes that affect the equilibrium values for both income and the rate of interest as being either *real* or *monetary* in origin. By real changes we mean those that originate in the goods sector and that thus come about because the IS curve has shifted.

Monetary changes, on the other hand, refer to developments emanating from the monetary sphere and, consequently, manifest themselves through a change in position of the *LM* schedule.[4] Examination of the major sources of shifts in both the *IS* and *LM* curves will provide us with the necessary background for a discussion of contemporary economic policy and its application to fluctuations in income and employment.[5]

Shifts in the *IS* Curve

The fundamental explanation for a rightward shift in the *IS* curve is an increase in aggregate demand. Four major explanations for an upward movement of the aggregate demand curve can be distinguished. First, there may be an autonomous increase in investment demand. In this instance, curve *I* in part A of Figure 6–1 shifts to the right; this indicates a higher level of investment spending at all ranges of the interest rate. Second, there may be an autonomous increase in government spending for goods and services. If such an increase takes place with no increase in taxes, the maximum shift in the aggregate demand curve will be obtained. However, even if taxes are increased in an amount equal to an increase in government spending for goods and services, the balanced budget theorem (explained in Chapter 9) indicates that the aggregate demand curve will still be displaced upward. Third, there may be an autonomous upward shift in the income-consumption relationship, the consumption function as Keynes called it. This could come about because of an increase in transfer payments, a reduction in personal income taxes, or a general tax reduction with no change in the level of either government expenditures or investment outlays. It might also result from changing attitudes toward thrift, which would have the effect of reducing the propensity to save at all income levels. Finally, the aggregate demand curve may shift because of an increase in exports relative to imports. This may result from an absolute increase in exports or a decrease in imports. (Refer again to Figure 6–1 and determine how each of the foregoing changes affects the position of the aggregate demand curve and, consequently, the position of the *IS* curve. Keep in mind at all times that the *IS* curve shows a series of equilibrium values for the output level at alternative values for the rate of interest, given all the underlying relationships that enter into the determination of the level of aggregate demand.)

Within the framework of our general equilibrium model, the effect on income of an upward shift in the aggregate demand curve depends on (1) the

---

[4] One should be careful not to confuse this use of the terms ''real'' and ''monetary'' with the distinction between real and nominal values. In the above discussion we are using real and monetary as a way to distinguish between the two spheres of the economy found in the income-expenditure analysis. In the other usage, the term ''real'' refers to values corrected for changes in the price level, whereas ''nominal'' refers to values not so corrected. One should always be aware of this distinction.

[5] In the discussion that follows we shall focus our attention on shifts to the right in both the *IS* and *LM* curves. The same reasoning and explanations apply with respect to shifts in the opposite direction.

extent to which the *IS* curve is displaced to the right (the distance *ab* in part A of Figure 6–9) and (2) the impact that a rising rate of interest will have on forces that determine equilibrium in the goods sphere (the distance *cd* in the same figure). The factors that govern the magnitude of the shift in the *IS* curve are those which influence the size of the multiplier effect, given an increase (or decrease) in aggregate demand. The size of the multiplier depends on all the factors that determine the extent of leakages from the income stream. These are matters that we shall examine in detail in Chapters 7 through 10.

If there is no change in the position of the *LM* curve with a given shift to the right in the *IS* curve, there will be a rise in the rate of interest. This happens because *any* increase in aggregate demand that causes a rightward shift in the *IS* curve will mean that more money is needed to carry out an increased volume of income and product transactions. If the monetary authority—the Federal Reserve System in the United States—does not increase the money supply to accommodate a higher level of aggregate demand (total spending), the additional money needed to sustain more economic activity can only come from drawing down the money balances that people have who are holding money as an asset. But to do this, as Keynes's liquidity preference theory of interest shows, interest rates will have to go up. The only other alternative is an increase in the velocity, the rate of turnover, of money, which may or may not happen. In any event, the overall impact of the rise in the interest rate is to dampen the income-increasing effect of the rightward shift in the *IS* curve. The magnitude of this dampening effect depends on both the steepness of the *LM* curve at the point of shift in the *IS* curve and the interest elasticity of the investment component of the aggregate demand function. In later discussions of policy, we shall return to this point.

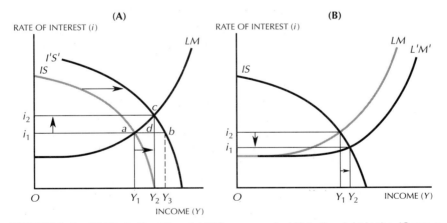

FIGURE 6–9   Shifts in the *IS* and *LM* Curves.   A shift to the right in the *IS* curve will result in higher levels of income (*Y*), but interest rates also will be higher. A shift to the right in the *LM* curve may also lead to higher levels of income (*Y*), but interest rates in this case may be lower.

Shifts in the *LM* Curve

The effect of a rightward shift in the *LM* curve on both equilibrium income level and the equilibrium value for the rate of interest is depicted in part B of Figure 6–9. This shift could take place because of an autonomous increase in the money supply. The reasons why an increase in the money supply shifts the *LM* curve were touched on in the discussion in conjunction with Figure 6–5. A change in the money supply is most likely to be the source of a shift in the *LM* curve. The *LM* curve might shift to the right because of a downward shift in the demand for money as an asset component of the total demand for money. This would be the result of a general decline in the demand for liquidity throughout the economy. The effect of a downward shift in the liquidity preference function is to release funds from idle balances, which spill over into the bond market, push up the prices of the latter, and thereby reduce interest rates. It follows from this that monetary equilibrium in relation to any given income level will be achieved at a lower rate of interest.[6]

In general, the effect on the equilibrium income level of a shift to the right in the *LM* curve depends on (1) the extent to which the rate of interest declines as a result of the shift in the *LM* curve and (2) the responsiveness of forces in the goods sphere to a decline in the rate of interest. The latter is primarily a matter of the interest elasticity of investment demand, although other components of aggregate demand may be affected by a change in the rate of interest. We shall elaborate further on this in our subsequent discussion of policy and its application.

In connection with shifts in the *LM* curve, one additional point should be noted: With the exception of changes taking place in the range of interest rates equal to or below the horizontal portion of the *LM* curve, a shift to the right in the *LM* curve will always reduce the rate of interest. The significance of this is that the full multiplier effect will follow; there will be, in other words, no offsetting changes in the rate of interest as is the situation confronting the economy when the *IS* curve shifts.

The Price Level and the *IS-LM* Model

Now that we have constructed the basic *IS-LM* model of the macroeconomy, it is appropriate to expand the model and at the same time make it more realistic by bringing the price level into the analysis. Up to this point the price level has been taken as given and constant. This basic assumption has had the effect of putting the analysis in *real* or constant price terms.

Now our objective is to demonstrate how the output (and employment) level may be affected by a change in the price level. The income-expenditure analysis pursued up to this point focuses on the demand side. It has been

---

[6] A third possibility involves a decline in the general price level, a possibility which will be explained in a later section.

explicitly assumed that output responds to any change in the level of aggregate demand. As a matter of fact, the constant price assumption means that the only way by which the economy can respond to shifts in the aggregate demand function is through output changes, that is, adjustments in the level of *real* GDP. To a degree this is a reasonable approach, but it is not adequate to deal with the full complexity of the real-world economy. We must recognize that in reality changes in aggregate demand lead to changes in both output and the price level. We must further recognize—as is the case with interest and income (output) in the general *IS-LM* model—that output and the price level are also determined simultaneously.

To resolve these problems, we shall proceed, first, by the introduction of the price level into the *IS-LM* model as an *exogenous* variable. This is necessarily an oversimplification, but it is a useful way to proceed. It is useful because from this perspective we can move to the treatment of the price level as an *endogenous* variable—which is the real-world situation—by the use of aggregate demand and supply curves that link the price level to both the supply of output (the GDP) and the total demand for that output. These are the Keynesian-classical aggregate demand and aggregate supply curves developed in Chapter 4. Recall that these particular concepts of aggregate demand and aggregate supply are analogous to the concepts of individual demand and supply that microeconomic analysis uses to explain the determination of the price and quantity produced or supplied of an individual good or service. This is what gives them a *classical* flavor. It is important to stress at this point that we shall still be operating within the fundamental framework of macroeconomics, which holds that output, employment, and the price level are best explained by the interplay between aggregate demand and aggregate supply. At this point in our analysis we shall be looking at these latter relationships from a somewhat different perspective than we did earlier in Chapter 4, but conceptually the approaches are the same.

The Price Level as an Exogenous Variable

To introduce the price level as an exogenous variable into the basic *IS-LM* model, we need to make two simplifying assumptions. The first is that of flexible prices, which is to assume that all prices move freely upward and downward in response to changing economic conditions. Reality, of course, is quite different, but this assumption will enable us to develop our model. The *IS-LM* model with flexible prices has been described as the *neoclassical synthesis,* because it combines classical principles of demand and supply operating in competitive markets with Keynesian principles of output determination.[7] The fully developed neoclassical model also requires that we graft a classical model of the labor market onto an *IS-LM* model with flexible prices.

The second simplifying assumption is that when the price level changes,

[7] Samuelson, *Economics, An Introductory Analysis,* 6th ed., (New York: McGraw Hill, 1955), p. 337.

all prices change in the same proportion. This, too, is not necessarily true in reality, but it is a useful technique because it enables us to trace through in the most direct fashion how a change in the price level will affect the *IS* and *LM* curves.

Now to proceed. It should be clear that all the key variables that lie behind the *IS* curve—consumption, investment, government spending, and net exports—are measured in real terms. This is how we have proceeded earlier in this chapter to build up all the variables that enter into the economy's aggregate demand schedule. This also means that households, business firms, and governments do not suffer from a money illusion. To put it differently, we are assuming that the key economic actors in our macroeconomic drama—the households, business firms, and governments in the United States and the rest of the world—clearly understand that the value of money is not stable. Consequently, the relationships that enter into the construction of the aggregate demand schedule are framed in real, not nominal, terms. This being the case, there is no reason why the rise or fall in the general price level should shift any of the underlying real functions—the consumption function or the investment demand function, for example—which determine the position of the *IS* curve. Consequently, we shall assume initially that the *IS* curve does not shift as a result of a change in the general price level.

It is a different story with respect to the *LM* schedule. The demand for money balances is a demand for real balances, but the amount of money in existence (which is money being held) can only be denominated in nominal terms, as money is the basic unit in which all else is measured. The important question is what happens to the real value (the purchasing power, in other words) of such balances when the price level changes, all else remaining constant? If prices go up, this means that the *real* value of nominal money balances has declined. But this will be the same in an economic sense as a decline in the money supply, since persons and firms find themselves with less money available to carry on economic transactions. Thus, an increase in the price level, *ceteris paribus,* will pull money out of asset balances into active circulation and thereby cause an increase in the interest rate. There is no difference in this effect between an increase in the price level and a decrease in the money supply, *ceteris paribus.* Since this takes place at any or all values for output, the *LM* curve will lie to the left of the position it would occupy at a lower price level. An increase in the price level, in other words, shifts the *LM* curve to the left. A fall in the price level, on the other hand, has the same effect, *ceteris paribus,* as an increase in the money supply. Thus, introduction of a price level variable into the analysis results in a series of *LM* schedules, each one associated with a different price level. These are depicted in Figure 6–10 as $LM(p_3)$, $LM(p_2)$, and $LM(p_1)$.

What we now have in our general equilibrium model is not a single set of equilibrium values for interest and income, as shown earlier in Figure 6–6, but a series of equilibrium values, each one uniquely associated with a different level of prices. But we have something more than this. We now have

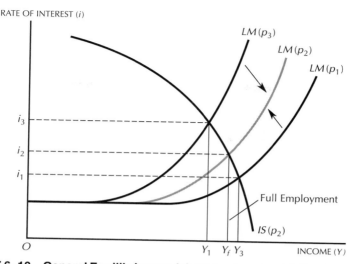

FIGURE 6–10   General Equilibrium and the Price Level. A falling (rising) price level has the same effect as an increase (decrease) in the money supply: it shifts the *LM* curve to the right (left) and causes a rise (fall) in the equilibrium value of income (Y).

a mechanism to ensure that equilibrium in the goods market (*IS*) and in the money market (*LM*) is brought into balance at an assumed full-employment level. This mechanism is the price level, if we assume *flexibility* in all prices, including money wages.

Turn again to Figure 6–10. If we assume that Y_f is the full-employment output level and that momentarily the price level is at p_1, we now have a disequilibrium condition in terms of the model.[8] This is because, given the price level p_1, the *IS* and *LM* curves will intersect at an income level equal to Y_2. But this is not possible if we assume Y_f is the full-employment real income. Y_2 is an income level in which aggregate *money* demand is in excess of aggregate full-employment supply. Consequently, in this situation, the adjusting factor must be a rise in the price level from p_1 to p_2 if we assume no changes in the underlying determinants of the system. The income-expenditure model shows, in other words, that, if conditions in the monetary and goods spheres are such that the *IS-LM* equilibrium output lies beyond the full-employment level, then rising prices are inevitable.

If the price level happens to be p_3, we have an opposite situation. Now the equilibrium output for *IS* and *LM* is Y_1, which represents a level of aggregate money demand below the full-employment output level Y_f. Now what will happen? Just the reverse of what took place in the opposite situation. Prices will fall, and they will continue to fall until the system reaches a full-em-

---

[8] In the full neoclassical synthesis, it is the labor market that ultimately determines the level of output.

ployment equilibrium. In Figure 6–10 this will be at the price level p_2. Flexibility in prices ensures an automatic adjustment of the economic system to full employment.

At this point an important word of caution is in order. The assumption of price flexibility is just that—an assumption. It is not a common characteristic of the real economic world. It is an assumption, however, that is critical to those analytical perspectives—primarily monetarism and the new classical economics—that argue that the economic system when left alone is self-adjusting, that market forces tend automatically to move the economy toward a condition of full employment. In the real economic world, price rigidity, particularly downward rigidity, is the common situation. Moreover, whatever flexibility exists for real economic world prices is mostly upward, as the fact of the economy's almost continuous inflation since the end of World War II demonstrates. For theoretical completeness, it is necessary to understand how our macroeconomic model would work *if* all prices were completely flexible. It is also important to remember at all times that the theoretical models used in all branches of economics are not precise descriptions of economic reality. They always are intellectual constructs that help toward a better understanding of reality. That is their real value.

The Keynes and Pigou Effects

In the foregoing discussion, it is price flexibility per se that forces the system to adjust to a stipulated full-employment output, given a fixed quantity of money in nominal terms. We have not to this point identified any specific mechanisms through which these results might be achieved. There are, however, two possible mechanisms by which these results can in theory be brought about—mechanisms which in the literature of economics have come to be known as the *Keynes effect* and the *Pigou effect*. These mechanisms are illustrated in Figure 6–11.

The Keynes effect, shown in part A of the figure, works through the impact that lower prices have on the real value of the economy's money supply. Why is this called the "Keynes effect"? The answer is that a falling price level, which increases the *real* value of the nation's money supply, will, *ceteris paribus,* lower interest rates. Lower interest rates will, given the negative slope of the investment demand curve, increase investment spending—a change which will also bring the multiplier into play. Thus aggregate demand will increase—in terms of the *IS-LM* relationship this involves a movement along the *IS* curve—and the income level will rise. The price level effects that trigger this change are reflected in Figure 6–11 by rightward shifts in the *LM* curve. If we admit the possibility of a liquidity trap—the flat portion of the *LM* curves—there is a limit to the amount of expansion that can be obtained by reducing prices. In Figure 6–11, this limit is the income level Y'. Since, at this income level, the *IS* curve intersects the *LM* curve in the flat portion of the latter, a further reduction in the price level from p_2 to p_1 will

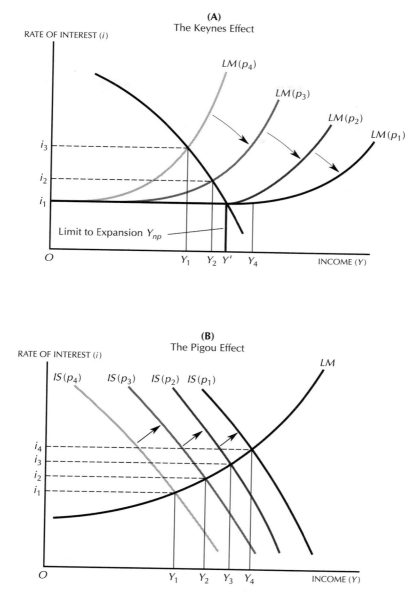

(A)
The Keynes Effect

(B)
The Pigou Effect

FIGURE 6–11 The Keynes and Pigou Effects. The Keynes effect works through the impact that a falling price level has on the *real* value of money, a development which lowers interest rates and thereby increases investment spending and the equilibrium income level (*Y*). The Pigou effect works by shifting the consumption curve upward because a falling price level increases the *real* value of assets held by consumers.

not lead to any additional increase in income, even though the *LM* curve would be pushed farther to the right.

A word of caution is in order here. This mechanism is called the "Keynes effect" because it works through the basic Keynesian propensities involving investment and consumption (i.e., the multiplier), but this does not mean that Keynes advocated such a course of action. As a matter of fact, he strongly opposed wage and price deflation as a means of increasing output and employment; he believed on practical grounds that an increase in the money supply could achieve the same result with far less resistance and social disharmony. What the idea of the liquidity trap did in this situation—granted that Keynes was dubious about its real existence—was to provide theoretical ammunition for Keynes's attack in the 1930s on the prescription of the classical economists that the way out of the depression was to slash wages and prices.

The argument embodied in the Pigou effect (which is also known as the real balance effect) is of a different sort and, in principle at least, does not run into any limit on the extent to which output can be expanded by reducing the general level of prices.[9] The Pigou effect asserts that a falling price level will shift the income-consumption curve upward, because lower prices increase the real value of the consumer's stock of liquid assets and thus lessen the need to save. Hence, real consumption will be higher at all income levels. In terms of the general equilibrium model, this means that the *IS* curve will shift to the right, or upward, as the price level drops. Thus, as shown in part B of Figure 6–11, the Pigou effect postulates a series of *IS* curves, each associated with a different level of prices. As a theoretical proposition, the Pigou effect is logical, but most economists do not believe it has any great practical value. Certainly the experience of past depressions and recessions does not offer any convincing evidence that a falling price level will stimulate demand in this fashion. Furthermore, the idea of a *falling price level* is almost wholly an academic question. As noted, at no time since World War II has the price level (as measured by the CPI) actually declined. What has happened, of course, is that the *rate* of inflation has dropped, especially since 1980. In our development in Chapter 12 of an aggregate supply relationship which has its roots in modern microeconomic theory, we shall take this into account.

There is another side to the Pigou effect that works in an opposite manner. It is true that a falling price level increases the real value of assets, which are normally denominated in money terms. But at the same time it increases the real burden of debts, since their monetary value does not change when the price level falls. Debtors are always hurt by falling prices. It is theoretically— and practically—conceivable that as far as debtors are concerned, a falling price level will force them to consume less in order to service their debts, the

---

[9] A. C. Pigou, "The Classical Stationary State," *Economic Journal*, December 1943, and "Economic Progress in a Stable Environment," *Economica*, August 1947. The latter is reprinted in *Readings in Monetary Theory* [New York: McGraw-Hill (Blackiston), 1951], pp. 241–251.

monetary value of which has not changed. Irving Fisher, the United States' leading economist at the time of the 1929 crash, was concerned about this, since he was doubtful that the positive side of the real balance effect would be strong enough to restore full employment.

The Price Level as an Endogenous Variable

The preceding analysis has shown how the *IS-LM* model can be modified to take into account changes in the general level of prices, as well as changes in output and the rate of interest. A problem remains: the model is still basically indeterminate, because the price level is treated as an *exogenous* variable. As with the earlier version of the *IS-LM* model, which included only the goods and money market and in which output and the rate of interest were determined simultaneously, we now have a model in which output, the rate of interest, *and* the price level are treated simultaneously.

One way to improve on the situation is to modify the model so that the price level becomes an *endogenous* variable. This can be accomplished by the use of Keynesian-classical aggregate demand and aggregate supply curves that relate the demand for and the supply of output to the general price level. As noted earlier, curves of this type are analogous to the kind of demand and supply curves used to explain how the prices and output level for individual goods and services are determined.

The question is this: What specific uses can be made of these curves? What, in other words, can we show about the economy's performance by using these curves that we cannot show with the standard *IS-LM* analysis? There are two broad answers to this. First, the Keynesian-classical aggregate demand and aggregate supply curves provide a convenient mechanism for showing the effect of policy decisions on prices as well as on output and employment. Second, this simplified model involving the price level as well as output and employment provides a good introduction to the development later of an aggregate supply curve which embodies Keynes's ideas about the aggregate supply price and the expectation of proceeds, and which also has its roots in contemporary microeconomic theory. As we shall learn in Chapter 12, the Keynesian-based aggregate supply curve is not only suitable for explaining the inflation and stagnation of the 1970s, but also provides an appropriate and realistic means of introducing the price level into the income-expenditure model.

In Figure 6–12 we bring together in a single diagram the Keynesian-classical curves of aggregate demand and aggregate supply. In principle, as we shall explain in detail in the next section, we could move the economy to a full-employment output level either by monetary policy, which shifts the *LM* curve, or by fiscal policy, which shifts the *IS* curve. Let us duplicate these policy changes in terms of the Keynesian-classical aggregate demand and aggregate supply curves shown in Figure 6–12. In this figure we assume that initially output is at the level Y_1 and the price level is at p_1. This is less than the full-employment output, which we shall designate in the figure as Y_2. To

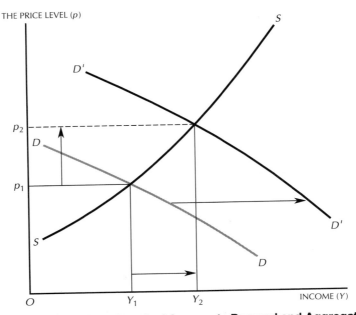

FIGURE 6–12   Keynesian-Classical Aggregate Demand and Aggregate Supply Curves.   A shift to the right in the *LM* curve in the *IS-LM* model can be depicted as an increase in the aggregate demand curve (*DD*) in the Keynesian-classical model, a change that results in both a higher income level (*Y*) and a higher price level (*p*).

move the economy to this level of output, we simply have to bring about a rightward shift in the aggregate demand curve to the position shown by the curve $D'D'$. How is this to be done, and how will such a shift affect the price level? These are the key questions.

In principle this shift in aggregate demand can be brought about by either monetary or fiscal actions. Let us look first at monetary action in the form of an increase in the money supply. Given an initial level of prices (p_1), an increase in the money supply will shift the *LM* curve to the right. *Ceteris paribus*, an increase in the money supply causes the rate of interest to fall, which, in terms of the basic *IS-LM* model, leads to an increase in aggregate demand and a move down the *IS* curve. The equivalent of this in terms of Figure 6–12 is a shift to the right in the aggregate demand curve (*DD*). The policy problem is to increase the money supply sufficiently so that the Keynesian-classical aggregate demand curve in Figure 6–12 shifts just enough to bring the economy to the full-employment output level (Y_2).

What makes the policy problem more complicated than in the earlier *IS-LM* model is the positive slope to the aggregate supply curve (*SS*), depicted in Figure 6–12. This means that, when total effective demand is increased, not only will the output level rise, but prices will also rise. The extent to which both output and the price level respond to an increase in aggregate demand depends on the elasticity of aggregate supply. The less elastic aggregate supply is, the less responsive output and employment are to an increase in the money supply and the greater will be the extent to which more spending dissipates itself in rising prices. The supply curve *SS* is constructed on the assumption of a fixed money wage. This is not an absolute requirement. What is necessary is that prices rise faster than the money wage, for only if this happens, will *real* wages decline. The latter is necessary if employers, given the classical production function, are to increase both employment and output.

We can, in effect, go behind the curves shown in Figure 6–12 and, using *IS-LM* diagrams, depict what happens when aggregate demand is shifted by either monetary or fiscal actions. This is done in Figure 6–13. In part A of the figure the results of monetary action are shown. Initially output is at the level Y_1 and the rate of interest is i_3, so equilibrium is less than the full-employment output of Y_2. The price level associated with this $LM(p)_1$ curve is p_1. Now the money supply is increased, with prices momentarily unchanged at p_1; this shifts the *LM* curve to the level indicated by $LM(p_3)$. If prices remained stable, the interest rate would fall to i_1, and the equilibrium income level would rise to Y_3. But this is not possible because of the upsloping aggregate supply curve shown in Figure 6–12. Therefore, as expenditure increases because of the rightward shift in the *LM* curve, the price level also begins to rise. For the reasons discussed earlier in conjunction with Figure 6–10, a rising price level has the effect of shifting the *LM* curve to the left. Ultimately, a new equilibrium will be established by the intersection of $LM(p_2)$ and the *IS* curve, which is the full-employment output Y_2. The price level will now be p_2, the rate of interest will be i_2, and the money supply will be greater.

The alternative to monetary moves for shifting the aggregate demand schedule to the $D'D'$ level is fiscal action. Let us assume that this takes the form of an increase in government spending, which will shift the *IS* curve to the right. Again the policy problem is to increase government spending by an amount sufficient to bring output to the full-employment level Y_2 as depicted in Figure 6–12. The complicating factor as before is the price level, since any increase in aggregate spending will cause it to rise. What happens is shown in part B of Figure 6–13. As indicated, the *IS* schedule shifts from IS_1 to IS_2—a direct result of the increase in government spending. If the price level remained at p_1, output would rise to a new equilibrium at Y_3, and interest rates would also rise to the level of i_2. But the price level does not remain still. More spending causes it to rise, and as it rises, the *LM* curve shifts to the left. What this does is raise the interest rate even further—a development which will have the effect of reducing investment spending. To sum up, the net effect of fiscal action in the form of increased government spending with respect to the output level will be smaller than otherwise would be the case because of rising prices. As long as the money supply remains fixed, there is no offset to the impact that rising prices have on interest rates through a change in the position of the *LM* curve. Thus, the final equilibrium position of Y_2, which we assume is a full-employment equilibrium, will be one at

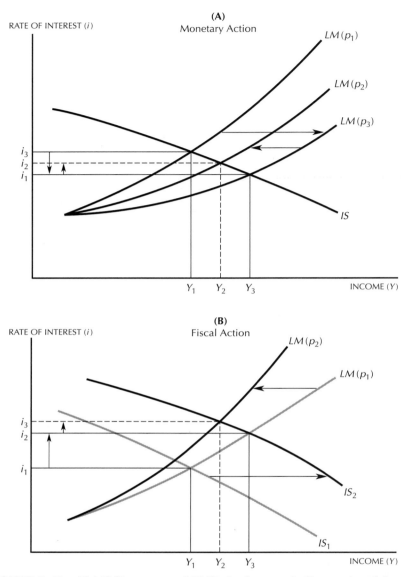

FIGURE 6–13   *IS-LM* Changes and Shifts in Aggregate Demand and Aggregate Supply.   When the *LM* curve is shifted to the right by an increase in the money supply, income (*Y*) will increase, but also because the aggregate supply curve is positively sloped (Figure 6–12), the price level will rise, even though more money tends to lower interest rates. If the economy is stimulated by a shift to the right in the *IS* curve, there will be a similar impact on the price level, but interest rates will also rise.

which interest rates are higher and investment spending is smaller than would be the case if prices had remained stable.

Public Policy and the *IS-LM* Model

Although we shall defer to Chapter 15 a full discussion of the theory and practice of modern macroeconomic policy, at this point we can draw on the analysis in this chapter to review the principles of monetary and fiscal policy, which were introduced initially in Chapter 4. The *IS-LM* model offers us a succinct and useful vehicle for doing this.

Monetary policy works primarily through controls exercised over the supply of money. In an advanced economy this basically means control over the volume of bank lending. In the United States the Federal Reserve System is the chief agency through which such control is exercised. The objective in controlling the money supply, including bank lending, is indirectly to control spending. More specifically, and within the income-expenditure framework, changes in the money supply will result in changes in interest rates, which, in turn, will have an impact on spending. The brunt of this impact will be borne by investment expenditure, as neither the consumption nor the government expenditures component of aggregate demand is linked strongly to the rate of interest. Thus, the question of the efficacy of monetary policy as an instrument of economic stabilization largely turns on the issue of the shape of the investment demand curve, about which economists are not in full agreement. This is a question taken up in Chapter 8. To some modern monetarists, though, this is not the relevant question, for, as we shall see in Chapter 11, they argue that monetary policy works through the impact of changes in the money supply on money balances and the further impact of this on spending for output. Furthermore, the real public policy issue in their view is, in the final analysis, one of persuading the monetary authorities to allow the money supply to grow at a constant rate and do nothing more.

Fiscal policy, on the other hand, involves deliberate changes in government expenditures and taxes as a means of controlling economic activity. The budget of the national government is the key instrument through which fiscal policy is effected. Government expenditures for goods and services directly affect the level of economic activity because such expenditures are a component part of the aggregate demand function; transfer expenditures and taxes, on the other hand, affect disposable income and thus indirectly influence the other two major components of aggregate demand, consumption and investment spending. Fiscal policy therefore works through changes in the government's budget which, in turn, increase or decrease the level of spending in the economy.

Figure 6–14 shows how the economy can move from an underemployment equilibrium by the application of either fiscal or monetary policy or a combination of the two. Let us assume that initially the economy is at an under-

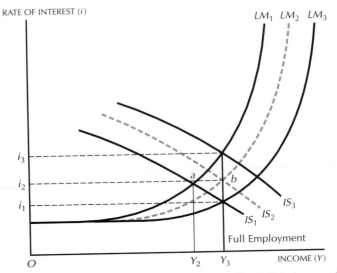

FIGURE 6–14   **Fiscal Policy, Monetary Policy, and Full Employment.**   Fiscal policy operates by shifting the *IS* curve to the right to raise income (*Y*). Monetary policy operates by shifting the *LM* curve to the right to raise income (*Y*).

employment equilibrium given by the intersection at point *a* of *IS* and *LM* curves designated as IS_1 and LM_1. Fiscal policy measures have the effect of shifting the *IS* curve to the right. If fiscal policy alone is used to get the economy to the full-employment income level of Y_3, the *IS* curve must shift to the position designated in the diagram as IS_3.

The extent to which the *IS* curve shifts as a result of a given change in either government expenditures *G* or net taxes *T* depends on the value of the multiplier. It is the multiplier in combination with the shift in the aggregate demand curve that determines, *ceteris paribus,* the amount by which equilibrium income changes (see Chapter 7). However, the shift in the *IS* curve is not the only factor to be taken into account. If there is no change in the money supply curve, then the interest rate will increase as a consequence of a higher level of real output. At IS_3 and LM_1 the equilibrium interest rate has risen to i_3. A rise in the interest rate, *ceteris paribus,* tends to reduce investment outlays and offsets to some extent the effect of more government expenditures for goods and services or of lower taxes on the economy's equilibrium position. Thus, policymakers must take interest rate changes as well as the value of the multiplier into account in trying to estimate the net effect of a fiscal change on output and employment.

If monetary rather than fiscal policy is chosen as the means to move the economy to the full-employment output Y_3, then the *LM* curve must shift to the position designated as LM_3 in Figure 6–14. This can be brought about by a rightward shift in the money supply curve. For any given shift to the right in the *LM* curve, the response of real output is governed by the interest elasticity of the *IS* curve. This depends primarily on how investment expenditures respond to a change in the rate of interest. If they are sensitive to such changes, then a shift to the right of the *LM* curve will, via the investment multiplier, have a highly favorable effect on real output. It should be noted, too, that the interest rate effects of monetary policy are the opposite of those associated with fiscal policy changes. Thus, in Figure 6–14, a full-employment equilibrium resulting from the intersection of IS_1 and LM_3 will lower the rate of interest to the equilibrium value of i_1.

The examples just cited show the effects in isolation of fiscal or monetary policy on real output. Reality is more complex; it may involve a combination of both monetary and fiscal action. It is possible, in principle at least, to move the economy to the full-employment output of Y_3 without any change in the rate of interest. This outcome is shown by the intersection of the dashed curves IS_2 and LM_2 at point *b*. A combination of fiscal and monetary action means that less-stringent measures of either type have to be taken than would be the case if either policy approach is applied separately and in isolation. For the sake of simplicity in the exposition we have assumed that the *IS* and *LM* curves are independent of one another. In reality this may not be true—a fact which complicates the application of either fiscal or monetary policy. We shall return to this point in Chapter 15.

Summary

1. The model of general equilibrium in terms of two curves, the *IS* curve and the *LM* curve, is the central theme of the chapter.

2. Equilibrium in the goods sphere (the *IS* curve) refers to a balance between the demand for and the supply of total output. It means that aggregate demand and aggregate supply are in balance. For every equilibrium value of output in the goods sphere, there is a specific value for output and for the rate of interest. The *IS* curve shows all possible equilibrium values for output (and employment) in terms of alternative values for both income and the rate of interest.

3. Equilibrium in the monetary sphere (the *LM* curve) refers to a balance between the demand for money and the supply of money. This equilibrium, like equilibrium in the goods sphere, can be defined in terms of unique values for both income and the rate of interest. The *LM* curve links all possible equilibrium values for the demand and supply of money to the level of income and the rate of interest.

4. General equilibrium in both the goods and monetary spheres is attained by bringing together the *IS* and *LM* curves in a single diagram. This diagram shows how general equilibrium in the system is possible only if we have equilibrium in both the goods and the monetary spheres. There is, in other words, only one unique value for both money and income that is compatible with equilibrium in the goods and the monetary spheres. Changes in equilibrium are explained by shifts in either the *IS* or the *LM* curve.

5. The basic *IS-LM* model can be expanded by bringing government expenditures (G) and the net export balance $(X - M)$ into the analysis. These variables have their impact on the level of aggregate demand; this means they move the *IS* curve to the right of where it would be in the absence of a public sector or international economic relationships. When government (G) and the export-import balance $(X - M)$ are factored into the analysis, we have an open economy model.

6. The *IS-LM* model was initially constructed in constant prices; hence, it deals on the *IS* side only with *real* magnitudes. It can be modified, however, to bring in price level changes and thus made more realistic. Price level changes operate in the model through the *LM* curve and have effects on the curve similar to changes in the money supply. As developed initially, the price level is treated as an exogenous variable.

7. An alternative way to handle the price level is to treat it as an endogenous variable. This is done by developing aggregate demand and aggregate supply curves that relate output to the price level, rather than to expenditures and receipts as in the usual income-expenditure approach. When this is done, a more realistic analysis of fiscal and monetary policies can be undertaken, an analysis that involves changes in the inflation rate as well as in output and employment levels.

8. One major use of the *IS-LM* model is to explain the workings of monetary and fiscal policies. Such policy changes can be represented by shifts in the *IS* and *LM* curves with resulting changes in the equilibrium values for income and the rate of interest. The *IS-LM* model is also useful in showing the conditions under which the effectiveness of monetary and fiscal policies is limited.

Exploring the Foundations of Aggregate Demand and Aggregate Supply

7 Consumption, Saving, and the Multiplier

IN PART II WE ESTABLISHED the fundamental principle that in the short run aggregate demand is the key to the level of income and employment. The reason is that aggregate demand determines the extent to which the economy's productive capacity will be utilized. The aggregate demand schedule is a summation of the decisions made to use the economy's output; that is, it reflects demand for the various categories of goods and services that enter into the national output. Structurally, aggregate demand is the sum of expenditures for consumption goods and services (C), investment or capital goods purchases (I), government spending for collective goods and services (G), and the balance on international transactions in goods and services ($X - M$). As we also learned in Part II, the behavior and level of the aggregate demand function is influenced strongly by money and the forces that affect the demand for money and the rate of interest. We brought this part of our analysis to a conclusion by constructing the *IS-LM* model, a useful theoretical exercise designed to bring together as succinctly as possible the key forces that explain macroeconomic behavior in a system of market capitalism.

Now in Part III we turn to a different task. We shall dig more deeply into our basic model and explore what lies behind each of the component parts that enter into our general analysis. We shall proceed, in other words, from the whole to the parts. In this chapter we shall, figuratively speaking, put consumption spending under our analytical microscope. It is appropriate to begin with consumption because, as we have already seen, consumption spending is the largest spending component that enters into the aggregate demand function. Then, in Chapters 8 through 12, we shall analyze all the other component parts of aggregate demand and aggregate supply.

The Determinants of Consumption Expenditure

Keynes's basic hypothesis with respect to the volume of consumption expenditure in the economy is that _income is the prime determinant of consumption expenditure_. That is the case for the individual and for the economy as a whole. Keynes stated that "aggregate income . . . is, as a rule, the principal variable upon which the consumption constituent of the aggregate demand function will depend."[1] To say that income is the prime determinant of consumption expenditure is not to say that there may not be other determinants. For the moment, however, we shall put aside any other possible determinants and concentrate on income.

Which particular measure of income is appropriate for our analysis? Should we regard consumption as a function of GDP, national income, personal income, or some other income measure? Since we are concerned primarily with consumer behavior, the income concept most appropriate to our analysis is one that most nearly approximates the idea of take-home pay. If there is validity to the hypothesis that income is a prime determinant of consumption expenditure, income in this context must mean the income that is wholly at the disposal of the consumer for consumption expenditure. Within the framework of national income aggregates, the particular measure that meets this requirement is _disposable income,_ which is defined as the income remaining to individuals after deduction of all personal taxes. It is the closest approximation to take-home pay at the national level. Accordingly, income and employment theory has generally formulated the consumption function in terms of the relationship between disposable income and consumption expenditure. Consumption is thus held to be a function of disposable income.

If we assume that all saving other than capital consumption allowances originates in the household sector, disposable income will be equal to the net national product minus taxes and plus transfer payments. In equation form we have

$$Y_d = Y_{np} - TX + TR. \tag{7-1}$$

In the discussion that follows in this and ensuing chapters, _net national product_ (Y_{np}) will be used as our basic income measure rather than gross domestic product, primarily because use of the latter in the algebraic formulations re-

---

[1] Keynes, _The General Theory,_ p. 96.

quires making the extreme assumption that saving even in the form of capital consumption allowances originates in the household sector. Use of net national product does not in any way change the basic analysis or principles.

The Keynesian Consumption Function

In *The General Theory* Keynes established two basic ideas concerning the relationship between consumption and income. These ideas, which we examined briefly in Chapter 4, form the underpinning of the modern theory of consumption and saving. First, Keynes asserted that consumption expenditure is related to income in a systematic and dependable way. Symbolically, we have the equation

$$C = f(Y_d). \tag{7-2}$$

Keynes defined the functional relationship between a *given* level of income and the consumption expenditure out of that income as *the propensity to consume*.[2] (It may be noted that the functional relationship posited by Keynes is one between real consumption and real income.)

The second key idea is known as Keynes's *fundamental psychological law*.

> The fundamental psychological law, upon which we are entitled to depend with great confidence both *a priori* from our knowledge of human nature and from the detailed facts of experience, is that men are disposed, as a rule and on the average, to increase their consumption as their income increases, but not by as much as the increase in their income.[3]

What Keynes meant is that when an individual's income increases, the individual will spend more for consumption because of the increase, but will not spend the whole of the increase. Some portion of the increase, in other words, will be saved. Keynes believed that this was especially true in the short run, for our consumption standards tend to become habitual and are not quickly adjusted either upward or downward. If income rises, spending, and our standard of consumption, may not immediately adjust upward to a new and higher level. The reverse, it may be noted, will be the case when income falls.

In modern income and employment theory these two Keynesian ideas with respect to income and consumption are brought together in the concept of the *consumption function,* which may be defined as *either a schedule or a curve showing the amounts that will be spent for consumer goods and services at different income levels.* The consumption function shown in Figure 7–1 is a curve. This figure is essentially the same as Figure 4–5 in Chapter 4, except

[2] Ibid., p. 90.

[3] Ibid., p. 96.

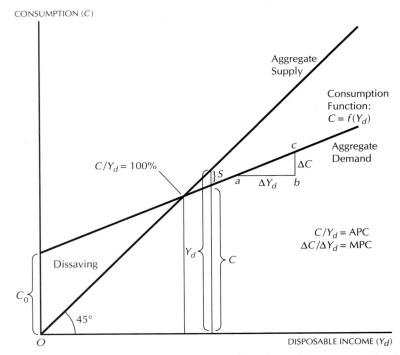

FIGURE 7–1　The Consumption Function.　The slope of the consumption function is less than 45°; this reflects Keynes's basic idea that when income increases, consumption also increases, but not as much as income.

it is more detailed. Aggregate real disposable income is measured on the horizontal axis and real consumption expenditure on the vertical axis. The curve $C = f(Y_d)$ represents the Keynesian consumption function; this curve shows the amount of consumption expenditure forthcoming at any and all income levels.

Depicting the consumption function as a curve follows logically from Keynes's definition of the propensity to consume as the functional relationship between income and consumption. This curve shows the range of values over which the dependent variable (consumption) moves as a result of changes in the independent variable (income). It is the usual practice in macroeconomics to use the Keynesian term *consumption function* to signify the entire range of values for income and consumption.

It should be noted that the curve depicting the consumption function is quite similar to the ordinary demand curve. The latter is the graphic representation of a schedule showing the amounts of a commodity or service that buyers are willing to purchase at any and all possible prices within a specified period of time. The ordinary demand schedule embodies the idea that quantity demanded is a function of price. Thus, it is correct to state the law of demand in the form of an equation, such as $q = f(p)$, in which q represents quantity demanded and p represents the price of a good or service. So it is with the consumption function, except that the two variables are disposable income (the independent variable) and consumption expenditures (the dependent variable).

The consumption-income curve, like all similar relationships in economic analysis, is an *ex ante* phenomenon. The curve shows intended values, that is, the levels to which consumers plan to adjust their consumption expenditures on the assumption that any particular income level is achieved and maintained for a reasonable period of time. The consumption function is presumed to define the normal relationship of consumption to income.

Technical Attributes of the Consumption Function

The consumption function has two key attributes, the average propensity to consume and the marginal propensity to consume. The *average propensity to consume* (APC) is the ratio of consumption to income, C/Y_d, at a specific level of income. It is the proportion of a given income that is spent for consumption purposes. This is the first significant attribute of the function. The average propensity to consume may vary as the income level varies. In Figure 7–1, for example, the average propensity to consume is 100 percent at the point at which the consumption function $C = f(Y_d)$ crosses the aggregate supply function OZ. At this point, consumption is exactly equal to income. To the left of this point, the average propensity to consume will be more than 100 percent because at every possible intended income level, consumption is greater than income. Thus, the ratio C/Y_d will be greater than 100 percent. To the right of the point of intersection, on the other hand, the average propensity to consume will be less than 100 percent, because at every income level above that at which consumption and income are equal, intended consumption is less than income.

The second important attribute of the consumption function is the *marginal propensity to consume* (MPC). This concept is the formal expression of Keynes's fundamental psychological law, which, the reader will recall, states that people are disposed to increase or decrease their consumption by less as their income increases or decreases. We may define the marginal propensity to consume as the ratio of a change in consumption (ΔC) to a change in income (ΔY_d). With an increase in income, the marginal propensity to consume gives, in percent, the amount by which consumption will increase. If income declines, the marginal propensity to consume measures, again in percent, the amount by which consumption expenditure will decline. If, for example, the marginal propensity to consume of the economy is 0.75 (that is, 75 percent), consumption expenditure will increase by $75 with every increase of $100 in the income level and fall by the same amount with every $100 decline in the income level.

In Figure 7–1 the marginal propensity to consume is measured by the slope of the consumption function, because, in mathematical terms, the slope of a line is determined by the ratio of the vertical distance to the horizontal distance (when movement takes place horizontally). Since consumption (C) is measured on the vertical axis and income (Y_d) on the horizontal axis, the marginal propensity to consume must necessarily be the same thing as the slope of the curve. In Figure 7–1 the marginal propensity to consume can be depicted by reference to the triangle abc. The vertical side of the triangle is the change in consumption expenditure ΔC, and the horizontal side is the change in income ΔY_d. The reader should note carefully that as long as the consumption function is assumed to be linear, that is, drawn as a straight line, the marginal propensity to consume will have a constant value. The basic reason for this is that all triangles formed by ΔY_d and ΔC will be similar (in a geometric sense) to the triangle abc, and consequently the ratio of their vertical sides to their horizontal sides will always be the same. The marginal propensity to consume and its constant value are to be contrasted to the changing value of the average propensity to consume.[4]

In an analytical view, Keynes's fundamental psychological law established limiting values for the slope of the consumption function. In *The General Theory* Keynes held that normally the marginal propensity to consume is positive, but its value is less than unity. This means that the slope of the consumption function will normally be less than 1. The marginal propensity to consume relates to consumption expenditure that is *induced* by a change in income. Such a change can be viewed geometrically as a movement along a known consumption function and should not be confused with the change that may come about as a result of a shift in the consumption function itself. Keynes assumed that normally the consumption function is stable, so that most changes in consumption are induced by income changes. This means that fluctuations in the income and employment level are not likely to have their origins in the consumption component of the aggregate demand schedule.[5] Whether or not this particular conclusion is warranted remains to be seen; for the moment, though, our chief concern is with the marginal propensity to consume as a phenomenon having to do with induced changes in consumption expenditure. The analytical significance of the idea of induced consumption expenditures is that we find in such phenomena the basis of the theory of the multiplier, an aspect of modern income and employment theory that we shall develop in full detail later in this chapter.

Our discussion of the consumption function would not be complete without

---

[4] The above remarks do not necessarily imply that the income-consumption relationship must be linear. The consumption function may have a shape such that both marginal and average propensities to consume decline as the income level rises. For reasons of simplicity in analysis, however, most economists operate on the assumption that the consumption function is linear.

[5] This comment needs to be qualified. Contemporary policymakers clearly understand that one way to influence consumption spending (and with it the overall level of economic activity) is by changing taxes. A tax reduction, for example, will increase disposable income [Equation (7–1)], which should lead to higher consumption spending. The Kennedy-Johnson administration did this in 1964, as did the Ford administration in 1975, the Carter administration in 1977, and the Reagan administration in 1981. The mechanics of tax changes and the income and employment effects are analyzed in Chapter 9.

the algebraic expression of this relationship. If we assume the function is linear, as we did in Figure 7–1, the consumption function can be stated as

$$C = C_0 + aY_d.^6 \qquad (7\text{–}3)$$

In the above expression, C is the level of consumption, C_0 is the amount of consumption when income is zero, and a is the marginal propensity to consume. Geometrically, C_0 is the point at which the consumption function cuts the vertical axis, and a is the slope of the consumption function. The value of C_0 at zero income is wholly hypothetical, as there is no known instance of zero income for an entire society for any significant period of time. Students of algebra will recognize this equation for the consumption function as the formula for a graph of a straight line of the type depicted in Figure 7–1. A consumption function that has the characteristics of Equation 7–3 is usually described as a *cyclical* function, because the pattern of actual data for the short term fits such a schedule (see Figure 7–3, period 1929–40).

The Saving Function

The counterpart to the consumption function is the *saving function,* which we may define as a *schedule or curve showing the amounts that income recipients intend to save at different levels of income.* Saving is the nonconsumption of current income; because we are not at the moment concerned with any disposition of income other than consumption or saving, it logically follows that saving, too, is a function of income. In algebraic terms,

$$S = f(Y_d). \qquad (7\text{–}4)$$

Since we are assuming for the moment that consumption and saving are the only alternative uses of income, the saving curve can be derived directly from the consumption function. At each income level intended saving will equal the difference between the aggregate supply value and the consumption value, and these are the amounts that should be plotted to derive a curve as shown in Figure 7–2.

Since the saving function is conceptually similar to the consumption function, it is characterized by similar technical attributes. Thus, the *average propensity to save* (APS) may be defined as the ratio of saving to income, S/Y_d, at a given level of income. It is the proportion of any given income that is saved. Like the propensity to consume, the ratio of saving to income may vary as the income level changes, and as with income and consumption, the

---

[6] The reader may note that this algebraic expression of the consumption function is different from the expression used where we first introduced the concept in Chapter 4 (page 115). There we stated that $C = a + bY$, where a was the amount of consumption when income was zero and b was the slope of the consumption function. It is more useful for our subsequent analysis, however, to designate the amount of consumption that is *independent* of the income level as C_0 rather than a. C_0 is, therefore, consumption that is autonomous with respect to income.

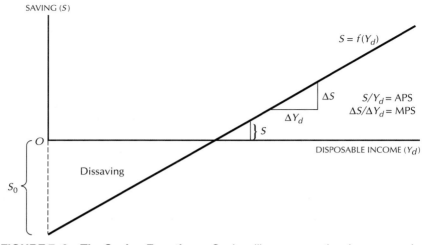

FIGURE 7–2   The Saving Function.   Saving, like consumption, increases when income increases and decreases when income decreases.

term *saving function* as used in macroeconomics refers to a range of values for income and savings. At the intersection of the saving function and the horizontal axis (point *s* in Figure 7–2), the volume of saving is zero; hence, the average propensity to save is zero. To the left of this point, the saving function drops below the horizontal axis; this means that saving is negative, or that dissaving is taking place. If this is the case, the saving-income ratio S/Y_d will be negative, which is as it should be, since the consumption-income ratio C/Y_d and S/Y_d must add up to unity. To the right of point *s*, the average propensity to save is not only greater than zero, but increases in value as the income level rises. The proportion of income saved increases as the income level increases.

The counterpart of the marginal propensity to consume is the *marginal propensity to save* (MPS). It is defined as the ratio of a change in saving ΔS to a change in income ΔY_d. Analogous to the representation of the consumption function, the marginal propensity to save is depicted graphically by the slope of the saving schedule. If this schedule is assumed to be linear, the marginal propensity to save will have a constant value. Numerically, the marginal propensity to save is equal to 1 minus the marginal propensity to consume. This is true only so long as we adhere to our assumption that all income must be either consumed or saved. A marginal propensity to consume of 0.75 would mean a value of 0.25 for the marginal propensity to save, because if $75 is spent for consumption purposes out of an additional $100 of income, the balance of $25 is by definition saving. The ratio $\Delta S/\Delta Y_d$ must equal 0.25.

As with the consumption function, our discussion of the income-saving relationship will not be complete without a statement of the algebraic form of this relationship. With a linear saving function as shown in Figure 7–2,

Are Americans Failing to Save Enough?

MIT economist Lester Thurow is the best known and most vociferous advocate of the view that Americans do not save enough. In his book, *The Zero-Sum Solution: Building a World-Class American Economy,* Professor Thurow argues that in order to compete with the Japanese, Americans ought to save at a rate at least three times greater than what they are now doing.

There are problems with Thurow's argument in particular and the savings argument in general. Thurow focuses on personal savings, that is, savings by persons and families, which, it is true, have declined somewhat in recent years. However, what is of greater importance in the U.S. economy is business saving. This is not in decline. As a share of the gross domestic product (GDP), business saving has actually grown in recent years.

The savings-investment-productivity argument implies that the rate of productivity growth is falling because of inadequate saving. What are the facts?

The table below shows averages for five-year intervals since 1950 for gross private savings, investment in new equipment, and productivity growth.

Period	Net Savings as a Percent of GDP*	Investment in New Equipment†	Rate of Growth of Productivity
1950–54	15.7%	5.8%	3.1%
1955–59	16.7	5.9	2.1
1960–64	16.4	5.7	3.0
1965–69	16.7	6.7	1.8
1970–74	17.1	6.6	1.2
1975–79	18.1	7.4	1.0
1980–84	17.8	7.4	1.0
1985–90	15.3	7.0	0.9
1990–94	12.6	6.7	1.5

*GNP used for 1950s data. GDP used after 1950s.

†Percent of GNP or GDP.

Source: Economic Report of the President, 1995, pp. 274, 308, 329.

What do these figures tell us? A major point is that until the last half of the 1980s and the 1990s, there was no major decline in the net savings (business plus personal savings minus the government deficit) rate. When the rate finally did decline, the decrease was caused by the combination of a drop in personal savings and large federal deficits, not by a drop in business savings.

A second point concerns investment spending for new equipment. This average dropped in the 1990s, primarily because of the 1990–91 recession, but there was no significant fall-off in this figure during the 1980s. Investment in equipment is the kind of investment that leads to productivity growth.

So we are left with a minor mystery. Productivity growth has definitely slowed since the early 1950s, as the figures in the third column show. But this cannot be attributed primarily to either inadequate saving or inadequate investment, at least from the perspective of the share of the GDP being saved and invested in equipment. We need look elsewhere for an explanation of the productivity decline, a matter we take up in Chapter 13.

the relationship may be stated as

$$S = -S_0 + sY_d, \qquad \text{or} \qquad S = sY_d - S_0. \tag{7-5}$$

In the above expression, S is saving, S_0 is the amount of saving when income is zero, and s is the marginal propensity to save. S_0 is negative because at zero income consumption is positive; this means saving must be negative (see Figure 7–2).

Empirical Verification

Up to this point in our analysis we have advanced two general propositions. The first of these is that consumption (and saving) is primarily a function of income, and the second is that the functional relationship between consumption (and saving) tends (in the short run) to assume the shape and character depicted by the schedules shown in Figures 7–1 and 7–2. But how well do these propositions accord with the facts of experience? In other words, do the statistical data pertaining to income and consumption expenditures tend to confirm the existence of the kind of behavior pattern embodied in the notion of the consumption function? Table 7–1 gives data on disposable income and personal consumption expenditures for the U.S. economy for the period 1929 to 1994. The table also shows the percentage of disposable income spent for consumption goods and services in each of these years. The data are computed in 1982 prices; thus, we are dealing with real income and real consumption expenditures. A careful inspection of the data reveals a rather general tendency of consumption expenditure to conform to the pattern suggested by the Keynesian hypothesis.

For example, from 1929 to 1933 disposable income declined, but the average propensity to consume rose. This is the type of behavior pattern for consumption expenditure suggested by the consumption function in Figure 7–1. From 1933 to 1941, a period in which disposable income was rising, the average propensity to consume underwent a decline. Between 1941 and 1945 the figures lose much of their value, since these were mostly war years, and consumption expenditures as a percentage of disposable income fell sharply because of wartime rationing, cutbacks in the production of consumer durables, pressures on the consumer to save and purchase war bonds, and general shortages of consumer goods and services. For the postwar period, beginning in 1946, disposable income has risen in relatively steady fashion. Consumption expenditure too has increased, but the average propensity to consume has shown, particularly in recent years, a greater tendency toward a constant value than during the prewar years. Note that in 1970 and 1971 the average propensity to consume fell slightly, a consequence (some economists believe) of the temporary surcharge on the personal income tax in effect at that time. Between 1972 and 1976 the propensity to consume also fell slightly, even during the 1974–75 recession. Some economists believe that continued inflation in these years led to a somewhat higher savings ratio. Somewhat the same seemed to happen in 1981–82, another recession period, but also one

TABLE 7–1 Disposable Income and Personal Consumption Expenditure: 1929–1994 (in billions of 1982 dollars)

(1) Year	(2) Disposable Income	(3) Personal Consumption Expenditure	(4) = (3) ÷ (2) Average Propensity to Consume (in percent)	
1929	$498.6	$471.4	0.945	
1930	459.2	439.7	0.958	⎫
1931	438.7	422.1	0.962	⎬ Depression
1932	380.2	384.9	1.012	
1933	370.8	378.7	1.021	⎭
1934	392.1	390.5	0.996	⎫
1935	427.8	412.1	0.963	⎬ Recovery
1936	479.1	451.6	0.943	
1937	494.7	467.9	0.946	⎭
1938	462.3	457.1	0.989	⎫ Depression
1939	499.5	480.5	0.962	⎭
1940	530.7	502.6	0.947	⎫
1941	604.1	531.1	0.879	
1942	693.0	527.6	0.761	⎬ War Years
1943	721.4	539.9	0.748	
1944	749.3	557.1	0.743	⎭
1945	739.5	592.7	0.801	
1946	723.3	655.0	0.906	
1947	694.8	666.6	0.959	Recession
1948	733.1	681.8	0.930	
1949	733.2	695.4	0.948	Recession
1950	791.8	733.2	0.926	
1951	819.0	748.7	0.914	
1952	844.3	771.4	0.914	
1953	880.0	802.5	0.912	
1954	894.0	822.7	0.920	Recession
1955	944.5	873.8	0.925	
1956	989.4	899.8	0.909	
1957	1,012.1	919.7	0.909	
1958	1,028.8	932.9	0.907	Recession
1959	1,067.2	979.4	0.918	
1960	1,091.1	1,005.1	0.921	
1961	1,123.2	1,025.2	0.913	Recession
1962	1,170.2	1,069.0	0.914	
1963	1,207.3	1,108.4	0.918	
1964	1,291.0	1,170.6	0.907	
1965	1,365.7	1,236.4	0.905	
1966	1,431.3	1,298.9	0.907	
1967	1,493.2	1,337.7	0.896	
1968	1,551.3	1,405.9	0.906	
1969	1,599.8	1,456.7	0.911	
1970	1,668.1	1,492.0	0.894	Recession
1971	1,728.4	1,538.8	0.890	
1972	1,797.4	1,621.9	0.902	
1973	1,916.3	1,689.6	0.882	

TABLE 7–1 (Continued)

(1)	(2)	(3)	(4) = (3) ÷ (2)
		Personal	*Average Propensity*
	Disposable	*Consumption*	*to Consume (in*
Year	*Income*	*Expenditure*	*percent)*
1974	1,896.6	1,674.0	0.883 } Recession
1975	1,931.7	1,711.9	0.886
1976	2,001.0	1,803.9	0.901
1977	2,066.6	1,883.8	0.912
1978	2,167.4	1,961.0	0.905
1979	2,212.6	2,004.4	0.906
1980	2,214.3	2,000.4	0.903
1981	2,248.6	2,042.2	0.900 } Recession
1982	2,261.5	2,050.7	0.907
1983	2,331.9	2,146.0	0.920
1984	2,469.8	2,249.3	0.911
1985	2,542.8	2,354.8	0.926
1986	2,635.3	2,446.4	0.928
1987	2,670.7	2,515.8	0.942
1988	2,800.5	2,606.5	0.931
1989	2,869.0	2,656.8	0.926
1990	2,893.3	2,682.2	0.927 } Recession
1991	3,011.0	2,780.4	0.923
1992	3,114.3	2,865.0	0.920
1993	3,175.4	2,962.6	0.933
1994	3,295.2	3,074.4	0.932

Source: Economic Report of the President, 1991, p. 317; 1994, pp. 278, 307.
Source: Economic Report of the President, 1995, pp. 278, 306.

of high inflation, at least in 1981. From 1982 through 1986 the inflation rate came down. The rate accelerated again after 1986, reached 5.4 percent in 1990, and then fell to 2.6 percent in 1994. Nevertheless, the postwar data appear to be roughly in line with the consumption function hypothesis.

A better view of the extent to which actual data conform to the Keynesian hypothesis can be obtained if we plot the data of Table 7–1 on a graph. This is done in Figure 7–3, wherein disposable income is measured on the horizontal axis and personal consumption expenditures on the vertical axis. When all the points representing consumption expenditure associated with disposable income for specific years are plotted, we have what statisticians term a *scatter diagram.* Such a diagram is highly useful for it helps us to determine whether or not values for two variables are related. If they are independent, then the value of one of the variables will be associated equally with large and small values for the other variable. In such a case the points will spread over the scatter diagram as if they were thrown there at random. On the other hand, if the value of one of the variables is uniquely determined by the value of the other variable, the points will fall on a line or curve that represents the *perfect* relationship between variables. Such a line, or curve, is said to describe a perfect relationship in the sense that this would be the way in which

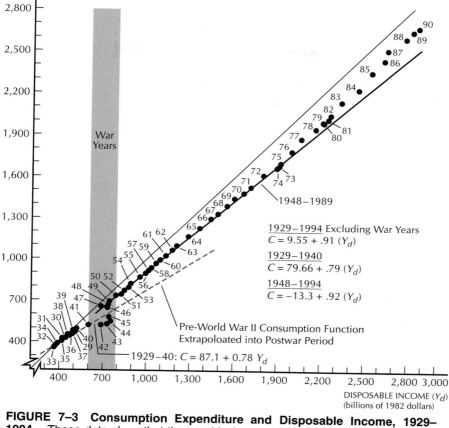

PERSONAL CONSUMPTION EXPENDITURES (*C*)
(billions of 1982 dollars)

War
Years

1948–1989

1929–1994 Excluding War Years
$C = 9.55 + .91 (Y_d)$

1929–1940
$C = 79.66 + .79 (Y_d)$

1948–1994
$C = -13.3 + .92 (Y_d)$

Pre-World War II Consumption Function
Extrapoloated into Postwar Period

1929–40: $C = 87.1 + 0.78 \, Y_d$

DISPOSABLE INCOME (*Y_d*)
(billions of 1982 dollars)

FIGURE 7–3 Consumption Expenditure and Disposable Income, 1929–1994. These data show that the empirical consumption function has shifted upward during the post-World War II era as compared with the prewar period.
Source: Economic Report of the President, 1991, p. 317; 1995, p. 307.

the two variables were related if the value of one of the variables were determined solely by the value of the other variable. This, of course, is rarely the case with any two variables in the real world.

The data plotted in Figure 7–3 fall into three distinct periods: 1929 to 1940 (the depression years), 1948 to 1994 (the post-World War II era), and 1929 to 1994 (the entire period). World War II was an abnormal period, because consumption expenditures as percentages of disposable incomes dropped well below prewar averages; the prime reason was the lack of consumer durables during the war. Thus, it is appropriate to look at the pre- and postwar periods separately. Keynes argued that the stability of the consumption function depended on the existence of normal conditions, by which he meant the absence of wars, revolutions, or any form of social upheaval that might seriously distort the income-consumption relationship.

If we fit curves to the pre- and post-World War II data of Figure 7–3, we obtain two distinct schedules, one appropriate to each of these periods. Inspection of these curves shows, first, that the fit is not perfect, as all the points do not lie on the curves, but, second, that there is a tendency for the data to be in accord with the consumption function hypothesis.[7] The general shapes and slopes of the curves are similar to those of the hypothetical consumption function of Figure 7–1. The fact that the fit of the curves is not perfect suggests that other factors besides income play a role in the determination of the level of consumption expenditure in the economy. There is nothing surprising in this, for neither Keynes nor any other modern economic theorist seriously maintains that income is the sole determinant of consumption expenditure. When we posit the notion of a functional relationship between income and consumption, we are saying in effect that, of the many factors that probably influence the level of consumption expenditure, income has the most strategic significance. Later on we shall analyze some of the other factors.

Before we conclude our discussion of the empirical validity of the consumption function hypothesis, let us consider an additional fact revealed by the data plotted in Figure 7–3. It is apparent that these two curves differ from each other in both level and slope. In order to compare the curves, we have extended the straight-line curve that best fits the data for 1929 to 1940 beyond the period to which the data apply (dashed lines in Figure 7–3). Note that the extension lies below the curve fitted to the data for 1948 to 1994. What is the significance of this? One possible answer is that the empirical data suggest that the consumption function tends to shift upward over time. The 1948-to-1994 curve, for example, lies above the extended 1929-to-1940 schedule. There are good reasons why this may happen, but we shall defer any further consideration of this point until later in this chapter when we discuss recent theoretical efforts to deal with the phenomenon of the shifting consumption function. If we calculate the consumption-disposable income relationship for the entire period, 1929 to 1994, excluding the war years (1941 to 1945), the resulting schedule shows that $C = 9.55 + 0.91Y_d$.

The Equilibrium Income Level

The consumption function is important as an analytical tool because it helps us determine the equilibrium income level. To see how this relationship comes about, let us examine a hypothetical economy in which there are only two

---

[7] In Figure 7–3 the schedules are fitted to the plotted data simply by drawing them in such a manner that they pass as closely as possible to all the dots. There are, of course, more exact and specialized statistical techniques for fitting a curve to data, but the approximation method employed here is adequate for our purposes. The lines that relate consumption to disposable income are called *regression lines*. Expressed as an equation, they take the form $C = C_0 + aY_d$ [Equation (7–3)]. The empirical consumption functions for the three periods calculated from the data in Table 7–3 are shown in the figure.

categories of output or expenditure, consumption and investment. Table 7–2 gives data pertaining to this hypothetical economy. Column 1 in this table lists possible income levels for the economy (from $0 to $6,000 billion), whereas column 2 represents the economy's consumption function, the intended consumption associated with these income levels.[8] The consumption function in this model is $C = \$1,200 + 0.75Y_{np}$. This consumption function is also shown graphically in part A of Figure 7–4. The 45° aggregate supply curve (OZ in the figure) shows that the analysis is in real terms because output in constant prices is measured on both the horizontal and the vertical axes.

We shall assume that investment expenditure is autonomous with respect to the income level, that is, that the amount of investment expenditure is independently given, not determined by any of the other variables that enter into our hypothetical economic system. We are not implying that economic analysis has nothing to say about the determinants of investment spending. Rather, for the sake of convenience and analytical simplicity, we assume its value as given in the same sense that the schedule for the consumption function is given. Furthermore, we assume that the amount of investment expenditure will not change as the income level changes. Column 4 of Table 7–2 is this autonomous investment schedule. The values shown are *ex ante*.

TABLE 7–2 The Process of Income Determination
(in billions of constant 1987 dollars)

(1) Income Y_{np}	(2) Planned Consumption C	(3) Planned Saving S	(4) Planned Investment I	(5) Aggregate Demand C + I	(6) Unplanned Inventory Change
$ 0	$1,200	$−1,200	$200	$1,400	$−1,400
4,500	4,575	−75	200	4,775	−275
4,600	4,650	−50	200	4,850	−250
4,700	4,725	−25	200	4,925	−225
4,800 ⟷ 4,800		—	200	5,000	−200
4,900	4,875	25	200	5,075	−175
5,000	4,950	50	200	5,150	−150
5,100	5,025	75	200	5,225	−125
5,200	5,100	100	200	5,300	−100
5,300	5,175	125	200	5,375	−75
5,400	5,250	150	200	5,450	−50
5,500	5,325	175	200	5,525	−25
5,600	5,400 ⟶ 200 ⟵ 200			5,600	—
5,700	5,475	225	200	5,675	25
5,800	5,550	250	200	5,750	50
5,900	5,625	275	200	5,825	75
6,000	5,700	300	200	5,900	100

[8] Since the hypothetical economy has only the two categories of output, consumption and investment, there are neither taxes nor transfer expenditures. Consequently, net national product and disposable income are identical: $Y_{np} = Y_d$. The consumption function is constructed such that the marginal propensity to consume has a value of 0.75.

PLANNED CONSUMPTION (C),
INVESTMENT (I) EXPENDITURES
(billions of constant 1987 dollars)

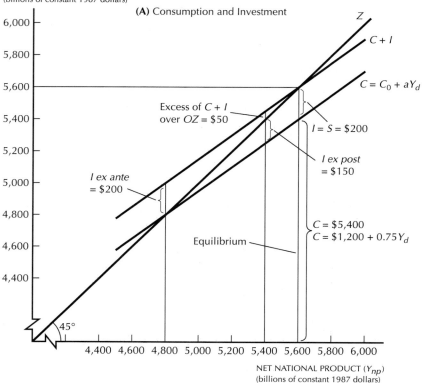

(A) Consumption and Investment

Z

C + I

C = C₀ + aY_d

Excess of C + I
over OZ = $50

I = S = $200

I ex post
= $150

I ex ante
= $200

Equilibrium

C = $5,400
C = $1,200 + 0.75Y_d

45°

NET NATIONAL PRODUCT (Y_np)
(billions of constant 1987 dollars)

PLANNED SAVINGS (S) AND INVESTMENT (I)
(billions of constant 1987 dollars)

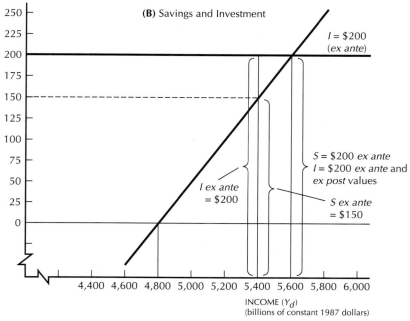

(B) Savings and Investment

I = $200
(ex ante)

I ex ante
= $200

S = $200 ex ante
I = $200 ex ante and
ex post values

S ex ante
= $150

INCOME (Y_d)
(billions of constant 1987 dollars)

Since the schedule of aggregate demand consists of the sum of *ex ante* consumption and *ex ante* investment expenditure, we can construct this schedule for our hypothetical economy by adding an amount equal to autonomous investment to the consumption function. In Table 7–2 the results of this procedure are shown in column 5. In part A of Figure 7–4 we derive aggregate demand diagrammatically by drawing $C + I$ parallel to the consumption function and at a distance equal to the assumed value for autonomous investment expenditure. Thus, aggregate demand is equal to the consumption function plus autonomous investment. We can express this idea algebraically as

$$DD = (C_0 + aY_d) + I. \qquad (7\text{–}6)$$

Given the fact that we have established an aggregate demand curve, $C + I$, for this hypothetical economy, the process by which an equilibrium income level is attained is as described in Chapter 4. The equilibrium income (and employment) level is to be found at the point of intersection of the aggregate demand and aggregate supply curves. On the basis of the data contained in Table 7–2, the income equilibrium is $5,600 billion. It is at this income level that the aggregate demand curve of Figure 7–4 intersects the aggregate supply schedule. If actual income is below the $5,600 billion level in any income period, a disequilibrium situation in which aggregate demand is in excess of aggregate supply will result. This will set in motion forces that tend to drive the income level higher. As long as aggregate demand is in excess of aggregate supply, income and employment will continue to rise toward the equilibrium position. Conversely, an income level above $5,600 billion cannot be sustained because aggregate supply then runs ahead of aggregate demand— a condition that will lead to unwanted inventory accumulation and eventual cutbacks in output. A downward adjustment of income and employment levels will continue until output is once again in balance with total demand. Equilibrium is a situation in which producing and spending intentions coincide, and, given the assumed schedules of consumption and investment for this hypothetical economy, the only income level at which such coincidence is possible is $5,600 billion.

Part B of Figure 7–4 shows as a counterpart to the consumption function the aggregate savings curve and the investment demand curve. As in part A of the figure, the values shown in both schedules are *ex ante*. Investment *(ex ante)* is assumed to be autonomous at the level of $200 billion, whereas *ex ante* saving rises as the level of output (net national product) rises. Part B of Figure 7–4 is important for understanding the issue of the *identity* between saving and investment, a topic to which we now turn.

FIGURE 7–4   (left) The Process of Income Determination; Saving and Investment. This figure shows graphically what Table 7–2 shows numerically, namely, how the equilibrium income level is determined, given the consumption function and a fixed level of investment. The figure also shows how equilibrium between saving and investment is reached.

The Identity of Saving and Investment

In the discussion of equilibrium in the goods sphere in Chapter 6, we pointed out that equilibrium could be defined in terms of equality between saving and investment in an *ex ante* sense. It is appropriate here to explore in greater depth this question of the identity between saving and investment, a subject that is often a source of confusion for the student of macroeconomics.

It will be recalled that in the discussion of the relationship between income and wealth in Chapter 2, the statement was made that saving and investment are necessarily identical when conceived of in an *ex post* sense. This *ex post* equality (or accounting identity of saving and investment as it is sometimes called) logically follows from the way in which we defined saving and investment. The basic identity equations for a single economy in which consumption and investment are the only categories of output permit us to demonstrate that saving and investment must be equal. This equality holds true all the time.

There is, however, a condition in which saving and investment are not necessarily always equal. This is when saving and investment are conceived of in an *ex ante* sense, which means planned saving and investment. The claim that in one sense saving and investment are always equal and that in another sense they are not necessarily equal may at first glance seem to be logically impossible. For a number of years after the publication of Keynes's *The General Theory,* lively controversy raged among professional economists over the exact meaning of these concepts and the sense in which they were equal or not equal. Actually, however, it is not difficult to reconcile the seemingly contradictory claims.

Let us assume that the economy in Table 7–2 and Figure 7–4 has not yet attained an equilibrium income level. Income in the current period, let us say, is at the level of $5,400 billion. We know that this particular level cannot be maintained, but for the moment that is not of primary concern to us. We want to understand what is taking place during the current income period, irrespective of how income may change in subsequent periods. Consumption will be $5,250 billion. This is planned consumption expenditure, since the consumption function is an *ex ante* phenomenon. If planned consumption is $5,250 billion, then it follows logically that *ex ante* saving must equal $150 billion, because the saving function is the counterpart of the consumption function and is derived (in this hypothetical economy) by subtracting the consumption function from the aggregate supply curve. But since the actual income level must always lie on the aggregate supply curve, this is tantamount to saying that the *ex ante* saving is equal to the distance between actual income and *ex ante* consumption. In part B of Figure 7–4 the amount of *ex ante* saving is shown as the distance between the horizontal axis and the saving curve at the income level $5,400 billion. This distance corresponds to the distance between the aggregate supply curve *(OZ)* and the consumption function $(C_0 + aY_d)$ at the income level \$4,000 billion, shown in part A of the figure.

But what of investment? Column 4 of Table 7–2 has already been described as the autonomous investment schedule. This is depicted in part B of Figure 7–4 as the horizontal line of the \$200 billion level. This means that the unchanging level of *ex ante,* or planned, investment expenditure, is \$200 billion. But if investment *ex ante* is equal to \$200 billion, while saving *ex ante* is equal to \$150 billion, we have a situation in which these two entities are not equal. The failure of *ex ante* saving and investment to be in balance is a prime indicator of the existence of a disequilibrium condition with respect to the income and employment level; income equilibrium must be defined in terms of equality between *ex ante* saving and *ex ante* investment.

There is nothing mysterious about the notion that saving and investment *ex ante* are not always equal, because there is no inherent reason that the intentions or plans of savers in the economy should always coincide with the intentions or plans of those undertaking investment expenditure. They may coincide, of course, although it is more likely that they will not.

Returning now to the idea that saving and investment *ex post* must always be equal, let us see how this concept of the identity between saving and investment can be explained through reference to the data of Table 7–2. By definition, saving is the nonconsumption of current income, so in this hypothetical economy saving *ex post* (or actual) must also be equal to \$150 billion at the income level of \$5,400 billion. Investment has been defined as the net addition to the economy's stock of wealth that results when the whole of current income (i.e., output) is not consumed. Thus, *actual* investment in an income period is the difference between income and consumption. In the income period that we have under consideration, actual, or *ex post,* investment equals current income (\$5,400 billion) minus current consumption (\$5,250 billion), or \$150 billion. This is the same as *ex post* saving during the income period.

At this point the reader may wonder how to reconcile *ex post* investment of \$150 billion with *ex ante* investment of \$200 billion. Since our analysis is constructed to rule out any change in the general level of prices, if planned investment runs ahead of actual investment, the difference between planned *(ex ante)* and actual *(ex post)* investment represents the portion of total demand that is satisfied through sales from *existing* stocks of goods. In Figure 7–4 it can be seen that at the \$5,400 billion level of income this difference of \$50 billion between investment *ex ante* and investment *ex post* is the identical amount by which the aggregate demand schedule exceeds the aggregate supply schedule. This \$50 billion represents the amount of inventory *disinvestment* that has taken place in the income period because aggregate demand is in excess of aggregate supply. This inventory disinvestment is unplanned and comes about primarily because producers (in the aggregate) have underestimated the level of aggregate demand. It is *unplanned* investment or investment in stocks that is the balancing item between planned and actual investment.[9] Column 6 in Table 7–2 shows this magnitude for all income levels.

From the foregoing discussion we emerge with the important conclusion that equilibrium requires that saving and investment *ex ante* be equal. Equilibrium also means that *ex ante* and *ex post* values coincide. Disequilibrium exists if saving and investment are not equal in an *ex ante* sense, and, whenever this is the case, forces are set in motion that make for a change either upward or downward in the income and employment level. This also brings us to another extremely important point, one which in a fundamental way distinguishes the Keynesian analysis from the classical model. What brings about the equality between saving and investment in *both* the *ex ante* and *ex post* senses are changes in income (and employment). As the system moves toward an equilibrium ($5,400 billion in Figure 7–4), the income changes cause planned *(ex ante)* saving to rise until finally at the $5,400 billion output level, saving and investment are in balance. In contrast, in the classical theory, it is changes in the rate of interest which equilibrate *ex ante* saving and investment (see Chapter 3, pages 84 and following).

The Theory of the Multiplier

In Chapter 4 we pointed out that changes in the income and employment level can be of two distinct types. In the one instance, we have the kind of change just discussed which involves adjustment toward a specified equilibrium level, given known positions for the schedules that enter into the structure of aggregate demand. There is also the kind of change that takes place when an existing equilibrium situation is disturbed as a result of a shift in the position of the aggregate demand schedule. A change of this type can be brought about by a shift in any of the schedules that constitute the aggregate demand schedule. This includes the consumption function, although most economists believe it to be highly stable under normal conditions. The implications of shifts in the aggregate demand schedule lead us to the consideration of one of the most significant facets of modern income and employment theory, the *multiplier* process.

Let us assume, using data for the consumption function from Table 7–2 and Figure 7–4, that the autonomous investment schedule shifts upward by $50 billion. This means simply that at all the relevant income levels, business executives are prepared to spend for investment goods at an annual rate of $250 billion rather than $200 billion. Table 7–3 contains data for this new

---

[9] It is possible that there can be unplanned saving as well as unplanned investment. Unplanned saving can come about if consumption expenditure lags behind changes in income. In our analysis, however, we are assuming that consumption expenditure adjusts immediately to any change in income. This is not necessarily the case in reality.

TABLE 7-3   Increased Investment and the Income Equilibrium
(in billions of constant 1987 dollars)

(1)	(2)	(3)	(4)	(5)	(6)
	Planned	Planned	Planned	Aggregate	Unplanned
Income	Consumption	Saving	Investment	Demand	Inventory
Y_{np}	C	S	I	C + I	Change
$ 0	$1,200	$-1,200	$250	$1,450	$-1,400
4,500	4,575	-75	250	4,825	-325
4,600	4,650	-50	250	4,900	-300
4,700	4,725	-25	250	4,975	-275
4,800	4,800	—	250	5,050	-250
4,900	4,875	25	250	5,125	-225
5,000	4,950	50	250	5,200	-200
5,100	5,025	75	250	5,275	-175
5,200	5,100	100	250	5,350	-150
5,300	5,175	125	250	5,425	-125
5,400	5,250	150	250	5,500	-100
5,500	5,325	175	250	5,575	-75
5,600	5,400 ⟶ 200		250	5,650	-50
5,700	5,475	225	250	5,725	-25
5,800	5,550 ⟶ 250 ⟵ ⟶ 250			5,800	—
5,900	5,625	275	250	5,875	+25
6,000	5,700	300	250	5,950	+50

situation. Inspection of this table reveals that the effect of this increase in autonomous investment expenditure has been to shift the aggregate demand schedule upward by a like amount, namely $50 billion. These new data for our hypothetical economy are plotted in Figure 7–5.

What has been the consequence for the income equilibrium of this upward shift in the schedule of autonomous investment expenditure and the upward shift in the aggregate demand schedule? If we look at the numerical data of Table 7–3 and the graphic presentation of these data in Figure 7–5, we are struck by the fact that the equilibrium income level has risen not by $50 billion, but by $200 billion. Here is a clear illustration of the multiplier process: An autonomous change in one of the variables that enters into the structure of aggregate demand has brought about a change in the income level several times greater than the amount of the initiating change. Technically, the multiplier can be defined as the *coefficient* that relates an increment of expenditure to an increment of income.[10] Keynes discussed the multiplier process entirely in terms of an *investment multiplier,* which he designated by the symbol k. The investment multiplier "tells us that, when there is an in-

---

[10] Basically the multiplier process is concerned with real changes. We are assuming that any change in expenditure for either consumption or investment goods leads to a corresponding increase in the output of these goods. This does not mean that a multiplier effect in purely monetary terms cannot take place in the economy. If, for example, there would be an increase in expenditure when the economy is at a level of full employment, the multiplier would still come into play, but the ensuing income changes would be wholly the result of changes in the general level of prices.

CONSUMPTION (C) AND INVESTMENT (I)
(billions of constant 1987 dollars)

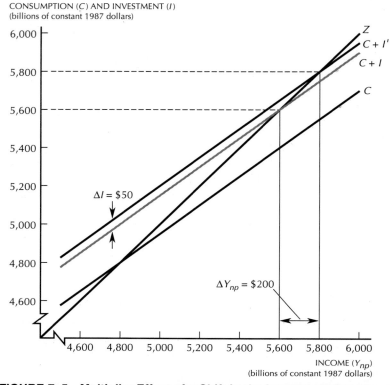

FIGURE 7–5 Multiplier Effect of a Shift in the Investment Function. When autonomous investment increases, the aggregate demand curve shifts upward and leads to an increase in output (and more employment) which is several times greater than the original increase in investment spending.

crement of aggregate investment, income will increase by an amount which is k times the increment of investment."[11] In algebraic form this idea is expressed as

$$\Delta Y_{np} = k\Delta I. \qquad (7\text{--}7)$$

From this equation we can define the investment multiplier as a ratio of a change in income ΔY_{np} to a change in investment ΔI. Thus,

$$k = \frac{\Delta Y_{np}}{\Delta I}. \qquad (7\text{--}8)$$

[11] Keynes, *The General Theory*, p. 115. The net national product Y_{np} equals disposable income Y_d, for in the simple system under discussion, which has neither taxes nor transfers, the two measures of income are identical.

Although Keynes analyzed the multiplier process almost entirely in terms of the relationship between changes in investment and changes in income, the reader should not be misled into thinking that the multiplier effect is limited to changes in investment expenditure. Actually it is a coefficient that links *any* autonomous shift in aggregate demand to the consequent change in income. This point is emphasized because it is usually most convenient to introduce and discuss the theory of the multiplier through analysis of changes in the investment component of the aggregate demand structure.

What lies behind the fundamental idea of the multiplier that any change in the expenditure rate for any of the component parts of the aggregate demand schedule will have magnified effects on the overall income level? To answer this, let us go back and trace what happens in the economy when, as is assumed in Table 7–3, there is an increase in the rate of investment expenditure equal to $50 billion. For the moment we need not be concerned with the means by which this extra $50 billion of investment expenditure is financed; all that interests us is that business executives have increased their spending for investment goods by $50 billion.

When this happens, the first discernible result is that the producers or suppliers of investment or capital goods will find that their incomes have risen by $50 billion, because increased spending for investment goods will lead to an increase in their production and, as more output is generated, incomes will rise. Thus, the primary effect of the increased spending for investment goods will be to create an equal amount of new income (in the form of wages, rents, interest, and profits), which will accrue to resource owners in the capital-goods-producing sector of the economy. What will happen after this? For the answer to this question we return to Keynes's assertion that whenever income increases, there will be a strong tendency for the beneficiaries of such increases to step up their expenditures for consumption goods and services. In the case of our hypothetical economy, the beneficiaries of the initial increase in spending are those engaged in the production of investment goods. Since the members of this group have experienced a rise in their incomes, it is to be expected that they will spend some part of this additional income for consumption goods and services. There will be, in other words, *induced* changes in consumption expenditure. These induced changes can be described as a *secondary* effect flowing from the increased spending for investment goods.

We have been able to isolate and describe two major effects associated with an increase in expenditure of the kind that leads to an increase in output and increased incomes for the producers of the output. These effects are a *primary,* or initial, effect, which is associated with the initial change in income, and a *secondary,* or induced, effect, which arises out of the fact that the original recipients of the increased income will in turn spend some portion of this increase for consumer goods and services. It is in this secondary effect that we have the key to the multiplier process, because, in the absence of any induced or secondary changes in spending, the impact of increased investment expenditure (or any other form of spending) on the income level could be no greater than the amount of the initial change in income. The multiplier effect results from the sum of the initial and induced changes in expenditure (and output) that ensue from a change in the rate of expenditure for any of the component parts of the aggregate demand structure.

What, however, determines the amount of induced spending? The answer is simple: the *marginal propensity to consume*. Once we know what proportion of an increment of income will be spent for consumption goods and services, we are in a position to determine how great will be the secondary or induced effects resulting from autonomous increases in expenditure. The marginal propensity to consume provides the analytical key to the increases in secondary spending and, consequently, to the numerical value of the multiplier.

The Formal Multiplier Process

To understand the multiplier process clearly, the first step is to trace in detail the effects of the increase in investment expenditure of $50 billion. The hypothetical consumption function presented in Tables 7–2 and 7–3 is constructed in such a way that it has a slope of 0.75; this means that the marginal propensity to consume a is 75 percent: out of every $100 increment of income, $75 will be spent for consumption. On the basis of this and given our assumed increase in investment outlays of $50 billion, we have constructed Table 7–4 to show how this initial increment in investment expenditure will generate a whole chain of respending. The first column, which contains only the figure

TABLE 7–4   The Multiplier: With a Single Initiating Increase in Investment Expenditure (in billions of constant 1987 dollars)*

(1) Initiating Increase in Expenditure ΔI	(2) Income Recipients	(3) Income Changes ΔY_{np}		(4) Induced Consumption ΔC	(5) Algebraic Derivation of ΔC
$50	1st Group	$ 50	↙	$ 38	$\Delta I a$
	2nd Group	38	↙	29	$\Delta Y_{np} a$
	3rd Group	29	↙	22	$\Delta Y_{np} a^2$
	4th Group	22	↙	17	$\Delta Y_{np} a^3$
	5th Group	17	↙	13	$\Delta Y_{np} a^4$
	6th Group	13	↙	10	$\Delta Y_{np} a^5$
	7th Group	10	↙	8	$\Delta Y_{np} a^6$
	8th Group	8	↙	6	$\Delta Y_{np} a^7$
	9th Group	6	↙	5	$\Delta Y_{np} a^8$
	*n*th Group	5	⟶	4	$\Delta Y_{np} a^n$
$50		$\Sigma = \$200$†		$\Sigma = \$150$†	

*All data rounded to the nearest whole number.

†After an infinite number of spendings and respendings.

of $50 billion, represents the *initiating* increase in expenditure. The second column represents groups of income recipients, designated by numbers, and the third column records the increments of income that accrue to each of these groups as a result of successive rounds of spending. The fourth column shows the *induced* consumption spending that results from the income increases experienced by each successive group. The fifth column shows the algebraic derivation of the change in consumption for each group, based on the initiating increase in investment expenditure of $50 billion. It is the change in income for each group times the marginal propensity to consume (a). Breaking the process of income change down into separate groups of income recipients is an artificial simplification, but it does enable us to analyze clearly how an initial increase in spending has multiple effects.

The initial increase in investment expenditure accrues as income to the first group, which then increases its consumption expenditures by $38 billion (75 percent of $50 billion). The spending will accrue as income to the suppliers of these consumption goods and services, namely, the second group, which also increases its consumption expenditures by 75 percent of the rise in its income, and so provides additional income for yet a third group. And so forth. We can thus see that the initial increase in expenditure will generate a series of spending and respending, which, if carried far enough, will raise income by some multiple of the original increment. The data in Table 7–4 show that ultimately the sum of induced consumption expenditure will total $150 billion, which, with the original increase in investment expenditure of $50 billion, will add up to a total increase in income of $200 billion, or four times the initiating increase. The value of the multiplier in this case is 4. Students familiar with mathematics will recognize that the total change in income (ΔY_{np}) involves a geometric progression of infinite sequence in which the initial change in investment (ΔI) is the first term and the marginal propensity to consume (a) is the common ratio or fixed number by which each preceding number in the sequence is multiplied.

Two further aspects of Table 7–4 should be noted. First, the multiplier has a time dimension, since it would be quite impossible in reality for the whole series of spendings and respendings to occur simultaneously. This point is stressed because in theoretical analysis we often ignore, for reasons of simplicity, the time element in the multiplier process. Second, the data of Table 7–4 show only what happens with a single, nonrecurring increment of investment expenditure. If we extended our example over a greater time span, income, which at first rose, would gradually fall back to its original level. The total increase in income spread over the whole time period in which the multiplier process was at work would, of course, equal the $200 billion shown in Table 7–4, but this would not be a permanent change. In order for the equilibrium income level to rise permanently to a new and higher level—which is the situation depicted in Table 7–3 and Figure 7–5—the increase in expenditure that initially triggers the expansion must be a *sustained* increase. Investment expenditure would have to expand from $200 billion to $250 billion and remain at that level if an enduring increase in the income level from $5,600 billion to $5,800 billion were to be brought about.

The nature of the multiplier process, given the assumption of a sustained increase of $50 billion in investment expenditure, is shown in Table 7–5. The data shown for period 0 pertain to the equilibrium existing prior to the increase in investment expenditure by $50 billion. In period 1 investment expenditure increases by $50 billion—a development that amounts to a shift upward in aggregate demand from $5,600 billion to $5,650 billion. In this table we are operating on the assumption that output cannot respond instantaneously to an increase in expenditure; consequently, output does not rise to the level of aggregate demand of period 1 until period 2. In period 2 the actual increase in output of $50 billion—column 4 in the table—induces additional consumption expenditure in the amount of $38 billion as shown in column 6. This is because the assumed value for the marginal propensity to consume is 0.75. Aggregate demand in period 2, therefore, is equal to the total of planned consumption expenditure ($5,438 billion) and planned investment expenditure ($250 billion). Output in this period has risen in response to the level of aggregate demand of the previous period, but aggregate demand has risen even higher because of the phenomenon of induced consumption expenditure. Gradually, the increments of induced consumption become smaller and smaller as the new equilibrium level of $5,800 billion is approached. In theory, this level will be reached only at the expiration of an infinite number of income periods, but, as a practical matter, the increments of both income and consumption expenditure will become insignificantly small after a finite number of periods. Once the new equilibrium income level has been attained, consumption expenditure will total $5,550 billion and investment expenditure will be $250 billion. There has been a multiplier effect of 4, because the initial increase of $50 billion in investment expenditure has brought about a total increase in income of $200 billion. In examination of this adjustment process, special note should be taken of the figures in columns 8, actual investment, and 9, planned saving. They reflect the facts, first, that investment output cannot respond instantaneously to changed overall investment spending and, second, that planned saving rises gradually *as income increases* to the new equilibrium value of $5,800 billion. This illustrates the point made earlier (page 230) that in the Keynesian system changes in the *ex ante* value of saving are brought about by changes in income, *not* the rate of interest as in the classical analysis.

Algebraic Statement of the Multiplier

Now that we have examined by means of a numerical example the multiplier process, let us formalize the concept by stating it in terms of some relatively simple algebraic formulas. From our investigation of the multiplier process we have discovered that the magnitude of the multiplier effect depends on the sum of *initial* and *secondary* effects. We saw that the key to the magnitude

TABLE 7-5 The Multiplier: With a Sustained Increase in Investment Expenditure (in billions of constant 1987 dollars)*

(1) Period	(2) Aggregate Demand C + I	(3) Aggregate Supply Y_{np}	(4) Actual Increase in Output ΔY_{np}	(5) Planned Consumption C	(6) Induced Consumption ΔC	(7) Planned Investment I	(8)† Actual Investment I'	(9) Planned Saving S
0	$5,600	$5,600	—	$5,400	—	$200	$200	$200
1	5,650	5,600	—	5,400	—	250	200	200
2	5,688	5,650	$50	5,438	$38	250	212	221
3	5,717	5,688	38	5,467	29	250	221	221
4	5,739	5,717	29	5,488	22	250	229	229
5	5,755	5,739	22	5,505	17	250	234	234
6	5,768	5,796	17	5,518	13	250	278	278
7	6,059	5,809	13	5,528	10	250	281	281
8	6,069	5,819	10	5,536	8	250	283	283
9	5,792	5,827	8	5,542	6	250	285	285
10	5,797	5,833	6	5,547	5	250	286	286
∞	5,800	5,800	—	5,550	—	250	250	250

*For simplicity, all numbers have been rounded to the nearest whole number.

†Actual (ex post) investment is the difference between aggregate supply (column 3) and planned consumption (column 5).

of the secondary effect is the marginal propensity to consume. Let us begin our algebraic analysis with the basic identity equation.

$$Y_{np} = I + C = Y_d. \tag{7-9}$$

The above equality is true because we are assuming the absence of taxes and transfer payments (see footnote 8). In the following algebraic discussion, the multiplier is defined in relation to net national product, which is the same as disposable income, given the foregoing assumption. From the above identity it follows that

$$\Delta Y_{np} = \Delta I + \Delta C. \tag{7-10}$$

In the preceding analysis it was concluded that induced consumption expenditures depend on the value of the marginal propensity to consume. In Equation (7–3) the marginal propensity to consume out of disposable income ($\Delta C/\Delta Y_d$) was designated as a. Since Y_d and Y_{np} are assumed to be equal, we can substitute $a\Delta Y_{np}$ for ΔC in Equation (7–10). We now have

$$\Delta Y_{np} - a\Delta Y_{np} = \Delta I. \tag{7-11}$$

Let us manipulate this equation algebraically as follows:

$$\Delta Y_{np} - a\Delta Y_{np} = \Delta I, \tag{7-12}$$

$$\Delta Y_{np}(1 - a) = \Delta I, \tag{7-13}$$

$$\Delta Y_{np} = \Delta I \times \frac{1}{1 - a}, \tag{7-14}$$

$$\frac{\Delta Y_{np}}{\Delta I} = \frac{1}{1 - a}. \tag{7-15}$$

The left-hand side of Equation (7–15) is what was defined in Equation (7–8) as the multiplier, the ratio of a change in income to a change in investment. From this we may conclude that in a formal, mathematical sense the multiplier is equal to the *reciprocal of 1 minus the marginal propensity to consume*.[12] In our simple and hypothetical economy the multiplier would also be equal to the reciprocal of the marginal propensity to save, for as long as saving and consumption are viewed as the only alternatives for the disposition of income, it is a simple matter of arithmetical truth that 1 minus the marginal propensity to consume, $1 - \Delta C/\Delta Y_d$, equals the marginal propensity to save, $\Delta S/\Delta Y_d$. But one must be careful here not to generalize that the value of the multiplier is always equal to the reciprocal of the marginal propensity to save. It is equal to this only in the absence of taxes and foreign trade.

---

[12] The theoretical limits to the value of the multiplier are 1 and infinity (∞). If the value of the marginal propensity to consume is 0, then the multiplier will have a value of 1; if, on the other hand, the value of the marginal propensity to consume is 1.00 (100 percent), the multiplier will have a value of ∞. The reader should work out the simple arithmetic to be convinced that this is true.

Now that we have defined the multiplier algebraically, we shall review the process and apply the formula to the data of our hypothetical economy. Originally, the income equilibrium level was $5,600 billion, given the consumption function and a level of investment expenditure of $200 billion (Table 7–2). The marginal propensity to consume is 0.75, which yields a numerical value for the multiplier of 4. All that is necessary is to apply this coefficient to the change in investment expenditure, $50 billion. A change of investment expenditure of this amount will cause income to rise by $200 billion ($k \times \Delta I = 4 \times \$50$ billion $= \$200$ billion). As a result of this $200 billion increase in income, consumption expenditure will rise by $150 billion.

Summary Remarks on the Theory of the Multiplier

Before we discuss other important aspects of consumption theory, it is important to summarize the salient features of the multiplier concept.

First, the multiplier is a device for explaining why a change in spending may have cumulative effects on the income level. The multiplier is associated with any autonomous change in expenditure in the economic system; it is not limited, as in our example, to changes in investment expenditure.

Second, the multiplier is properly regarded as an aspect of consumption theory, since its value depends on induced consumption spending.[13] The amount of induced, or secondary, consumption spending that will ensue depends on the marginal propensity to consume, the slope of the consumption function.

Third, the magnitude of the multiplier effect is inversely related to the total of *leakages* from the current income stream. Income that is not spent for currently produced consumption goods and services may be regarded as having *leaked out* of the income stream. Most economists regard the marginal propensity to consume as normally having a value of less than 1, because it is felt that some leakages are bound to be present. In this chapter, saving represented the only form of leakage from the income stream. Actually, there are other forms of leakages. Tax collections and expenditures for imported goods and services are leakages. A leakage is any factor that reduces the tendency toward the spending or respending of income on currently produced domestic goods and services; the greater such leakages, the smaller will be the multiplier effect. It is for this reason that we cannot claim that the multiplier is always equal to the reciprocal of the marginal propensity to save. If we could determine and measure all leakages as marginal propensities, then we could state comprehensively that the multiplier has a value equal to the reciprocal of the sum of all leakages expressed as marginal propensities.

---

[13] It should be noted that consumption expenditure is not the only type of expenditure that may be induced through a change in income. It is possible for investment expenditure to be induced. When there is a rise in induced investment, the result is what is called a *supermultiplier*, because of the combined effect of both induced consumption and induced investment. This is a matter that we shall discuss in the following chapter.

Putting Theory into Practice: The 1964 Kennedy-Johnson Tax Cut

When John F. Kennedy became President, one of the challenges facing the new administration was to get "the economy moving again." In the hard-fought 1960 campaign, Kennedy hit again and again on the sluggishness of the economy during the waning years of the Eisenhower presidency. Once in office, he and his administration worked to deliver on their campaign promise that they could dramatically improve the economy's performance.

The strategy devised—a strategy which was the brainchild of Walter Heller, Kennedy's chief economic adviser and professor on leave from the University of Minnesota—was drawn almost directly from the pages of Keynes's *The General Theory.* The Keynesian multiplier was the key factor in this strategy, although private investment spending was not to be the primary instrument through which the multiplier would work its magic on output and employment.

Put concisely, what the administration proposed was a tax cut—a relatively large tax cut for that time and one which flew in the face of the conventional economic wisdom. The economy, though sluggish, was not in a recession, and there was a sizable deficit in the federal budget. The conventional view was that tax cutting and increasing the federal deficit should be done only during a recession. Heller disagreed. Further, he was successful in persuading President Kennedy to ask the Congress for an overall tax cut of $13.5 billion; $11 billion would go to individuals and the rest to business.

The logic of the Heller-Kennedy proposal is spelled out in almost textbook fashion in the 1963 *Economic Report of the President.* The proposed reduction in the personal income tax, the report said, ". . . will directly add to the disposable income of households. . . ." Since consumers typically spend from 92 to 94 percent of their disposable income (see Table 7–1), there will be an immediate and sizable increase in the buying of consumer goods and services. What the tax reduction will do is ". . . start a process of cumulative expansion throughout the economy. . . . The additional increases in spending will stimulate production and employment, generating additional incomes." The Keynesian multiplier will be at work.

But, the report went on to say, the expansion generated by the tax cuts will not proceed without limit. There will be leakages, not only because households will save some of their increased disposable income, but because of retained corporate earnings and a return flow of excise and income tax revenues to government. Taking into account all the leakages that could be identified, the Council of Economic Advisers estimated that the multiplier effect associated with a tax reduction "works out to roughly 2." For every dollar of added consumption spending that resulted from the tax cut, the gross national product (GNP) would rise by two dollars.

President Kennedy did not live to see his proposed tax cut translated into reality, but the Johnson administration was able, in the wake of the Kennedy assassination, to get a substantial tax reduction bill—$11 billion for individuals and $3 billion for corporations—enacted in early 1964.

Did the tax cut work? We cannot be 100 percent certain, but the *ex post* evidence suggests it did. In its 1966 *Economic Report,* the Council of Economic Advisers presented statistical evidence to show that the tax cut was responsible for most of the $30 billion gain in the GNP the economy experienced by the end of 1965. By current levels of GNP, $30 billion may seem miniscule, but it was 4.3 percent of the GNP in 1965, a major increase in output.

Finally, we must be very careful to note that the computation of a numerical value for the multiplier depends on accurate knowledge of the economy's consumption function and marginal propensity to consume. The empirical data examined earlier suggest that consumers tend to behave in the fashion indicated by the consumption function hypothesis, but this does not mean that it is easy to construct a statistical consumption function that will determine the exact value of the multiplier for the economy. In essence, we are cautioning against an overly simple interpretation of the multiplier phenomenon. If we recognize and understand this limitation, we are still left with a concept of great value for analysis of the process of change in the income and employment level.

Consumption and the Multiplier in the *IS-LM* Model

So far in this chapter we have developed the Keynesian theory of the consumption function, a theory which shows the linkages between current income and consumption. We have also developed fully the basic theory of the multiplier, another of Keynes's major contributions to macroeconomics. The theory of the multiplier explains how autonomous changes in spending translate into proportionally larger changes in the national output (GDP). Later in the chapter we shall look at other developments in the theory of consumption, developments that show the effect of relative and expected income as well as wealth on consumption spending.

At this point we will use the Keynesian consumption function and the multiplier to further develop the *IS-LM* model introduced in Chapter 6. Specifically, we shall examine how changes in the marginal propensity to consume (MPC) affect the *IS-LM* model. Why the marginal propensity to consume? The reason is that up to this point in our analysis it is the value of the MPC that governs the size of the multiplier. When the marginal propensity to consume increases, the multiplier will increase. The greater the multiplier, therefore, the greater is the impact of *any* autonomous change on income. The *IS-LM* model provides a clear and convenient way to show why this is true.

Figure 7–6 traces the impact of an increase in the value of the marginal propensity to consume on the *IS* curve in the *IS-LM* model. We begin with

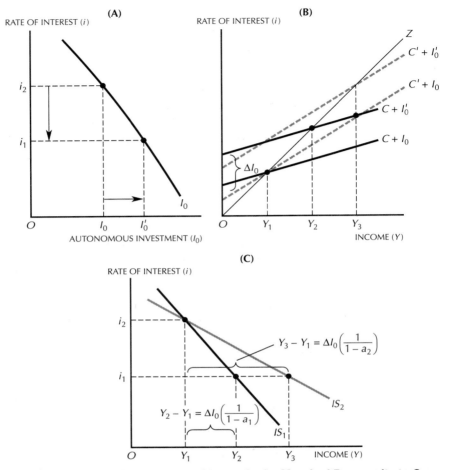

FIGURE 7–6   The *IS* Curve and a Change in the Marginal Propensity to Consume.   When the MPC increases, the multiplier becomes larger. Therefore, the national income is more sensitive to changes in the rate of interest. A steeper slope for the aggregate demand curve *(C + I)* and a less steep slope for the *IS* curve result from an increase in the value of the MPC.

part A in the upper left-hand corner of the figure, where we find a standard investment demand curve, which shows investment as an inverse function of the rate of interest $[I = f(i)]$. If the rate of interest is i_2, investment spending will be I_0. This amount of investment, when added to a Keynesian consumption function, gives us the aggregate demand schedule shown in part B of the figure and labeled $C + I_0$. The slope of the aggregate demand curve depends on the slope of the underlying consumption function, which, the reader will recall, is measured by the value of the marginal propensity to consume. The equilibrium level of income is Y_1.

Now let us see what happens if the interest rate is lowered to i_1. This causes, in turn, investment spending to increase to I_0'. In part B of the figure this change is seen as an upward shift in the aggregate demand curve to the level $C + I_0'$. The precise amount by which the equilibrium income level changes depends, as we know, on the numerical value of the multiplier, a value which is governed by the slope of the underlying consumption function.

In part C of Figure 7–6 we have the *IS* curve. The solid line labeled IS_1 is constructed as was done in Chapter 6 by linking each equilibrium income level as determined by the intersection of aggregate demand and aggregate supply to the rate of interest associated with each and every equilibrium level of income. The solid line reflects the relationships and changes sketched out above.

Now we are in a position to see what happens if there is a change in the economy's marginal propensity to consume (MPC). We shall assume that the MPC increases, which means a steeper slope for the underlying consumption function. What then follows logically is a steeper slope for the aggregate demand curve, irrespective of the level of investment spending that is autonomous with respect to income. The effect of the increase in the marginal propensity to consume is shown in part B by the dotted-line curve labeled $C'+ I_0$. Now if the interest rate falls from i_2 to i_1, investment will still rise from I_0 to I_0'. Income, however, will increase from Y_1 to Y_3—a larger increase than in the previous case. The same change in investment spending leads to a larger increase in output, because with a higher value for the MPC, the multiplier is greater.

The impact of the foregoing on the *IS* curve is shown by the dotted line labeled IS_2 in part C of Figure 7–6. The net effect of an increase in the MPC gives us an *IS* curve that is less steep than the previous curve. In a practical sense, the meaning of the foregoing is that the economy has greater sensitivity to a change in interest rates. This is simply because there will be a larger multiplier effect associated with any autonomous change in investment—or any other spending—that results from a change in interest rates.

In *The General Theory* Keynes saw in the value of the multiplier a clue to what he called the "paradox of poverty in the midst of potential plenty."[14] In a rich country, like the United States, the value of both the average and the marginal propensity to consume may be low as compared with a poor country, like Mexico. But if the values of both the APC and MPC are low, so will be the size of the multiplier. Hence, in a recession or depression it will take a very large spending stimulus to bring the economy out of a slump. In a poor country with higher values for both the APC and MPC there is also a higher value for the multiplier. Under such circumstances, as Keynes pointed out, a "very modest measure of investment will be sufficient to provide full employment."[15]

[14] Keynes, *The General Theory*, p. 32.
[15] Ibid., p. 33.

Income, Consumption, and Saving in the Long Run

There is another aspect of the income-consumption relationship that has intrigued economists for a number of years. The consumption function depicted in Figure 7–1 is one in which the average propensity to consume falls as the income level rises. The slope of a function of this type is such that it intersects both the aggregate supply curve and the vertical axis. Since this schedule pertains to the behavior of consumption expenditure over relatively short periods of time, it is usually described as a short-run, or Keynesian, cyclical function. The statistical data shown in Table 7–1 and plotted in Figure 7–3 tend to confirm the existence of this type of relationship.

However, a dilemma is created by the fact that statistics on income, consumption, and saving over long periods of time show that the consumption-income ratio, C/Y, tends to be constant. In some path-breaking studies published just after World War II, Nobel laureate Simon Kuznets showed that, for 60 years (1869 to 1929), the ratio between consumption and income

TABLE 7–6   Net National Product and Consumption Expenditures in the Long Run (in billions of 1929 and 1982 dollars)

(1) Decade	(2) Net National Product	(3) Consumption Expenditures	(4) Average Propensity to Consume (3) ÷ (2)
1869–78	$ 9.3	$ 8.1	87.1
1874–83	13.6	11.6	85.2
1879–88	17.9	15.3	85.5
1884–93	21.0	17.7	84.2
1889–98	24.2	20.2	83.5
1894–1903	29.8	25.4	85.2
1904–13	45.0	39.1	86.9
1909–18	50.6	44.0	86.9
1919–28	69.0	62.0	89.8
1924–33	73.3	68.9	94.0
1929–38	72.0	71.0	98.7 Great Depression
1950–59*	927	848	91.5
1960–69*	1,342	1,211	90.2
1970–79*	1,939	1,738	89.6
1980–89*	2,565	2,334	91.0
1990–94*	3,004	2,785	92.7

*1950–59, 1960–69, 1970–79, 1980–89, and 1990–94 data are for disposable income rather than net national product and are in 1982 dollars. Kuznets' figures are in 1929 dollars. The income and consumption figures are rounded to the nearest whole numbers.

Sources: Decades for 1869–78 through 1929–38 from Simon Kuznets, National Product Since 1869 (New York: National Bureau of Economic Research, 1946), p. 119. Decades 1950–59, 1960–69, and 1970–79 from Economic Report of the President, 1991, p. 317; 1990–1994, 1995, pp. 276, 279, 307.

tended to be constant.[16] Kuznets' data are shown in Table 7–6. Also shown in this table are post-World War II data for 1950–59, 1960–69, 1970–79, 1980–89, and 1990–94. These data are not strictly comparable with the earlier data developed by Kuznets, primarily because he computed consumption as a percentage of net national product, whereas the postwar figures relate consumption to disposable income. Furthermore, Kuznets employed definitions of both the net national product and consumption different from those currently used by the Department of Commerce. Nevertheless, both the pre- and post-World War II data show that over long periods of time the ratio between consumption and income (however defined) tends to be constant. The only exception to this for the period covered by the data in Table 7–6 is the decade 1929–38 (Kuznets' data), when the ratio of consumption to income rose to nearly 100 percent. The reason for this is that this period includes the years of the Great Depression.

The upshot of all this is that, over the long run, consumers spend about the same proportion of their income, even though they have experienced a steady rise in the level of real income. As a matter of fact, in the years covered by Kuznets' data when the propensity to consume remained practically constant, *real* income rose nearly eightfold. Diagrammatically, the long-term (or *secular*) consumption function appears as a straight line whose slope is such that the marginal and average propensities to consume are equal. Such a consumption function is shown in Figure 7–7. The Kuznets data are also shown in this figure. It is called a secular function because it pertains to the behavior of consumption expenditures in relation to income over long periods of time.

The dilemma faced by economists is how to reconcile statistical evidence on the long-run constancy of the average propensity to consume with equally worthy statistical evidence that shows that in the short run the consumption-income ratio is not a constant. Actually, we have already suggested one solution to this dilemma, for in our earlier discussion of the empirical validity of the consumption function hypothesis, we pointed out that the short-run data on income and consumption suggest that over time the consumption function may actually be shifting upward.

Expanded Theories of Consumption

The upward drift of the consumption function over time is clearly seen in Figure 7–3, in which data are extrapolated from the 1929–40 period into the

[16] Simon Kuznets, *Uses of National Income in Peace and War* (New York: National Bureau of Economic Research, 1941), p. 31, Table 2, and p. 35, Table 6. See also Kuznets, *National Product Since 1869* (New York: National Bureau of Economic Research, 1946), p. 119. Similar results were found by Raymond Goldsmith; see his *A Study of Savings in the United States* (Princeton, N.J.: Princeton University Press, 1955), pp. 22, 78.

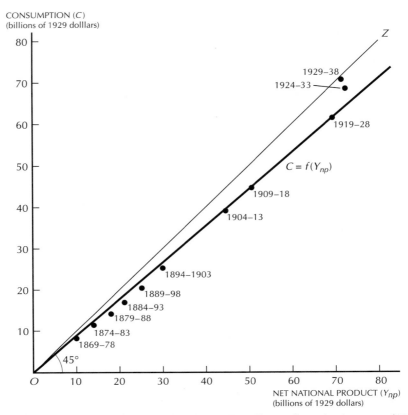

FIGURE 7–7   The Secular Consumption Function. Over the long run (1869 to 1938) the average propensity to consume tends to be constant—a fact depicted by the straight line intersecting the vertical axis at the zero level.

Source: Kuznets, *National Product Since 1869.*

post-World War II era. The extrapolated curve (the dashed line extension in Figure 7–3) lies below the curve that fits measured data in the 1948–94 period. Thus, it may be argued that the measured consumption function has shifted upward.

The observed difference between the income-consumption ratio in the long- as compared to the short-run presents an interesting, and puzzling, theoretical problem. It can be argued that the *real* relationship between income and consumption is one of proportionality (as revealed by long-term data), but that in the short run, *cyclical* factors distort this relationship and result in the kind of income-consumption pattern shown in Figure 7–1. What is the explanation for these differences in empirical findings? Unfortunately, contemporary income theory does not have a precise answer to this question. Research since Keynes first proposed the basic relationship between income and consumption has led to three hypotheses that attempt to explain the observed data. These are known as the *relative* income, the *permanent* income, and the *life-cycle* income hypotheses. We shall briefly examine each of these arguments, and then conclude this chapter with a short discussion of variables other than income that influence consumption.

The Relative Income Hypothesis

James S. Duesenberry, professor emeritus of Harvard University and former member of the President's Council of Economic Advisers, developed this hypothesis shortly after the end of World War II.[17] Duesenberry's thesis is based on two key ideas. First, consumer preferences are interdependent; this means that a family's level of consumption depends on not just its income, but its income as compared to the income of other families. Consumption spending, in other words, is *emulative*; it is influenced by the consumption of families further up the income distribution ladder. This relationship is dominant at a time when incomes generally are rising.

Duesenberry's second idea is that a family's consumption spending in a period when incomes generally are falling is strongly influenced by the household's peak income, that is, the income attained before incomes began to fall. This idea springs directly from Keynes's belief that a family's habitual standard of living has first claim on its income. Thus, when income falls, efforts will be made to preserve the standard of living to which the family has become accustomed. This will cause the observed propensity to consume to rise. When faced with a decline in income, families, to the extent possible, will sacrifice saving in an effort to maintain their living standards. Of course, as a slump continues, consumption spending will necessarily fall, but not as rapidly as income.

Slumps eventually end, and when this happens, the family's income will start to rise back toward the level it had attained before the slump—the family's prior peak income. What happens during the recovery period when the economy's income and the incomes of many families are climbing back to the levels attained before the slump? Duesenberry argues that the propensity to consume will decline, partly because families seek to restore their savings to the level that prevailed earlier and partly because they will not adjust their consumption upward quite as rapidly as income increases until they are reasonably certain that their incomes gains will last.

Now the stage is set for reconciling the observed difference between the propensities to consume in the short- and long-runs. Once the recovery is complete and incomes for most families begin to rise above the levels they attained during the last period of prosperity, Duesenberry says that consumption will increase proportionally to income, along the path shown in Figure 7–7. Why? In part, this is because incomes are continually rising to a new peak, so income is allocated between consumption and saving in a constant

---

[17] James S. Duesenberry, *Income, Saving and the Theory of Consumer Behavior* (Cambridge, Mass.: Harvard University Press, 1949), pp. 17–46. See also Duesenberry, ''Income-Consumption Relations and Their Implications,'' in *Income, Employment and Public Policy: Essays in Honor of Alvin H. Hansen* (New York: Norton, 1948), pp. 54–81.

ratio, the one regarded as normal at the prior highest income level. Further, if the distribution of income remains stable during an expansion, the average propensity to consume for the whole economy should remain stable, since the *relative* position of all families would not change. Over time, the short-term consumption function shifts upward and gives rise to a *ratchet effect* that tends to boost consumption spending to ever-higher levels of what consumers come to regard as normal.

The Permanent Income Hypothesis

The other two hypotheses we shall discuss have one major idea in common—individuals and families plan their consumption not on the basis of current or recent income as Keynes and Duesenberry suggest, but on the basis of long-term or even lifetime income expectations. Consumers, it is assumed, look beyond current income and into the future in deciding how to allocate their income between consumption and saving. The fundamental relationship between consumption and income is one of proportionality, even though short-term (or cyclical) factors can cause the average propensity to consume to depart from its long-term norm. We shall examine first the *permanent income* argument.

The best-known exposition of the permanent income hypothesis is that developed by Professor Milton Friedman, also the foremost proponent of modern monetarism (see Chapter 11).[18] In Friedman's analysis, *permanent income* is roughly akin to lifetime income, which depends on the real and financial wealth of an individual plus the value of that person's human capital in the form of inherent and acquired skills and training. The average expected return on the sum of all such wealth would be an individual's permanent income.

The foregoing is the concept. Measurement is something else. The income that an individual actually receives in a given year is called *measured income* by Professor Friedman. Over a lifetime, measured income ought to coincide with permanent income, but in any one year measured income will not equal permanent income because of cyclical fluctuations and other random changes. The best practical measure of permanent income is a weighted average of past and present measured income, with less weight attached to measured income the further it lies in the past. In any single year, Professor Friedman calls the difference between measured income and permanent income *transitory income*. It may be positive or negative in any single year, but over an individual's lifetime it is necessarily zero.

The key idea in this hypothesis is that an individual's permanent consumption is proportional to her or his permanent income. In other words, the consumer or family expects over a lifetime to consume or save a fixed proportion of its lifetime or permanent income. Practically, this means that sav-

---

[18] Milton Friedman, *A Theory of the Consumption Function* (Princeton, N.J.: Princeton University Press, 1957).

ings will increase (or decrease) whenever there is an increase (or decrease) in the *transitory* component of income. This is what accounts for short-term fluctuations in the savings-income (or consumption-income) ratio as depicted in the short-term, or cyclical, function. The idea that all transitory increases in one's income are saved may seem contrary to ordinary observations, as people often use windfall gains to buy a durable consumer good, car, color TV, or stereo outfit. But, in concept at least, this difficulty disappears if durable goods purchases are viewed as additions to private wealth and their services viewed as consumption.

How does Friedman's hypothesis square with reality? As is often the case with theoretical propositions in economics, the empirical evidence is mixed. One major difficulty is measuring permanent income, because the concept includes all future income that an individual expects to receive. A weighted average of past measured income is probably the only way to get at permanent income, but such an average is not always a reliable guide to future income.

Federal tax changes offer insights into the validity of the permanent income hypothesis. For example, in June 1968 the Congress passed a 10 percent surcharge to the personal income tax to dampen consumer spending and lessen inflationary pressures caused by the Vietnam War. Seven years later in March 1975, the Ford administration and the Congress agreed on a $21 billion tax cut package to stimulate consumption and the economy. In both instances, consumption spending failed to respond as expected, in large part because the tax changes were widely advertised as temporary. Thus, it can be argued that because permanent income was not affected by these temporary changes in measured income, consumers did not change their consumption significantly as a result of the tax changes.

The Life-Cycle Income Hypothesis

In the 1950s and 1960s Franco Modigliani and some colleagues developed what is now known as the *life-cycle* hypothesis.[19] Their basic argument is simply stated. Consumers, it is held, plan their consumption spending essentially over their lifetimes, rather than only on the basis of incomes received in the current period. In this context, "lifetime" means an individual's expected remaining years of work and life. Consumption depends on the individual's total resources, which consist of personal wealth or property, income from work, and income expected from work. It is also presumed that consumption over one's lifetime will be proportional to income from resources owned and labor expended.

---

[19] For details of the life-cycle hypothesis, see Franco Modigliani and Richard Brumberg, "Utility Analysis and the Consumption Function: An Interpretation of Cross-Section Data," in K. Kurihara, ed., *Post Keynesian Economics* (New Brunswick, N.J.: Rutgers University Press, 1954); A. Ando and F. Modigliani, "The Life-Cycle Hypothesis of Saving," *The American Economic Review*, March 1963; and Franco Modigliani, "The Life Cycle Hypothesis of Saving, the Demand for Wealth and the Supply of Capital," *Social Research*, June 1966.

The lifetime pattern of income and consumption seen by Modigliani is as follows. In the early years for an individual or a family—the years of household formation and heavy borrowing—consumption will run ahead of income, and in the later years—those of retirement—consumption will also run ahead of income. During the in-between years, though, consumption will be less than income, as these are the years when debt is being retired and saving is taking place in anticipation of retirement. This is a reasonable picture of the way people behave.

This hypothesis provides an explanation for many individual budget studies that show, as Keynes postulated for the economy overall, that at low income levels the average propensity to consume is higher than at high income levels. At any given moment, individuals in either the young adult or the retirement years will tend to have incomes lower on the average than the incomes of persons in the middle, working years. Consequently, at any particular time and for any given distribution of the age structure, the pattern for society as a whole will be one in which the propensity to consume is higher at lower levels of income and lower at higher levels of income. Family budget studies in combination with the life-cycle hypothesis confirm the Keynesian argument that the short-term income-consumption relationship is as shown in Figure 7–1 and Equation (7–3) (pages 214 and 217).

How, we may ask, does Modigliani reconcile the short- and long-term empirical findings on the propensity to consume? This can be explained by reference to the following algebraic statement of the life-cycle income hypothesis:

$$C = f(W + Y_1 + Y_e). \tag{7-16}$$

In the equation, W equals personal wealth, Y_1 equals current earnings, and Y_e equals future or expected labor earnings. For the individual's whole span of life and work, consumption will be proportional to these variables—the consumer's total resources—but in the short run it is a different story. In any single income period, future income from work is not realized; it is only something expected. Therefore, its influence can only affect the propensity to consume out of current income. This means that an increase (or decrease) in current income will have to continue for several income periods before it has a significant effect on expected income. From this is follows logically that when income changes in any single period, consumption will change less than when consumers see their total resources change and adjust their consumption to a proportional relationship to those resources.

Essentially, the life-cycle hypothesis says that in the short term the path of consumption will be along a Keynesian consumption function (Figure 7–1), whose point of intercept with the vertical axis is determined by wealth holdings (W). Over time, as wealth holdings increase, the short-term cycle will drift upward and then the life-cycle path of consumption will be along the long-term schedule as depicted in Figure 7–7. It is at this point that an essential difference between these two hypotheses becomes apparent. For the Friedman analysis, variations in the short-run income-consumption relationship happen because of essentially random variations in a family's transitory income. However, in the Modigliani argument, these short-run variations happen because expected income and wealth holdings do not increase fast enough for families to adjust their consumption spending to what ultimately may turn out to be changes in their anticipated lifetime income. Actually, both hypotheses account for short-term fluctuations in the income-consumption ratio in similar fashion, but with a slightly different perspective as to how changes in the ratio come about.

The problem with both the permanent and life-cycle income hypotheses is not with the idea that families and individuals plan ahead. Most economists would concede that they do. The real problem in this age of family instability and rapidly changing notions about what constitutes a family is how we get a firm measure of the time horizon within which *any* family does its income planning and makes its consumption decisions. To plan effectively over a long term—forty to fifty years might not be unrealistic for a stable family—expectations about future family income would have to be correct. It is doubtful that many families in today's volatile economic environment have the skill and information needed for such long-term projections.

Which Hypothesis?

So we are left with a question: Which of the expanded theories of consumption we have just been discussing offers the best, or most appropriate, explanation of consumer behavior? Unfortunately, no precise answer can be given to this question, as each represents a view that is reasonably in accord with observed experience. There are elements of truth in all these approaches to understanding the relationship between income and consumption (or saving). Over the years, literally hundreds of econometric consumption functions have been developed and tested, without any wholly conclusive results. Econometric testing, in other words, has not come up with a definitive consumption function, one that will always yield precise predictions of how consumption will respond to any given change in income. What is most crucial is the realization that both analysis and empirical observation point strongly to the conclusion that income is the dominant factor in explaining consumption behavior in the national economy. Furthermore, the *observed* relationship between income and consumption seems to adhere to a Keynesian-type path over the short term, even though this relationship is a proportional one when a longer span of time is taken into consideration. There is no general agreement among economists as to which of the three hypotheses offers the best explanation for the upward drift of the cyclical consumption function. Nevertheless, there is agreement that the cyclical function does shift upward over time. The economy would be violently unstable if it did not.

Other Influences on Consumption

One reason that it has been so difficult to derive an acceptable econometric consumption function is that income is not the only determinant of consumption spending. There are many other variables that influence consumption decisions, but most of them are not subject to quantification and precise measurement. The general practice in analysis of consumer spending is to treat variables other than income as *parameters,* whose values determine the level and slope of the income-consumption curve. Analytically, this means that changes in any of these parameters will result in a shift in the curve, rather than a movement along it. Let's take a brief look at the most important of these variables and how they may influence consumption.

Attitudes toward Thrift

In a general way, we can group together in the category of thrift the psychological attributes of human nature that lead people to save rather than spend some part of current income, as well as various business practices and institutional arrangements of a society that make for saving. Cultural factors that condition a society's attitudes toward thrift and spending are deeply rooted in its past and not readily subject to change. Installment purchasing and other forms of borrowing that raise the propensity to consume are to some extent offset by developments of modern life that tend to raise the propensity to save. The twentieth century has seen a powerful tendency toward the institutionalization of saving through commitments of income to life insurance, private pension plans, and long-term mortgages on private homes. The average person does not usually think of premiums on life insurance, payroll deductions for a pension plan, or monthly amortization of home loans as forms of saving, yet they represent saving from the viewpoint of the whole economy. Moreover, most saving of this type is contractual in nature and thus cannot readily be changed.

Asset Holdings by the Consumer

Another factor believed by many economists to exercise a powerful influence on consumer spending patterns has to do with assets held by the consumer, including both financial assets in the form of cash on hand, bank accounts, bonds, stocks, and other claims and physical assets in the form of stocks of durable goods owned by the consumer.

Financial Assets. The most plausible hypothesis that we can advance regarding the influence of financial assets on expenditures is simply that spending will vary directly with the value of private holdings of financial assets. Such holdings, particularly if they are easily converted into purchasing power, constitute a reserve of spending power that the consumer can draw on in emergencies. As a consequence, there is less need to save out of current income in order to build such a reserve. This means that an increase in holdings of liquid assets by consumers would, other things being equal, shift the consumption function upward. This, it will be recalled, is the argument of the life-cycle income hypothesis.

The hypothesis of a direct relationship between consumer spending and holdings of financial or liquid assets is subject to some reservations. For one thing, the distribution of ownership of liquid assets will have a bearing on their overall impact on consumer spending. If, for example, ownership is concentrated in the upper-income groups, it is doubtful that the size or value of such holdings will have much influence on the level of consumption for the whole economy, since high-income earners as a group tend to save a large proportion of their income at all times.

In addition to the distribution of ownership, changes in the real value of liquid assets may exercise an influence on the consumer's spending-saving decisions. For example, if the general price level rises, the real value of financial assets in the form of bank deposits, bonds, and other financial resources may decline. If this happens, consumers may be induced to save more out of their current income in order to recoup a desired position with respect to asset holdings. The possibility of a unique relationship between the real value of the stock of liquid assets and the position of the consumption function was encountered in Chapter 6 as the *Pigou effect*. Generally, the Pigou effect is not taken seriously because ownership of liquid assets is not widespread in the U.S. economy. There is one exception to this. Lenders have discovered a new asset basis for consumer borrowing, namely, the equity that homeowners have built up in their homes. Consumers are urged not to deny themselves what they want—a winter cruise, a new boat, a family swimming pool—by borrowing on the equity in their homes. How much this type of borrowing has sustained consumer spending in recent years is not really known, but it undoubtedly has had some effect.

Stocks of Durable Goods. The second type of asset that may affect the spending-saving pattern of consumers consists of the stock of durable goods in their possession. As a general proposition, a large stock of durable goods in the hands of consumers may, other things being equal, have a tendency to depress consumption spending. Such goods represent a capital investment for the consumer, and they provide a stream of services as long as the goods are in existence. The person who owns an automobile, for example, need not spend much of her income for other forms of transportation. Similar results flow from the ownership of other types of durable goods, such as television sets and radios, home laundry equipment, and various other household appliances. It should be recognized, though, that ownership of durables may stimulate other expenditures. The owner of an automobile, for example, must purchase large quantities of gasoline, new tires, and spare parts. She is, moreover, a purchaser of insurance and other services that stem directly from her

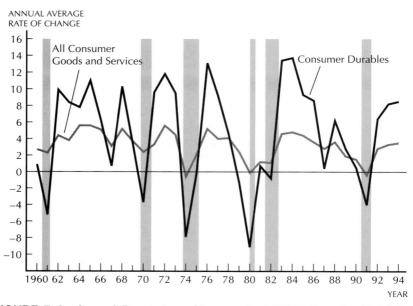

FIGURE 7–8 Annual Percentage Changes in 1987 Dollars for Total Consumer Spending for Goods and Services and Consumer Spending for Durable Goods, 1960–1994. Consumer spending for durable goods is much more volatile than consumer spending in general; spending on durables is usually postponable. Shaded areas are recessions.

Source: Economic Report of the President, 1995, p. 276.

ownership of an automobile. On balance, it is difficult to say which of these influences is the strongest.

The chief conclusion we can draw concerning the influence of the stock of consumer durables on consumer spending is that such goods by their very durability introduce elements of uncertainty into consumer spending. Consumer spending for durable goods is more volatile than consumer spending in general—a fact reflected in Figure 7–8. This shows for the period 1960 through 1994 annual percentage changes in consumer spending for durable goods in constant 1987 dollars and for total consumer spending, also in constant 1987 dollars. Note especially how consumer spending for durables dropped sharply in each of the post-World War II recessions marked on the figure. Consumer spending for durable goods as a percentage of disposable income has risen over the periods shown in Figure 7–8. It averaged 9.6 percent in the 1960s, 11.2 percent in the 1970s, and 13.1 percent in the 1980s and early 1990s.[20] Aside from income itself, the most important determinant of consumer spending for durables appears to be consumer credit. Not unexpectedly, studies have found that consumer spending for durable goods varies positively with consumer credit.

---

[20] *Economic Report of the President*, 1991, pp. 296, 316; 1995, p. 293.

The Distribution of Income

Economists regard the distribution of money income of a society as one of the important parametric determinants of the consumption-income relationship. This particular influence on consumption is thought to be stable, as the pattern of income distribution in any society is determined by a complex of institutional factors, including the structure of property rights, the distribution of ownership of productive assets, the tax system, and the social security system, all of which appear to change with relative slowness. This stability is reflected in the data in Table 7–7, which shows for selected years from 1947 to 1992 the distribution of money income to families by quintiles, or fifths. Over most of the post-World War II period, income distribution was relatively unchanged, but since 1980 there has been a measurable shift toward greater inequality. In 1992 the share of income going to the top 20 percent of families was the highest since 1947, and the share going to the bottom 20 percent was the lowest since 1955.

Insofar as the pattern of income distribution has an influence on the level and slope of the consumption function, other things being equal, a movement toward more equality in the distribution of income will raise the level, and possibly the slope too, of the consumption function, whereas any movement toward greater inequality in the distribution of income will have the opposite effect. This deduction is based on the fact that studies of income and its disposition at the level of the household show that families in the lower-income brackets have a higher average propensity to consume than families in the higher-income brackets.

The Rate of Interest

At one time many economists would have been inclined to list the rate of interest as probably the most important determinant of consumption and saving. According to pre-Keynesian thought, to save is to exchange present satisfactions (gained from consumption) for future satisfactions, but a price must be paid to persuade people to make such an exchange. This price is interest.

TABLE 7–7   Money Income Distribution to Families in the United States: 1947–1992 (percent)

Income Rank	1947	1955	1965	1975	1980	1985	1992
Total families	100.0	100.0	100.0	100.0	100.0	100.0	100.0
Lowest fifth	5.0	4.9	4.8	5.5	5.1	4.7	4.4
Second fifth	11.9	12.3	12.3	11.8	11.6	10.9	10.5
Third fifth	17.0	17.8	17.8	17.6	17.5	16.8	16.5
Fourth fifth	23.1	23.7	24.0	24.1	24.3	24.1	24.0
Highest fifth	43.0	41.3	41.3	41.1	41.6	43.5	44.6
Top 5 percent	17.5	16.4	15.9	15.5	15.3	16.7	17.6

Source: U.S. Bureau of the Census, *Current Population Reports,* P-60, No. 184, 1993.

The higher the price, the greater the willingness of people to postpone consumption; the lower the price, the smaller their willingness. As a consequence, interest was regarded as a prime determinant of the amounts that families and spending units would save out of their incomes.

Today many economists do not believe that the rate of interest exercises any appreciable effect one way or the other on the level of consumption or saving. From a deductive point of view it is possible to show that increases in the level of interest rates may actually reduce saving. A rise in interest rates means that, if people save in order to amass a sum designed to yield them some specific annual income, a smaller absolute sum would yield an identical annual income at higher interest rates as a larger sum at lower rates. If, for example, the rate of interest rose from 10 to 15 percent, a saver would have to amass only $13,333 rather than $20,000 in order to obtain an annual interest income of approximately $2,000. A rise in the rate of interest also may tend to reduce some types of contractual saving, such as life insurance. At higher interest rates a *fixed* amount of life insurance requires smaller premiums.

Price Changes and Consumer Expectations

Changes in the general level of prices and shifts in consumer expectations for the future are two additional and related factors that economists recognize as potential influences on spending and saving levels. Our knowledge of the impact of these variables is more speculative than empirical. There is a presumption that a rise in the level of all prices will raise the average propensity to consume, if we assume (somewhat tenuously) that money income does not change in the same degree. The increase in prices leads real income to decline and thus causes a higher consumption-income ratio. It is also possible, in the face of a falloff in real income, that consumers will attempt to maintain the same absolute level of real consumption. This would result in a shift upward of the consumption function, for consumption spending would absorb a higher proportion of an absolutely lower real income level.

Consumer expectations concerning future income may also be of significance and affect the slope rather than the level of the consumption. The slope of the function is the marginal propensity to consume, which specifies the way in which consumers react to a change in their incomes. Logically, one would expect that an individual (or spending unit) would react differently to an increase (or decrease) in income, depending on whether or not the change was expected to be permanent. To illustrate, if a change in income is seen as temporary, consumption spending probably would not change to the same degree as it would if the income change were viewed as permanent. As we noted earlier in our discussion of the 1968 tax increase, consumption spending did not decline as expected because of the widespread knowledge that the tax increase was temporary.

Consumer Credit

The significance of consumer credit on consumption is readily apparent; the availability of credit permits more spending for consumption purposes than would be possible if current income were the only source of purchasing power. The practical importance of consumer credit as a factor in consumer expenditure in the United States is enormous. In December 1994 the volume of outstanding consumer credit of all types was $911 billion, an amount that had grown 31 times since 1952. Moreover, the volume of credit extended to consumers has increased in every year except 1991 since World War II, including the recession years of 1949, 1954, 1958, 1970, 1970–74, and 1981–82.[21]

The obvious fact concerning consumer credit is that borrowed funds represent additional financial resources that can be used for current consumption expenditures. If consumers borrow sufficiently so that the total of their indebtedness increases—that is, new borrowings exceed repayments—the consumption function would tend to shift upward. Total consumption spending would rise relative to income, since borrowing has given the consumer control over financial resources greater than the amount represented by current income. It is interesting to note that ever since 1946 consumers have added to their borrowings at a greater rate than they have repaid their obligations. Consumer credit in this period thus created upward pressure on the consumption component of aggregate demand.

Although an initial extension of credit to the consumer tends to raise the propensity to consume, the subsequent effects of such credit extension may depress consumption expenditure. Such loans must be repaid. If Mr. Jones, for example, borrows $9,000 to help finance the purchase of a new automobile, his expenditure of the proceeds of the loan will take an item of current output off the market. Subsequently, though, a portion of Mr. Jones's current income will no longer be available to spend for currently produced goods and services, since he must repay the loan. If he arranges to repay the $5,000 at the rate of $300 a month, then for a period of 30 months (ignoring interest and other charges that are connected with the loan) the amount of current income that he can spend for currently produced goods and services will be $300 less than usual.

What lesson does this hypothetical example hold for the economy as a whole? Unless there are new borrowings sufficient to offset the repayment of old borrowings, any stimulus to consumption expenditure that comes from an extension of credit to the consumer will be short-lived. If borrowing by the consumer tends to raise the level of the consumption function, repayment of loans has the opposite effect. Economists interested in the influence of consumer credit on consumption expenditure are more concerned with the relationship between the rate of new borrowing and the rate of repayment

[21] *Economic Report of the President*, 1991, p. 374; 1995, p. 364.

than with the absolute amount of consumer credit outstanding at any particular time.

The rate at which consumers increase their indebtedness is no doubt in some way tied in with expectations. Again there is scant empirical evidence to help us determine the precise nature of this relationship. It does not require any great feat of the imagination to see how disastrous it could be for the economy if consumers decided all of a sudden to reduce drastically their rate of new borrowing. This result would be a precipitous fall in the level of the consumption function.

A Concluding Comment

In this chapter we have examined in detail the findings of modern economic analysis with respect to the determinants of consumption expenditure. The impetus for study and analysis of this key component in the structure of aggregate demand comes from Keynes's *The General Theory*. Keynes's belief in the existence of a functional relationship between real income and real consumption has been formalized in the concept of the consumption function. This has become one of the key analytical tools of modern income and employment theory. In retrospect, we can say that, although economists are no longer as sure as they once were of either the stability or the simplicity of the consumption-income relationship, they do regard its embodiment in the formal body of economic analysis as one of the major achievements of economic science within the last several decades.

Summary

1. The consumption function, a fundamental principle, holds that consumption, other things being equal, is determined primarily by income.

2. There are two important technical attributes of the income-consumption relationship: (1) the *average* propensity to consume *(C/Y)* and (2) the *marginal* propensity to consume ($\Delta C/\Delta Y$).

3. The marginal propensity to consume reflects Keynes's fundamental psychological law, which states that when income changes, consumption changes, but not as much as does income. This is the basis for the theory of the multiplier.

4. The theory of the multiplier relates any exogenous change in one of the spending components, such as investment, to a total and larger change in income. The multiplier results because any initial or exogenous change induces additional changes in consumption and investment.

5. The value of the multiplier depends directly on the *marginal* propensity to consume (and its converse, the *marginal* propensity to save), and it is equal to the reciprocal of 1 minus the marginal propensity to consume.

6. Several hypotheses have been developed that expand on the basic income-consumption relationship. These include the *relative* income hypotheses, as well as the *permanent* income and *life-cycle* hypotheses. No one is wholly satisfactory, but all throw light on the income-consumption relationship.

7. There are also other important influences on consumption, including attitudes toward thrift, asset holdings by consumers, the distribution of income, the rate of interest, and expected prices.

8 Investment and Finance

I N THIS CHAPTER we turn to the second major category of expenditure entering into aggregate demand: investment expenditure. There are three basic reasons why investment expenditure occupies a highly significant role in the functioning of the economy. First, the demand for investment goods is a large and important part of the total demand picture. In 1994, for example, *real* gross private domestic investment was $955.5 billion, an amount equal to 17.9 percent of *real* GDP. Second, investment expenditures play a strategic role in the economy, because changes in both income and employment are more likely to result from fluctuations in spending for capital goods than from fluctuations in spending for consumer goods. Changes in spending for consumer goods generally come about as a result of changes in the income level, rather than the other way around. In Keynes's *The General Theory* investment expenditures are volatile. In 1991, for example, investment spending in constant 1987 dollars dropped 8.5 percent from the 1990 level, but in the recovery year of 1993 it jumped 12.9 percent. Students of change and growth have long been aware that fluctuations in capital goods production are more violent than fluctuations in the production of consumer goods and services. This is true both in a relative sense and in an absolute sense. Investment expenditures not only initiate change in income and employment levels, but also act to exaggerate the effects. As Keynes saw it, the basic reason for the volatility

TABLE 8–1   Ratio of Stock of Business Equipment and Structures to GDP and to Employed Workers: Selected Years, 1950–1994

Year	Stock of Equipment*	GDP	Ratio	Employment	Equipment per Worker
1950	$2,250.2	$1,470.9	1.53	59,918	$37,555
1955	2,591.2	1,749.5	1.48	62,170	41,679
1960	2,948.1	1,970.8	1.50	65,778	44,819
1965	3,431.2	2,470.5	1.39	71,088	48,268
1970	4,250.1	2,873.9	1.48	78,678	54,401
1975	5,170.6	3,221.7	1.60	85,846	60,023
1980	6,263.6	3,776.3	1.66	99,307	63,076
1985	7,388.5	4,279.8	1.73	107,150	68,954
1990	8,459.1	4,897.3	1.74	117,914	71,739
1994	9,158.9	5,342.3	1.71	123,060	74,264

*In billions of dollars.

Sources: Survey of Current Business, 1992, p. 122; Economic Report of the President, 1995, pp. 276, 312.

of investment is that it depends on our expectations about the future. But the future is something about which we know very little.[1]

Finally, investment expenditures are significant because of their impact on the economy's productive capacity. Investment expenditures involve the acquisition of capital goods, the procreative element in an industrial society. Their function is to produce other goods and services. Even though investment expenditures play a key role in determining current levels of income and employment, their influence reaches beyond the present because of their impact on capacity. Investment expenditures are thus vital factors in economic growth, which depends to a great extent on how rapidly productive capacity is being enlarged.

Table 8–1 contains data that bear on the foregoing in an important way. There are two sets of figures in the table. The first shows the ratio of the gross stock of fixed reproducible tangible wealth in the form of business equipment and structures to the gross domestic product. Both are measured in 1987 dollars, so the comparison is between *real* values. The Bureau of Economic Analysis in the U.S. Department of Commerce compiles the data on the nation's stock of all forms of fixed, reproducible wealth, including not only equipment (machines), but also structures, business and residential. This ratio tells us the approximate quantity of fixed capital in the form of machines needed per dollar of gross national output. In 1950, it required $1.53 worth of capital for each dollar of output. By 1994 the ratio had climbed to $1.71 per dollar of output. Economists describe this ratio as the *capital-output ratio*. Symbolically, it is equal to *K/Y*. What the figures in Table 8–1 show is that the U.S. economy is being increasingly capitalized, which is to say it now requires more capital in the form of equipment or machinery per dollar of

---

[1] John Maynard Keynes, "The General Theory of Employment," *Quarterly Journal of Economics,* February 1937, p. 221.

output than it did 44 years ago. During this period the ratio jumped 11.7 percent. What these figures do not reveal are the qualitative changes in equipment that have taken place during this period, so not only are business firms using more capital for every unit of output produced, but they are also using better capital.

The second set of figures in the table tells us how much capital in the form of equipment (or machinery) is available for each worker employed. These figures, too, are measured in 1987 dollars. They also reflect the increasing capitalization of the economy. Whereas in 1950 the constant dollar value of equipment per worker was $37,555, by 1994 this figure had increased to $74,264, a 97.7 percent increase. Behind these figures lies an important and baffling economic puzzle. In some of these years when the ratio of equipment capital to output and the quantity of real capital per employed person were increasing, the annual average rate of growth in the nation's productivity was in decline. From 1970 through 1994 productivity, output per hour for all persons, grew at a mere 1.2 percent annually. In the 20-year period from 1950 to 1969, however, the annual average rate of growth in productivity was 2.5 percent, a rate twice the rate of the more recent period. We shall return to the discussion of the great productivity puzzle in Chapter 13.

The Investment Decision

There is one basic fact about investment spending in a market system that one should never forget: Business firms invest in equipment and buildings in order to make money. It is as simple as that. All investment expenditure is undertaken in the expectation of profit. In actuality it is often difficult in an enterprise to separate expectations of profit from actual (or current) profitability, which is dependent on current levels of output, sales, and costs. Expected profits obviously will be influenced by current profits, as well as other variables. This is common sense, but it does not mean that investment will take place only when current profits are satisfactory, because in many instances firms with low profit margins will invest in money-saving equipment in an effort to reduce costs.[2]

Generally speaking, there are two ways in which investment in capital will improve the profitability of the firm's operations. First, investment in new and improved equipment is a means of reducing production costs. Capital equipment is productive partly because it can supplement or take the place of other resources, particularly labor. Capital goods are tools. Through their use the effectiveness in production of both labor and natural resources may be enormously enhanced. It is estimated, for example, that machines in a

---

[2] Walter W. Heller, "The Anatomy of Investment Decisions," *Harvard Business Review,* March 1951. This article by the late Walter Heller, economic adviser to President Kennedy, is one of the best descriptions of business decision making for investment spending ever written.

modern factory supply from 30 to 70 times as much energy as could be provided by human muscle. Capital is also productive because it frequently represents the means by which new methods or techniques of production are introduced into the economic process.

The second way in which investment in capital equipment may improve the profitability of the firm's operations centers on market conditions. Frequently, the firm will be confronted with an opportunity to increase its profits either by introducing a new product or by expanding the output and sales of existing products. In either case, added capacity may be required if the firm is to exploit fully the profit potential of a favorable market situation; investment in new equipment and plants is necessary to provide this added capacity. In the quest for greater profitability, many firms engage extensively in product research and sales promotions. Both these activities frequently force a firm to invest in more plant and equipment.

Now that we have examined briefly the reasons investment expenditure cannot be separated from profitability in the operation of the firm, let us examine the nature of the investment decision. How does the entrepreneur look on an item of capital equipment? What factors does the entrepreneur have to take into account when contemplating the purchase of additional capital equipment? These questions lie at the heart of the investment decision, and investment theory must provide at least tentative answers to them.

Investment and Expected Income

Since the entrepreneur undertakes investment expenditure in the expectation that it will be profitable, she sees an item of capital equipment essentially as a stream of expected income, or, as Keynes described it, "a series of prospective returns, which she expects to obtain from selling its output, after deducting the running expenses of obtaining that output, during the life of the asset."[3] To the business executive, the value of a capital good lies in the stream of net income that the asset is expected to yield over its life. What the business executive does in essence is convert money (the firm's or borrowed money) into capital goods (equipment and buildings) that are expected to generate a cash flow over their lifetime. The investment process in a market society is one that moves from money to goods and back to money. The stream of income, or cash flow, is an *expected* stream primarily because capital is durable and yields value to its user only over a relatively long period of time. The size of the expected income stream depends on, first, the physical productivity of the capital instrument, second, the price at which the output produced with the aid of the capital equipment can be sold (which is primarily a matter of future demand and market conditions), and, finally, the nature and amount of other expenses in the form of wages and material costs that may be incurred from the use of additional amounts of equipment. These expenses,

[3] Keynes, *The General Theory*, p. 135.

too, depend on future market conditions. Keynes said that the considerations on which "expectations of prospective yields are based on partly existing facts ... and partly future events which can only be forecasted with more or less confidence. ... The *outstanding fact is the extreme precariousness of the basis of knowledge on which our estimates of prospective yields have to be made.* Our knowledge of the factors which will govern the yield of an investment some years hence is usually very slight and often negligible."[4] Here in a nutshell is why investment spending is so much less stable than consumption spending, why expectations are subject to sudden and frequent change.

In analyzing the investment decision, the usual practice is to think of the stream of expected income associated with the use of additional amounts of capital as being net of all other expenses that the firm may incur as a result of using more capital. Added expenditures for labor and materials, as well as any other additional operating expenses, are deducted from the contemplated income stream or from prospective returns on the capital good. This is done because the entrepreneur is primarily interested in what the equipment will yield him in the way of income over and above any additional expenses that may be involved in its operation.

Having stripped the stream of expected income of all costs incidental to the process of producing additional output, the entrepreneur is faced with the question of whether the investment is worthwhile. Will it, in other words, be profitable? As has just been stressed, the business executive in modern industrial society obtains a profit by converting money, which is the most liquid of all assets and which can always be loaned out at interest, into a less liquid form, that of a capital asset. Through the sale of its output, the capital asset is converted back to monetary form. This movement from money to capital asset and back to money will be profitable to the entrepreneur only if the asset yields more than the cost of its acquisition. *Here is the nub of the investment decision.* The entrepreneur will find an investment worthwhile if it yields a stream of income greater than what the entrepreneur must pay to acquire the asset. The investment decision involves balancing expected gain against the costs of acquiring the gain.

The Costs of Investment

What are the costs that the entrepreneur has to take into account in estimating the profitability of an investment expenditure? If we ignore momentarily the element of risk present in the acquisition of any capital asset, we can distinguish two fundamental types of costs that enter into the investment decision: the cost of producing under current market conditions the capital asset itself and the cost involved in the use of money or funds to acquire the asset.

The cost of the capital good under current market conditions is called the

---

[4] Ibid., pp. 147, 149 (italics added).

supply price of the asset. This is the price that would induce the manufacturer of any particular type of capital asset to produce one additional unit of the capital asset in question. The supply price for a particular capital asset is not the current market price of existing assets of that kind, but, basically, the cost of producing a new unit. It is the price that lies somewhere on a supply curve for the kind of capital equipment under discussion. From a monetary standpoint this represents what the entrepreneur must spend in order to acquire the asset. It also represents the absolute, irreducible minimum that the entrepreneur expects to get back from the purchase and utilization of a capital good. In a world dominated by the profit motive, no entrepreneur would contemplate the purchase of a new capital asset unless the entrepreneur believed that the asset would yield a stream of income whose present value, in the very least, would be equal to the supply price of the asset. In actuality, the entrepreneur would expect more, but this notion of a kind of irreducible minimum gives us a point of departure.

The above statements would be all that need be said if the use of money did not involve any costs. Then we could say that it would be profitable to acquire a capital asset whenever the value of the stream of expected income was greater than the current supply price. This, though, is not the case. In a monetary society there is always a cost involved in the use of money. The entrepreneur contemplating the acquisition of a capital asset faces a second choice. Since the asset cannot be obtained without money, the entrepreneur must either borrow the necessary funds to finance its purchase or else draw on accumulated reserves. If borrowing, the entrepreneur must pay the current market rate of interest appropriate to a loan of the type and duration necessary. The interest rate reflects the *financial cost* of the investment decision. Even if the entrepreneur uses private funds to finance the purchase of capital equipment, the interest rate reflects financial costs. In this event, the financial cost is implicit, since by using private funds for the purchase of a capital instrument, the return on which is uncertain, the entrepreneur forgoes the possibility of securing a return on these funds equal to the current market rate of interest, which could be obtained by lending the funds. It is only proper for the entrepreneur to treat such forgone interest income as a cost element in the acquisition of a capital asset. The market rate of interest is a measure of the opportunity cost involved in the use of funds to purchase an item of capital in preference to lending such funds to someone who is willing to pay the going rate to secure their use.

The essential point of the foregoing paragraph is that capital assets, no matter what their physical nature or durability, must be financed, which is to say that business firms have to acquire money before they can acquire more capital assets. Where do firms get the money? They may get it from their earnings (ploughing a part of profit back into new capital), by selling additional shares in the stock market (equity financing), or by borrowing (through bank loans or by issuing bonds or other types of debt instruments). In all three cases the current rate of interest represents either the implicit or the explicit cost to the firm of using money however obtained to purchase additional capital assets.[5] Borrowing to obtain funds is not only a common practice, but presents for the business firm problems of a different sort than it may encounter when it uses its own resources or sells shares to obtain money.[6] The reason is that a loan arrangement sets up a stream of cash payments that have to be met in order to pay off the loan. Normally this cash flow of required payments is contractual in nature, which means the firm is legally committed to make payments to its creditors until the loan is paid off or refinanced with a new loan. When funds are obtained internally or by the sale of shares, no such contractual pledge exists, although the owners will expect a return on the money (i.e., dividends) they have put into the firm by the purchase of its shares. As we shall see subsequently, the size of the contractual flow of payments that confronts a firm as a result of debt financing of new capital assets may affect significantly its willingness to invest in such assets.

The preceding remarks describe the factors that enter into the investment decision when the business firm is contemplating newly produced capital assets. From the perspective of the whole economy, decisions by business firms that lead to more investment spending—that is, the production of more capital goods—are what counts. There are times, however, when a business firm contemplating a major expansion in its capacity may find it cheaper to acquire through a buy-out or merger the assets of an existing firm, rather than to expand by acquiring newly produced machines and structures. This often happened in the buy-out and merger mania that swept over U.S. business in the 1980s. For the firm, the same factors discussed above enter into the investment decision, but with a buy-out or merger, no new investment spending takes place in the economy overall. In the 1980s, for example, the collapse of oil prices from the extreme highs they had reached in the 1970s made it cheaper for some major oil companies to acquire more oil reserves by buying out smaller companies, rather than by investing in exploration for and development of new wells.

The Basic Framework of Investment Theory

Now that we have examined the essential character of the investment decision, let us develop a formal framework for investment theory. In the preceding discussion it was emphasized that an excess of expected revenues from the use of a capital good over its supply price means that the good yields a

---

[5] In the case of the use of internal funds, the firm would expect to get back through the profitability of the capital a return at least equal to what the firm could have obtained by lending. If shares are sold, the purchasers will also expect a return in the form of dividends that also is at least equal to what they could have obtained by lending their money. There is no guarantee that the firm will earn such a return from the capital assets so acquired, but this is the expectation.

[6] It is estimated that more than three-quarters of investment expenditure (equipment, buildings, and inventories) that is financed externally is financed by borrowing. See Frank J. Jones, *Macrofinance* (Cambridge, Mass.: Winthrop Publishers, 1978), pp. 263 ff.

prospective profit. This is true, regardless of the financial costs of the invest-ment, as long as the expected income stream is greater than the supply price. The excess of the expected yield over the cost of the capital can be expressed as a rate; more specifically, this excess is a rate of return over cost, in which the net return per unit of time is shown as a percentage of the original cost. For example, a machine might cost an entrepreneur $10,000 and yield a net annual return of $1,000. Without at this moment considering the question of the useful life of the machine, we can say that such a machine yields *an annual rate of return over cost* of 10 percent.

The rate of return over cost relates the expected yield of a capital good to its supply price. It is this relationship that Keynes, in *The General Theory*, called the *marginal efficiency of capital.*

> The relation between the prospective yield of a capital asset and its supply price or replacement cost, i.e., the relation between the prospective yield of one more unit of that type of capital and the cost of producing that unit, furnishes us with the *marginal efficiency of capital* of that type. More precisely, I define the marginal efficiency of capital as being equal to that *rate of discount* [italics added] which would make the present value of . . . the returns expected from the capital asset during its life just equal to its supply price.[7]

The above definition emphasizes the word "marginal." We are interested in the expected rate of return on additional units of capital, not the rate of return now being earned on existing capital. Keynes defined the marginal efficiency of capital as a *rate of discount*; specifically, as the rate of discount that will make the present value of the income stream derived from the capital good just equal to its supply price.

What is a rate of discount? It is a rate used to determine the present value of a sum that will not be received until sometime in the future. In the real economic world it would be the rate of interest appropriate to the type or form of capital being acquired. For example, $100 due one year from today is worth less than $100 now on hand, because $100 on hand can be loaned at interest. Thus, in one year the $100 will be worth more than $100 because of interest. Therefore, $100 due in a year must be worth less than $100 in hand. When we allow a sum to grow over time at a fixed rate of interest, this is known as compounding, that is, growing at a constant rate. Discounting is just the opposite of compounding. It means shrinking at a constant rate.

The Discount Formula

The discount formula is a technique for finding the present value of an ex-pected future income. It applies a rate to some expected future sum that will cause it, as it were, to shrink in value. The usual procedure for determining the present value of some expected income stream is to discount it at the

[7] Keynes, *The General Theory*, p. 135.

current rate of interest. As indicated above, this would be the rate appropriate to the kind of capital involved. To see how this works, let us assume that we have an asset that will yield an income of $3,000 per year for a three-year period ($9,000 over its total life span). We want to know the present value of this asset. The discount formula for finding the present value of a future income is

$$V_p = \frac{R_1}{(1 + i)} + \frac{R_2}{(1 + i)^2} + \cdots + \frac{R_n}{(1 + i)^n}, \qquad (8\text{--}1)$$

where V_p is the present value; $R_1, R_2, \ldots, R_n$ is the expected income stream in absolute amount; and i is the current rate of interest. The numerical subscript appended to each R represents the year in which each of the specific sums that are a part of the total is due. If we assume that the current rate of interest is 10 percent, we can apply the above formula to find the present value of our asset:

$$V_p = \frac{\$3,000}{(1.10)} + \frac{\$3,000}{(1.10)^2} + \frac{\$3,000}{(1.10)^3}.$$

Clearing fractions, we obtain

$$V_p = \$2,727 + \$2,479 + \$2,256 = \$7,462.$$

The present value of the series is thus $7,462, an amount less than the sum of the absolute amounts to be received in the three years. The process we have just described is also called *capitalization*. When we use the rate of interest to find the present value of an income stream, we are said to have *capitalized* the income stream. Present value is found, in other words, by capitalizing expected cash flows.

Our example shows that the more remote the date in the future at which the income is expected, the less its present value; $3,000 due in three years, for example, has a lower present value than $3,000 due in one year. Again when we leave aside any question of uncertainty, simple arithmetic tells us that if we lend the sum of $2,727 for a period of one year at a rate of interest of 10 percent, we will get back $3,000 which includes the original sum and interest. This being the case, no one would be willing to pay more than $2,727 for an asset that would yield a total return of $3,000 one year hence. By the same reasoning, if we lend $2,479 for a period of two years at a rate of interest of 10 percent, we will get back $3,000, for $2,479 compounded at a rate of 10 percent for two years equals $3,000. Thus, no one would be willing to pay more than $2,479 for an asset that yields a total return of $3,000 two years hence. The same reasoning applies to the third sum in our series, namely $2,254 if it is made available as a loan for a three-year period at the rate of 10 percent.

The foregoing example underscores the fact that the more remote in the future is the expected income, the less is its present value. It is also true that the higher the rate of interest used to determine present value, the lower will be the present value of the expected income stream. If, for example, we had used a 15 percent interest rate to determine the present value of the income stream of $3,000 spread over three years, the result would be

$$V_p = \frac{\$3,000}{(1.15)} + \frac{\$3,000}{(1.15)^2} + \frac{\$3,000}{(1.15)^3}.$$

Clearing fractions, we get

$$V_p = \$2,609 + \$2,272 + \$1,974 = \$6,856.$$

Earlier it was pointed out that any expected income stream rests on an extremely precarious foundation, which introduces a high degree of volatility into the investment decision. It should also be noted at this point that interest rates also are volatile, as is shown in Figure 8–1. This figure traces since 1978 the behavior of three key rates, namely the rate for high-grade corporate bonds (a long-term rate), the rate on Treasury bills (a short-term rate), and the Federal Reserve discount rate (the rate at which the Federal Reserve lends to commercial banks and also a short-term rate). As the figure shows, interest rates generally rise during a boom and fall during a recession. As will be recalled from our discussion in Chapter 1, the economy experienced recessions in 1980, 1981–82, and 1990–91, and these downturns were preceded by substantial increases in each of these interest rates.

The Marginal Efficiency of Capital

Let us now return to the concept of the marginal efficiency of capital. Examination of the discount process shows that there has to be some rate of discount that will make the present value of prospective returns from a capital good equal to its supply price. This is the rate that Keynes calls the marginal efficiency of capital, which we shall designate by r. Let us now modify the foregoing discount formula by substituting the current supply price of the capital instrument K_s for present value V_p and also by substituting the marginal efficiency of capital r for the current rate of interest i. The formula now appears as

$$K_s = \frac{R_1}{(1 + r)} + \frac{R_2}{(1 + r)^2} + \cdots + \frac{R_n}{(1 + r)^n}. \qquad (8-2)$$

The expected income stream (or series of R's) is the same as in Equation (8–1). The current supply price K_s is a known value in contrast to the unknown present value V_p in the earlier equation. In the above formulation the unknown

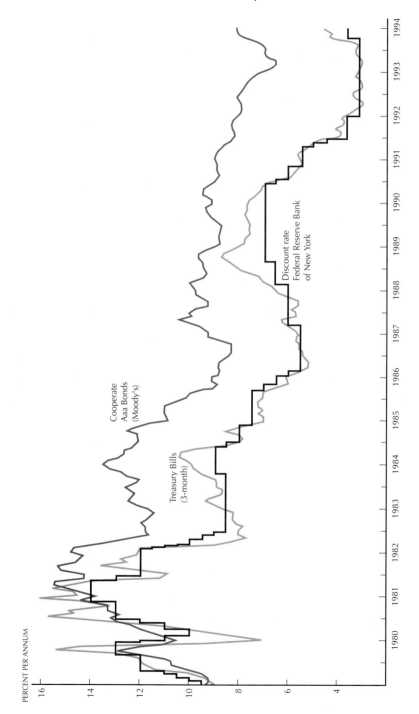

is the marginal efficiency of capital r, or discount rate, which will make the present value of the expected income stream $R_1, R_2, \ldots, R_n$ equal to the supply price K_s. The equation must be solved for the unknown r.

As long as the computed value of the marginal efficiency of capital is positive, we know that the capital asset in question will yield some rate of return. This means the income stream expected from the use of the capital asset is at least large enough to cover the supply price. But the current supply price of the asset represents only a part of the cost of acquiring an added unit of capital. In addition to the supply price, there is the financial cost that arises from the use of money funds in the acquisition of the asset. Since this cost element is measured by the current rate of interest, we can compare it directly with the marginal efficiency of capital; both are rate phenomena.

If such a comparison is made and we find that the marginal efficiency of capital is greater than the current rate of interest, the situation is favorable to investment. The income stream expected from the use of an additional unit of capital exceeds *all* the costs of acquiring the capital. Consequently, the capital instrument will be purchased. An entrepreneur may, in practice, require a substantial margin of safety between the rate of interest and the marginal efficiency of capital before investment is actually undertaken. Of course, an entrepreneur could use resources to purchase a financial asset rather than an item of capital equipment and presumably will do so whenever the marginal efficiency of capital falls below the current rate of interest.

The idea that, other things being equal, investment expenditure will take place whenever the marginal efficiency of capital is greater than the current rate of interest is the key element in the theory of investment. It is the formal, theoretical expression of the view that profitability is the dominant factor in the investment decision. Unless the prospects are such that the expected yield of a new item of capital exceeds its supply price plus financial cost, it will not be purchased by the business firm. When we say that the marginal efficiency of capital r is greater than the rate of interest i, we are also saying the the present value V_p of the capital asset (which is obtained by discounting its expected income at the current rate of interest) is greater than its supply price K_s.

Keynes's Investment Demand Schedule (Curve)

The foregoing discussion brings together the key elements involved in decisions at the firm level to increase the use of capital goods relative to other resources. In *The General Theory* Keynes said it is possible (in principle) to build up a schedule for each type of capital, showing how much its marginal

FIGURE 8–1   (left)   Key Interest Rates, 1979–1994.   Interest rates are not only volatile, but in general they rise and fall together, even though there is a spread between the various types of rates.

Sources: *Current Economic Indicators,* February 1995; and *Economic Report of the President,* 1995.

efficiency will fall as investment in it is increased within a given period. Further, he went on to say, "We can then aggregate these schedules for all the different types of capital, so as to provide a schedule relating the *rate* of aggregate investment to the corresponding marginal efficiency of capital in general which that rate of investment will establish. We shall call this the investment demand schedule. . . ." He continued, ". . . the rate of investment will be pushed to the point on the investment demand schedule where the marginal efficiency of capital in general is equal to the market rate of interest."[8]

Figure 8–2 depicts an investment demand curve as visualized by Keynes in his classic book. In design, it is quite similar to the classical demand for savings for investment curve developed in Chapter 3 (page 85), although Keynes ties investment spending directly to the expected profitability of new capital as reflected in his concept of the marginal efficiency of capital.

In algebraic terms the relationship embodied in investment demand is given by the equation

$$I = I_0 - ci, \qquad\qquad (8–3)$$

where I_0 is investment expenditure that will take place at zero rate of interest and c is the coefficient relating investment expenditure to the rate of interest. The fact that c has a negative value reflects the inverse correlation between investment and the rate of interest, which is to say that the greater the value of i, the smaller will be the value of I.

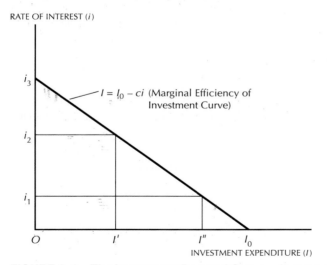

FIGURE 8–2   The Investment Demand Curve.   Investment spending varies inversely with the rate of interest; it falls when the latter goes up, and rises when the latter goes down.

---

[8] Ibid., pp. 156, 157. Keynes is using the word "schedule" as we have been using the word "curve."

At this point the student should note carefully the similarity of our treatment of investment expenditure with our earlier analysis of consumption expenditure. Compare, for example, Equation (8–3) with Equation (7–3). What this means, essentially, is that at this point, investment is made a function of a single variable, namely, the rate of interest. This does not mean, however, that other variables are not also important as determinants of the aggregate level of the investment demand function. This procedure is identical to what we followed in the analysis of the consumption function and is a standard analytical technique in economics.

Shifts in the Keynesian Investment Demand Schedule (Curve)

As with any demand curve, the investment demand curve depicted in Figure 8–2 is subject to either upward or downward shifts. These shifts are to be explained in terms of the fundamental determinants that lie behind the schedule. To clarify this, let us refer once again to Equations (8–1) and (8–2). They serve to underscore the two major sources of a shift in the investment demand curve. When we speak of a shift in a demand curve, it means that there will be more or less of the variable shown on the horizontal axis associated with any specific value for the variable shown on the vertical axis. In the case of investment demand, it means more investment spending for a given rate of interest if the demand curve shifts upward and less if it shifts downward.

The two major sources of a shift in the curve are a change in the expected yield of capital [the R series in Equations (8–1) and (8–2)] and a shift in the supply curve for capital goods. Suppose there is a sharp decrease in expected yields for new capital (the R series in the equations), resulting from a wave of pessimism sweeping over the business community. In terms of Equation (8–1) this would reduce the present value of any capital asset a firm contemplated acquiring if we assume no change in market rates of interest, and in terms of Equation (8–2) it would reduce the marginal efficiency for that type of capital. But since it assumed that interest rates are unchanged, this latter change would cause the marginal efficiency of investment curve [the investment demand curve (Figure 8–1)] to shift to the left. Similar results would follow from a shift in the supply curve for newly produced capital goods. A shift in the supply curve means that the schedule of prices for all possible quantities of capital the capital goods industry can produce will change, either upward or downward. If the supply curve shifts upward, it means in terms of Equation (8–2) a rise in the value of K_s, the current supply price. But with no change in the expected income stream (the series of R's), the marginal efficiency of capital must decline. This is tantamount to a shift to the left of the investment demand curve. At any given rate of interest, there will be less investment.

This, then, is the formal model of investment spending as developed originally in Keynes's *The General Theory*. But the abstract, formal model does not capture the full spirit of how Keynes thought about investment spending. What really counts is the volatility of the investment demand curve: it is highly unstable, depending on expectations of the yield to be derived from capital goods whose useful life may stretch far into an uncertain future. As was pointed out earlier, Keynes believed that the basis of the knowledge on which business executives form their expectations of prospective yields is extremely precarious, subject to sudden and unforeseen changes as the climate of business opinions fluctuates. The world is little different today in this respect than it was when Keynes wrote in the 1930s. In *The General Theory* Keynes devoted an entire chapter to this theme,[9] a chapter in which he reminds us that "human decisions affecting the future, whether personal or political or economic, cannot depend upon strict mathematical expectation, since the basis for making such calculations does not exist; and that it is our innate urge to activity which makes the wheels go round, our rational selves choosing between the alternatives as best we are able, calculating when we can, but often falling back for our motive on whim or sentiment or chance."[10] Developing a curve in which we link investment spending to a single variable like the rate of interest is a highly useful analytical technique, but we must not allow our preoccupation with the technique itself to cause us to lose sight of the more fundamental economic forces at work in any economic situation. Often the latter are not readily reduced to a quantitative, functional relationship.

The Shape of the Keynesian Investment Demand Schedule (Curve)

Even though the Keynesian investment demand curve may be subject to frequent and unpredictable shifts, economists are also interested in its shape. Technically, this is a matter of the *interest elasticity* of investment expenditure, by which we mean the responsiveness of aggregate investment expenditure to a change in the rate of interest. Specifically, the interest elasticity of investment demand, which we shall designate as e_i, is equal to the ratio of a percentage change in investment expenditure to a percentage change in the rate of interest. In algebraic terms the interest elasticity of the investment demand schedule is given by

$$e_i = \frac{\Delta I / I}{\Delta i / i} = \frac{\Delta I}{I} \times \frac{i}{\Delta i} = \frac{\Delta I i}{I \Delta i}. \tag{8–4}$$

An investment demand function that is relatively *elastic* will have a coefficient of elasticity whose absolute value is greater than 1, whereas an investment demand curve that is relatively *inelastic* will have a coefficient of elasticity whose absolute value is less than 1.

The question of how investment spending responds to a change in the rate

---

[9] Ibid., Chap. 12, "The State of Long-Term Expectation," pp. 147–164.
[10] Ibid., p. 162.

of interest is an important one, especially for policy purposes. Monetary policy, for example, works through changes in the money supply which, in turn, may affect the rate of interest. Whether investment spending responds to such changes is, therefore, an important policy consideration. Basically, two sets of circumstances determine how responsive investment spending may be to changes in the rate of interest, one of which is external to the business firm and the other internal. Let us examine these, again using Equations (8–1) and (8–2) as our frame of reference. We shall assume a decline in interest rates.

A decline in interest rates, *ceteris paribus,* should favor more investment spending because after the decline the marginal efficiency of capital momentarily becomes greater than the rate of interest. A decline in interest rates also increases the present value (V_p) of any capital asset that the firm contemplates purchasing [Equation (8–1)]. Thus, investment spending should increase, but how much investment spending actually increases depends in part on a factor external to the business firm. This is the shape of the supply curve for the production of new capital. As more new capital is produced, the supply price (K_s) normally rises also. But as Equation (8–2) shows, a rise in the supply price (K_s) will, *ceteris paribus,* cause the marginal efficiency of capital (r) to fall. This is where the elasticity of the supply function for capital goods becomes crucial. The more *elastic* this function, the more the production of capital assets can be increased without sharp rises in their prices; therefore, the more investment spending can respond to any given decline in the rate of interest. On the other hand, if the supply function for capital goods is *inelastic,* then any increase in demand for such goods will cause their prices to move up sharply and so limit the effectiveness of a decline in interest rates on investment spending. In sum, elasticity in the supply function for capital assets makes for elasticity in investment demand, and inelasticity in the supply function for capital assets makes for inelasticity in the demand for capital.

The other factor that governs the elasticity of the investment demand function is essentially internal in that it pertains to the physical life of the capital asset that the firm contemplates purchasing. The effect of physical life on investment spending can readily be seen by examining the variables in Equation (8–1). The longer the physical life of a unit of capital, the smaller will be the expected net return on the asset in any single year (R_1 in the equation, for example). But the smaller the net return in a single year, the more pronounced is the impact on present value (and hence the marginal efficiency of capital) of a given change in the rate of interest. It follows from this that the more durable the capital asset—that is, the longer its expected physical life— the more sensitive investment spending for that type of asset will be to changes in the rate of interest. The less durable the asset, the less will be the response of investment spending to any change in the rate of interest.

The practical import of the foregoing is that business structures and residential constructions, since they are relatively long-lived, are most likely to be sensitive to changes in the rate of interest. Equipment is normally less long-lived than structures, and inventories are the least durable of all forms of business investment. Thus it follows that the demand for structures—both business and residential—should be more elastic than the demand for either equipment or inventories. Undoubtedly, the latter are the least sensitive to interest rate variations of any of the forms of investment spending.

Thus, we have the argument, but what of the reality? Does investment spending, in other words, actually respond significantly to changes in the rate of interest? Unlike statistical findings with respect to the income-consumption relationship, the results of empirical research in this area have not been either fruitful or conclusive. An early and classic British study that took the form of asking business executives about the influence of the rate of interest on their investment decisions found that, in general, changes in short-term interest rates did not directly affect either inventory or other forms of investment. But there was some indication that, in the manufacturing industry in particular, investment in equipment and structures was influenced by changes in the long-term rate of interest.[11] The latter is usually measured by the rate on corporate bonds of high quality. An early U.S. study, for example, found an interest elasticity coefficient for investments in plant and equipment equal to 0.65. This means that for 1 percentage change in the rate of interest as measured by the rate on long-term bonds, investment spending would change by 0.65 percent. More recent studies have found investment elasticities to be even lower. One such study computed the interest elasticity of investment in equipment spending for the entire economy to be 0.36, which again means that a 1 percent change in the rate of interest would lead to a 0.36 percent change in investment spending. A series of studies made in the 1960s and early 1970s found that, in general, a 1 percent change in the yield on long-term corporate bonds changed fixed business investment between 1/4 to 1/2 percent.[12] The data in Table 8–2 show that investment in equipment and structures is even less sensitive to changes in the real prime rate. The elasticity coefficient for these data is 0.13 percent; this means that a 1 percent change in the real prime rate causes only a 0.13 percent change in equipment spending.

Housing may be the most sensitive of all forms of investment spending to changes in the rate of interest. Table 8–3 rearranges the data from Table 8–2 to show linkages between nominal mortgage rates and housing starts for five different periods between 1970 and 1993. The periods are not of the same length, but represent years in which the nominal mortgage rates—actual rates not adjusted for inflation—were either moving upward or downward. What these data show is that through 1989 housing starts and interest rates moved

[11] T. Wilson and P. W. S. Andrews, eds., *Oxford Studies in the Price Mechanism* [London: Oxford University Press (Clarendon), 1951], pp. 27 ff.

[12] Edwin Kuh and John R. Meyer, ''Investment, Liquidity, and Monetary Policy,'' in *Impacts of Monetary Policy,* Commission on Money and Credit (Englewood Cliffs, N.J.: Prentice-Hall, 1963), p. 381; Charles W. Bischoff, ''Business Investment in the 1970s: A Comparison of Models,'' *Brookings Papers on Economic Activity.* Vol. 1 (Washington, D.C.: Brookings Institution, 1971), p. 30. See especially S. J. Nickell, *The Investment Decisions of Firms* (London: Cambridge University Press, 1978), p. 299.

TABLE 8–2 Interest Rates and Investment Activity: 1970–1994

Year		Nominal Prime Rate	Real Prime Rate*	Fixed Investment (in billions)†	Nominal Mortgage Rate	Real Mortgage Rate*	Housing Starts (in thousands)
	1970	7.91%	2.21%	$292.0	8.45%	2.75%	1,469
	1971	5.72	1.32	286.8	7.74	3.34	2,085
	1972	5.25	2.15	311.6	7.60	4.40	2,379
Recession	1973	8.03	1.83	357.4	7.96	1.76	2,058
	1974	10.81	−0.97	356.5	8.92	−7.08	1,353
	1975	7.86	−1.24	316.8	9.00	−0.10	1,171
	1976	6.84	1.04	328.7	9.00	3.20	1,548
	1977	6.83	0.33	364.3	9.02	2.52	2,002
	1978	9.06	1.46	412.9	9.56	1.96	2,036
	1979	12.67	1.37	448.8	10.78	−0.42	1,760
	1980	15.27	1.77	437.8	12.66	−0.84	1,292
Recessions	1981	18.87	8.57	455.0	14.70	4.40	1,084
	1982	14.86	8.66	433.9	15.14	8.94	1,062
	1983	10.79	7.59	420.8	12.57	9.37	1,703
	1984	12.04	7.74	490.2	12.38	8.08	1,750
	1985	9.93	6.33	521.8	11.55	7.95	1,742
	1986	8.33	6.43	500.3	10.17	8.27	1,805
	1987	8.21	4.61	497.8	9.31	5.71	1,621
	1988	9.32	5.22	530.8	9.19	5.09	1,488
	1989	10.87	6.07	540.0	10.13	5.33	1,376
	1990	10.01	4.61	546.5	10.05	4.65	1,193
Recession	1991	8.46	4.26	515.4	9.32	5.12	1,014
	1992	6.25	3.25	525.9	8.24	5.24	1,200
	1993	6.00	3.00	591.6	7.20	4.20	1,288
	1994	7.15	4.55	672.4	7.49	4.79	1,455

*Nominal rate minus inflation rate (CPI).

†In 1987 dollars.

Source: *Economic Report of the President*, 1995, pp. 276, 336, 346, 358.

in opposite directions, but that after the 1970s housing starts became much less sensitive to changes in interest rates than previously. From 1990 through 1994 housing starts on the average did not respond favorably to a decline in mortgage rates. This was due in part to the 1990–91 recession, when housing starts dropped by 26.3 percent in two years, and due as well to other factors, such as population trends. The baby-boomer bulge in the population was moving beyond the home-buying stage. Nominal rather than real mortgage rates are used in these comparisons because consumers probably pay more attention to the former. This is because in home buying what counts is the monthly payment a family will have to make in relation to its income. It is the nominal rate that directly affects the size of the monthly mortgage payment. Concern and uncertainty about inflation led to the development of adjustable rate mortgages for home financing in the early 1980s. These permit annual adjustments in interest rates on long-term home loans in accordance with fluctuations in short-term interest rates. This will presumably minimize

TABLE 8–3   Nominal Mortgage Rates and Housing Starts: 1970–1993

Period	Average Annual Percentage Change in Nominal Interest Rates	Average Annual Percentage Change in Housing Starts
1. 1970–1972	− 5.1%	+28.0%
2. 1973–1979	+ 7.3	−56.0
Includes Recovery from 1973–74 Recession		
3. 1980–1989	− 7.8	+ 8.0
Includes 1980 and 1981–82 Recessions		
4. 1989	+10.2	− 7.5
5. 1990–1994	− 6.0	− 5.3
Includes 1990–91 Recession		

Source: Table 8–2.

the impact of inflation on home financing. The majority of home mortgages are still of the standard, fixed interest rate type.

The foregoing studies and comments are useful in that they point to the fact that the sensitivity (i.e., elasticity) of investment spending to changes in interest rates increases the more long-lived the type of investment, as with housing. But they are limited because they simply do not reflect fully the unprecedented rise in interest rates that has taken place since the mid-1960s. Between 1965 and 1981, for example, the rate of interest on long-term corporate bonds of the highest quality (AAA) rose by 222.0 percent, whereas the rate of interest on prime commercial paper—a good measure of the cost of short-term borrowing by business firms—rose by 271.8 percent. These sharp increases came following a period of relative stability in interest rates, both for the short and the long terms. From 1945 through 1964, the long-term corporate bond rate (AAA) averaged 3.40 percent, while the yearly average on prime commercial paper for the same years was 2.44 percent. By 1994, however, the corporate bond rate dropped to 7.97 percent, a 45.8 percent decline from its 1981 high of 14.17 percent. Commercial paper rates followed, dropping to 4.93 percent by 1993, a 76.6 percent decline from their 1981 postwar peak of 14.76 percent.[13]

No dramatic and wholly clear-cut conclusion follows from these data, but it does appear that housing is sensitive to nominal as well as real rates, at least more so than investment spending for equipment and structures. It is possible, too, that business executives are more sensitive than home buyers to real as compared with nominal changes. Perhaps the soundest conclusion is that rising interest rates, both nominal and real, will ultimately choke off investment spending, but the degree of sensitivity (i.e., elasticity) of investment spending to interest rate changes remains uncertain.

---

[13] *Economic Report of the President,* 1995, p. 358.

Current Income and Investment Expenditure

Although the central idea in the standard Keynesian theory of investment is the inverse relationship between investment expenditure and the rate of interest, economists also argue that *income* is a major determinant of investment expenditure. This approach involves *induced* investment, which we shall designate as I_i. In algebraic terms, $I_i = f(Y)$; this means that investment outlays will increase as income increases. The income measure appropriate to this relationship is the net national product.[14]

In Equation (8–3), it was stated that $I = I_0 - ci$. Let us designate $I_0 - ci$ as I_0' and define it as all investment expenditure that is autonomous with respect to the income level. We can then postulate the identity

$$I = I_0' + I_i. \tag{8–5}$$

This equation simply states that total investment consists of the two major categories of autonomous and induced investment. Since the latter is a direct function of income, we can transform Equation (8–5) into

$$I = I_0' + bY_{np}. \tag{8–6}$$

In the above expression b is the *marginal propensity to invest,* which we may define algebraically as

$$b = \frac{\Delta I_i}{\Delta Y_{np}}. \tag{8–7}$$

The student will note that we defined the marginal propensity to invest in a fashion analogous to the marginal propensity to consume and the marginal propensity to save, namely, as the ratio of a change in investment to a change in income (net national product). The marginal propensity to invest concept implies that some portion of any increased income will be directed toward investment expenditure, an outcome of the assumption that current investment expenditure is linked functionally to the current income level. The marginal propensity to invest also measures the slope of the curve that relates induced investment to income. A curve of this type is displayed in Figure 8–3. Net national product is measured on the horizontal axis and investment on the vertical axis. Because investment is an increasing function of income, the curve slopes upward to the right. The level at which the curve intersects the vertical axis equals I_0', investment which is independent of the income level.

---

[14] Net national product Y_{np} and disposable income Y_d remain equal because we are still assuming that neither taxes nor transfer payments are present in the system.

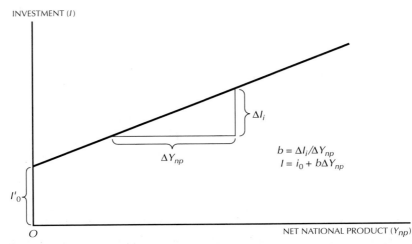

INVESTMENT (I)

ΔI_i

ΔY_{np}

$b = \Delta I_i / \Delta Y_{np}$
$I = i_0 + b\Delta Y_{np}$

I'_0

O

NET NATIONAL PRODUCT (Y_{np})

FIGURE 8–3 Investment and the Income Level.   Investment spending varies directly with the income level; it rises as the latter rises and falls as income falls.

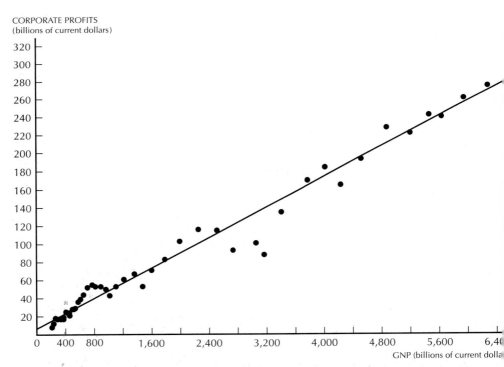

CORPORATE PROFITS
(billions of current dollars)

GNP (billions of current dollar

FIGURE 8–4 Corporate Profits after Taxes and Gross National Product 1946–1994.   Since the GNP is strongly influenced by investment spending and since investment spending depends on expected profits, it follows that there is a strong correlation between corporate profits after taxes and the GNP.

Sources: Economic Report of the President, 1991, 1995; and Current Economic Indicators, February 1995.

The assumptions embodied in this relationship are, first, that investment depends on profitability and, second, that profitability is directly linked to the current income level. There is a sound empirical basis for the second assumption, as is demonstrated in Figure 8–4. The figure contains a scatter diagram showing a close correlation between the level of the nation's gross national product and corporate profits after taxes for the period 1946 through 1993. GNP is used because the series for GNP extends back to 1946 and earlier. As the level of the GNP rose, there were parallel increases in the level of corporate profits. The latter are a good proxy for all profits in the economy. In *The General Theory* Keynes explained that, in general, there is a strong tendency within the business community to assume that the existing state of affairs will continue, *unless* there is a specific reason to expect a change. This, Keynes said, constitutes a kind of convention that enables business executives to cope with the reality that their knowledge of the factors that govern the prospective yield on a new investment "is usually very slight and often negligible."[15] Consequently, if current net profits have been favorable, expectations for future profits will be favorable, and we can expect investment expenditure to rise *in response to a rising income level*. This, of course, is an oversimplification of a complex relationship. But the proposition that investment is a direct function of income enables us not only to deal with the phenomenon of induced investment in a direct way, but also to incorporate investment expenditure into the equilibrium income determination process and the theory of the multiplier far more readily than when we consider investment expenditure as a function of the rate of interest.

The Marginal Propensity to Invest and Equilibrium Income

Let us examine how the concept of the marginal propensity to invest may be incorporated into our formal equilibrium diagram. In Figure 8–5 the 45° line *OZ* again represents the aggregate supply function; the line labeled *C* is the consumption function. The basic difference between this figure and Figure 7–4 (page 226) is that the aggregate demand curve does not lie parallel to the consumption function; investment expenditure is not autonomous with respect to the income level, but increases as the income level increases. We construct the aggregate demand curve by adding an investment function of the kind shown in Figure 8–3 to the consumption function. Equilibrium is attained at the point of intersection of the aggregate demand and aggregate supply curves. However, because we have included induced investment, the equilibrium level is higher than otherwise would be the case.

This can be seen clearly by contrasting an aggregate demand curve, constructed with an autonomous investment function, with the aggregate demand curve constructed with a function involving induced investment. In Figure

[15] Keynes, *The General Theory,* p. 149.

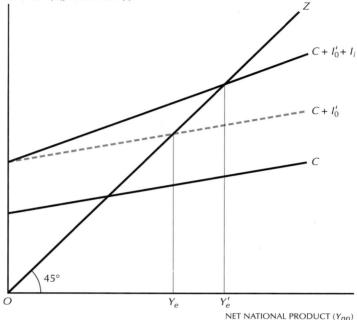

CONSUMPTION (C), INVESTMENT (I)

NET NATIONAL PRODUCT (Y_{np})

FIGURE 8–5 Induced Investment and Aggregate Demand. Once induced investment expenditure is introduced into the analysis, total investment spending will rise as the income level rises—a development which will raise the equilibrium income level above what it would have been in the absence of induced investment spending.

8–5 the dashed line $C + I_0'$ is an aggregate demand curve of the former type, whereas curve $C + I_0' + I_i$ on the other hand incorporates the phenomenon of induced investment. $C + I_0' + I_i$ intersects the aggregate supply curve at a higher income level than $C + I_0'$, and it should be noted that the slope of $C + I_0' + I_i$ is equal to the sum of the marginal propensity to consume and the marginal propensity to invest. The sum of these two marginal propensities can be defined as the *marginal propensity to spend,* a concept particularly relevant to multiplier analysis because, as was shown earlier, the value of the multiplier depends on the amount of additional spending that is *induced* by an exogenous change in spending.

Induced Investment Expenditure and the Multiplier

Let us explore how induced investment expenditure may be incorporated into multiplier theory. To facilitate the exposition, we shall break the investment component of the aggregate demand schedule into two subcategories: autonomous investment, which we have already designated as I_0' in Figure 8–5, and induced investment, represented symbolically by I_i. We assume that investment and consumption are the only expenditure categories and that changes in the income level are initiated as the result of shifts in the autonomous investment function. Given these basic assumptions, we can postulate the following two definitional equations:

$$Y_{np} = I_0' + I_i + C, \tag{8–8}$$

$$k' = \frac{\Delta Y_{np}}{\Delta I_0'}. \tag{8–9}$$

Equation (8–8) is the basic identity equation, which states that income (net national product) is equal to the sum of consumption and investment, except that investment is broken down into its two subcategories. Equation (8–9) is the basic definition of the multiplier k, except that in this instance we are using the symbol k' to indicate the multiplier because we incorporate into it the phenomenon of induced investment.

From Equation (8–8) we get the following identity pertaining to a change in the income level:

$$\Delta Y_{np} = \Delta I_0' + \Delta I_i + \Delta C. \tag{8–10}$$

Since the change in induced investment expenditure ΔI_i depends on the value of the marginal propensity to invest b and since the change in consumption expenditure depends on the value of the marginal propensity to consume a, we have

$$\Delta I_i = b \times \Delta Y_{np} \tag{8–11}$$

and

$$\Delta C = a \times \Delta Y_{np}.\text{[16]} \tag{8–12}$$

If we substitute the above values for ΔI_i and ΔC in Equation 8–10, we have

$$\Delta Y_{np} = \Delta I_0' + b\Delta Y_{np} + a\Delta Y_{np}. \tag{8–13}$$

This equation can be manipulated algebraically as follows:

[16] $\Delta Y_{np} = \Delta Y_d$ when taxes and transfers are zero.

$$\Delta Y_{np} - a\Delta Y_{np} - b\Delta Y_{np} = \Delta I_0', \tag{8-14}$$

$$\Delta Y_{np}(1 - a - b) = \Delta I_0', \tag{8-15}$$

$$\Delta Y_{np} = \Delta I_0' \times \frac{1}{1 - a + b}, \tag{8-16}$$

$$\frac{\Delta Y_{np}}{\Delta I_0'} = \frac{1}{1 - (a + b)}. \tag{8-17}$$

Thus, we can define k', the effective multiplier, as the reciprocal of 1 minus the marginal propensity to consume and the marginal propensity to invest. A quick examination of the algebra shows that by introducing an additional kind of induced spending, induced investment spending, into our analysis, we will get a larger ultimate increase in spending for an initial exogenous increase in spending. As a parenthetical note, k' is sometimes called the *supermultiplier*.

In the foregoing discussion we assumed a constant value for the marginal propensity to invest b, which in turn enables us to compute an exact value for the multiplier k'. Reality is not so accommodating. It is most unlikely that the marginal propensity to invest will have a constant value for any significant length of time. This particular approach to induced investment rests on the assumption that current profits are sufficient to engender favorable expectations with respect to the profitability of additional capital equipment. If the current profit picture is not satisfactory, however, there is no reason to believe that any amount of investment expenditure will be induced by the current income level. Thus, there is no real assurance that the value of the marginal propensity to invest will remain stable, and, for that matter, there is no positive assurance that it will remain above zero.

Investment and the *IS-LM* Model

Investment spending, as we learned in Chapter 6, is a crucial element in the construction of the *IS* curve, the curve which depicts equilibrium in the goods sphere for various values of the rate of interest (i) and the level of income (Y). We do not need at this point to repeat the steps by which the *IS* curve is constructed, although it should be reviewed (see pages 178–80 and Figure 6–1). What we need to know now is how the matters we have just been discussing affect the model. Specifically, these are the elasticity of the investment demand schedule and induced investment.

Consider first the question of elasticity, that is, the sensitivity of investment spending to changes in the rate of interest. If investment spending is *inelastic* with respect to the rate of interest, then the investment demand function (Figure 8–2) is depicted with a steep slope. If investment spending is thought to be interest-elastic, then the function is depicted with a more gradual slope. The significance of elasticity is that it governs how much investment spending will change given a change in the rate of interest. With a given value for the multiplier, the greater the change in investment spending, the greater the change in the equilibrium income level. Therefore, an *inelastic* investment demand schedule means a much steeper slope for the *IS* curve. The *LM* curve is not affected by the elasticity of the investment demand function. If the latter function is thought to be *elastic,* then the slope of the *IS* curve will be much more gradual. To summarize: a steep slope for the *IS* curve depicts a system in which it is not easy to influence output (Y) by changing the rate of interest. The less steep the slope for the *IS* curve, however, the easier it is to change output through changes in the rate of interest.

What of induced investment? Here the story is slightly different for there are not two alternative and opposing possibilities. Given *any* value for the multiplier, the effect of induced investment is *always* to increase the impact on income (Y) resulting from a change in investment brought about by a change in the rate of interest. The higher the value of the marginal propensity to invest (b), the greater is this effect. As far as the *IS* curve is concerned, the existence of induced investment will reduce the slope of the curve—make it less steep—irrespective of the inelasticity or elasticity of investment demand.

The Acceleration Principle

A much more complex analysis of the phenomenon of induced investment is based on the *acceleration principle*. In its original formulation, the principle asserted that net investment is a function of the *rate of change* in final output rather than of the absolute level of output. This is an important distinction. The concept of the acceleration principle was developed in 1917 by Professor John Maurice Clark in a renowned article, ''Business Acceleration and the Law of Demand: A Technical Factor in Economic Cycles.''[17] Clark set out to show, first, that a special and technical relationship exists between the demand for a final product and the demand for the capital equipment necessary to produce the final product and, second, that this technical relationship is of such a character that it can be employed to explain not only the nature of the demand for new capital instruments, but also why the demand for capital fluctuates much more violently than the demand for final goods. Since the publication of Clark's historic article, many economists have analyzed and refined this principle and used it to explain the apparent cyclical nature of much economic activity.

In our discussion of the acceleration principle we shall use the income symbol Y to designate *output of final goods and services* and the symbol K to designate *capital stock.* The technical relationship existing between a given

---

[17] Reprinted in *Readings in Business Cycle Theory* [New York: McGraw-Hill (Blakiston), 1944].

level of output and the quantity of capital necessary to produce that output is the *capital-output ratio*. We shall designate this ratio by the capital letter A.

$$A = \frac{K}{Y}. \tag{8–18}$$

If we assume no change in the technical conditions under which resources are combined in order to obtain a given output, it is reasonable to assume that an increase in output once full capacity has been achieved will require additional capital equipment in the proportion indicated by the capital-output ratio. For example, if we find that, on the average, it requires capital equipment in the amount of $3 for each $1 of output, then, as long as there is no change in the technical conditions under which capital is combined with other resources in the productive process, every $1 increase in output above the level of existing capacity will require $3 worth of additional capital equipment. Formally, we may say that, given constant technical conditions of production, the marginal capital-output ratio will equal the average capital-output ratio. When the average and the marginal capital-output ratios are equal,

$$A = \frac{K}{Y} = \frac{\Delta K}{\Delta Y}. \tag{8–19}$$

By definition, though, the change in the capital stock ΔK is the same thing as net investment in the economy I_n. Substituting I_n for ΔK in the algebraic formula and transposing ΔY to the left-hand side of the expression, we have

$$A = \frac{I_n}{\Delta Y}, \tag{8–20}$$

$$I_n = A \times \Delta Y. \tag{8–21}$$

Equation (8–21) is the formal algebraic expression of the acceleration principle. It tells us that there exists some coefficient A which, when multiplied by the change in output, will yield the required net investment expenditure. To put the matter the other way around, we can say that, if output is to increase by an amount equal to ΔY, then additional capital equipment in the amount I_n is required. This is necessary because, as can readily be seen from the formula, the larger the absolute change in output, the larger the amount of induced investment, if we assume that initially capacity was fully utilized.

If we set this analysis within a time sequence, it is relatively easy to see why the acceleration principle makes induced investment expenditure a function of the *rate* at which output is increasing (or decreasing). Net investment in the current income period (designated by the symbol t) is equal to the difference between the capital stock of the current period, K_t, and the capital stock of the previous period, K_{t-1}. Thus,

$$I_t = K_t - K_{t-1}. \tag{8-22}$$

The change in income in the current period, ΔY_t, is equal to the difference between current income Y_t and the income of the previous period, Y_{t-1}. Therefore, we have

$$\Delta Y_t = Y_t - Y_{t-1}. \tag{8-23}$$

The rate at which income (or output) changes between one period and the next is measured by the ratio of ΔY_t to Y_{t-1}. For example, if income in constant dollars rose by \$45 billion between the present and the past income periods and if Y_{t-1} was \$900 billion, then the rate of income increase, $\Delta Y_t / Y_{t-1}$, will be 5 percent. The importance of this is that the rate of change in income depends on the absolute change in income in a period relative to the income level of the previous period. The larger the absolute change relative to income of the previous period, the larger will be the rate of change. But the acceleration formula, Equation (8-21), shows that, given a fixed technical relationship between capital and output, the amount of induced investment will vary directly with the size of the absolute change in output. Consequently, the acceleration principle means that *induced net investment is a function of the rate of change of final output.*

A Practial Use for the Acceleration Principle

The acceleration principle helps to explain a phenomenon long observed by economists, namely, that the output of capital instruments fluctuates much more violently than the output of goods in general. The exaggerated impact of an increase (or decrease) in demand for final output on the demand for capital goods can be illustrated by means of a simple arithmetical example. Let us imagine a hypothetical industry whose output of final goods is 100 units per income period (see Table 8–4). The capital-output ratio for this industry is assumed to be 3, which means 300 units of capital are required to produce this output. These units of capital have an average economic life of 10 income periods, so the normal replacement demand for capital equipment

TABLE 8–4 The Acceleration Effect and the Demand for Capital

Income Period	Capital Stock	Output	Replacement Demand	Demand for New Capital	Total Demand for Capital
1	300.0	100.0	30.0	0.0	30.0
2	330.0	110.0*	30.0	30.0	60.0
3	346.5	115.5†	30.0	16.5	46.5
n‡	346.5	115.5	34.6	0.0	34.6

*A 10 percent increase in final demand.
†A 5 percent increase in final demand.
‡When capital added in periods 2 and 3 begins to be replaced.

is 30 units per income period. Let us now see what will happen if, first, there is a 10 percent increase in demand for the final product. A 10 percent increase in demand will mean the production of 10 additional units of final product per income period. But if the industry is operating at its capacity level prior to this increase in demand, then the production of 10 additional units of final product per income period will require 30 additional units of capital. Now if this increase in demand of 10 percent for the final product is presumed to take place within the confines of a single income period, the demand for capital goods will increase by 100 percent in this same income period. The reason for this is that the 30 units of capital needed to provide an additional 10 units of output are added to the normal replacement demand of 30 units; this makes a 100 percent increase in demand for capital goods in period 2.

Let us go on to period 3, in which the demand for final output is still rising, but at a slower pace than earlier. In this period the increase in final demand is 5 percent. Assuming that the capital stock was adjusted upward in the prior period to reflect the change in final demand, what happens now? Since demand has increased once again, more capital is needed, but not as much as in the previous period. Net investment will again increase, but the absolute amount will be less than in period 2. Thus, we find that the *total* demand for capital will be smaller than previously. This is because the *rate* of increase in final demand between periods 2 and 3 has slowed down. Total investment will rise to a peak and then fall back to a level determined wholly by replacement needs. Net investment will rise from zero to a peak and then fall back eventually to zero.

Our hypothetical example demonstrates the most important single fact about the acceleration principle: There will be induced investment expenditure only so long as final demand is increasing. Once the latter stabilizes at a new and higher level, induced investment expenditure will cease. Expressed in formal terms, the absolute level of induced net investment will enlarge as long as final demand is increasing at an increasing rate; once the rate of increase of final demand begins to slow down, the absolute level of induced net investment will decline. The reader should also note that the more durable the capital instrument, the greater will be the fluctuation in the demand for capital instruments relative to the demand for final output. If, in our hypothetical example, the capital units had an average economic life of 20 rather than 10 income periods, a 10 percent increase in demand for final output would have brought about a 200 percent increase in demand for capital instruments (15 replacement units plus 30 additional units of capital). This would be true as long as the capital-output ratio remained equal to 3.

Limitations of the Acceleration Principle

The acceleration principle of the foregoing analysis is sometimes described as the *simple* accelerator. Although it is useful in explaining the cyclical and sharp fluctuations in capital goods spending, the accelerator model that relates new investment spending to changes in the rate of output is subject to several important limitations. For one thing, most economists recognize that the acceleration principle is too mechanical to serve as an explanation of such a complex phenomenon as the investment process in a modern economy. One criticism is that the acceleration principle has little or no motivational content. The entrepreneur is presumed to act as a thermostat, note when capacity is overtaxed and then take the necessary steps to overcome this deficiency. A more serious criticism concerns the matter of productive capacity. In a strict sense, the acceleration principle is effective only when an industry or the economy as a whole is operating at a level of full utilization of existing capacity. Since the principle is based on a technical relationship between capital and output, it follows that additional capital will not be required to make possible additional output unless existing productive capacity is being fully utilized. If surplus capacity exists in the economy, the principle breaks down because added output can be supplied from the untapped capacity. This has led some economists to conclude that, insofar as business cycle analysis is concerned, the principle may operate during the upswing (when rising demand eventually presses hard against existing capacity), but not in the downswing or depression phase of the cycle (when excess and idle capacity are the most common features of the economy).

A related objection concerns the sticky matter of the definition of capacity. There is little, if anything, in the voluminous literature that has grown up around the acceleration principle that attempts to define precisely the meaning of such terms as "capacity" and "surplus capacity." In a literal sense, the acceleration principle asserts that net investment is induced, or more capital is created, because output has risen. Because of the technical relationship between capital and output fundamental to the acceleration principle, additional output can be forthcoming only if the stock of capital has already been increased. This is the dilemma that faces us if we interpret both the acceleration principle and its underlying assumption of full-capacity production quite literally. The only way out of this dilemma is to interpret the notion of capacity somewhat freely and suggest that at some point the entrepreneur will reach the conclusion that existing facilities will be overtaxed if there is an attempt to provide for an expected demand without expansion.

The Flexible Accelerator Hypothesis

The foregoing problem has led to the development of a less restrictive, a more relaxed, version of the accelerator, called the *flexible accelerator hypothesis.* Simply put, this version of the accelerator links investment spending to a gap between the desired capital stock and the actual capital stock, but recognizes that it is unlikely that this gap will be wholly closed in a single income period. As one analyst phrased it:

> In a situation of short capacity a tendency of plant expansion may be expected. But an immediate full adjustment is neither technically necessary nor considered possible or advisable from an economic point of view. There may be checks from the side of

finance or the lumpiness of capital goods. Moreover, the high level of output may be expected to be temporary, in which case a "wait and see" policy will be followed.[18]

In equation form, the flexible accelerator hypothesis is

$$I_n = \alpha(K^* - K_{t-1}), \tag{8-24}$$

where the coefficient α represents the proportion of the gap between the desired capital stock (K^*) and the capital stock of the past income period (K_{t-1}) that can be closed in the current income period. Thus, it reflects the point stressed above, namely, that it is neither likely nor particularly desirable that net investment in a single income period increase by the full amount of the shortfall in the desired stock of capital. What the flexible accelerator hypothesis suggests is that the adjustment process involved, when there is a change in demand that requires more capital goods, will be spread over a number of income periods. There is still an accelerator effect, but there is also a lagged response of investment to the change in output.

Theory and Reality

From the foregoing discussion of investment three variables emerge as prime determinants of investment spending in the economy. They are, first, the rate of interest; second, the level of income; and third, the quantity of capital required to produce a particular level of ouput. The most basic idea, of course, is that investment spending is undertaken in the expectation of profit and that such expectations are always tied to an elusive and unknown future. Formal investment theory attempts to cut through the difficulties involved in dealing with the uncertainties that surround expectations and tie investment spending to variables that are observable and measurable. The basic question, then, is which approach has the greatest validity?

In spite of the enormous and growing volume of economic literature that embodies empirical investigations into the determinants of investment spending, no definitive answer to this question has emerged.[19] As we found true in the case of different hypotheses about consumption spending, there are elements of value in each of the foregoing approaches to the complex problem of investment behavior. The empirical evidence now available offers support

---

[18] L. M. Koyck, *Distributed Lags and Investment Analysis* (Amsterdam: North-Holland, 1954), p. 63.

[19] For a recent survey of this literature, see Dale W. Jorgenson, "Econometric Studies of Investment Behavior: A Survey," *Journal of Economic Literature,* December 1971, pp. 1111–1147. In the bibliography which is a part of this survey, 109 articles and books dealing with the investment question are listed. For a more recent econometric study of investment spending, see S. J. Nickell, *The Investment Decisions of Firms* (London: Cambridge University Press, 1978). See also Ben Bernanke, "The Determinants of Investment: Another Look," *American Economic Review, Papers and Proceedings,* May 1983.

for the ideas discussed in this chapter. In these studies real output emerges as the most important single determinant of investment expenditure. This ties in with the analysis of induced investment spending. In the 1970s studies of manufacturing industries found a 1 percent change in output led to a 1.5 to 2.0 percent change in investment spending within a two-year period.[20]

The relationship may be stronger than these figures suggest. For the 34 years from 1960 through 1994, analysis of the changes in real output (GDP) and changes in nonresidential investment (producer's equipment and structures) shows that investment responds to all changes in output, but that the response is stronger when changes in the rate of output are increasing compared to when they are declining. During this period (1960 to 1994), there were 18 years in which the rate at which output changed rose compared to the prior year and 17 years in which the rate dropped. In the years in which the output rate increased, a 1 *percentage point* change in real GDP led to a 4.1 *percentage point* change in nonresidential investment within two years. Most of the increase in investment spending—72 percent—came in the same year that output rose. In the 17 years in which the rate of change for output dropped compared to the prior year, a 1 *percentage point* decline in real GDP led to a 2.1 *percentage point* drop in nonresidential investment spending within two years. Again, most of the decline—75 percent—came in the year the rate of output fell.[21]

As we saw earlier in this chapter, even though there is no agreement on the precise value for the coefficient of elasticity for investment spending in relation to the rate of interest, in practically every empirical study in which the interest rate was included as a variable, interest was found to be of some significance, especially for investment spending in capital that is long-lived. Evidence on the validity of the accelerator is at best mixed; some studies find support for such a relationship and others reject it. In general, however, empirical studies support the flexible rather than the simple version of the accelerator principle. Although it is encouraging that empirical research (to date) tends to support the basic ideas about the determinants of investment spending that emerged from *The General Theory,* it is unlikely that even the most painstaking econometric research will uncover the definitive investment function. The reason is rooted in the uncertainty and precariousness that surround *all* efforts to gauge the income stream that a new item of capital will yield. This is unlikely to change, no matter how sophisticated our econometric techniques.

---

[20] Michael K. Evans, *Macroeconomic Activity: Theory, Forecasting, and Control* (New York: Harper & Row, 1969), p. 138. See also Peter K. Clark, "Investment in the 1970s: Theory, Performance, and Prediction," *Brookings Papers on Economic Activity,* Vol. 1 (Washington, D.C.: Brookings Institution, 1979), p. 103.

[21] *Economic Report of the President,* 1995, p. 277. Note that these findings apply to changes in the *rate* at which output and investment change in any one period compared to the prior period. A decline in the rate of change for output does not mean output has fallen. In the 17 years during the period 1960 to 1994 in which the rate of change for real GDP dropped, there were only six years (1970, 1974, 1975, 1980, 1982, and 1991) in which the fall in the rate of change for output was negative, indicating an actual decline in real GDP, not just a decline in its rate of change.

Financing Investment

Investment spending, as we have seen, is an unstable component in the structure of aggregate demand in a market economy, basically because of the uncertainty that surrounds estimating the present value of an expected income stream. This is the essence of the contemporary view of investment. The instability may be exaggerated by how a business firm finances its acquisition of new capital assets: this makes it important to pay careful attention to the financing side of the investment decision, a topic to which we now turn.

Earlier it was pointed out that there are basically three ways firms can get the money needed to purchase new capital assets. These are (1) retaining earnings (the internal cash flow of the firm), (2) selling shares in the firm (equity financing), and (3) borrowing (issuing bonds or other forms of debt). Although the first two means of investment finance are not in any sense problem free, the funds obtained through borrowing are of major significance in linking finance to the volatility of investment spending. Thus, we shall concentrate most of our analysis on this type of finance. Some idea of the magnitude of debt financing is found in the fact that in 1993 net new security issues of all types of U.S. corporations totaled $764.5 billion, of which $641.5 billion (or 83.9 percent) were either bonds or short-term notes (promises to pay).[22]

Financial Instruments and Real Capital Assets

Professor Hyman Minsky, formerly of Washington University and a leader in the Post Keynesian perspective, suggests that it is necessary to adopt a Wall Street point of view if we are to understand fully the crucial role that finance plays in investment behavior.[23] By suggesting such a point of view, he means that we are dealing not only with a monetary economy with highly sophisticated financial institutions, but one in which money and debts are the key instruments through which ownership or control of *real* capital assets is acquired. Thus, the instruments of finance (including money) become in their own right a powerful factor in the investment equation, especially because a market system attaches values, that is prices, to such instruments just as it does to real capital assets as well as goods and services in general. Keynes

---

[22] *Federal Reserve Bulletin,* February 1995, p. A-34. This does not measure the amount of debt financing for new capital assets, as it includes borrowings for all purposes by corporations, not just the acquisition of new physical capital.

[23] Hyman P. Minsky, *John Maynard Keynes* (New York: Columbia University Press, 1975), p. 73. This section draws heavily on Professor Minsky's analysis of the role of debt finance in the investment decison. See also his *Stabilizing an Unstable Economy* (New Haven, Conn.: Yale University Press, 1986) for a complete discussion of his ''financial instability hypothesis'' by means of which he seeks to explain the behavior of modern market economies.

described this intermingling of money, the instruments of finance, and real capital as follows:

> There is a multitude of real assets in the world which constitute our capital wealth—buildings, stocks of commodities, goods in the course of manufacture and of transport, and so forth. The nominal owners of these assets, however, have not infrequently borrowed *money* in order to become possessed of them. To a corresponding extent the actual owners of wealth have claims, not on real assets, but on money. A considerable part of the ''financing'' takes place through the banking system, which interposes its guarantee between its depositors who lend it money, and its borrowing customers to whom it loans money wherewith to finance the purchase of real assets. The interposition of this *veil of money* [italics added] between the real asset and the wealth owner is a specially marked characteristic of the modern world.[24]

Keynes wrote that in 1931. If anything, it describes more accurately the contemporary paper world of money and finance than it did the conditions when first set into print.

What happens when a firm borrows to finance the purchase of real capital?[25] Basically by issuing debts (bonds), the firm gets the cash necessary to buy the desired capital asset. By issuing bonds, the firm creates for itself a contractual obligation not only to repay the sum borrowed at some future data, but to meet periodically the interest payments on the debt. The firm, in other words, obligates itself to a flow of cash payments which stretch into the future for the lifetime of the debt. Over and against this cash outflow commitment the firm must balance the expected cash inflow that stems from the assets purchased with the proceeds of the loan. Professor Minsky says that the fundamental speculative decision of a business firm centers on how much of the firm's income from normal operations can be pledged to pay the interest and principal on the liabilities incurred in order to acquire income-producing (capital) assets.[26] The firm, in adding to its liability structure, is ''betting that the ruling situation at the future dates (when payments come due) will be such that the cash commitments can be met; it is estimating that the odds in an uncertain future are favorable.''[27]

Pricing Financial Assets

To understand how the firm makes this fundamental speculative decision, we must look again at the discount (capitalization) process. As we saw earlier, the investment decision in its most basic sense involves comparing the present

[24] John Maynard Keynes, ''The Consequence to the Banks of the Collapse of Money Values,'' in *Essays in Persuasion* (New York: Norton, 1963), p. 169.

[25] The analysis to follow applies primarily to investment in long-term capital—plant and equipment. Inventories are normally turned over in a very short time; hence, immediate sales prospects are the key factor in the investment-in-inventories decisions.

[26] Minsky, *John Maynard Keynes,* p. 86.

[27] Ibid., p. 87.

value of the expected income stream produced by a capital asset with its supply price. When we introduce a contractual cash flow commitment into the picture, the comparison has to be between the present value of the expected income stream and the present value of the contractual cash flow. The latter covers both the supply price of the capital—what the firm has to pay for a newly produced unit—and the interest charges on the borrowed money.

Present value, let us recall, is determined by capitalizing a payments flow at *some* rate of interest. Unless a firm experiences a complete financial collapse, its long-term obligations (bonds) are secure because they are contractual. Thus, the present value for the debts issued by a firm normally would be found by discounting their contractual cash flows at the prevailing market rate of interest.[28] If the world were free of risk and the future not characterized by uncertainty, the same capitalization (of discount) rate could be applied to the stream of income expected from the capital assets whose purchase is being contemplated. Then it would be necessary only to compare two present values: if present value for the expected income stream were greater than present value for the cash flow commitment from a newly issued debt, then the investment decision could be positive.

But the world is not like this. Risk is present and the future is uncertain. This means that much greater certainty attaches to income derived from a contractual cash commitment such as a bond provides than to income derived from a newly produced item of capital. But the less certain the future income stream, the less its present value. Since greater uncertainty (and risk) attaches to the prospective yield on capital, a higher rate of discount must be used to determine its present value as compared with the going rate for money loans. The difference between these two rates must reflect the state of uncertainty existing at any particular time. The key question thus becomes: What determines this uncertainty?

In *The General Theory* Keynes dealt with this question by distinguishing between two types of risk: borrower's risk and lender's risk. As Keynes phrased it:

> Two types of risk affect the volume of investment which have not commonly been distinguished, but which it is important to distinguish. The first is entrepreneur's or borrower's risk and arises out of doubts in his own mind as to the probability of his actually earning the prospective yield for which he hopes. If a man is venturing his own money, this is the only risk which is relevant.
>
> But where a system of borrowing and lending exists, by which I mean the granting of loans with a margin of real or personal security, a second type of risk is relevant which we may call the lender's risk. This may be due to either a moral hazard, i.e., voluntary default or other means of escape, possibly lawful, from the fulfillment of the obligation; or the possible insufficiency of the margin of security, i.e., involuntary default due to the disappointment of expectation.[29]

---

[28] This would also be the rate of interest that the bond pays, since the decision or comparison being discussed is made when new debt is being issued.

[29] Keynes, *The General Theory,* p. 144.

Borrower's risk is essentially subjective; it exists primarily in the mind of the borrower and never appears explicitly in a contract. Lender's risk, on the other hand, is objective and shows up in various ways in financial contracts—higher interest rates, shorter terms to maturity, or pledges of specific assets as collateral for loans.[30] Borrower's risk is the key to the difference between the discount rate appropriate to a firm's debt structure and the rate used to determine present value for uncertain yields from new capital assets. Borrower's risk, in other words, is the focal point through which uncertainty makes itself felt.

Basically, the process works as follows. As a firm increases the proportion of new capital assets financed by debt relative to either internal funds or equities, the firm's basic financial position becomes increasingly risky. The reason is simply that it finds itself in a situation in which the cash flow obligations it must meet grow because of its debt structure, while the prospective yields become less and less certain as the firm continues to acquire new capital assets. Thus, the discount rate used to determine the present value of expected yields must rise to reflect the increasing uncertainty that follows from a rise in the ratio of debt to other forms of financing. But this means, of course, that the demand price for new capital will decline as uncertainty increases.[31] As the demand price for capital (the present value of the expected yield) falls, the less favorable are the prospects for continued investment spending, particularly since normally the supply price for new capital assets is positive. Since borrower's risk is highly subjective, it may increase quite suddenly and thus cause a collapse in the demand price for capital, followed by a sharp drop in investment spending.

Boom Conditions, Asset Values, and Investment Spending

Boom conditions may provide a setting for this sequence of events. A factor that strongly influences borrower's risk is the past performance of the economy. Thus, in the early stages of a boom, when the economy is picking up steam, borrower's risk is likely to be low; furthermore, the debt-financing ratio may be low. In a boom period, past estimates of the prospective yield for capital assets may turn out to have been too low—actual yields are higher than anticipated. This leads to capital gains—increases in the value of the firm and the firm's assets because of the higher-than-anticipated earnings on newly acquired assets. As a consequence, both borrower's and lender's risks are reduced—a development which pushes the firm further into debt financing. As the boom proceeds, firms become more and more willing to resort to debt financing. Boom conditions lead to a layering of debt, which means using actual or anticipated capital gains as a source of more borrowing power. But as this process continues, the firm's cash commitments due to its liabilities

---

[30] Minsky, *John Maynard Keynes,* p. 110.
[31] Ibid., p. 109.

Speculation versus Enterprise

In Chapter 21 in his 1936 classic, *The General Theory of Employment, Interest and Money,* John Maynard Keynes spoke of the difference between enterprise and speculation. It is a distinction as important today as then. Perhaps even more so.

Enterprise, according to Keynes, is economic activity that ultimately leads to the creation of new, real wealth. Building a factory, adding onto an existing plant, developing a new product are examples of enterprise. Enterprise adds to our real standard of life because it makes more things available for everyone.

Speculation, on the other hand, refers to economic activity that looks to increases in the monetary value of things that already exist. Buying land or shares of stock in anticipation of an increase in their value are speculative activities.

Speculative activity, which is both widespread and legal, adds to the financial wealth of individuals. But it does not add to the real wealth of a nation. That real wealth is a nation's stock of productive capital, which can be used to produce the goods and services that we actually consume.

What concerned Keynes in his 1936 excursion into the distinction between enterprise and speculation was the relationship of the stock market to these two vastly different types of economic activity. This relationship, Keynes felt, was crucial to understanding the behavior of the capitalistic system.

What the stock market does is make it easy for any person or other entity such as a bank, an insurance company, or pension fund to buy or sell ownership rights in corporate business. And like the market for many goods, the prices paid for the stock being bought and sold fluctuates, sometimes quite widely.

In principle, our highly organized securities markets ought to promote enterprise. Firms wishing to build a new plant, expand their facilities, or develop a new product can sell new shares and thereby get the needed money.

Unfortunately—and this is what disturbed Keynes—most buying and selling of stocks on the great exchanges does not take place in the furtherance of enterprise. Rather, the bulk of buying and selling is undertaken in anticipation of changes in the value, that is the prices, of shares that already exist. This activity is purely speculative.

When people want to get rich in a hurry, speculative activity crowds out enterprise; the result is such spectacles as the great "bull" market of the late 1920s. Buyers seeking instant wealth frantically outbid each other and push prices ever higher. A collapse of stock value, like the one in 1929, can be anticipated because no growth in real wealth undergirds the boom. It is all paper.

We have witnessed a dramatic plunge in stock value in our own time. On October 19, 1987, prices on the New York Stock Exchange dropped 508 points, a one-day record that translated into a 22 percent drop in overall value. In one sense, the modern-day collapse was worse than in 1929; the speedy transfer of data today meant near-simultaneous drops in other major financial markets. But in another sense, October 19 proved that the 1987 economic climate could (probably) withstand such a shock.

Nevertheless, speculation is cause for concern. "When the capital development of a country," Keynes said in a masterpiece of understatement, "becomes the by-product of the activities of a casino, the job is likely to be ill-done."

(debts) may begin to mount faster than the income the firm gets from its operations and assets it may own. In terms of the factors that enter into the investment decision, the cash flow commitments from newly issued debt begin to outpace the proceeds expected from the capital assets financed by the debt. The optimism of the boom often leads a firm to overcommit itself to debt financing; this results in a situation in which its cash payment obligations exceed cash receipts flowing in from current operations. If the firm gets itself into this situation, both borrower's risk and lender's risk will rise sharply, especially borrower's risk. The consequence is a drastic fall in the demand price for new capital relative to its supply price, followed by a collapse in investment spending. With the latter, the boom will also collapse. A process of debt deflation may follow, a period in which firms attempt to scale down their debt structure, using whatever internal funds they can muster to service existing debts. They will try and reduce their cash flow commitments by replacing short-term debt with long-term debt as the former matures, a process called refunding. It does not reduce the total debt-based cash commitments of the firm, but it can reduce the size of the more immediate, short-term cash obligations confronting the firm. During the debt deflation process borrower's risk remains high—a development which keeps investment spending for new capital low and the economy in a depressed condition.[32]

---

[32] The U.S. economy has not experienced a serious debt-deflation-induced depression since the 1930s, but Professor Minsky believes that the economy has come close on at least five occasions in recent years—in 1966, 1970–71, 1974–75, 1979–80, and 1981–82. In each of these periods trouble developed in the financial sector of the economy because too many leading financial institutions had used short-term debt to finance their holdings of longer-term assets, which could not be readily sold to meet short-term cash commitments. They engaged, in other words, in speculative finance, expecting to be able continuously to renew ("roll over" is the term the financial community uses) short-term debt as it came due. When this proved difficult, they found themselves in deep trouble. What saved the economy from going through the wringer of a full-blown debt inflation and the ensuing depression was the high level of government spending, which sustained incomes, and the willingness of the Federal Reserve System to provide the funds necessary to prevent collapse in the financial system. In the late summer of 1990 the economy was perilously close to a debt-induced recession, or even depression, given the enormous growth in both private and public debt during the 1980s. Once again, because of timely action by the Fed, the 1990–91 recession did not become a debt-deflation-induced depression. See Hyman P. Minsky, "Financial Markets and Instability, 1965–1980," *Nebraska Journal of Economics and Business,* Autumn 1981, pp. 5–16; "How 'Standard' Is Standard Economics?" *Society,* March–April 1977, pp. 24–29; and *Stabilizing an Unstable Economy,* Chaps. 2–4, pp. 13–98.

The Supply Curve for Finance

Before we look briefly at some other factors that may influence the business firm's investment decision, some comments are in order on how firms typically view the costs of alternative forms of finance. The prior discussion centered around debt finance, primarily because this particular type of financing plays a crucial role in the volatility of investment spending. But firms also finance new capital assets from retained earnings and from issuing additional shares of the stock of the firm. The explicit or implicit cost of funds obtained from the three possible sources of finance is an important factor in the investment decision. For the typical firm contemplating the purchase of real capital assets, the supply curve for finance appears as shown in Figure 8–6.

Essentially, the supply schedule for finance has three segments, each of which relates to a different source of finance. In the figure the first segment (designated A) is retained earnings. There is no lender's risk involved in getting funds from this source, and if we assume that borrower's risk is a constant, then the rate appropriate for funds from this source is the interest rate forgone by not lending (i.e., purchasing securities) the retained earnings. Thus, this segment of the curve is perfectly elastic (horizontal) at the current rate for outstanding long-term debts (i.e., bonds). The next segment (designated B) represents funds obtained by borrowing. This portion of the curve slopes upward to the right, reflecting the fact that, as the firm borrows more, the cost of borrowing will rise. This is primarily due to lender's risk, since this will get larger the more heavily indebted the firm becomes. Finally, there is a range in which the firm will resort to equity financing; this is to say it

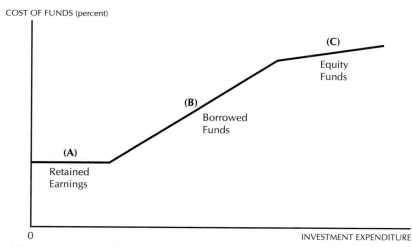

FIGURE 8–6 The Supply Curve for Finance. In a general way the supply curve for finance for investment spending has a positive slope as is true for supply curves in general, but the level and slope of the curve vary with the source of the financing.

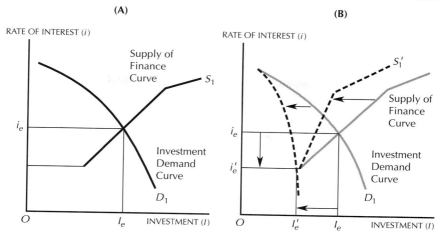

FIGURE 8–7   Investment Demand and the Supply of Finance Curves. An increase in borrower's risk may cause the demand for funds for investment to collapse (a shift to the left in the investment demand curve), whereas an increase in lender's risk may cause the supply curve for external finance to shift upward.

will issue new ownership shares to obtain the money needed to finance investment outlays (segment C in Figure 8–6). This type of financing is generally regarded as more costly than borrowing, even though there is no obligation to pay out dividends to the shareholders. The reason for this is the differential treatment under the income tax laws for interest and dividend payments. Interest is a deductible expense in computing the tax liability of a business corporation, whereas dividends are not. The equity portion of the finance curve also slopes upward. This is because if a firm issues new shares, the increased supply of its stock may depress the market price of shares outstanding and thus cause their yields to rise.[33]

If we bring together the supply curve for finance shown in Figure 8–6 and the investment demand curve developed earlier (Figure 8–4), we can show how the interaction between the marginal efficiency of capital and the cost of finance determines the rate of investment. This is done in Figure 8–7, part A. We can also use this diagram to show the impact of a change in both borrower's and lender's risks on the rate of investment. This we find in part B of Figure 8–7. In this part of the figure the original demand and supply curves shift to the positions indicated by the dashed curves in the diagram. The investment demand schedule collapses because of a rise in borrower's risk. The impact of increased lender's risk is shown by an upward shift in the supply of funds curve. The resulting outcome—investment outlays decline to I_e'—is one in which investment spending is limited by the amount of internal

---

[33] The foregoing analysis of the supply schedule for finance is drawn primarily from the approach found in Evans, *Macroeconomic Activity*, pp. 86 ff.

finance available, because firms hesitate to resort to debt financing of capital
outlays until they have reorganized and scaled down their debt structure.

Other Influences on the Investment Decision

Within the basic analytical framework of the capital and investment demand
curves, other determinants of investment are treated as parametric factors
whose basic role is to determine the positions of these curves. Changes in the
value of any of these factors cause a shift in their positions or slopes. As was
true with the consumption function, many of these factors are subjective and
hence not capable of exact quantitative measurement. We can, however, summarize here the way in which three major variables other than interest and
income may affect investment spending, even though the way in which these
factors are linked to investment cannot be reduced to a precise mathematical
formula. The variables are government, technology, and market structure.

The Role of Government

There has been an enormous expansion in the role and influence of the public
sector in this century, a development that could not help but have far-reaching
repercussions on the investment decision and the level of investment expenditure. Government units purchase an important part of the final output of
goods and services in the economy, and, as we have seen, demand for final
output has a direct effect on investment outlays.

Probably the most important influence that public activity has on investment expenditure operates through taxes and the tax laws. The marginal efficiency of capital is concerned with the profitability of additional amounts
of capital to the business enterprise, so it is to be expected that the business
executive or entrepreneur would be acutely aware of the influence of taxation
on the expected rate of return on capital assets. Investment expenditure depends on the expected rate of return over cost, and it can thus be presumed
that taxes, because they lower the expected returns, will lower investment
expenditures.

Specifically, two techniques have been used by the federal government in
recent years to influence investment spending in the economy. These are
accelerated depreciation accounting and the investment tax credit. We shall
examine each of these briefly.

Accelerated depreciation is an administrative technique that permits a firm
to depreciate a capital asset at a more rapid pace than usual. Since the Internal
Revenue Service allows business firms to treat depreciation as an expense of
doing business, acceleration will reduce the taxable income of the firm during
the earlier years of the asset's life. Overall, taxes should not be changed, only
deferred. But this will have two advantages for the firm. First, it will get for
a time the use of money that would otherwise go to the government. Second,

reduced taxes in the early years of the asset's life will increase its present value during those years, because its net after-tax income will be higher. Later, of course, the net after-tax income will go down, but since a dollar of expected income in the near future is worth more than a dollar due in the more distant future, the present value of the asset should be greater.

The investment tax credit as a device to stimulate investment spending was first introduced in 1962 by the Kennedy administration. An investment tax credit allows a firm to deduct a certain percentage of its investment outlays from its income tax liability. What this does, in effect, is to lower the supply price for a new item of capital and thereby raise its effective marginal efficiency [the r of Equation (8–2)]. When first introduced the tax credit was 7 percent. The investment tax credit was suspended in 1966, put back into effect in 1967, terminated by the Tax Reform Act of 1969, and reinstated again in 1971. In the spring of 1975 the rate was raised to 10 percent as part of a tax package designed to bring the economy out of the 1974–75 slump. It remained at this level until eliminated entirely in 1986 by the Tax Reform Act. Evidence is mixed on the effectiveness of the investment tax credit as a stimulus to investment.

The Role of Technology

Among the possible factors that enter into the investment process, many economists would rate changing technology near the top in terms of influence and importance. This is true even though technology is a concept that cannot be measured with precision. Moreover, there is much obscurity in economic analysis with respect to the specific manner in which the investment decision is affected by technology.

Technology as a concept deals with the productive process; the usual definition of *technological change* is a change involving a shift in the production function. The production function involves the technical relationship between inputs of economic resources, in the form of land, labor, and capital, and the output of product. Any particular combination of economic resources will embody a particular level of technology, and a change in technology means either more product from the same quantity and combination of resources or else the same amount of product with a smaller quantity of resources. The critical question is: how does technological change affect the demand for capital instruments? The traditional view is that technological change is highly favorable to investment spending. Some would argue that because capital goods are the physical embodiment of new production techniques, the latter cannot be introduced without at the same time creating more capital. It is also maintained that the adoption of techniques that shift the production function requires that the ratio of capital to other resources be increased and that technological change render existing capital goods obsolete. Both of these tendencies, if present in the economy, would link the demand for capital very closely to the rate of technological change.

Although many economists would agree that technological change is an important factor in the investment decision, there are reasons to doubt that the relationship between technological change and the investment decision is as simple and as direct as suggested by the traditional view. Howard R. Bowen, for example, questioned the view that technological change will require more capital relative to other resources and that technologically induced obsolescence will increase the demand for capital.[34] Does technological change raise the capital-output ratio? If it does, then clearly technological change will increase the demand for capital. But, as Bowen pointed out, many innovations of a technological character are capital-saving in the sense that they reduce the capital-output ratio. If technological change tends to be capital-saving rather than capital-using, its effects on the demand for capital may be reduced.[35] Bowen also argued that a rapid rate of technological change may be inimical to a high level of investment expenditure because it increases the risk of obsolescence. If technological change makes existing capital obsolete, it may create a demand for new capital. But because obsolescence raises the element of risk in all investments, the entrepreneur may demand higher rates of return from prospective capital investments than otherwise would be the case. Thus, it is entirely possible that technological change can inhibit, as well as spur, investment expenditure.

The Role of Market Structure

The term "market structure" is used in reference to the kind and degree of competition characteristic of the industrial environment within which the firm functions. Traditionally, economists have argued that a competitive economic environment is highly conducive to both economic progress and a high rate of investment expenditure. This view rests on the assumption that, since business firms seek to maximize profits, a major way of achieving this objective is to reduce production costs. In an environment of rigorous competition, firms will be forced, if they are to survive, to seize every opportunity for the introduction and exploitation of cost-reducing techniques. Since this requires investment, it follows that a competitive market structure is favorable to a high level of investment activity.

Other economists maintain that monopoly may be just as conducive to innovation as competition, technological change, and a high rate of investment expenditure. The ability, for example, of a firm to invest successfully depends to a large degree on its entrepreneurial and managerial capacity and

---

[34] Howard R. Bowen, "Technological Change and Aggregate Demand," *American Economic Review,* December 1954.

[35] If the amount of capital required per unit of output is reduced, it does not necessarily follow that the demand for capital has been reduced. A reduction in the capital-output ratio means that the productivity of capital has been increased, and this may lead to an increase in the demand for capital. On this point see especially the article by Robert Eisner, "Technological Change and Aggregate Demand," *American Economic Review,* March 1956. See also John La Tourette, "Sources of Variations in the Capital-Output Ratio in the United States Private Business Sector, 1909–1959," *Kylos,* Fasc. 4, 1965.

its financial power. If this is true, the monopolistic firm will be better off than the typical small firm in a highly competitive industry; the small firm will have neither the ability to attract outstanding entrepreneurial talent nor the financial power to undertake the investment that is often necessary for the introduction of new techniques. It can be argued that only financially powerful firms, found in industries characterized by monopoly and oligopoly, can afford to underwrite the extensive, formalized research that is the necessary precursor to new developments in production and products in a world of rapid technological change.

We can best sum up this discussion of market structure and investment by pointing out that the traditional view that an economy dominated by the competition of many small units is most conducive to economic progress is not particularly appropriate in a world in which research and technological change have become dominant factors in the competitive position of the firm. Competition remains necessary and desirable, but it is a different type of competition than that envisaged in the model of a purely competitive market economy. It is, rather, the competition of a relatively few large economic units with the ability and power to bring together the human talent and other resources necessary for performing the increasingly specialized functions of research and introduction of the fruits of research into the economic process.

A Summary View

We have sought in this chapter to examine and analyze the most important things that contemporary economic theory has to say about the determinants of investment expenditure. The investment decision remains one of the most involved problems relating to the operations of the modern economy, chiefly because the factors that enter into it are more varied and less predictable than, say, those that enter into the consumption-saving decision. In the area of consumption theory the economist has at least the solid fact of income on which to build an analysis; no matter what other influences may be involved, it is impossible to ignore or overlook the dominant role that income plays as a determinant of consumption expenditure. In investment theory, however, there is no such prime determinant to provide a foundation for analysis. In the early days of Keynesian analysis, economists believed that the rate of interest could occupy the same role in investment theory that income occupies in consumption theory, but research into the mechanics of the investment decision has tended to undermine faith in this view. Modern investment theory is cast in the framework of the investment demand schedules. But, at best, this approach is a device to organize our thinking, a means of getting started, not a complete theory that adequately explains the fluctuating phenomenon of investment. Many of the more important determinants are to be found in the area that we have labeled "other influences," and the major difficulty here is not that their existence and importance go unrecognized, but that they are highly subjective. Most of the time these other determinants cannot be measured quantitatively, and there is no easy way to assess their relative impacts on the level of investment expenditure.

Summary

1. Investment is a key determinant of the income level and a major source of instability in the economy. It is volatile because it depends on uncertain expectations about the future.

2. The investment decision involves weighing the expected gains from the acquisition of more capital (structures and equipment) by the firm against the costs of acquiring the capital, including the finance costs.

3. The marginal efficiency of capital is basic to the formal theory of investment and is a percentage measure of the rate of return over cost expected from new investment. It is compared with the rate of interest to determine whether the investment should be made.

4. The expected rate of return on capital can be expressed as a schedule, called the "investment demand schedule," showing how the rate of return declines as the volume of investment output is increased. This schedule is subject to sudden and unforeseen shifts because of changes in expectations with respect to the expected profitability of new capital.

5. Investment expenditure may be linked to income as well as to the rate of interest. This is done through the concept of the *marginal* propensity to invest and the accelerator. Both concepts add to the theoretical understanding of the investment process.

6. In addition to the income level, another key factor in the determination of investment spending is the source of finance. Financing may be a source of instability, particularly when it involves debt financing.

7. Investment is also influenced by many other factors, including government policy, technology, and the kinds of markets in which the business firms operate.

9 Public Expenditures, Taxes, and Finance

IN THIS CHAPTER our focus is on how government expenditures, taxes, and other sources of finance for government activities affect the economy's aggregate demand. Government purchases of goods and services exert a direct influence on the level of the aggregate demand because they are a part of the demand for final output; government transfer expenditures and taxes exert an indirect influence because their impact is on the nongovernmental components of the function, consumption and investment.

Government Purchases of Goods and Services and the Income Level

To show how the purchase of goods and services by government units enters into the structure of aggregate demand, let us again make use of data pertaining to a hypothetical economy, as was done in Chapter 7 (pages 224–27). These data for our hypothetical economy are shown in Table 9–1. Our economy is still closed, which is to say it has no economic ties with any other nation, but now we have assumed that there are three, rather than merely two, categories of output (or expenditure): consumption C, investment I, and government G. The consumption function is given in column 2 and shows the intended consumption expenditures at income levels ranging from $0 to

TABLE 9–1   A Closed Economy with Three Categories of Output (in billions of constant 1987 dollars)

(1) Net National Product Y_{np}	(2) Consumption C	(3) Investment I	(4) Government Expenditures G	(5) Aggregate Demand C + I + G
$ 0	$1,150	$200	$810	$2,160
4,500	3,400	650	810	4,860
4,600	3,450	660	810	4,920
4,700	3,500	670	810	4,980
4,800	3,550	680	810	5,040
4,900	3,600	690	810	5,100
5,000	3,650	700	810	5,160
5,100	3,700	710	810	5,220
5,200	3,750	720	810	5,280
5,300	3,800	730	810	5,340
5,400	3,850	740	810	5,400
5,500	3,900	750	810	5,460
5,600	3,950	760	810	5,520
5,700	4,000	770	810	5,580
5,800	4,050	780	810	5,640
5,900	4,100	790	810	5,700
6,000	4,150	800	810	5,760

$6,000 billion. The marginal propensity to consume of this schedule is 0.5, or 1/2. Investment expenditure, shown in column 3, includes both autonomous and induced investment outlays. The marginal propensity to invest is 0.1, or 1/10. Government purchases of goods and services are shown in column 4. For the sake of analytical simplicity we assume that government expenditures are autonomous with respect to the income level. Although it is likely that government expenditures increase as income increases, the nature of any such relationship is not known exactly.

Once we have assumed values for the investment function and autonomous government expenditures, the aggregate demand curve is obtained by adding these to the consumption function, the position and slope of which are given by the parameters C_0, consumption at zero income, and a, the marginal propensity to consume. The parameters for the investment function are I_0', investment expenditure that is autonomous with respect to the income level, and b, the marginal propensity to invest. The results of this addition are given in column 5, which now shows the aggregate demand schedule, $C + I + G$.

This is shown graphically in Figure 9–1. The aggregate demand schedule, $C + I + G$, or DD, is derived by adding to the consumption function the appropriate values for investment and government expenditures. The process of income determination that results from the construction of an aggregate demand curve that includes government expenditures is identical to the process discussed in earlier chapters. Equilibrium income is at the point of in-

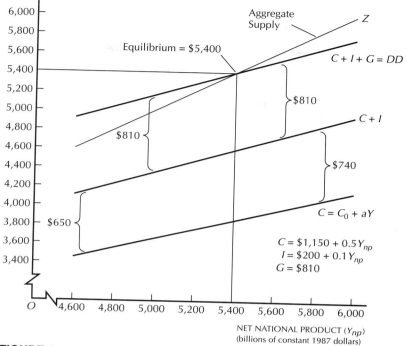

CONSUMPTION (C), INVESTMENT (I),
GOVERNMENT EXPENDITURES (G)
(billions of constant 1987 dollars)

FIGURE 9–1   The Process of Income Determination: Government Expenditures and Aggregate Demand.   By adding an autonomous level of government spending for goods and services (G) to the consumption plus investment schedule, the level of aggregate demand and the equilibrium level of income are increased.

tersection of $C + I + G$, aggregate demand, and OZ, aggregate supply. In this instance, equilibrium is at $5,400 billion. This is the only output level at which the three major expenditure categories will add up to an amount identical with aggregate supply. At any output level greater than $5,400 billion $C + I + G$ would fall short of output, and we would have a disequilibrium situation in which aggregate supply OZ would be greater than aggregate demand DD. Consequently, the income level would fall. At any income level below $5,400 billion the reverse would be the case. Aggregate demand DD would run ahead of aggregate supply OZ, and the income level would rise.

The reader will recall that an income equilibrium is defined not only in terms of an equality between aggregate demand and aggregate supply, but also as a situation in which saving and investment *ex ante* are equal (pages 228–30). It is possible, given the data assumed for our hypothetical economy, to construct saving and investment schedules and show why the point at which they are equal must necessarily be the equilibrium income level (Figure 7–4, page 226). When we include government purchases of goods and services in

**TABLE 9–2   Equilibrium of _S_ and _I_ + _G_
(in billions of constant 1987 dollars)**

(1) Net National Product Y_{np}	(2) Saving S	(3) Investment plus Government Expenditures I + G
$ 0	$-1,150	$1,010
4,500	1,100	1,460
4,600	1,150	1,470
4,700	1,200	1,480
4,800	1,250	1,490
4,900	1,300	1,500
5,000	1,350	1,510
5,100	1,400	1,520
5,200	1,450	1,530
5,300	1,500	1,540
5,400	1,550	1,550
5,500	1,600	1,560
5,600	1,650	1,570
5,700	1,700	1,580
5,800	1,750	1,590
5,900	1,800	1,600
6,000	1,850	1,610

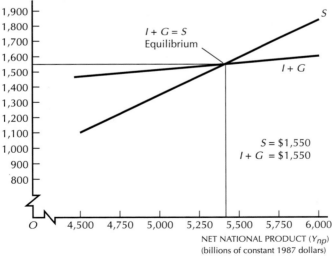

FIGURE 9–2   Equilibrium of _I_ + _G_ and _S_.   With government spending for goods and services (_G_) added to the analysis, the level of _ex ante_ saving (_S_) must now equal _I_ plus _G_ at the equilibrium income level.

the analysis, the definition of an equilibrium in terms of equality between saving and investment must be modified to take into account these purchases. This is done in Table 9–2.

In Table 9–2, column 3 is the sum of the investment and government expenditure totals of Table 9–1. Column 2 is obtained by subtracting intended consumption as shown in Table 9–1 from each income level. The difference between income and consumption we shall still define as saving, simply because at the moment we are not concerned with taxes. They will be brought into our analysis shortly. It may be noted, however, that taxes are similar to saving in their economic effects because they also represent a leakage from the current income stream (page 239). In a closed economic system, income not consumed must be disposed of either as saving or as taxes. Consumption, saving, and taxes are the only three alternatives for the disposition of income in a closed economy. In an open economy, the purchase of imported goods and services is a fourth alternative. Returning to Table 9–2, we see that the equality between S and $I + G$ exists when income is $5,400 billion.

The data of Table 9–2 are plotted graphically in Figure 9–2. The equilibrium level of income is determined by the intersection of the two curves. At the equilibrium income level of $5,400 billion, $I + G$ *ex ante* is equal to S *ex ante*. Leakages out of the current income stream through saving are just being offset by expenditures for investment goods and government purchases of goods and services. This being the case, income must be in equilibrium.[1]

Government Expenditures and the Multiplier

Since the public sector buys a part of the national output in the same manner as consumers and business firms, the economic impact of government expenditures for goods and services is essentially the same as that associated with either consumption or investment expenditure. Consequently, a change in government purchases of goods and services will shift the aggregate demand curve in exactly the same manner as either an autonomous change in investment spending or an autonomous shift in the consumption function. It follows that there will be a multiplier effect associated with the change in government expenditures that is identical in concept with the general multiplier effects discussed earlier.

In Table 9–3 we have assembled another set of data pertaining to our hypothetical economy. The only difference between these data and those of Table 9–1 is that the level of autonomous government expenditures G has risen from $810 billion to $890 billion. It is now labeled G'. We leave aside temporarily the question of how these increased government expenditures are being financed; for the moment it suffices to point out that if, prior to this change, saving was equal to the sum of investment and government expen-

---

[1] The manner in which G is financed as discussed later.

TABLE 9–3 Results of an Expansion in Government Expenditures (in billions of constant 1987 dollars)

(1) Net National Product Y_{np}	(2) Consumption C	(3) Investment I	(4) Government Expenditures G′	(5) Aggregate Demand C + I + G′
$ 0	$1,150	$200	$890	$2,240
4,500	3,400	650	890	4,940
4,600	3,450	660	890	5,000
4,700	3,500	670	890	5,060
4,800	3,550	680	890	5,120
4,900	3,600	690	890	5,180
5,000	3,650	700	890	5,240
5,100	3,700	710	890	5,300
5,200	3,750	720	890	5,360
5,300	3,800	730	890	5,420
5,400	3,850	740	890	5,480
5,500	3,900	750	890	5,540
5,600	3,950	760	890	5,600
5,700	4,000	770	890	5,660
5,800	4,050	780	890	5,720
5,900	4,100	790	890	5,780
6,000	4,150	800	890	5,840

ditures, the expansion of government expenditures by the amount of $80 billion means that new funds are being injected into the income stream. The data of Table 9–3 show that the increase in government expenditure by this amount has, *ceteris paribus,* brought about a rise in the equilibrium level of income to $5,600 billion. There is an increase of $200 billion in the income total as a result of an autonomous change in government expenditures of $80 billion. Thus, we have a multiplier of 2.5. Figure 9–3 shows these results graphically.

The underlying logic of the multiplier effect associated with changes in government expenditures is the same as that of the multiplier effect in conjunction with changes in investment expenditure or autonomous shifts in consumption (page 239). The multiplier effect results from the combined impact of the initial (or primary) change in spending (which in this instance is the amount by which government purchases of goods and services have increased) and the induced (or secondary) spending that is a consequence of the increased income resulting from the original increase in expenditures. Induced spending is in the form of purchases of consumer goods and services and additional investment outlays.

The multiplier effect associated with the change in government expenditures can be explained through a series of simple algebraic formulas. In a formal sense, and as was the case with investment changes, we define the multiplier as the ratio of a change in income ΔY_{np} to a change in government

CONSUMPTION (C), INVESTMENT (I),
GOVERNMENT EXPENDITURES (G)
(billions of constant 1987 dollars)

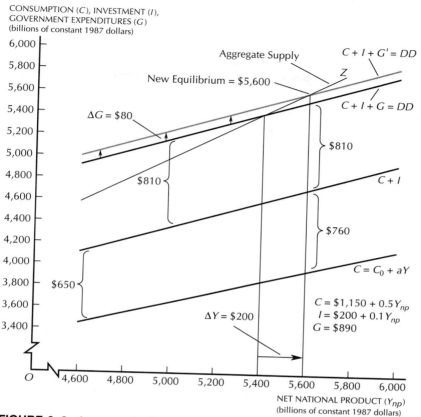

FIGURE 9–3   Increase in Government Expenditure.   An increase in government spending for goods and services (ΔG) has a multiplier effect on the equilibrium income level that works in the same way as the previously discussed increase in autonomous investment spending (ΔI).

expenditures for goods and services ΔG. As the income variable relevant to our analysis is net national product, we have

$$k' = \frac{\Delta Y_{np}}{\Delta G}. \tag{9-1}$$

In a closed economy, output consists of three categories: consumption C, investment I, and government purchases of goods and services G. Consequently, we begin with the following identity:

$$Y_{np} = C + I + G. \tag{9-2}$$

From the above it follows that a change in income must be composed of a change in government expenditures ΔG, a change in consumption expenditures ΔC, a change in investment expenditures ΔI, or some combination of all three. This gives us the additional identity

$$\Delta Y_{np} = \Delta C + \Delta I + \Delta G. \tag{9-3}$$

Since the change in government expenditures is the autonomous change, it follows that changes in either consumption expenditures or investment expenditures will be of an induced nature. Induced consumption depends on the value of the marginal propensity to consume, whereas induced investment depends on the value of the marginal propensity to invest. The former, it will be recalled, is designated by a and the latter by b. Induced consumption ΔC will be equal to $a \times \Delta Y_{np}$, on the assumption that taxes and transfers are still zero, and induced investment ΔI_i will be equal to $b \times \Delta Y_{np}$. If we substitute these values for ΔC and ΔI_i in Equation (9–3), we have

$$\Delta Y_{np} = \Delta G + a\Delta Y_{np} + b\Delta Y_{np}. \tag{9-4}$$

This expression may now be manipulated algebraically as follows:

$$\Delta Y_{np} - a\Delta Y_{np} - b\Delta Y_{np} = \Delta G, \tag{9-5}$$

$$\Delta Y_{np}[1 - (a + b)] = \Delta G, \tag{9-6}$$

$$\Delta Y_{np} = \Delta G \times \frac{1}{1 - (a + b)}, \tag{9-7}$$

$$\frac{\Delta Y_{np}}{\Delta G} = \frac{1}{1 - (a + b)} = k'. \tag{9-8}$$

Equation (9–8) tells us that the value of the multiplier in a closed economy, with investment and government spending for goods and services, is equal to the reciprocal of 1 *minus* the marginal propensity to consume plus the marginal propensity to invest. It should be noted at this point that the mathematical expression $1 - (a + b)$ is a measure of leakages expressed as marginal propensities. The formal mathematical statement of the multiplier relationship just developed underscores once again the fundamental ideal that the overall magnitude of the multiplier effect associated with any shift in the aggregate demand function depends on the total *secondary* spending induced by such a shift.

Transfer Expenditures and the Income Level

Unlike government purchases of goods and services, which are a part of the aggregate demand function, transfer expenditures exert an indirect influence on aggregate demand. It is primarily by their impact on the volume of consumption expenditures that transfer payments influence the level of aggregate demand. To a lesser degree they may affect investment expenditures as well, but our analysis is directed basically toward the manner in which they affect expenditures for consumer goods and services.

To understand the influence of transfer expenditures on aggregate demand, it is necessary, first, to recall that the crux of the income-consumption relationship is that the amount of spending for consumption purposes is determined by the income level. In our discussion of the empirical validity of the consumption function hypothesis, we concluded that the most meaningful income measure appropriate to this relationship is that of *disposable income* (page 212). Since we assumed a linear relationship between income and consumption, the consumption function in equation form is

$$C = C_0 + a(Y_d). \qquad (9\text{–}9)$$

Disposable income was defined in Chapter 5 as the net national product minus taxes (direct and indirect) paid by the owners of economic resources plus transfer payments received by individuals and households. Since we assumed that all saving (other than capital consumption allowances) originates with individuals or households and that government is the only source of transfer payments, disposable income was defined as

$$Y_d = Y_{np} - TX + TR. \qquad (9\text{–}10)$$

In Equation (9–10), Y_{np} is the net national product; TX the total of all taxes, including indirect taxes; and TR the total of all transfer expenditures. The consumption function can now be written as

$$C = C_0 + a(Y_{np} - TX + TR). \qquad (9\text{–}11)$$

It is apparent from Equation (9–11) that transfer expenditures influence consumption expenditure and thus indirectly the level of aggregate demand by affecting the amount of disposable income in the hands of individuals and households. A change in transfer expenditures will bring about a change in disposable income, which in turn will induce a change in consumer spending, since the amount of disposable income constitutes the point of origin of spending for consumer goods and services. Schematically, the chain of causation appears as

$$\Delta TR \rightarrow \Delta Y_d \rightarrow \Delta C.$$

Let us refer once again to the data of the hypothetical economy for a demonstration of how this chain of causation may work. To show the relationships involved, we shall turn to Table 9–4 and Figure 9–4 and confine the analysis initially to the impact of transfer expenditures on the consumption function. In column 2 of Table 9–4 the consumption function for the hypothetical economy is as set forth in Table 9–1. This curve appears as the solid line C in Figure 9–4. We may note that Table 9–1 contained no transfer

TABLE 9–4 Results of an Increase in Transfer Expenditures (in billions of constant 1987 dollars)

(1) Net National Product* Y_{np}	(2) Consumption C	(3) Change in Disposable Income† ΔY_d	(4) Disposable Income Y_d	(5) Change in Consumption‡ ΔC	(6) New Level of Consumption C'
$ 0	$1,150	$80	$ 80	$40	$1,190
4,500	3,400	80	4,580	40	3,440
4,600	3,450	80	4,680	40	3,490
4,700	3,500	80	4,780	40	3,540
4,800	3,550	80	4,880	40	3,590
4,900	3,600	80	4,980	40	3,640
5,000	3,650	80	5,080	40	3,690
5,100	3,700	80	5,180	40	3,740
5,200	3,750	80	5,280	40	3,790
5,300	3,800	80	5,380	40	3,840
5,400	3,850	80	5,480	40	3,890
5,500	3,900	80	5,580	40	3,940
5,600	3,950	80	5,680	40	3,990
5,700	4,000	80	5,780	40	4,040
5,800	4,050	80	5,880	40	4,090
5,900	4,100	80	5,980	40	4,140
6,000	4,150	80	6,080	40	4,190

*Net national product = disposable income when taxes and transfers are zero.

†This is equal to the increase in transfer expenditures.

‡The marginal propensity to consume is 0.5.

expenditures, and consequently net national product and disposable income are equal prior to the introduction of transfer expenditures. They appear in column 1.

What impact does the introduction of transfer expenditures into the analysis have on the level of consumption? Let us assume that the government of our hypothetical economy undertakes transfer expenditures of $80 billion. (We shall not concern ourselves at this point with the manner in which this new expenditure is financed.) The immediate effect of this new expenditure is to increase disposable income at all possible income levels, as shown in column 4 of the table. This is the same at all income levels because the assumed increase in transfer expenditures of $80 billion must have the same effect on disposable income *irrespective of the actual income level*. The impact of this increase in disposable income on consumption expenditure depends on the value of the marginal propensity to consume. Our original consumption function was drawn with a slope such that the marginal propensity to consume had a value of 0.5. If we assume that the introduction of transfer expenditures into the analysis in no way affects the slope of the schedule, it follows that consumption expenditures at each and every possible level of income will increase by $40 billion, one-half the increase in disposable income. This change is shown in column 5 of Table 9–4.

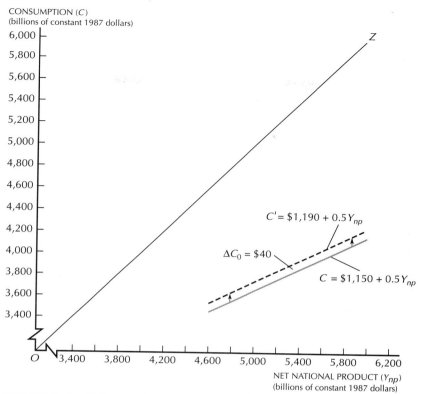

CONSUMPTION (C)
(billions of constant 1987 dollars)

$C' = \$1,190 + 0.5Y_{np}$

$\Delta C_0 = \$40$

$C = \$1,150 + 0.5Y_{np}$

NET NATIONAL PRODUCT (Y_{np})
(billions of constant 1987 dollars)

FIGURE 9–4   Shift in the Consumption Function.   The effect of an increase in transfer spending (ΔTR) is to shift the consumption function upward by an amount equal to $a \, \Delta TR$. Recall a is the marginal propensity to consume.

The overall impact of the introduction of transfer expenditures may be described as *a shift in the position of the consumption function*. The consumption function has shifted upward because of the added factor of transfer expenditures. As a consequence, consumption expenditures are higher at all levels of the net national income. This shift is shown graphically in Figure 9–4. The new and higher consumption function is labeled C'. Thus, transfer expenditures constitute one of the key factors that influence the level of the consumption function. In a technical sense transfers exercise their influence through the parameter C_0, which determines the level of the function. A change in transfer expenditures will, therefore, bring about a shift in the position of the curve and in this way affect consumption spending and the level of aggregate demand.[2]

Let us refer once again to the data of Table 9–1 and the income equilibrium level associated with these data. On the assumption that government expen-

---

[2] It is possible, too, that a change in transfers may affect the slope of the function, but this is precluded in our example.

ditures for goods and services totaled a constant $810 billion, the equilibrium income is $5,400 billion, given the original position of the consumption function as shown in column 2 and the investment function shown in column 3 of Table 9–1. What will happen to the equilibrium income if an additional $80 billion in government transfer expenditures are injected into the picture? The immediate result is to shift the consumption function upward, as we have done in Table 9–4. This means, in turn, an equal upward shift of the aggregate demand curve. The immediate (or initial) increase in spending that this change entails is equal to the amount by which both the consumption function and the aggregate demand curve have shifted upward. This is $40 billion, and if we multiply this change by the general multiplier of 2.5, we find that the new equilibrium level will be $100 billion higher than previously. This value of 2.5 for the general multiplier is based on our assumed value of 0.5 for the marginal propensity to consume and 0.1 for the marginal propensity to invest. The effect on the income level of a change in transfer expenditures is shown numerically in Table 9–5 and graphically in Figure 9–5. In the table the original position of the consumption function is given in column 3 and its position after the introduction of transfer expenditures by column 7. The aggregate demand function, $C' + I + G$, at the new and higher level of the

**TABLE 9–5   Transfer Expenditures and Aggregate Demand
(in billions of constant 1987 dollars)**

	Before Transfers				After Transfers*		
(1) Net National Product Y_{np}	(2) Dispos- able Income Y_d	(3) Consump- tion C	(4) Aggregate Demand $C + I + G^†$	(5) Net National Product Y_{np}	(6) Dispos- able Income Y_d	(7) Consump- tion C'	(8) Aggregate Demand $C' + I + G^†$
$ 0	$ 0	$1,150	$2,160	$ 0	$ 80	$1,190	$2,200
4,500	4,500	3,400	4,860	4,500	4,580	3,440	4,900
4,600	4,600	3,450	4,920	4,600	4,680	3,490	4,960
4,700	4,700	3,500	4,980	4,700	4,780	3,540	5,020
4,800	4,800	3,550	5,040	4,800	4,880	3,590	5,080
4,900	4,900	3,600	5,100	4,900	4,980	3,640	5,140
5,000	5,000	3,650	5,160	5,000	5,080	3,690	5,200
5,100	5,100	3,700	5,220	5,100	5,180	3,740	5,260
5,200	5,200	3,750	5,280	5,200	5,280	3,790	5,320
5,300	5,300	3,800	5,340	5,300	5,380	3,840	5,380
5,400	5,400	3,850	5,400	5,400	5,480	3,890	5,440
5,500	5,500	3,900	5,460	5,500	5,580	3,940	5,500
5,600	5,600	3,950	5,520	5,600	5,680	3,990	5,560
5,700	5,700	4,000	5,580	5,700	5,780	4,040	5,620
5,800	5,800	4,050	5,640	5,800	5,880	4,090	5,680
5,900	5,900	4,100	5,700	5,900	5,980	4,140	5,740
6,000	6,000	4,150	5,760	6,000	6,080	4,190	5,800

*Transfers = $80.
†$I + G$ are the same as in Table 9–1.

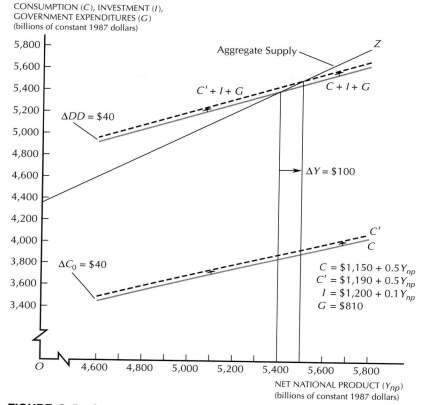

CONSUMPTION (C), INVESTMENT (I),
GOVERNMENT EXPENDITURES (G)
(billions of constant 1987 dollars)

Aggregate Supply

Z

$C' + I + G$

$C + I + G$

$\Delta DD = \$40$

$\Delta Y = \$100$

C'

C

$\Delta C_0 = \$40$

$C = \$1,150 + 0.5Y_{np}$
$C' = \$1,190 + 0.5Y_{np}$
$I = \$1,200 + 0.1Y_{np}$
$G = \$810$

O 4,600   4,800   5,000   5,200   5,400   5,600   5,800

NET NATIONAL PRODUCT (Y_{np})
(billions of constant 1987 dollars)

FIGURE 9–5 Aggregate Demand and a Shift in the Consumption Function. The effect of a shift upward in the consumption function brought about by an increase in transfer spending is to shift the aggregate demand curve upward by a like amount and thus lead to the usual multiplier-based increase in output (ΔY).

consumption function is shown in column 8. The new equilibrium income level is $5,500 billion.

Transfer Expenditures and the Multiplier

There is a multiplier effect associated with a change in the level of transfer expenditures similar in a fundamental conceptual sense to all the multiplier effects previously discussed. An increase (or decrease) in transfer expenditures will lead to an increase (or decrease) in the income level that is some multiple of the initial change in consumption resulting from the change in transfers. This is identical to what takes place when there is an autonomous change in investment outlays or government purchases of goods and services. But there is an important difference between the multiplier effect associated with transfers and that associated with the G or I components of the aggregate demand schedule. Normally, the multiplier effect associated with transfer expenditures will be *smaller* than the multiplier effect of a change in either investment or government expenditures. Let us see why this is true.

The multiplier phenomenon results from the combination of initial and induced changes in spending. But a change in transfer expenditures does not operate directly on aggregate demand in the same way as does a change in either investment expenditures or government purchases of goods and services. Additional transfer expenditures trigger, first, a change in disposable income and then, via the marginal propensity to consume, a new level of consumption spending. But so long as Keynes's fundamental psychological law holds true—that is, that normally the marginal propensity to consume is less than 100 percent—consumption cannot rise (or fall) by the full amount of the change in transfer expenditures. Consequently, *the shift in the aggregate demand curve,* which equals the initial or primary change in spending that gives rise to the multipler process, *must always be smaller than the change in transfer expenditures.* It follows that, if the initial effect of any given change is smaller, then the induced effect will also be smaller. Thus, the multiplier effect will be smaller for transfers than for investment or government expenditures.

Taxes and the Income Level

Our detailed analysis of the way in which transfer expenditures affect the income level by their influence on disposable income and consumption spending makes it relatively easy for us to consider the impact of taxes on the income level. Once we realize that taxes are, in a sense, nothing more than negative transfers, it can be seen that they will affect the income level in a manner exactly the reverse of transfers. Taxes, *ceteris paribus,* have the effect of reducing disposable income, as we saw in Equation (9–10). Thus, an increase in taxes would tend to reduce consumption spending because it would reduce disposable income. On the other hand, a decrease in taxes would have the opposite effect of increasing consumption spending because it would increase disposable income. The foregoing remarks apply primarily to a situation in which taxes increase (or decrease) by a specific amount. Changes in taxation that may accompany changes in the income level present a more complex problem, as we shall see shortly.

In view of the above similarities between the impact of transfers and taxes on the income level, let us assert as a general principle that the absolute level of taxes is a factor which, like the absolute level of transfer expenditures, influences the level of the consumption function. This statement applies to that part of the tax total that is independent of income level. Given this general principle, it follows that any increase in taxes that is autonomous with respect to the income level will, *ceteris paribus,* shift the consumption function downward. On the other hand, an autonomous reduction in the level of taxation will, *ceteris paribus,* shift the consumption function upward. As is the case with transfer expenditures, the amount by which the consumption function shifts as a result of change in taxation depends on the value of the marginal propensity to consume. Taxes change disposable income, and consumption spending will change in accordance with whether the value of the marginal propensity to consume is high or low.

Let us refer once again to the data of our hypothetical economy to analyze the impact of an introduction of taxes into the system. We shall assume that a flat total of taxes in the amount of $160 billion is imposed. The effect of this change on disposable income and the consumption function is shown in Table 9–6. Essentially, the effect of new taxes in the amount of $160 billion is, first, to reduce disposable income by a like amount at all levels of the net national product and, second, to reduce consumption spending in accordance with the value of the marginal propensity to consume. This value is 0.5, which means, in effect, that at all levels of the net national product consumption spending will decline by $0.5 \times \Delta TX$. This is $80 billion; thus, we have an autonomous downward shift in the consumption function in the amount of $80 billion. The new schedule of consumption is shown in column 6 of Table 9–6.

The data contained in Table 9–7 indicate the effect of the introduction of

TABLE 9–6   Results of the Introduction of Taxes (in billions of constant 1987 dollars)

(1) Net National Product* Y_{np}	*(2)* Consumption* C′	*(3)* Change in Disposable Income† ΔY_d	*(4)* Disposable Income Y_d	*(5)* Change in Consumption ΔC	*(6)* New Level of Consumption C″
$ 0	$1,190	$−160	$−160	$−80	$1,110
4,500	3,440	−160	4,420	−80	3,360
4,600	3,490	−160	4,520	−80	3,410
4,700	3,540	−160	4,620	−80	3,460
4,800	3,590	−160	4,720	−80	3,510
4,900	3,640	−160	4,820	−80	3,560
5,000	3,690	−160	4,920	−80	3,610
5,100	3,740	−160	5,020	−80	3,660
5,200	3,790	−160	5,120	−80	3,710
5,300	3,840	−160	5,220	−80	3,760
5,400	3,890	−160	5,320	−80	3,810
5,500	3,940	−160	5,420	−80	3,860
5,600	3,990	−160	5,520	−80	3,910
5,700	4,040	−160	5,620	−80	3,960
5,800	4,090	−160	5,720	−80	4,010
5,900	4,140	−160	5,820	−80	4,060
6,000	4,190	−160	5,920	−80	4,110

*Same as column 6 of Table 9–4 and column 7 of Table 9–5.

†This is equal to the increase in taxes ($160 billion) and is applied against the disposable income shown in column 6 of Table 9–5.

TABLE 9–7   Taxes and Aggregate Demand (in billions of constant 1987 dollars)

(1) Net National Product Y_{np}	(2) Net Taxes $T*$	(3) Disposable Income $Y_d{}^\dagger$	(4) Consumption C''	(5) Aggregate Demand $C'' + I + G^\ddagger$
$ 0	$80	$ −80	$1,110	$2,120
4,500	80	4,420	3,360	4,820
4,600	80	4,520	3,410	4,880
4,700	80	4,620	3,460	4,940
4,800	80	4,720	3,510	5,000
4,900	80	4,820	3,560	5,060
5,000	80	4,920	3,610	5,120
5,100	80	5,020	3,660	5,180
5,200	80	5,120	3,710	5,240
5,300	80	5,220	3,760	5,300
5,400	80	5,320	3,810	5,360
5,500	80	5,420	3,860	5,420
5,600	80	5,520	3,910	5,480
5,700	80	5,620	3,960	5,540
5,800	80	5,720	4,010	5,600
5,900	80	5,820	4,060	5,660
6,000	80	5,920	4,110	5,720

$*T$ = net taxes = $TX - TR$ = ($160 − $80) = $80.
$^\dagger Y_d = Y_{np} - T.$
$^\ddagger I + G$ is the same as in Table 9–1.

taxes into the system on aggregate demand and the equilibrium income level. Prior to this change, the equilibrium income was $5,500 billion and the position of the consumption function was given by column 7 of Table 9–5. The initial impact of the added taxes is to reduce autonomously the consumption function by $80 billion, as we have just seen, and, if it is assumed that no change in either government purchases of goods and services or investment follows, this means, too, that aggregate demand shifts downward by $80 billion. When the general multiplier of 2.5 is applied against this shift, the ultimate decline in the net national product is $200 billion. Thus, the new equilibrium position is depicted in Table 9–7 as being at the $5,300 billion level. These changes are depicted graphically in Figure 9–6.

In Table 9–7 the concept of net taxes is introduced. This concept should be carefully noted, as it is crucial to a clear understanding of the algebraic derivation of the multiplier in a system that incorporates changes in *both* taxes and transfer expenditures as the net national product changes. Net taxes are defined as total taxes less transfer payments; they represent the net withdrawal of income from the income stream as a result of the combined effect of both taxes and transfer payments. In symbolic terms, we have

$$T = (TX - TR). \qquad (9\text{–}12)$$

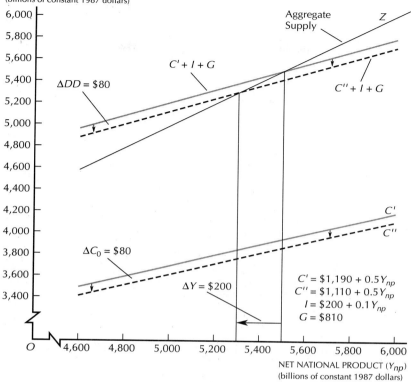

CONSUMPTION (C), INVESTMENT (I),
GOVERNMENT EXPENDITURES (G)
(billions of constant 1987 dollars)

$C' = \$1,190 + 0.5Y_{np}$
$C'' = \$1,110 + 0.5Y_{np}$
$I = \$200 + 0.1Y_{np}$
$G = \$810$

NET NATIONAL PRODUCT (Y_{np})
(billions of constant 1987 dollars)

FIGURE 9–6 Effect of Taxes on the Aggregate Demand Curve. An increase in taxes (ΔTX), *ceteris paribus,* has the opposite effect of an increase in spending; it causes the consumption function to shift downward by an amount equal to $a\,\Delta TX$.

From this it follows that the consumption function can be written

$$C = C_0 + a(Y_{np} - T). \tag{9–13}$$

Earlier in this chapter we pointed out that taxes are a leakage from the income stream in the same sense as saving. This being true, equilibrium requires that leakages in the form of net taxes plus saving must be offset by investment expenditures and government purchases of goods and services. Now that net taxes have been introduced into our analysis, we can plot *ex ante* values for $I + G$ and $S + T$ and show that equilibrium is obtained at the intersection of these curves. This is done in Figure 9–7.

Transfers, Taxes, and the Multiplier

We shall now proceed to derive algebraically the multiplier in a system that includes both transfers and taxes, as well as induced investment. In Equation

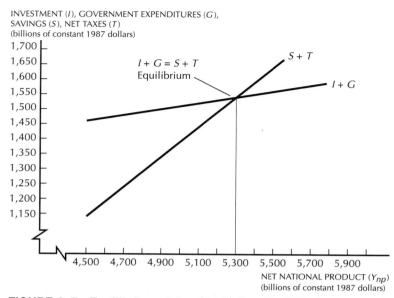

INVESTMENT (I), GOVERNMENT EXPENDITURES (G),
SAVINGS (S), NET TAXES (T)
(billions of constant 1987 dollars)

NET NATIONAL PRODUCT (Y_{np})
(billions of constant 1987 dollars)

FIGURE 9–7   Equilibrium of $I + G$ and $S + T$. With the introduction of both taxes (TX) and transfer spending (TR) into the analysis, the offset to $I + G$ at the equilibrium income level is $S + T$, where T is net taxes ($TX - TR$).

(9–12) we defined net taxes T as the difference between total taxes and transfer payments. We may also define net taxes as

$$T = T_0 + tY_{np}. \tag{9–14}$$

In this equation, T_0 represents net taxes that are independent of the income level, and t may be defined as the net marginal propensity tax out of net national product. It is equal to $\Delta T / \Delta Y_{np}$. The value of t may increase, remain the same, or decline as Y_{np} rises, depending on the nature of the rate structure for the tax system, a topic we shall discuss shortly. Equation (9–14) is the net tax function.

The consumption function shown in Equation (9–13) can be further modified by the substitution of the net tax function given above for T in the equation. This gives

$$C = C_0 + a[Y_{np} - (T_0 + tY_{np})], \tag{9–15}$$

$$C = C_0 + aY_{np} - aT_0 - atY_{np}, \tag{9–16}$$

$$C = C_0 - aT_0 + (a - at)Y_{np}. \tag{9–17}$$

We shall designate $(C_0 - aT_0)$ as C_0'. This represents consumption that is independent of the level of the net national product. The expression $(a - at)$

is the marginal propensity to consume out of the net national product.[3] We shall designate this as a'. We now have the equation

$$C = C_0' + a'Y_{np}. \tag{9-18}$$

Since both transfer payments and taxes have been introduced into our analysis, there no longer is equality between disposable income and the net national product. The multiplier formula must take this into account. We shall continue to designate the multiplier, which reflects the effect of both transfers and taxes as well as induced investment, as the *effective* multiplier, again using k' as the symbol for the multiplier. Recall, too, that k' is sometimes called the supermultiplier. Algebraically, the effective multiplier is

$$k' = \frac{\Delta Y_{np}}{\Delta D}. \tag{9-19}$$

In the equation, ΔD refers to any autonomous shift in the aggregate demand function. To complete our analysis, let us assume that it is an increase in government purchases of goods and services that is the source of an autonomous shift in the aggregate demand function. Then, $\Delta G = \Delta D$. If this happens, it follows that

$$\Delta Y_{np} = \Delta G + \Delta C + \Delta I. \tag{9-20}$$

By substitution we have

$$\Delta Y_{np} = \Delta G + a'\Delta Y_{np} + b\Delta Y_{np}, \tag{9-21}$$

$$\Delta G = \Delta Y_{np} - a'\Delta Y_{np} - b\Delta Y_{np}, \tag{9-22}$$

$$\Delta G = \Delta Y_{np}(1 - a' - b). \tag{9-23}$$

If we substitute the right-hand portion of Equation (9–23) for ΔD in Equation (9–19), we get

$$k' = \frac{\Delta Y_{np}}{\Delta Y_{np}(1 - a' - b)} = \frac{1}{1 - a' - b}. \tag{9-24}$$

When a' is replaced with $(a - at)$ in the above expression, the equation defining the effective multiplier becomes

$$k' = \frac{1}{1 - (a - at) - b} = \frac{1}{1 - a + at - b}. \tag{9-25}$$

---

[3] See the Appendix for an algebraic proof that $a' = a - at$.

By careful examination of the above equation, the student can see clearly the effect of both transfer payments and taxes on the value of the multiplier and hence on income changes as a result of an autonomous shift in aggregate demand. Any development that increases the value of the net marginal propensity to tax t will have the effect of reducing the size of the effective multiplier; any development that reduces t will have the opposite effect.

Government and the *IS-LM* Model

We can use the *IS-LM* model to show in a single diagram how government spending for goods and services, government transfer spending, and taxes affect the income level. This is done in Figure 9–8. For the sake of clarity and simplicity in the analysis at this point, both the *IS* and *LM* curves are depicted by straight lines, even though curves as shown in the earlier graphic representation of the model (Figure 6–6, page 186) are more realistic.

The initial position of the economy is given by the intersection of the two heavily lined curves labeled *IS* and *LM*. This gives an original equilibrium income level of Y_e and rate of interest (i_e). Now what happens if government

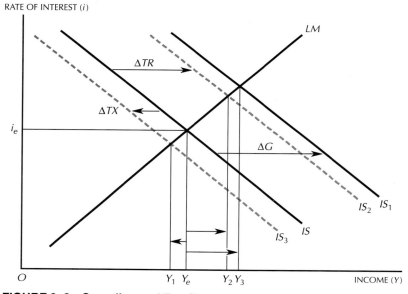

FIGURE 9–8   Spending and Tax Changes and the *IS-LM* Model.   An increase in government spending for goods and services (ΔG) will shift the *IS* curve to the right and cause a rise in the equilibrium income level (Y_e). An increase in taxes (ΔTX) will shift the *IS* curve to the left and cause the equilibrium income level (Y_e) to fall.

spending for goods and services (G) is increased? This will shift the IS curve to the right—a shift depicted by the IS curve labeled IS_1. Income will rise to a new equilibrium, depicted as Y_{3e}. The same thing will happen if there is an increase in transfer spending (TR), although in this case the shift in the IS curve is smaller. In the figure this change is depicted by the shift of the IS curve to the position indicated by the dotted-line schedule labeled IS_2. Since the shift in the IS curve is smaller, the increase in equilibrium income is also smaller. Income only rises to the Y_{2e} level. An increase in taxes (TX), other things being equal, will cause income to fall. This is depicted by a shift to the left in the IS curve to the position depicted by the curve labeled IS_3. The income level now falls to Y_1.

The perceptive reader will note at this point that nothing has been said about the rate of interest, although close examination of the diagram shows that the two rightward shifts of the IS curve will be accompanied by a rise in interest rates, whereas a leftward shift in the IS curve will bring about a decline in interest rates. No mention is made at this point of the precise interest rate changes that may follow from shifts in the IS curve for two reasons. The first is simply to keep the figure clear of too much clutter, as the objective is to show the effects of changes in spending and taxes. The second and more important reason is that the interest rate effects—at least as far as rightward shifts in the IS curve are concerned—depend on how the spending increases are financed, a topic we discuss later in this chapter in the section on the role played by finance in government spending. At that time we can examine the interest rate effects in terms of the IS-LM model.

The Federal Budget

The combination of theoretical ideas of an essentially Keynesian nature concerning taxes and government spending in combination with post-World War II experience with actual policy measures has enlarged significantly our understanding of how the federal budget affects the economy. To the extent that we look to tax and expenditure changes at the national level as a means of influencing output and employment, the federal budget is the instrument for the exercise of fiscal policy. There are four important concepts to examine in this context: (1) the full- or high-employment budget, (2) structural and cyclical budgets, (3) automatic (or built-in) stabilizers, and (4) the balanced budget thesis.

The mechanics of fiscal policy are relatively simple. If we let G represent *federal* spending for goods and services and T *net federal* taxes (total federal taxes minus federal transfers), then the federal budget is in deficit when $G > T$ and in surplus when $T > G$. As a general proposition, a deficit has an expansionary or inflationary effect, because with a deficit the federal government is putting more money into the income stream through its spending than it is pulling out through taxes. If there is a surplus, the effect is the opposite, namely, a tendency toward contraction or deflation: more money is being pulled out of the income stream than is being put in.

The foregoing analysis is correct as far as it goes, but the fact that at any particular time the federal budget is in either deficit or surplus does not tell us whether or not the government is pursuing an active fiscal policy. In other words, a deficit or surplus may be a wholly *passive* development, in that it comes about because the general level of economic activity is changing, not because the government is trying through spending or tax changes to influence the level of economic activity. The growing deficits that the Reagan administration wrestled with in the winter and spring of 1982 are a prime example. They came about because the recession caused spending to rise (more unemployment and welfare payments) and tax revenues to fall. The deficit was not deliberately engineered as a way to stimulate the economy.

The Full-(High-)Employment Budget

In the early 1960s a technique emerged for determining whether a particular surplus or deficit was the result of deliberate policy actions, whether, in other words, the surplus or deficit was the consequence of an *active* fiscal policy. This technique led to the concept of the full-employment (or high-employment) budget, an idea developed for policy purposes in the early days of the Kennedy administration. The man most responsible for this development was the late Walter Heller, professor of economics at the University of Minnesota and chairperson of the Council of Economic Advisers under President Kennedy. In explaining how the administration developed this concept, Heller said:

> As part of the reshaping of stabilization policy, then, our fiscal policy targets have been recast in terms of "full" or "high" employment levels of output, specifically the level of GNP associated with a 4-percent rate of unemployment. *So the target is no longer budget balance every year or over the cycle* [italics added], but balance . . . at full employment. And in modern stabilization policy . . . even this target does not remain fixed.[4]

Simply put, the full-(or high-)employment budget does not measure the actual budget surplus or deficit in any single year; rather, it is a measure of the surplus or deficit that would exist *if the economy were actually operating at a full-employment level.* This will give a much better indication of the active fiscal influence of a particular budget. For example, if the calculations show that at full (or high) employment a proposed budget will be in deficit,

[4] Walter W. Heller, *New Dimensions of Political Economy* (New York: Norton, 1967), p. 66. What Heller meant by the full-employment target not being fixed was that the economy would grow over time, since a growing labor force and a rising productivity for the labor force would increase continuously the output level associated with a 4 percent unemployment rate.

this is a clear indication that the budget will be expansionary (or inflationary). Note that deficit or surplus figures in the full-(or high-)employment budget are hypothetical, not realized. They are deficit or surplus figures that will be realized only if the economy reaches the full-employment level. Measuring the full-(or high-)employment deficit or surplus requires, first, estimating the economy's full-employment output potential (see Chapter 1) and, second, determining the amount of revenue the federal tax system will generate at this level of output, as well as the amount of expenditures forthcoming. The basic rationale for this budget concept is that the true inflationary or deflationary potential of any proposed federal budget is apparent only when the economy is at full employment. Figure 9–9 illustrates the concept of the full-(or high-)employment budget.

In the figure, real output, as measured by net national product, is shown on the horizontal axis and possible budget deficits or surpluses are shown in dollar amounts on the vertical axis. Two curves are shown in the figure, one labeled budget A and the other budget B. These curves are obtained by subtracting expenditures for goods and services by the federal government (G) at various output levels from the net taxes (T) appropriate to each income level. The curves slope upward to the right because, with a fixed level of

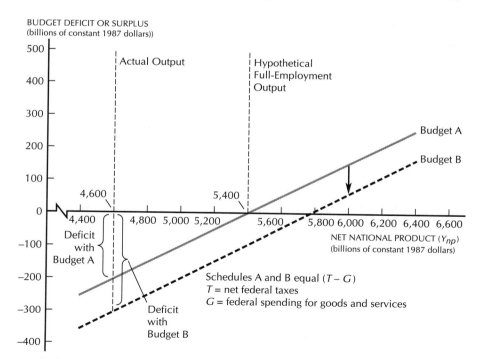

FIGURE 9–9 The Full-(or High-)Employment Budget Concept. The curves appropriate to the different budgets show how with a fixed structure of spending for goods and services, taxes, and transfers, the deficit will decline or the surplus increase as the income level rises.

expenditures and a fixed rate structure for the federal government, net taxes (T) will automatically rise as output rises and thus lead to a surplus (or a smaller deficit) at higher levels of income and the reverse at lower levels of income. In the figure the curve labeled budget A represents a combination of taxes and expenditures designed to balance at the full-employment output of $5,400 billion. If the actual output falls below the full-employment level, the budget will be in deficit, but the deficit will be of a *passive* nature, induced by the failure of the economy to attain full employment. In the figure actual output is shown at $4,600 billion; the result is a deficit of $200 billion. This will be the measured budget deficit found in the national income accounts. What the curve labeled budget B represents is a deliberately engineered full-employment deficit, the purpose of which is to provide the economy with a strong fiscal stimulus. The curve will shift down either because expenditures are increased with no change in taxes or because taxes are reduced with no change in expenditures. In either case the effect will be to create a deficit under full-(or high-)employment conditions, a development that sends a clear signal to policymakers that fiscal policy has turned *active*. It should be noted parenthetically that the level labeled "Hypothetical Full-Employment Output" in the figure is not fixed. As the economy grows, this will shift upward— to the right on the graph—and as this happens, budget A will automatically generate a surplus. We shall return to this possibility later (see Chapter 15).

Table 9–8 compares actual and full-(or high-)employment deficits and surpluses from 1960 through 1988. The data in the table for the high-employment budget figures are from a revised series developed by the Department of Commerce. Up until 1980, the President's Council of Economic Advisers provided estimates of the high-employment budget, but beginning in 1981, these estimates were made by the Department of Commerce, and found in the November issue of the Department's monthly magazine, *Survey of Current Business*. Unfortunately, the Department of Commerce stopped publication of this series after 1988; this is a loss of a valuable statistical tool for economic analysis and policy formulation.

The figures shown in Table 9–8 are useful because they illustrate clearly the difference between a budget deficit that is passive and one that results from an active fiscal policy. A passive deficit arises in an economic downturn because revenues fall and expenditures rise (see the following section on built-in stabilizers), whereas an active deficit is a result of a deliberate reduction in taxes or increase in spending for the purpose of stimulating output and employment. Examine, for example, what happened between 1972 and 1975; keep in mind that 1974 and 1975 were recession years. Between 1973 and 1975 the actual budget deficit rose sharply and reached $69.4 billion in 1975, a figure which was the largest on record until the more recent deficits of the Reagan and Bush administrations. The full-employment deficit, however, was in decline between 1972 and 1974—a fact that reflects the restrictiveness of actual budget policy. In these years the change in the full-employment budget gives a clue to the direction that fiscal policy is moving. The swing from a minus $11.4 billion in the column in 1972 to a positive $6.0 billion in 1974

TABLE 9–8 Actual and Full-(or High-)Employment Federal Government Surplus or Deficit: 1960–1988 (billions of current dollars)

Calendar Year	Actual Surplus or Deficit		Change		Full- (or High-) Employment Surplus or Deficit		Change	
1960	$	3.5	$	6.1	$	11.1	$	6.7
1961		−2.6		−6.1		6.7		−4.4
1962		−3.4		−2.8		2.1		−4.6
1963		1.1		4.5		6.8		4.7
1964		−2.6		−3.7		0.4		−6.4
1965		1.3		3.9		0.4		−
1966		−1.4		−2.7		−6.5		−6.9
1967		−12.7		−11.3		−16.0		−9.5
1968		−4.7		8.0		−11.3		4.7
1969		8.5		13.2		4.9		16.2
1970		−13.3		−21.8		−3.4		−8.3
1971		−21.7		−8.4		−9.6		−6.2
1972		−17.3		4.4	Falling	−11.4	Restrictive	−1.8
1973	Rising	−6.6		10.7	Deficit	−9.0	Budget	2.4
1974	Actual	−11.6		−5.0		6.0		15.0
1975	Deficit	−69.4		−57.8		−25.2		−31.2
1976		−52.9		16.5		−18.8		6.4
1977		−42.4		10.5		−22.0		−3.2
1978		−28.1		14.3		−13.4		8.6
1979		−15.7		12.4		5.4		18.8
1980		−60.1		−44.4		−17.1		−22.5
1981		−58.8		1.3		4.5		21.6
1982		−135.5		−76.7		−32.6		−37.1
1983		−180.1		−44.6	Rising	−90.8	Expansive	−58.2
1984		−166.9		13.2	Deficit	−129.7	Budget	−38.9
1985		−181.4		−14.5		−171.9		−42.2
1986		−201.0		−19.6		−185.4		−13.5
1987		−151.8		49.2		−159.5		25.9
1988		−136.6		15.2		−172.5		−13.0
1989		−122.3		14.3		NA		NA

Note: Detail may not add to totals because of rounding.

Sources: Economic Report of the President, 1994; and *Survey of Current Business,* November 1980, 1983, 1984, 1989.

reflects a shift from an expansive to a restrictive stance as far as the federal budget is concerned. The $69.4 billion actual deficit recorded in 1975 is of a passive character, since it came about because federal spending rose and taxes fell as a result of the recession.

The direction of change recorded in the last column of the full-employment portion of the table tells us whether or not the budget is becoming more or less restrictive (or expansionary). Positive values in this column mean that the deficit is declining or the surplus (if one exists) is increasing *under full-employment conditions.* When this happens, the budget is restrictive. We can easily trace, for example, the policy changes of the Carter administration by looking at these data. In 1977, President Carter's first year in office, the administration pursued a mild expansionary policy, since it believed that its primary objective ought to be to get the unemployment rate down. Thus, there was a slight increase ($3.2 billion) in the full-employment deficit in this year. Thereafter, and as inflation began to supersede unemployment as an administration priority, the budget became more restrictive. Between 1977 and 1979, the full-employment deficit dropped from $22.0 to $5.4 billion—an exceedingly sharp shift from an expansionary to a restrictive budget stance. This shift in budgetary policy by the Carter administration was a factor in the recession of 1980. The enormous jump in the actual deficit between 1979 and 1980 (from $15.7 to $60.1 billion) again reflects a *passive* budgetary change, brought on by the recession.

What about the Reagan administration? The actual budget deficits were most in the public eye, but again it is the high-employment deficit that tells us more about the economic impact of these deficits. Unlike the Carter administration, the Reagan high-employment deficits have been wholly expansionary, at least through 1985—a fact which supports the point that the recovery from the 1981–82 recession was largely Keynesian in origin. This conclusion stems from the fact that the 6 percent unemployment trend rate for the GDP budget deficit steadily increased from 1981 through 1985. Further, the direction of change in the last column was negative in these years; this also indicates that the high-employment deficit was expansive. After 1985 the overall expansionary effect was relatively mild. The actual budget deficits for 1981 to 1988 are partly *passive,* a consequence of the 1981–82 recession, and partly *active,* a consequence of the 1981 tax cut. The sharp drop in the high-employment deficit in 1987 ($25.9 billion) was the result of the Tax Reform Act of 1986, an act which broadened the corporate income tax base by ending or reducing the scope of a number of corporate loopholes. The high-employment deficit rose again in 1988, although the actual deficit declined in that year. Because the Department of Commerce estimates of the 6 percent unemployment budget—or cyclically adjusted budget, as it is also called—are no longer available, precise estimates of the extent to which fiscal policy in the Bush and Clinton administrations was actually expansive or restrictive are not readily available. Using national product and employment data, the authors estimate that in 1989 the high-employment budget turned sharply restrictive, eased toward expansion in 1991 and 1992, and then turned restrictive again in 1993, the first full year of the Clinton administration.

Structural and Cyclical Deficits

In recent years the terms ''structural'' and ''cyclical'' have come into use to describe the difference between a deficit that results from a downturn in the economy and a deficit that is a result of deliberate policy action. In the prior section the focus was on the overall budget and what its effect would be on the economy in terms of either a deficit or surplus, depending on where the economy stood in relation to a full-(or high-)employment level. As developed originally by Walter Heller and other economists in the Kennedy-Johnson era, the full-employment budget was seen essentially as a planning tool designed to measure the fiscal stimulus (or lack thereof) of the federal budget in a particular year.

The focus when the deficit (rather than the total budget) is viewed in a structural or cyclical context is somewhat different. The focus is not so much on planning as on determining what part of a deficit is due to structural factors and what part is due to cyclical elements. In this context, *structural* means the part of the deficit that would exist even if the economy were operating at its full potential, that is, at a full- or high-employment level. If a deficit exists under those conditions, it must be the result of deliberate policy decisions involving taxes and expenditures. The *cyclical* component of the deficit, on the other hand, is that part of the deficit which can be attributed to the normal ups and downs of the economy. In a period of economic downturn, the cyclical proportion would increase. In an economic upswing the reverse would happen.

How are structural and cyclical deficits determined? The procedure is quite simple, for basically all that has to be done is subtract from the total deficit recorded in any one year the full- or high-employment deficit computed for that same year. The difference represents the cyclical component in the total deficit. Viewed in this manner, the structural and cyclical components of the deficit are being measured *ex post* (after the fact). They can also be estimated *ex ante* and used for planning.

Built-in Stabilizers

The foregoing discussion pertains primarily to recent experience with *deliberate* changes in taxes as a technique for economic management by the federal government. But there is another way in which both taxes and transfer payments may play an important role in the functioning of the economy. Both taxes and transfer payments may vary (or change) as a consequence of changes in the income level. Changes of this type are the basis for *passive* budgetary shifts, but they are also the basis for *built-in stabilizers,* also called automatic fiscal stabilizers. The term ''stabilizers'' is used because these features of the economic system operate in a manner that counteracts fluctuations in economic activity. They are described as built-in because they come into play automatically as the income level changes. These built-in stabilizers do not depend, in other words, on discretionary action by the monetary and fiscal authorities.

To illustrate, taxes may act as a stabilizing influence on the economic system if the tax structure is designed so that the amount of taxes collected by the government rises with an increase in the net national product. If this is the case, the effect will be to lessen the expansion in disposable income that accompanies any autonomous shift in aggregate demand. From a stabilizing point of view, the consequence of this will be a less rapid rise in induced consumption spending than would be the case in the absence of this tax system. If the tax system is constructed so that the percentage of income going to taxes increases with an increase in net national product, the stabilizing impact will be even greater. This situation will prevail if the rate structure for the tax system is progressive, because then the effective rate at which income is taxed increases as the level of income increases. In terms of our analysis (see page 322) such a system is one in which the value of the net marginal propensity to tax is an increasing function of the income level. Stabilizing effects of a reverse character come into play when the income level declines. The fiscal system, in short, operates in a countercyclical or stabilizing fashion if its overall effect is to insulate to a degree disposable income from changes in the net national product.

The foregoing analysis is predicated on prices' being reasonably stable, because sharp and continued inflation can cause the stabilizers to work in a perverse fashion. One of the unhappy consequences of the serious inflation the nation experienced in the 1970s (annual rates from 3.3 percent to double-digit levels) was to thrust many families into higher brackets, even though their money incomes were not rising any faster than the price level. Thus, the combination of inflation and a progressive tax structure brought them an actual decline in *real* income, not just a slowing down in the rate at which their income was rising. In 1974 *real* per capita disposable income actually declined—a factor that contributed to the severity of the recession in this year. The movement of a taxpayer into a higher tax bracket solely because of income gains that merely keep pace with inflation is known as *bracket creep*. The purpose of indexing the tax system in the 1981 law was to end such a phenomenon.

The discussion of built-in stabilizers has concentrated on taxes, but the reader should be aware that various forms of transfer expenditures affect the economy in a similar countercyclical fashion. If transfer payments are to have a stabilizing effect, they must decrease in absolute amount when the net national product (or national income) increases and increase when the reverse happens. Transfers in the form of unemployment compensation payments provide a good example of this kind of behavior. When output and employment are falling, payments to the unemployed automatically increase and thus insulate disposable income to a degree from a decline in earned income. When unemployment declines with a recovery from a recession or depression, transfer payments fall off and, thus, disposable income does not rise as rapidly as would be the case otherwise.

How effective are the built-in stabilizers? It is instructive to look at some figures from five recent recessions, 1969–70, 1974–75, 1980, 1982, and 1990–91. These are given in Table 9–9, which shows the percentage changes in both federal tax receipts and transfers to persons for the period 1968 through 1993. They are derived from current dollar figures, not data corrected for changes in the price level. According to the theoretical propositions set forth in this chapter, we should expect the rate of tax collections to fall off and the rate of transfer outlays to rise during a recession. This is exactly what happened. There was a mild recession in 1969–70 (unemployment rose to 4.9

TABLE 9–9   Changes in Federal Tax Receipts and Transfer Payments to Persons: 1968–1994 (annual percentage change)

Year	Tax Receipts	Transfers to Persons
1968	15.8%	14.7%
1969	12.9	10.0 ⎫ Recession
1970	−2.2	21.3 ⎭
1971	3.7	18.5
1972	14.6	10.8
1973	13.6	15.9
1974	11.5	22.7 ⎫ Recession
1975	0.3	27.7 ⎭
1976	15.3	8.5
1977	12.9	6.8
1978	14.9	7.2
1979	14.4	12.7
1980	9.7	20.1 Recession
1981	15.5	14.2
1982	−0.7	12.1 Recession
1983	3.9	7.5
1984	10.0	1.2
1985	8.6	6.5
1986	5.0	5.3
1987	3.7	4.1
1988	6.7	5.8
1989	7.7	7.9
1990	4.9	8.8 ⎫ Recession
1991	1.5	10.8 ⎭
1992	4.4	9.6
1993	7.4	5.4
1994	8.7	3.8

Source: Economic Report of the President, 1991, p. 381; 1995, p. 374.

percent of the labor force in 1970 compared to 3.6 percent in 1968), a sharp recession in 1974–75 (when unemployment hit 8.9 percent), another sharp but short recession in 1980, and a severe recession in 1981–82, when unemployment reached 9.7 percent of the civilian labor force. Although officially the 1990–91 recession ended in March 1991, the unemployment rate continued to rise through 1992, when it reached 7.3 percent. The recovery from the 1990–91 recession was sluggish compared to prior recoveries. The data in the table also show clearly that transfer expenditures behaved in the expected countercyclical fashion: they rose sharply during the recession years and fell back to more moderate rates of gain in the nonrecession years. For the nonrecession years shown in the table, tax receipts grew at an annual average rate of 9.4 percent and transfers at an annual average rate of 9.1 percent. Compare these averages with the figures for the recession years, when taxes grew at an annual average rate of 5.2 percent, but transfers exploded to a 17.5 percent growth rate.

The behavior of the built-in stabilizers has been analyzed by many economists. One study of the experience of the 1950s concluded as follows:

> On the average a fall in national income has led to a rise in transfer payments and a fall in tax collections, totaling a swing of approximately 50 percent of the decline in national income. During upswings the automatic stabilizers have exhibited a swing to increases in national income of slightly less than 30 percent on the average. Thus, assuming a $10 billion increase in national income, disposable income will rise by $2.8 billion less than it would have had automatic stabilization been inoperative. Had national income fallen by $10 billion, the induced drop in disposable income would have been $5.1 billion less as a consequence of the presence of automatic stabilizers.[5]

Another study estimated the extent to which the stabilizers reduced the potential change in income during three recessions and three expansions. In this instance it found that the stabilizers are capable of reducing declines in the national income by about 50 percent if the values for the marginal propensity to invest out of retained corporate earnings are close to 0.9 to 0.5, respectively. (Note that the higher the value of the marginal propensity to consume out of disposable income, the greater is the impact of transfer expenditures in maintaining disposable income in the face of a decline in the national income.) It was also found that during expansions the stabilizers would prevent over 40 percent of the potential increase in income if the values for the marginal propensity to consume out of disposable income and the marginal propensity to invest out of retained corporate earnings were as above and, furthermore, if government spending on goods and services remained unchanged.[6]

In 1963 the Council of Economic Advisers had the following comments about built-in stabilizers:

> Thus the tax-and-transfer response narrows fluctuations in income caused by irregularities in the strength of demand. The sharper the response of tax collections to changes in GNP, the stronger the stabilization effect. Although the tax-and-transfer response cannot prevent or reverse a movement in GNP, it can and does limit the extent of cumulative expansions and contractions. At least with respect to contractions, this is clearly an important service to the economy.
>
> Automatic fiscal stabilizers have made a major contribution in limiting the length

---

[5] M. O. Clement, "The Quantitative Impact of Automatic Stabilizers," *Review of Economics and Statistics,* February 1960, p. 60.

[6] Peter Eilbott, "The Effectiveness of Automatic Stabilizers," *American Economic Review,* June 1966, p. 463. See also George E. Rejda, "Unemployment Insurance as an Automatic Stabilizer," *Journal of Risk and Insurance,* June 1966, pp. 195–208.

and severity of postwar recessions. Each of the four postwar recessions—1948–49, 1953–54, 1957–58, and 1960–61—has been both short and mild.[7]

Few economists would argue that the stabilizers by themselves can smooth out fluctuations in income and employment in the complex economy characteristic of a modern nation, but most would probably agree that they are a vital and effective complement to discretionary action. Perhaps the best evidence in support of this is the fact that only once (1949) during the whole post-World War II period did disposable income in current dollars decline, and even then the amount of the decline was negligible. Without the impact of built-in stabilizers it is unlikely that the economy could have gone this long without a major depression. Because the effectiveness of built-in stabilizers has become so widely accepted among economists, they are seldom in the news. Attention was drawn to them once again in 1995 during the debates on the balanced budget amendment to the Constitution. A number of economists pointed out that such an amendment would nullify the stabilizers, because during a downturn the government would be forced to raise taxes and cut spending to keep the budget in balance—behavior that would worsen not improve economic conditions.

Before concluding this discussion of built-in stabilizers, one further comment is in order. Although they work through the theoretical structure designed by Keynes, they are not a product of *The General Theory*. They exist because of the growth of the Western welfare state, which developed independently of Keynesian ideas, and progressiveness in income taxes, an idea much older than *The General Theory*. To the extent that the Reagan and Bush administrations cut back on welfare spending and reduced income tax progression, the effectiveness of the stabilizers was reduced.

The Balanced Budget Thesis

In this era of chronic federal deficits—the last time the federal budget was in balance was 1969—it may seem quixotic to speak of a *balanced budget thesis*. Yet for the sake of theoretical completeness we need to examine the special case in which an increase (or decrease) in government spending is matched by an equal increase (or decrease) in taxes. This is a special situation because, contrary to what one might think at first glance, a tax-financed increase in such expenditures *may* be expansionary. This possibility has come to be known as the *balanced budget thesis*. It is derived from the fact that the multiplier effect associated with changes in both taxes and transfers is normally smaller than the multiplier effect associated with changes in government expenditures for goods and services.

To illustrate the nature of this thesis, let us refer once again to the data of Table 9–3. We made the assumption there that government exhaustive ex-

---

[7] *Economic Report of the President*, 1963, p. 67.

penditures increased by $80 billion. Let us now assume further that taxes are simultaneously increased by an equal amount so that the new and higher level of government expenditures can be financed. Our problem is to determine how the combined impact of the increase in both government expenditures and taxes will affect the income level. Contrary to what might be assumed at first, a change of this type is not neutral in its effects on the income level.

The effect of simultaneous change in both government expenditures and taxes depends on the combined impact of the increase in government expenditures and the increase in taxes on the aggregate demand function. In our example let us assume, as earlier, that the marginal propensity to consume out of disposable income a is 0.5, the marginal propensity to invest b is 0.1, and the marginal propensity to tax t is 0.2. The value of the effective multiplier, according to Equation (9–25), is thus 2. The shift in the aggregate demand function will equal the increase in government expenditure ΔG less the autonomous shift downward in the consumption function that results from the tax increase. This latter shift is designated as ΔC_0. In algebraic terms we have

$$\Delta D = \Delta G - \Delta C_0. \qquad (9\text{–}26)$$

But ΔC_0 depends on the value of the marginal propensity to consume (out of disposable income) and the change in disposable income. The latter is the same as the increase in taxes. Thus, we have

$$\Delta C_0 = a\Delta Y_d = -a\Delta TX.$$

Given a value of 0.5 for a, we find that ΔC_0 is equal to minus $40 billion. The combined effect of the increase in government purchases of goods and services and the increase in taxes will be to shift the aggregate demand function upward by $40 billion. When the effective multiplier of 2 is applied against this increment in aggregate demand, the final change in the net national product is $80 billion, which is just equal to the amount by which government expenditures for goods and services increased. The significant point to note is that the expansion of these expenditures, even though accompanied by an equal increase in taxes—the balanced budget thesis—was not neutral with respect to its impact on the output level. In other words, an expansion of government purchases of goods and services under balanced budget conditions may cause a rise in the output level; if the expansion were to occur with full-employment conditions, the result would be a significant increase in pressure on the price level.

In the foregoing example the student will note that the net national product increased by an amount just equal to the increase in government expenditures, namely, $80 billion. If the marginal propensity to tax t were 0 rather than 0.2, the increase in the net national product would have been $100 billion rather than $80 billion. On the other hand, if the value of the marginal propensity to tax is greater than 0.2, the increase in the net national product will be less than $80 billion, but will still be greater than zero. It would be a useful exercise to compute, if we assume different values for the marginal propensity to consume out of a disposable income a, how large a tax increase would have to be to prevent any increase in the net national product, given an $80 billion increase in government outlays. The student should note carefully, too, that the shift in the aggregate demand function, given the amount of the tax increase, is governed by the value of the marginal propensity to consume out of disposable income, whereas the size of the ultimate change in the net national product, given both the increase in taxes and the value of a, depends on the value of the marginal propensity to tax t.

The Debt and the Deficit in the 1980s and Beyond

One of the consequences unintended and unforeseen by the architects of the Reagan economic program was an unprecedented growth of both the federal debt and the federal deficit in peacetime and under high-employment conditions. There is a close link between the two.

In 1980 the gross federal interest-bearing debt was $906.4 billion. Fifteen years later it stood at $4,689.5 billion, a 417.3 percent, or more than fivefold, increase. The federal deficit on a national income accounts basis—total federal expenditures less total federal receipts—was $60.1 billion in 1980. It rose to a peak of $282.7 billion in 1992 then dropped back to $172.5 billion in 1994.[8] These absolute increases in both the debt and deficit during the 1980s made the headlines and caught the public eye. However, absolute figures don't tell the full story of the deficit and its significance for the economy.

A more useful way to approach this question is to look at the size of the deficit relative to the gross national or domestic product (GNP or GDP). This is done in Table 9–10, showing the average ratio of the federal deficit to the GNP or GDP from the 1930s through the 1980s. The table also indicates what major events influenced the economy's behavior during each of these decades. Two facts are especially important. First, in *every* decade since 1929 the federal budget has, on the average, been in deficit. Second, and except for the period which included World War II, the deficits of the Reagan-Bush era were larger relative to the GDP than in any other decade since 1929.

As a consequence of the continued growth in both the debt and the deficit, the deficit issue came to dominate federal policymaking to an unprecedented degree during the 1980s. Passage of the Gramm-Rudman-Hollings (GRH) bill in December 1985 reflected this. This act sought to achieve by legislative fiat the balanced budget that continued to elude the normal legislative process. Gramm-Rudman-Hollings failed totally in attaining the balanced budget sought after, but it succeeded almost every year in bringing a near shutdown

---

[8] *Economic Report of the President,* 1995, p. 371.

TABLE 9–10   **Federal Surplus or Deficit (−) as a Percent of the GNP or GDP: 1930s–1990s**

Decade	Surplus or Deficit (−)*	Comment
1930s	−3.39%	Great Depression
1940s	−9.99	World War II
1950s	−0.42	Korean War, two recessions (1953, 1958)
1960s	−0.83	Kennedy-Johnson tax cut, Vietnam War
1970s	−2.51	Two recessions (1970, 1974–75), oil shocks
1980s	−4.10	Reagan tax cut, two recessions (1980, 1981–82)
1990s	−4.16	Recession (1990–91)

*Percent of GNP through 1970s and of GDP for 1980s and 1990s.

Source: Economic Report of the President, various years.

of the federal government as the Congress and the administration struggled to find a way to avoid the across-the-board cuts mandated by the act.

Not all economists are convinced that the deficits of the 1980s and 1990s are nearly so threatening to the economy's basic health as media reporting and the conventional wisdom believe them to be. For one thing, it is not so easy as one might think to determine the exact size of the deficit. The *official* deficit—the measure used to calculate the percentage figures shown in Table 9–10—is the difference between the government's total receipts and total expenditures. Some economists, however, argue that a *net* deficit figure is the appropriate measure.[9] Since a significant portion of the federal debt is held by the federal government itself in so-called trust funds for Social Security, Medicare, highway and airport construction, and other purposes, it is appropriate to adjust the official deficit to reflect this fact. In 1994, for example, the gross debt was $4,689.5 billion, of which $1,224.0 billion was held within the federal government. The net debt, therefore, was equal to $3,465.5 billion.[10] The net deficit is equal to the change in the government's net debt during a year.

Yet another possible measure is the *national* or *economic* deficit. This is the federal deficit adjusted for the deficits or surpluses incurred by state and local governments. The reasoning behind this version of the deficit is that what counts economically is the overall deficit (or surplus) for the entire public sector, not just the federal segment. Since state and local governments had surpluses for *every* year since 1967,[11] making this adjustment reduces significantly the size of the overall, nominal deficit associated with government activity.

By far the most thorough critique of the conventional measurement of the

[9] Robert Heilbroner and Peter Bernstein, *The Debt and the Deficit: False Alarms/Real Possibilities* (New York: Norton, 1989), pp. 71 ff.

[10] *Economic Report of the President,* 1995, pp. 376, 378.

[11] Ibid., p. 372.

Gramm-Rudman-Hollings: A Balanced Budget by Fiat

Like a King Canute ordering the tide not to come in, the Congress by legislative fiat decreed that the federal budget shall be balanced. This is the essence of the Gramm-Rudman-Hollings bill, passed in December 1985.

Described as "a bad idea whose time has come" by Senator Warren Rudman, one of the bill's sponsors, this piece of legislation mandated that the federal budget deficit be cut over a period of years and reach a balanced state by fiscal year 1991. The official name of GRH was the Balanced Budget and Emergency Deficit Control Act of 1985.

As originally passed, the legislation required that the federal budget be cut automatically to reach the deficit target if in any single year the Congress failed to come up with a budget that met the GRH target. In July of 1986, however, the Supreme Court ruled that the automatic triggering mechanisms of the act were an unconstitutional delegation to the executive of the congressional budget authority.

Congress amended the act in 1987 to correct the deficiencies found by the Supreme Court and thereby kept alive the idea that a balanced budget could be mandated by legislation. It also extended the targeted deadline for achieving a balanced budget to fiscal year 1993. When fiscal year 1993 ended the deficit was not zero, but $254.7 billion. *Sic transit gloria GRH* (thus passes the glory of GRH)!

"Recent history," Princeton University economist and member of the Council of Economic Advisers Alan S. Blinder said, "has proved what he (Senator Rudman) should have known: The right time for a bad idea never comes."

deficit has been made by Northwestern University professor Robert Eisner. In his 1986 book, *How Real is the Federal Deficit?*, Professor Eisner argues that the conventional and official measure of the deficit vastly overstates its size; the consequence of this has been serious errors in economic policy. The essence of his argument is that the deficit should reflect the changing *real* value of the federal government's outstanding debt. The real market value of the debt changes because of both inflation and changes in interest rates. As Professor Eisner observes, "the market values of existing debts fall as interest rates rise, and their real values fall still further as prices rise. If we want measures of deficits that are equal to the *real, market value* of debt, then we must adjust our measures to incorporate these changes in real market values due to inflation and changing interest rates."[12]

Figure 9–10 compares the official deficit with Professor Eisner's inflation-adjusted deficit on a high-employment basis for both deficit measures. The period covered is 1955 through 1984. It is, the reader will recall, the high-(or

---

[12] Robert Eisner, *How Real is the Federal Deficit?* (New York: Free Press, 1986), p. 12.

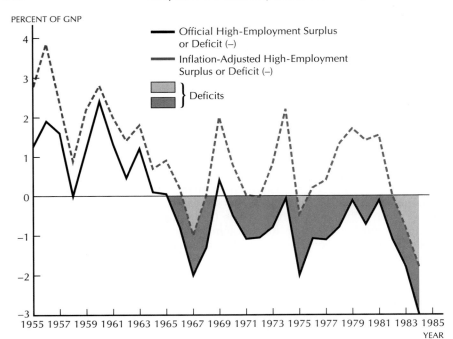

FIGURE 9–10   Official and Price-Adjusted High-Employment Budget Surplus.   The solid line in the figure traces the path of the official high-employment budget surplus (or deficit) for the period 1955 through 1984. The upper dotted line is the path of Professor Eisner's price-adjusted surplus (or deficit). Through the 1970s it registered a surplus, whereas the official budget was in deficit.

Source: Robert Eisner, *How Real is the Federal Deficit?* (New York: Free Press, 1986).

full-)employment deficit (or surplus) which provides the best measure of the impact of fiscal policy on the economy. The most striking contrast between these two measures of the deficit emerges during the 1970s, years in which the official high-employment federal budget was in deficit. Yet throughout the 1970s, Professor Eisner's budget calculations adjusted for inflation almost always show a *surplus*.

What this means, Professor Eisner suggests, is that "some significant rewriting of recent economic history is perhaps in order. Inflation could hardly be ascribed to excess demand associated with increasing fiscal ease and stimulus if, at least by the appropriately corrected high-employment budget measure, there was no such movement to fiscal ease."[13] This is an important point. One of the key arguments in the monetarist challenge to Keynesian economics was its alleged inability to explain the simultaneous appearance of inflation and high unemployment in the 1970s. True, there were both excessive inflation and unemployment in the 1970s, but as will be shown later

[13] Ibid., p. 87.

(Chapter 12), this was not because of the inadequacy of Keynesian theory, but because of a failure to pay heed to what Keynes said in *The General Theory* about the price level and how it is determined.

The failure to perceive that the high-employment budget was in a surplus state, not in deficit, was especially damaging, Professor Eisner asserts, in the late 1970s. Viewing the official rather than inflation-adjusted data, the Carter economists believed that the economy was "suffering from too much fiscal stimulus. Both the deficits and the stimulus had to be reduced to curb inflation."[14] This belief helped pave the way for the tight money policy initiated by Chairperson Paul Volcker and the Federal Reserve in October 1979. The combination of tight money and a tight fiscal policy pushed the economy into the recessions of 1980 and 1981–82.

What conclusions are to be drawn from the foregoing? The first, and perhaps most obvious, is that there is no single *correct* measure of either the debt or the deficit. All the measures that we have discussed have their uses, especially the inflation- and interest-rate-corrected measure devised by Professor Eisner. Second, policymakers in the nation's capital ought to employ *all* the measures we have been discussing in their formulation of policy actions. Unfortunately to date this has not happened. Official neglect of the Eisner approach is particularly serious, as it can lead to doing the wrong thing at the wrong time.

The Role of Finance

In our earlier discussions in this chapter of the impact on output and employment of an increase in government expenditures (or the reverse) or a decrease in taxes, questions pertaining to how the government finances added expenditures or how it responds to a revenue loss following a tax cut were deferred. Now it is appropriate to deal with these questions. As we have just seen, if government expenditures are increased and the added expenditures are financed by an equal increase in taxes, there will be some impact on output and employment, but the effect will be minimal. Much the same will be true if a tax cut is accompanied by an equal reduction in government expenditures, so that the overall budget position of the government is left unchanged.

Finance enters the picture when the government either increases its expenditures without an offsetting tax increase or reduces taxes without cutting back on its outlays. Then a deficit is created, or an existing deficit is enlarged. In either event the government will have to resort to more borrowing; the deficit must be financed. This is the crucial point, for the ultimate impact of the fiscal action—increasing government expenditures or cutting taxes—will also depend on how the deficit is financed.

[14] Ibid., p. 23.

If we assume that the government will not simply resort to the printing press to finance its deficit, it has basically two choices: (1) It can borrow from the public (this is done by selling government bonds to the public),[15] or (2) it can borrow directly from the central bank (the Federal Reserve System in the United States). We shall examine each of these alternatives.

Borrowing and the Crowding-out Phenomenon

When the government obtains funds by borrowing directly from the public, the effect may be to lessen the stimulative impact of either an increase in spending or a reduction in taxes. This may happen either because households and business firms decrease some of their spending for goods and services in order to buy government bonds—the bonds are not purchased at the expense of either household or business saving—or because increased demand by government for credit causes interest rates to rise. This would lead to a reduction in private borrowing with a subsequent decline in private spending. It is possible in principle that private spending would fall sufficiently to nullify wholly the economic impact of more public spending or a tax cut.

If this happens, then the economy will have experienced the phenomenon known as *crowding out.* This term refers to the failure of any expansionary fiscal action by government (spending increases or tax cuts) to stimulate the overall level of economic activity. The crowding-out thesis originated with a paper published in 1968 by the Federal Reserve Bank of St. Louis.[16] Essentially, the thesis argues that, overall, the level of aggregate demand remains unchanged, because the stimulus coming from government action (more spending or a tax cut) is offset by unplanned reductions in private spending elsewhere in the economy. As suggested above, the latter may stem from higher interest rates or a decrease in spending resulting from the sale of bonds to the public. In either case, the expansionary effects are nullified. Since it was first formulated about three decades ago, the crowding-out thesis has generated considerable controversy among economic theorists, plus no small amount of empirical research, but no agreement has been reached on either the magnitude or certainty of this effect. With the enormous deficits of the Reagan administration plus the growing foreign trade deficit, the crowding-out argument is back in the daily news. The full dimensions of the controversy will be discussed in Chapter 11.

Monetizing the Debt

A different picture emerges if the government chooses to finance its deficit by borrowing from the central bank (the Federal Reserve System). Techni-

---

[15] The term "public" includes banks, insurance companies, and other firms, as well as persons.

[16] For a good summary, see "Crowding Out and Its Critics," *Review,* Federal Reserve Bank of St. Louis, December 1975.

The Checkered History of U.S. Income Taxes

The massive revision of the federal income tax code in 1986 is the latest chapter in a stormy story of income taxation that dates back to the Civil War. It will not be the last.

The nation's first venture into taxing income came during the Civil War. Up until that time, the federal government had depended mostly on tariffs for its relatively modest revenue needs. No more. War is expensive, and the Civil War—the first of the modern wars involving the large-scale mobilization of men and material—proved no exception to this rule. So an income tax was enacted. By today's standards it was relatively modest, as the top rate was 10 percent. It lasted 10 years.

For a while the issue of federal taxation of income was put to rest when the Supreme Court in 1895 held that such a tax was unconstitutional, being in violation of Article I, Section 8 of the U.S. Constitution which says, "No Capitation, or other direct Tax, shall be laid, unless in Proportion to the Census or Enumeration herein before directed to be taken." However, in 1909 the Congress was able to levy a tax of 1 percent on corporate income without running up against the constitutional question.

The question of constitutionality was settled (save for the ranting of fringe groups on the far right) by the adoption of the 16th Amendment to the Constitution. This amendment says that the "Congress shall have the power to lay and collect taxes on income from whatever source derived. . . ." After the amendment was approved, the Congress enacted an individual income tax of 1 percent for most taxpayers and a top rate of 7 percent. Capital gains, which are increases in the value of assets bought and sold by the taxpayer, were fully taxed as ordinary income at that time. It was only later that capital gains began to receive more-favored treatment in the income tax laws.

World War I led to the next big changes in the income tax. Corporate profits were taxed at a 12 percent rate, double the rate that had prevailed just before the United States entered the war. The rate on individual income went to a high of 77 percent in 1917, up from 15 percent in 1916.

In 1921, the first preferential rate was adopted for capital gains, and rates on individual incomes were reduced from the high levels that prevailed during World War I. The *marginal* rate—the rate applied to additional income—fell from a high of 77 percent in World War I to a low of 24 percent in 1929.

War again brought major changes in both individual and corporate income taxes. During World War II, the marginal rate for individuals went to 94 percent for the highest bracket, and the corporate tax rate rose to 40 percent on profits above $40,000. During the Korean War, the tax on corporate incomes rose again to a top rate of 52 percent on income above $25,000.

In the post-World War II period two trends dominated the income tax picture. Individual and corporate rates were cut from their wartime highs, and two new devices were introduced into corporate taxation to bolster investment spending. These were accelerated depreciation and the investment tax credit. The latter was eliminated, and the former cut back by the 1986 Tax Reform Act.

And what does the future hold? The only certainty is that conflict over the form and rate of income taxation will continue and that practically everything proposed will be proposed in the name of either fairness or simplicity.

cally, the U.S. government is limited by law in the amount the Treasury can borrow directly from the Federal Reserve; the limit is $5 billion. But there is a way around this because there is no limit on the amount of Treasury debt (bills and bonds) that the Federal Reserve can buy in the open market for government securities. When the Federal Reserve purchases Treasury obligations in the open market, this, of course, increases the supply of money and credit. In effect, the Federal Reserve is indirectly financing the government's deficit through an expansion of the money supply. If the deficit is financed in this fashion—described as *monetizing* a part of the government's debt—there will not be the same pressure on interest rates as occurs when the government borrows directly from the public. In fact, the added supply of money and credit could cause lower rates and thus lead to an increase in private spending. The upshot of all this is that private spending is much less likely to be curtailed if this is the route chosen by the government for the financing of its deficit.

Government Borrowing and the *IS-LM* Model

The way in which government borrowing *may* affect the economy can be shown in a single diagram, again using the *IS-LM* model. The key is the different effects of the crowding-out phenomenon and monetizing the debt. Figure 9–11 shows this.

As in Figure 9–8, the initial position of the economy is given by the intersection of the two heavily lined curves labeled *IS* and *LM,* giving the initial equilibrium income level (Y_e) and interest rate (i_e). An increase in government spending (ΔG) is shown by a shift in the *IS* curve to the right; the new position is shown by the curve labeled IS_1. What happens to the income level depends on how the increased government spending is financed.

If the added expenditure is financed by borrowing from the public, then *crowding out* may occur. This leads to a rise in interest rates, shown in Figure 9–11 by the shift of the interest rate to the level i'_e. Complete crowding out does not occur in the figure, because the income level rises from Y_e to Y_1. If there had not been any crowding out because of a rise in interest rates, the full effect of the shift in the *IS* curve would have been felt and income would have risen to the Y_2 level. What is assumed here, although it is not shown in the figure, is that some private investment has been crowded out by the rise in interest rates. Consequently, the overall change in income is less than it would have been without the increase in interest rates induced by crowding out.

The result is different if the government monetizes the debt created by the borrowing associated with the added government spending (ΔG). The effects in this case are the same as an increase in the money supply. Hence, in the *IS-LM* model the *LM* curve is shifted to the right; its new position is shown by the curve labeled LM_1. Since in this simplified example there is no increase

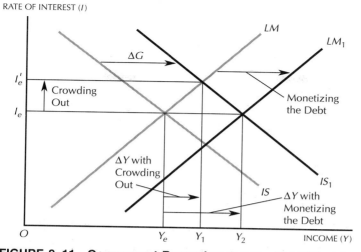

FIGURE 9–11   Government Borrowing and the *IS-LM* Model. If there is an increase in government spending (Δ*G*), the *IS* curve will shift to the right. If this added spending is financed by borrowing from the public, the income level will only rise to Y_1. But if the added debt is monetized, the *LM* curve will shift to the right, there may be no increase in interest rates, and the full effect of the increased government spending on income will result.

in interest rates because the additional debt has been monetized, the full effects of the shift in the *IS* curve are realized. The new equilibrium income level is now Y_2.

Budget Surpluses

To this point the discussion has centered on the financing problems associated with a deficit that results from either increased public expenditures or a tax cut. But, as the analysis undertaken earlier in this chapter suggests, fiscal action may move in either direction. That is, the government may reduce its expenditures or increase its taxes. If expenditures are reduced without a corresponding cut in taxes, or taxes are increased without an increase in expenditures, the government will have a surplus.[17] A surplus obviously does not pose a financing problem, as does a deficit, but it may have consequences for the general level of economic activity. Other things being equal, a surplus tends to be deflationary, because its existence means the government is taking more out of the income stream through taxes than it is putting back in through

---

[17] Discussion of the economic effects of a budget surplus may seem academic, as there have been only four years since 1960 when the federal government had a surplus. These years were 1960, 1963, 1965, and 1969.

expenditures. But the impact of the surplus on aggregate demand will depend on the disposition the government makes of its surplus.

In principle, two options are available to the government. First, it may elect to use the surplus to retire debt held by the public. If it does this, it is, in effect, transferring the surplus revenues received to the public, which may or may not spend them. If the funds received by the public when debt is retired are spent, then the deflationary impact of the government's surplus is reduced. It is not too likely that this will happen, however, as many of the holders of government obligations are in the upper-income brackets; they will probably use the checks they receive from the government to purchase other securities. The alternative to debt retirement is for the government simply to continue to hold the surplus funds idle; then there cannot be any offsetting private expenditures at all. This is possible in principle, but the chances that it would actually happen are exceedingly remote.

Summary

1. Government expenditures for goods and services are a major element in the aggregate demand function. As with investment expenditure, there is a multiplier effect associated with changes in government spending for goods and services.

2. Transfer expenditures are basically different from the purchase of goods and services by government because they do not enter directly into aggregate demand. They do so indirectly by their effect on disposable income.

3. The multiplier effect associated with changes in transfer expenditures is smaller than the multiplier associated with the direct purchase of goods and services by government. This is because changes in transfer expenditures first affect disposable income and only then is total spending affected through the consumption function.

4. Taxes affect the income level in the same manner as transfers do, except in the opposite direction. They affect disposable income first and then indirectly consumption. As with transfers there is a multiplier effect smaller than the multiplier effect associated with a change in government spending for goods and services.

5. The full-(high-)employment budget calculates what the federal surplus or deficit would be under full-(high-)employment conditions; it emerged in the 1960s as an important analytical tool for policymakers. It has been used in varying degrees by recent administrations, depending in part on their activist propensities, but is no longer calculated by the U.S. Department of Commerce.

6. More recently, the concepts of cyclical and structural deficits have been developed to show how the state of the economy affects the government's financial situation. A cyclical deficit results from an economic downturn, whereas a structural deficit exists even under full-(high-)employment conditions. Hence it is a consequence of policy actions.

7. Built-in stabilizers are the features of the tax and transfer structure of the federal government that come into play automatically during cyclical swings and tend to either dampen or stimulate the economy, depending on the stage of the business cycle in which the economy finds itself.

8. The balanced budget thesis shows how a balanced budget may be expansionary because of the fact that expenditures for goods and services have a greater direct affect on aggregate demand than do taxes.

9. The financing of government expenditures plays an important role in the impact of the government's actions on the economy's performance. Under some circumstances, spending financed by borrowing may crowd out private borrowing and thus be less expansionary than expected.

Appendix

Formal Proof That $a - at = a'$, the Marginal Propensity to Consume out of Net National Product

(1) $a = \dfrac{\Delta C}{\Delta Y_d}$
    The marginal propensity to consume out of disposable income

(2) $a' = \dfrac{\Delta C}{\Delta Y_{np}}$
    The marginal propensity to consume out of net national product

(3) $t = \dfrac{\Delta T}{\Delta Y_{np}}$
    The net marginal propensity to tax out of net national product

(4) $1 - t = \dfrac{\Delta Y_d}{\Delta Y_{np}}$
    The net marginal rate of retention of income

This is derived as follows:

(a) $Y_{np} = Y_d + T$

(b) $\Delta Y_{np} = \Delta Y_d + \Delta T$

Divide both sides of (b) by ΔY_{np}:

(c) $1 = \dfrac{\Delta Y_d}{\Delta Y_{np}} + \dfrac{\Delta T}{\Delta Y_{np}}$

(d) $\dfrac{\Delta Y_d}{\Delta Y_{np}} = 1 - \dfrac{\Delta T}{\Delta Y_{np}} = 1 - t$

(5) $(1 - t) \times a = \dfrac{\Delta C}{\Delta Y_{np}} = a'$

This is derived as follows:

(a) $\dfrac{\Delta Y_d}{\Delta Y_{np}} \times \dfrac{\Delta C}{\Delta Y_d} = \dfrac{\Delta C}{\Delta Y_{np}} = a'$ (by substitution)

Therefore:

(b) $a' = a(1 - t) = a - at$

10 The International Economy

U P TO THIS POINT in Part III we have examined the foundations of aggregate demand through the analysis of consumption, investment, and government spending. It is now time to move beyond that and bring the international economic transactions of a nation into the analysis. Our focus in this chapter is on the *open economy*. Specifically, we shall examine how changes in the international economic position of a nation affect its internal economy and, then, how internal changes affect the nation's international economic position.

As in the prior chapters on consumption, investment, and government spending, the fundamental analytical tool through which we approach these objectives is the schedule of aggregate demand, the key thread that runs through all macroeconomics. Our analysis of how the domestic economy fits into the larger scene of the international economy must be undertaken against the backdrop of profound changes and upheavals that have and are continuing to take place in the international economy. Among the most important of these are the following:

1. The rise and fall during the 1970s of OPEC (the Organization of Petroleum Exporting Countries), a development which drove the world price of petroleum to unprecedented levels, was a major factor in the rampant inflation of the decade, brought about an enormous transfer of wealth from the United

States and the nations of Western Europe to a small group of oil-rich countries, and, finally, contributed to stagnating conditions in Western Europe which lingered into the 1990s. The Iraq invasion of Kuwait on August 1, 1990 and the short Gulf War of early 1991 again thrust the Middle East and its instabilities into the forefront of the international economic picture. Uncertainties with respect to the price of oil and its availability because of continued political, social, and economic turmoil in this region remain an ever-present concern to the world economy.

2. The end of the Bretton Woods system of fixed exchange rates. Between 1945 and 1971 the world economy operated under a system of relatively fixed rates of exchange (that is, prices) for the various national currencies. In this system, which was constructed toward the end of World War II at an international conference in Bretton Woods, New Hampshire, the U.S. dollar played a key role; most other major currencies were tied to the dollar in terms of their exchange values and to gold through the dollar. This system came to an end in 1971, when President Nixon ended the convertibility of foreign official holdings of dollars into gold. For a quarter century since Nixon's historic decision, exchange rates have been free to fluctuate in response to market forces, but there is growing dissatisfaction in the world economic community with this post-Bretton Woods system. Increasingly the freely floating exchange rate system serves the whims and desires of speculators at the expense of the more serious needs of trade and commerce. No agreement yet exists on the shape of a revamped international monetary system, but the forces demanding change are gathering strength.

3. The world economy has become more integrated and more competitive than at any time in modern history. We are living in a global economy in which all parts of the world are tied together economically. Competition has also become truly international, as witnessed by the fact that products from Japan, West Germany, Korea, Hong Kong, and nearly every other part of the globe now play major roles in U.S. life. U.S. manufacturing, which once dominated the globe, is now hard-pressed and fighting in some areas for survival against aggressive foreign competition. The changed structure of the world economy means that all nations, including economic giants like the United States, have far less scope than once was the case to manage their domestic economies without reference to international economic events. The means do not yet exist, however, by which the major economic powers can cooperate and coordinate in economic policymaking, either for domestic or for international economic objectives.

4. In the 1980s the international economic position of the United States underwent a drastic change. Since 1980 the nation has moved from being the world's leading creditor nation with net foreign-held assets in excess of $140 billion to the leading debtor country. By the end of 1993 net foreign claims against the United States equaled $556 billion, a figure that will probably continue to grow. This change in the nation's international economic position is tied closely to key macroeconomic developments, including the deficits of

the federal government, the explosive growth of imports, and the fluctuations in the foreign exchange value of the dollar.

5. The continuing economic unification of Western Europe and the emergence of market-oriented economies in Eastern Europe will influence significantly the nature and scope of international macroeconomics in the 1990s and into the 2000s. Unified markets in Western Europe, while competitively challenging U.S. business, will also create the need for new and workable institutions for international policy coordination and cooperation. Rebuilding the economies of Eastern Europe requires huge volumes of global capital; this may strain the world's capital markets, although eventually enlarging the world's potential for output and employment growth.

We shall begin with some general comments on the characteristics of an open economy, followed by an analysis of the key macroeconomic relationships that enter into the aggregate demand function in an open economy. Then we shall conclude the chapter by bringing these relationships together in an open economy, *IS-LM* model.

The Open Economy

In macroeconomic analysis the term ''open economy'' is used to mean an economy that has significant economic relationships with other nations. Economists find it analytically useful to examine, as we have done to a degree in the prior chapters, how economies behave at the macroeconomic level by assuming there are no economic ties with other nations. This is the closed economy assumption. As we saw in Chapter 2, a closed economic system defines output (Y) as being equal to $C + I + G$. There are no exports (X) or imports (M).

What distinguishes an open from a closed economy is the existence of trade between nations, flows of financial capital between nations, and a mechanism (the foreign exchange markets) whereby the domestic monetary systems of different countries are linked together. At the empirical level it is essentially a matter of the importance of trade, capital flows, and foreign exchange links *relative* to the size of the domestic economy that determines whether the economy ought to be viewed primarily as closed or open. The determination is made by the exercise of judgement, not the mechanical application of any arithmetic formula.

Until relatively recently, for example, foreign trade did not play a significant role in the U.S. economy, so for all practical purposes the economy could be analyzed in the macroeconomic sense as if it were a closed system. This is no longer true. Between 1960 and 1994 the ratio to the GDP of a combined total for exports and imports rose from 9.4 to 22.8 percent—a rise that indicates the relative importance of foreign trade to the U.S. economy grew by 142.5 percent in this period. In constant dollar volume the total for exports and imports combined increased more than 7.8 times, compared with a 2.7-fold increase in the GDP.[1]

Moreover, the financial markets of the major trading nations have become so closely coordinated as to become, in the view of one international economist, "... inseparable. Funds flow so swiftly and smoothly from one financial center to another that interest rates tend to be speedily equalized throughout the world."[2] Consequently, it is increasingly difficult, if not impossible, for nations to pursue either fiscal or monetary policies in isolation. Policy actions taken in one country are transmitted almost instantly to other countries, sometimes with disruptive effects. When the foreign exchange value of the U.S. dollar soared to unprecedented levels in the late 1970s and early 1980s, the flood of imports that ensued had devastating effects on U.S. agriculture and manufacturing in steel, automobiles, and electronics. The foreign exchange markets, which are global in scope and in which the currencies of all the major nations are continuously traded, exceed in size the largest of the financial markets, such as the stock exchanges in New York, London, or Tokyo.[3]

We also saw in Chapter 2 (page 69) that we can move from the idea of a closed to the idea of an open economy by adding exports (X) and imports (M) to the basic macroeconomic identity equations developed in that chapter. Another way to illustrate the nature of an open economy is to expand the simplified circular-flow diagram developed in Chapter 2 (Figure 2–1) to bring the trade balance, financial flows, and foreign exchange markets into the model. This is done in Figure 10–1. The circular-flow model of the domestic economy developed earlier is expanded by adding a box designated "Markets for Goods and Services," which links the spending and selling activity of households and business firms (producing units), and a box designated "Markets for Economic Resources," which links the selling of the services of economic resources by households and the purchase of these services by business firms. In the diagram the solid lines represent real, or goods, flows, and the dotted lines money flows.

Added to this basic model in the lower part of the diagram is a box designated "Rest of the World" (ROW) and two smaller boxes designated, each "Foreign Exchange Market." Figure 10–1 is still highly simplified, but it does enable us to see the essential ways in which the domestic economy fits into the global picture. Let us trace through some of these ways. For example, when U.S. firms export goods and services to the rest of the world (ROW), other countries must ultimately pay for these goods in U.S. dollars. They get dollars by exchanging their own currencies for dollars in the foreign exchange markets. Thus, the money counterpart of the outward flow of goods and services from the United States is an inward flow of money to the country, either

---

[1] *Economic Report of the President,* 1995, pp. 274–277.

[2] Thomas F. Dernburg, *Global Macroeconomics* (New York: Harper & Row, 1989), p. 5.

[3] Ibid.

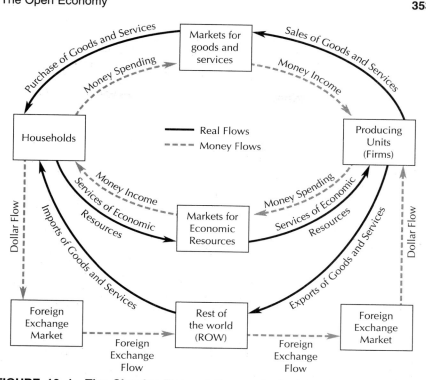

FIGURE 10–1   The Circular Flow of Economic Activity in a Global Context.   In the context of the global economy, the circular flow of output matched by money flows is augmented by adding in exports, imports, and the corresponding monetary flows of domestic and foreign currencies. In this way domestic economic activity is tied in with international economic activity.

dollars or foreign currencies. If U.S. banks, which are a part of the global foreign exchange market, want to increase their inventories of foreign currencies in anticipation of selling those currencies to Americans in the future, then U.S. exports provide a means for doing this.

Turn now to the other side of the coin, imports of foreign-made goods and services by U.S. households. These imports must ultimately be paid for in the currency of the country selling to the United States. Japanese firms, for example, expect eventually to be paid in yen for their exports. Americans get the foreign currency needed to finance their imports by exchanging dollars for foreign currencies in the foreign exchange markets. Here, the money counterpart of the inward flow of goods and services into the United States is an outward flow of money, either dollars or foreign exchange itself. As in the case of U.S. exports, the foreign banks that are a part of the global foreign exchange market may want to build up their inventories of dollars for the same reason that U.S. banks may build up their inventories of foreign exchange. The essential point is that the real flows of goods and services into and out of a country—its imports and exports—are matched by money flows in which the foreign exchange markets play a major role, not only in converting national currencies from one to another, but also in building up inventories of the major national currencies that can be drawn on to finance trade.

While this diagram accurately depicts the linkages of the domestic economy, through trade, money flows, and the foreign exchange markets, to the global economy, it does not capture the full flavor of the forces that have emerged to dominate these linkages in recent years. Microelectronics has created a worldwide network of instantaneous communication, which has made it possible for money and credit to be moved almost immediately to any spot on the globe. As a consequence, trillions of dollars—money that is largely beyond the reach of any national authority—continuously moves across the globe in search of profit in foreign exchange, bond, and stock markets, wherever profit exists. Figure 10–1 implies that money flows through the foreign exchange markets in response to the real flows of exports and imports. This is true, but not the full story. In today's world the flow of money capital across the globe overshadows the real flow of goods and services. This is a fundamental fact of life in the highly integrated, intensely competitive global economy that has been emerging since the early 1970s. Now we shall turn to a more detailed analysis of the primary elements that enter into a country's international transactions and to how these are measured.

The Nature of a Nation's Foreign Balance

A nation's international economic balance involves all the economic transactions that residents of the nation enter into with residents of all other nations during some specific period of time. The most important tool for analysis of the internal economic position of a nation is the balance of payments statement.[4] This accounting statement records (in principle) all the economic transactions that residents of one country make with residents of foreign countries during a given period of time, normally the calendar year. Since an economic transaction generally consists of a payment or a receipt in exchange for a good, service, or some type of financial asset, the balance of payments statement constitutes a record of payments made by residents of a country to foreigners and payments made by foreigners to residents of the country in question.

In balance of payments accounting practice, transactions that require foreigners to make payments to residents of the domestic economy or, alterna-

---

[4] For the purpose of balance of payments accounting the word "residents" is interpreted to mean not only physical persons, but also business firms, governments, and international agencies. Persons are considered residents of the country in which they normally reside. Residents are not necessarily or always citizens. In the United States balance of payments statistics are compiled by the Department of Commerce.

tively, provide residents of the domestic economy with the means to make payments to foreigners are treated as *credit* entries in the balance of payments statement. Thus, an export of merchandise by a U.S. firm to the United Kingdom and a loan extended by a British bank to U.S. residents would be credit entries in the U.S. balance of payments statement. On the other hand, transactions that require residents of the domestic economy to make payments to foreigners or, alternatively, provide foreigners with the means to make payments to residents of the domestic economy are treated as *debit* entries in the balance of payments statement. Imports and loans extended to foreigners would fall into the category of debit transactions in the balance of payments statement of the domestic economy.[5] Balance of payments accounting is often confusing and complex. However, if the following key rule is kept in mind, it will be easier to understand:

A credit (+) is any transaction that results in a receipt from residents in the rest of the world (foreign residents), and a debit (−) is any transaction that requires a payment be made to residents in the rest of the world.

The Structure of the Balance of Payments Statement

A nation's balance of international payments statement normally consists of several component parts, sometimes called *accounts*. There are basically two major accounts plus one or more measures of the nation's external balance. The latter vary with individual governments and the particular national purposes that balance of payments statements may be designed to serve. In the United States the most important parts of our balance of payments statement consist of the *current* account, the *capital* account, and the *balance of official reserve transactions*. Table 10–1 contains balance of payments data for the United States in 1993. We shall interpret some of these data following discussions of the major parts of the balance of payments statement.

The Current Account

The current account section of the balance of payments records all *current* transactions, which are transactions that involve either the export or the import of goods (i.e., merchandise) and services. Under services are grouped income from transportation, banking, and insurance; income in the form of interest and dividends from various financial assets; and expenditures by tourists. Transactions involving services are sometimes described as *invisible* items, whereas transactions in goods or merchandise are classified as *visible* items. In general, goods and services exported by the domestic economy are a part of the national output, but goods and services imported constitute a form of

---

[5] For a more extended discussion of the mechanics of balance of payments accounting see Wilfred J. Ethier, *Modern International Economics,* 3rd ed. (New York: Norton, 1995), Chap. 12.

**TABLE 10–1   Balance of Payments of the United States in 1993
(in billions of current dollars)**

Item	Credits (+) (Receipts)	Debits (−) (Payments)	Balance
Current account			
Trade in goods	$456.8	$589.4	$−132.6
Investment income*	113.8	109.9	3.9
Current services†	—	—	56.9
Unilateral U.S. grants	—	—	−32.1
Balance on current account	—	—	$−103.9
Capital account			
Capital outflows (net increase in U.S. assets abroad)			
1. U.S. official reserves‡		$−1.4	
2. Other U.S. government assets		−0.3	
3. Private assets		−146.2	
Total		$−147.9	
Capital inflows (net increase in foreign assets in the U.S.)			
1. Foreign official assets	$ 71.7		
2. Private assets	159.0		
3. Statistical discrepancy	21.1		
Total	$251.8		
Balance on capital transactions			$103.9

*Includes military spending.

†Includes travel, transportation, insurance, and other private services.

‡Includes gold, special drawing rights in the International Monetary Fund (IMF), convertible currencies, and U.S. reserves in the IMF.

Source: Current Economic Indicators, June 1994.

disposition of the national income. There are exceptions to this principle, but they are for the most part of minor significance. The current account section also includes unilateral (one-way) transfers by private individuals and governments (see below).

The difference between the export (or credit) items and the import (or debit) items in the current account represents its net balance. If the credit transactions exceed the debit transactions, it is customary to describe the current account balance as *active*. On the other hand, an excess of debit over credit transactions is usually spoken of as a *passive* balance on the current account. In Chapter 2 we pointed out that the net foreign investment component of the GDP can be *approximately* defined as the net difference between a nation's export of goods and services and its imports of goods and services, because any excess of receipts from exports over payments for imports, or vice versa, reflects a net change in the international asset position of the nation concerned. The word "approximately" is emphasized because the Department of Commerce defines net foreign investment as the difference between exports and imports *plus* transfer payments to foreign residents.

The current account has special significance for the purposes of this text. This is because the transactions recorded in this portion of the balance of payments statement are linked closely to the determination of the national output and the employment level. Exports of goods and services enter directly into the aggregate demand schedule and hence become one of the determinants of output in an open economy. Imports of goods and services are, on the other hand, a form of disposition of the national income, analogous in their economic effects to saving and taxes.

Special mention needs to be made of one type of transaction normally found in the current account. This is the category of unilateral transfers. Included in this category are all transfers, gifts, or donations, both public and private, made either by U.S. residents, including the U.S. government, to the rest of the world or by foreign residents to the United States. The United States, for example, gives military and economic aid to some foreign nations. This is a unilateral (government) transfer from this country to the rest of the world. In the current account, the amount of such a transfer in any one year would be recorded as a debit $(-)$ item, and the goods or services that were exported because such a transfer was made would be recorded as a credit $(+)$ item. The latter presumes that the proceeds of the transfer were spent by the recipient country.

The Capital Account

The capital account represents the financial counterpart of transactions involving currently produced goods and services that are recorded in the current account. Let us assume, for example, that a nation has in the current income period an excess of exports (of goods and services) over imports. Since exports generate payment claims against foreign residents, it can readily be seen that the export surplus increases the claims of the domestic economy against the rest of the world. An import surplus would, of course, have just the opposite effect. Within the context of the current income period, settlement of the net export surplus can be effected in a number of ways. Foreigners, for example, may borrow the needed funds from residents of the domestic economy. If this is done, there will be a net increase in the foreign claims or internationally held assets of residents of the domestic economy. A transaction of this type is called a *capital export,* and in the balance of payments statement of the domestic economy it is recorded as a debit item since it provides foreign residents with the means to make payments to residents of the domestic economy. Alternatively, it is possible that foreign residents may finance the aforementioned export surplus of the domestic economy by drawing down bank balances they may hold in the banks of the domestic economy. If this is done, it means there has been a *net decrease* in the liabilities owed by domestic residents to foreign residents because a bank deposit is a liability of the bank.

The capital account section of the balance of payments statement basically reflects the net change during the accounting period in the claims and liabilities (real and financial) of the domestic economy vis-à-vis the rest of the world. But this net change can take the form of a capital export, an increase in claims (or decrease in the liabilities) of domestic residents relative to foreign residents; conversely, it can take the form of a capital import, a decrease in the claims (or increase in the liabilities) of domestic residents relative to foreign residents.

International Equilibrium and the Balance of Payments

As an accounting instrument, the balance of payments statement must necessarily be in balance; for every credit entry there has to be an offsetting debit entry. But this does not mean that an *equilibrium* exists with respect to a nation's international economic position. Although there is no clear-cut and universally accepted method of determining economic equilibrium with respect to a nation's international payments position, the state of a nation's international *reserves* is a good indication of its international economic situation. For the nation, international reserves consist primarily of gold, national currencies widely accepted as money in international transactions (the U.S. dollar has been such a currency throughout most of the post-World War II period), special drawing rights, and other borrowing rights in the International Monetary Fund.[6] An important measure of the international economic position of the United States is the *balance of official reserve transactions,* the third important component in the nation's balance of international payments structure. This indicates the net change in the country's international reserves, including its holdings of gold, foreign currencies, and borrowing rights in the International Monetary Fund.

The normal meaning of an international equilibrium for a nation is that it is paying its way internationally, which is to say that it is obtaining sufficient foreign exchange on a sustainable basis to meet its needs to make payments abroad. Normally a nation obtains foreign exchange through its exports or by borrowing abroad on a long-term basis. But increasingly since World War II grants by governments and international agencies have become important as sources for certain currencies, particularly the dollar. Disequilibrium in a nation's balance of payments implies a condition that is not sustainable; one or more items in either the current account or the capital account must undergo change if an equilibrium condition is to be restored, and this can affect income and employment levels in the domestic economy.

Changes in the current or capital account may be described as either autonomous or induced. An *autonomous* change in the current account is one that is not the consequence of a change in the capital account; an *induced*

---

[6] For the United States, of course, dollars would not count as a part of its international reserves, but they would for other nations because the dollar is widely accepted as an international medium of exchange. Foreign currencies held by the United States do count, however, as part of its international reserves.

change in the current account is one that follows from a change in the capital account. For example, a nation may find as a result of events abroad that its exports increase, and an export surplus develops in the current account. If imports remain unchanged, then this development requires an offsetting transaction in the capital account. This offsetting transaction, which will take the form of an outflow of capital, is properly described as induced because it is a consequence of a change that has already taken place in the current account. On the other hand, a nation may undertake lending operations abroad (i.e., a capital export) quite independently of any current account developments. If such autonomous capital transactions take place, they must be followed by offsetting transactions in the current account. In this event, changes in the current account would be of an induced nature. From an examination of the statistical data contained in a balance of payments statement, it is not always possible to determine whether the recorded changes are autonomous or induced, but these concepts are nonetheless useful for economic analysis.

Table 10–1 contains a simplified statement of the balance of international payments for the United States for 1993. The student should study these data carefully, although a few comments on particular items in the statement are in order. Overall, there was a deficit in the current account in 1993. One item of particular interest in the capital account is the large sum ($21.1 billion) labeled ''Statistical discrepancy.'' Although there is no way to account for precisely all international economic transactions, this particular item reflects a large movement of financial capital into the United States. The other item of major interest in the table is the financing of the current account deficit in the U.S. balance in 1993. Simply put, the financing of the deficit was done in part by foreigners increasing their holdings of assets in the United States ($159.0 billion) by an amount ($12.8 billion) greater than Americans increased their holdings of foreign assets. This reflects the fact that the United States has become a net debtor nation.

The Exchange Rate

Besides knowledge of the balance of payments, some understanding of foreign exchange rates is needed for a full appreciation of the manner in which international economic transactions interact with the domestic economy. The rate of exchange is simply the price of one national currency measured in terms of another national currency. For example, the dollar-pound rate of exchange on September 14, 1994 was $1.88 = £1; this meant that it cost U.S. residents $1.88 to obtain 1 unit of British currency. The exchange rate is important because exports, imports, and all possible financial transactions are affected not only by the levels of real income and prices that prevail in different countries, but also by the prices at which their currencies exchange for one another. To illustrate, Americans might increase their imports from Great Britain because, for one reason or another, the prices for certain goods in

Britain were lower than in the United States. Or they might buy more from the United Kingdom because British currency had fallen in price in terms of U.S. dollars.

Exchange rates may be either *fixed* or *flexible* (floating). A fixed exchange rate system is one in which the rate—or price—at which different currencies exchange for one another simply does not change or at most changes infrequently. The gold standard system of the nineteenth century worked in this way. For the first 28 years (1945 to 1973) of the post-World War II period, exchange rates between the major world currencies were relatively fixed. This was the Bretton Woods system, so named because of the 1944 wartime conference held in Bretton Woods, New Hampshire, which led to the establishment of the International Monetary Fund. Under the initial agreement, exchange rates were set using the U.S. dollar as the key, or benchmark, currency. Signatories also agreed to rather stringent conditions for changes in exchange rates, which were to be carried out under the auspices of the International Monetary Fund. The individual currencies were linked to gold by virtue of the fact that the U.S. dollar maintained a basic gold parity ($35 per ounce), and the U.S. government agreed to convert dollars held by foreign official holders (foreign central banks and international organizations like the IMF) into gold at this price. Thus, dollars were regarded as good as gold and, for this part of the post-World War II period, nations were content to hold their international monetary reserves as dollars.

A fixed exchange rate system is conducive to stability in the international economy because participants at least know the price they must pay to obtain foreign currencies. When exchange rates fluctuate, this condition no longer exists.

The alternative to a fixed exchange rate system is one in which rates are free to fluctuate (or float) on the basis of the interplay of demand and supply forces for different currencies. In any system in which exchange rates are not tied to gold or some other standard (such as the U.S. dollar), there are two basic possibilities. One is that rates be *absolutely* free to fluctuate in accordance with market forces. This would be a true *flexible* exchange rate system. The other alternative is for the exchange rate to be free of any tie to gold or another currency, but for governments to intervene in the market for exchange rates and attempt to keep fluctuations moderate or within a desired range. If this happens, the system is characterized as one with a *managed* or *dirty* float. For most countries this has been the kind of system in effect since 1973. Central banks all over the world intervene almost daily in foreign exchange markets to dampen fluctuations in the rate of exchange for their currencies.[7] Figure 10–2 traces the fluctuations in the foreign exchange value of the U.S.

---

[7] In recent years there have been periodic meetings between the heads of the central banks in the United States, Britain, France, Germany, and Japan, the so-called Group of Five. Their usual purpose is to try and coordinate policies to stabilize exchange rates, an objective for which they have had some success, as exchange rates for the U.S. dollar are more stable at time of writing than they were in the 1980s.

dollar (in terms of an index) since 1967. After the effective end of the Bretton Woods system in 1971, the dollar underwent a series of drastic fluctuations.

It is worth noting that the present system of flexible exchange rates with a managed (or dirty) float did not come into existence by design, but because of the gradual breakdown of the Bretton Woods system of fixed exchange rates caused by imbalances in the international economic accounts of the United States throughout the post-World War II period. During most of this period the outflow of dollars from the United States due to the combined impact of our import purchasing, our lending, and our unilateral transfers (one-way grants) exceeded the inflow derived from exports and loan repayments. In the 1950s, the era of the worldwide dollar shortage, most nations were content to have dollars as international reserves and see their dollar holdings grow. But this was not so from 1960 onward. As the dollar outflow continued because of international economic disequilibrium, more and more nations became uneasy and worried about the convertibility into gold of their growing stock of U.S. currency. Thus, they increasingly exercised their right to convert official holdings into gold; the result was a drastic drain of gold from the United States. From a peak of $25 billion in 1949, the U.S. gold stock dropped to near $10 billion at the end of the 1960s. The continued

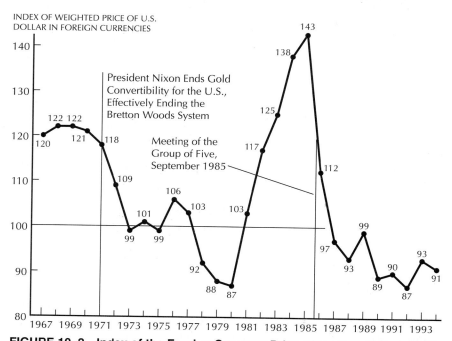

FIGURE 10–2   Index of the Foreign Currency Price of the U.S. Dollar; 1967–1994. Ever since the end of the Bretton Woods system in 1971, the index that measures the foreign exchange value of the U.S. dollar has fluctuated wildly, from a low of 87 in 1980 (March 1973 = 100) to a high of 143 in 1985.

Source: Economic Report of the President, 1995.

pressure on the dollar and unceasing gold loss led President Nixon on August 15, 1971 to abandon all convertibility of the dollar into gold. Thus, the cornerstone of the Bretton Woods system crumbled. From there it was but a short step to the present system of fully flexible exchange rates. In December 1971 the dollar was devalued in terms of gold (its official price was raised from $35 to $38 an ounce), and most of the major currencies were revalued in terms of the dollar. But this arrangement lasted only until February 1973, when once again the dollar was devalued in terms of gold (the price went to $42.22 per ounce), and shortly thereafter all efforts to maintain fixed exchange rates between the major currencies were ended. Now, there is no fixed price for the dollar in gold. Because a system of fixed exchange rates no longer exists, and because, too, the exchange rate has become a major factor in how international economic transactions interact with the domestic economy, it is vital to understand the forces that determine both the level and changes in exchange rates. It is to this topic that we now turn.

Determination of the Exchange Rate

Chapter 5 included a model of the foreign exchange rate (page 169). This model is built around the idea that the exchange rate is simply the price of one national currency in terms of another. Foreign exchange is purchasing power delineated in a foreign currency. Since the exchange rate is a price, we can use supply and demand curves to explain how it is determined and how it behaves. We did this in the model developed in Chapter 5. In the model, it will be recalled, the supply curve for foreign exchange slopes upward. This is because as the price of foreign exchange increases, the effective price for domestically produced goods is lower. Foreign residents, therefore, will supply more foreign exchange because they want to buy more domestically produced goods. Conversely, the demand curve for foreign exchange slopes downward to the right. As the price of foreign exchange falls, the effective price of foreign-produced goods also falls. Hence, the quantity of foreign exchange demanded by domestic residents will increase because they want to import more foreign-made goods. The equilibrium price of foreign exchange is determined by the interaction of the demand and supply schedules for foreign exchange.

As is the case for any supply and demand model in economics, price and quantity changes come about either through movement of the variables involved toward an equilibrium position or through shifts in the schedules that enter into the model. This is true for foreign exchange rates. In foreign exchange markets, two principal factors account for *shifts* in the supply and demand curves. These are price differentials between countries and *real* interest rate differentials between assets in different countries. These two factors largely account for changes in the foreign exchange value of the dollar that have taken place since the ending of the Bretton Woods system in 1973. Most economists believe that price differentials are responsible for long-run exchange rate movements, whereas interest rate differentials are more important in explaining short-term variations in exchange rates. The next two sections take up, first, price differentials and the important theory of purchasing power parity and, second, interest rate differentials.

The Theory of Purchasing Power Parity

A well-known explanation developed by economists to account for the effect of price differentials on exchange rates is called the *theory of purchasing power parity*. This theory holds that when the prices charged for essentially the same goods in different countries diverge, exchange rates will move in the opposite direction and equalize the *effective* prices between the two countries. To show how this would work, let us assume that the United States and Canada produce identical bushels of wheat and that, initially, the exchange rate is $1.00 Canadian for $1.00 U.S. However, the market price of wheat in Canada is $3.00 per bushel, and in the United States $2.50 per bushel. Under these circumstances, Canadians would import the cheaper U.S. wheat. In doing this, they would increase the supply of Canadian dollars and thereby cause a reduction in the value of the Canadian dollar relative to the U.S. dollar. The Canadian dollar, in other words, would *depreciate* relative to the U.S. dollar. This process would also increase the effective price of U.S. wheat for Canadians, but the increased demand by Canadians for U.S. wheat would also push up the price of U.S. wheat. Over time, the depreciation of the Canadian dollars and the increase in the price of U.S. wheat would combine to bring about a single price for both U.S. and Canadian wheat. This is why the theory of purchasing power parity is also described as the *law of one price*.

Figure 10–3 uses the foreign exchange market model to show how this process works. The process is viewed from the perspective of the U.S. economy, so the exchange rate shown on the vertical axis is the price of Canadian dollars in U.S. currency. The increase in the Canadian demand for U.S. wheat, which stems from the lower market price for wheat in the United States, is seen in the model as a *shift* to the right in the supply curve for foreign exchange, that is, Canadian dollars. This is because Canadians are offering more of their dollars in exchange for the U.S. dollars they need to buy more wheat. The end result will be a fall for U.S. residents in the price of foreign exchange, the Canadian dollar. Ultimately, a new equilibrium will be established, one in which the price in U.S. dollars of the Canadian dollar is lower, and more Canadian dollars are available to U.S. residents. This is shown in the figure by FX_{P_1} and Q_2.

The full impact of the increase in demand for U.S. wheat is broader than is indicated here, for in our model we are tracing the results of just the changes that flow from an initial difference between the market price for wheat in the United States and in Canada. The fact that this leads to a fall in the price of the Canadian dollar relative to the U.S. dollar may lead to further changes, as Americans now find Canadian goods (and services) are cheaper than they

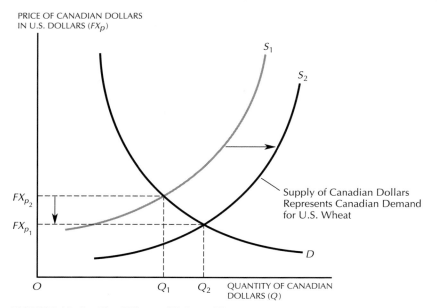

FIGURE 10–3   **The Effect of Price Differences on the Exchange Rate.**   If the market price for wheat in the United States is below the market price of wheat in Canada, Canadians will increase their demand for U.S. wheat. This will shift the supply curve for foreign exchange (Canadian dollars) to the right (S_1 to S_2) and bring about a fall in the price in U.S. dollars of Canadian currency (FX_{p_2} to FX_{p_1}). The value of the U.S. dollar in Canadian dollars will have risen.

were previously. The reader may want to explore, for example, why the changes just described might lead in time to more Americans vacationing in Canada and what the effects of this would be on exchange rates.

Is this the way the world really works? Examine again Figure 10–2 (page 361), which traces fluctuations in an index of the foreign exchange value of the U.S. dollar since 1967.[8] When the index falls, the price of foreign currencies for Americans—that is, the price of foreign exchange—is rising, and when the index rises, the price of the dollar for foreigners is increasing. Since the Bretton Woods system of relatively fixed exchange rates ended in 1971, Figure 10–4 covers 23 years in which exchange rates fluctuated freely on the basis of supply and demand forces. This index shows that from 1971 through 1994 the international value of the dollar was extremely volatile; it rose to a high of 143 in 1985 and dropped to a low of 87 in 1980 and rising to 91 by 1994.

Does the purchasing power parity theory explain these wide swings in the foreign exchange value of the dollar? It does in part, at least in the first half

---

[8] The exchange rate data is the Federal Reserve's measure of the value of the dollar in 10 industrialized countries, weighted by trade. The countries are Belgium, Canada, France, Germany, Italy, Japan, the Netherlands, Sweden, Switzerland, and the United Kingdom.

of the period. From 1970 through 1982, consumer prices in the United States were, on average, higher than in Europe, although the gap in prices between the two areas steadily narrowed over these 12 years. Figure 10–4 shows a downward trend in the foreign exchange value of the dollar from 1970 through 1980, which is what the purchasing power parity theory would lead us to expect. Higher prices in the United States as compared to those in Europe led to a reduced demand for dollars and hence a fall in the dollar's exchange value. So there is some empirical support for this theory.[9]

However, to explain the strong upsurge in the international value of the dollar between 1980 and 1985—the dollar's foreign exchange value jumped by 64.4 percent—we have to go beyond the theory of purchasing power parity. True, European prices became higher than U.S. prices after 1982, and this

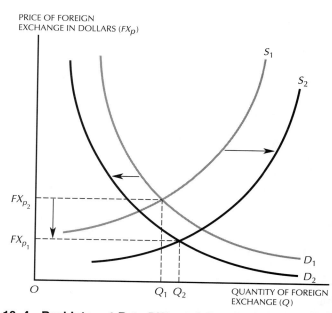

PRICE OF FOREIGN
EXCHANGE IN DOLLARS (FX_p)

FIGURE 10–4 Real Interest Rate Differentials and the Price of Foreign Exchange. When U.S. real interest rates rise relative to foreign real interest rates, the supply curve for foreign exchange shifts rightward as foreign investors exchange their currency for dollars to be used to buy U.S. financial instruments. The demand curve for foreign exchange shifts leftward as returns on foreign financial instruments appear inferior from the perspective of U.S. investors. U.S. investors buy fewer foreign financial instruments and, thus, demand less foreign exchange.

[9] In 1970, consumer prices were 45 percent higher on average than in European Community countries (Belgium, Luxembourg, Denmark, France, Greece, Ireland, Italy, the Netherlands, the United Kingdom, Germany, Portugal, and Spain), but by 1982 the difference had narrowed to 5 percent. After 1982, European prices began to rise faster than prices in the United States; this led to a differential of nearly 10 percent by 1992. For the entire period, 1983 through 1992, consumer prices in these European countries averaged 6.1 percent more than similar prices in the United States. See *Economic Report of the President*, 1994, p. 392.

increased the foreign exchange value of the U.S. dollar. But price differentials between the two areas were not great enough to explain fully the unprecedented surge in the dollar's international value. A more powerful factor in the form of interest rate differentials entered the picture after 1980, overshadowing by far purchasing power parity as a cause of the explosive growth in the dollar's foreign exchange value. We shall examine the impact of interest rate differentials momentarily, but first some additional remarks are in order on other limitations to the purchasing parity doctrine.

Economists are aware of a number of reasons why *all* fluctuations in exchange rates are not explained by purchasing power parity. First, and for purchasing power parity to work smoothly and completely, *arbitrage* in commodities must be possible. Arbitrage involves the act of buying something in one market and simultaneously selling it in another market. It works primarily in markets in which near-identical commodities (like wheat) are bought and sold and the possibility exists for *forward* sales, that is, selling a commodity for future delivery at a specified price. Foreign exchange and commodity markets have these characteristics. There are many goods that enter into a nation's price level, but are not suitable for arbitrage. French wine is not interchangeable with New York wine, nor is a Chevrolet Lumina the same as a Volkswagen Passat. To the extent that perceived or real differences in quality exist, commodity arbitrage is reduced and thus exchange rates will not necessarily change enough to equalize prices across international borders.

Another reason why the theory of purchasing power parity cannot fully explain short-period exchange rate changes is that there are many goods that are *nontradables*. As Reuven Glick of the San Francisco Federal Reserve Bank puts it, ". . . many goods and services (the prices of which are included in a country's price level) are not traded across borders. Housing, land, and services such as haircuts and golf lessons, for example, are not traded internationally. Commodity arbitrage will equalize prices of internationally traded goods but not of nontraded goods."[10]

Finally, real shocks can prevent prices from being equalized across international borders. These would include productivity differences, varying rates of technological change and capital accumulation, conflicting fiscal and monetary policies, and real interest rate differentials. For all these reasons exchange rates may be slow to adjust to price differences between nations.

Real Interest Rate Differentials

Interest rate differentials on international investments are the second major determinant of exchange rate changes. Because real interest rate differences between countries can change over short periods of time, economists tend to view them as the major cause of exchange rate changes in the short run. Craig Hakkio of the Kansas City Federal Reserve bank concluded that real interest

[10] Reuven Glick, "How Good is PPP?" *Weekly Letter,* Federal Reserve Bank of San Francisco, June 9, 1989.

rate differentials overcame price differentials as the major factor influencing exchange rates in the 1980s.[11]

In today's highly fluid international economic environment, people are able to buy and sell financial assets in many different countries with little regard for national borders. The motivation for international investment is the higher interest rate the investor seeks in financial markets across the globe. Money capital flows ceaselessly, 24 hours a day, from nation to nation. For our purposes it must be recognized that whenever financial capital moves from one nation to another, matching flows of exchange rates are involved. Once again, we can use the model of the foreign exchange market to show how this works. This is done in Figure 10–4.

As before we shall examine what happens from the perspective of the U.S. economy. This means that on the vertical axis the price of foreign exchange is measured in terms of the U.S. dollar. Foreign exchange in this context means any or all foreign currencies offered in exchange for U.S. dollars in the world's foreign exchange markets. Assume now, that U.S. real interest rates are higher than those in other countries. The *real* rate of interest, it will be recalled, is the nominal (current or actual) rate minus the inflation rate. Attracted by the relatively higher rates of return to be earned in the United States, foreign residents will want to buy financial assets in this country— primarily debt instruments in the form of short-term notes and bonds. However, in order to purchase financial assets in the United States, the foreign residents must exchange their currency for dollars. Thus, the supply curve for foreign exchange will shift to the right, from S_1 to S_2; this indicates that more foreign exchange than previously is being offered on the market in exchange for dollars. Further, because the higher real interest rates in the United States make foreign financial instruments less attractive to U.S. residents, the U.S. demand curve for foreign exchange may shift to the left, from D_1 to D_2.

As a result of both of these possible shifts, the price Americans must pay for foreign exchange falls. The dollar has *appreciated* in value relative to foreign currencies, while foreign currencies have *depreciated* in value relative to the dollar. As with our earlier example involving wheat, there may ultimately be further effects on the domestic economy because of the change in foreign exchange rates, but at this point we are only concerned with the initial change. As a generalization the following holds: Ceteris paribus, *the higher domestic real interest rates are relative to foreign real interest rates, the higher will be the foreign exchange rate for the domestic currency.*

Does empirical evidence confirm this relationship—a relationship which indicates that real interest rate differentials and the foreign exchange value of the dollar ought to move together? Figure 10–5 shows that at least during the 1980s this has been approximately true. In the figure, the difference between U.S. and foreign real interest rates for 6 industrialized countries is plotted along with the Federal Reserve System's weighted-average index of

---

[11] Craig S. Hakkio, "Interest Rates and Exchange Rates—What is the Relationship?" *Economic Review,* Kansas City Federal Reserve, November 1986, pp. 33–43.

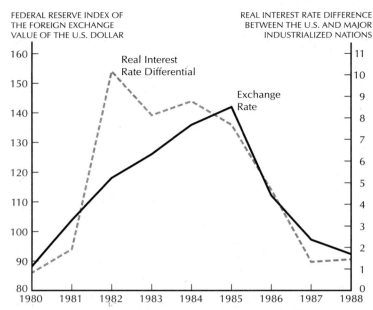

FEDERAL RESERVE INDEX OF
THE FOREIGN EXCHANGE
VALUE OF THE U.S. DOLLAR

REAL INTEREST RATE DIFFERENCE
BETWEEN THE U.S. AND MAJOR
INDUSTRIALIZED NATIONS

FIGURE 10–5 The Exchange Rate and the Real Interest Rate Differential. During the 1980s there was a close correlation between differences in the real rate of interest in the United States and other countries and the foreign exchange value of the dollar. When the real interest rate differential rose, so did the foreign exchange value of the dollar. When the differential fell, the foreign exchange value of the dollar fell.

Sources: The International Monetary Fund; *International Financial Statistics;* the Board of Governors of the Federal Reserve System; Hakkio, "Interest Rates and Exchange Rates—What is the Relationship?" pp. 33–43.

the exchange value of the dollar compared with the currencies of 10 major industrial nations.[12] From 1980 through 1984 real interest rates in the United States were significantly higher compared with those in other industrialized nations. The real interest rate differential peaked in 1982, when the U.S. rate was 10.2 percentage points higher than its foreign counterpart.

As the theory suggests, the dollar price of foreign exchange fell, which is to say that there was a strong appreciation in the foreign exchange value of the dollar. Among the consequences of this was a surge in U.S. imports in the early 1980s; the appreciation of the dollar made foreign-made goods cheaper in the United States. After 1984, the gap between real interest rates in the United States and abroad narrowed sharply; the decline in U.S. real interest rates was paralleled by a 33 percent drop in the foreign exchange

---

[12] The foreign real interest rate measure is the average real interest rate on 10-year government bonds of Canada, France, Germany, Italy, Japan, and the United Kingdom. The exchange rate data is the Federal Reserve's measure of the value of the dollar in 10 industrialized countries, weighted by trade.

value of the U.S. dollar between 1985 and 1988. Note, however, that not all of the drop in the foreign exchange value of the dollar after 1985 can be attributed to the changes in the interest rate differential. Some of it is due to the agreement reached in September 1985 by the Group of Five (see footnote 7, page 360) to take action to bring down the foreign exchange value of the dollar.

Income Changes and Central Bank Intervention

Brief mention needs to be made here of two additional determinants of the price of foreign exchange, both of which are discussed in detail subsequently. These are the level of income in the domestic economy and direct intervention by the central bank (the Federal Reserve System in the United States) in the foreign exchange markets.

When an economy expands, people in the economy have more disposable income. Some of this added income will spill over into the purchase of imported goods, a process we shall examine closely in the next section. This may result in an increased demand for foreign exchange and an increase in the price of foreign exchange measured in domestic currency (a devaluation or depreciation in the currency of the domestic economy). It is also true, as we have just seen, that imports may increase because the foreign exchange value of the domestic currency has appreciated.

Ever since the demise of the Bretton Woods system, an important determinant of the foreign exchange rate has been intervention in foreign exchange markets by central banks. When countries attempt to control the exchange value of their currency, they do so by making purchases or sales of that currency in the foreign exchange market. If, for example, the Federal Reserve believes that the dollar's foreign exchange value is too low, it can increase the dollar's value by buying dollars in the foreign exchange markets. This presupposes, of course, that the central bank, the Federal Reserve in this case, has sufficient foreign exchange on hand to do this. Such action would increase the supply of foreign exchange, reduce its price, and simultaneously increase the foreign exchange price of the dollar. After the Group of Five agreed in September 1985 to bring down the foreign exchange value of the dollar, they did so by selling dollars in the foreign exchange markets of the world.

Since 1973 central bank intervention in the foreign exchange markets has become an important macroeconomic policy tool. We shall examine fully the policy implications of intervention in the foreign exchange markets in Chapter 15. Now we turn our attention to another key concern of this chapter, the analysis of how changes in the nation's international economic position affect its domestic economy and how changes in the domestic economy affect the nation's international economic situation. This will round out our understanding of how Keynesian aggregate demand analysis applies within the context of the emerging global economy, one of the dominant economic facts of our time.

Exports, Imports, and the Structure of Aggregate Demand

To analyze the manner in which exports and imports of goods and services fit into the structure of aggregate demand, let us begin with a review of the basic identity equations appropriate to an open economy. In an open economy, exports of goods and services enter directly into the aggregate demand function because they represent the portion of the demand for the national output that originates abroad. The demand for a nation's exports X is as much a part of the demand for its output as is the demand for consumption goods and services C, investment goods I, or social goods G. In an open economy, M is the domestic demand for imports. Thus, the origin and component parts of the net national output can be summed up in the following identity equation.[13]

$$Y_{np} = C + I + G + X - M. \tag{10-1}$$

What determines the level of exports for a nation? We shall not try to answer this question at this point, but only make the assumption that expenditures for exports are autonomous with respect to output and employment levels in the domestic economy. This is not an unrealistic assumption, although we shall need to modify it later. Since export expenditures constitute demand for domestic output originating outside the nation, their level will not be significantly affected by changes in the domestic income and employment

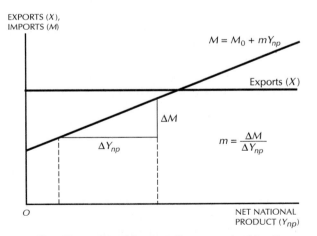

FIGURE 10–6   The Export and Import Curves.   In this diagram the level of exports (X) is depicted by a horizontal line, because exports are autonomous with respect to domestic output (Y_{np}). In contrast, imports (M) are shown as varying directly and positively with income (Y_{np}), because import spending depends on income produced in the domestic economy.

[13] See the earlier discussion on identities in the Appendix to Chapter 2, pages 67–70.

levels. Thus, the export function may be shown as a horizontal line in Figure 10–6.

Imports of goods and services do not represent an expenditure for any part of the domestic or national output, but they do represent a disposition of the money income created as a consequence of current productive activity, specifically the part of the domestic income that is directed toward the purchase of the output of other nations. In this sense, imports are a form of leakage from the domestic income stream and analogous in their economic effects to saving and taxes.

With respect to the level of imports M, we are on surer ground than with exports. Since imports are a form of disposition of domestic income, a reasonable hypothesis is that the level of imports of a nation is basically a function of the general level of economic activity within the nation. Specifically, this means that imports are a function of the income level, as in

$$M = f(Y_{np}). \tag{10-2}$$

In most societies an important share of the import total will consist of consumer goods and services. Given this, we would expect a society's expenditures on imported consumption goods to rise as its income level rises. Equation (10–2) is therefore nothing more than an extension of consumption theory to the situation of an open economy. We can also expect that expenditures for imported goods which enter into the investment and government expenditures components of aggregate demand will rise along with rising levels of income and employment.

Since imports are analogous in their economic effects to saving and taxes, it follows that the import-income relationship can be shown as a curve that slopes upward to the right in Figure 10–6. For the sake of simplicity, the import function, $M = f(Y)$, is presented as a straight line, although in reality the relationship between imports and the national income is not necessarily linear. The point at which the import curve crosses the vertical axis indicates the amount of expenditures on imports at a zero income level. This, of course, is primarily a theoretical rather than a practical proposition. Algebraically the import function may be defined as

$$M = M_0 + mY_{np}. \tag{10-3}$$

The technical attributes of this function are conceptually similar to those associated with both the consumption and the saving functions. M_0 represents import expenditures at zero income. The ratio between the level of imports M and the level of income Y at any and all possible income levels is the *average propensity to import*. This ratio shows the proportion of any given income level that is being spent for imported goods and services. Like the average propensity to consume and its counterpart, the average propensity to save, the ratio M/Y will vary as the income level varies. The ratio of a change in imports ΔM to a change in the income level ΔY is the *marginal propensity to import.* This ratio measures the slope of the import curve (as shown in Figure 10–6) and indicates how (in percentage terms) imports will vary as the income level shifts. From the standpoint of the impact of changes in the export-import balance on the level of income and employment in the domestic economy, the marginal propensity to import *m* is a vital concept.

Income Equilibrium in an Open Economy

Determination of the equilibrium level in an open economy is essentially a matter of fitting both exports and imports into the kind of analytical structure that we have developed in earlier chapters. Table 10–2 gives data pertaining to a hypothetical economy. These data are similar to those in Chapter 9, except that now a column representing the value of the economy's exports is included. For the moment we shall assume that imports are zero. The export figures shown in column 6 are the same for all income levels because of the autonomous nature of exports relative to the net national product. Investment and government purchases of goods and services are the same as in Table 9–3, and the consumption function is drawn from Table 9–7. Aggregate demand for this hypothetical—and open—economy is obtained by adding the stated values for investment, government expenditures, and exports to consumption at each indicated level of the net national product. This result is shown in column 7. Given this aggregate demand schedule, we find that the equilibrium income level for this open economy is $5,500 billion. Notice that Table 10-2 also contains an aggregate demand schedule for a closed economic system—that is, no exports or imports. This is shown in column 5. In the absence of exports, the equilibrium level of the net national product is $5,300 billion. The upward shift of the aggregate demand function by $80 billion, the amount of the exports, has the effect of increasing the equilibrium value of the net national product by $200 billion. Thus, a change in the foreign balance can exercise a multiplier effect on the domestic economy. We shall discuss shortly the operation and value of the multiplier in an open economy.

The process of income determination is shown graphically in Figure 10–7. Aggregate demand *DD* now includes exports *X* as well as the other components of output included heretofore. As in our previous analysis, the income equilibrium is determined at the point of intersection of the aggregate demand *DD* and aggregate supply *OZ*. This, according to the figure, is an income level of $5,500 billion. Given the position of the aggregate demand schedule, it is the only possible income level at which our four major expenditure categories will add up to an amount equal to aggregate supply.

For simplicity's sake we assumed in the foregoing example that imports were zero. We can now make our hypothetical model more realistic by intro-

TABLE 10–2 Exports, Aggregate Demand, and Equilibrium Income (in billions of constant 1987 dollars)

(1)	(2)	(3)	(4)	(5)	(6)	(7)
Net National Product Y_{np}	Consumption* C"	Investment† I	Government Expenditures† G	Aggregate Demand C" + I + G	Exports X	Aggregate Demand C" + I + G + X
$ 0	$1,110	$200	$810	$2,120	$80	$2,200
4,500	3,360	650	810	4,820	80	4,900
4,600	3,410	660	810	4,880	80	4,960
4,700	3,460	670	810	4,940	80	5,020
4,800	3,510	680	810	5,000	80	5,080
4,900	3,560	690	810	5,060	80	5,140
5,000	3,610	700	810	5,120	80	5,200
5,100	3,660	710	810	5,180	80	5,260
5,200	3,710	720	810	5,240	80	5,320
5,300	3,760	730	810	5,300	80	5,380
5,400	3,810	740	810	5,360	80	5,440
5,500	3,860	750	810	5,420	80	5,500
5,600	3,910	760	810	5,480	80	5,560
5,700	3,960	770	810	5,540	80	5,620
5,800	4,010	780	810	5,600	80	5,680
5,900	4,060	790	810	5,660	80	5,700
6,000	4,110	800	810	5,720	80	5,800

*From Table 9–7.
†From Table 9–1.

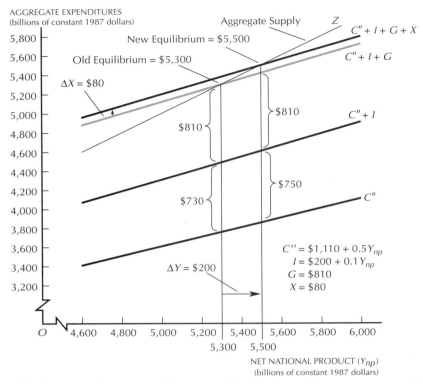

FIGURE 10–7   Exports and Aggregate Demand.   Adding an autonomous level of exports (X) raises the level of aggregate demand by the amount of exports and also raises the equilibrium income level above what it would be in the absence of an export demand.

ducing an import function into the analysis. This is done in Table 10–3, in which the import function is shown in column 5. In our example, imports M are equal to $27 billion plus $0.01\, Y_{np}$. In other words, M_0 is equal to $27 billion and the marginal propensity to import m equals 0.01. The aggregate demand function now becomes the sum of the four expenditure categories contained in Table 10–3 less imports ($C'' + I + G + X - M$). This new aggregate demand schedule is shown in column 6 of Table 10–3. Since imports constitute, in effect, a leakage of income from the domestic income stream, the effect of the introduction of an import function is to lower overall the level of the aggregate demand function. A comparison of the data in Tables 10–2 and 10–3 will show that at each possible value for aggregate supply—column 1 in each table—aggregate demand is less in Table 10–3 than it is in Table 10–2.

The data of Table 10–3 are plotted in Figure 10–8. A comparison of this diagram with Figure 10–7 shows clearly that the introduction of the import

TABLE 10-3 Exports, Imports, Aggregate Demand, and Equilibrium Income (in billions of constant 1987 dollars)

(1)	(2)	(3)	(4)	(5)	(6)
Net National Product Y_{np}	Consumption* C''	Investment and Government Expenditure $I + G$	Exports X	Imports† M	Aggregate Demand $C'' + I + G + X - M$
$ 0	$1,110	$1,010	$80	$27	$2,173
4,500	3,360	1,460	80	72	4,828
4,600	3,410	1,470	80	73	4,887
4,700	3,460	1,480	80	74	4,946
4,800	3,510	1,490	80	75	5,005
4,900	3,560	1,500	80	76	5,064
5,000	3,610	1,510	80	77	5,129
5,100	3,660	1,520	80	78	5,182
5,200	3,710	1,530	80	79	5,241
5,300	3,760	1,540	80	80	5,300
5,400	3,810	1,550	80	81	5,359
5,500	3,860	1,560	80	82	5,418
5,600	3,910	1,570	80	83	5,477
5,700	3,960	1,580	80	84	5,536
5,800	4,010	1,590	80	85	5,595
5,900	4,060	1,600	80	86	5,654
6,000	4,110	1,610	80	87	5,713

*Same as Table 10-2.

†$M = \$27 + 0.01 Y_{np}$.

function shifts the aggregate demand curve below the position given by the data of Table 10-2. The equilibrium level of net national product is now $5,300 billion rather than $5,500 billion. To avoid unnecessary clutter in the figure, the $(C'' + I)$ and $(C + I + G)$ curves are omitted.

The equilibrium level of the net national product in our open system can also be explained in terms of schedules that represent *ex ante* values for expenditures other than consumption (investment, government purchases of goods and services, and exports) and leakages out of the domestic income stream (saving, net taxes, and imports). Equilibrium exists at the point at which these expenditures $(I + G + X)$ just offset the leakages from the current income stream $(S + T + M)$. The sum of the expenditure items $(I + G + X)$ is shown in column 2 of Table 10-4 and the sum of leakages $(S + T + M)$ is given in column 3 of the same table. Equality between the two exists at the $5,300 billion level of the net national product. Curves for the sum of these variables are plotted in Figure 10-9, which depicts graphically the determination of the equilibrium level of the net national product in terms of the *ex ante* values for $I + G + X$ and $S + T + M$. Income equilibrium

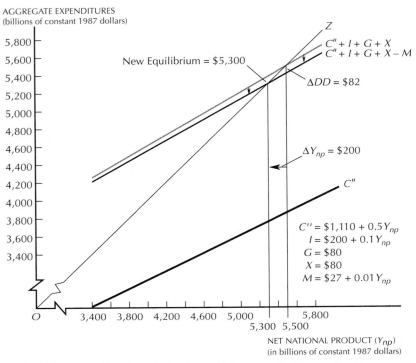

FIGURE 10–8   Exports, Imports, and Aggregate Demand.   In an open economy in which demand for imports (*M*) varies directly with income, aggregate demand will not rise as rapidly as it would if there were no import demand. Imports
have a dampening effect on aggregate demand in the same way as saving and
taxes.

requires that *ex ante* values for all leakages be offset by *ex ante* expenditures.
At any level of the net national product at which $S + T + M$ is greater than
$I + G + X$, aggregate supply will be in excess of aggregate demand and
output will fall. If the reverse situation prevails, output and employment will
rise.

Foreign Trade and the Multiplier

An important implication of the preceding analysis is that income equilibrium
in an open economy also means that equilibrium exists in the nation's balance
of payments situation. Equilibrium in the nation's international economic position does not require that exports and imports be exactly in balance, but it
does require that any imbalance between exports and imports be offset by
other international transactions, such as loans or grants. (See the discussion

TABLE 10–4 Equilibrium of $I + G + X$ and $S + T + M$ (in billions of constant 1987 dollars)

(1)	(2)	(3)
Net National Product Y_{np}	Investment, Government Expenditures, and Exports $I + G + X$	Saving, Net Taxes, and Imports $S + T + M$
$ 0	$1,090	$-1,023
4,500	1,540	1,212
4,600	1,550	1,263
4,700	1,560	1,314
4,800	1,570	1,365
4,900	1,580	1,416
5,000	1,590	1,467
5,100	1,600	1,518
5,200	1,610	1,569
5,300	1,620	1,620
5,400	1,630	1,671
5,500	1,640	1,722
5,600	1,650	1,773
5,700	1,660	1,824
5,800	1,670	1,875
5,900	1,680	1,926
6,000	1,690	1,977

INVESTMENT (I), GOVERNMENT EXPENDITURES (G),
EXPORTS (X), SAVINGS (S), NET TAXES (T), IMPORTS (M)
(billions of constant 1987 dollars)

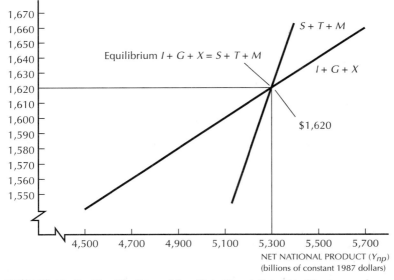

FIGURE 10–9 Equilibrium of $I + G + X$ and $S + T + M$. In an open economy the equilibrium condition requires that expenditures for investment (I), goods and services by governments (G), and exports (X) be offset by the sum of saving (S), net taxes (T), and imports (M).

of the role of the capital account in the discussion of the balance of payments in the beginning of this chapter.) A change in a nation's international economic position affects the export-import balance either directly or indirectly. When this happens, the position of the aggregate demand curve is altered. As we know from our previous study, a change in the position of the aggregate demand curve will have a multiplier effect on the income and employment levels within the domestic economy. Since a change in the export-import balance affects aggregate demand, there will be a multiplier effect associated with such a change. Some writers prefer to talk of the *foreign trade,* or the *open system,* multiplier when discussing this phenomenon, but actually what is involved is nothing more than the application of the general theory of the multiplier to shifts in aggregate demand that have their origin in a change in the nation's international economic position. We saw in Table 10–2 that an autonomous increase in exports in the amount of $80 billion led to an ultimate increase in the net national product of $200 billion. Of course, an autonomous increase in imports could have the opposite effect.

To derive algebraically the multiplier in an open economy, let us begin, as in Chapter 9, with our basic definition of the effective multiplier k'. This is

$$k' = \frac{\Delta Y_{np}}{\Delta D}. \tag{10-4}$$

In an open economy it follows from Equation (10–1) that

$$\Delta Y_{np} = \Delta C + \Delta I + \Delta G + \Delta X - \Delta M. \tag{10-5}$$

By substitution we then have

$$\Delta Y_{np} = a'\Delta Y_{np} + b\Delta Y_{np} + \Delta G + \Delta X - m\Delta Y_{np}. \tag{10-6}$$

If we assume that $\Delta G = 0$, we have

$$\Delta X = \Delta Y_{np} - a'\Delta Y_{np} - b\Delta Y_{np} + m\Delta Y_{np}, \tag{10-7}$$

$$\Delta X = \Delta Y_{np}(1 - a' - b + m). \tag{10-8}$$

Since the change in aggregate demand ΔD is the same as the change in exports ΔX, we can substitute the right-hand portion of Equation (10–8) for ΔD in Equation (10–4). We get

$$k' = \frac{\Delta Y_{np}}{\Delta Y_{np}(1 - a' - b + m)} = \frac{1}{1 - a' - b + m}. \tag{10-9}$$

Equation (10–9) gives us the value of the multiplier in an open economy. It includes not only the marginal propensity to import, but also the marginal propensity to tax. The latter is the case because $a' = a - at$. By further substitution, we can define the multiplier in an open economy as

$$k' = \frac{1}{1 - a + at - b + m}. \tag{10–10}$$

Graphic Illustrations of the Multiplier in an Open Economy

Figure 10–10 depicts the effects on the net national product and imports that result from an autonomous change in exports. We assume a simplified economy that has neither investment and saving nor government expenditures and taxes. In such a system the necessary condition for equilibrium is that exports *ex ante* and imports *ex ante* be equal, because only when they are equal will leakages, represented by imports M, be just offset by expenditures originating outside the economy, that is, exports X. In Figure 10–10 the equilibrium income level is determined by the intersection of the curve of *ex ante* exports (depicted by the lower horizontal line) and the curve representing the import function, $M = M_0 + mY_{np}$. At this income level, exports and imports are in balance.

A shift upward in the export curve from X to the new level X' causes a movement of the equilibrium net national product from Y_{np} to Y'_{np}. The mag-

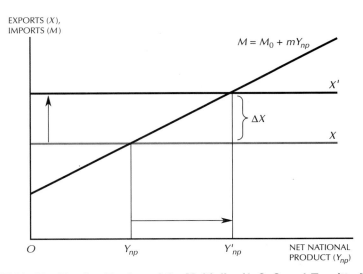

FIGURE 10–10   Foreign Trade and the Multiplier (I, G, S, and T omitted).   An autonomous increase in exports (ΔX), *ceteris paribus,* will raise the income level (Y_{np}) by a multiple of the change in exports; thus, the foreign trade multiplier has the same impact on output as the investment or government spending for a goods and services multiplier.

nitude of this change depends on the value of the multiplier, which in this instance is determined solely by the value of the marginal propensity to import *m*. The important point to note is that, as the multiplier process works itself out and the income level rises, the volume of imports will also continue to rise. This is true because we have assumed a positive value for the marginal propensity to import. In our hypothetical system, in which there are no leakages other than expenditures for imports, the import level will have to continue to rise until once again it is equal to the volume of exports. The autonomous increase in exports disturbed a preexisting balance in the current account of our hypothetical economy, but the increase in income that was generated by the change in exports induced a significant rise in imports to restore the export-import balance. At the new equilibrium income level, exports *X* and imports *M* are once again in balance. Changes in the opposite direction would, of course, take place if the economy experienced a decline in exports.

A more realistic picture appears if we reintroduce both investment and saving as well as government expenditures and taxes into the analysis. This is done in Figure 10–11. The initial income equilibrium Y_{np} is at the point of intersection of the $I + G + X$ curve and the $S + T + M$ curve. The diagram is drawn so that, at the initial equilibrium income level, exports *X* and imports *M* are in balance, although it should be noted that this does not necessarily

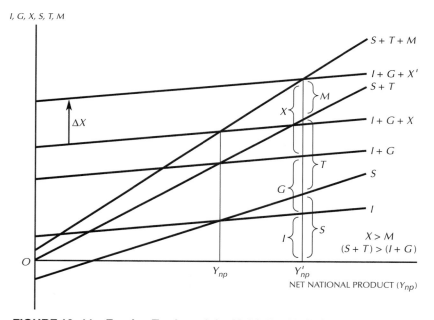

FIGURE 10–11   Foreign Trade and the Multiplier (*I, G, S,* and *T* included).   In an open system which includes both exports (*X*) and imports (*M*), the increase in income (ΔY_{np}) resulting from an increase in exports (ΔX) will be smaller than in a system without imports, because as income rises, some of the increased spending leaks out of the domestic income stream through spending on imports (*M*).

have to be the case. From the standpoint of the income equilibrium, all that is required is that $I + G + X$ *ex ante* be just equal to $S + T + M$ *ex ante,* not that I be exactly offset by S, G be exactly offset by T, or X be exactly offset by M.

Let us examine the impact on the economy of an increase in exports. This change will shift the entire $I + G + X$ schedule upward. The new position of the schedule is given in Figure 10–11 by the line labeled "$I + G + X'$." The increase in exports ΔX will, via the multiplier process, drive income to the new and higher equilibrium level of Y'_{np}. The rise in the income level brought about by the increase in exports also induces in this instance not only an increase in imports, but additional saving and taxes as well. At the new and higher income equilibrium Y'_{np}, the sum of $I + G + X'$ is again in balance with the sum of $S + T + M$. Imports have not risen sufficiently to restore equality in the nation's export-import balance because leakages in the form of both taxes and saving also rise as the income level rises. The amount by which exports and imports differ at the new and higher income level will be just offset by the difference between domestic investment and saving or government expenditures and taxes or both. Since $X > M$, then $S + T$ must be greater than $I + G$ by a like amount.

☐ Income Changes and the Export-Import Balance

Our analysis has been largely directed toward the effect of a change in exports or imports on income and employment levels in the domestic economy. It is appropriate that we look at the other side of the coin and analyze how internal changes in the income level may affect a nation's export-import balance.

Income equilibrium in an open economy requires equality between $I + G + X$ *ex ante* and $S + T + M$ *ex ante*. For the sake of simplicity let us assume that government expenditure G and net taxes T are equal (and therefore eliminate them from the foregoing equality). Thus, in our equilbrium condition, $I + X = S + M$. Transposing the terms in this equation, we get

$$X - M = S - I. \tag{10–11}$$

The meaning of the above equation is that *ex ante* the current account balance must be equal to the difference between saving and investment if an income equilibrium is to exist. Since the values that we have been discussing in this context are *ex ante* in nature, we can express $X - M$ and $S - I$ in the form of schedules that link both of these to the income level. This is done in Figure 10–12. Net national product is measured on the horizontal axis; the net differences between exports and imports, $X - M$, and between saving and investment, $S - I$, are measured on the vertical axis. The $X - M$ schedule slopes downward to the right because, even though the level of exports is presumed to be autonomous with respect to the domestic income level, the

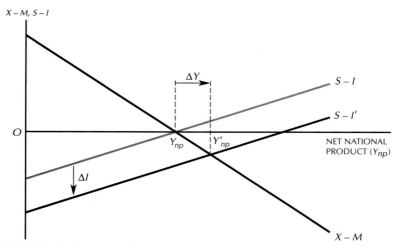

FIGURE 10–12   Income Changes and the Foreign Balance.   The trade balance $(X - M)$ can be offset by a change in income. If income increases, *ceteris paribus,* this will cause imports to rise and thus lead to a deficit in the nation's export-import balance. If income falls, the opposite effect will take place.

level of imports will rise as the domestic income level rises. Thus, as the economy moves from a lower to a higher income level, the export-import balance will shift from a positive to a negative value. The $S - I$ schedule slopes upward to the right because saving increases as the income level rises if investment expenditure is a constant or the marginal propensity to invest is less than the marginal propensity to save.

To illustrate the impact of a change in domestic income on the export-import balance, let us start the analysis with equality between exports and imports. This is shown in Figure 10–12 at the income level Y_{np}. The $X - M$ curve and the $S - I$ curve intersect so that the net difference between exports and imports, $X - M$, and saving and investment, $S - I$, is zero. The effect on the domestic income level as well as the balance of trade of an *increase* in the level of autonomous investment is depicted by a shift downward in the $S - I$ curve.[14] The new and higher equilibrium income level occurs at Y_{np}', a point determined by the intersection of curve $X - M$ and the new and lower curve $S - I'$. The point of intersection of these two curves now lies below zero on the vertical axis; this means that $X - M$ is now negative, or that imports exceed exports. We can therefore conclude that a change in the domestic income level, in this instance an increase, has induced an increase in imports sufficient to cause an adverse balance to develop in the nation's balance of trade.

The preceding discussion of the impact of a change in the domestic income level on the balance of trade position has been worked out on the assumption

---

[14] The reason for this is that, at every income level, $S - I$ will be less than it was prior to the increase in autonomous investment. This presumes, of course, that the saving function is unchanged.

of an increase in the income level, leading to a worsening of the export-import balance. This, of course, is not the only possibility, as study of Figure 10–12 reveals. The income level may fall, for example, as a result of a shift upward in the saving curve. This will raise the $S - I$ curve and cause it to intersect with the $X - M$ curve at a lower income level. This change will lead to an export surplus in the current account. In reality, though, it is unlikely that such a surplus could be maintained for long because the decline in imports may have repercussions abroad that are likely to be felt in the domestic economy.

Starting from a balanced trade position, an increase in the domestic income level will, *ceteris paribus,* lead to an import surplus and weaken the nation's international payments position. If the trade deficit can be financed on a sustaining basis, no serious problem results. If not, the disequilibrium in the nation's international accounts may sooner or later force a downward adjustment in the domestic income level. What will happen if, starting from a balanced position, the domestic income level falls? Precisely the opposite of what we have just described will occur.

Exchange Rates and the Export-Import Balance

It is now time to bring foreign exchange rates in the analysis, as it makes a great deal of difference to a nation and its international economic position whether it operates with a system of fixed or flexible exchange rates. We shall consider the consequences of each of these alternatives.

A system of fixed exchange rates not only ties a nation's domestic situation closely to its international economic position, but also makes it difficult to secure simultaneously a full-employment equilibrium in the domestic economy and equilibrium with respect to its international economic transactions. A review of the situation shown in Figure 10–12 will clarify this.

As already pointed out, a rise in domestic investment (depicted by a shift downward in the $S - I$ curve in Figure 10–12) causes a disequilibrium in the nation's export-import balance. If the nation is able to borrow at long term (experience a capital inflow), no serious problems will result and the exchange rate can remain fixed. But if long-term capital inflows are not forthcoming, the situation is quite different. As long as the exchange rate is fixed and in the absence of induced (or accommodating) capital transactions, the nation will experience a loss of its international reserves (gold, foreign exchange, and drawing rights in the International Monetary Fund). There is no other way in which a nation can get the necessary foreign exchange to finance an excess of imports.

The continued loss of international reserves by a nation ultimately will force changes in its international economic position.[15] This is so because

---

[15] There is no generalization about the link between international reserves and a nation's money

sooner or later a nation will exhaust its international reserves, including its drawing rights in the International Monetary Fund. What then? The most likely result would be an official devaluation of its currency, a reduction in its price as measured in other national currencies. This was the remedy nations generally opted for during the Bretton Woods era, 1944 to 1971. Since a currency devaluation makes a nation's exports cheaper (in terms of other currencies) and its imports more expensive, exports should rise and imports should fall; this tends to restore balance in the nation's international economic position. Refer once again to Figure 10–12. If devaluation works as just described, the $X - M$ schedule will shift upward—a change that has the effect of not only increasing the net national product, but also restoring international economic equilibrium. But there is a catch: As the national income rises, imports will also rise; this tends to nullify somewhat the impact of the devaluation. Furthermore, these developments can take place *only* if the economy is at less than full employment when devaluation takes place. In Figure 10–12, in other words, Y'_{np} must be a less than full-employment net national product. If this were not the situation, an increase in export demand would cause output to bump up against the full-capacity ceiling, after which prices would rise. But a rise in the price level would also nullify the effect of the devaluation (in whole or in part), since it would make the nation's exports more expensive. Imports would become more attractive for the nation's residents.[16]

The upshot of all this is that a system of fixed exchange rates makes it unlikely that a simultaneous equilibrium for a full-employment output and the balance of international payments is attained. The two may not be compatible; this means the nation would have to choose one at the expense of the other. Of course, if all prices, including the prices of factors of production as well as of goods and services, were flexible both upward and downward, the foregoing conclusion would not hold. Any shift in demand in a nation away from domestic output toward imports would cause the price of the former to fall relative to the latter and thus tend to restore balance between exports and imports. But the real world is simply not like this; most prices are flexible in only one direction—up! Thus, the basic problem remains that, with a fixed exchange system, the nation may have to choose between the pursuit of domestic stability and full employment at the cost of international balance, or the pursuit of balance of payments equilibrium at the cost of full employment at home. Since most Western nations have committed themselves to main-

---

supply that is valid for all countries. For some nations, especially those which have used the U.S. dollar as a reserve currency, the link may be quite close, as the central banks of such countries are likely to loosen or tighten the money supply on the basis of changes in the nation's inventory of international reserves. For other nations, this is not the case. The United States is in the latter category.

[16] If devaluation fails to correct a trade imbalance, then a nation may have to resort to more direct restrictive measures, such as tariffs or quotas. Most economists prefer devaluation to quantitative restrictions on imports (such as quotas) because the former acts through price and permits more scope for consumer choice.

taining full employment (e.g., the U.S. Employment Act), the realities of politics mean they select the first alternative.

If exchange rates are fully flexible, the situation should be quite different. In principle, it is impossible for there to be an imbalance between imports and exports, except as a result of lags and other imperfections in the market. The reason is that the rate of exchange would be continuously adjusting to changes in the demand and supply of exports and imports. Thus, if a nation increases its demand for imports relative to the foreign demand for its exports, the foreign exchange value of its currency will fall, and this would cause an immediate increase in the price of imports and a corresponding decrease in the price (for foreigners) of its exports.

Turn once again to Figure 10–12. A fully flexible exchange rate system means that the $X - M$ line becomes horizontal; it coincides with the horizontal axis in the diagram. If this were the situation, then an increase in domestic investment (depicted by the downward shift of the $S - I$ curve) would cause the net national product to rise without any impact on the foreign balance. Under such circumstances equilibrium in the output level would be restored at the point of intersection of the $S - I'$ schedule and the horizontal axis. The multiplier effect of a change in investment is much greater in this situation, simply because none of the increase in income is drawn off into import purchases. This is well and good if the new equilibrium is at or below the full-employment level of net national product, but if beyond it, then prices will go up.

Unhappily, the real world of international trade and payments does not behave this way. The United States, for example, has had almost continuous deficits in its current account transactions since the early 1970s. The international value of the dollar has been free to fluctuate for this same period, but this has not led to a continuous fall in the foreign exchange value of the dollar, as the theory of flexible exchange rates suggests. As we have seen, the dollar's foreign currency value has gyrated rather wildly since 1970 (Figure 10–2). How then, one may ask, has the United States been able to accommodate continuous deficits in its current account transactions with the rest of the world? The answer is a large and continuous influx of capital from abroad, an influx which has taken the form of dollars that foreigners acquired from the nation's payments deficits on current transactions and used to buy U.S. securities (stocks and bonds) and real fixed assets in the Unites States (land, office buildings, shopping malls, and factories). The United States is now the world's leading debtor nation (see box, page 386).

The Balance of Payments Curve

In this section we bring together all the aspects of international economic transactions analyzed in this chapter to present a complete model of an open economy. To do this, we must, first, construct a *balance of payments (BP)*

Living beyond Our Means: Foreign Borrowing and the U.S. Economy

By any measure $556 billion is a lot of money. That is the amount that Americans owed foreigners in excess of what foreigners owed Americans by the end of 1993. The United States is now the world's largest debtor nation!

There are two questions of major importance surrounding this $556 billion figure. Only a few years ago (1984) Americans owned $234 billion more in assets abroad than foreigners owned here, so how did the situation get turned around so fast? Second, how is the United States going to repay the debt represented by these assets, not to mention meet the annual interest commitments to foreigners?

The story of how we drifted in just a few years from being a net creditor to a net debtor nation is simple, although many of the details are complex. For the past eight years the nation has been living beyond its means in the context of the world economy and with respect to private and public spending. Roughly speaking, we have been doing this to the tune of about 1.4 percent of our GDP—this is the nation's real income—and the difference has been supplied by borrowing from abroad.

In 1993, the federal deficit was $254 billion, and the trade deficit in merchandise reached a level of $132 billion. Foreign funds financed a substantial part of the federal government's excess of spending over income and the consumers' splurge of the last few years.

The reason foreigners continue to lend to the United States is simple. Until 1990 interest rates in the United States were higher than interest rates abroad; thus they acted as a strong lure for foreign money seeking an outlet in areas where the return was greatest. So foreign funds poured into the economy. They were used primarily to finance our overblown military budget and consumer spending.

The United States was a net debtor nation before World War I and during most of the nineteenth century. Then, however, the nation used foreign capital to build up its infrastructure—its network of roads, canals, railroads, water systems, and other public utilities, all things that added to productive capacity. In recent years foreign debt has financed a consumption and military spending boom. There is a difference.

Now we arrive at the tough question. How will the nation both service and repay this debt? In the international economy the day will come when the piper has to be paid. Our choices are limited.

There are three. The United States can, of course, continue to borrow. This means that foreigners will have to be willing to give us real goods and services in exchange for paper claims in the United States. The indications are that they are less and less willing to do this.

A second choice is inflation, the historic preference of all debtors. Through inflation, a debt is repaid with cheaper dollars. With inflation, the foreign exchange value of the dollar will also fall and thus make it easier to export and harder to import. But foreign nations are not likely to go along, since their own prosperity is tied up with their ability to export to the United States.

Finally—and this is the most difficult choice of all—Americans will have to tighten their belts and learn how to export more than they import. This requires a reduction in our standard of life and learning to live internationally within our means. Can we make this choice?

---

curve, and, second, combine this with the *IS* and *LM* curves. The *BP* curve represents an overall equilibrium in the nation's balance of payments and shows how this equilibrium is related to income and interest rates. Equilibrium exists when any imbalance between exports (X) and imports (M) is offset by an appropriate volume of capital flows. Equilibrium in the balance of payments may be defined algebraically as

$$BP_e = Xf(FX_p) - Mf(FX_p, Y_{np}) + K_g f(i_d) = 0. \qquad (10\text{--}12)$$

In the equation,

FX_p = the real exchange rate,
Y_{np} = real net national product,
K_g = net global capital flows,
i_d = the difference between domestic and global interest rates.

The equation includes the key relationships discussed in this chapter. Exports (X) are positively related to the price of foreign exchange (FX_p). If the price of foreign exchange increases, the international value of the domestic currency drops. Thus, domestic goods become cheaper for foreigners and exports increase. Imports (M) are positively related to the level of real net national product (Y_{np}) and inversely related to the price of foreign exchange (FX_p). A fall in the price of foreign exchange (an appreciation in the international value of domestic currency) will make imports cheaper and thus lead to an increase in imports. Imports also will increase, as we saw earlier, from a rise in the net national product (Y_{np}). Finally, global capital flows (K_g) are positively related to the difference between domestic and global interest rates (i_d).

Equation (10–12) reflects the fact that any difference between exports and imports—the net export balance—must be offset by net flows of global capital. For example, if the domestic economy is running a current account surplus ($X > M$), there must be an outflow of capital to offset the surplus. If, on the other hand, there is a current account deficit ($M > X$), then an inflow of global capital is required to counter the deficit.

We can utilize a four-quadrant diagram to show how a balance of payments (*BP*) curve can be developed. This is done in Figure 10–13. Normally, the *BP* curve slopes upward to the right, for reasons that will become clear as we

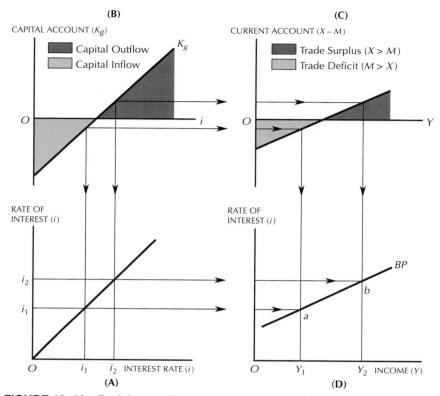

FIGURE 10–13 Deriving the Balance of Payments (*BP*) Curve. (B) At interest rate i_1 there is an outflow of capital. (C) This coincides with a current account surplus. (D) This current account surplus is consistent with the income level Y_1. As the income level rises to Y_2, a current account deficit appears, and the interest rate must rise to i_2 to generate the inflow of capital necessary to sustain the import surplus. The *BP* schedule shows balance of payments equilibrium for all possible values of *Y* and *I*.

explain how the curve is derived. In part B, capital inflows or outflows are linked to the domestic rate of interest. When domestic interest rates are low, funds will flow out of the country as holders of money seek higher returns abroad. In panel C the current account surplus or deficit is tied to the level of income. Part A contains a 45-degree line, which connects both axes to the rate of interest. In the basic *IS-LM* model, it will be recalled, low values for income (Y_{np}) are associated with low values for the rate of interest (i).

To construct the *BP* curve, let us begin with low values for both income and interest in the domestic economy. At the income level Y_1, the current account shows a surplus (part C). This is because a low level of income leads to a low level of imports relative to exports. Since the level of interest i_1 presumably is low relative to global interest rates, financial capital (funds) flow out of the domestic economy. The current account surplus ($X > M$) is offset by a capital outflow. In part D the export-import balance and capital flows connect to give us a point (*a*) on the balance of payments schedule (*BP*). This point is one of equilibrium in the balance of payments, an equilibrium defined in terms of income (*Y*) and the rate of interest (*i*).

Let us now consider what happens when the income level (*Y*) increases. This is depicted in part C. As income rises, the current account shifts from a surplus to a deficit. As the trade balance worsens, the domestic interest rate must rise *relative* to interest rates abroad to attract the financial capital necessary to finance the deficit. This is depicted in part B. At the income level Y_2 and the interest rate i_2 we have a second point (*b*) on the *BP* curve. Thus, the *BP* curve is the locus of all possible values for income (*Y*) and interest (*i*) at which the nation's overall flow of international payments is in balance.

The Slope and Position of the Balance of Payments Curve

A balance of payments curve as constructed in Figure 10–13 rests on three givens. These are the level of exports and autonomous imports, the exchange rate, and the values of interest rates abroad. What we need to know concerning the curve is what determines its slope and its level. The slope, that is, the steepness of the curve, depends on the sensitivity of global flows of financial capital to international interest rate differentials. This is a matter of elasticity. If global capital is highly sensitive to small changes in relative interest rates, then the *BP* curve will be relatively flat. This means, as far as the domestic economy is concerned, that a relatively large trade deficit could be financed with a relatively small increase in interest rates. On the other hand, if international capital flows are not responsive to relative interest rate differentials, the *BP* curve will be steep. This would mean that large increases in interest rates would be required to attract the global capital needed to finance a balance of trade deficit.

The level of the *BP* curve depends on the three givens noted above. This being the case, any changes in these givens will bring about a shift in the overall position of the curve. The possibilities may be summarized as follows:

1. *Net exports.* If exports fall or autonomous imports rise, net exports (*X − M*) will decline and an increased flow of global capital will be needed to maintain balance of payments equilibrium. This can be attained only by higher domestic interest rates, which will require a shift upward and to the left in the *BP* curve. If exports rise or autonomous imports fall, net exports (*X − M*) will decline and an outflow of capital will be necessary. This, in turn, will require a reduction in interest rates, depicted through a shift downward and to the right in the *BP* curve.

2. *Exchange rates.* If the international value of domestic currency depreciates—the price of foreign exchange goes up—there will be an increase in net exports and the current account will move toward a surplus. This will require an outflow of capital brought about by lower interest rates and a shift downward and to the right in the *BP* curve. If the price of foreign exchange falls, imports will increase—net exports (*X − M*) will decline—and the cur-

rent account will move toward a deficit. Now a capital inflow will be required; this means domestic interest rates must rise. Such a rise is depicted by a shift upward and to the left in the *BP* curve.

3. *Foreign interest rates.* When foreign interest rates change relative to domestic interest rates, the inflow or outflow of capital will be affected. If foreign interest rates rise, there will be a capital outflow. To offset this, domestic interest rates must rise. The *BP* curve shifts upward and to the left. If foreign interest rates fall relative to domestic interest rates, opposite conditions will result. The influx of global capital will require an offsetting decline in domestic interest rates, depicted by a shift downward and to the right in the *BP* curve.

A General Equilibrium Model in an Open Economy

Development of the balance of payments (*BP*) curve enables us to expand the basic *IS-LM* model to include international economic transactions. When this is done, the result is a model in which overall (or general) equilibrium requires a state of balance in not just two but three spheres of activity—the goods sphere, the monetary sphere, and now the international sphere. This is done by adding the *BP* curve to the basic *IS-LM* model, as shown in Figure 10–14. General equilibrium exists at the point of intersection for the three curves—the *IS* curve, the *LM* curve, and the *BP* curve. The meaning of the figure is that the income level Y_e and interest rate i_e are the *only* values for

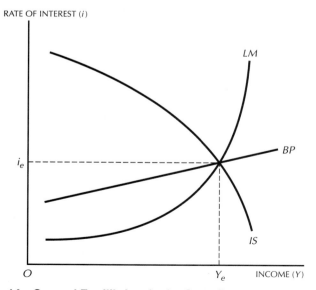

RATE OF INTEREST (*i*)

FIGURE 10–14 General Equilibrium in the Open Economy. The open economy general equilibrium model includes the *BP* as well as the *IS-LM* curves. Equilibrium in the goods sphere, the monetary sphere, and the balance of payments is found at the point where all three curves intersect.

both income and interest compatible with equilibrium in all three spheres of the economy. At any other level of income there will be disequilibrium, a situation that will require either interest rates, output itself, or exchange rates to adjust in order for equilibrium to be restored.

Let us note an extremely important point. Our model as such does not tell us *anything* with respect to how any of these adjustments are to be brought about. They may come about automatically as a result of market forces, or they may be brought about by deliberate policy actions by a central government, a central bank, or even an international institution such as the International Monetary Fund. The model itself is neutral. That is the point. Economists may and do disagree strongly on the question of the self-adjusting nature of the economic system. But this disagreement should not stand in the way of using the model both for analysis and for understanding how the economy works.

To illustrate this, let us examine what might happen to the U.S. economy if a serious recession developed in Europe, assuming the existing system of flexible exchange rates. We can use the model to show how such a recession could spread to the United States and, further, what course economic events might follow. Figure 10–15 illustrates these events. Let us assume initially that exchange rates, while flexible, do not change immediately. This is an important assumption, one which we shall drop shortly, but which is essential to start with in order to see precisely how events might work themselves out.

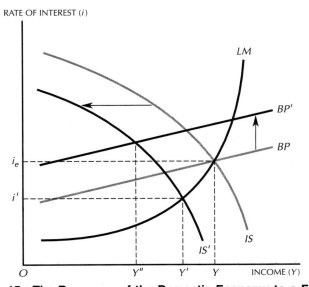

FIGURE 10–15   The Response of the Domestic Economy to a Foreign Recession.   The initial effect of a recession abroad is to shift both the *IS* and *BP* curves to the left and upward. This causes income to decline and leads to a trade imbalance. Flexible exchange rates may offset these developments by tending to shift the schedules back to their original position.

The recession in Europe will reduce the demand for U.S. goods—a change depicted in Figure 10–15 by a leftward shift in the *IS* curve to the position indicated by *IS'*. Why this shift? Exports are a part of the United States' aggregate demand, so consequently they are included in the *IS* curve. The shift to the left in the *IS* curve leads to a fall in income in the United States to the level *Y'*.

Now we have a disequilibrium situation. Although momentarily the domestic economy is in equilibrium at the income level *Y'*, there is disequilibrium in the international sphere. This is because with the decline in income in the United States, a trade imbalance develops, still assuming no change in the exchange rates. The market response to this disequilibrium would be a rise in interest rates, as foreign funds were sought to cover the newly emerged deficit in the trade balance. In Figure 10–15 this leads to a shift upward in the *BP* curve to the *BP'* level. This shift in itself, *if nothing else happened,* would push income in the United States to an even lower level, namely *Y"* in the figure.

Let us now return to our starting assumption, namely, that foreign exchange rates are flexible. How would the events described above unfold if exchange rates were allowed to adjust to these events? This will change the picture significantly. When Europe's demand for U.S. goods drops, the foreign exchange value of the dollar will also drop. This is because in the world's foreign exchange markets there will be less demand for the U.S. dollar. Thus, its price will fall. As we have seen from our earlier analysis, a fall—or depreciation—in the foreign exchange value of the U.S. dollar makes U.S. goods cheaper for residents of other nations. This should lead to an increase in Europe's demand for U.S. goods and thereby shift the *IS* curve back toward its original position. If the trade balance improves, the differential between U.S. and foreign interest rates will narrow—a development which could push the *BP* curve back to its original position. It is theoretically possible that through exchange rate flexibility the United States might be partly insulated from the European recession.

Roughly, something like this happened between 1989 and 1993. The European Community nations moved into a recession as their growth rates dropped from an average of 3.5 percent in 1989 to minus 0.3 percent in 1993. The index of the foreign exchange value for the dollar also fell, from 98.6 in 1989 to 93.2 in 1992, a decline which helped turn the United States' trade with Europe from a $4.0 billion deficit in 1989 to a $3.1 billion surplus in 1992.[17] Note, however, that a flexible exchange rate did not prevent a recession from starting in the United States. The shift in the trade balance with Europe from a deficit to a small surplus merely mitigated the severity of the recession that began in July 1990 and ended in March 1991.

Suppose we look at the foregoing from a different perspective, assuming the world economy still had a system of relatively fixed exchange rates as in the Bretton Woods era. How would things work out then, again assuming a

---

[17] *Economic Report of the President*, 1995, pp. 397, 402, 403.

recession starting in Europe? As in our earlier example, the impact of the recession would be to shift both the *IS* and *BP* curves to the left and upward. The dollar would still be under pressure, even though its exchange rate was fixed by international agreement. To defend the foreign exchange value of the dollar, the United States' central bank (the Federal Reserve System) would have to buy dollars with its reserves of foreign currency. This would, in effect, reduce the domestic money supply. In Figure 10–15 the *LM* curve would shift to the left and raise interest rates and depress even further the level of income (*Y*).

Critics of the fixed exchange rate system (i.e., Bretton Woods) maintain it causes a nation to lose control of its domestic money supply, which is determined by balance of payments considerations rather than internal needs for high employment and moderate inflation. These are essentially the same arguments Keynes used in the early 1930s, when he urged that Britain abandon the gold standard. The theoretical answer that our model supplies for the foregoing is an expansionary fiscal policy that would push the *IS* curve enough to the right to counteract the above effects. Under a system of flexible exchange rates, what saves the day (the employment level) is expanded exports brought about by a depreciation in the foreign exchange value of the domestic currency. With a system of fixed exchange rates, what saves the day is an expansionary fiscal policy.

What is the point of this analysis? In principle the argument suggests that through flexibility in exchange rates an economy can insulate its domestic economy from foreign shocks. Is this realistic? Probably not. Even in a textbook example, it takes time before the full effects of exchange rate adjustments worked themselves out. In the meanwhile, there will be significant disturbances to output and employment in the domestic economy. Events of the last 10 to 15 years have shown that even with flexible exchange rates there is far less independence among nations than the theory suggests. The world economy is becoming more integrated, more interdependent, not less so. Some of the reasons for this will become evident as we now turn to a discussion and analysis of recent macroeconomic developments in the international economy. We shall examine these developments primarily from the perspective of the United States.

Recent Developments in International Macroeconomics

The increasing interdependence between the domestic economy—even for a nation as large as the United States—and the international economy is made dramatically evident by developments since the late 1970s. Figure 10–16 is a flow-type diagram, which shows graphically key developments and how they interact with one another. The centerpiece in the drama depicted in Figure 10–16 is the deficit of the federal government. In the 13 years from 1981 through 1993 the cumulative deficit was $2,224.9 billion, a figure unprece-

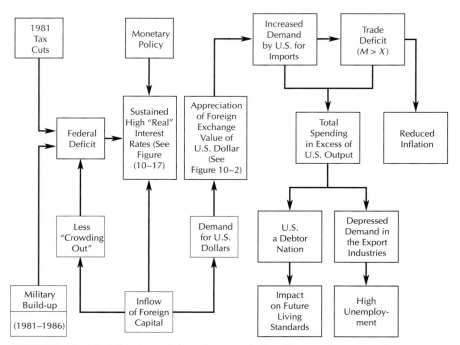

FIGURE 10–16 The Interdependence of the Domestic and International Economies. Tax cuts in 1981 plus the military buildup (1981–86) have contributed to the federal deficit, which, in turn, sustained real interest rates at levels above those in foreign countries (Figure 10–17). Consequently, there has been an influx of foreign funds into the United States, which has tended to drive up the foreign exchange value of the U.S. dollar—a development that stimulated imports and depressed demand in some of the nation's export industries.

dented in peacetime.[18] The deficit is a direct consequence of macroeconomic policy decisions made in 1981, namely the tax cuts embodied in the Economic Recovery Tax Act of 1981, and the long-term buildup in military spending also initiated by the Reagan administration in 1981. Between 1980 and 1986 military spending grew by 87.5 percent, and the increases were not offset by cuts elsewhere in the federal budget. Overall, cumulative military spending from 1981 through 1992 (the Reagan and Bush administrations) totaled $3,465.5 billion in current dollars.[19] Monetary policy, which became tight in 1979 and continued tight until mid-1982, contributed indirectly to the size of the deficit by plunging the economy into the 1981–82 recession. As usual in a recession, tax collections lagged and expenditures grew; this added to the deficit.

[18] Ibid., p. 371.

[19] *Economic Report of the President*, 1994, p. 371.

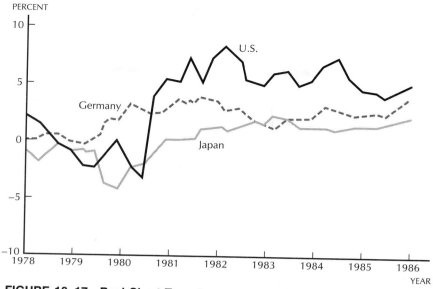

FIGURE 10–17   Real Short-Term Interest Rates in the United States, West Germany, and Japan: 1978–1986.   Higher short-term interest rates in the United States as compared particularly with West Germany and Japan contributed to the appreciation of the foreign exchange value of the dollar in the early 1980s, a development which led to continuing deficits in the merchandise trade balance of the United States.

Source: Federal Reserve Bank of Philadelphia.

The combination of a growing federal deficit and tight money kept interest rates, especially real interest rates, higher in the United States than abroad, particularly in West Germany and Japan, two of the nation's major competitors in the international economy. Figure 10–17 shows the course of real interest rates in the United States, West Germany, and Japan from 1978 through early 1986. Real interest rate differentials between these three countries *narrowed* appreciably afer 1986. The real rate of interest is the nominal (or market) rate adjusted for inflation. The consequences of this inflow of foreign funds (i.e., capital) into the United States, as foreigners took advantage of the higher rates of return on financial investments (bonds, stocks, etc.) in the United States, were twofold. First, it eased the crowding-out problem discussed earlier (page 342). Although the deficit tended to drive interest rates higher, *ceteris paribus,* the availability of foreign funds lessened somewhat the pressure on interest rates because foreign funds added to the general pool of money available for lending. Second, the influx of foreign funds led to an increase in the foreign-based demand for U.S. dollars, because dollars were needed for the purchase of financial investment instruments in the United States. This is what drove up the foreign exchange value of the dollar between 1980 and late 1985 (see Figure 10–2).

Two results flowed directly from the dollar's appreciation. Imports became cheaper, because as the dollar's foreign exchange value increased, every dollar commanded more units of a foreign currency in exchange. Thus, the price of imported goods and services fell, and U.S. spending on imports rose. In the national income accounts, spending for imported goods and services rose by 53.6 percent between 1980 and 1986, whereas the sale of U.S. exports and services increased by only 14.3 percent in the same period.[20] The appreciation in the foreign exchange value of the dollar meant that U.S.-made goods and services were more expensive internationally. The overall consequence of this was a merchandise trade deficit, which worsened steadily from 1981 through 1987.

After 1987 the situation changed, although not as dramatically as one might have thought, given the sharp fall in the foreign exchange value of the U.S. dollar ushered in by the Group of Five meeting in September of that year. By 1994 the foreign exchange value of the dollar had dropped 33.1 percent below its peak in late 1985.[21] Even though this fall raised the cost to Americans of imported goods, imports continued to climb. They increased in value by 96.0 percent between 1985 and 1994. Quality factors as much as price accounted for this persistent growth in imports in spite of the dollar's fall. As expected, the depreciation helped exports; they rose by 137.1 percent during these years. As a result the overall trade deficit improved; it dropped slightly from $115.6 billion in 1985 to $102.1 billion in 1994.[22]

The national income and accounting identities discussed earlier (pages 68–70) can be drawn on to summarize the linkages between total output for the U.S. economy and its trade balance and total spending. Recall that our basic identity equation in an open economy is

$$\text{GDP} = C + I + G + X - M. \tag{10–13}$$

If we rearrange this identity, we have an equation that relates total spending and the volume of goods and services available to the economy:

$$\text{GDP} + M = (C + I + G) + X. \tag{10–14}$$

In the above expression, and in plain English, the left-hand side represents the total volume of goods and services available to the country—domestic production (GDP) plus imports—whereas the right-hand side necessarily equals total spending within the domestic economy $(C + I + G)$ plus purchases by foreigners (X). We may term $C + I + G$ "Gross Domestic Spending (GDS)" to distinguish it from Gross Domestic Product (GDP). Therefore,

[20] Ibid., p. 275.
[21] Ibid., 1995, p. 402.
[22] Ibid., p. 275.

it follows that

$$GDP - GDS = X - M. \qquad (10\text{--}15)$$

A country's trade balance (on goods *and* services) is, therefore, simply the difference between its total production of goods and services (GDP) and its total domestic spending (GDS). As far as the United States is concerned, the last 12 years (1982 through 1993) saw total domestic spending outrun domestic production. Put another way, a significant proportion of U.S. spending has been met by foreign production—a development which has had a depressing effect on U.S. industry generally and the export industries in particular. This has kept unemployment unnecessarily high in the United States, as well as been responsible for the change in the last few years of the United States' status from a net creditor to a net debtor nation. The ultimate impact of the latter lies in the future (see Figure 10–16), because sooner or later the United States will have to develop an export surplus of goods and services to both service and repay its growing foreign-held debt. Thus, the long-term impact of the trade deficit will be on the nation's real standard of living, since a part of the domestic output will have to be used for the foregoing purpose.

A Summary Comment on the Determination of Aggregate Demand

In this and the three preceding chapters our concern has been with analysis of the component parts of the economy's structure of aggregate demand. As stressed in Chapter 4, the central thesis of modern employment theory is that, in the short run, when the economy's capacity to produce is relatively fixed, the key to both the income and employment level is demand for the economy's whole output or, more simply, aggregate demand. Expectation of demand leads to the creation of output—and income. Thus, if we can analyze what determines the level of demand for the output of the whole economy, we learn something about the determination of income and employment.

As a result of theoretical developments stemming from the work of Keynes and others and of advances in the field of national income accounting, it is possible to identify the four major components of the economy's aggregate demand structure: *consumption, investment, government purchases of goods and services,* and the *export-import balance.* Our purpose has been not only to tie these four forms of demand together in a single integrated structure representing the demand for the economy's total output, but to analyze, too, the determinants of the level of each of these individual parts of the aggregate demand function. Moreover, we have sought to show how changes in the income (and employment) level are linked to changes in the economy's aggregate demand function and how changes in this function are the result of shifts in any or all of its component parts.

Summary

1. The performance of the domestic economy is affected by the economic transactions undertaken with the rest of the world. These transactions are reflected formally in a nation's balance of payments statement, which is an accounting statement that records exports, imports, international transfers, and all major financial transactions with foreign nations.

2. The United States, like most modern nations, has become increasingly a part of the global economy. A major indication of this is the extent to which international commerce (defined as one-half a nation's exports and imports) has grown for most nations as a proportion of their gross domestic products.

3. The foreign exchange rate, another major factor affecting the domestic economy through the international sphere, measures the price of the domestic currency in terms of foreign currencies. As this price changes, a nation's export-import balance changes and thereby affects the domestic economy.

4. Exports are an important element in a nation's aggregate demand structure. In theory, they are generally treated as an exogenous variable, similarly to the way investment expenditure is treated. Imports, a function of domestic income, must be subtracted from exports because they represent expenditure directed abroad.

5. In an open economy, both exports and imports must be fitted into the analytical structure involving aggregate demand and aggregate supply. Exports represent a direct demand for domestic output, whereas imports are, like saving and taxes, a leakage out of the current income stream. In an open economy, aggregate demand (DD) is equal to $C + I + G + X - M$.

6. As with investment and government expenditure, there is a multiplier effect associated with changes in the export-import balance. An increase in exports, other things being equal, will increase income by some multiple of the initial increase in exports. An increase in imports will also have a multiplier effect, but in the opposite direction.

7. The line of causation discussed in most of this chapter is from changes in the export-income balance to changes in output and employment. However, changes in the domestic economy will also affect the export-import balance. Other things being equal, a rise in income tends to bring about a trade deficit or a reduction in a trade surplus; a fall in income has the opposite effect.

8. A balance of payments (BP) schedule can be constructed, relating both income and the rate of interest to the overall balance in a nation's international accounts. By adding this schedule to the basic IS-LM model, it can be shown how equilibrium in the goods and monetary spheres in the domestic economy is linked to equilibrium in the international sphere.

9. The influence of the foreign exchange rate on the domestic economy depends in part on whether a nation is operating with a system of fixed or flexible exchange rates. In principle, a flexible exchange rate system will insulate the domestic economy from economic upheavals abroad, but in practice this insulation is less than complete.

Money and Output

IN CHAPTERS 7 THROUGH 10 we analyzed the major forms of spending that, when added together, represent total demand for the output the economy is capable of producing. This, as we have seen, pertains to the real, or goods, sphere of the economy, the arena of economic activity where the forces of aggregate demand and supply determine the conditions under which an equilibrium of output and employment is achieved. In Chapter 5 we examined the most important characteristics of money, followed by an analysis of how money and interest are linked through the loanable funds and liquidity preference theories. This set the stage for showing why there also exists a monetary sphere of economic activity, an area in which the forces at work focus on the demand for and the supply of money. The basic *IS-LM* model shows the interaction between these two fundamental spheres of activity in the domestic economy.

In this chapter we shift the analysis back to the monetary sphere. Since Keynes wrote about money in the 1930s, it has been apparent that what happens in the economy's monetary sphere can have a profound impact on *real* activity, that is on the level of output and employment. Money has been present throughout the analysis to this point, but its role has been primarily to serve as a unit of measurement. This is because the spending and output magnitudes we have been discussing must be measured in monetary terms.

Our task in this chapter is twofold. First, we shall analyze the forces that surround the demand and supply of money, which takes the form of an in-depth analysis of the monetary sphere of the economy. Here, in other words, we shall describe and discuss the economic principles that govern behavior that is reflected in the demand for and supply of money. Second we shall show how events in the monetary sphere affect the level of aggregate demand and, thereby, output and employment. Chapter 6 addressed this generally, when we showed through the *IS-LM* general macroeconomic model how output and employment depend on the interaction between the goods and monetary spheres of the economy. Now it is essential to explore these relationships in greater depth. We shall use both of the two major theoretical approaches that seek to understand the role money plays in the performance of the economy—the Keynesian and the modern quantity theory developed largely by Milton Friedman.

The Role of Money in Keynesian Theory

As noted in Chapter 5 (page 146), several years before *The General Theory* appeared, Keynes wrote an article in which he explained why money was not neutral. In what he described as a "monetary economy," money plays a role of its own, being "one of the operative factors" in the way the economy performs. It is from this perspective that we undertake our analysis of the theoretical foundations of the Keynesian demand for and supply of money. Specifically, we shall look first at the demand for money, follow this with comment on some theoretical questions involving the supply of money, and conclude this section with a restatement of the reasons why money plays such a crucial role in the way systems of market capitalism work in the real economic world.

The Demand for Money

We start with the demand for money because the primary means by which money is introduced into economic analysis *in a causal sense* is through the demand side. Before we examine how economists have approached this question, some preliminary observations are in order. First, when we speak of the *demand* for money, we are speaking of a demand for real balances. People basically want money because of its purchasing power, for what it will buy. This means that we approach the demand for money within the same frame of reference used in analyzing the determinants of aggregate demand, namely, in terms of *real* rather than *nominal* values. Second, the demand for money focuses on the basic question of why people (and institutions) choose to hold money rather than some other type of asset. Money, let us recall, is a stock phenomenon, which means that the amount in existence at any time must be held by someone or some entity, irrespective of its ultimate use.

The Reasons for Holding Money

In *The General Theory* Keynes provides an excellent framework for analyzing the question of why people want to hold money. Money, after all, is in a sense barren, because it does not yield a rate of return, as do most financial assets, and it does not provide directly for the satisfaction of wants. In Chapter 5 we examined the major functions that money serves. What Keynes did in *The General Theory* was to go behind these functions and probe into the motives that govern the desire to hold money.[1] Keynes suggested three primary motives for holding money: the transactions motive, the precautionary motive, and the speculative motive.

The Transactions Motive. The transactions motive relates to the need to hold some quantity of money balances to carry on day-to-day economic dealings. Practically all transactions in a money-using economy involve an exchange of money, and, since the receipt of income is not synchronized exactly with all transactions involving money outlays, it is necessary that some money be held in order to meet this need.

Money held to satisfy the transactions motive is related primarily to the medium of exchange function. Money balances held idle in response to this motive provide a means of payment for transactions which will take place in the future. The amount of money in relation to income that people and business firms find it necessary to hold to satisfy the transactions motive depends on the time interval within which income is received relative to the income. To illustrate with a simple example, let us assume an individual has an annual income of $25,000. If this individual is paid only once a year and, further, if the whole income is spent during the year, the money balance will be $25,000 at the beginning of the year and zero at the end of the year. The individual's *average* holding of money during the year will be $12,500, or 50 percent of the income. Now let us consider what happens if this individual's employer decides to pay out income twice a year. Every six months the individual will receive $12,500 and will spend the whole of this before the beginning of the next pay period. The money balances will total $12,500 at the beginning of the six-month period and zero at the end, Thus, the average money balance will total $6,250 in each pay period during the year. This means that a person paid twice a year must, on the average, hold but 25 percent of the annual income as money balances in order to satisfy the transactions motive. The more frequent the pay period, the smaller is the proportion of an individual's annual income that must be held to carry on day-to-day transactions.

---

[1] Keynes, *The General Theory*, pp. 194–199.

The Precautionary Motive. The precautionary motive is the desire to hold some quantity of money balances to meet unforeseen emergencies or contingencies. It is, in other words, a desire to set aside some money balances to provide for a rainy day. The need to hold money to satisfy this particular motive arises out of the fact that we do not have certain knowledge concerning future transactions; a situation may arise in which the need for money balances is much greater than the amount required to carry on normal day-to-day transactions. For the individual this may be the result of unemployment, illness, or some other form of economic misfortune, although it should be stressed that all unforeseen developments that require extraordinary expenditures on the part of either individuals or business firms are not necessarily of an adverse character.

The Speculative Motive. The speculative motive is the most complex and the most important of the three major sources of demand for cash balances postulated by Keynes. Fundamentally, the speculative motive relates to the desire to hold a part of one's assets in the form of cash in order to take advantage of future market movements. It involves, according to Keynes, holding money balances with the objective of "securing profit from knowing better than the market what the future will bring forth."[2] The speculative motive shifts the emphasis from the medium of exchange function of money, which dominated classical thinking and which underlies the transactions and precautionary motives, to the store of value function. Under the speculative motive, money is wanted as an asset rather than as a medium of exchange that can be drawn on as needed at some future date. Money is being held in preference to holding assets in some other form.

Since idle money balances do not, like debt or equity instruments, yield income, why would an individual or a business firm wish to hold on to them? We posed this question earlier (page 146) and answered it partly in Keynes's own words. The question is of such momentous importance for understanding the peculiar role played by money in the way that market capitalism works that it is well worth our while to ponder again Keynes's thoughts on the matter. He wrote:

> Money, it is well known, serves two principal purposes. By acting as a money of account it facilitates exchanges without it being necessary that it should ever itself come into the picture as a substantive object. In this respect it is a convenience which is devoid of significance or real influence. In the second place, it is a store of wealth. So we are told without a smile on the face. But in the world of the classical economy, what an insane use to which to put it! For it is a recognized characteristic of money as a store of wealth that it is barren; whereas practically every other form of storing wealth yields some interest or profit. *Why should anyone outside a lunatic asylum wish to use money as a store of wealth?*
>
> Because, partly on reasonable and partly on instinctive grounds, our desire to hold

---

[2] Ibid., p. 170.

money is a barometer of the degree of distrust of our own calculations and conventions concerning the future. Even though this feeling about money is itself conventional or instinctive, it operates, so to speak, at a deeper level of our motivation. It takes charge at the moments when the higher, more precarious conventions have weakened. *The possession of actual money lulls our disquietude; and the premium which we require to make us part with money is the measure of our disquietude.*[3]

Basically, the transactions and precautionary motives center on the medium of exchange function of money, whereas the speculative motive relates to money in its role as a store of wealth or value.

The foregoing is essentially descriptive, setting forth what Keynes believed were the three basic reasons why people want to hold money. For analytical purposes, we must go beyond description and put these basic motives into the context of functional relationships that represent the demand for money. It is to this that we now turn.

The Transactions and Precautionary Demands for Money

Both logically and for the sake of simplicity in the analysis, the transactions and precautionary demands for money should be lumped together, because both motives involve holding money to bridge the gap between income and expenditures, either relatively soon for transactions or later for a rainy day. In any case, the demand for money rooted in these two motives must be related primarily to the medium of exchange function of money. Let us call the combined demand for money to satisfy the transactions and precautionary motives the *transactions demand* and designate it by the symbol L_t.[4]

Given the existence of some kind of a normal ratio with respect to the *proportion* of income that the public wants to hold as idle money balances in response to L_t, the actual amount of money held to satisfy this motive will vary directly with income. Thus, L_t is, *ceteris paribus,* a function of income. Algebraically we have

$$L_t = f(Y). \tag{11–1}$$

The fundamental reason for this is not difficult to see. In a complex society the volume of economic transactions of all kinds varies directly with the income level. Consequently, the absolute quantity of money balances needed

---

[3] John Maynard Keynes, "The General Theory of Employment," *Quarterly Journal of Economics,* February 1937, pp. 215, 216 (italics added). No better example of what Keynes meant exists, perhaps, than the run on U.S. banks during the early months of 1933, a crisis which finally led to the temporary closing of the banks. Because their fears about the continued solvency of the banking system were so great, people panicked and sought to withdraw their funds. They wanted cash money because they feared for the safety of any other form of money, including demand deposits and savings deposits.

[4] The analysis that follows is cast in real terms; that is to say the demands for money are for real quantities. This follows because it is presumed that any change in the price level will cause the demand for nominal money balances to change in the same proportion. Thus, it is ultimately real changes that are significant.

to carry on these transactions also varies directly with the income level. The amount of money that can be held strictly in response to the precautionary component of the transactions demand schedule is for most people a residual sum, which also will vary with income. The higher the income level, the easier it will be for individuals and firms to hold idle balances to meet unforeseen contingencies.[5]

The functional relationship between the transactions demand for money L_t and the income level is depicted in Figure 11–1. The transactions demand L_t is shown on the vertical axis, and the income level Y on the horizontal axis. The transactions function is the curve labeled $L_t = f(Y)$. It is a straight line, drawn so that its slope is less than 45°. This indicates, first, that the ratio of money balances held for transactions purposes to income, L_t/Y, is normally less than unity (100 percent) and, second, that this ratio is assumed constant. Given these assumptions, the figure shows that the amount of money demanded for transactions purposes L_t varies directly with the income level Y. For example, at the income level Y_1 the transactions demand is L_{t_1}, and at the income level Y_2 the transactions demand is L_{t_2}.

Since idle money balances do not yield any income, should not the amount of money people are willing to hold as balances be related to interest rates? As a matter of fact, this is the crucial relationship insofar as the demand for money to satisfy the speculative motive is concerned. But most economists

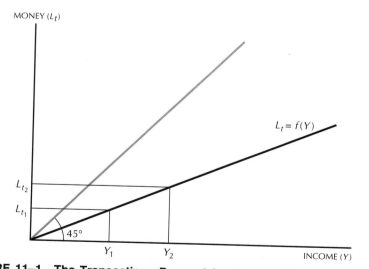

FIGURE 11–1   The Transactions Demand for Money.   The curve $L_t = f(Y)$ shows that the demand for money for transactions purposes (L_t) will increase as the level of income increases. The value of the coefficient linking the transactions demand for money (L_t) to income (Y) is normally less than 1.

---

[5] This should not be confused with saving. Funds held idle to satisfy the precautionary motive may represent one way in which savings are disposed of, but they are not to be mistaken for the act of saving itself.

believe the transactions demand is relatively unresponsive to the rate of interest, except, perhaps, at very high interest rates. Then there would be a strong incentive to economize on holding money for ordinary transactions. There is evidence that high interest rates during 1973–74 and 1979–80 did exactly that.[6] Nevertheless, linking the demand for money in response to the combined transactions and precautionary motives to income is a useful, working hypothesis. The response of money demand to a change in income measures the *income elasticity* of the demand for money.

The Asset Demand for Money

The other type of demand for money balances stems from the speculative motive. This is the motive that lies behind the liquidity preference theory of interest, whose basic features were sketched out in Chapter 5 (pages 146–47). Here we shall probe into the theoretical bases of this motive. The essential feature that distinguishes this demand from the categories considered previously is that it represents demand for money to hold *as an asset*. In our analysis we will call this demand the *asset demand* and designate it by the symbol L_a.

The essence of the asset demand for money is that money is regarded as a way of holding economic value over time, which is preferable to debt instruments and equity instruments.[7] Debt instruments normally yield the holder a fixed income in the form of interest, whereas equity instruments yield the holder an uncertain income in the form of profit. Although profit can be expressed as a rate of return and thus compared directly with the income derived from a debt instrument, we will simplify our analysis at this stage by assuming that the person who wants to hold economic value over time considers only *two* alternatives: holding money or holding debt instruments. We shall use bonds to represent debt instruments.[8]

Why would an individual hold money, which yields no return, in prefer-

---

[6] See Richard Porter, Thomas Simpson, and Ellen Mauskopf, "Financial Innovation and Monetary Aggregates," *Brookings Papers on Economic Activity,* Vol. 1 (Washington, D.C.: Brookings Institution, 1979).

[7] A person holding either a debt or an equity instrument may experience either a capital gain or a capital loss because of unforeseen changes in the current market value of the asset. The possibility of a capital loss is a risk a debt or equity instrument holder assumes.

[8] Equity instruments involve considerations of future values for the rate of return over cost (the marginal efficiency of capital) as well as for the rate of interest. If persons and firms turn to equities as a means of holding economic value over time, they will have to make judgments about the future yields of capital assets and compare these expected yields with the anticipated return from bonds. Holding equities means, too, that economic value may be tied up in real capital assets; thus, in principle wealth holders should take into account the future value of such capital assets as well as the current rate of return in reaching decisions about the form in which they want to hold economic value through time. Highly organized markets for buying and selling equities such as the New York Stock Exchange tend to blur the distinction between debts and equities. Nevertheless, a rational wealth holder would allocate holdings among the three basic forms in which economic value can be held through time—money, debts, and equities—so that at the margin there would accrue the same money return, or satisfaction in the event money is held, from each type of holding.

ence to a fixed-income debt instrument? The answer, as Keynes pointed out, lies in the fact of uncertainty with respect to the future market value of the debt instruments. The corollary of this is that the income forgone by holding money in preference to a fixed-income obligation such as a bond becomes the *opportunity cost* of holding money. If we limit the alternative forms in which economic value may be held to money and bonds, then the rate of interest is the cost of holding money as an asset in satisfaction of the speculative motive, since interest is the income forgone when one chooses to hold money in preference to bonds. This implies that the amount of money held as an asset is a function of the rate of interest, although an *inverse* one. Thus, we have algebraically

$$L_a = f(i). \tag{11-2}$$

The higher the rate of interest, the more costly it becomes to hold money rather than bonds and, consequently, the smaller will be the amount of money held as an asset.

To comprehend fully the nature of the asset demand function, it is essential to understand how Keynes believed people acted when they had to decide between holding money or holding bonds. What is involved in this decision, according to Keynes, is a relationship between the current interest rate, the interest rate that people regard as normal, and, finally, the current market value of bonds. Normal in this context means the level of interest rates that seems appropriate because of past experience. It cannot be defined in an exact numerical manner because of the changing nature of experience. When the decision has to be made between holding money and holding bonds, the wealth holder will be guided by his or her perception of whether the *current* rate of interest lies above or below what is regarded as the *normal* rate. To illustrate, if the wealth holder believes that current market rates are *below* the normal level of interest rates, the decision will be to hold cash. The reason is this: Believing that current market rates are below normal levels is the same as saying that market rates are expected to rise in the future. But if this happens, bond prices will fall. Hence, it would be unwise to hold bonds since this entails the risk of a capital loss. It is preferable for the wealth holder to hold cash and wait to see if bond prices actually fall. If the latter happens, then it is appropriate to move from holding cash to holding bonds. On the other hand, if the current interest rate lies *above* a rate that is perceived to be normal, the wise thing is to move from holding cash to holding bonds. In this scenario, market rates of interest are expected to fall in the future—or bond prices to rise—and thus the wealth holder who moves into bonds has the opportunity for capital gains, as well as for deriving interest income from the bond.

The foregoing should help explain a vital point about the functional relationship suggested between the demand for money as an asset and the rate of interest. It is not just the fact that it becomes more costly to hold money as an asset as interest rates go up (remember interest is the opportunity cost of holding money); that is important, but expectations about what is going to happen to future interest rates also enter into the relationship. Since expectations are often fragile and based on highly uncertain knowledge about what may happen in the future, they tend to be volatile. Thus, the entire functional relationship embodied in Equation (11–2) may also be volatile.

In a formal sense, the functional relationship between the asset demand for money and the rate of interest is represented by a curve as drawn in Figure 11–2. Theoretically, this is the same demand for money as an asset curve contained in Figure 5–4 (page 160). Our concern now is for Keynes's thinking with respect to the fundamental theoretical justification for the existence of the relationship depicted by the curve. The demand for money as an asset L_a appears on the horizontal axis, and the rate of interest i on the vertical axis. The curve $L_a = f(i)$ shows the quantity of money that people and firms want to hold *as an asset* at different rates of interest. The curve depicts the basic relationship discussed earlier, namely, the more costly it is to hold money in terms of interest income forgone, the smaller will be the quantity of money that people want to hold. As depicted in Figure 11–2, every point on the curve represents a consensus of opinion about the desirability of holding cash, given actual market interest rates (current bond prices) and expectations about future rates (future bond prices). If there is a basic and, perhaps, sudden change in expectations on the part of wealth holders, the entire curve shown in Figure 11–2 will shift. Thus, the volatility of expectations for future interest rates relative to notions of what constitutes a normal interest rate means that the kind of asset demand schedule for money that Keynes envisaged in *The General Theory* is volatile.

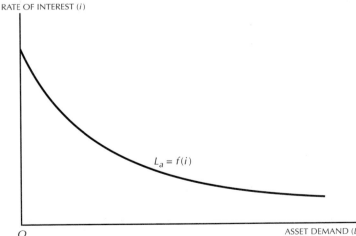

FIGURE 11–2 The Asset Demand for Money. The asset demand for money (L_a) is inversely related to the interest rate (i); it increases when the interest rate falls and declines when the interest rate goes up.

To illustrate, let us suppose a development that causes wealth holders in general to believe that future interest rates will be higher than previously expected. Such a development occurred, for example, in the spring of 1982 when it became increasingly clear to the financial community that the deficit of the federal government for the upcoming fiscal year was going to be far larger than originally forecast. A development of this sort has the effect of shifting upward the entire demand schedule for money as an asset. Changes in the budgetary outlook changed people's minds about the relative desirability of holding cash and bonds. The expectation that *future* interest rates would be higher than previously anticipated increases the demand for cash. As people shift from holding bonds to holding cash, the price of bonds will decline (current interest rates will rise) and thus help bring about the conditions anticipated by the changed expectations.

As was noted in Chapter 5, the graphic representation of the asset demand function is also called a *liquidity preference curve*. Since money is the most liquid of all assets, the demand for the money as an asset is necessarily a demand for liquidity. Although Keynes tended to use the term "liquidity preference" rather loosely to mean the demand for money for all reasons, modern usage restricts the term to the demand for money as an asset. There is one further aspect of the demand for liquidity (money as an asset) that needs to be explored. As drawn in Figure 11–2, the asset demand curve tends to become perfectly elastic—that is, horizontal—at very low rates of interest. This condition is described as the *liquidity trap*. Keynes suggested that it was theoretically possible for the demand for liquidity (money) to "become virtually absolute in the sense that almost everywhere one prefers cash to holding a debt."[9] What Keynes meant by this was a situation in which expectations about the future value (price) of all income-earning assets have become so pessimistic that no one would hold such an asset because of the risk of a severe capital loss. Thus, the demand for liquidity becomes absolute. Keynes also said that he did not know of any historical examples of the demand for liquidity becoming virtually absolute, but it was a possibility.[10] Although no significant empirical evidence exists to support the existence of an actual liquidity trap, the concept is drawn on to demonstrate the theoretical possibility of a situation in which monetary authorities have lost all practical control over the rate of interest.

The Total Demand for Money

Up to this point we have considered the transactions demand for money L_t and the asset demand for money L_a as separate functions. This is logical because the determinants of the amount of money held are, in the first instance, income and, in the second, interest. It is possible in theory, though,

---

[9] Keynes, *The General Theory*, p. 207.
[10] Ibid.

to combine these two demand functions and obtain a total demand for money. First, we posit the following identity:

$$L = L_t + L_a. \tag{11-3}$$

This equation states that the total demand for money is equal to the sum of the transactions demand and the asset demand. This being true, we can posit the functional relationship

$$L = f(Y, i). \tag{11-4}$$

In this equation the total demand for money L is a function of both the income level Y and the rate of interest i.

The combined transactions and asset demands for money are illustrated in Figure 11–3. The rate of interest is measured on the vertical axis, the total demand for money on the horizontal axis. Income as a variable influencing the level of the overall demand for money is introduced by adding the transactions demand L_t *appropriate to each income level* (see Figure 11–1) to the asset demand function $L_a = f(i)$. The result is a total demand function for money $L = f(i, Y)$, which combines the asset and transactions demands. As income rises, we get a series of demand curves for total money balances, each of which is associated with a different level of income. The student should note that the L curves shown in Figure 11–3 are drawn so that they begin to bend backward at the upper ranges of the interest rate. This is because even

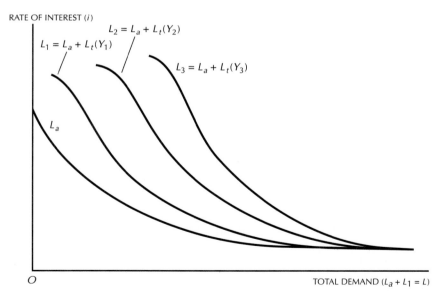

FIGURE 11–3 The Combined Asset and Transactions Demands for Money. The curve that links the total demand for money (L) to the rate of interest (i) will necessarily shift upward as the income level (Y) changes, because a higher income level increases the need for money to carry out transactions.

the transactions demand for money becomes sensitive to the rate of interest at very high interest levels.

At this point the reader may want to refer back to Figure 6–3 and the discussion relating to it (pages 181–86). Figure 11–3 explains more precisely than the earlier figure why the curve representing the demand for money as an asset shifts upward when the income level increases. In Figure 11–3 this results because the transactions demand has been factored into the overall picture. In the earlier analysis (Figure 6–3) the curve shifted because *all* demand curves tend to shift to the right with an increase in income. Conceptually, however, the results in both cases are the same: a series of curves that relate the demand for money to the rate of interest, with each individual curve linked to a unique income level.

Modifications to the Keynesian Conception of Money Demand

Before we analyze the supply of money and bring the demand for and supply of money together, it is important to discuss some important modifications that have entered the picture. The Keynesian ideas about money and its demand traced out in the preceding pages are essentially macroeconomic in character; that is to say they are put in the context of the overall (or total) demand for money. Since Keynes's pathbreaking work on the speculative demand for money, there have been theoretical refinements to the general subject of the demand for money that are closer to the spirit of microeconomics. That is, they begin with the individual (business firm or wealth holder) and treat the demand for money as a theoretical question similar to the demand for any good or service. The results are then generalized to apply to the economy as a whole. Two economists who have made important contributions to our understanding of the demand for money through this approach are Professors James Tobin of Yale and William Baumol of Princeton. Their findings are generally in harmony with Keynes's views.

One basic difficulty inherent in the Keynesian explanation of the schedule of liquidity preference and the available supply of money for asset purposes is that it presupposes that persons in the money market will either hold bonds if their expectations are bullish with respect to future bond prices or hold cash if their expectations are bearish. "Bullish" expectations means they believe bond prices will be higher in the future; therefore, capital gains can be expected from holding bonds. "Bearish" expectations means just the opposite with respect to future bond prices. Consequently, holding cash is preferred to holding bonds so that capital losses may be avoided. Individuals will behave in this fashion if their expectations concerning future movements of bond prices (interest rates) are *certain*. But if not, what then? The fact that there may be uncertainty about what will happen to bond prices (interest rates) in the future may lead an individual to hold both bonds and money, to diversify the portfolio. As a matter of fact, this is the reality, for the personal wealth portfolio of most people includes at any one time both money and other types of financial assets.[11] What is needed is an explanation for this fact, as well as an explanation of why people shift from holding one type of asset to another.

Professor Tobin utilizes the concept of risk to explain, first, how it is possible that an individual's asset portfolio may be divided between bonds and cash and, second, why the liquidity preference function (the asset demand) is negatively sloped.[12] Tobin reaches virtually the same conclusion as Keynes with respect to the shape of this function, but his explanation is formulated primarily in terms of attitudes toward risk rather than expectations with respect to future bond prices. Tobin's analysis, unlike that of Keynes, does not depend on the notion of a normal rate of interest for understanding why people may choose to hold money rather than bonds (or vice versa). This aspect of Keynes's analysis has been criticized on the grounds that in time the current rate, if we assume it is reasonably stable, may come to be regarded as normal. If this happens, then a key motive for holding assets in money form disappears. Tobin shows that the asset demand for money will still be inversely related to the rate of interest even if the concept of a normal rate is discarded.

In Tobin's view the world of wealth holders consists of two kinds of people: risk lovers and risk averters. These terms come from the fact that, whenever a person holds bonds in preference to cash, the risk of a capital loss or gain is incurred because of uncertain knowledge concerning future bond prices. The larger the proportion of assets held as bonds in preference to money, the greater the risk. The risk lovers do not have to be induced by higher interest rates to hold bonds instead of cash; they will maximize both risk and interest income by holding all their assets in bonds.[13] If all participants in the money market were risk lovers, an asset demand schedule of the kind shown in Figure 11–2 could not exist.

It would appear, however, that more people in the market are risk averters than risk lovers. The risk averter will, first of all, diversify asset holdings. More important, the risk averter will assume more risk—that is, hold a greater proportion of the portfolio in bonds—only as the rate of interest increases. Higher interest rates are necessary, in other words, to compensate for the additional risk assumed when more bonds and less cash are held. Since this is the case, the asset demand curve assumes the shape shown in Figure 11–2. In reality both attitudes toward risk and expectations with respect to future

---

[11] Equities, too, may be included in an individual's portfolio. For purposes of the exposition, though, we will continue to assume the choice is between money and bonds (consols).

[12] James Tobin, ''Liquidity Preference as Behavior Towards Risk,'' *Review of Economic Studies,* February 1958, pp. 65–86; see also David E. W. Laidler, *The Demand for Money: Theories and Evidence,* 3rd ed. (New York: Harper & Row, 1985), pp. 59 ff.

[13] This is an oversimplification, even though useful for understanding Tobin's basic ideas: It has been shown, however, that even risk lovers would hold both money and bonds when confronted with uncertainty with respect to both prospective income and expenditure flows. See Roger N. Waud, ''Net Outlay Uncertainty and Liquidity Preference as Behavior Toward Risk,'' *Journal of Money, Credit, and Banking,* November 1975, pp. 499–506.

movements of bond prices—or interest rates—constitute forces at work that determine the nature of the asset demand for money.

Professor Baumol's analysis is addressed to the transactions demand for money. Keynes, as did his classical predecessors, treated the transactions demand (including money held in response to the precautionary motive) as determined essentially by the general level of economic activity (see page 404). Baumol, however, approaches the matter as a problem in inventory management; the inventory is the stock of money the individual or business firm chooses to keep on hand for transactions purposes.[14] It costs something to hold any inventory, including an inventory of money. Thus, the firm or individual will attempt to minimize the cost of holding money in response to the transactions demand.

The amount of money an individual needs to hold for transactions purposes depends on the total values of transactions undertaken over a period of time and the frequency of those transactions. Since the receipt of income for an individual or a business firm does not coincide exactly with expenditures, there must be an inventory of cash on hand. This inventory can be obtained from either holding some portion of income received in the form of cash balances—that is, saving and holding the savings in the form of immediate liquid command over goods and services, namely, money—or converting an interest-earning asset (a bond or consol) into cash. These two sources for cash inventory needed for transactions purposes can be related directly to the costs for maintaining such an inventory—costs which the individual or firm seeks to minimize.

First there is an opportunity cost involved in holding an inventory of cash. This is represented by the current rate of interest i. This cost exists simply because cash held idle forgoes the opportunity to earn an income through lending at the current rate (purchase of a bond or consol). The larger the inventory of cash held, the greater will be this part of the overall costs for such an inventory. But there are also noninterest transactions (withdrawal) costs which occur each time an income-earning asset is converted into cash. These are broker's fees, as well as any other noninterest cost which may be associated with a conversion-to-cash transaction (postage, telephone bills, bookkeeping charges, etc.). The more frequently conversion transactions to obtain cash for the inventory are undertaken, the greater will be this aspect of the overall inventory cost. Thus, the total cost for the inventory of cash held for the transactions motive is the sum of interest (opportunity) and transactions (withdrawal) costs.

Now we get to the nub of the problem. If the firm or an individual holds large cash balances, then there will be few withdrawals to get more cash and, hence, transactions costs will be small. But the opportunity costs of forgone

---

[14] W. J. Baumol, "The Transactions Demand for Cash: An Inventory Theoretic Approach," *Quarterly Journal of Economics,* November 1952, pp. 545–556. In his analysis, money held in response to both the speculative and precautionary motives is not considered.

interest become large. On the other hand, the latter are reduced by holding down the size of the cash inventory, but this may necessitate more frequent withdrawals and thus raise the transactions part of total inventory cost. To solve the problem, Baumol developed a formula to determine the size of cash withdrawals (conversion of bonds to money) that would minimize the total cost of maintaining an inventory of cash large enough to finance the volume of transactions over a stipulated period of time.[15] Essentially, the formula shows that the demand for cash balances for transactions purposes will vary positively with both the volume of transactions and transactions costs, but inversely with the opportunity costs (the rate of interest). This finding is also in harmony with earlier conclusions about the nature of the transactions demand (page 404). The Baumol formula also implies that the demand for cash balances will rise less than in proportion to the increase in transactions—a finding which suggests that there are economies of scale in the use of money. The meaning of this is that the richer or more prosperous an individual or business firm is, the greater is the ability to economize in the use of cash. This should not be confused with the tendency of individuals and firms to reduce their cash holdings in response to a rise in interest rates. Both effects may be at work in the modern economy.

Some Empirical Findings

The preceding analysis essentially tells us that the real demand for money will vary inversely with the rate of interest and positively with the level of output. Does the demand for money behave in this fashion? Since Keynes's *The General Theory* first appeared, there have been a large number of empirical investigations into the demand for money relationship. No study has yet been able to come up with an exact statement of this relationship, one that could be used without question for predictive purposes. But most of the studies that have appeared do tend to confirm the general theoretical statements made about the demand for money. They show, first, that the demand for money balances is linked positively to the level of real income and, second, that the relationship between changes in interest rates and the demand for money is an inverse one.

Technically, the magnitude of these relationships is a matter of the elasticities of the demand for money with respect to the two key variables, namely, income and interest. The income elasticity of the demand for money is the ratio of the percentage change in money demand to the percentage change in income, and the interest elasticity of the demand for money is the ratio of the percentage change in money demand to the percentage change in

---

[15] The formula for the optimum size of withdrawal is $C = 2bT/i$. C is the optimum withdrawal of cash, T the total transactions in the period, b the costs associated with the conversion of earning assets into cash, and i the appropriate market rate of interest.

the rate of interest. The main empirical findings on the demand for money may be summarized as follows:[16]

1. The demand for money balances is a demand for *real* balances. This is demonstrated by the fact that studies show that the demand for *nominal* money balances rises in proportion to changes in the price level. The practical meaning of this is that people are not victims of a *money illusion.*[17] They will, in other words, adjust their nominal holdings of money whenever the price level changes.

2. The demand for real money balances is related negatively to the rate of interest; this means that, when interest rates rise, less money will be held and, when interest rates fall, more money will be held. The interest elasticity of the demand for money balances is low, ranging in the short run from −0.12 to −0.15 and in the long run from −0.2 to −0.6, depending on the definition of money used and the rate of interest selected.[18] To illustrate, an interest elasticity of demand for money of −0.5 means that the demand for idle balances would *decline* by 0.5 percent for every 1 percent increase in interest rates. Empirical studies have not turned up any significant evidence supporting the existence of a liquidity trap. In summary, the demand for money balances responds to the rate of interest in the manner suggested by Keynes, but is less sensitive to interest rate changes than Keynes envisioned.

3. The demand for real money balances responds positively to changes in *real* income. Although the income elasticity of demand for money is not particularly high, ranging from 0.19 to 0.68, the empirical findings support the Keynesian hypothesis that income is the primary determinant of the quantity of money held in response to the transactions and precautionary motives. If the income elasticity of demand for money balances were 1.0, this would mean that the demand for money balances would grow in direct proportion to the growth of real output. In general, however, the empirical evidence suggests that the income elasticity is less than 1; this means that, while real balances grow as real output expands, they do not grow as rapidly. As far as income elasticity is concerned, the evidence is the long-run elasticity is

[16] Interested students should consult the following studies on this question. H. Latane, "Income Velocity and Interest Rates: A Pragmatic Approach," *Review of Economics and Statistics,* November 1960; C. Christ, "Interest Rates and Portfolio Selection Among Liquid Assets in the U.S.," in C. Christ et al., *Measurement in Economics* (Stanford, Calif.: Stanford University Press, 1963); R. Teigen, "The Demand for and Supply of Money," in Warren L. Smith and Ronald L. Teigen, eds., *Readings in Money, National Income, and Stabilization Policy* (Homestead, Ill.: Irwin, 1965); H. R. Heller, "The Demand for Money: The Evidence from Short-Run Data," *Quarterly Journal of Economics,* May 1965; Tong H. Lee, "Alternative Interest Rates and the Demand for Money," *American Economic Review,* December 1967; and Stephen Goldfeld, "The Demand for Money Revisited," *Brookings Papers on Economic Activity,* 1973:3. For a comprehensive summary of practically all empirical work on the demand for money, see David E. W. Laidler, *The Demand for Money,* pp. 115–162.

[17] The term "money illusion" was coined by the American economist Irving Fisher and refers to "a failure to perceive that the dollar or any other unit of money expands and shrinks in value." See his *The Money Illusion* (New York: Adelphi, 1928), p. 4.

[18] Laidler, *The Demand for Money.*

greater, roughly by a factor of 3.5.[19] The practical meaning of this is that over time the sensitivity of the amount of money people want to hold as idle balances increases with respect to income. The long run in this context is approximately two years.

4. There is some evidence that the demand for money is influenced by changes in the expected rate of inflation. If the inflation rate is expected to accelerate in the future, this will reduce the demand for real money balances. The reason is that a higher-than-expected inflation rate increases the opportunity cost of holding money, because the higher rate reduces the *real* value of an individual's nominal money holdings. In effect, this means that the implicit yield on money has been reduced relative to other assets, so less of it will be held. The implicit yield of money is the satisfaction (or utility) that an individual derives from holding money in preference to another asset. Keynes, as we have seen, saw this arising out of the uncertainty which surrounds the future market value of other forms for holding wealth. The general message conveyed by Figure 11–2 is that the higher the opportunity cost of holding money, the less will be held. In the figure opportunity cost is measured by the rate of interest, but the idea applies to opportunity cost, however measured.

5. Like the Keynesian consumption function, there have been a number of attempts by economists to test empirically the demand for money concepts we have been discussing. The statistical demand for money functions growing out of this research sought to link the demand for money to both the rate of interest and the level of income. Usually such studies employed a short-term interest rate, like the rate on U.S. Treasury bills, and either current or constant GDP. The choice of the GDP measure depended on whether money was needed for carrying out current transactions or money was viewed as a form of holding wealth, which was expected to increase as income rose. Until the early 1970s the money demand functions predicted money growth quite accurately, but after 1973 they no longer worked. During the 1970s the predicted money supply fell far short of the actual money supply, but in the 1980s predicted money exceeded the actual money supply. These empirical findings suggest that the demand for money function is far less stable than once believed, a conclusion supported by similar findings about unforeseen changes in the 1980s for the velocity of the circulation of money.[20]

The Supply of Money

One of the most firmly established propositions in economics, both theoretically and empirically, involves the process of deposit creation by depository institutions within the nation's banking system.[21] As we saw in Chapter 5

---

[19] Goldfeld, "The Demand for Money Revisited," pp. 602, 606.

[20] Thomas Mayer, James S. Duesenberry, and Robert Z. Aliber, *Money, Banking, and the Economy,* 5th ed. (New York: Norton, 1995), pp. 291ff.

[21] It was an American economist, Chester Arthur Phillips, who was among the first to discover and

(pages 148–50), the commercial banks and other depository institutions are able to expand the money supply on the basis of their reserves. The key to this is the *principle of fractional reserves,* an idea that dates back to at least the goldsmiths of medieval Europe (see the box in Chapter 5, page 144). In exploring more fully the nature of the money supply in the modern economy, we shall consider two major issues. The first is the relationship between the monetary base (the reserves of the banking system plus currency in circulation) and the amount of money in circulation. Formally, this relationship is called the "money multiplier" and is designated as km'. The second is whether the money supply should be treated as an exogenous variable—independent, that is, of the other variables that enter into the *IS-LM* model—or as an endogenous variable—dependent on the other variables in the system. The latter is an important question, not yet resolved by economists, but one which has significant implications for the practice and effectiveness of monetary policy.

The Money Multiplier

To consider the relationship between high-powered money (the monetary base) and money actually in circulation it is not necessary to undertake a complete review of the process by which commercial banks expand the supply of bank credit (deposit money) on the basis of their reserves, but some summary comments on the key principles involved in the process may prove helpful.[22] The comments apply primarily to M1, the concept of money most appropriate to the basic theme of this text—understanding output, employment, and the price level in the modern market economy.

Since a major part of money in circulation consists of deposit money, which can be transferred by check, the key to understanding how the money supply changes is the *principle of fractional reserves.* This principle is at the heart of the money supply question in all modern market economies. In essence, it states that normally a bank need only keep a fraction of its total deposit liabilities on hand to meet the withdrawal of deposits by its customers. Reserves not needed for this purpose become excess reserves; they can be used by the bank as a basis for new loans. Banks and other financial institutions are in business to make money, and they do so primarily by lending money, most of which is created by the process of lending excess reserves.

There is, of course, a catch to this. Any single bank in the financial system is limited in its lending—and, hence, money-creating power—to its own excess reserves. But for all banks together the increase in the money supply through the creation of new demand deposits as loans are made is a *multiple*

---

formalize in a systematic sense the relationship between bank credit—"credited money"—and the reserves of the banking system. See his *Bank Credit* (New York: Macmillan Co., 1920).

[22] Most principles-of-economics texts contain a detailed explanation of the process of the money-creation process as it takes place through the nation's commercial bank system. See, for example, Campbell R. McConnell and Stanley L. Brue, *Economics,* 12th ed. (New York: McGraw-Hill, 1993), Chap. 16.

of the reserves banks are required to keep on hand. It is this process that elementary textbooks explain in detail when they describe how the money-creating process takes place in the nation's banking system. The amount of reserves in the form of currency and deposits of the banks with the Federal Reserve System that the banks must maintain is established by the central bank.[23] What is important to understand, however, is that the fractional reserve principle permits the banking system to expand its deposit liabilities—that is, to create "money"—by some multiple of the total reserves in the system. It is this fact, a principle as old as banking itself, that makes it appropriate to describe reserve money as high-powered money. Because of the fractional reserve principle there is a *money multiplier* associated with any change in the reserves that banks hold against their deposit liabilities.

Formally, this relationship is defined as the ratio of a change in the money supply (M) to a change in the monetary base (M_b). Or,

$$km' = \frac{\Delta M}{\Delta M_b}. \qquad (11-5)$$

Determination of the theoretical value of the money multiplier is explained in the box on page 420. Table 11–1 shows empirical values for the money multiplier for 1960 through 1994. The money multiplier for each year, shown in the third column in the table, is obtained by dividing the money supply by the monetary base. At the beginning of the period (1960) the money multiplier was 3.43; at the end of the period (1994) it had fallen to 2.74. What this means is that the Federal Reserve System had slightly less control over the effective money supply at the end of the period than it did at the beginning. To put it differently, there was less leverage associated with a dollar of high-powered reserves in 1994 than there was in 1970.

What accounts for this decline in the numerical value of the money multiplier (km')? The primary reason is an increase during this 35-year period in the proportion of the total money supply (M1) that the public chooses to hold as currency (in cash). In the 1960s the average ratio of currency to deposit money was 21.2 percent. During the 1970s this ratio rose to an average of 24.7 percent, during the 1980s it climbed a bit further to an average of 25.1 percent, and in the 1990s jumped to 29.5.[24] If the public chooses to hold more cash, then whenever a bank makes a loan, a smaller proportion of the amount loaned will show up as deposits in another bank. It is of course the latter that

---

[23] Before the Monetary Control Act of 1980 was passed, all banks that were members of the Federal Reserve System (primarily national banks, which are banks chartered by the federal government) were required to hold varying reserve percentages for different types of deposits, but nonmember banks did not have to hold any reserves on deposit with the Federal Reserve System. The new law, which was phased in gradually, has varying reserve requirements that apply to *all* deposit institutions. A primary purpose of the 1980 act was to give the Federal Reserve better control over the money supply.

[24] *Economic Report of the President*, 1995, pp. 353, 354.

TABLE 11–1 The Money Supply, the Monetary Base, and the Money Multiplier: 1960–1994*

Year	Money Supply (M1)	Monetary Base	Money Multiplier	Currency	% of M1
1960	$140.7	$41.0	3.43	$28.7	20.4
1961	145.2	41.9	3.47	29.3	20.2
1962	147.8	43.0	3.44	30.3	20.5
1963	133.3	45.0	3.41	32.2	21.0
1964	160.3	47.2	3.40	33.9	21.1
1965	167.9	49.6	3.39	36.0	21.1
1966	172.0	51.6	3.33	38.0	22.1
1967	183.3	54.6	3.36	40.0	21.8
1968	197.4	58.4	3.38	43.0	21.8
1969	203.9	61.6	3.31	45.7	22.4
1970	214.4	65.0	3.30	48.6	22.7
1971	228.3	69.1	3.30	52.0	22.8
1972	249.2	75.2	3.31	56.2	22.6
1973	262.8	81.1	3.24	60.8	23.1
1974	274.3	87.5	3.13	67.0	24.4
1975	287.5	93.9	3.09	72.8	25.3
1976	306.3	101.5	3.02	79.5	25.9
1977	331.1	110.3	3.00	87.4	26.4
1978	358.2	120.4	2.98	96.0	26.8
1979	382.5	131.1	2.92	104.8	27.4
1980	408.5	142.0	2.88	115.4	28.2
1981	436.3	149.0	2.93	122.6	28.1
1982	474.4	160.1	2.96	132.5	27.9
1983	521.2	175.5	2.97	146.2	28.1
1984	552.4	187.2	2.71	156.1	28.3
1985	620.1	203.6	3.04	167.9	27.1
1986	724.5	223.7	3.24	180.8	25.0
1987	750.0	239.9	3.13	196.9	26.3
1988	787.1	256.9	3.06	212.3	24.2
1989	794.2	267.7	2.96	222.7	28.0
1990	825.9	293.2	2.82	246.7	29.8
1991	897.3	317.2	2.83	267.2	29.7
1992	1,024.4	350.6	2.92	292.8	28.6
1993	1,128.6	385.9	2.92	322.1	28.5
1994	1,147.8	418.2	2.74	354.5	30.9

*All dollar amounts are in billions. Totals are for December of each year.
Source: *Economic Report of the President,* 1995, pp. 353, 354.

leads to a multiple expansion of the money supply. To put it differently, an increase in the holding of cash by the public drains some potential reserves out of the banking system and thereby reduces the effectiveness of the control over the total money supply that the Federal Reserve can exercise.

Why there has been this large increase in currency holdings relative to deposit (checking account) money is not entirely clear. Some observers at-

Calculation of the Money Multiplier

The theoretical value of the money multiplier (km') depends on two things: (1) the relationship between demand deposits (D_d) and the required reserves of the banking system (R_r), a relationship defined by the required reserve ratio for the banking system (rr), and (2) the proportion (cr) of the total money supply (M) the public wants to hold as currency (C_u). The total money supply (M) is equal to demand deposits (D_d) plus currency (C_u), and the monetary base (M_b) is equal to required reserves in the banking system (R_r) plus currency (C_u). Since the money multiplier (km') is defined as the ratio of a change in the total money supply (ΔM) to a change in the monetary base (ΔM_b), we have by substitution

$$km' = \frac{\Delta M}{\Delta M_b} = \frac{\Delta C_u + \Delta D_d}{\Delta R_r + \Delta C_u}. \tag{B-1}$$

The value of ΔC_u is equal to cr times ΔD_d, and the value of ΔR_r is equal to rr times ΔD_d. By substitution of these in Equation (B–1), we get

$$km' = \frac{cr\ \Delta D_d + \Delta D_d}{rr\ \Delta D_d + cr\ \Delta D_d} = \frac{\Delta D_d(1 + cr)}{\Delta D_d(rr + cr)}. \tag{B-2}$$

By further simplification, we have

$$km' = \frac{1 + cr}{rr + cr}. \tag{B-3}$$

Inspection of the above shows how the public's attitude toward holding cash will influence the ability of the Federal Reserve to affect the total money supply through its control over the reserves of the banking system. If, for example, the value of cr—the proportion of the money supply the public wants to hold as cash—increases, the power of the Fed over the money supply is reduced. A decline in cr would have the opposite effect.

tribute it to the emergence of an *underground economy* brought about by inflation (in the 1970s) and crime (in the 1980s and 1990s). The underground economy includes all transactions that are not traceable. In other words, they take place in cash and are not reported to the government. Drug deals, tax evasion, and other criminal activity dominate in the underground economy. However, this argument becomes somewhat less plausible when we look at the ratio of cash (currency) to the GDP. This ratio fell from 1960 through 1989, and then rose again in the 1990s. Although in the 1970s the ratio of cash to GDP averaged 5.2 percent, it fell rather sharply to 4.5 percent, then still further in the 1980s to 4.2 percent. From 1990 to 1994, however, it rose to an annual average of 4.9 percent.[25] Some of the decline in this ratio may be explained by the increasing use of credit cards for more and more transactions, although there is no obvious reason why the ratio would go up again in the 1990s.

To sum up our discussion of the money supply to this point, it is through the reserves of financial institutions, especially their excess reserves, that the central bank (the Federal Reserve) gets its leverage over the nation's monetary system. By pumping reserves into or out of the banking system, it creates the necessary conditions for either an expansion or a contraction of the money supply. Note carefully that the Federal Reserve System cannot force an *increase* in the money supply. It can put more reserves into the banking system, but this does not mean that the public will increase its borrowings. Only if the latter happens will deposits (and the money supply) increase. Contraction is a different story. If the Federal Reserve System puts the squeeze on the reserves of the commercial banks of the system, they will be forced to reduce their liabilities—call in loans when possible and not renew loans as they are paid off—and this will reduce the money supply. Thus, the powers of the central bank to force a contraction in money are greater than its powers to force an expansion.

There are three basic means by which the Federal Reserve can affect reserve money in the banking system. They are changing the required reserve ratio (rr); changing the rate it charges commercial banks when it makes loans to them (the discount rate); and, through open market operations, buying and selling government securities. When the Federal Reserve buys government securities, the effect is to pump more reserves into the system; when it sells in the open market, the effect is the opposite. Open market buying and selling is by far the most frequently used control instrument. Lending by the Federal Reserve (discount rate policy) has been especially important during periods of financial crises, such as those in 1966, in 1970, during the 1974–75 recession, and again in 1980 and 1981–82, at which time the Federal Reserve was called on at times to open the discount window and play the role of lender of last resort.[26] Changes in the reserve requirements are the least used of the means available to the Federal Reserve System to influence the size of the commercial banking system's reserves of high-powered money.

---

[25] Ibid., pp. 274, 353.

[26] The lender-of-last-resort concept refers to the ultimate responsibility of the Federal Reserve System for the health of the nation's financial system. Thus, when the Franklin National Bank of New York, with assets of over $5 billion, failed in late December 1973, the Federal Reserve provided emergency loans to other financial institutions whose financial health was threatened by the Franklin National collapse. It is a matter, essentially, of providing emergency credit. This is what is meant by the phrase "opening the discount window." Other recent instances in which the Federal Reserve System intervened in financial markets in its lender-of-last-resort role include the Penn-Central Railroad financing in 1970, the Real Estate Investment Trust (R.E.I.T.) debacles of 1974–75, the failure of the First Pennsylvania Bank in 1980, the refinancing of Chrysler Corporation also in 1980, and the collapse of the Penn Square Bank in Oklahoma in 1982. When the stock market collapsed in 1987, the Federal Reserve poured money into the banking system, and thus prevented any serious collapse in the nation's financial system.

The Money Supply: Exogenous or Endogenous?

The second important theoretical issue involving the money supply is whether money should be treated as an endogenous or exogenous variable. Up to now and primarily for simplicity in analysis, the money supply has been regarded as exogenous (see Figure 5–4, page 160, and Figure 6–3, page 182). Reality is not this simple. In general, economists in the classical tradition, including current followers of Milton Friedman, view the money supply as exogenous, meaning that its value is determined independently of the other variables that enter into the income system. From this perspective, it is an increase (or decrease) in bank reserves, which leads in turn to an increase (or decrease) in the money supply. When there is an increase in money, spending will increase, either directly because there is more money available or indirectly because more money leads to a lower rate of interest. As we shall note later, Keynes treated the money supply as an exogenous variable when explaining the mechanism through which changes in the money supply affected aggregate demand.

The trend in recent analysis is to treat the money supply endogenously, as a variable functionally related to other variables in the income system. Economists working in the Post Keynesian tradition (see Chapter 18) are among the strongest advocates of an endogenous view of money creation. Whereas in the classical and modern quantity theory approach the line of causation is from money to spending, the Post Keynesians stress a "reverse causation," wherein, for example, businesses desire to spend more for investment, and so require finance. If the banking system accommodates the demand for finance, the money supply (demand deposits) will increase and make more spending possible. The causal sequence is from the desire for spending to changes in the money supply rather than the reverse.[27] There is much to be said in favor of this viewpoint. What the Federal Reserve can do is control the reserves in the system, but it cannot compel people to borrow, which is how excess reserves become money in circulation. People must want to spend and be willing to borrow so they can spend if the money supply is to increase whenever the Fed pumps more reserves into the system.

The late Professor Ronald Teigen of the University of Michigan developed an endogenous approach to the money supply which reflects both the facts that commercial banks are profit-maximizing private businesses and that the Federal Reserve is a public body whose primary interest is ensuring that the nation has a safe, adequate, and dependable money supply. His theory of the money supply was based on the view that

> commercial banks act in a profit-maximizing way in response to changes in the return from lending relative to the cost. Both the return and the cost are represented by short-term interest rates: in principle, the return is the yield on loans, and the cost is measured

---

[27] L. Randall Wray, "Commercial banks, the central bank, and endogenous money," *Journal of Post Keynesian Economics*, Vol. 14, No. 3 (Spring 1992), pp. 297–310.

by the cost of acquiring the reserves necessary to support the new loans. When it becomes more profitable to make loans, banks are assumed to be willing to supply more deposits and to increase the money stock. However, member banks are constrained in supplying deposits by the reserve requirements imposed by the Federal Reserve System, and if excess reserves are scarce, member banks will tend to increase their borrowings.[28]

In formal terms this hypothesis is expressed as an equation in which the ratio of the existing money supply to money based on unborrowed reserves is equated to the rate of return on loans and the cost of acquiring reserves. Specifically, Teigen's money supply function is

$$\frac{M}{M*} = f(r - r_d).^{29}$$ (11–6)

In the equation, M is the existing stock of money (currency plus demand deposits) and $M*$ is the amount of money that could be supported by unborrowed reserves, given the reserve requirements and other institutional characteristics of the Federal Reserve System. Unborrowed reserves are reserves created at the initiative of the Federal Reserve System rather than from member bank borrowing. The significance of $M*$ in the equation is that it represents the monetary policy variable through which the central bank can affect the money supply. An increase in $M*$ as a result of Federal Reserve open market operations will lead ultimately to an increase in the money supply (M) if we assume no change in either the rate of return from lending (r) or the cost of borrowing from the Federal Reserve by the commercial banks (r_d). This presumes, of course, that the commercial banks are profit maximizers seeking to increase their loans, whenever excess reserves become available. The variables on the right-hand side of the equation reflect market forces that operate directly on the commercial bank's willingness to expand or contract the money supply. An increase in the return (r) on lending, *ceteris paribus,* should lead the banks to expand their loans, and hence the money supply, whereas a rise in the cost of borrowing (r_d) from the Federal Reserve, *ceteris paribus,* should have the opposite effect.

Overall, the general tenor of Professor Teigen's analysis is to suggest that if the supply of money responds positively to the rate of interest, the multiplier effect associated with any shift in the aggregate demand schedule will be larger than it would be with a fixed money supply. This is so because any increase in aggregate demand, *ceteris paribus,* tends to raise interest rates— a development which will normally depress investment spending and dampen the multiplier effect. But if the money supply also increases as interest rates

[28] Teigen, "The Demand for and Supply of Money," p. 60.

[29] Ibid., p. 62. Professor Teigen's use of r should not be confused with our earlier use of this letter to stand for the marginal efficiency of capital. In his equation M represents money, not imports as M is generally used in this text.

rise, the ultimate increase in the rate of interest will be smaller and thus the adverse effect on investment spending—and the multiplier—will be lessened.

Monetary Equilibrium

In Chapter 6 it was explained (pages 182–84) that a condition of *monetary equilibrium* existed when the total amount of money that people want to hold for whatever reason is just equal to the amount of money actually in existence. Now we can pull together the material we have discussed that pertains to both the demand for and supply of money to show in a full theoretical sense the nature of monetary equilibrium in the modern economy. We shall also show how the rate of interest is simultaneously determined, given the fact that the level of interest depends on the interplay between the demand for and supply of money. The interest rate is the link between the demand for money and its supply and thus makes possible equilibrium in the monetary sphere.

The matter of interest rate determination would be relatively simple if there were but a single demand-for-money schedule. This, however, is not the case. The reader will recall that we constructed the total demand for money by adding the transactions demand prevailing at any given income level to an asset demand curve (see Figure 11–3). What Figure 11–3 shows is that we do not have a single curve which relates the total demand for money to the rate of interest and which is independent of the income level. The asset demand for money may be independent of the income level, but the transactions demand is not. Thus, we have a series of curves as shown in Figure 11–3, the position of any one of which is determined by the income level.

We need at this point to add to the diagram showing the total demand for money appropriate to different income levels an *endogenous* money supply curve. By an endogenous money supply curve we mean one showing that the supply of money is a positive function of the rate of interest, a conclusion reached in our earlier discussion (page 422). This is done in Figure 11–4. This curve is labeled M^0 and it slopes upward to the right. Let us examine carefully the significance of this diagram.

Basically, as explained above, monetary equilibrium requires that the total demand for money be equal to the supply. But if we have a series of demand curves for money such as depicted in Figure 11–4, then there is no single equilibrium rate of interest and no single equilibrium point that equates the total demand for money to the supply. Rather, we have, as Figure 11–4 suggests, a series of equilibrium values with respect to both the rate of interest and money demand and supply, no one of which can be determined until we know the precise level of the total demand curve for money. This, however, requires that we know the income level. This is the point at which a major complicating element in the macroeconomic theory is encountered. It underscores the way in which all the key variables that enter into the determination

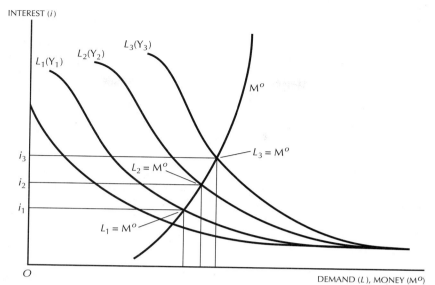

INTEREST (i)

$L_1(Y_1)$ $L_2(Y_2)$ $L_3(Y_3)$

M^o

i_3 $L_3 = M^o$

$L_2 = M^o$

i_2

i_1

$L_1 = M^o$

O DEMAND (L), MONEY (M^o)

FIGURE 11–4   The Demand for Money, the Supply of Money, and the Rate of Interest.   Monetary equilibrium equates the total demand for money (L) and the total supply of money (M^o) at a particular rate of interest, but because the position of the demand for money curve depends on the income level (Y), equilibrium values for the demand and supply of money and the rate of interest cannot be determined independently of the income level.

of income and employment are interrelated. It is why the basic *IS-LM* model developed in Chapter 6 is such a useful analytical tool for understanding how the economy works at the macroeconomic level. Interest and income (and employment) are not separate and distinct variables. They are variables whose values are determined *simultaneously* by the interplay of forces at work in the three fundamental spheres of activity in the economy—the goods, the monetary, and the international.

Money and Market Capitalism

In the 1933 article (page 146) in which Keynes distinguished between a *real exchange economy* and a *monetary economy,* he concluded by saying that the next task for economic theory was to work out a "monetary theory of production," a goal toward which he believed he was moving. As we have also noted, Keynes said a monetary economy is one in which money, in effect, occupies central stage, follows its own rules of behavior, and affects the way things turn out in the real economy of production and exchange.[30]

---

[30] Keynes, "On the Theory of a Monetary Economy," p. 9.

But more is involved than this. The late University of Maryland Professor Dudley Dillard said a monetary theory of production is "... a model of production in which business firms ... produce output and try to convert it into money. Emphasis is on money's special properties that inhibit the easy conversion of output into money. Profits are *real*-ized when ... real output is converted by sale into a greater sum of money than the cost of producing the output."[31] In his later life and after *The General Theory* was published, Keynes was even more pointed. "The firm," he said, "is dealing throughout in terms of sums of money. It has *no object in the world* except to end up with more money than it started with. This is the essential characteristic of an entrepreneur economy."[32]

To put the matter somewhat differently, a monetary economy is one in which the flow of events is from money to goods and then back to money (symbolically, $M \rightarrow G \rightarrow M$). A real exchange economy—Keynes's label for the classical system—is one in which the flow of events is from goods to money and then back to goods (symbolically, $G \rightarrow M \rightarrow G$). In the monetary economy, as we saw earlier in Chapter 5 (page 146), money is *not* neutral, but in a real exchange economy it is. Market capitalism is a system, as Hyman Minsky puts it, that operates from a Wall Street perspective, by which he means that goods, especially capital goods, are valuable not because they possess utility or are productive in a physical sense, but "... because they yield profits."[33]

Later in Chapter 18 we shall explore all the important implications of this view. At this point it will suffice to say that understanding the institution of money and everything that revolves about it is crucial to understanding how systems of market capitalism really work. This was what Keynes was striving to achieve in *The General Theory,* with its emphasis on such novel ideas as liquidity, uncertainty, the nonneutrality of money, and the division of economic activity into what we have described as real and monetary spheres.

Classical economics, as we have seen, regarded money as little more than a convenience, a means of exchange. Certainly, the classical economists failed to see or understand the distinction that the iconoclast economist Thorstein Veblen saw between making money and making goods. Making money, however, is the all-powerful, central motivating force in market capitalism. Money is the common denominator for all economic activity. The marketplace itself is indifferent, inherently unable to distinguish between productive and nonproductive activity. Most of the time, fortunately, making goods and making

---

[31] Dudley Dillard, "The Evolutionary Economics of a Monetary Economy," *Journal of Economic Issues*, Vol. 21, No. 2 (June 1987), p. 580.

[32] John Maynard Keynes, *The General Theory and After, A Supplement*, Vol. 19: *The Collected Writings of John Maynard Keynes*, Donald Moggridge, ed. (London: Macmillan & Co., Cambridge University Press, 1979), p. 89 (italics added).

[33] Hyman P. Minsky, *Stabilizing an Unstable Economy* (New Haven, Conn.: Yale University Press, 1986), p. 204.

money coincide, as Adam Smith recognized a long while ago. But not always. This is a fact we should not forget, and it is why money is important.

The Modern Quantity Theory Challenge to Keynesian Economics

For more than three decades after 1936 the income-expenditure, or Keynesian, approach to output determination dominated income and employment analysis. Keynesianism became in this period the reigning orthodoxy, just as the classical theory was in the era prior to the Great Depression. But the commanding position that the Keynesian revolution established in macroeconomics has not gone unopposed. Beginning in the 1960s a formidable challenge to the Keynesian orthodoxy surfaced in the form of a modernized version of the classical quantity theory. *Monetarism*, as the modern quantity theory has come to be known, springs largely from the thinking of Milton Friedman, long-time professor at the University of Chicago, now retired. Even though monetarism did not succeed in displacing Keynesian theory as the dominant approach in macroeconomics, it stands as one of the major theoretical developments in aggregate economics since the publication of *The General Theory*. This is true in spite of the fact that the economy in the 1980s and early 1990s did not behave according to the monetarist scenario. Nevertheless, monetarism helped pave the way for an even more formidable theoretical critique of Keynesian economics—the new classical economics that challenges every fundamental aspect of Keynesian thought. Thus, it is essential to understand the circumstances that gave rise to Milton Friedman's modern quantity theory, as well as its key theoretical points and policy recommendations.

Origins of the Modern Quantity Theory

The appearance of a significant challenge to the income-expenditure analysis followed a pattern similar to the one involved in the Keynesian displacement of the classical orthodoxy. First, an important social problem emerged that appeared invulnerable to solution by established theory, and, second, an alternative body of theoretical ideas came into prominence at approximately the same time. In the case of the Keynesian revolution, the critical social problem was, of course, mass unemployment, and the body of theoretical ideas waiting in the wings to displace classical thinking was the system of thought Keynes brought together in *The General Theory*.

To critics the issue that justified the search for a new theory was the resistance of rapid and persistent inflation to control by conventional policy measures derived from the Keynesian income-expenditure approach to the economy's management. This has become the conventional wisdom with respect to the inflationary experience of the 1970s, a point of view challenged in Chapter 12. Nevertheless, between 1967 and 1981 consumer prices rose 172 percent, even though the economy slid through three recessions in this period. In spite of the Johnson administration tax surcharge in 1968 and restrictive fiscal and monetary policies pursued by the Nixon, Ford, and Carter administrations, inflation continued unchecked, reaching double-digit rates in 1974, 1979, and 1980. The combination of rising unemployment and continued inflation gave birth to the unlovely term "stagflation" to describe the condition of the economy.[34] Even the Nixon administration's experiment with comprehensive wage and price controls failed to crush the inflation. The pattern of behavior established during this period shows quite clearly that, prior to the advent of the Reagan administration, recessions had the effect of slowing the inflation rate, but once recovery came, inflation accelerated once again. In 1981, the Reagan administration, with the full cooperation of the Federal Reserve System, pursued a policy of monetary stringency with predictable results. The economy was plunged into another recession, the fourth in little more than a decade and the most severe since the 1930s. Once again the inflation rate fell, this time more rapidly than in the earlier recessions. The inflation rate which averaged 7.1 percent annually in the 1970s, dropped to an annual average rate of 5.6 percent in the 1980s and still lower to an annual average rate of 3.6 percent for 1990 through 1994.[35]

There are, however, other points worth noting that weaken the analogy with the 1930s. For one thing, many economists are not convinced that the policy prescriptions which flow from the Keynesian analysis are fundamentally flawed. It may be argued with considerable justification that the 1970s malaise (excessive unemployment and excessive inflation) resulted not from a basic error in theory, but from a failure to apply the policy prescription at the appropriate time. The 1968 surcharge on the income tax is a case in point. Professional economic opinion was nearly unanimous that the tax increase was needed in 1966, once it became apparent that a massive military buildup was being imposed on a fully employed economy. In 1966, for example, military outlays jumped $11.7 billion ($59.6 billion in 1994 prices), while the civilian unemployment rate stood at 3.8 percent. No better formula for economic and social disaster could have been devised than to have stepped up unproductive military outlays under full-employment conditions without a corresponding (and offsetting) increase in taxes.[36] The story of the 1970s might have been quite different if the Johnson administration and the Con-

---

[34] In the 1969–70 recession, for example, unemployment reached 4.9 percent of the civilian labor force and the inflation rate (rise in the consumer price index) was 5.7 percent. In the more serious 1974–75 recession (until the 1982 recession, the worst economic downturn since the 1930s), unemployment climbed to 8.5 percent of the civilian labor force and the inflation rate hit 11.0 percent. In the short but sharp 1980 (Carter) recession, unemployment hit 7.1 percent and the inflation rate was 13.5 percent.

[35] *Economic Report of the President*, 1995, p. 345.

[36] Recall the discussion on the balanced budget thesis in Chapter 9. This suggests that taxes should have been increased by even more than the increase in government outlays if inflationary consequences were to be avoided.

gress had been willing to apply Keynesian restraints before the economy became overheated and hard-to-control inflationary forces were unleashed.

There is a second point to consider. In the 1930s there was no doubt that mass unemployment was the single, critical economic problem confronting the economy. Among professional economists there was probably as much unanimity on this as there has ever been on any single subject. But this is not true with respect to inflation. Many economists, of course, view persistent inflation as an important social and economic problem, but not necessarily a more serious social evil than unemployment, even when the latter does not approach the magnitudes experienced in the 1930s. The larger society also reflects this ambivalence. Both the Nixon and Ford administrations tended to view inflation as the more serious problem, but neither was willing to put the economy through the wringer of a massive, 1930s-style depression in order to break the upward spiral of prices. When unemployment rose as a result of the recession that was brought on by stringent monetary and fiscal policies, both administrations reversed their course in an effort to relieve the unemployment problem. The Carter administration came into office vowing to reduce unemployment, so in its first two years it sought to stimulate the economy through monetary and fiscal actions. But when this led to a new surge of inflation in 1979 and 1980, the monetary and fiscal brakes were applied promptly, again plunging the economy into recession. The Reagan administration did not fit the pattern of any of its predecessors. In pursuit of the goal of ending inflation, it stuck with tight money even though this brought about the most severe recession since the 1930s. Only after the unemployment rate surged past 10 percent in mid-1982 did the Federal Reserve reverse course and allow the rate of growth of the money supply to accelerate.

Nobel laureate Milton Friedman believes that the Keynesian income-expenditure approach is not only an inadequate theoretical instrument for dealing with inflation, but is, also, a cause of continuous inflation. For a quarter of a century Friedman and his followers in the Chicago school worked on both theoretical and empirical levels to develop a modernized version of the quantity theory of money, capable of explaining fluctuations in income, employment, and the price level. The labels, the *modern quantity theory,* or *monetarism,* are attached to Friedman's work mainly because he believes that change in the money supply is the single most important determinant of change in the level of aggregate money income.[37] Until the late 1960s the modern quantity theory was viewed seriously only by Professor Friedman and his most ardent disciples. In the 1970s it won wide acceptance within the economics profession, only to see that acceptance fade in the 1990s, partly because economic events departed widely from the theory and partly because of the emergence of new classical economics. Monetarism was also bolstered

---

[37] Professor Friedman's views on monetarism have appeared in a wide variety of publications, including for a time a column in *Newsweek* magazine. The most authoritative statement of his position is the article, "The Quantity Theory of Money: A Restatement," in Milton Friedman, ed., *Studies in the Quantity Theory of Money* (Chicago: University of Chicago Press, 1956).

Guru for the Conservatives: Milton Friedman

Probably no contemporary economist, with the possible exception of John Kenneth Galbraith, has been more vocal and more controversial than Milton Friedman. Practically single-handedly he challenged the post-World War II Keynesian orthodoxy and created modern monetarism. Outside the economics profession he is best known for his outspoken and continuous opposition to government intervention in the workings of the market economy.

Born in 1912, Milton Friedman grew up in New York City, took his undergraduate degree at Rutgers University, and became a graduate student in economics at the University of Chicago in the early 1930s. After getting an M.A. from Chicago, he worked in Washington, D.C., for the National Resources Committee; he returned later to New York City to become a member of the research staff of the National Bureau of Economic Research. In the early 1940s he worked for the Treasury Department and then enrolled at Columbia University. After receiving his Ph.D. from Columbia in 1946, he began his long career at the University of Chicago.

At Chicago, Professor Friedman created the famous Chicago Money and Banking Workshop. For 25 years (1952 to 1977) the workshop served as a forum for graduate students and visitors to present papers and benefit from Professor Friedman's reactions and critiques. It was here that the main ideas of contemporary monetarism were pulled together. Professor Friedman's seminal thinking on money is found in his *Studies in the Quantity Theory of Money* (1956), his massive *A Monetary History of the United States, 1867–1960* (1963), coauthored with Anna Jacobson Schwartz, and his 1967 presidential address to the American Economic Association, "The Role of Monetary Policy." It was for his ideas on money that Professor Friedman received the Nobel Prize for Economics in 1976, the year before he retired from the University of Chicago.

Like his prime intellectual protagonist, John Maynard Keynes (the two never met), Professor Friedman also wrote extensively for noneconomists; he sought, as Keynes did, to persuade the public of the rightness or wrongness of policy actions by governments. For many years he wrote a column for *Newsweek,* pieces of which have been collected in a paperback called *An Economist's Protest.* He also produced a 10-week series called "Free to Choose" for public television in 1980 and wrote a book by the same name that was read by millions.

Beyond his views on money and its role in the economy, Professor Friedman is clearly the most powerful and influential spokesperson for libertarian economics. Although perhaps more a philosophy than a system of thought, the bedrock idea of libertarianism is that there is almost nothing that the market cannot do better than governments can do, including educating the young and getting people to serve in the armed forces. The Reagan administration with its oft-stated belief that government is not the solution to our problems, but that government is the problem, represented, perhaps, the high-tide mark of the influence of Professor Friedman's modernized version of *laissez faire* on public policy. Deregulation of transportation, banking and finance, and industry, the current system of flexible exchange rates, and the volunteer army are specific policy actions which owe much to his libertarian approach.

Monetarism, especially following the disappointments of the 1980s, may be on the wane, but nevertheless, Professor Friedman's place in the history of economic thinking is secure. He did not succeed in overthrowing Keynes and the Keynesian revolution, but nonetheless his ideas have had a powerful impact on the times in which we live. Only a few economists have achieved this.

---

in the 1970s by a heavy flow of supporting empirical research, particularly from the staff of the St. Louis Federal Reserve Bank.[38]

From the perspective of economic policy, Friedman's monetarism had a major influence on the policies pursued by the Federal Reserve in the waning days of the Carter administration and during the Reagan administration. Beryl Sprinkle, a strong monetarist, was chairperson of the Council of Economic Advisers in the second Reagan administration. He argued that there is a "... well-established causal link between money growth and inflation over the long run that has been supported by empirical evidence for the United States as well as many other countries."[39]

When the Federal Reserve, under the leadership of Chairperson Paul Volcker, decided in October 1979 to concentrate on the growth of the money supply as a policy target rather than the level of interest rates, it was widely hailed in the press and among academic economists as a victory for the monetarist point of view. This policy triumph was short-lived, for in October 1982 the Fed announced it was abandoning temporarily its monetary targets. In reality, the Fed since then has been much more pragmatic in policy, paying attention not only to the money supply, but also interest rates, exchange rates, and macroeconomic conditions generally. In the early 1990s under Allen Greenspan, the Federal Reserve's major target was interest rates. The Fed cut rates to bring the economy out of the 1990–91 recession and raised rates to slow the economy down in 1993 and 1994 when it feared a return of inflation.

The Basic Nature of the Monetarist Challenge

A fundamental point common to the Keynesian and monetarist analyses is that, in the short run, the economy's output and variations in that output must be explained in terms of total expenditure and *changes* in expenditure.

---

[38] See Michael W. Keran, "Monetary and Fiscal Influences on Economic Activity: The Historical Record," *Review*, Federal Reserve Bank of St. Louis, November 1969; Darryl R. Francis, "Has Monetarism Failed: The Record Examined," *Review*, Federal Reserve Bank of St. Louis, March 1972; Leonall C. Andersen, "The State of the Monetarist Debate," *Review*, Federal Reserve Bank of St. Louis, September 1973; Lawrence H. Meya and Chris Vavores, "A Comparison of the St. Louis Model and Two Variations: Predictive Performance and Policy Implications," *Review*, Federal Reserve Bank of St. Louis, December 1981; and Dallas S. Betten and Courtney C. Stone, "Are Monetarists an Endangered Species?" *Review*, Federal Reserve Bank of St. Louis, May 1983.

[39] *Economic Report of the President*, 1986, p. 27.

The crucial difference between monetarism and Keynesianism centers on the issue of what causes changes in expenditures. In the Keynesian model, changes in expenditure, that is aggregate demand, may be brought about by a variety of factors, including autonomous shifts in the consumption function, increases or decreases in investment as a result of varying interest rates, and tax and public expenditure changes deliberately engineered by public policy measures. But in modern monetarist theory what really matters are changes in the quantity of money. Money is the key variable. The central idea in the monetarist thesis, in other words, is that changes in the money supply explain changes in money income, real output (in the short run), and the price level. To the modern quantity theorist, the notion that such Keynesian relationships as the consumption function, the investment demand schedule, or the combined transactions and asset demand for money function may shift exogenously and thereby cause changes in output and employment is unacceptable. On the contrary, they hold to the view that any such changes are necessarily endogenous, triggered by prior changes in the quantity of money. The belief that there exists a direct—and causal—link between changes in the quantity of money and changes in money income has been the focus of a major portion of empirical research by contemporary monetarists, including the massive *A Monetary History of the United States, 1867–1960* by Professor Friedman and his co-worker Anna Jacobson Schwartz.[40]

The modern quantity theory is essentially short term, for in the long run monetarists do not believe that real economic aggregates such as output and employment are influenced by the money supply. In the long run what counts are changes in such real factors as the labor force, supplies of natural resources, investment in capital goods, and technology. But in the short run, in the monetarist view, the money supply can be, and is, a "powerful lever for determining income, employment, and the price level."[41] This may happen under two sets of circumstances. If the output can be expanded, then the increase in money expenditures triggered by an increase in the money supply may expand both output and employment. On the other hand, if output cannot be expanded, then money changes will affect only the price level, not such real values as output or employment. How the monetarists explain these relationships is the matter to which we now turn our attention. What, in other words, is the theoretical framework through which Professor Friedman and other monetarists explain the how and why of the impact of changes in money on the performance of the economic system?

[40] Milton Friedman and Anna Jacobson Schwartz, *A Monetary History of the United States, 1867–1960* (Princeton, N.J.: Princeton University Press, 1963). See also Anna Jacobson Schwartz, "Why Money Matters," *Lloyds Bank Review*, October 1969.

[41] David I. Fand, "Monetarism and Fiscalism," *Banca Nazionale Del Lavoro, Quarterly Review*, September 1970. For a concise survey of the essentials of monetarism, see Thomas Mayer, *The Structure of Monetarism* (New York: Norton, 1978), pp. 1–46.

The Structure of Monetarist Theory

In a nutshell we may characterize income-expenditure theory as a theory of the demand for output as a whole cast in the framework of the aggregate demand function ($C + I + G$ in a closed economy). By analogy, modern monetarist theory can be characterized as a similar theory cast in the framework of a demand for money function that explains how the money supply affects the performance of the economic system. The demand for money is the fundamental behavioral relationship in monetarist theory.

We shall, first, examine the process by which changes in the money supply affect money income and the price level and, second, analyze in detail Friedman's demand for money function. The latter is the key to the entire process, since the monetarists believe that the functional relationship between the quantity of real money people want to hold and its determinants—primarily income and wealth—is highly stable. Two other assumptions are needed, though, to complete the general picture of how changes in the money supply can influence the current level of economic activity: (1) that the velocity of money is also stable and (2) that the central bank (the Federal Reserve System in the United States) can control the quantity of money. Professor Friedman believes that the relationship between the quantity of money demanded and the variables that determine it in the modern quantity theory is more stable than the relationship between consumption and its determinants in the income-expenditure (i.e., Keynesian) theory. The practical meaning of this is that the velocity of money is believed to be consistently more stable than the Keynesian multiplier k, so that there is a closer relationship between changes in the stock of money and changes in income than there is between changes in investment outlays (and other autonomous expenditures) and changes in income.[42]

What will happen if there is a change in the money supply? Suppose the Federal Reserve creates more money through its open market operations. The initial effect will be to increase money balances in the hands of individuals in the economy. But because an increase in the amount of money will not change the quantity of money that people want to hold in relation to such fundamental determinants as income and wealth, they will seek to readjust their money balances back to the relationship that existed before the Federal Reserve expanded the money supply. To do this, they must dispose of the excess money balances, either by spending them or by lending them. As they do this, the added spending will bid up prices, expand output, or do both, until the desired balance is restored between money being held and the general level of economic activity. The process just described would, of course, be reversed if the Federal Reserve System chose to reduce the money supply. It

---

[42] Milton Friedman and David Meiselman, "The Relative Stability of Monetary Velocity and the Investment Multiplier in the United States, 1897–1958," in Commission on Money and Credit, *Stabilization Policies* (Englewood Cliffs, N.J.: Prentice Hall, 1963), p. 186.

is generally agreed by proponents of the modern quantity theory that a lag of six months to a year exists between the initiation of a change in the money supply and its ultimate effects on money income and the price level.

The essential difference between the Keynesian, or income-expenditure, approach and the modern quantity theory approach to the impact of a change in the money supply on the economy can be illustrated with the aid of a simple diagram, Figure 11–5. In the figure it is assumed that the Federal Reserve is the initiating force for a change in the money supply, a change that in both models works its way into the economic system via the effect of open market operations on the reserves of the commercial banks. Beyond this point, however, the two models display decidedly different *transmission* mechanisms. In the Keynesian model the increase in the money supply operates through the liquidity preference function to influence the rate of inter-

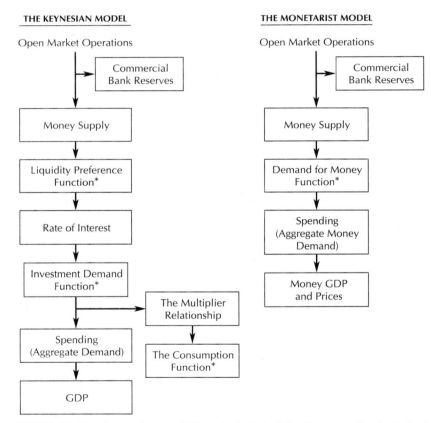

FIGURE 11–5 Keynesian and Monetarist Models Compared. In both the Keynesian and monetarist approaches, changes in the money supply ultimately affect the economy through their impact on spending, but in the Keynesian analysis money works through its impact on the rate of interest and investment spending, whereas in monetarist theory it works through the demand for money function.

*Key functional relationships.

est. Changes in the rate of interest, in turn, impinge on investment spending via the investment demand function. The ultimate change in total spending—and hence the output level—will depend on the value of the multiplier (whose size depends on the consumption function) and the amount by which investment spending changes. A key to the way in which the transmission mechanism works in the Keynesian model is the sensitivity of interest rates to the demand for cash. More money will prompt firms and households to exchange some of the excess money for income-earning assets—a process that pushes down interest rates. Indirectly, then, the demand for real output may be stimulated. But the latter cannot take place in the Keynesian model without a prior adjustment in the financial portfolio of the firm or household.

Monetarism tells a different story, one involving a much shorter transmission mechanism with respect to changes in the money supply and aggregate spending for output. In a nutshell, the monetarist's position is that any increase in the money supply spills over directly into the market for goods and services. The how and the why of this process depend on Friedman's theory of monetary demand analyzed in the next section. The modern quantity theory with its direct links between money and spending offers a much simpler explanation than does the Keynesian analysis for fluctuations in the general level of economic activity—a fact which, perhaps, accounted for some of its appeal.

The Friedman Theory of the Demand for Money

The point of departure for Friedman's analysis is the fact that people desire to hold money. Friedman is concerned primarily with the factors that determine how much money people want to hold, not, as in the Keynesian analysis, with their motives for holding it. His theory also differs in another significant way from the Keynesian analysis in that he employs a special definition of money. In his view money is anything that will serve as a *temporary abode for generalized purchasing power,* a definition that may cover some types of earning assets, such as time deposits, that do not serve as a medium of exchange.[43] This is not a matter of basic importance for our purpose, except that some critics of monetarism claim that Friedman's empirical findings verifying his analysis depend on his special definition of money.

Friedman identifies three major determinants of the amount of money that households and business firms will hold at any given time. These are (1) the total wealth in all forms of the household or business firm, (2) the opportunity cost of holding money, and (3) the tastes and preferences of the wealth-holding unit. Money in his analysis is viewed as any other commodity or good that yields some utility through its possession. Consequently, the gain, or utility, to be gotten from its possession has to be balanced against the utility forgone by not holding other forms of wealth. In a conceptual sense

[43] Stephen W. Rousseas, *Monetary Theory* (New York: Knopf, 1972), p. 161.

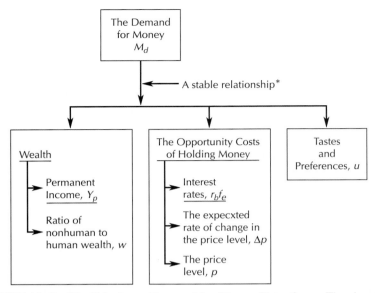

FIGURE 11–6   The Friedman Demand for Money Function.   The demand for money in Friedman's analysis depends ultimately on the amount of wealth held, the opportunity costs of holding money as compared with other assets, and individual tastes and preferences.

*In equation form, the relationship is $M_d = f(Y_p, w; r_b, r_e, p, \Delta p; u)$.

this view is quite similar to the Keynesian idea that money, through its liquidity, offers utility to its possessor; where it differs significantly is in its specification of the variables that determine the amount of money held.

To flesh out this bare-bones explanation of the quantity of money that households and business firms will hold at any one time, we need to look at all the variables that enter into the three major determinants Professor Friedman postulates. This we can do with the aid of Figure 11–6, which presents in schematic form a formal structure of the variables that determine the demand for money.

The meaning of these variables may be stated as follows:

1. M_d = the demand for nominal money balances. Although the basic functional relationship is expressed in nominal terms, this does not mean that the holders of money are subject to the money illusion. Monetarists view the demand for money balances as ultimately a demand for real balances; this means that nominal balances must be adjusted for changes in the price level.[44]

---

[44] In some versions of Friedman's basic equation (shown in the figure) the demand for money is shown as a demand for real balances; this can be done by dividing both sides by p.

2. Y_p = money income in Professor Friedman's permanent sense (see Chapter 7).

3. w = the ratio of nonhuman wealth to human wealth.

4. r_b = the rate of return on bonds.

5. r_e = the rate of return on equities.

6. p = the general price level.

7. Δp = the expected change in the price level.

8. u = the tastes and preferences of the wealth-holding units.

Essentially Professor Friedman holds that, first, the above variables which determine the amount of money that people want to hold do not change much in the short run and, second, the relationship between the demand for money balances and these key determinants is highly stable. Let us see specifically how these variables enter into the analysis.

First, there is the matter of wealth. Total wealth in all forms enters into the demand for money that can be held. No one, in other words, could hold more money than an amount equivalent to the total of the individual's financial worth in all forms. Professor Friedman's concept of wealth includes more than just assets such as cash, bonds, and equities. He also includes in it various types of tangible capital (such as producer and consumer durable goods) and human capital. The latter, as was pointed out in Chapter 7 (pages 248–49), is the worth of an individual's inherited and acquired skills and training. In principle, the value of human capital would be equal to the discounted value of the future income stream that an individual could expect to obtain from all inherited and acquired skills, which would, obviously, include education and training in all forms. The reader will recall from our discussion in Chapter 8 (pages 266–69) that the present value, or worth, of any asset is found by discounting its expected future income by the appropriate rate of interest.

In Friedman's words, "From the broadest and most general point of view, total wealth includes all sources of 'income' or consumable services."[45] Included in the latter is the productive capacity of human beings, as well as various physical and financial assets (nonhuman wealth) that an individual may own. The rub in this is the extreme difficulty involved in the measurement of human wealth. Therefore, Friedman uses permanent income (Y_p) as a proxy for wealth in his demand for money function. As the reader will recall from the discussion in Chapter 7 (pages 248–49), permanent income is defined as the expected average annual return that an individual would get from the sum of all her or his wealth, including human capital.[46]

---

[45] Friedman, "The Quantity Theory of Money," p. 4.

[46] Recall, too, from the discussion in Chapter 7 that there is no precise and readily available practical measure of permanent income. Friedman uses a weighted average of past and present measured income (the income an individual actually receives in a year), with less weight attached to measured income the further it lies in the past.

Given the foregoing, how does the demand for money vary with the stock of wealth? Professor Friedman believes that the holding of money balances should be regarded as a luxury, much like the demand for education and recreation. Consequently, he maintains that the amount of money the public wants to hold not only will increase as wealth, that is, permanent income, increases, but it will increase more than in proportion to the increase in the stock of wealth. This means in technical terms that the income elasticity of demand for real cash balances is greater than 1. In testimony before the Joint Economic Committee of the Congress, Professor Friedman suggested that past experience in the United States (at least prior to World War II) indicates that a 1 percent increase in real income per capita tends to be accompanied by nearly a 2 percent increase in the quantity of real cash balances held.[47] In his analysis of the demand for money balances, Professor Friedman clearly regards wealth as a factor that overshadows all the other determinants.

One may ask at this point why is a variable w representing the ratio of nonhuman to human wealth included in the analysis? Since we do not provide a market for human capital that would establish a rate of return on such capital (this would be possible in a slave society, but we, fortunately, do not live in such a society), there is no simple way in which we can include a variable that represents any direct measurement of human wealth in the analysis—a point of difficulty mentioned earlier. But the individual has some opportunity through education and training to substitute human capital for nonhuman capital (and vice versa) in the total stock of personal wealth. This, though, is a process that takes place only with a considerable lapse of time; hence, in the short term the ratio w will be relatively stable. Since as a practical matter it is difficult to turn wealth in the form of human capital into cash—one cannot easily borrow on the strength of future earning power—Friedman argues that this will be compensated for by a greater demand for cash as the human component in the total stock of an individual's wealth increases. Thus, the relationship between M_d and w is an inverse one.

What is the cost of holding money? This portion of Friedman's demand function for money is remarkably similar to the Keynesian liquidity preference function, except that Friedman introduces changes in the price level into the analysis in addition to the rate of interest. Basically, in Friedman's analysis, the cost of holding money is twofold: (1) the rate of interest that could be obtained if bonds or equities were held instead of money and (2) the effect of changes in the price level on nominal money balances. The underlying theoretical relationship is inverse, which is to say that when the cost of holding money rises, less will be held and when it falls, more will be held.

How this works with respect to the rate of interest should be clear from

---

[47] Milton Friedman, ''The Supply of Money and Changes in Prices and Output,'' in *The Optimum Quantity of Money and Other Essays* (Chicago: Aldine, 1969), p. 175. Friedman's views do not agree with other and more recent findings. For example, a 1973 Brookings Institution study found that the income elasticity of demand for money was less than unity. See Stephen M. Goldfeld, ''The Demand for Money Revisited,'' *Brookings Papers on Economic Activity,* 1973:3.

our earlier discussion of the liquidity preference function. In the income-expenditure approach, it will be recalled, the demand for money for asset purposes (the speculative demand) varies inversely with the rate of interest. Moreover the interest elasticity of the demand for money balances is relatively high. As a consequence, any change in the money supply will significantly affect the rate of interest and, indirectly, the level of investment spending. Professor Friedman and other monetarists do not deny that interest rates have an influence on the amount of money held, but, unlike the Keynesians, they maintain that the effect is relatively small.[48] The monetarists, in other words, argue that the interest elasticity of demand for money balances is quite low. Furthermore, they do not make the distinction found in the income-expenditure approach between money held as an asset and money held for normal transactions purposes.

What about expected changes in the price level? They work in a different fashion. An expected increase in the price level, for example, has the effect of making it more costly to hold money, since both the real value of nominal money balances will be lessened and the market value of other assets will rise. Thus, there will be a smaller demand for nominal money balances. The reverse would take place if the price level was expected to fall.

The matter is quite straightforward with respect to the price level. Since the demand for money function as shown in Figure 11–6 (see also footnote 44) is formulated in nominal terms, an increase in the price level p will result in a proportionate increase in M_d. This must occur if money balances in real terms are to remain constant. Professor Friedman believes that this factor is not particularly significant when price changes are small, a few percent a year, but it becomes of major importance when changes in the general price level are large and continue for a long period of time.

The third major determinant is designated as u in the basic schema presented in Figure 11–6. As Friedman says, ''The tastes and preferences of wealth-owning units . . . must in general simply be taken for granted in determining the form of the demand function. . . . it will generally have to be supposed that tastes are constant over significant stretches of space and time.''[49] The meaning of this is that no significant change in the amount of money people wish to hold can be expected in the short term as a result of any basic change in their attitude toward holding money as compared to other forms of holding wealth.

As a practical matter, Professor Friedman's theory of the demand for nominal money balances can be reduced to the proposition that there are really four major determinants of this demand. These are (1) wealth or permanent income, (2) the price level, (3) the rate of interest, and (4) the rate of increase in the price level. In its most elementary form, his theory holds that the demand for money varies directly with the first two and inversely with the

[48] Friedman, ''The Supply of Money and Changes in Prices and Output,'' p. 176.

[49] Friedman, ''The Quantity Theory of Money,'' p. 8.

latter two. If we transpose his theory into a demand for real balances, it says, in effect, that this demand varies positively with wealth (permanent income) and inversely with the cost of holding money (interest and expected inflation rates).

Now that we have analyzed the essentials of Friedman's theory of the demand for money, we are in a position to examine more carefully how the modern quantity theory works—how, in other words, we get from changes in money to changes in spending for output. The first point to note is the presumed stability of the money demand relationship; this means that if (for any reason) this relationship is disturbed, an effort will be made by persons and firms to restore the relationship. Since the money demand relationship concerns the amount of real cash balances people and firms desire to hold, anything that increases or decreases these holdings will cause them to try and return to the level of holdings desired on the basis of the enumerated determinants of these holdings. *This is why velocity becomes so important.* The stability of the Friedman demand for money relationship requires that the velocity of money be stable. If velocity is not stable, then a disturbance to the existing cash balances position (more or less money becoming available) may be offset by a change in velocity. If this were to happen, then the close link between the demand for money balances and the other variables is broken. This point can, perhaps, be more clearly seen if it is put in the context of the original quantity theory based on the equation of exchange ($MV = pY$). If we think of the quantity theory as a theory of the demand for money (as Friedman does) rather than as a theory of the price level, we have

$$M = (1/V)pY. \tag{11-7}$$

In this equation, the reciprocal of velocity ($1/V$) is a coefficient that links the demand for nominal money balances to nominal income. If there is to be a stable relationship between the demand for money and the general level of economic activity, *then V must be stable.* If it is not, then there is no possibility for the kind of relationship suggested by the modern quantity theory— a point to which we shall return subsequently.

A second basic point concerns monetarism's concept of what should be included in the portfolio of persons and firms. It differs from the ideas found in the Keynesian approach. The reason is because Friedman in his theory of the demand for money balances defines wealth to include *all* assets held, including both producer and consumer durable goods. In contrast, the Keynesian approach limits the portfolio of a person or a firm to idle money balances and financial assets (primarily bonds). This is why Friedman's point about the low interest elasticity of demand for money balances becomes crucial. A low interest elasticity of demand for money balances simply means that the willingness of people to hold money as an asset is not especially responsive to the rate of return being obtained on other financial assets, especially bonds. In Keynesian analysis, however, this is a key point, because it is the sensitivity of the demand for money balances to the rate of interest that accounts for the action people or firms take when their monetary equilibrium is disturbed. But if the quantity of money that people want to hold as an asset is not particularly sensitive to changes in the yield on bonds, then excess cash balances are just as likely to be spent for goods and services as for bonds. As a matter of fact, Friedman and the monetarists believe that any excess money balances will spill over directly into the spending stream for goods and services, primarily because the substitution effect between money and the range of financial assets available to the firm or the household is small. Critics of monetarism maintain that the monetarists have not yet demonstrated conclusively the sequence of events whereby excess money finds its way into spending channels. This issue is unresolved.

☐ Policy Implications of the Modern Quantity Theory

Although the theoretical differences between the Keynesian income-expenditure approach and the monetarist position are subtle and complex, the policy implications of these two visions of how the economy really works are, perhaps, even more important.

The modern quantity theory has a deep kinship with classical economics not only because of its stress on the importance of the money supply, but also because it reverts back to the classical idea that a market economy is inherently stable, which is to say that it is not subject to abrupt and wide fluctuations in employment and output. One of the leading proponents of the monetarist point of view has succinctly summarized the monetarist position on this point as follows:

> A central monetarist proposition is that the economy is basically stable and not necessarily subject to wide variations in output and employment. In other words, the economy will *naturally* move along a trend path of output determined by growth in its productive potential. Exogenous events such as wars, droughts, strikes, shifts in expectations, changes in preferences, and changes in foreign demand may cause variations in output around the trend path. Such variations will be mild and of relatively short duration. The basic stability is brought about by market forces which change rates of return and the prices of goods and services in response to these exogenous events.[50]

But are exogenous events the only cause of fluctuations in output and employment? The answer is no, because the monetarists hold that the *major* source of short-run economic instability is mismanagement of the money supply by the monetary authorities, which in the United States is the Federal Reserve System. In sum, exogenous events over which we have no control emerge in the monetarist view as the explanation of long-term fluctuations in

---

[50] Leonall C. Andersen, "A Monetarist View of Demand Management: The United States Experience," *Review,* Federal Reserve Bank of St. Louis, September 1971. See also Mayer, *The Structure of Monetarism,* pp. 14, 15.

output and employment, whereas government action is seen as the cause rather than the cure for short-term economic instability. It almost goes without saying that this is a point of view 180 degrees out of phase with the Keynesian vision of what the economy is really like. Since the 1930s the fundamental thrust of aggregate theory has been that the private market economy is inherently unstable, primarily because of the volatility of investment spending. Accordingly, government should play a stabilizing role, not only by varying its taxes and expenditures to offset fluctuations in private spending, but also by actions that will influence both private spending for consumption and investment in ways favorable to stabilization.

The monetarist's faith in the underlying stability of the economic system stems from a point already mentioned: the belief that significant variations in real economic variables such as output and employment cannot take place if the trend line of growth for the underlying real determinants—labor, capital, and technology—is stable. And monetarists think this is the case. Professor Friedman stressed essentially this idea in his 1967 presidential address to the American Economic Association in speaking of the natural rate of unemployment, a rate determined by relationships among such underlying real factors as real wages, the rate of capital formation, and technological change.[51] It is his firm belief that the economy will over time adjust to the level of output and employment determined by the rate of growth of these underlying real factors. Furthermore, he believes that the process is essentially smooth, except when disturbed by outside forces, including government. The clear implication of his analysis is that changes in any of the important real aggregates of the economy are beyond the reach of the short-term policy instruments of government, fiscal or monetary.

But if this is the case, what policy is appropriate? Given the stable demand function for money, and given, too, the strong belief that only such nominal variables as money GDP and the price level are affected by the money supply, then money alone becomes the appropriate policy instrument for affecting economic activity. Central bank control of the money supply is, in the monetarist's view, the single most powerful means we have to influence the overall level of economic activity, far more powerful in the monetarist's view than fiscal measures involving changes in taxes or public expenditures.

How should the central bank proceed in the conduct of monetary policy? As the monetarist's basic theoretical proposition—the demand function for money—indicates, the price level is clearly something that the monetary authority can control. But Professor Friedman and the monetarists reject using the price level as a guide for policy, partly because the link between policy decisions by the central bank and the price level is more indirect than the link between these policy decisions and the quantity of money.[52] The more important reason is the existence of time lags of an unpredictable length between

---

[51] Milton Friedman, "The Role of Monetary Policy," *American Economic Review,* March 1968, p. 8.
[52] Ibid., p. 15.

changes in the money stock and the variables affected by such changes, including the price level. Therefore, in Professor Friedman's words, "We cannot predict at all accurately just what effect a particular monetary action will have on the price level and, equally important, just when it will have that effect. Attempting to control directly the price level is therefore likely to make monetary policy itself a source of economic disturbance because of false stops and starts."[53]

The time lags are the real rub and, because they exist, the central bank should not attempt to pursue a countercyclical stabilization policy of varying the money supply in response to its reading of current economic conditions. What the monetary authority should do is adopt a rule that would allow the money supply to grow at a rate of between 3 and 5 percent a year, adhere strictly to this rule, and ignore the current state of the economy. Professor Friedman has never ceased to argue for this policy and has even gone so far as to suggest that there should be a legislated rule requiring the Federal Reserve System to increase the money supply at a specified rate. *This has been and remains the essence of the policy recommendations of the modern quantity theory.*[54] From October 1979 to mid-1982, the Federal Reserve under Chairperson Paul Volcker pursued such a policy, but after mid-1982 the Fed eased up on the money supply and returned to considering the interest rate and the exchange rate as target variables.

The Outcome of the Monetarist Challenge

What has been the outcome of the monetarist challenge to the essentially Keynesian structure of modern income and employment theory? In answering this question, it is important to caution the reader that many of the issues raised by the resurgence of the quantity theory in a modern guise have by no means been settled. The main theoretical structure of monetarism was largely in place by the end of the 1960s. Nevertheless, the exact and proper role of money in modern theory remains in an unsettled state.

The issues raised by the monetarist challenge are both theoretical and empirical, although Professor Friedman believes they are more empirical than theoretical. In any event, there has been a rash of empirical studies since the mid-1960s that aim either to refute or to uphold the contention that the modern quantity theory offers a better guide to the explanation and determination of the income level than the more standard income-expenditure analysis.

Out of the swirl of controversy that has engulfed the economics profession for more than two decades, several major issues have emerged and been clarified, if not resolved—issues important to both the monetarist and the income-expenditure positions. These include (1) the question of whether

---

[53] Ibid.

[54] Mayer, *The Structure of Monetarism,* pp. 33–35.

changes in the money supply or autonomous changes in the Keynesian variables are most important in bringing about shifts in aggregate demand that change output, employment, and the price level in the short term; (2) the validity of the monetarist claim of a strong short- and long-term link between the money supply, nominal GDP, and the price level; (3) the basic stability of the monetarist demand function for money, a matter primarily of the stability of velocity; (4) the interest elasticity of the demand for money; and (5) the ability of the central bank to control the supply of money. The next five sections examine the impact of each of these issues.

What Causes Short-Term Changes in Aggregate Demand?

During the 1960s and 1970s supporters of both monetarism and the Keynesian perspective undertook extensive research and econometric testing as they tried to determine whether the money supply or Keynesian variables (consumption, investment, and government spending) were the key to shifts in aggregate demand. On the monetarist side, Professor Friedman and his colleague David Meiselman, in a 1963 study for the Commission on Money and Credit, used two simplified one-equation models to test empirically the validity of the Keynesian and monetarist theories. Not surprisingly, perhaps, Friedman and Meiselman reported:

> The empirical results are remarkably consistent and unambiguous. The evidence is so one-sided that its import is clear without the nice balancing of conflicting bits of evidence, the sophisticated examination of statistical tests of significance, and the introduction of supplementary information that the economic statistician repeatedly finds necessary in trying to decide questionable points. . . .
>
> The income velocity of circulation of money is consistently and decidedly stabler than the investment multiplier except only during the early years of the Great Depression after 1929. . . . Moreover, such relationship as there is between autonomous expenditures and consumption seems simply to reflect the influence of money in disguise. . . .[55]

A second major effort to demonstrate the validity, as well as the superiority, of the monetarist model came a few years after the Friedman-Meiselman study appeared. This was by the staff of the Federal Reserve Bank in St. Louis. In 1968 two economists from this staff, Leonall C. Andersen and Jerry L. Jordan, published a study which was similar in design to the Friedman-

---

[55] See Friedman and Meiselman, op. cit., "The Relative Stability of Monetary Velocity." The monetarist equation was $Y = a + V'M$, and the Keynesian equation was $Y = \alpha + k'A$. In these equations Y represents income over time. The monetarist equation expresses income as a linear function of the stock of money M. V' equals income velocity. The Keynesian equation expresses income as a linear function of autonomous expenditures A. k' is the multiplier. These equations were their departure point. They were modified before having actual statistical data fitted to them. The Commission on Money and Credit was established in 1957 by the Committee on Economic Development, a private research organization. The basic purpose of the commission was to undertake studies into the monetary and financial systems of the United States.

Meiselman study and in which they sought to do two things: first, test the relative effectiveness of monetary and fiscal policies and, second, develop a basic monetarist model for predicting aggregate demand.[56] What they found was that the monetary (as compared to fiscal) actions were generally larger, more predictable, and faster—findings which they believe vindicated the monetarist position.

As one would expect, Keynesian economists reacted strongly to these models, producing their own empirical and econometric studies in support of the Keynesian relationships. Some were highly critical of the Friedman-Meiselman methodology and analysis,[57] while others developed much more complex econometric models, involving many more equations than found in either the Friedman-Meiselman or St. Louis Federal Reserve models. One of the most widely used Keynesian models is the one developed jointly by the Federal Reserve System and the Massachusetts Institute of Technology, generally known as the FR/MIT model. In contrast to the monetarist position, of which critics say the transmission mechanism is ill-defined (a sort of black box whose workings are hidden from view), the FR/MIT model identifies three channels through which monetary policy works.[58] These include the cost of capital, which affects primarily spending for equipment, business structures, and housing; the net worth of consumers, which affects consumer spending; and, finally, credit rationing, which refers to a situation in which lenders ration credit by various nonprice means. It emerges whenever interest rates fail to respond quickly to market forces. Credit rationing was found to be especially important with respect to the link between savings institutions and the housing market.

Not only is the FR/MIT econometric model different in structure from the one developed by the St. Louis Federal Reserve Bank, but the results from the use of the model are also decidedly different. Essentially, simulation experiments with the FR/MIT model show that the economy will respond, as the Keynesian analysis suggests, to an expansion of government expenditures that is sustained. It also shows that the impact of changes in the money supply

[56] Leonall C. Andersen and Jerry L. Jordan, ''Monetary and Fiscal Actions: A Test of Their Relative Importance in Economic Stabilization,'' *Review*, Federal Reserve Bank of St. Louis, November 1968. The Andersen and Jordan paper is reprinted along with other papers on monetarism in the October 1986 issue of *Review* of the Federal Reserve Bank of St. Louis.

[57] Albert Ando and Franco Modigliani, ''The Relative Stability of Monetary Velocity and the Investment Multiplier,'' *American Economic Review,* September 1965, p. 693. In their article, Ando and Modigliani also argue that a properly constructed income-expenditure model meets the test of statistical correlation just as well as does the more simple monetarist model. See also Michael de Prano and Thomas Mayer, ''Tests of the Relative Importance of Autonomous Expenditure and Money'' in the same issue of *American Economic Review.* There were also responses by Friedman and Meiselman in this issue. For a recent summary of the controversy, see Laurence Harris, *Monetary Theory* (New York: McGraw-Hill, 1981), pp. 414–428.

[58] For details on the FR/MIT models, see Frank de Leeuw and Edward Gramlich, ''The Federal Reserve-MIT Model,'' *Federal Reserve Bulletin*, January 1968, pp. 11–40, and ''The Channels of Monetary Policy,'' *Federal Reserve Bulletin*, June 1969, pp. 472–491. See also Richard G. Davis, ''How Much Does Money Matter? A Look at Some Recent Evidence,'' *Monthly Review*, Federal Reserve Bank of New York, June 1969, pp. 119–131.

is much smaller than the impact shown in the Andersen-Jordan (St. Louis Federal Reserve) study and that monetary policy works more slowly than fiscal policy, because it takes time before open market operations are reflected in changes in long-term interest rates.

Where does the above leave the matter? Basically still unresolved, as the econometric and empirical tests devised to date have not been able to demonstrate conclusively that either the money supply or the Keynesian autonomous variables are the most important determinants of changes in aggregate demand. Certainly the debate will continue. Monetarists still believe that money is the key to these changes, but Keynesian economists argue that, although money has a role to play, its importance is vastly overrated by the modern quantity theory approach to economic stabilization and management. Perhaps we can put the controversy into somewhat better perspective if we keep in mind that *neither* fiscal nor monetary policy in isolation was adequate to cope with the problem of stagflation in the 1970s.

The Money Supply, Nominal GDP, and Inflation

The situation is much more clear-cut with respect to the monetarist claim of a strong link between the money supply, nominal GDP, and inflation. The economy's behavior in the 1980s and early 1990s did not treat monetarism kindly, leaving even such a staunch monetarist as Beryl Sprinkle to doubt the validity of the money supply and nominal GDP and price level relationships.[59] Figures 11–7 and 11–8 tell this story.

Figure 11–7 plots the annual rate of change in the money supply (M1) and the annual rate of change in nominal GDP for the period 1960 through 1994. As the figure shows, for much of this period there was a rough correlation between the ups and downs of the money supply and the ups and downs of nominal GDP. But after 1980 this relationship went awry. In numbers, from 1960 through 1980, the money supply grew at an annual average rate of 5.3 percent, while nominal GDP grew annually at an average rate of 8.5 percent. Statistically, over these years, for every 1 percentage point increase in the money supply (M1), nominal GDP rose by 1.6 percentage points.

After 1980, this relationship changed dramatically. Between 1981 and 1994, the annual rate of growth of the money supply rose to 7.8 percent, a 47.2 percent increase in the rate, but the annual rate of growth for nominal

---

[59] *Economic Report of the President*, 1988, p. 34.

FIGURE 11–7(right) Rate of Change in M1 and Nominal GDP: 1960–1994. Up until 1980 there was a rough correlation between the annual rate of change in the money supply (M1) and in nominal GDP, but since then the paths of these two variables have moved in opposite directions—a development that casts doubt on the basic monetarist hypothesis.

Source: Economic Report of the President, 1995, pp. 275, 353.

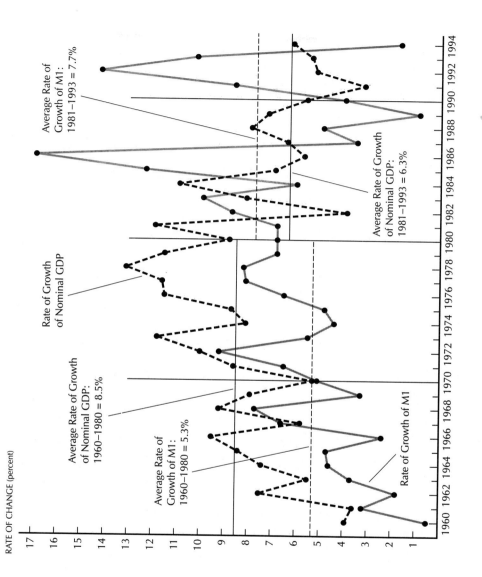

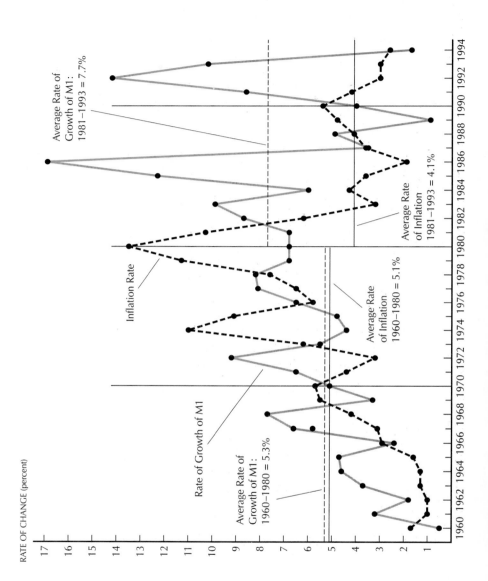

GDP dropped to 6.8 percent, a 20 percent decline in the rate. There is an even more fundamental difficulty with this relationship, one which critics describe as the problem of reverse causation. It is true that historically, as Friedman argues, changes in the money supply and changes in nominal income are correlated. But it is just as plausible to argue that changes in income caused changes in money—after all, more money is needed when income goes up— as it is to argue that changes in money caused the changes in income. Statistical correlation does show how two variables may move together, but it cannot tell which variable is the cause and which is the effect. As one critic has said, "theoretical issues cannot be resolved by playing the game of 'correlation, correlation, who's got the highest correlation?' "[60]

More devastating to the monetarist thesis is what happened to prices in relation to the money supply after 1980. As Figure 11–8 shows, the correlation between these two variables was quite close from 1960 through 1980. In percentage terms, the money supply as measured by M1 grew at an annual average rate of 5.3 percent, while prices rose on the average by almost the same annual rate—3.1 percent. From 1981 through 1994 it was an entirely different story. As noted above, the growth in the money supply jumped to an annual average rate of 7.8 percent during these years (a 47.2 percent increase), but the rate of inflation dropped to a 4.3 annual average rate, a 19.9 percent decline. In 10 of the 14 years from 1981 to 1993, money changes and price changes moved in opposite directions.

Stability of the Demand for Money Function

The third critical issue in monetarism involves the stability of the income velocity of money (GDP/M1). This is crucial. As we saw earlier (page 440), if the income velocity of money is not stable, then the stability of the demand function for money—the fundamental tenet of monetarism—breaks down. Friedman argues not that the velocity of money can never change, but that if it does change, the change will be gradual and predictable. This may have been the case at times in the past, but it has not been the situation for more than thirty years. Figure 11–9 traces the path of the income velocity of money (GDP/M1) from 1960 through 1994. The figures on the trend line indicate the actual rate of change in velocity in each year.

[60] Rousseas, *Monetary Theory*, p. 185.

FIGURE 11–8(left)   The Rate of Growth of the Money Supply (M1) and the Inflation Rate (CPI): 1960–1994.   Like the movement between money and nominal GDP (Figure 11–7), the rate of growth of the money supply (M1) and the inflation rate (CPI) moved closely together up until 1981, but after that date the rate of growth in money accelerated, whereas the inflation rate declined.
*Year to year.
Source: Economic Report of the President, 1995, pp. 346, 353.

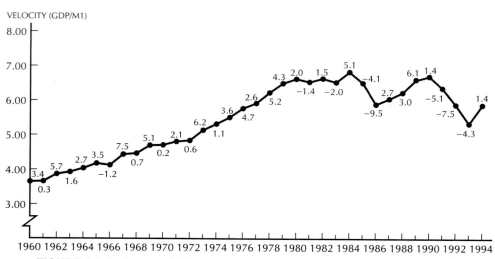

FIGURE 11–9 Income Velocity of Money (GDP/M1): 1960–1994. Since the early 1970s the income velocity of money (nominal GDP/M1) has been rising, but after 1980 velocity became increasingly erratic, dropping early in the 1980s, rising in the latter part of the 1980s, and then turning sharply down in the early 1990s.
Source: Economic Report of the President, 1995, pp. 274, 353.

Figure 11–9 tells us two important things about the behavior of money in recent years. First, it is clear that there has been a significant increase in the velocity of money since 1960, an increase that accelerated in the 1970s. In the 1960s, velocity grew by 33.1 percent, and in the 1970s by 38.6 percent. Second, after 1980 the picture changed dramatically, and the behavior of velocity became increasingly erratic. It fell sharply after 1980, rose unevenly in the middle and late 1980s, and then dropped sharply in the early 1990s. While there is no obvious explanation for this erratic behavior, it severely undermines faith in the stability of the monetarist's demand function for money.

The Interest Elasticity of the Demand for Money

If no final consensus has been reached among economists on either the relative importance of fiscal versus monetary measures or the basic stability of the demand for money function, this is not the situation with respect to the link between the rate of interest and the demand for money. On the issue of the interest elasticity of the demand for money, the evidence, as one critic puts it, is overwhelmingly "in favor of the proposition that the demand for money is *stably and negatively* related to the rate of interest. Of all the issues in monetary economics, this is the one that appears to have been settled most decisively.''[61] This finding tends to weaken the monetarist argument that the demand for money is not significantly affected by interest rates. On the other hand, the evidence from the same empirical studies casts doubt on the Keynesian notion that at very low rates of interest the demand for money balances becomes highly elastic. There is no empirical support for the idea of a liquidity trap, in other words. In sum, the evidence suggests that the demand for money is sensitive to the rate of interest, but not nearly so sensitive as the early Keynesian analysis indicated.

The Central Bank's Control of the Money Supply

Finally we turn to the money supply. Here the weight of the evidence is that over the long run the monetary authorities can control with reasonable accuracy the total money supply (M1), but they are less able to do so in the short term. As we saw earlier (pages 417–21), the money multiplier is not constant; it reflects among other things changing attitudes on the part of the public with respect to the relative desirability of holding currency as compared to demand deposits. The central bank can exercise firm control over the monetary base; this is what gives it control over the money supply in the longer run. But it is also true that the money supply responds positively to the rate of interest. The implication of this is that the money supply can accommodate itself to changes in the level of money GDP, as well as influence money GDP—a point of view not favored by the monetarist school. These comments need to be tempered in light of the internationalization of the commercial banking system by the enormous growth in the last three decades of *Eurodollars,* or *offshore deposits,* as they are sometimes called. A Eurodollar is a dollar-denominated deposit in a bank located outside the United States. As one economist describes this development, ''Eurodollars represent the first truly supranational form of money. Their growth and evolution is completely in the hands of the private banking system and they answer to no government or public authority—whether national or international.''[62] Estimates place the total of Eurodollars and other offshore deposits at more than a trillion dollars—money that flows continuously from nation to nation through modern mechanisms of electronic transfers. Money scholars do not agree on just how much the existence of this vast system of ''stateless'' money dilutes central bank control over the domestic money supply, but there is little doubt that it weakens this control.[63]

---

[61] David E. W. Laidler, *The Demand for Money,* 3rd ed. (New York: Harper & Row, 1985), p. 134 (italics added).

[62] Howard M. Wachtel, *The Money Mandarins* (New York: Pantheon Books, 1986), p. 92.

[63] Mayer, Duesenberry, and Aliber, *Money, Banking, and the Economy,* pp. 130–131.

☐ A Concluding Comment

The high-water mark for the influence of monetarism on public policy in the United States was from late 1979 to middle 1982, the short period of time when the Federal Reserve adopted the money supply rather than interest rates as its policy target.[64] Although this shift took place initially, though reluctantly, under the presidency of Jimmy Carter, monetarism was embraced with great enthusiasm by the Reagan administration. Not only were prominent monetarists appointed to key positions after the Reagan administration took office, but the administration's basic economic document, *A Program for Economic Recovery*, was explicit in making a reduced rate of monetary growth a key element in the scheme for economic recovery.

Once the new administration was in office, the Federal Reserve moved quickly to implement the policy of reduced monetary growth. From an annual rate of increase of more than 10 percent in January 1981, the rate of growth for M1 was reduced to a negative 0.1 percent by September 1981. This sharp reduction in monetary growth was expected, in accord with monetarist doctrine, to bring about an equally sharp break in expectations for continued inflation, a development that was supposed to lead to immediate and significant reductions in interest rates. This did not happen. By the end of 1981 triple-A-rated corporations, which had been paying less than 10 percent for long-term borrowing before the start of the monetarist experiment, found their borrowing rates had climbed to over 14 percent.

The short-term results of the Reagan experiment with monetarism were not a triumph. As in 1969, 1973, and 1980, a substantial slowdown in the rate of monetary growth pushed the economy into a recession, which in terms of the unemployment rate turned out to be the most severe of all the post-World War II recessions. As is usually the case (see Figure 1–8), recession brought relief from inflation, but the price for monetarism was the abandonment of its policy centerpiece, the targeting of the money supply.

Perhaps the most appropriate note on which to conclude this chapter is reference to a comment to the effect that the real differences between Friedman and the Keynesians are more ideological than theoretical.[65] This is probably true, for in a fundamental sense the monetarist counterrevolution is an attack on the basic Keynesian notion that a market economy is inherently unstable and, if it is to work at all well, government must play a stabilizing

---

[64] For an interesting account of how the Federal Reserve under Paul Volcker came to adopt a monetarist stance in late 1979 see Alfred L. Malabre, Jr., *Lost Prophets: An Insider's History of the Modern Economists* (Boston: Harvard Business School Press, 1994), pp. 162–172. Malabre is economics editor of the *Wall Street Journal*. The editorial page of the *Journal* was a major force in bringing about this shift in public policy, just as it was later in leading the Reagan administration to adopt supply-side economics.

[65] Rousseas, *Monetary Theory*, p. 196.

role and use to the best of its ability monetary and fiscal means to attain this objective. The Keynesian attack on the classical theory demolished the intellectual foundations for *laissez faire* as acceptable public policy. While the monetarist counterrevolution which sought to restore those foundations did not succeed, it did pave the way for yet another effort in this direction, the new classical economics, which we shall discuss in Chapter 16.

Summary

1. The two key objectives of this chapter are to explain the principles that govern the demand for and supply of money and to show how what happens in the monetary sphere affects the level of aggregate demand. As our frame of reference for these objectives, we use both Keynesian theory and the modern quantity theory of money developed by Milton Friedman.

2. The demand for money is crucial because the primary way in which money in a causal sense is introduced into the analysis is through demand. Analysis of the demand for money involves understanding why money is held and how the demand is linked to variables such as income and the rate of interest.

3. Two important theoretical explanations of the demand for money are the Keynesian theory revolving around the demand for money for transactions and the demand for money as an asset, and the modern quantity theory with its roots in the classical quantity theory of prices.

4. From a theoretical perspective there are two important issues relating to the supply of money. These are the formal theory of the money multiplier and the basic question of whether the money supply is exogenous or endogenous. For the sake of simplicity in analysis, the money supply is often treated as an exogenous variable, although in reality it is endogenous.

5. Monetary equilibrium, the counterpart in the monetary sphere of equilibrium with respect to the output level in the goods sphere, is a condition in which the total demand for money—the amount of money that people want to hold for various reasons—is in balance with the total supply. Changes in the monetary sphere react on the equilibrium of aggregate demand and aggregate supply (the goods sphere), and vice versa.

6. In systems of market capitalism, the institution of money plays a critical and strategic role. Money is the common denominator for all economic activity, and the pursuit of money is an all-powerful, motivating force in how capitalism works.

7. The modern quantity theory emerged in the late 1960s and early 1970s as a major theoretical challenge to the dominance of the Keynesian income-expenditure approach to output and employment determination. Milton Friedman, the primary architect of the modern classical theory, developed and perfected his ideas during his long tenure as professor of economics at the University of Chicago.

8. The key element in the modern quantity theory is Professor Friedman's theory of the demand for money. The demand for money is a stable function that depends on permanent income, wealth held by customers, including human wealth, the rate of interest, and expected changes in the general level of prices. Velocity is assumed to be stable.

9. Given the stable nature of the monetarist's demand function for money, a change in the quantity of money will disturb the balance between the amount of money being held in response to the variables included in the demand function for money and the money supply. Consequently, individuals and firms will seek to restore the desired balance in their holdings by either spending the excess of money or reducing their spending when the reverse is the case. In either event, imbalance in the demand for and supply of money spills over into spending and thereby affects output, employment, and the price level.

10. Contemporary monetarists do not believe in either activist monetary or activist fiscal policy. On the contrary, they regard the economy as inherently stable and believe attempts to influence it by an active fiscal or monetary policy are the cause of cyclical fluctuations. Therefore, they propose a monetary rule that requires the central bank (the Federal Reserve System) to allow the money supply to grow at a fixed rate based on the underlying real needs of the economy. The central bank should do nothing more.

11. The outcome of the monetarist challenge to the income-expenditure explanation of macroeconomic behavior remains inconclusive. Empirical tests have not shown conclusively that the money supply is a more important determinant of changes in output, employment, and the price level than are the basic Keynesian variables. Contemporary monetarism has had support in the economics profession and was a major influence on the Federal Reserve from 1979 to 1982. The Reagan administration and the Thatcher government in Great Britain embraced monetarism in the late 1970s and early 1980s, but by the mid-1980s this experiment with monetarism had ended quietly and with little success.

12 Output, Employment, and Inflation

Monetarism's failure to account for changes in the price level by changes in the money supply leaves the problem of the price level unresolved. Even though the inflation rate in 1994 fell to 2.7 percent, the Federal Reserve under Alan Greenspan's leadership raised short-term interest rates seven times during 1994 and early 1995. The Fed's fear was that the recovery that began in the spring of 1991 would unleash another surge of inflation, even though 7.5 million Americans (5.7 percent of the civilian labor force) were unemployed in January, 1995 and another 4.4 million who wanted full-time employment worked only part time.

The Fed's preoccupation with inflation is only one-half of a problem that has plagued the economies of the Western world ever since the end of World War II—how can contemporary systems of market capitalism such as that of the United States reach full employment without having to endure unacceptable rates of inflation? In this chapter we shall examine this problem carefully, placing strong emphasis on the ideas that Keynes developed in *The General Theory* with respect to how output, employment, *and* the price level relate to one another.[1] Having said this, we also want to stress that there is *no* single

---

[1] At this point the reader is advised to review the material on both the Keynesian aggregate supply curve (pages 103–11), which by its nature has prices built into it, and the Keynesian-classical aggregate supply curve (pages 132–38), which links output directly to the price level. Much of the material in this chapter involves an amplification of these relationships.

theory of the price level on which economists have reached agreement, just as there is no universal agreement on the causes of unemployment. It is crucial to keep in mind that inflationary and employment processes in the real world are exceedingly complex, involving at any one time a variety of forces. But it is appropriate to underscore once again our belief that the Keynesian income-expenditure approach involving interaction between aggregate demand and aggregate supply schedules is the best analytical approach to dealing with major macroeconomic problems, including the price level as well as output and employment levels.

A Short History of the Price Level in the United States

Let us begin by looking at what has happened to the price level throughout U.S. history, especially since World War II. We shall be concerned primarily with inflation, because inflation rather than deflation has been most characteristic of the era after World War II. Our discussion begins with some brief comments on the very long run, namely, what has happened to prices in the United States since the middle of the eighteenth century. Figure 12–1 shows for the period 1750 to 1994 an index of wholesale prices (now called the producer price index) with the average of 1947–49 as the base year. There are two things to be said about this long view of what has happened to prices in the United States. First, it is dramatically evident that before 1940, war was the main factor in inflation. During every war in U.S. history, prices rose sharply and fell just as sharply after the war. The years after World War II were the exception to this pattern. The reason for the behavior of prices in wartime is not hard to discover. As a nation, we have chosen to pay for our wars not by taxing ourselves, but by running the printing press or engaging in somewhat more sophisticated forms of debt financing. In either case, the economic effects have been the same. Prices rise dramatically as the government bids resources away from civilian use to fight a war. The second point is that historically inflation has *not* been the norm for the economy. There have been long periods of falling prices, notably during all the nineteenth century, save for the War of 1812 and the Civil War. As Figure 12–1 shows, the average level of wholesale prices in 1900 was below its level at the beginning of the nineteenth century. Deflation also has often meant hard times (see the box). From 1854 (the earliest year for which there are accurate records) onward, there were 20 periods of economic downturn with an average duration of 22 months each.[2]

The period after World War II has been different. Not only did prices fail to collapse after the war, as happened following every previous war in the

---

[2] See Table 14–1.

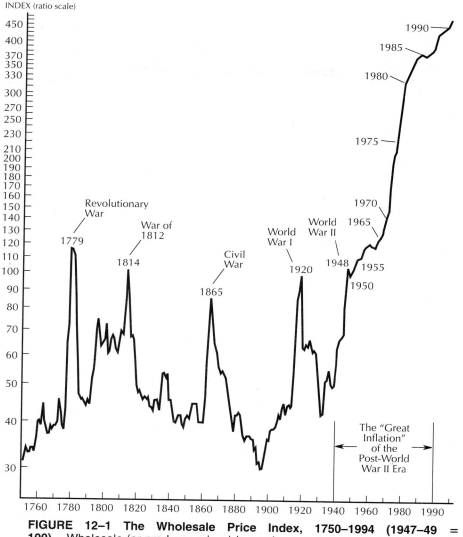

INDEX (ratio scale)

FIGURE 12–1 The Wholesale Price Index, 1750–1994 (1947–49 = 100). Wholesale (or producer prices) have shown great volatility since the mid-eighteenth century, although prior to the "Great Inflation" of the post-World War II period their trend was mostly downward, save during wartime. The producer price index includes only finished goods, not services.

Source: Historical Statistics of the United States; Economic Report of the President, 1991, 1995.

nation's history, but they have risen continuously since 1946, the first normal postwar year. Figure 12–2 traces the post-World War II inflation, using the GNP implicit price deflator as a measure of the inflation rate. This index includes both goods and services. In the 49-year period for 1945 through 1994, prices jumped over 9 times, or by 832.5 percent; this makes the period

INDEX OF THE PRICE LEVEL
(GNP deflator, 1945 = 100, semilog scale)

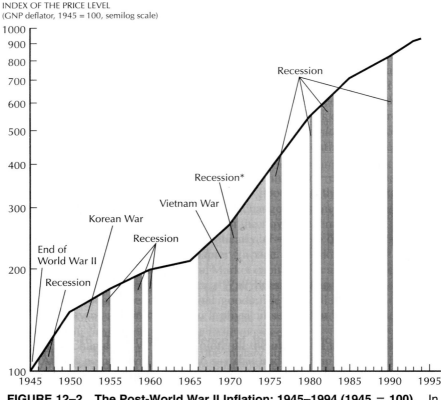

FIGURE 12–2   The Post-World War II Inflation: 1945–1994 (1945 = 100). In the post-World War II era the price level (measured by the GNP deflator) has moved steadily upward, although not always at the same pace. Recessions did slow the inflation rate, but at no time in this period did prices overall actually fall.

*1970 Recession came during Vietnam War years, 1966 to mid-1974.

Source: Economic Report of the President, 1991, p. 291; 1995, p. 278.

one of the longest and most severe inflationary eras in our history.[3] If the 1930s are known as the years of the Great Depression, it is possible that historians someday will call the era after World War II the time of the "Great Inflation."

The price explosion from 1946 through the 1990s is the third major such explosion in Western history. In the twelfth and thirteenth centuries (from 1150 to 1275 A.D.), prices rose fourfold, or 300 percent, whereas in the sixteenth century, there was a sixfold, or 500 percent, increase in prices. The first explosion was associated with the onset of the commercial revolution and growth of cities, whereas the second reflected the growth of capitalism

---

[3] GNP instead of GDP is used in Figures 12–2 and 12–3 because GDP data have not yet been extended back to before 1959. As noted in Chapter 2, the differences between GNP and GDP for the United States are minimal, especially in most post-World War II years.

and the vast influx of gold and silver from the Western Hemisphere. During much of the rest of Western history, prices have been either relatively stable or even declining.[4]

Although the general trend in prices was upward throughout the post-World War II period, the rate at which prices advanced was by no means even. To some extent what happened was in line with our historic experience, since there were sharp price increases because of war. When price controls were removed prematurely after World War II, the price level measured by the CPI jumped 23.6 percent in two years (1947–48). During the Korean War (1950–53) prices rose by 12.2 percent, even though price controls were imposed in 1951. In the years of the Vietnam War buildup (1966–69), prices rose by 16.5 percent. But the really explosive price increases came during peacetime. In the era of the first OPEC oil price explosion (1973–76), prices in the United States shot up by 38.1 percent, while during the two-year, second OPEC price increase era (1979–80) they rose by another 26.4 percent. Prices might have risen even further in these two periods if there had not been recessions in 1973–74 and 1980. Unlike all experience before World War II, prices did not fall during any of the postwar recessions, even though recessions brought a slowing in the inflation rate.[5]

Figure 12–3 offers some additional empirical insight into price behavior in the post-World War II era. Figure 12–3 is a scatter diagram that plots an index for *real* GNP, using 1945 as the base year, against an index for the price level, also using 1945 as the base year and using the implicit GNP price deflator as a measure of the price level. This figure tells us two things of importance. First, it shows that over time, increases in real GNP are accompanied by significant increases in the price level. Thus, the data in the figure provide some rough empirical verification for the type of theoretical aggregate supply curve developed earlier, one which relates real income (Y) to the price level (p). Second, these data show that the slope of the aggregate supply curve increased in the 1970s, a fact that reflected the economy's vulnerability to inflation. In the 1980s and early 1990s, however, inflationary pressures lessened; this is reflected in a less steep slope for the curve.

The Rate of Inflation

We have used the terms "inflation" and a "rise in the price level" in a manner that suggests they are synonymous. This is not quite correct. While inflation normally involves an upward movement in the general level of prices, all price level increases are not of the same magnitude, nor are their economic consequences and durations always the same. This is readily seen if we examine the data in Table 12–1. The periods shown are, of course,

---

[4] See David Warsh and Lawrence Minard, "Inflation Is Now Too Serious a Matter to Leave to the Economists," *Forbes,* November 15, 1976, pp. 121–41, and E. H. Phelps Brown and Sheila V. Hopkins, "Seven Centuries of Building Wages," *Economica,* August 1955, pp. 195–206.

[5] All percentages calculated from the *Economic Report of the President,* 1991, p. 351; 1995, p. 341.

INDEX OF THE PRICE LEVEL
(GNP deflator, 1945 = 100, semilog scale)

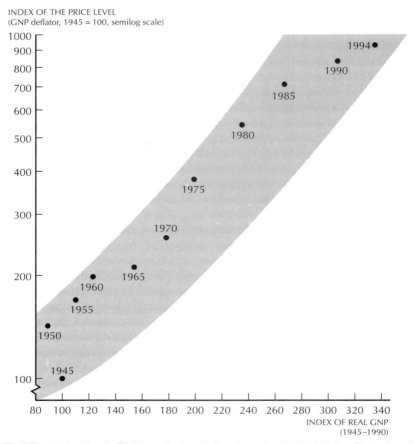

FIGURE 12–3   Real GNP and the Price Level: 1945–1994. Data for the changes in real GNP and the price level for the post-World War II period reflect the fact that, in general, over this period increases in output have been accompanied by increases in the price level. Thus, the shaded curve in the figure provides empirical support for ideas about the shape of the economy's aggregate supply curve.

Sources: Economic Report of the President, 1991, 1995. pp. 288, 290; 1994, pp. 276, 278.

arbitrary, but they permit us to be more specific about what the term "inflation" means. They correspond to the broad divisions established for discussion of post-World War II policy actions.

As data in the table indicate, there were wide variations in the rate at which prices went up during this period. The index used is the consumer price index (CPI). Many people would say that for all practical purposes we had price stability in the Kennedy era. The rate of increase was a modest 1.2 percent, and given the fact that there was undoubtedly some improvement in the quality of the goods and services produced in these years, inflation in a real sense was probably close to zero. The more recent data also show that the rate at

TABLE 12–1   Inflation Rates in the Post-World War II U.S. Economy (annual average percentage increase in the CPI)

Period	Inflation Rate (%)
Truman-Eisenhower Years (1948–60)	2.2
The Kennedy Era (1961–65)	1.2
Vietnam Buildup (1966–69)	3.9
The 1970s (1970–80)	7.7
Reagan Administration (1981–88)	4.1
Bush and Clinton Administrations (1989–94)	4.5
47-Year Average (1948–94)	4.1

Source: Economic Report of the President, 1991, p. 356; 1995, p. 339.

which prices are going up has accelerated. In the 1970s the rate was more than three times what it was in the first half of the postwar period. For the period as a whole, prices went up at an annual average rate of 4.1 percent. During this 47-year period, there were 25 years in which prices rose at a rate higher than the average for the whole period, 21 years in which the rate was below the average, and 1 year in which it was the same as the average.

What is the moral of this? Essentially—and in the absence of any techniques whereby price changes can be corrected for quality changes—it is that we cannot define inflation in terms of any *specific* rate of change in the price level. We simply have to fall back on the commonsense idea that inflation is a persistent or sustained rise in the general level of prices. This is a less satisfactory situation than exists with respect to full employment, for at least there is agreement among economists that full employment lies somewhere between a 4 and 5.5 percent unemployment rate. By the standard just enunciated, we thus had inflation even during the Kennedy era, although it was much more moderate—and hence easier to live with—than what we have experienced in recent years. An official definition of an appropriate inflation rate is given by the Full Employment and Balanced Growth Act of 1978, which stipulated as a national goal the reduction of the inflation rate to no more than 3 percent annually within five years after enactment of the act. Unfortunately, this remains a pious statement of intent rather than a program for action, since the act contained no effective machinery for its enforcement.

What Is Wrong with Inflation?

It is not necessary to belabor the point that a hyperinflation, such as Germany had in the 1920s, is a major social disaster. Many historians believe this inflation helped destroy the Weimar Republic and pave the way for Hitler and the ascent of Nazism.[6] However, this is not the kind of inflation we face.

---

[6] For a discussion of the link between the German hyperinflation of the 1920s and the rise of Hitler, see L. E. Hill, C. E. Butler, and S. A. Lorenzen, "Inflation and the Destruction of Democracy: The Weimar Republic," *Journal of Economic Issues,* June 1977, pp. 299–313.

Deflation and the Economy: A Mixed Blessing

In 1986 the rate of increase in the consumer price index (CPI) fell to 1.1 percent, the lowest inflation rate in 25 years. For all practical purposes this meant no inflation, a development welcomed by most Americans. But not all. Deflation, like inflation, is a mixed bag; some people benefit, some people do not.

The consumer price index is an average, and like all averages sometimes it conceals more than it reveals. When the inflation rate is calculated for a given year, it does not mean *all* prices included in the index change by the same amount. Not at all. Some prices go up and some prices go down. From this perspective, 1986 was no different than any year with a moderate to zero inflation rate: There were ups and downs for individual prices.

For a large part of the nation, a decline in the inflation *rate* translated into falling prices for a broad array of goods. Historically, deflation has meant hard times for farmers, miners, and most producers of the basic commodities that are the raw material inputs for industry. The period 1981 to 1986 was no exception to this pattern. Prices for crude materials dropped 14 percent.

"The Deflation Belt" was the name *Business Week* gave to the vast heartland area of the United States hit hardest by falling prices. Falling prices for farm products and collapsing values for agricultural land plunged most of the nation's farm economy into depression conditions. Banks failed, farmers left the land in ever-greater numbers, and net agricultural income in constant dollars in 1986 was only about one-half its 1981 level.

The impact of falling prices was not limited to agriculture. Mining was equally troubled. In Montana, Anaconda Minerals closed its giant Butte mine, unable to compete with lower-cost, equally high-grade copper from Chile. The story was much the same in Minnesota, Wyoming, Arizona, and other mining states. Falling prices, exhaustion of the best grades of ore, and declining world demand for basic commodities took their toll. Three states—Texas, Oklahoma, and Louisiana—were especially hard hit by the worldwide collapse of oil prices. OPEC (Organization of Petroleum Exporting Countries) could not stem the decline. When we add to these developments the damage done to many manufacturing areas by the overvalued U.S. dollar, most of the nation's midsection was battered by depressed economic conditions during the first half of the 1980s.

Not all economists or other observers lamented the hard times that buffeted agriculture and other commodity-producer areas. Some argued that agriculture, oil, and other commodity-based sectors were only experiencing a "well-earned hangover," following a decade of government or cartel (OPEC) action to pump up agricultural and commodity prices to unjustified levels. Further, it was argued that because the United States is rapidly becoming a service economy, the deflation of commodity prices is a normal part of this transition.

Others are not so sure. As Harold Breimyer, distinguished agricultural economist at the University of Missouri, pointed out, the United States by allowing its basic commodity activities to deteriorate, was crippled in areas where its worldwide competitive advantage remained large. "This is a built-in advantage that we have," Breimyer said; he noted further that, "it's almost impossible to retain a competitive advantage in high tech. We're no smarter than the Japanese or Germans."

Even so, we need to understand why, next to persistent unemployment, persistent inflation is a social problem of serious proportions. Keynes has said that "there is no subtler, no surer means of overturning the exising basis of society than to debauch the currency. The process engages all the hidden forces of economic law on the side of destruction, and does so in a manner which not one man in a million is able to diagnose."[7] Let us examine some of the things Keynes may have had in mind.

We must always be careful about making generalizations on the basis of a limited number of observations. Nevertheless, the experience of the 1970s strongly suggests that persistent inflation may loom as a major barrier to high employment and prosperity. An unchecked inflation may choke off a business boom if too many people find that their money incomes are not keeping pace with soaring prices. Thus, *real* incomes fall, buying is curtailed, and an economic collapse is triggered. For example, in the year (1974) following the first OPEC oil crisis in 1973, consumer prices jumped 11.0 percent, and in the year (1980) following the second OPEC fourfold increase in oil prices in 1979, prices shot up 13.5 percent. Between 1973 and 1980 the real value of the average weekly wage of the U.S. worker dropped by 13 percent—a loss in purchasing power that has never been made up.[8] Among expert observers— economists, business forecasters, and corporate executives—there was near unanimous belief that inflation was one of the prime causes of the 1974–75 economic collapse.[9]

Inflation also redistributes income and wealth in an arbitrary, capricious, and usually unjust fashion. "Throughout history," it has been said, "inflation, social injustice, and political upheaval have been strongly correlated; this association is neither coincidental nor arbitrary, but has much to do with the impact of inflation on the distribution of income and wealth between the various classes of society."[10] More often than not the redistribution wrought by inflation is from the poor to the affluent, from the ordinary citizen to the government, a fact not widely understood.

Among the groups that suffer the most in an inflation are the aged and the poor. The aged suffer because many of them are on fixed incomes, incomes

---

[7] John Maynard Keynes, *Essays in Persuasion* (New York: Norton, 1963), p. 78.

[8] *Economic Report of the President*, 1995, p. 395. The loss in the real value of the U.S. worker's wage has continued, in spite of real growth in the economy since 1973. By 1994, the real value of the weekly wage was 18.2 percent below its 1973 level!

[9] *Wall Street Journal*, April 25, 1975.

[10] Sylvia Ann Hewlett, "Inflation and Inequality," *Journal of Economic Issues*, June 1977, p. 353.

that are derived from savings, private pensions, insurance, or Social Security benefits. Since 1972 the latter have been *indexed,* which is to say that benefits are adjusted upward along with changes in the consumer price index. Since the income many retired couples get from Social Security is quite low, indexing does not always solve the inflation problem for the aged. The poor also suffer from inflation because all prices do not rise at the same rate. In the 1970s prices for basic necessities—food, shelter, medical care, and transportation—went up faster than most other prices. Since families of low or moderate means spend on the average three-fourths of their budget for such necessities, this aspect of inflation may be especially devastating.

Workers, too, are often among the losers in an inflation, even though some workers through unions may be able to protect themselves somewhat against inflation by cost of living agreements (or COLAs) in their wage contracts. The U.S. Department of Labor estimates that about 50 percent of all workers with collective bargaining agreements are covered by COLAs. Usually they provide for automatic wage increases based on changes in the consumer price index, although COLAs do not always allow for increases equal to the full change in the price index. From 1960 to 1994 average weekly earnings for all nonagricultural workers in current dollars rose by 376.9 percent. In constant dollars, however, weekly earnings in 1994 were 14.9 percent *below* their 1969 level.[11] What such clauses do is allow the better-organized workers to secure gains at the expense of the less organized, one example of how inflation redistributes income perversely.

But inflation may play a cruel joke on all workers, organized or unorganized, by thrusting them into a Catch 22 situation. In the past many families have found themselves in this situation. Because their money incomes went up during inflation, they were pushed into a higher tax bracket. But the increase in their money incomes was not sufficient to keep pace with both rising prices and rising taxes. This was known as *bracket creep.* During the 1974–75 economic slump, taxes as a percent of personal income rose from 13.2 percent of personal income as compared to 12.8 percent in 1974, even though the real value of personal income dropped by 1.1 percent between 1974 and 1973. Taxes as a percent of personal income also rose again in 1981 to 14.2 percent, as compared to 13.8 percent in the prior year.[12] Rising prices plus increased taxes caused the consumer's *real* take-home or spendable income to drop off in 1974 for the first time since 1949. This perverse working of the tax system—a feature of its progressive character—tended to offset the stabilizing effects of built-in stabilizers. The Reagan administration's Economic Recovery Tax Act, which became law in August 1981, provided for indexing the personal income tax, effective in 1984. This is supposed to eliminate bracket creep.

It is not just income which is rearranged in a capricious and usually unjust

[11] *Economic Report of the President,* 1995, p. 326.

[12] Ibid., p. 306.

fashion by inflation. The same thing happens to personal wealth, especially monetary wealth in the form of savings deposits, cash holdings, bonds, life insurance policies, pension rights, and other claims on present and future purchasing power. Basically, inflation redistributes wealth from creditors to debtors, provided debts are stated in fixed money terms, as is often the case. The reason there is redistribution is that inflation enables debtors to pay off their obligations in money whose real value has declined.

Professor G. L. Bach of Stanford University investigated how much redistribution of wealth resulted from inflation following World War II. From the end of the war until the beginning of the 1970s, Bach found that there was a massive transfer of wealth from households—ordinary citizens, in other words—to governments and to business. The magnitude of this transfer was staggering—between one-half and two-thirds of a trillion dollars.[13] The reason why the transfer was *from* households to government and business is because households were net creditors in this era. Their assets exceeded their liabilities. This wealth transfer undoubtedly continued through the 1970s, given the extremely high inflation rates that prevailed during that decade.

This is not the whole story. Inflation has also been responsible for significant transfers of wealth *between* households. Bach found these to be of two kinds. First, wealth was transferred from both the very poor and the very rich to households in the middle-income range. This happened because the latter are often, on balance, debtors, especially for houses and automobiles. The poor, on the other hand, have few debts and usually do not own assets whose value appreciates in an inflation (land or houses), whereas the rich are usually without debts simply because they are rich. Also their assets are often of a monetary nature (such as bonds) and hence vulnerable to inflation. What few assets the poor have are also in monetary form. Second, there was a large transfer of wealth from the old to the young, because young families are often heavily in debt. They borrow to set up a household, to buy houses and cars, and to finance education. On balance, a large proportion of the assets of the old are in a fixed value form. To a degree, this is offset by the fact that the Social Security System transfers income from the working population to the aged. This is a growing problem for the future as the proportion of retired people in the population grows.

The foregoing represent concrete, measurable ways in which inflation is damaging. But its ultimate threat is more intangible, more subtle, though nonetheless real. It arises out of the fact that modern society is a future-oriented society. No individual, no family, no business, or no government lives wholly in the present, disregarding the future. More perhaps than many realize, money and assets valued in money are the link that our economy has to the future. This, perhaps, is the most insidious danger of inflation. Between 1946 and 1993—47 years—the U.S. dollar lost 84.4 percent of its purchasing power. Since 1970 alone the value of the dollar shrank 63.3 percent.

---

[13] G. L. Bach, "Inflation: Who Gains and Who Loses?" *Challenge*, July–August 1974, pp. 48–55.

Destruction of the value of a nation's currency is serious. Besides being a link to the future, money is part of the glue holding a society together. When confidence in the value of money erodes, a pernicious and corrosive element enters into the nation's economic life. People are robbed of a dependable yardstick for understanding and evaluating what is happening around them. Further, there tends to be within a society a subtle but dangerous tilt away from productive activities toward those which are primarily speculative. Inflation provides an ideal milieu for the fast-buck operator; often more money can be made by dealing in things that already exist than by producing new wealth. It is also true that inflation exacerbates the struggle over the distribution of income. As individuals and families catch on to the adverse effects that inflation has on relative income positions, they become aroused, aggressive, and angry, ready to deploy all the economic power they command to protect or enlarge their share of the income pie. A vicious circle ensues. Inflation worsens income distribution, but the struggle over distributive shares that it unleashes feeds the inflationary spiral.

The Inflationary Process

Since the end of World War II there has been much discussion concerning the cause and cure of the persistent inflationary trend that has characterized the economies of most nations. Yet there does not exist today any single theory of inflation widely accepted in the economics profession. There have emerged, however, from analysis and empirical research, two basic approaches to the problem of inflation, within which a variety of factors that affect the price level can be analyzed. They may be described as the *demand-pull* approach and the *cost-push* approach. We shall examine each in turn, but the reader is cautioned at the outset that these approaches are not mutually exclusive and that neither of them will suffice to explain the inflationary process. The upward trend of the general price level that is an important characteristic of most modern economies is neither wholly understood nor readily controlled.

Demand-Pull Inflation

Demand-pull relates to what may be called the "traditional" explanation for inflation. The theory holds that inflation is caused by an excess of demand (spending) relative to the available supply of goods and services at existing prices. In both the traditional and modern quantity theories the factor of key significance is the money supply; only an increase in the money supply is capable of driving the general price level upward. In income-expenditure theory, demand-pull is interpreted to mean an excess of aggregate money demand relative to the economy's full-employment output level. The basic idea is that whatever upward pressure may exist on the price level emanates from demand. The theory further presumes that prices for goods and services as well as for economic resources are responsive to supply and demand forces and will thus move readily upward under the pressure of a high level of aggregate demand.

The Vietnam inflation experience provides an almost perfect textbook example of demand-pull inflation. During 1965 the economy was near full employment—at the end of the year the unemployment rate had dropped to 4.1 percent of the civilian labor force—and the price level was nearly stable. In 1966, however, and as part of the Vietnam military buildup, expenditures for goods and services for military purposes jumped $11 billion, followed by increases of $11.4 billion in 1967 and $5.7 billion in 1968. The total increase of $28 billion in three years is equal to $137 billion in 1994. During these three years of the Vietnam buildup, the unemployment rate averaged 3.7 percent, below the rate of 4.0 percent that the Kennedy administration set for a full-employment economy. With no offsetting tax increases, and accommodating increases in the money supply in 1967 and 1968, these billions in increased federal spending started the economy on an inflationary spiral that was still going strong at the beginning of the 1970s.[14] Given the upward slope of the aggregate supply curve, any excess of aggregate demand will drive up the price level, even if the economy is not initially at the full-employment level. An initial increase in prices and costs does not mean that all prices and wages are affected equally. There will be some groups that register a net gain from the initial inflationary spurt in the economy because their money incomes have increased more than the prices of things they buy. Other groups find their real position unchanged; their money incomes and the prices of the things they buy have changed in the same proportion. Still others are net losers because prices increased more swiftly than their money incomes.

The extent to which an upward movement in the price level generated initially by aggregate demand continues depends basically on whether or not all groups in the economy attempt to maintain their real income and expenditure positions. If all groups, in the face of inflation, are able to maintain real expenditure positions, real aggregate demand is unaffected by changes in the price level. But real expenditure positions can be maintained only if aggregate money demand, that is expenditure, continues to rise at the same rate as the general price level. For example, if the groups that initially saw their real economic position adversely affected by the original inflationary spurt succeed in raising either the prices of the things they sell or their money wages, their real income and expenditure position remains intact. But this, of course, will boost prices to still higher levels and thus require additional upward adjustments in money income and expenditure on the part of still other groups that now seek to maintain intact their real expenditure positions. From the viewpoint of the whole economy, an added increase in the level of aggregate money expenditure is inevitable if the level of real aggregate de-

[14] *Economic Report of the President*, 1991, p. 287; 1995, p. 279.

mand is to remain constant.[15] For this to happen, it is necessary for the monetary authority, the central bank, to accommodate this situation by increasing the money supply. This is precisely what the Federal Reserve did following the initial upward surge in consumer prices in 1966.

The presumed cure for inflation in the demand-pull category is clear. If there is an excess of spending, it must be cured by the vigorous pursuit of monetary and fiscal policies that will reduce total spending and thus lessen the upward pressure on the price level. The demand-pull argument presumes, too, that prices and other costs are flexible downward as well as upward. Therefore, the policy measures necessary to reduce total spending will not adversely affect employment levels. However, if money wages and prices are not flexible downward, then it is not possible to control excess spending without significant reductions in employment. This point was verified by the experiences in 1969–70, 1974–75, 1980, 1981–82, and 1990, when the fiscal and monetary brakes were applied successively by the Nixon, Ford, Carter, Reagan, and Bush administrations. The results were recessions but continued inflation, although the rate was slowed. In the case of the Reagan administration, the recession was severe enough not only to reduce the inflation rate, but to keep it below the high rates of the 1970s. The administration did not deliberately seek to stimulate output to bring the unemployment rate down— civilian unemployment reached 10.7 percent of the work force in December 1982—but after the tax cuts of 1981, the administration found itself (in effect unwittingly) stimulating the economy with Keynesian-style fiscal policies, even though the tax cuts were supposed to raise output by giving workers and business firms more incentives to produce. In any event, the deficits that followed on the Reagan tax cuts—the federal deficit rose from $74.0 billion in 1981 to a peak of $221.2 billion in 1986—were a major factor in bringing the economy out of the nation's worst recession since the 1930s.

Cost-Push Inflation

The cost-push explanation of the source of inflation has come into favor since World War II, especially in the 1970s.[16] This theory finds the basic explanation for inflation in the fact that some producers, groups of workers, or both

---

[15] In a dynamic setting in which output is rising, aggregate real demand must rise, not remain constant. The student should note most carefully at this point that the analysis is attempting to spell out the circumstances under which the price level will continue to rise, given an initial excess of aggregate demand over supply at current prices. A continued expansion of demand is much the simpler case. Recent experience provides empirical verification on the point. Aggregate real demand slowed sharply in 1969 and actually declined in 1970, but money national income continued to rise in both years. The same thing happened again in 1974, 1975, 1980, 1982, and 1990. In all these years real GDP fell, but GDP valued in current prices continued to rise. This happened even though the 1981–82 slump was the most severe since the Great Depression of the 1930s. In the second and third quarter of 1990 as the recession developed, real GDP dropped by 0.7 percent and 3.2 percent respectively, but nominal GDP continued to rise by 3.1 percent in the third quarter and 1.0 percent in the fourth quarter.

[16] This type of inflation is also described as market power inflation, income share inflation, and administrative inflation.

succeed in raising the prices for either their products or their services above the levels that would prevail under more competitive conditions. It may also originate with forces outside the economic system, such as the oil shocks of the 1970s. Inflationary pressure begins, in other words, with supply rather than demand and spreads throughout the economy. An inflation of this type is possible in theory because in the aggregate, prices and wages are not only costs as seen from the standpoint of buyers, but also income when viewed from the standpoint of sellers of goods and labor. For any single commodity or factor service an increase in its price will reduce the quantity of the good or service demanded, but this is not necessarily true for the whole economy.

Inflation of the cost-push variety is most likely to originate in industries which are relatively concentrated and in which sellers can exercise considerable discretion in the formulation of both prices and wages. Competitive conditions must be such that either business firms or trade unions have some control over the prices of their products or services. Cost-push inflation would not be possible in an economy characterized by pure competition. If prices and money wages, for example, go up in one industry, demand for the output of that industry and the labor used in it will shift elsewhere and thus bring prices and wages back to their initial levels. A purely competitive economy, let it be recalled, is one in which both prices and money wages are flexible upward and downward.

The results are different if money wages and prices are not particulary sensitive to a change in demand, even though aggregate real demand is adversely affected by a general upward movement of the price level. Under these conditions the economy no longer contains any kind of internal corrective factor to limit the extent to which an initial excess of aggregate demand can push up the price level. A reduction in real aggregate demand, given inflexible wages and prices, leads chiefly to a reduction in employment and to excess capacity. Prices and wages will not decline, and thus the inflation may continue. If unemployment and idle capacity lead to demands from organized labor and business that the government adopt monetary and fiscal policies that will increase aggregate money demand sufficiently to restore real aggregate demand to its prior level, a cost-push type of inflationary process is possible. This clearly was the case in early 1971, at which time the Nixon administration junked the game plan that called for a gradual slowdown in the pace of economic activity in the hope of containing inflation. The same scenario was played over again in the spring of 1975 when the Ford administration changed its policy stance and called for a tax cut as part of a package to stimulate the economy. The Carter administration did the same in the spring of 1977, even though the economy then was in the recovery stage from the 1974–75 recession. As noted earlier, the Reagan administration did not follow this pattern as the 1981–82 recession unfolded. Its 1981 tax cut package of a 5 percent reduction in 1981, followed by a 10 percent reduction in both 1982 and 1983, was originally proposed to the Congress and to the public as a supply-side measure that would raise productivity and production. Ironically, however, as the recession dragged on through 1982, the tax cut came to be viewed even by the business community from a Keynesian perspective. For example, a *Business Week* ''Commentary'' in March 1983 argued that, in fact, Reaganomics had in early 1983 become more Keynesian than supply side.[17]

In general, however, the circumstances described above may set the stage for a continuous upward movement of the price level, particularly because all groups do not share equally in the initial round of price increases. When the price level begins to rise, aggregate real demand may fall. But this does not bring down prices. As a consequence, groups that did not gain from the initial price rise now seek to boost their money incomes to maintain real expenditure positions. This creates more upward pressure on the price level and, indirectly, puts pressure on government to take the necessary steps to sustain aggregate real demand and prevent unemployment. Both the 1970 and 1974–75 recessions and the sluggish recoveries that followed these economic downturns illustrate this process. As Table 12–2 shows, hourly earnings in current dollars continued to rise in the recession years at rates that were only slightly less than those in the preceding boom periods. In 1970, for example, gross hourly earnings in private nonagricultural activity increased by 6.6 percent, compared to 6.7 percent in 1969, a year of fiscal and monetary restraint, and 6.1 percent in 1968, a boom year. Again in 1974, a recession year, hourly earnings rose more rapidly than they did in 1972 and 1973, both boom years. The pattern was not quite so clear-cut during the 1981–82 recession, although hourly wages continued to rise in spite of the recession. The rates of increase in money wages after the recovery in 1983 were relatively moderate during the Reagan expansion that lasted through 1989, a result of both the severity of the 1981–82 slump and the extremely hostile attitude of the Reagan administration toward organized labor.

In the situation described above, both the elasticity of the price level and the elasticity of money wages have values that are high with respect to any increase in aggregate money demand, but low with respect to a decrease in aggregate real demand.[18] Beyond this, the mechanism must exist through which pressure can be generated to raise the level of aggregate money demand and thus prevent unemployment and idle capacity from developing. It is clear from recent experience that the political process provides that mechanism.

The phenomenon of inflation in the modern economy cannot be fully ex-

---

[17] ''Reaganomics II: More Keynes than Laffer,'' *Business Week,* March 21, 1983. The ''Laffer'' in the *Business Week* headline refers to Arthur Laffer, economist from the University of Southern California who gained fame and influence in the late 1970s and 1980s as a key architect of supply-side economics, the philosophical foundation of the Reagan tax cuts. The supply siders tried to show that through massive tax cuts work incentives would be stimulated enough so that the economy would grow fast enough not only to increase government revenues, but even to generate a surplus. None of this happened after the early 1981 tax cuts. For details of the ''supply-side revolution,'' see Chapter 16.

[18] The elasticity of money wages is the ratio of a percentage change in money wages to a percentage change in aggregate money demand, and the elasticity of the price level is the ratio of a percentage change in prices to a percentage change in aggregate money demand.

TABLE 12–2 Annual Average Increase in Hourly Earnings in Nonagricultural Employment: 1968–1993

Year	Economic Conditions	Percentage Increase in Hourly Earnings	Unemployment Rate
1968	Boom	6.3%	3.6%
1969	Boom + restraint	6.7	3.5
1970	Recession	6.3	4.9
1971	Recovery—slow	6.8	5.9
1972	Boom	7.2	5.6
1973	Boom + restraint	6.5	4.9
1974	Recession	7.6	5.6
1975	Recession + stimulus	6.8	8.5
1976	Recovery—slow	7.2	7.7
1977	Expansion	8.0	7.1
1978	Expansion	8.4	6.1
1979	Slowdown in expansion	8.2	5.8
1980	Recession	8.1	7.1
1981	Recession	8.9	7.6
1982	Recession	5.9	9.7
1983	Recovery	4.4	9.6
1984	Boom	3.7	7.5
1985	Moderate expansion	3.0	7.1
1986	Slow expansion	2.2	6.9
1987	Moderate expansion	2.5	6.1
1988	Moderate expansion	3.3	5.4
1989	Slow expansion	4.1	5.2
1990	Start of Recession	3.6	5.1
1991	Recession	3.0	6.6
1992	Slow recovery	2.4	7.3
1993	Modest expansion	2.5	6.7
1994	Strong expansion	2.7	6.1

Source: *Economic Report of the President*, 1995, pp. 277, 326.

plained in terms of either the demand-pull or the cost-push approach. The major distinction between these two views of the inflationary process centers on the sensitivity of both money wages and prices to changes in demand. Those who believe that significant price and wage flexibility exists in the economy would generally argue in favor of the demand-pull thesis as the basic cause of inflation because such flexibility makes it virtually impossible for any cost-induced inflationary trend to sustain itself if the level of aggregate real demand is sensitive to a rising price level. On the other hand, economists who are skeptical concerning the extent of wage and price flexibility in the economy are inclined to place more emphasis on cost-push as basic to an explanation and understanding of inflation. Such theorists do not deny the importance of demand factors, but they take the view that the basic insensitivity of wages and prices to demand conditions means that a substantial— and probably intolerable—level of unemployment and idle capacity would be required before the general price level was stabilized. In essence, the cost-push advocates see inflation as a consequence of market power, a phenomenon that cannot be dealt with by traditional fiscal and monetary tools.

In a cost-push situation the pressure on the price level does not have to come solely from wages or other costs. It may originate with prices themselves, given the existence of market power in key sectors of the economy. Many large trade unions have the power to push wages up in the face of a falling demand, but many large corporations have the same power with respect to prices. In a 1974 report on the causes of the economy's inflation, the Joint Economic Committee of the Congress said that "increasingly, a significant part of the current inflation can be understood only in the context of administered prices in concentrated industries which typically increase despite falling demand."[19] Concentrated industries, the committee asserted, have the power to resist competitive forces and achieve a target rate of return on investment in good times and bad. To do this they must have power to control prices. To cope with inflation caused by private market power, administrative and legislative action should be taken to break up such power and to eliminate, as well, government regulations and practices that restrict competition. This was a key recommendation of the committee. Among economists, John Kenneth Galbraith and the late Gardner C. Means are probably the best-known advocates of the thesis that concentrated market power in the oligopolistic sectors of the economy is a major factor in inflation, particularly inflation when unemployment is high.[20] Both argued that the basic remedy is for the government to control prices in the few hundred giant corporations that dominate the U.S. economy. Means was willing to experiment with policies that would reduce market power by breaking up oligopolistic enterprises, but Galbraith remains skeptical of this approach.

Toward a Keynesian Theory of the Price Level

There is a dual aspect to the Keynesian analysis of the price level—the short term and the long term.

Prices in the Short Run

For the short term, Keynes's theory is rooted in standard textbook analysis of cost behavior at the level of the individual firm. In Chapter 21 of *The General Theory*, Keynes succinctly summed up the basic linkage between

---

[19] "An Action Program to Reduce Inflation and Restore Economic Growth," Joint Economic Committee, Congress of the United States (Washington, D.C.: U.S. Government Printing Office, September 21, 1974), p. 3. See also Howard M. Wachtel and Peter D. Adelsheim, "How Recession Feeds Inflation: Price Markups in a Concentrated Economy," *Challenge,* September–October 1977.

[20] The best statement of Galbraith's position on this question is found in his *Economics and the Public Purpose* (Boston: Houghton Mifflin, 1973), especially Chaps. 19 and 26. See also Gardner C. Means, "Simultaneous Inflation and Unemployment," in *The Roots of Inflation* (New York: Burt Franklin, 1975), pp. 1–30.

what happens at the level of the firm or industry and of the economy as a whole with respect to prices:

> In a single industry its particular price-level depends partly on the rate of remuneration of the factors of production which enter into its marginal cost and partly on the scale of output. There is no reason to modify this conclusion when we pass to industry as a whole. The general price level depends partly on the rate of remuneration of the factors of production which enter into marginal cost and partly on the scale of output as a whole, i.e., (taking equipment and technique as given) on the volume of employment.[21]

By "scale of output" Keynes means all those factors that influence the shape of the cost curves of business firms as the output level changes. By "remuneration of the factors of production," Keynes is pointing to all the forces that may cause the prices business executives have to pay (wages, interest, rents, etc.) to get resources to rise as they use more resources. These forces influence the levels of the cost curves in either perfectly or imperfectly competitive industries.

In the development of his theory of the price level, Keynes starts with a change in the money supply. This does not mean, as classical economics argues, that the money supply is the prime determinant of the price level. Rather, it is simply a convenient way to begin the analysis. This technique permitted Keynes to bring into the analysis of the price level all the key elements that enter into his explanation of the level of output and employment. By starting with money, Keynes was able to show that the determination of the price level involves not only his basic theory of output determination, but also standard microeconomic ideas about how individual prices are determined. Money is the link between his theory of output and employment and his theory of the individual industry or firm.

Keynes began his analysis by asking the question of how and by what process does a change in the money supply get into the price level? The answer he gave runs as follows. A change in the money supply will affect, first, the rate of interest. How the interest rate changes depends on the schedule of liquidity preference, which in turn depends on expectations concerning the future as well as the current level of economic activity. Next, a change in the interest rate will lead to a change in investment spending. How much investment spending changes is a matter of the sensitivity of the latter to changes in the rate of interest. This question involves *all* the variables entering into the investment demand schedule (see Chapter 8), including expectations and the state of business confidence. A change in investment spending will lead to a change in aggregate demand, but the magnitude of the latter depends on the value of the multiplier. This, it will be recalled, is determined by the various leakages from the income stream (Chapters 7, 9, and 10). Once aggregate demand has increased, it *must* exhaust itself in either an increase in

---

[21] Keynes, *The General Theory*, p. 294.

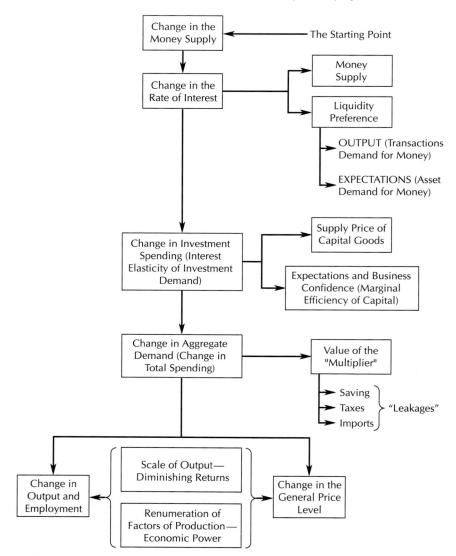

FIGURE 12–4   **The Keynesian Theory of the Price Level.** If a change in the money supply is used as a convenient starting point, how the price level is affected depends first on how aggregate demand changes in response to lower interest rates, higher investment spending, and the multiplier and then ultimately on the play of diminishing returns and the remuneration of the factors of production.

output (and employment), an increase in the price level, or both. This brings us full circle to Keynes's basic argument: The way in which more spending in the short run divides itself between higher prices and more output depends on the strength of the underlying forces which affect the scale of output and which determine the rate of remuneration for the factors of production. Figure 12–4 shows these relationships.

In the short run Keynes believed strongly that the principle of diminishing returns (or productivity) was a major factor in explaining why marginal and variable costs rise as output expands, because technology and equipment (i.e., capital) are fixed. In this respect he was very much a classical economist. To see how this works requires a brief review of cost behavior for the typical business firm as normally explained in microeconomics. This will enable us to see how Keynes incorporated these costs into the aggregate supply curve, which together with aggregate demand, determines in the short run not just output and employment but also the price level.

For the business firm, costs and their behavior are the key to the prices the firm must receive to justify production at any given level. Most economists believe short-term cost curves confronting the typical business firm are U-shaped, as shown in Figure 12–5. Why is this? Essentially there are two reasons, both stressed by Keynes in his theory of the price level. The first of these is the classic *principle of diminishing returns*. Even if we assume that all resources are homogeneous, using additional units of a variable resource such as labor eventually leads to a less than proportionate increase in output as long as productive capacity is fixed. This is the essence of the principle of diminishing returns. If the price of a variable resource like labor is fixed— the money wage is constant—then diminishing returns translates into a rise in labor costs per unit produced. In the figure, costs per unit produced for all resources used rise because of diminishing returns. This is what Keynes meant

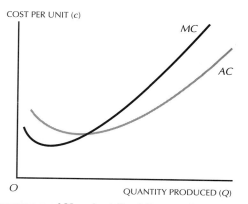

FIGURE 12–5   Average and Marginal Cost Curves for the Typical Firm.   The short-term cost curves for the typical business firm are U-shaped because of the operation of the principle of diminishing returns and the nonhomogeneity of resources used in production.

by reference to "the scale of output"—behavior of unit costs of production as more (or less) resources were used within the limits of existing capacity.

Aside from diminishing returns, Keynes strongly stressed another reason why unit costs increase as the scale of production increases. In the real world, resources are nonhomogeneous: labor and other variable inputs are not fully interchangeable in the production process. Take the matter of labor. An expansion of output within the limits of existing productive capacity may require the firm to employ labor that is less and less efficient in relation to the going money wage. This will cause an increase in the labor cost per unit of output even though the firm's stock of capital equipment—its capacity—is not fully utilized.[22]

Now we can return to the task of showing how Keynes integrated standard microeconomic (or classical) theory about the firm and its costs into his aggregate supply schedule. As we noted in Chapter 4 (page 103), Keynes defined the aggregate supply price of the output resulting from a given volume of employment as " . . . the expectation of proceeds which will just make it worth the while of the entrepreneur to give that employment." Keynes meant a curve showing the volume of receipts from the sale of the output that would be needed to justify employing the people needed to produce different outputs. The receipts would have to be sufficient to cover all costs incurred by business firms plus a profit.

Figure 12–6 shows a Keynesian aggregate supply curve drawn in such a way as to include the impact of diminishing returns and the nonhomogeneity of labor and other resources on the volume of expected receipts necessary to justify varying amounts of real output. The latter is shown on the horizontal axis, while the money value of expected receipts is shown on the vertical axis. In the diagram, the curve OZ is the path that expected receipts would follow if all resources were homogeneous and diminishing returns did not exist. But resources are not homogeneous and diminishing returns do exist. Therefore, the path of expected receipts will follow the curve OZ', which shows that because of these two factors, expected receipts (the aggregate supply price) must rise proportionately more than output if the costs associated with increases in output are to be covered. The curve OZ' means that price level will rise as output rises, a relationship verified empirically in Figure 4–2 (page 106) and Figure 12–3 (page 460). It is not the money supply that causes prices to increase as output increases, but the well-established classical law of diminishing returns to scale! As a practical matter more money will no doubt be needed to sustain more output, but this simply re-

---

[22] The relationship between marginal and average costs as shown in Figure 12–5 is important to understand. The marginal cost curve *always* intersects the average cost curve at the latter's low point—the bottom of the U. This is because marginal cost is the cost of producing one more unit of output. As long as marginal cost is below average cost, producing one more unit of output will lower the average cost. When marginal cost is above average cost, producing one more unit of output will raise average cost. Readers will recall from their principles course that normally the business firm is operating to the right of the low point of the two cost curves, so additional output leads to an increase in average cost.

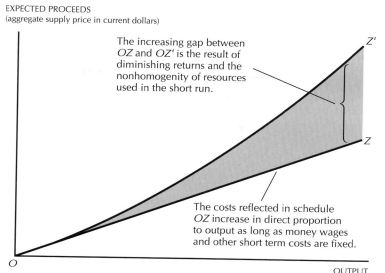

EXPECTED PROCEEDS
(aggregate supply price in current dollars)

The increasing gap between
OZ and OZ' is the result of
diminishing returns and the
nonhomogenity of resources
used in the short run.

Z'

Z

The costs reflected in schedule
OZ increase in direct proportion
to output as long as money wages
and other short term costs are fixed.

O

OUTPUT
(billions of constant dollars)

FIGURE 12–6 Expected Proceeds and Output. The figure shows the relationship between different levels of output and the expected proceeds required to cover all costs associated with each level of output. Curve OZ shows how expected proceeds would relate to output if diminishing returns did not exist and all resources were homogeneous. Curve OZ' shows the path of expected proceeds in relation to output with diminishing returns and the nonhomogeneity of resources.

flects—and reinforces—the view that generally the money supply responds to changes in economic activity, not the other way around.

Expected proceeds (including profit margins) shown on the vertical axis in Figure 12–6 are stipulated in money (or nominal) values. This is realistic because it is money profits that business firms seek and it is money costs that they have to deal with. As we saw in Chapter 4, this presents a potential problem, since the components of aggregate demand are developed in real— or constant dollar—terms. This problem was resolved by converting the aggregate supply schedule into constant dollars; (the nominal aggregate supply schedule embodies changes in the price level, but the changes are removed when the current value variables are converted to constant dollar values.) What is important to keep in sight is the fact that Keynes's approach to the aggregate supply schedule is not only rooted in standard microeconomic theory, but is also realistic in the sense that it is the expectation of money profits that motivates business firms.[23]

---

[23] For a much more detailed explanation and analysis of the microeconomic roots of Keynes's aggregate supply schedule, see Victoria Chick, *Macroeconomics after Keynes: A Reconsideration of the General Theory* (Cambridge, Mass.: MIT Press, 1983), Chap. 5, pp. 82–98.

Prices in the Long Run

For the long run, Keynes's explanation of the behavior of the price level is less theoretical, more pragmatic and empirical. As he put it in *The General Theory*, " . . . the long-run stability or instability of prices will depend upon the strength of the upward trend of the wage-unit (or, more precisely, of the cost-unit) compared with the rate of increase in the efficiency of the productive system."[24]

The British economist, the late Joan Robinson, called the idea that in an industrial economy the level of prices is determined primarily by the level of money wages "the other half of the Keynesian Revolution"; the first half is the principle that aggregate demand determines the level of output. She believed that this view seriously undermines the neoclassical belief that the economy is inherently stable, tending toward an equilibrium of full employment. "The level of money wages in any country at any time is more or less a historical accident going back to a remote past and influenced by recent events affecting the balance of power between employers and trade unions in the labor market.[25] Another economist, the late Professor Sidney Weintraub of the University of Pennsylvania, has drawn on Keynes's basic analysis to develop a theory which is particularly appropriate to the pricing process in concentrated industries. Weintraub argues that typically the large firms add a standard markup to their wage bill; the markup is large enough to cover all other costs and ensure the firm of a target rate of return on its investment.[26] Thus, when wages go up as a result of collective bargaining, prices will follow accordingly. This approach presumes that both trade unions and firms have sufficient economic power to push up both wages and prices even when aggregate demand is depressed.

Confirmation of Keynes's view about the longer-term relationship between money wages and the price level is found in Table 12–3, which gives in index number form the link since 1960 between increases in hourly compensation (money wages plus employer contributions to public and private benefit programs for workers), productivity, unit labor costs, and the price level. If money wages go up faster than productivity (Keynes's "the rate of increase in the efficiency of the productive system"), unit labor costs will rise. If there is a markup factor at work as Weintraub suggests, then prices ought to rise at about the same pace as unit labor costs. This is almost precisely what happened in the 1960s. Money compensation grew by 61.9 percent, but because of the growth in productivity by 26.7 percent, unit labor costs rose by

---

[24] Keynes, *The General Theory*, p. 309. By the "wage-unit" Keynes means the money wage. The cost-unit would be all unit costs. But money wages are of major importance; they account for two-thirds to three-fourths of production costs.

[25] Joan Robinson, "What Has Become of the Keynesian Revolution?" *Challenge,* January–February 1974, pp. 9, 29.

[26] Sidney Weintraub, *Classical Keynesianism, Monetary Theory, and the Price Level* (Philadelphia: Chilton, 1961), especially Chap. 3, "The Theory of the Price Level and the Analysis of Inflation."

only 27.9 percent, which was almost equal to the 26.1 percent increase in consumer prices during the decade.

In the 1970s the picture changed dramatically. Productivity growth turned sluggish, rising by only 13.9 percent over the decade, while money compensation exploded, increasing by 122.3 percent. Consequently, unit labor costs

TABLE 12–3   Productivity, Wages, Labor Costs, and Prices: 1960–1994 (1960 = 100)

Year	Productivity*	Money Wages**	Unit Labor Costs	Consumer Prices†
1960 (R)	100.0	100.0	100.0	100.0
1961	103.3	103.6	100.0	101.0
1962	106.6	107.7	100.9	102.0
1963	110.3	111.3	100.9	103.4
1964	114.4	116.7	101.3	104.7
1965	117.0	120.3	102.8	106.4
1966	119.3	127.4	106.6	109.5
1967	121.9	135.1	110.7	112.8
1968	125.5	145.9	115.7	117.5
1969	125.5	155.4	123.9	124.0
1970 (R)	122.3	166.7	131.4	131.1
1971	132.3	177.5	135.5	136.8
1972	134.8	188.7	139.9	141.2
1973	137.9	204.5	148.1	150.0
1974 (R)	135.2	224.8	167.0	165.5
1975 (R)	138.3	247.3	178.6	181.8
1976	140.6	268.5	191.2	192.2
1977	144.0	290.1	200.9	204.7
1978	145.1	315.8	217.3	220.3
1979	142.9	345.5	241.5	245.3
1980 (R)	142.9	382.4	269.5	278.4
1981	142.9	418.9	292.8	307.1
1982 (R)	143.1	450.5	314.5	321.0
1983	146.6	468.5	319.2	336.5
1984	149.8	487.8	325.2	351.0
1985	151.1	508.1	335.9	363.5
1986	154.1	533.3	345.9	370.3
1987	155.4	551.8	354.7	383.8
1988	156.8	575.2	366.4	399.7
1989	155.4	590.1	382.1	418.9
1990	156.1	632.7	401.3	441.6
1991 (R)	158.4	658.6	415.4	460.1
1992	162.7	692.3	425.2	474.0
1993	165.2	715.3	432.4	488.2
1994	168.7	737.4	436.5	500.6

*Output per person in nonfarm business section.

**Total hourly compensation per person.

†The Consumer Price Index (CPI).

Note: (R) = recession year.

Source: Economic Report of the President, 1995, pp. 328, 341.

also rose sharply, increasing by 94.9 percent, while consumer prices in turn jumped by 97.8 percent.

The real-world events behind these changes were the Vietnam War and the fourfold surge in international oil prices in 1973, a by-product of the 1973 Arab-Israeli Yom Kippur War. What started out as a demand-pull inflation in 1966 turned into a wage-dominated, cost-push inflation at the end of the 1960s and all through the 1970s. A close look at the numbers in Table 12–3 shows that in 1967 money wage increases began to depart increasingly from productivity growth. Figure 12–7 shows just how dramatic this departure has been. Many economists believe the oil price increases in the 1970s—fourfold in 1973 and fourfold again in 1979—played a major role in the slowdown in productivity growth that began with the Vietnam War and has continued almost to the present.

In the 1980s and 1990s the situation changed again, although not necessarily for the better. Productivity growth slowed further, rising by only 8.7

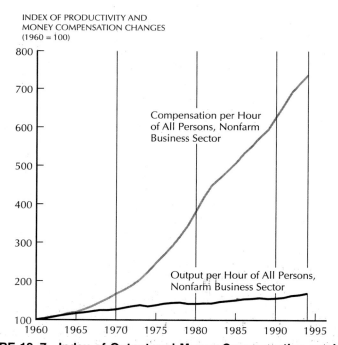

FIGURE 12–7   Index of Output and Money Compensation per Hour for All Persons: 1960–1994 (1960 = 100). These data show the explosive growth in money compensation (wages and salaries plus employer contribution to social insurance and private benefit plans) per person as compared to the near stagnation in output per person over this 34-year period. Whenever money wages and related benefits run significantly ahead of productivity gains, a rising price level is inevitable.

Source: Economic Report of the President, 1995.

percent over the years of the Reagan expansion (1983–89), while money compensation continued to rise, but not as rapidly as in the 1970s. Over the decade they grew by 70.1 percent, which brought a 58.2 percent increase in unit labor costs. Consumer prices, however, grew even more rapidly, rising by 70.8 percent during the decade. The pattern of prices rising significantly faster than unit labor costs continued into the 1990s—a development that suggests an increase by business firms in the markup rate applied to unit labor costs. The ratio of the rate of growth for prices to the rate of growth for unit labor costs was virtually unchanged in the 1960s and 1970s but rose significantly in the 1980s and early 1990s—a fact which supports this argument. See Table 12–4, which shows annual average rates of growth over the 1960 to 1994 period for the variables as in Table 12–3.

At this point, the reader may wonder: what in *real time* is the difference between the short and the long run? This is a valid question, but unfortunately one for which economics does not have a precise answer. The concepts of the short and long run trace back to the great English economist, Alfred Marshall (1842–1924). In his classic and widely used text, *Principles of Economics*, Marshall developed the notion of the short run as a period of time in which the individual business firm could vary its output *within* the limits of a fixed productive capacity. The long run, on the other hand, was a period of time long enough to enable the firm to enlarge its productive capacity. Marshall's definitions do not tell us how long these periods are in real time. His ideas are conceptual, not measured by any specific period of real time. That leaves us in a rather unsatisfactory situation. Because we live in a dynamic economy in which productive capacity is almost continually changing, the short run can only be a few years. Given that the average business cycle—from peak to peak or trough to trough—since World War II has averaged just about five years, it would not be too far off the mark to say that in real time the short run cannot be any longer than two to three years. This is a pragmatic, working definition.

TABLE 12–4 Annual Average Rates of Change in Percent for Productivity, Wages, Unit Labor Costs, and Prices: 1960–1994 (1960 = 100)

Period	Productivity*	Wages**	Unit Labor Costs	Consumer Prices[†]
1960s	2.6%	5.0%	2.4%	2.4%
1970s	1.3	8.3	6.9	7.1
1980s	0.8	5.5	4.7	5.5
1990s	1.7	4.4	2.7	3.5

*Output per person in nonfarm business sector.

**Total hourly compensation per person.

[†]The Consumer Price Index (CPI).

Source: Economic Report of the President, 1995, pp. 329, 345.

Output and Prices: Some Empirical Findings

There is an important aspect of the relationship between the price level and output (real GDP) that is *not* revealed by the data and the theory examined so far. This is that the output-price relationship is not reversible. This is a crucial finding. Prices rise when output rises, but they *do not fall when output falls.* As a matter of fact, prices continue to rise when output falls, even though the *rate* at which they are rising (the inflation rate) slows down. This has been the pattern ever since 1960. Whether or not it will continue to be the pattern in the future remains uncertain, although there is no evidence to suggest that the trend shown in Table 12–3 of money wages continuing to outrun productivity improvements is changing. Since 1982 the gap between the rate of increase in money wages and productivity has become smaller, but overall wage increases are still moving ahead faster than productivity gains. From 1983 through 1994, productivity grew at an annual average rate of 1.4 percent, but money wages (compensation) grew even faster at an annual average rate of 4.0 percent.

What the foregoing suggests is that when the economy is expanding, that is, when *real* GDP is rising, the price level moves upward in the fashion indicated by the Keynesian-classical aggregate supply curve (see Figure 4–10 pages 136–37). But when recession comes and real output falls, the entire price-output relationship may be displaced upward. The reason for this lies in a combination of rising labor costs per unit produced, as suggested by the data in Table 12–3, plus markup pricing, which is characteristic of large, oligopolistic firms. Thus, we find that the nonreversibility of the output-price relationship stems from periodic upward shifts in the aggregate supply curve, shifts that apparently take place whenever expansion is interrupted and the economy falls into a recession.

Is the foregoing simply hypothetical, or does evidence exist to support such an interpretation? The answer to the latter question is yes. Empirical evidence supporting this view is found in Figure 12–8, which shows a scatter diagram relating real output (measured in 1987 prices) to an index of the price level as measured by the consumer price index (1960 = 100). Beginning in 1960, the economy grew steadily through 1969, a 10-year expansion period. Real GDP rose by 50.4 percent and the price level rose by 24.0 percent. Then came the 1970 recession, when real GDP was unchanged. But prices continued to rise, and, when expansion resumed the following year, the process of both output and prices rising started from a new and higher price plateau. There was, in effect, a kind of ratcheting effect that, as Figure 12–8 suggests, can be interpreted as a leftward shift in the Keynesian-classical aggregate supply function. Then, in the 1971–73 expansion, the process repeated itself. Real output rose by 13.7 percent and the price level jumped another 20.9 percent. Output fell for two years (1974 and 1975), but the price level continued to rise. Consequently, once again the aggregate supply curve was dis-

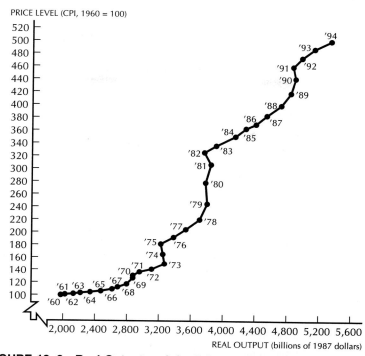

PRICE LEVEL (CPI, 1960 = 100)

REAL OUTPUT (billions of 1987 dollars)

FIGURE 12–8   Real Output and the Price Level: 1960–1994. Linking output (GDP) and the price level (CPI) reveals a ratchet effect, wherein prices may rise during an expansion and also continue to rise during a downturn, although at a slower pace.

Source: Economic Report of the President, 1995, pp. 276, 341.

placed leftward. In the third distinct expansion period shown in the figure (1976–79), output (real GDP) rose by 17.8 percent and prices climbed even more sharply, by 34.9 percent. After 1979 the pattern is more erratic, since there was a short but sharp recession in 1980 followed by barely a year of expansion (from mid-1980 to mid-1981), and then a new and deeper recession (1981–82), followed by a short and shallow recession in 1990–91. What the future pattern will be is uncertain. The strongest probability is that, once expansion is again underway, the price level will again rise, although whether prices will rise as rapidly as in the past is yet to be determined. Nothing has happened in the last few years to suggest any fundamental change in this pattern.

The explanation for the output-price relationship shown in Figure 12–8 lies in a combination of downward wage and price rigidity—at no time in the entire post-World War II period have average hourly wages dropped—and of the ability of workers and oligopolistic firms in the economy's central core to push up wages and prices under nearly all demand conditions. In spite of five recessions since 1965, wages and prices continued to rise, although the rate of increase was slowed by the recessions (Figure 12–8). Aside from the external shocks, such as came from OPEC-administered oil prices in the 1970s, the data from Table 12–3 and Figure 12–8 suggest that trade union pressure and administered prices based on markups are the basic source for the inflation side of the stagflation of the 1970s. As Joan Robinson said in her 1971 Ely Lecture to the American Economic Association, the "experience of inflation has destroyed the conventions governing the acceptance of the existing distribution [of income]. Everyone can see that his relative earnings depend upon the bargaining power of the group that he belongs to."[27]

The Phillips Curve

Another way in which the general level of activity in the economy is linked to prices and inflation is through the Phillips curve. This curve, however, describes a relationship between the inflation rate and the rate of unemployment. For a time in the 1960s it showed promise of being a highly useful policy tool, although theoretical developments and empirical events since then have cast doubt on its usefulness. The curve is named for a British economist, A. W. Phillips, who in a seminal article published in 1958 established for the British economy a statistical relationship between the annual average rate of unemployment and the annual average rate of change in money wages.[28] Because labor costs make up such a high proportion of total costs, there is a close correlation between changes in money wage rates and the inflation rate.

A theoretical Phillips curve is shown in Figure 12–9. It is the solid curve designated *aa*. The rate of change in money wages is shown on the vertical axis on the left side of the diagram, and the unemployment rate on the horizontal axis. The significance of this curve lies in the fact that the unemployment rate can be expected to decline as aggregate demand increases, but a fall in the unemployment rate will be accompanied by a higher rate of increase in money wages. This is the way Phillips posed the original relationship. The solid curve is drawn with a slope such that the rate of increase in money wages is 3 percent when unemployment reaches a level of 5 percent of the labor force. If the unemployment rate is reduced to 4 percent through an increase in aggregate demand, the rate of increase in money wages rises to 5 percent. The extent to which any particular rate of increase in money wages causes increases in the price level depends on the annual rate at which the average productivity of labor is increasing. If, for example, this rate were also 3 percent, then it would be theoretically possible for the economy to attain an unemployment rate of 5 percent of its labor force and have money wages

---

[27] Joan Robinson, "The Second Crisis of Economic Theory," *The American Economic Review*, May 1972, p. 9.

[28] A. W. Phillips, "The Relation between Unemployment and the Rate of Change of Money Wages in the United Kingdom, 1861–1957," *Economica*, November 1958, pp. 283–299.

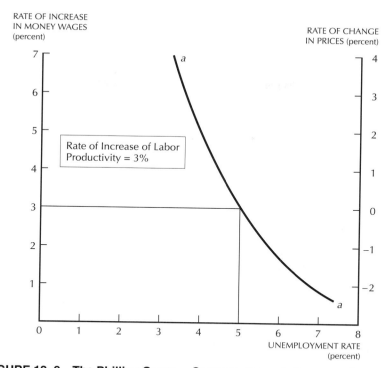

FIGURE 12–9   The Phillips Curve.   Curve *aa* connects the unemployment rate with the rate of increase in money wages, shown on the left-hand vertical scale, and with the inflation rate, shown on the right-hand vertical scale. Inflation rates associated with varying levels of unemployment are obtained by subtracting the rate of growth in productivity from the rate of increase in money wages.

increase at an annual rate of 3 percent without any increase in the general price level. Any reduction of the unemployment rate below the 5 percent level would generate upward pressure on prices. If we subtract the rate of productivity increase—3 percent—from the rate of increase in money wages as shown on the left-side vertical scale, we get rates of inflation associated with each level of unemployment. These rates are shown on the right-side vertical scale.

As we shall see, events of the 1970s cast deep doubt on the idea that there is a stable, trade-off relationship between unemployment and the price level. However, if we accept momentarily as a working hypothesis the notion of a stable Phillips curve, some policy problems of the modern economy can be illuminated. It means, for example, that policymakers must choose between more inflation and less unemployment or more unemployment and less infla-tion—an unhappy choice in any event. This difficulty implies that there are maximum rates for both unemployment and increases in the price level that are socially—or politically—acceptable. Rates above these maxima simply

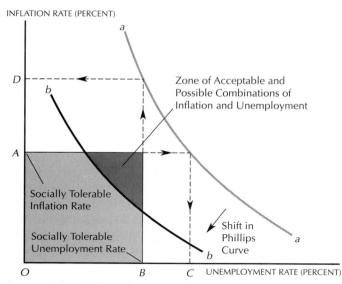

FIGURE 12–10   The Phillips Curve and Socially Tolerable Rates of Inflation and Unemployment.   If the Phillips curve lies along *bb* (dotted line), then it is possible to have both an unemployment and inflation rate that lies within limits that are socially tolerable. But if the Phillips curve lies beyond this zone, then there is no combination of unemployment and inflation that is socially and politically acceptable.

will not be tolerated. If such rates exist, this poses another difficult—or cruel—dilemma for policymakers.

The situation is illustrated in Figure 12–10. The shaded area represents a zone of socially tolerable outcomes, derived from the combination of the acceptable rate of inflation and the acceptable rate of unemployment. If the Phillips curve lies above and to the right of this zone, then there is *no* combination of unemployment and inflation that is politically or socially acceptable. It seems the economy has been in this fix much of the time in recent years. That is what the stagflation of the 1970s was all about. In the figure this is the situation depicted by the solid-line Phillips curve labeled *aa*. If the inflation rate is brought down to a level that the society is willing to tolerate—point *A* in the diagram—then the unemployment rate rises to an intolerable level, point *C* on the horizontal axis. On the other hand, if the unemployment rate is reduced to the tolerable level, as indicated by point *B* in the figure, then the inflation rate is pushed beyond an acceptable rate to point *D* on the vertical axis.

What is to be done? If it is impossible by means of fiscal and monetary policies to attain an acceptable combination of inflation and unemployment, then different policy alternatives must be found. Monetary and fiscal policies can move the economy along a given Phillips curve such as *aa*, but they cannot shift the curve downward and to the left into the zone representing an acceptable combination of unemployment and inflation rates. How can such a move be brought about? One approach is through adoption of an incomes policy, which is composed of measures designed to limit the rate at which wages and prices rise as the economy approaches full employment. In the late 1960s the Johnson administration developed an incomes policy in the form of wage-price guideposts, and the Nixon administration had its own incomes policy in the form of direct wage-price controls, beginning in mid-1971. The Carter administration also experimented briefly with an incomes policy in 1978. We shall discuss both forms of income policies later in the chapter. Another approach lies in the development of programs to train and retrain unskilled, semiskilled, and displaced workers so that the economy has a better supply of trained workers as it moves toward higher employment levels. If such policies succeeded, the Phillips curve might shift downward and to the left and thus make possible the attainment of some combination of unemployment and inflation that is socially acceptable. The dashed curve bb shows this. To date, however, such training programs have not demonstrated any spectacular successes.

Challenges to the Phillips Curve Analysis

Until the late 1960s the idea that the Phillips curve reflected a stable trade-off relationship between inflation and unemployment was not subject to serious question. This is no longer the case. For one thing, recent data on both inflation and unemployment cast doubt on the stability of this relationship. Figure 12–11 contains a scatter diagram relating the inflation rate as measured by the annual rate of change in the GDP price deflator and the unemployment rate for the period 1960 through 1994. The solid-line curve ee is sketched in to indicate that the data for the years 1960 through 1969 roughly approximate the behavior pattern suggested by the Phillips hypothesis. More specifically, there appears to be a close correlation between falling unemployment and a rising price level from the beginning of the decade through 1966. For the next three years, 1967 through 1969, prices rose very sharply with only minimal effects on the unemployment rate. But the most noticeable—and damaging—departure from the Phillips hypothesis occurred in the 1970 through 1993 period. In each of these years the unemployment rate was much higher for any given inflation rate than it ought to have been, given the relationship shown by the curve ee. What, therefore, are we to conclude? One possible explanation is that the data for 1970 through 1989 are to be found on Phillips curves that lie to the right of and above the curve ee. If this is the case, it means that there may not be one basically stable functional relationship between inflation and unemployment, but possibly a series of short-run Phillips curves of a volatile nature.

Bolstered by empirical findings that indicate a shifting Phillips curve, monetarists launched a strong theoretical attack in the late 1960s on one of the fundamental premises of the Phillips curve analysis, namely, that it is possible to reduce permanently the unemployment rate to some desired level by driv-

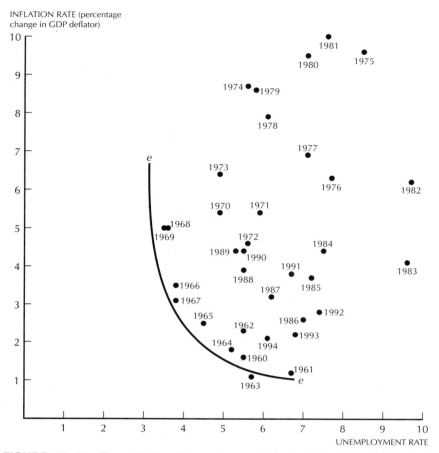

FIGURE 12–11   The Inflation-Unemployment Trade-Off, 1960–1994. Data from the 1960s yield a scatter diagram that fits the pattern of the Phillips curve relationship relatively well, but data in subsequent years do not fit the pattern. One explanation for this is that the curve itself has been shifting upward in recent years, so that any given unemployment rate will necessarily be associated with a higher inflation rate.

Source: Economic Report of the President, 1995, pp. 321, 345.

ing up the price level. On the contrary, according to the monetarists, there is no permanent trade-off between inflation and unemployment. Policy measures based on such an assumed trade-off will, in the long run, only result in an acceleration in the inflation rate, with no permanent change in the unemployment level.

As in the case of the controversy over the role of money in aggregate economic analysis, this monetarist challenge to the Phillips curve analysis was led by Milton Friedman. He argued, first, that there exists a *natural* unemployment rate, determined by underlying real factors such as capital formation and technological change and, second, that the Phillips curve is a short, transitory relationship, valid only as long as the wage earners adhere to the money illusion and have no expectations prices will continue to rise.

Once wage earners lose the money illusion and develop expectations about continued inflation, they begin to bargain for real wages by attempting to take the anticipated inflation rate into account in their wage negotiations. If, under these circumstances, an attempt is made to reduce the unemployment rate, all that will happen is an acceleration in the inflation rate, with no effect on the long-term natural rate of unemployment. It is for this reason that the monetarist critique of the Phillips curve theory is sometimes called the "accelerationist thesis."

The manner in which this works is shown in Figure 12–12. According to the accelerationist thesis, the Phillips curve becomes, in the long run, perfectly inelastic with respect to the rate of change in the price level at the natural rate of unemployment. This is the vertical line labeled the "Long-Run Phillips Curve" that intersects the horizontal axis at the natural rate of unemployment U_n. The curves PC_1, PC_2, and so on, represent a series of short-term Phillips curves, each of which incorporates a different *expected* rate of inflation. An increase in the expected inflation rate will cause the Phillips curve to shift upward. The point at which a particular short-term curve intersects the long-run curve represents equality between the expected and actual inflation rates. Let us suppose that the policy objective is one of reducing the unemployment rate to U_1, a level below the presumed natural rate. If we assume, further, that the economy was in equilibrium with stable prices, then aggregate demand would have to increase to bring the economy closer to the target level

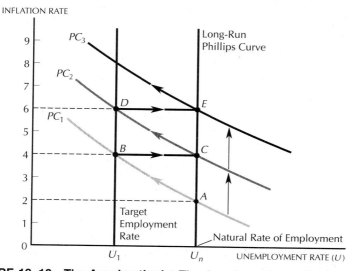

FIGURE 12–12 The Accelerationist Thesis. According to the natural rate of unemployment hypothesis, the long-run Phillips curve is vertical at the level of the natural rate. Consequently, any attempt by policy actions to push the unemployment rate below the natural rate will lead to an acceleration in the inflation rate.

of unemployment U_1. The increase in aggregate demand will trigger a rise in prices, which will be reflected in a movement of the economy along the short-term Phillips curve labeled PC_1. Prices must rise faster than money wages; that is, real wages must fall if unemployment is to be avoided.

According to the accelerationist thesis, however, the rise in the price level cannot keep the economy permanently at a level of unemployment below the natural rate. This is true for two reasons. First, money wages will begin to catch up with the price level and thus push the real wage back toward its original level. This tends to cause the unemployment rate to move back toward the natural rate U_n. But the inflation rate will have accelerated to 4 percent. Second, wage earners soon abandon the money illusion in the face of a rising price level and begin to bargain for money wages that take into account anticipated increases in the price level. If this happens, the short-term Phillips curve will shift upward in response to expectations that inflation will continue. It will now be at the level PC_2, a level which incorporates a new set of expectations (4 percent) about the inflation rate in the future. But the target goal of a reduction of unemployment to the level U_1 has not been reached. If aggregate demand is stimulated once again, the process will repeat itself, except this time the movement will be along the curve PC_2, and the inflation rate will rise to 6 percent. Once again employment will sink back to the natural rate as money wages catch up with the rising price level. But 6 percent now becomes the expected rate and the Phillips curve shifts once more, this time to the level PC_3.

The conclusion of the monetarists is quite clear: The unemployment rate can be kept below the natural rate only by a *continuously accelerating* inflation rate. The inflation and unemployment rates will follow the zigzag path marked *ABCDE*. What Figure 12–12 shows is that the short-term Phillips curve must move continuously upward for unemployment to remain at the level U_t. Since it is unlikely that a society will tolerate a continuous acceleration in the inflation rate for the sake of marginal gains in employment, the short-term Phillips curve should eventually stabilize. But when this happens, the unemployment rate will move back to its natural level and the inflation rate will be at a permanently higher level. In the figure this is 6 percent. This is the essence of the accelerationist thesis. In the view of Professor Friedman and other monetarists, the only way in which the unemployment rate can be permanently lowered is through structural changes that reduce the natural unemployment rate. These would include measures to improve the mobility of labor through better information systems relating to labor demand and supply, improved vocational and on-the-job training, less discrimination in hiring, the abolishment of legal minimum wages, and the reduction or elimination of import quotas and tariffs. Some of these measures tend to make the labor market more effective and others, such as the elimination of tariffs, put downward pressure on the domestic price level. It may be noted, too, that supporters of the Phillips curve hypothesis endorse some of these measures, for, as pointed out earlier, improvements in the skill and knowledge of the work force tend to push the curve to the left.

The Phillips Curve: Alternative Interpretations

The problem with both the early version of the Phillips curve and the accelerationist critique developed by the monetarists is that it does not adequately explain what happened in the 1970s or what has happened in the 1980s and 1990s. A more complete theoretical framework must take into account two additional variables: (1) the expected inflation rate and (2) the bargaining strength of workers. By adding these variables, we can develop an interpretation of the Phillips curve which is better suited to the facts of experience. We shall use the data in Table 12–5 for this purpose. This table shows (as did the original Phillips relationship) rates of increase in money wages and unemployment rates. The rates shown are annual averages at five-year intervals since 1960.

In *The General Theory* Keynes maintained that the wage bargains workers strike with their employers determine the level of nominal (money) wages in the economy. This is essentially correct, but wage bargains are always tempered by the general state of the economy, by whether labor markets are tight or loose. This is what the general Phillips curve analysis shows. But wage bargains also depend on the additional two factors mentioned above, namely, expected inflation and bargaining power. Thus, we can say that at any given time and given historical background of wage levels, the actual rate of increase in money wages (and hence prices) depends on an interaction between the following three factors: (1) the state of labor markets, (2) the expected inflation rate, and (3) the bargaining strength of workers. These are the loose ends that need to be pulled together to complete the basic theory of the price level.

Using the data in Table 12–5, we can draw on these factors to explain in a rough but reasonable way what happened over the long period from 1960

TABLE 12–5 Annual Average Rates of Money Wage* Increases and Unemployment at Five-Year Intervals: 1960–1994

Period	Rate of Money Wage Increase	Unemployment Rate
1960–1964	4.0%	5.7%
1965–1969	5.9	3.8
1970–1974	7.7	5.4
1975–1979	9.0	7.0
1980–1984	7.1	8.3
1985–1989	4.0	4.9
1990–1994	4.4	6.5

*Total hourly compensation as in Table 12–3.

Source: Economic Report of the President, 1995, pp. 321, 329.

through 1994. Between 1960 and 1969, as Figure 12–11 shows, there was a normal Phillips curve relationship in that the rate of money wage increases rose as the unemployment rate fell. The fit of the data in the 1960s was good because there was practically no inflation, labor markets gradually tightened as unemployment fell, and the bargaining strength of workers was high. In the 1970s, however, money wages rose as unemployment rose. This can be explained by bringing expected inflation rates into the wage bargain and by a continued strong bargaining position on the part of workers, even though economic conditions generally slackened. Since inflation generally accelerated in the 1970s, labor leaders included expected inflation in their wage bargaining; to assume otherwise, one would have to argue that trade union leaders were especially obtuse, hardly a realistic position. The evidence for continued bargaining strength is the fact that money wage gains ran well ahead of productivity gains (Table 12–3) all during the decade. Finally, we come to the 1980s and early 1990s, when there is a rough resumption of the normal Phillips curve relationship, although at levels of both inflation and unemployment far above those that prevailed in the 1960s. As compared with the 1970s, the rate of increase in money wages fell as the unemployment rate rose. The severity of the 1981–82 recession began to overwhelm the workers' bargaining strength—a development that continued through the 1980s and into the 1990s.

Recently a British economist and entrepreneur, Paul Ormerod, developed two new and novel interpretations of the Phillips curve, analyses that challenge Friedman and the acceleration hypothesis. Using U.S. inflation rate and unemployment data, Ormerod argues that over most of the post-World War II period, there has not been a single Phillips curve in the United States—a view also suggested by the data shown in Figure 12–11. What the United States has had over this period are at least three different Phillips curves, which have suddenly and markedly shifted their positions.[29] He reaches this conclusion by plotting in a scatter diagram the inflation rate in the current year against the unemployment rate in the prior year, and then noting that these observations fall into three different groups. Within these groups, the scatter points slope downward to the right, just as they are expected to do in a Phillips curve.

Figure 12–13 shows Ormerod's findings with the three groups he identifies: Group I, 1960–1970; Group II, 1974–1984; and Group III, 1985–1993. The years 1972 and 1973 do not fit readily into any of his three groups. The drastic shift upward in the array of points from Group I to Group II occurred because of the shock administered to the economy by the oil crisis of 1973–74. The shift downward to Group III from this level began in the mid-1980s, primarily as an aftereffect of the sharp recession that the Reagan administration put the economy through in the 1980s. This was the point made earlier in the discussion of bargaining strength and the Phillips curve. Ormerod concludes

---

[29] Paul Ormerod, *The Death of Economics* (London: Faber and Faber, 1994), pp. 127–131.

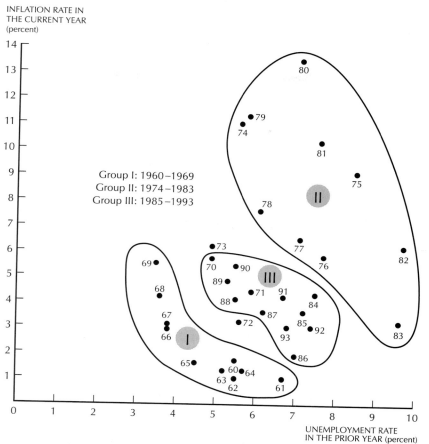

FIGURE 12–13   Inflation and Unemployment: 1960–1993. This scatter diagram plots the inflation rate in the current year against the unemployment rate in the prior year. Three scatter groups are shown, each of which has the Phillips curve characteristic of a negative relationship between the inflation rate and unemployment rate.

Sources: Paul Ormerod, *The Death of Economics* (London: Faber and Faber, 1994), and *Economic Report of the President,* 1995.

from these data that (1) Phillips curve relationships exist, but they are not stable over time; (2) because of this instability, the rate of inflation at any given *level* of unemployment is indeterminate; and (3) Friedman's natural rate of unemployment is also indeterminate, because it will shift with every shift in the short-term Phillips curve.

A second major point that Ormerod makes in his analysis is that the nature of the relationship between inflation and unemployment is not properly specified, either in the early Phillips curve models or by critics of these models. The underlying law that describes the link between inflation and unemployment is between *changes* in the rate of inflation and *changes* in the rate of

CHANGE IN THE INFLATION RATE
IN THE CURRENT YEAR (percentage points)

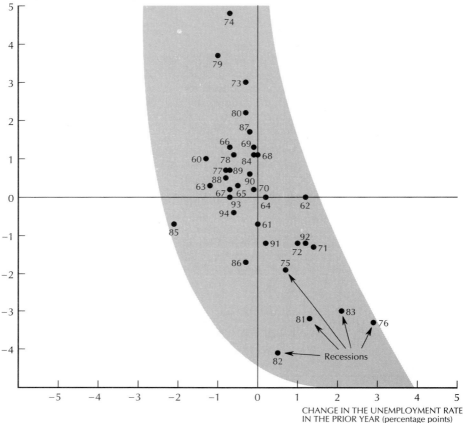

FIGURE 12–14   Changes in Inflation and Unemployment: 1960–1994. In this scatter diagram the percentage point change in the current year inflation rate is plotted against the percentage point change in unemployment in the prior year. The result is a scatter diagram with the negative Phillips curve relationship applicable to the entire period.

Sources: Paul Ormerod, *The Death of Economics,* and *Economic Report of the President,* 1995.

unemployment. Changes in this context mean percentage point changes. Figure 12–14 is a scatter diagram that links percentage point changes in the current inflation rate with percentage point changes in the unemployment rate in the prior year. In this diagram, the scatter of dots slopes unmistakably downward from the top left to the lower right, even though the scatter points do not lie on a curve with a perfect fit. Reductions in the unemployment rate are linked to increases in the inflation rate, and vice versa.[30]

What are the implications of Ormerod's analysis for economic policy?

[30] Ibid., p. 131.

First, governments should not ignore this linkage between inflation and unemployment, even though it cannot be reduced to a simple trade-off between the two, as was believed when the Phillips curve made its first appearance on the economic scene in the early 1960s. Governments must still reckon with the probability that reducing unemployment will raise the inflation rate.

Second, the primary aim of anti-inflation policy should be to shift the economy from a higher to a lower inflation-unemployment path—to shift the conventional Phillips curve downward. How can this be done? It is possible that draconian policy measures like a severe deflation might do the job, but a better way is to seek a social consensus that puts emphasis on the rights and responsibilities of both employees and employers in the matter of changes in money wages and prices. Germany, following OPEC's first oil price hike, offers an example of such a consensus. The real income of German workers fell because of OPEC, but German workers did not press for immediate wage increases, which in turn would have led to an inflationary spiral of still higher costs and higher prices. They did not do so because of a broad social contract—sometimes called the "social wage"—formed after World War II in which workers have the right to be consulted about a whole range of matters affecting their lives, including involvement in the decision-making processes in industry—a policy that is foreign to Britain and the United States.[31]

Incomes Policy in the 1960s

The emergence of the Phillips curve hypothesis in the early 1960s gave a strong impetus to the development of incomes policies as complements to the older and more traditional fiscal and monetary approaches to influencing the level of output and employment. In its essentials, an *incomes policy* deals with the creation of mechanisms through which money wage and price increases can be held within tolerable levels as an economy approaches full employment. The lesson of the Phillips curve analysis is that, unless something is done about the matter, the economy cannot expect to get to full employment without high—and probably unacceptable—rates of inflation.

In the United States the first serious attempt to develop an incomes policy was made in 1962, when the President's Council of Economic Advisers established a series of guideposts for noninflationary wage and price behavior.[32] The principles of the guideposts were relatively simple. The council asserted that if gains in wages and other forms of money incomes were to be noninflationary, then they should be no greater, on the average, than the annual average gain in productivity (output per worker-hour) for the economy as a whole. If all increases in money income were held within this limit, then factor costs per unit of output for the economy as a whole would be stabilized,

[31] Ibid., p. 134.

[32] *Economic Report of the President, 1962.*

and any tendency for market forces to bring about an increase in the general price level would be eliminated. In its analysis of the situation, the Council of Economic Advisers put primary stress on increases in money wages, since they account for 65 to 70 percent of the national income. The principle, though, could be applied to all forms of money income, including profits. At the time the guidepost policy was proclaimed, the council believed that productivity was rising on the average at a rate of 3.5 to 4 percent a year; hence, wages and other forms of income could advance at this rate without being inflationary.

How well did the guidepost policy work? From 1962 through 1965 it was moderately successful, as the data in Table 12–3 indicate. In these years, annual average percentage increases in compensation per worker-hour (wages and salaries plus employer contributions to social security and private benefit plans) were only slightly higher than the annual average gain in productivity, with consequent mild effects on unit labor costs. But beginning in mid-1966, when the unemployment rate fell below 4 percent of the civilian labor force and the expenditure buildup for Vietnam accelerated, the guidepost policy broke down as pressures mounted for wage and salary adjustments in excess of productivity gains. Since 1966 wage and salary adjustments have shown very little relationship to productivity changes.

One reason for the breakdown of the guidepost policy was the fact that the government had no effective means for forcing business and industry to adhere to productivity guidelines in wage and salary settlements. The government's power was largely limited to persuasion and exhortation, which derisively was termed *jawboning*. This apparently worked only as long as organized labor and the management of large and powerful business firms were willing to adhere voluntarily to the guidelines, a condition that rapidly evaporated when the economy began to heat up as a consequence of the expanded war in Vietnam.

Incomes Policy in the 1970s

Although the Nixon administration came to power in 1969 firmly convinced that an incomes policy was unnecessary and that inflation could be brought under control by the delicate applications of monetary and fiscal policy, in mid-1971 it completely reversed its stance. On August 15, 1971, the president announced to a startled nation his New Economic Policy, a program which, among other things, contained a 90-day absolute freeze on wages, prices, and rents. This date marks the beginning of the nation's most comprehensive and longest experiment with an incomes policy involving strong controls over wages and prices backed by the enforcement power of the federal government, an experiment that ran its full course by April 1974. Authority for the control system came from the Economic Stabilization Act, first passed in 1970 and extended in 1972 for another two years. The act has since expired, and thus a president no longer has the authority to impose wage and price controls without going to the Congress and asking for such authority.

Incomes policy during the Nixon administration was a rather hectic affair, evolving through four phases, as they came to be known to the public. The headline-catching element of phase I was a 90-day freeze on wages and prices, but the package also included tax cuts, a slowdown in federal spending and employment, and a devaluation of the dollar in foreign exchange markets. In November 1971, phase II went into effect. The freeze was lifted, but mandatory guidelines were set for wage and price increases. Wage increases of 5.5 percent and price increases of 2.5 percent were allowed. Phase II lasted until January 1973, at which time, to the public's great surprise, the administration announced phase III, a system of voluntary controls. The voluntary control program was short-lived, for in June 1973 the Nixon administration made another sharp reversal of policy, proclaiming a new 60-day freeze on prices. This was a stopgap measure, since in mid-July 1973, phase IV was put in place. This was a return to a tougher system, of mandatory controls administered on a selective basis. Phase IV ended in April 1974. By that time public support for Nixon's experiment in peacetime wage and price controls had largely evaporated.

Was the Nixon incomes policy successful? As one would suspect, the answer is mixed. A close examination of the path of the consumer price index over the control period suggests two things. First, it is apparent that the peak of the inflation induced by the Vietnam buildup (1966–69) was reached in January 1970, about 20 months before the August 1971 freeze was imposed. The reason for this was the recession of 1970, which followed the economic slowdown measures taken by the Nixon administration in 1969. The second point is that price data show that prices began to move strongly upward before phase II was dropped in favor of voluntary controls. They surged even more, however, after the controls were dropped in January 1973. Price and wage controls were applied in such an unpredictable, erratic fashion that a fair judgment on their effectiveness is nearly impossible. A cynic might point out they contained prices quite effectively during most of 1972, and this was helpful to Nixon's reelection campaign.

The last experiment in the United States with an incomes policy without actual controls came during the Carter administration. In its first year in office (1977) the administration, preferring to concentrate on bringing down the unemployment rate, paid little attention to prices. At the beginning of 1978, however, the administration began to show concern with inflation, as the rate of increase in the consumer price index went from 5.8 percent in 1976 to 6.5 percent in 1977. Consequently, in his 1978 economic report, President Carter called on the business community and the nation's workers to participate in a voluntary program to decelerate the rate of price and wage increases. No standards were established, but it was hoped that both wage and price increases would be kept below the rate at which they had risen in the previous year. The latter did not happen; by midyear consumer prices were advancing at near double-digit rates. Consequently, in October the administration announced a new program that included explicit wage and price standards. Wages and fringe benefits were to rise no more than 7 percent per year, and business firms were requested to keep their price increases to a rate 1½ percentage points below the annual average rate of increase in their prices during the period 1966 to 1977. Like the Johnson administration guideposts, the program was voluntary, except that the Carter administration sought to use the federal government's purchasing as a means to favor firms that complied with the program. There is no evidence that this approach was particularly successful. Furthermore, it aroused considerable resentment in the business community.

The Future of Incomes Policies

Do incomes policies have a future? In spite of the less than satisfactory experience to date in this country with incomes policies, it remains doubtful that modern economies can avoid indefinitely facing the fact that inflation has become endemic in the system and heats up once a recovery is underway. During the last year of the Reagan expansion (1990), consumer prices rose by 5.4 percent, from a low of a 1.9 percent gain in 1986.[33]

A major failure of post-World War II mainstream economics was not recognizing that a serious inflationary problem could arise out of the combination of sustained full employment and the concentration of economic power in strategically important areas of the economy. As the late Thomas Balogh, a leading British economist once pointed out, market power lodged in a giant corporation enables it to shift readily onto prices the burden of increased wages, which are determined in many instances under bilateral monopoly relationships.[34] What is called for under these circumstances and in the absence of any fundamental institutional changes that modify power relationships in the economy is a workable incomes policy.

An incomes policy is easy to define but difficult to implement. Essentially an incomes policy involves finding the means to keep increases in money incomes within the bounds set by productivity gains. Ideally, an incomes policy should encompass *all* forms of money income, including profits, but as a practical matter a workable incomes policy will probably be limited to changes in money wages. However, since wages make up nearly three-fourths of the national income and are thus the major element in production costs, an incomes policy built around wage income alone has the potential to control inflation.

Three approaches to the problem are worthy of mention, although there

---

[33] *Economic Report of the President,* 1995, p. 345.

[34] Thomas Balogh, ''Is Keynes Dead?'' *The New Republic,* June 7, 1980, p. 16.

are no immediate prospects for any being enacted as law. Two come under the rubric of tax-based incomes policies—or TIPs for short—because they propose using the tax system to restrain wage and price increases. The third approach involves a market-based anti-inflation program, known by the acronym MAP.

One TIP proposal was developed jointly by Henry C. Wallich, formerly a member of the Board of Governors of the Federal Reserve System, and the late Sidney Weintraub, professor of economics at the University of Pennsylvania. The other came from the late Arthur M. Okun of the Brookings Institution who was also chairperson of President Carter's Council of Economic Advisers. A MAP strategy was developed jointly by the late Abba Lerner and David Colander of Middlebury College.[35]

The two TIP plans are basically similar, except that the Wallich-Weintraub plan operates on a penalty principle, whereas the Okun plan operates on the basis of a reward. Both use taxes as the mechanism of control, but both also operate through the price system and thereby avoid the charge that any direct intervention into the wage- and price-setting process will impair efficiency and distort the allocation of resources. Both plans claim to be relatively inexpensive to administer because of the way in which they are tied into the tax system.

Keynes's belief that in the long run the prime factor in inflation is the relationship between money wages and efficiency, that is productivity, provides the theoretical jumping-off place for the Wallich-Weintraub approach. In their view, wage settlements in excess of productivity gains plus markup pricing in the economy's oligopolistic core are the sources of inflation. The remedy is to persuade corporate managements to resist wage settlements that exceed some set of noninflationary guidelines. To achieve this objective, Wallich and Weintraub would establish a system whereby the corporate tax rate is automatically increased for any firm whose wage settlements were in excess of the allowable amount. Suppose, for example, that noninflationary wage increases were pegged at 4 percent, but corporation X concluded a collective agreement with its workers for a 6 percent wage increase. The corporation's tax liability would then be increased automatically by some multiple of the amount by which the wage settlement exceeded the allowable increase. If this multiple were 4, then there would be a surcharge of 8 percent (4 × the 2 percent excess) added to the corporation's normal tax liability. The amount of the multiple would depend on how severe the government wanted the penalty to be for a wage settlement in excess of the guidelines. Since it is hoped that a TIP approach would lead to settlements within the guidelines, the administrative costs would be small. Neither organized labor nor business management has shown any great enthusiasm for such a plan. This, perhaps,

---

[35] For details on these and other plans, see Hugh Rockoff, *Drastic Measures: A History of Wage and Price Controls in America* (New York: Cambridge University Press, 1984).

is one of the major drawbacks to the Wallich-Weintraub approach, since the political support of both labor and management will be necessary to get any incomes policy put into effect.

The Okun plan is also based on the tax system, but rather than penalize firms that exceed the noninflationary guidelines for wage settlements, it would reward both workers and firms that followed the guidelines. At the start of the year the government would announce acceptable rates of increase for both money wages and prices. If a firm and its workers adhered to these guidelines during the year, the workers would receive a rebate equal to a certain percentage of their wage or salary, and the firm would receive a tax rebate calculated as a percentage of its tax liabilities. When Professor Okun first unveiled his scheme in 1977, he suggested that for 1978 an appropriate wage increase would be 6 percent and the price increase 4 percent. Workers who participated would get 1.5 percent of their wage or salary as a rebate, up to a maximum of $225, and firms would get a rebate equal to 5 percent of their tax liabilities.[36] These figures would have to be set anew each year, depending on inflationary conditions at the time the decision was made and the outlook for the coming year. The Carter administration tried unsuccessfully to develop a version of this type TIP with its proposal for real wage insurance. Employees would have received a tax credit if their wages rose no faster than a stipulated standard.

The Lerner-Colander MAP strategy would ration the right of business firms to raise wages, and thereby keep overall wage increases within the guideposts set by productivity gains. It would do this by having the government issue transferable coupons that a firm would need in order to raise wages. The money value of the coupons issued would be limited to the amount by which the economy's overall wage bill could increase without being inflationary— that is, as determined by productivity growth. Individual firms that wanted to raise wages beyond the productivity guidelines would have to bid in the marketplace for the coupons they needed for their wage increases.

A final comment on the incomes policy approach to inflation control is in order. The arithmetic behind this approach is irrefutable. If money incomes in all forms continue to exceed productivity gains, then, on the average, costs of production, especially labor costs, per unit produced will rise and inflation is inevitable. Consequently, the basic idea of a set of guidelines (or guideposts) that seek, on the average, to keep wage and salary incomes in line with productivity gains is sound. The real rub comes from the fact that it means that the *relative* income position of every group in the economy remains unchanged. If there is satisfaction with the existing distribution of income, then such a policy will work. But if such satisfaction does not exist, it will break down, once groups find that they can begin to exercise whatever economic power they can muster to improve their standing relative to the rest of

---

[36] Arthur M. Okun, "The Great Stagflation Swamp," *Challenge*, November–December 1977, pp. 6–13.

the economy. The fundamental lesson, then, that we should draw from our experience to date with an incomes policy is that no such policy can hope to succeed, no matter how it is designed, unless the income distribution issue is addressed at the same time.

Summary

1. Inflation remains one of the unsolved economic problems of market capitalism, as no modern industrial nation has been able to achieve both full employment and a low rate of inflation. Over the long term (since 1750), inflation has not been the norm for the U.S. economy, but since World War II the price level has risen almost continuously.

2. Inflation is bad because of its arbitrary and uneven impact on different groups in our society, especially those on fixed incomes and with little economic power. Inflation redistributes income and wealth in an unfair manner.

3. Economists are not in agreement on the causes of inflation, which may be many and varied, but they do agree on at least two approaches for understanding the inflation problem. These approaches are described as demand-pull and cost-push. They provide a framework in which forces responsible for inflation that originate on either the demand side or the cost side of the process can be examined.

4. The theory of the price level developed by Keynes in *The General Theory* argued that the price level depends on (1) the scale of output, which means diminishing returns play a key role, and (2) the remuneration of the factors of production. Thus, Keynes argues for the microeconomic roots of inflation; he asserts that the general price level can be explained by the same forces that explain how individual (or relative) prices are determined. In the long run, the level of prices depends on the relationship between productivity growth and increases in money wages. Empirical data on wages, prices, productivity, and output support the Keynesian view of how prices are determined overall, in both the short and the long runs.

5. The Phillips curve was developed in the 1950s and shows the relationship between the unemployment rate and the rate of increase in money wages (or the rate of increase in the price level). Until simultaneous inflation and unemployment at high rates for both appeared in the 1970s, economists generally thought that the Phillips curve provided guidance for a satisfactory trade-off between inflation and unemployment. This notion disappeared in the 1970s, especially in the face of challenges by monetarists to the effect that no such trade-off existed. Alternative interpretations of the Phillips curve relationship, which stress expected inflation rates and the bargaining strength of workers as well as current economic conditions, provide a reasonable interpretation of the events of the 1960 to 1993 period.

6. Out of the Phillips curve analysis and other theoretical developments in the post-World War II period, the idea of an incomes policy emerged. Such a policy is directed at keeping the rate of increase in money incomes, especially wage income, in line with productivity gains. The Kennedy-Johnson and the Carter administrations attempted an incomes policy, but without notable success. The Nixon administration experimented with mandatory wage-price controls from mid-1971 to early 1974 with mixed results. No administration subsequently has shown any interest in an incomes policy.

Growth, Fluctuations, and Public Policy

13 Productivity and Growth

W E TURN OUR ATTENTION in this part to some of the principles and problems of a growing economy. Up to this point we have examined output, employment, and the price level on the assumption of a relatively fixed productive capacity. This chapter shifts the analysis from an essentially static to a dynamic approach, seeking to understand what happens over time when there are continuous changes in both the economy's productive capacity and in its aggregate demand function. Chapter 14 will take up the fact that in the real world economic growth is never smooth, that, in fact, the economy moves up and down over time. This is the world of fluctuations in output, prices, and employment, the world of the business cycle. In Chapter 15 we shall take a long, backward glance to see how macroeconomic policy has unfolded and worked in the sixty years since Keynes published *The General Theory*.

We begin by approaching the problem of economic growth from two perspectives. First, we shall look at the supply side of the matter. This means we examine the basic determinants of the economy's productive capacity and how that capacity may change over time. We first encountered this issue in Chapter 2 when we discussed the relationship between employment and output. Now we shall explore this in depth. The analysis will focus, first, on the production function concept, which provides us with the formal, theoretical basis for identifying the sources of growth in the modern economy, and, second, on the concept of potential output, which provides a practical and useful way to translate the theoretical basis for output into a measured magnitude. In connection with this part of our discussion, we shall also examine what has been called the *productivity crisis* of the U.S. economy. This pertains to the falling rate of growth in U.S. productivity.

Second, if the productive capacity of the economy is growing over time, how can the use of this capacity—especially its full-employment use—be assured? This is the basic theoretical problem posed by growth, one that has been looked at in different ways in the post-World War II era. The quite simple but nonetheless fundamental fact about such an economy is that the economy's productive potential is utilized *only* if demand (actual or expected) exists for the goods and services produced. If there is no market for what is being produced, a market economy will not work—a point often neglected by supply-side theorists. Resources and technology make output possible, but it is through demand that potential output is transformed into actual output.

The Nature of Economic Growth

Economic growth is the expansion of a nation's capability to produce the goods and services its people want. Since the productive capacity of an economy depends basically on the quantity and quality of its resources as well as on its level of technological attainment, economic growth involves the process of expanding and improving these determinants of productive capacity. Actual growth depends not only on the change in the economy's potential for production, but also on the extent to which that potential is utilized. Economic growth involves, in other words, an increase over time in the actual output of goods and services as well as an increase in the economy's capability to produce goods and services.

Interest in economic growth stems from our concern with the material welfare of human beings. There is no acceptable set of criteria for measurement of such a subjective matter as welfare, but there is general agreement that material welfare (or well-being), in the last analysis, depends on the availability of goods and services. A rising level of economic well-being for any society requires an expansion in its output of goods and services.

If we are interested in economic growth because of its significance for our material well-being, then what counts is not just an increase in capacity and output per se, but output per capita—the availability of goods and services per person. It is reasonable to talk of an improvement in the material well-being of a people only if, over time, each person has a growing volume of goods and services at his or her disposal. Thus, the measure of economic growth that is most meaningful is the level of real output per capita. Analysis of economic growth on a per-person basis requires that we take into account not only changes in a nation's productive potential and its use of that potential, but also changes in its population. If population grows at a faster rate than either output or capacity, no improvement in the average standard of material well-being on a per capita basis is possible (see Table 13–1).

TABLE 13–1   Growth Trends in the U.S. Economy, 1839–1994 (average percentage increase per year)

	(1) Entire Period	(2)	(3)	(4)	(5)	(6)
		40-Year Subperiods				
	1839–1959	1839–79	1879–1919	1919–59	1960–94	1970–94
1. GNP/GDP in constant prices	3.7	4.3	3.7	3.0	3.0	2.5
2. Population	2.0	2.7	1.9	1.3	1.1	1.0
3. Per capita GNP/ GDP in constant prices	1.6	1.6	1.8	1.6	2.0	1.5
4. Price level	1.2	−0.2	1.9	1.4	5.3	5.8

Note: 1839 through 1959 are for GNP, while the data from 1960 through 1993 are for GDP.

Sources: Joint Economic Committee, Congress of the United States, *Staff Report on Employment, Growth and Price Levels,* 1960, p. 34; *Economic Report of the President,* 1995, pp. 277, 311, 345.

Why is economic growth important? Growth certainly is not an end in itself. It is a means to an end. It provides a society with the means—resources plus goods and services—whereby it can do more things for itself and for its citizens. Growth makes more goods and services available to consumers for their private use and more resources available to the public sector for its purposes and responsibilities. The ways in which private citizens and governments use the added output may be wise or foolish, but one cannot gainsay the fact that without economic growth prospects for a better life for everyone would be much grimmer. In the developed nations of the West, standards of life are affluent enough so that some of the population can afford the luxury of discussing whether or not more growth is desirable. But for most of humankind this is not possible. The overwhelming proportion of the world's people live in or on the edge of grinding poverty. For them growth is an absolute imperative if they are to survive.

The Growth Record of the U.S. Economy

A brief review of the growth record of the U.S. economy shows that over the long run its performance has been highly impressive. The overall record of growth for the period 1839 through 1993 is summarized in Table 13–1. The data for 1839 through 1959 are taken from an analysis of the U.S. economy prepared in 1960 for the Joint Economic Committee of the Congress. Separate data for the periods 1960 through 1994 and 1970 through 1994 are shown in columns 5 and 6 of the table. They are taken from the 1995 *Economic Report of the President.*

As the table shows, the data for 1839 through 1959 are broken down into three subperiods, each of 40 years length. The average annual rate of growth for the real GNP of the U.S. economy over the whole 120-year period (1839 through 1959) was 3.7 percent, a record unmatched by any other country for so long a period. These data also show that there was some slowing down in the rate of total real output in the third period, although when the data are reduced to a per capita basis, there does not appear to be any significant change in the long-term trends. Real GNP rose at an annual average rate of 4.3 percent during the first 40-year period (1839 through 1879). In the period 1879 through 1919 the growth rate fell to 3.7 percent per year, and then for the next 40 years (1919 through 1959) declined further to an annual average rate of 3.0 percent. The per capita data do not show the same long-term decline. During the first 40-year period GNP per capita in constant prices increased at an annual average rate of 1.6 percent. This period, though, was the one in which population increased most rapidly; population grew at an annual average rate of 2.7 percent, compared to 1.9 percent in the second 40-year period and 1.3 percent in the third 40-year period. The slower rate of population growth is reflected in the fact that real GNP per capita in constant prices actually increased at a more rapid rate in the second 40-year period (1.8 percent). During the third 40-year period (1919 through 1959) the rate declined to an annual average of 1.6 percent, the average of the whole 120-year period. This period includes the Great Depression years.

And what of the more recent period, 1960 through 1994? The data do suggest some shifts in the long-term trends, although it is, perhaps, premature to say that they are permanent. More likely they reflect in part some of the turbulence of the last three decades. Real GDP grew more slowly in 1960 through 1994 than the long-term historic average and still more slowly in 1970 through 1994, owing in part to four recessions. The most dramatic change is in the price level, as its rate of growth is significantly above the average for any of the pre-1960 periods covered by the data in the table. This clearly reflects both the severity of the 1970s inflation and its uniqueness compared to the nation's historical experience. The growth rate for population continued to decline—a development in line with past experience. Finally, real per capita GDP rose from 1960 through 1994 at a 2.0 percent annual rate, but fell back 1.5 percent in the 1970 through 1994 period. Was the gain in 1960 through 1994 real? Given the fact of an unpopular war and the social turbulence of the 1960s and early 1970s, one would, indeed, be bold to assert that this increase represented real gains in social and economic welfare.

Economic Growth and the Production Function

In Chapter 2, the idea of the production function was introduced, a concept which offers a useful way to organize thinking about the sources of growth in the modern economy. In a formal, theoretical sense, the production function

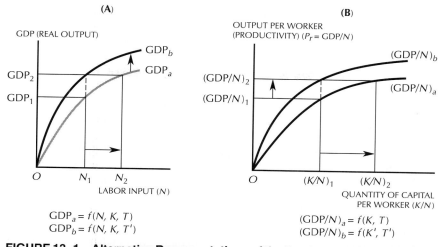

(A)

GDP (REAL OUTPUT)

GDP$_b$

GDP$_a$

GDP$_2$

GDP$_1$

O N_1 N_2

LABOR INPUT (N)

$$GDP_a = f(N, K, T)$$
$$GDP_b = f(N, K, T')$$

(B)

OUTPUT PER WORKER
(PRODUCTIVITY) ($P_r = $ GDP/N)

(GDP/N)$_b$

(GDP/N)$_2$

(GDP/N)$_a$

(GDP/N)$_1$

O (K/N)$_1$ (K/N)$_2$

QUANTITY OF CAPITAL
PER WORKER (K/N)

$$(GDP/N)_a = f(K, T)$$
$$(GDP/N)_b = f(K', T')$$

FIGURE 13–1   Alternative Representations of the Production Function. The production function can be represented as a relationship between labor input (N) and output (GDP) as in part A, or a relationship between the quantity of capital per worker (K/N) and the output per worker (GDP/N) as in part B.

sets forth the relationship between the quantities of resources used during a period of time and the output produced during the same period of time. Conceptually, the relationship applies to a single commodity or service or to the entire economy. Our concern is with the latter, namely, the relationship between the domestic output (GDP) and the resources needed to produce that output.

In the form presented originally in Chapter 2 (see pages 64–66), the production function showed how output (GDP) varied in response to changing levels of employment (N), given known values for the economy's stock of capital equipment (K), and the state of technology (T). Such a production function is shown in part A of Figure 13–1. As more people are employed (N), the level of output (GDP) rises, but not proportionally because the principle of diminishing productivity applies when only one input varies. In the diagram this is reflected in the gradual leveling off of the output curve. Note that the diagram shows that there are two possible ways in which output can be increased from GDP$_1$ to GDP$_2$. The first is simply by increasing the quantity of labor used from N_1 to N_2. This, of course, reflects the basic relationship represented by the production function. The other way comes from a shift upward in the entire function—from the curve GDP$_a$ to GDP$_b$ in the diagram—a development which comes about through either a change in the stock of capital, an improvement in technology, or some combination of both. An upward shift in the production function means that the economy has become more efficient—that there has been an improvement in the productivity of labor—since more output is being produced with the same quantity of labor. This is the basic meaning of an improvement in efficiency.

The foregoing represents a standard way of depicting the production function. Another useful way is to describe it in terms of a relationship between the quantity of capital per worker (K/N) and the output per worker (GDP/N). This approach puts the focus on a key concept, namely, the average productivity of labor. The productivity of labor is a convenient measure of the efficiency with which labor is being used in production. We must be cautious in the use of this concept, for it does not simply measure the average skill or efficiency of the individual worker as such; rather, it is a useful way to express in terms of the input of a single resource, namely labor, all the factors that have a bearing on the efficiency of the economic system. Output per worker can be measured on a worker-hour basis, when GDP is divided by total hours worked by the labor force, or on a worker-year basis, when GDP is divided simply by the number of people at work in a given year. In concept both are the same; only the time unit differs. If P_r stands for *output per worker-year,* then the economy's productive capacity is equal to $P_r \times N'$, the economy's fully employed labor force. We shall use this approach later in calculating a measure of the economy's potential output for different periods (see Table 13–3, page 516).

A key factor in determining worker productivity as defined above is the amount of capital per worker (K/N). If we think of capital essentially as tools—basically this is the nature of capital—then, in general, the more capital (tools) workers on the average have at their disposal, the more efficient each worker will be. It is reasonable, therefore, to conclude that the output per worker per unit of time will increase as the quantity of capital available per worker increases. This observation permits us to express the production function as a relationship between capital per worker (which is also called the ''capital-labor ratio'') and the productivity of labor. This version of the production function is shown in part B of Figure 13–1. On the vertical axis worker productivity is shown, and on the horizontal axis capital per worker. Note that the curve is similar in shape to the curve depicting how total output varies as the quantity of labor used in production increases (part A of Figure 13–1). The reason again is diminishing productivity. Worker productivity will increase as the capital-labor ratio increases, but not without limit. As long as all other resources and technology remain fixed, the gains in worker productivity attained by increasing the ratio of capital to labor will eventually level off. Two curves are also shown in part B of Figure 13–1, and they indicate that output per worker can be increased from GDP/N_1 to GDP/N_2 in one of two ways: The first is simply by increasing the capital-labor ratio from K/N_1 to K/N_2, a process precisely analogous to increasing employment from N_1 to N_2, as depicted in part A of Figure 13–1. Alternatively, the increase may come through an upward shift in the entire production function, a result that can come about only through an increase in the efficiency of capital, given no change in the quantity of labor being employed. This represents technological change, which has its impact primarily on the efficiency with which capital is used in the economy.

Theoretical Sources of Economic Growth

One important result that flows from the foregoing discussion of the production function is a precise identification of the primary sources of growth in the modern economy, of which there are basically three. First, there is growth in the supply of labor. As first discussed, the production function shows that output will increase as more labor is employed, *other things being equal*. The latter applies primarily to capital and technology. If we put this into the context of increases in the economy's productive capacity, designated by the symbol Q, then changes in the size of the labor force are an important source for such increases, again if we assume the stock of capital and technology to be a given.

A second major source of growth in the modern economy is physical capital—the tools with which the labor force has to work. Our analysis of the production function concept has shown that, as long as capital is growing more rapidly than the labor force, worker productivity will rise, even though at a decreasing rate because of diminishing returns. Other things being equal, however, this means that normally an increase in the capital stock will increase the economy's productive potential. As we have seen from our discussion of investment spending in Chapter 8, the factors that influence spending for capital goods in a market economy are both numerous and complex. But there is one basic point to be kept in mind: Ultimately it is the expected profitability of capital goods which determines whether or not they will be produced and used. This is true whether we approach the question from the capacity side or the demand side. More capital is created only through spending for capital goods by entrepreneurs, and more spending for capital goods takes place only if the profit prospects for the new capital are favorable.

The third and final source of growth is technological change, depicted in both types of the production function shown in Figure 13–1 by shifts in the functions. Technological change means that more output can be produced with the same quantity of labor, given the stock of capital (K), or that more goods and services can be produced with no change in capital per worker (K/N). To put the matter somewhat differently, technical progress means that more output can be produced with the same inputs. Like the determinants of investment spending, which adds to the capital stock, the determinants of technological change are many and complex. But two factors are of particular importance. The first is research and development, that is, the deliberate employment of scientific and engineering talent and other resources for the discovery and implementation of new knowledge. The second is capital. For analytical purposes it is useful, as we have done, to identify capital as a source of growth distinct from technological change. But in the real world this distinction is often blurred, if not impossible to make. The reason is that technical changes do not take place in the abstract; frequently, they must be embodied in new equipment if they are to become a viable part of the real-world economy.

Sources of Growth in the U.S. Economy

Now that we have examined the theoretical sources of growth for an advanced market economy, let us turn to this question: What do we know about the actual sources of growth for the U.S. economy, including their relative importance? A number of economists have investigated this question, but none more extensively than the late Edward F. Denison, long-time Senior Fellow with the Brookings Institution in Washington, D.C. In Table 13–2, adapted from Denison's study, the major sources of economic growth in the United States are identified. The data cover three periods, a 53-year span from 1929 to 1982 and two subperiods: 1948 to 1973, which is typical of the postwar "Age of Keynes," and 1973 to 1982, which reflects the upheavals and recessions of the 1970s, including the oil price increases in 1974 and 1979.

The first line in the table shows the annual average rate of growth for potential *real* national income for each of the periods. *Real* national income differs from *real* GNP because it excludes depreciation and indirect business taxes. For each period the growth rates shown are broken down, in terms of percentage points, into basic sources of growth. These consist of either more input of labor and capital or advances in output per unit of input (productivity). The latter reflects technological changes. These percentage points are then converted (columns 3, 5, and 7) into percentage figures showing the relative importance of each source, using the annual average rate of growth appropriate to the period as 100 percent. What do Denison's figures tell us about the sources of growth in the U.S. economy? For the longer period (1929 to 1982) slightly more than 63 percent of the growth in potential output came from using more resources, mostly labor. Somewhat surprisingly, only about 17 percent of growth is explained by the use of more capital, although we should not forget that the longer period includes the depression years, a time when capital investment was drastically curtailed. Improved productivity accounted for 36.6 percent of growth during this period, most of which was due to advances in knowledge. Better use of resources and economies of scale are

TABLE 13–2 Sources of Growth of Potential Real National Income in the United States: 1929–1982 (in annual average rates and in percentage distribution)

(1) *Source of* *Growth*	*(2)* *1929–82*	*(3)* *Percentage* *Distribution*	*(4)* *1948–73*	*(5)* *Percentage* *Distribution*	*(6)* *1973–82*	*(7)* *Percentage* *Distribution*
Rate of growth of real national income	3.20%	100.0%	3.89%	100.0%	2.61%	100.0%
Total factor inputs	2.03	63.4	2.23	57.3	2.53	96.9
1. Labor	1.49	46.6	1.46	37.5	1.86	71.3
2. Capital	0.54	16.8	0.77	19.8	0.67	25.6
3. Productivity	1.17	36.6	1.66	42.7	0.08	3.1

Source: Edward F. Denison, *Trends in American Economic Growth, 1929–1982* (Washington, D.C.: Brookings Institution, 1985), p. 112. Denison's study uses GNP, not GDP.

included under this category; they fit the concept of an improved technology since the latter means using resources more efficiently.

If we shift to the Age of Keynes period (1948 to 1973), the most important development is the increased role that technological change (improved productivity) played in the growth process. In this period, 42.7 percent of the growth in the economy's potential was due to greater output per unit of input, as contrasted to 36.6 percent for the longer period (1929 to 1982). Because of the overlap between the two periods, the contribution of advances in knowledge to growth—the knowledge explosion of the post-World War II period— was actually much greater after World War II than is indicated by these figures. In the period before the war (1929 to 1941), Denison found that improved productivity was responsible for only 28.6 percent of the growth in the economy's productive potential.[1] What is reflected in these figures is the gradual but continued transformation of the modern market economy in the direction that Harvard sociologist Daniel Bell describes as a "post-industrial society." The latter, according to Bell, is one in which improvements in knowledge increasingly loom more important in explaining growth than simply the use of more labor and capital.[2] This is a complicated matter since advances in knowledge also transform the nature of both capital and labor as resources (factor inputs)—a transformation that cannot be readily measured statistically. Nonetheless, it is the direction in which Denison's statistical findings point; this means that now and in the future research and development activity and education are of critical importance for continued growth in the economy's productive capacity.

After 1973, however, this process in which improved productivity was a source of economic growth slowed dramatically. It is this development that reflects the nation's productivity crisis, a topic we turn to shortly. What Denison's statistics show for the 1973 to 1982 period is that productivity as a source of potential growth for the economy dropped drastically. In these years it accounted for a mere 3.1 percent of the growth in output. The growth in output that took place in the period was due overwhelmingly to more inputs of labor and capital. Most of this came from labor, as added workers accounted for 71.3 percent of the growth and added capital accounted for only 25.6 percent. The total of these two inputs explained 96.9 percent of the growth in the economy's real national income in this period. After 1982 there was some improvement in the nation's productivity growth—a fact reflected in the 1994 *Economic Report of the President.* For the period 1973 to 1992, the President's Council of Economic Advisers found that productivity accounted for 17.7 percent of the annual growth rate, while inputs of labor and capital were responsible for 86.3 percent. The council also found that the annual real growth rate of productivity during this period was 1.0 percent.[3]

[1] Edward F. Denison, *Accounting for Slower Growth* (Washington, D.C.: Brookings Institution, 1978), p. 105.

[2] Daniel Bell, *The Coming of Post-Industrial Society* (New York: Basic Books, 1973), p. 112.

[3] *Economic Report of the President*, 1994, pp. 44, 323.

Both the Denison and council findings show a substantial drop in the rate of productivity growth after 1973, which reflects the nation's productivity crisis.

Measuring Potential Output

In a practical sense the most important use made of the foregoing theoretical and empirical material on the production function is in the form of statistical estimates of the economy's potential output. Two questions are involved here: (1) How is potential output measured? (2) What use has been made of measures of potential output?

It was in the early 1960s that the Kennedy administration through its Council of Economic Advisers started using potential GNP as a key policymaking tool. The Kennedy council used GNP, as the government did not shift to GDP until 1991. Basically two techniques have been used for the calculation of potential GNP. In its 1962 *Economic Report,* the Kennedy Council of Economic Advisers computed potential GNP by extrapolating a trend rate of growth for *real* GNP from a year which, in their judgment, represented a full-employment output. For the latter, the Kennedy Council used a 4 percent unemployment rate. The trend rate of growth used in their extrapolation was 3 1/2 percent, the real average rate of growth of the economy in the post-Korean War period. Mid-1955 was chosen as the starting point for the extrapolation, since unemployment stood at 4 percent at that time.[4] The result was the chart shown in Figure 13–2, which plots potential GNP through 1963, as determined by the method just described, and actual output through most of 1961. The basic point of this statistical exercise was to demonstrate the existence of a growing *gap* between the economy's potential and actual output, a gap in output caused by the failure of the economy to achieve and maintain a full-employment (4 percent unemployment) output level. The gap analysis developed in the 1962 *Economic Report* set the stage for the administration's later package of tax cuts, designed to stimulate growth, discussed fully in Chapter 15.

The alternative method for calculating potential output, a method favored by subsequent councils, adheres more closely to the theoretical material discussed earlier. Basically, this method involves multiplying the average productivity of labor (P_r)—measured on either a worker-hour or worker-year basis—by the fully employed labor force. In equation form, this is

$$\text{GDP}' = P_r \times N' . \tag{13–1}$$

In the equation, GDP′ represents potential output, P_r represents labor productivity, and N' represents the fully employed labor force. The values for P_r and N' will depend on assumptions made about the rate of technological growth, which govern the annual average rate of change in labor productivity, the appropriate measure of a fully employed labor force, and the rate at which the labor force is expected to grow.

---

[4] *Economic Report of the President,* 1962, p. 51.

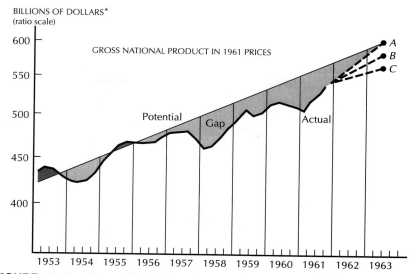

BILLIONS OF DOLLARS*
(ratio scale)

FIGURE 13–2   **Gross National Product (Actual and Potential), Kennedy Administration Estimates, 1953–1963.**   It was the gap analysis developed in the 1962 *Economic Report* that set the stage for the 1964 tax cut, designed to stimulate the economy's rate of growth.

*Seasonally adjusted annual rates.

Source: Economic Report of the President, 1962.

During the 1970s there were a number of revisions in estimates of the economy's potential GNP, primarily for two reasons. First, during the decade there was a sharp decline in the rate at which productivity was increasing, and, second, there were several upward revisions in the unemployment rate used to measure full or high employment. In 1977, for example, the Ford administration in its *Economic Report* revised downward the rate of growth of labor productivity to 2.0 percent and revised upward the full-employment benchmark for the labor force from 4.0 to 4.9 percent.[5] One consequence of these revisions was a reduction in the size of the GNP gap, a welcome political development. Subsequently, the Carter council in 1979 again revised downward its estimates of the rate of growth of productivity, while raising the benchmark unemployment rate to 5.1 percent.[6]

Table 13–3 shows the output potential calculated by the method reflected in Equation (13–1), the actual output, and the gap between the two. For the period 1970–1994 actual output per employed worker per year was calculated for each year by dividing real GDP (in 1987 prices) by the actual employment of that year. Then the average rate of growth of worker productivity for the entire period was determined and this percentage applied to determine

---

[5] *Economic Report of the President, 1977, pp. 53–54.*

[6] *Economic Report of the President, 1979, p. 75.*

TABLE 13–3 Potential and Actual GDP: 1970–1994 (billions of 1987 dollars)

(1)	(2) Output per Worker per Year*	(3)	(4) Potential	(5) Actual	(6)
Year		Employment†	Output	Output	Gap
1970 (R)	37,116	78.6	2,917.3	2,873.9	− 43.4
1971	37,354	80.2	2,995.7	2,955.9	− 39.8
1972	37,615	82.7	3,110.8	3,107.1	− 3.7
1973	37,863	84.9	3,214.6	3,268.6	− 5.4
1974 (R)	38,113	87.3	3,327.3	3,248.6	− 78.7
1975 (R)	38,365	89.1	3,418.3	3,221.7	−196.6
1976	38,618	91.4	3,529.7	3,380.1	−149.6
1977	38,873	94.1	3,657.9	3,533.3	−124.6
1978	39,130	97.2	3,803.4	3,703.5	− 99.9
1979	39,388	99.7	3,926.9	3,796.8	−130.1
1980 (R)	39,648	101.6	4,028.2	3,776.3	−251.9
1981	39,910	103.3	4,122.7	3,843.1	−279.6
1982 (R)	40,173	104.5	4,198.1	3,760.3	−437.8
1983	40,438	106.0	4,286.4	3,906.6	−379.8
1984	40,705	107.8	4,379.9	4,148.5	−231.4
1985	40,974	109.7	4,494.8	4,279.8	−215.0
1986	41,244	111.9	4,615.2	4,404.5	−210.7
1987	41,516	113.8	4,724.5	4,539.9	−184.6
1988	41,790	115.6	4,830.9	4,718.6	−112.3
1989	42,066	117.7	4,951.2	4,838.0	−113.2
1990 (R)	42,314	118.5	5,014.2	4,897.3	−116.9
1991	42,623	119.0	5,072.1	4,867.6	−204.5
1992	42,904	120.6	5,174.2	4,979.3	−194.9
1993	43,187	121.6	5,251.5	5,134.5	−117.0
1994	43,463	124.5	5,411.1	5,342.4	− 68.7

*Assumed to grow at an annual average rate of 0.66 percent.

†In millions; equals 95.0 percent of the civilian labor force.

Note: (R) = recession year.

Source: Economic Report of the President, 1995, pp. 276, 312.

the output per worker figure from 1969 onward. The latter year was taken as the starting point because it was a full-employment year (the unemployment rate was 3.5 percent). Output per worker per year grew during this period at an annual average rate of 0.66 percent; this was the figure used to calculate the productivity totals shown in column 2. Unemployment was assumed to be 5.0 percent, so the figures for total employment were obtained by multiplying the actual civilian labor force data for each year by 95.0 percent. This is shown in column 3. Potential output (column 4) is then obtained, as prescribed by Equation (13–1), by multiplying employment by the appropriate output per worker per year for each year. This figure is then compared with the actual output (column 5) and the gap between actual and potential calculated (column 6). These results are plotted in Figure 13–3. One main difference between this figure and the two previous ones is that the path of potential output (the solid line in the figure) shows slight fluctuations from

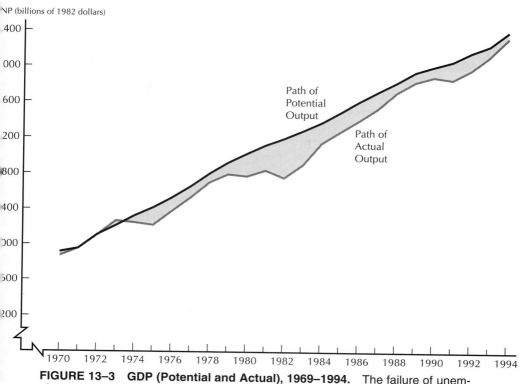

FIGURE 13–3   GDP (Potential and Actual), 1969–1994. The failure of unemployment to remain at or near the 5 percent rate led to a gap between actual and potential GDP. Expansion after the 1982 recession reduced the gap, but it rose again with the 1990-–1991 recession.

year to year. That is because of actual variations in the labor force; it has not grown at a precise rate each year in the period covered. In the two earlier figures, potential output is shown as a trend line, incorporating assumed and constant rates of growth for both productivity and labor from the base period used.

The figures shown in Table 13–3 are instructive in a number of ways. First, in every year from 1970 through 1994 there is a serious gap between the economy's output potential and its actual output. This gap rose sharply during recession years and improved during nonrecession years, but never disappeared. What is being documented here by comparing actual output with potential output is the economy's subnormal performance during these years. Although the 1980s are touted as the nation's longest period of peacetime prosperity, the economy's actual performance over this entire period is closer to Keynes's view that the economy is capable of remaining in a condition of subnormal activity for a long period of time.

The productivity growth rate used to calculate potential output per worker per year was 0.66 percent, a figure much lower than the actual growth in productivity of 2.5 percent a year from 1947 through 1969. The 5.0 percent figure used as a measure of full (or high) employment is a percentage point higher than the 4.0 percent rate used by the Kennedy-Johnson administration. But it is lower than the actual rate during these years, which averaged 6.7 percent. If the 2.5 percent productivity growth rate that actually prevailed from 1947 through 1969 had been used in calculating the output potential, the calculated output gap would have been far larger.

What the gap represents is output lost forever, output that could have been produced, but was not. To understand the magnitude of this loss, consider these numbers. For the entire period from 1970 through 1994, the total output lost was $3,990.1 billion, or an average of $159.6 billion per year. In this same period, military spending totaled $5,762.5 billion ($230.5 billion per year), while the cumulative federal deficit—the federal budget was in deficit every year from 1969 through 1993—totaled $2,921.7 billion, or an average of $116.9 billion per year. Imagine how drastically different our economic situation would be today if this output had not been lost, if the society had each year an additional $159.4 billion worth of goods and service and income to use for private and social purposes.[7]

From the time the concept of potential output was introduced into the reports of the Council of Economic Advisers by the Kennedy administration until the Carter administration left office in January 1981, every administration utilized the concept as a tool for economic policymaking. Primarily, the emphasis was placed on the growth of the economy's basic potential for production in relation to actual output; this set up a backdrop against which policies could be discussed for bringing the two trends—potential and actual output—closer together. With the advent of the Reagan administration, references to the economy's potential disappeared from the *Economic Report*. In view of the Reagan administration's strong philosophic thrust toward less government and basic distrust of the ability of the federal government to employ monetary and fiscal policies in the effective short-term management of the economy, such a development was not surprising. It was not used in the Bush administration, but the Clinton administration reintroduced potential growth into its *Economic Reports*. Potential GDP is an important analytical tool for policymaking purposes, one which complements and enlarges on the usual measures of GDP growth, unemployment, and the inflation rate used in the formation of economic policy.

The Productivity Crisis

Stanford University economist Paul Krugman says that productivity is not everything, "... but in the long run it is almost everything."[8] The rate of

---

[7] These totals are calculated from data in the *Economic Report of the President*, 1991, p. 339; 1995, pp. 277, 278, 365. Data are in 1987 dollars.

[8] Paul Krugman, *The Age of Diminished Expectations* (Cambridge, Mass.: MIT Press, 1990), p. 9.

growth of labor productivity is a major determinant of both the economy's productive potential and our material standard of life. The figure for labor productivity subsumes all the underlying real forces—technological change, the growth of capital, the skill and training of the labor force—that ultimately determine how rapidly the economy, real incomes, and money incomes can grow without causing inflation.

Table 13–4 illustrates some of these crucial relationships for specified intervals since 1948. It shows annual average rates of increase for worker productivity (output per hour for all persons); real compensation per hour for workers, which includes hourly pay plus all fringe benefits paid by both workers and employers; real weekly wages; labor costs per unit of output; and the inflation rate as measured by the GDP deflator.

The figures in Table 13–4 illustrate three matters of crucial importance. First, there is the serious decline in the rate of productivity growth over the period. This decline is the heart of the productivity crisis. The figures show a slight recovery in productivity growth in the early 1990s, but this was brought about more by worker layoffs as a result of corporate downsizing than by normal improvements in productivity growth from investments in capital and education. A second vital point is the close correlation between rates of growth in worker productivity and the real incomes of workers, both on an hourly and a weekly basis. The first three columns of the table reflect this correlation. Finally, there is a crucial link between productivity growth, money compensation to workers (shown in column 4 in the table), and the inflation rate. When money wages and the monetary value of fringe benefits run ahead of productivity gains, it is inevitable that labor costs per unit produced will rise. Since wages and salaries plus fringe benefits make up, on the average, 60 to 70 percent of business costs, and since, too, most firms set their prices on a markup-over-cost basis, higher unit labor costs are quickly translated into higher prices. The close correlation between inflation and unit

TABLE 13–4 Productivity, Worker Compensation and Wages, Labor Costs, and Inflation: 1948–1994 (annual average rates of change)

Period	(1) Productivity*	(2) Real Compensation per Hour†	(3) Real Weekly Wages	(4) Unit Labor Costs**	(5) GDP Deflator
1948–1959	2.6%	3.1%	2.4%	2.7%	2.9%
1960–1969	2.4	2.6	1.4	2.5	2.4
1970–1979	1.3	1.2	−0.3	7.3	6.7
1980–1989	0.8	0.1	−1.0	4.7	5.0
1990–1994	1.7	0.7	−0.5	2.7	3.1

*Output per worker in the nonfarm business sector.

†Hourly wages plus all fringe benefits, nonfarm business sector.

**Per unit of output, nonfarm business sector.

Source: *Economic Report of the President*, 1991, p. 336; 1995, pp. 278, 326, 329.

labor costs is shown in columns 4 and 5 of the table. This is particularly relevant for the 1970s, when increases in money wages consistently outran productivity gains.

Why Has Productivity Growth Slowed?

If we want to understand why productivity growth has slowed, we must look once again at the sources of growth identified earlier (Table 13–2). Essentially, they are three—capital, labor, and technology. Providing the work force with more and better machines, tools, and buildings—more capital, in other words—is essential to increasing productivity. Capital in this context must include public as well as private capital. It is a curious fact in modern economics that analysis of the role of the economy's performance is limited almost entirely to *private* capital. Yet, on the average since 1947, public capital has accounted for roughly $1 out of every $3 of the economy's total stock of physical capital.[9] The private production and distribution of goods and services would be almost physically impossible without a basic *infra-structure*—roads, airports, mass transit systems, water supply and sewage systems—most of which is supplied by public investment.

With respect to labor, the growth of total output, as Table 13–2 demonstrates, depends on increases in the labor force and the actual employment of labor in production. Since 1949 the labor force has grown at an annual average rate of 1.7 percent, while at the same time the proportion of the civilian noninstitutional population in the labor force has risen from an average of 59.3 percent in the 1950s to an average of 65.3 for the years 1980 through 1994.[10] More labor does not improve productivity per se; that requires greater skill in both the existing labor force and new entrants into the labor force, and that requires education and training, which economists call "investment in human capital."

"Technology" is a catchall term that describes the application of scientific knowledge to the production of goods and services. But technology does not exist in the abstract. It stems from research and development, from the ability and willingness of society to invest human and material resources in the discovery and advancement of new knowledge. To be effective in production, technology must become a part of physical capital, the skill and training of labor, or both. For example, the shift from the manual to the electric typewriter and then to the word processor reflects a changing technology that is embodied in increasingly sophisticated machines. Further, workers must have the necessary skill to take advantage of the improved technology. An illiterate person cannot use a typewriter, let alone a personal computer or word processor.

The foregoing provides a useful framework within which to consider some

[9] David Alan Aschauer, *Public Investment and Private Sector Growth* (Washington, D.C.: Economic Policy Institute, 1990), pp. 8, 9.

[10] *Economic Report of the President*, 1995, p. 312.

specific causes of the nation's slowdown in productivity growth. Before doing this, a word is in order about savings. For years the U.S. public has been told that our fundamental problem is that we are not saving enough—that Germany and Japan, our chief global competitors, save more than we do and have thus forged ahead in productivity growth. At best, this is a half-truth. Until the 1980s there was little change in the overall rate of savings in the United States by business firms and people. It is more important to understand that the role of savings in promoting investment in new capital is essentially *permissive*. It is not fundamental; that is to say while savings are necessary for investment, they do not *determine* investment. What counts is the expectation by business leaders that investing in new equipment and structure will be profitable. If there is a good prospect of profit, the necessary savings and finance will be found.

Turning to specific causes of the slowdown in productivity growth, let us look first at "military Keynesianism." This colorful term was coined by the late Joan Robinson, a student of Keynes and a distinguished British economist in her own right, in a 1971 address to U.S. economists to describe how military spending in the era of the Cold War (1950 to 1990) had become a major, perhaps dominant, force in the U.S. economy.

Table 13–5 shows by decade since 1950 to the early 1990s the proportion of federal spending for goods and services devoted to military purposes. Recall from the discussion in Chapter 2 (pages 44–45) that the output of the public sector is measured by what governments spend for goods and services, a figure that excludes transfer spending. Table 13–5 documents that for the forty years of the Cold War over three-fourths of the goods and services purchased by the federal government were for military purposes. A society that for nearly half a century devoted more than three-fourths of the output of its national government to military goods and services is a society dominated by military Keynesianism.

The crucial question is how has military Keynesianism affected both productivity and general economic growth? Lloyd J. Dumas of the University of Texas at Dallas, a careful student of military spending and the economy, argues that military budgets have had an "enormously negative long-term impact upon the functioning of the . . . economy," due in large part to the fact that from 30 to 33 percent of the country's scientific and engineering talent has been channeled into military activity. In Professor Dumas' view, this diversion of vital resources away from the civilian economy played a key role in the decline in the rate of productivity growth. Further, and contrary to

TABLE 13–5   Military Spending by Decades as a Percent of Total Federal Spending for Goods and Services: 1950–1994 (percent)

1950–59	1960–69	1970–79	1980–89	1990–94
85.4%	78.3%	70.1%	73.6%	70.2%

Source: Economic Report of the President, 1991, p. 287; 1995, p. 275.

the conventional wisdom, there is no longer any significant spin-off of military-related research into the civilian economy. As Professor Dumas concluded in his 1986 book, "The effects of severe structural damage to the competitiveness of United States industry by three decades of persistently high military spending surfaced with a vengeance in the 1970s. Collapsing productivity, high inflation, and high unemployment are the sad legacy of our participation in the international arms race."[11]

Two other economists, Professors Ann Markusen and Joel Yudken of Rutgers University, argue that spending for modern weaponry has created an "aerospace-communications-electronics complex (ACE)." These three industries plus those that supply ships, ordnance, and tanks have been the prime beneficiaries of the more than $5.5 trillion (in current dollars) spent on defense since 1950. The big firms of the ACE complex prospered, offering well-paid jobs to thousands of white- and blue-collar workers, while becoming strongly competitive in world markets. Unfortunately, Professors Markusen and Yudken found, much of the prosperity of ACE complex firms came at the expense of the rest of the United States' industrial base, including industries producing both capital and consumer goods. In the meanwhile, Germany and Japan pushed their resources, including engineering and scientific talent, into industries producing consumer goods. As a result, the United States was displaced from markets both at home and abroad for a long list of consumer products—automobiles, television sets, cameras, sewing machines, tape recorders, bicycles, calculating machines, and many more.[12]

A second important factor in the productivity slowdown, one neglected by mainstream economics, is a sharp decline in the nation's stock of nonmilitary public capital. Professor David Alan Aschauer of Bates College, a leading researcher into the link between public capital, the nation's infrastructure, and the growth in both total output and productivity, found that almost 60 percent of the drop in productivity growth is accounted for by the downturn in spending for public investment in the 1970s and 1980s.[13]

A third causal factor in the productivity slowdown stems from what happened to nonresidential private investment in the post-World War II period. Overall, the stock of private capital per employed person grew at about the same rate from 1947 through 1990. However, the composition of the stock of nonresidential private capital changed in a way that adversely affected productivity growth. The two components of nonresidential private capital

---

[11] Lloyd J. Dumas, *The Overburdened Economy* (Berkeley: University of California Press, 1986), pp. 56, 118, 206ff.

[12] Ann Markusen and Joel Yudken, *Dismantling the Cold War Economy* (New York: Basic Books, 1992), pp. 35, 51, 59.

[13] Aschauer, *Public Investment and Private Sector Growth*, pp. 3, 8, 9, and 16. See also David Alan Aschauer, *Back of the G-7 Pack: Public Investment and Productivity Growth in the Group of Seven* (Chicago: Federal Reserve Bank of Chicago, 1989), p. 8. Aschauer's work has not gone unchallenged by critics within the economic profession, but to date it has weathered this scrutiny successfully. See Alcia H. Munnell, "Is There a Shortfall in Public Capital Investment: An Overview," *New England Economic Review*, May–June 1991, pp. 23–35.

are structures and equipment. The latter is relatively more important from the standpoint of productivity, for it is primarily through new and better tools and machines that advances in technology enter into the economic system.

What happened after 1973 was a sharp slowdown in the rate of growth of equipment per employed worker, and an increase in the rate of growth in structures per employed person in the same time span. To be specific, equipment per worker grew at an annual average rate of 3.6 percent from 1947 through 1973, but at the much slower rate of 1.9 percent from 1974 through 1990. Structures grew at an annual average rate of 0.8 percent from 1947 through 1973, but jumped to a 2.0 percent annual growth rate for the period 1974 through 1990.[14]

Measured in constant 1987 dollars, equipment per worker totaled $34,510 in 1990, but if this variable had grown after 1973 at the same 3.6 rate that prevailed from 1947 through 1973, the amount of equipment per worker in 1990 would have been $45,704. The shortfall in the stock of private equipment per employed worker thus reached $11,194 in 1990. On the other hand, the stock of nonresidential buildings per worker reached $37,461 by 1990, $1,844 greater than what the figure would have been if growth in this variable had continued at the lower rate that prevailed from 1947 through 1973.[15]

What happened to private nonresidential investment after 1973 led to an *oversupply* of buildings—vacant office space and the overbuilding of shopping malls attest to this—and an *undersupply* of the tools and machines workers need to do their jobs. Redundancy of buildings and a shortage of equipment in the economy's private sector are important reasons for the slowdown in the economy's productivity growth. One possible explanation for these trends was the extension of the investment tax credit to buildings in 1981, a move which helped stimulate the office-building and shopping-mall boom of the 1980s.

The Productivity Crisis: What Can Be Done?

There is no quick or easy solution to the nation's productivity crisis, but one thing is certain: unless the nation's productivity growth rate improves (see Table 13–4), a long period of mediocre economic performance may lie ahead. This can only compound the difficult economic problems facing the nation, not the least of which is the increasing share of the national output that must be transferred to the "baby boomers" as they begin to retire early in the next century. The real answer to productivity growth is Keynesian, as it has always been—more and better investment. This must be investment in goods, in people, and in research and development.

---

[14] U.S. Department of Commerce, "Fixed Reproducable Tangible Wealth in the United States: Revised Estimates," *Survey of Current Business*, January 1992, pp. 130–137.

[15] Ibid.

Our current situation is unique because of the large shortfall in *public* capital, a deficiency that Professor Aschauer describes as the nation's "third deficit," comparable in magnitude to the twin deficits of the federal government and the balance of trade.[16] This calls for a massive program of infrastructure investment, carried out over a period of 10 to 15 years. Given the estimated shortfall in the nation's stock of public capital of approximately $1 trillion, a program of infrastructure investment in the range of $100 billion per year is in order. Is $100 billion an unreasonable figure? Not really. It is only 1.5 percent of the 1994 GDP of $6,737 billion (in current dollars). Furthermore, as infrastructure investment succeeds in stimulating both private investment and productivity growth, the percent of output devoted to this purpose will decline steadily.

Most investment in public capital takes place at the state and local level. In 1990, for example, the stock of federal nonmilitary capital was worth $540.8 billion (in 1987 dollars), an amount equal to 4.2 percent of the nation's total stock of fixed capital (equipment and structures). The latter was $11,957.5 billion in 1990.[17] State and local capital equals 24.7 percent of this total. Although ownership of most public capital is held at the state and local level, any infrastructure investment program on the order of $100 billion per year would have to be financed by the national government. This raises two difficult questions: first, where would the federal government find the money for such a program, and, second, is such a program politically possible?

Since fiscal year 1980, the federal deficit has averaged $187.3 billion annually, a figure which as a practical matter forecloses further borrowing by the federal government as a source of finance for a major infrastructure investment program.[18] If the United States had a capital budget, as do most states, all large businesses, and many foreign governments, the deficit picture would look entirely different. Unfortunately, this is not the case. Moreover, with a balanced-budget constitutional amendment still looming on the horizon, the possibility that the federal government would establish a capital budget is increasingly remote. Currently, 69 percent of the federal budget is now consumed by entitlement spending—Social Security, Medicare, Medicaid, federal pensions, and similar programs—plus interest on the federal debt.[19] There is no way these programs could be cut back sufficiently to free up the needed $100 billion.

This leaves only the military budget as a source of funds for an infrastructure investment program. The Clinton administration military budget projections for fiscal year 1995, which average 83.2 percent of Cold War spending, continue to fund nearly all the major and expensive new weapons systems begun during the Cold War, even though the former Soviet Union is in dis-

---

[16] Aschauer, *Public Investment and Private Sector Growth*, p. 11.

[17] U.S. Department of Commerce, "Fixed Reproducible Tangible Wealth in the United States: Revised Estimates," pp. 122, 130.

[18] *Current Economic Indicators*, February 1995, p. 32.

[19] Ibid.

array and the Cold War has been "won." There are probably sufficient resources locked up in military spending, which, if freed, could readily finance an infrastructure investment program of the magnitude suggested. This brings us to the second crucial question: is such a program possible politically? Given the changing political climate of the last few years, the answer is no. In the spring of 1993, President Clinton initially proposed in his first full budget (for fiscal year 1994) a modest $15 billion for infrastructure investment, but this was quickly lost because of the pressure for deficit reduction. The sweeping Republican victories in the 1994 congressional elections has turned the nation further away from an activist economic role for the federal government. How the swing to the right with its demand for a smaller federal government with drastically restricted economic powers will play itself out remains to be seen. What is now certain is that the massive deficits of the Reagan and Bush years effectively destroyed the federal government's ability to use fiscal policy as a tool for economic management. What is likely to happen as the economic power of the national government continues to be curtailed is examined again in Chapter 15.

Theories of Economic Growth

Over time the economy's potential for production expands, but the actual growth in output that follows from this is not necessarily smooth. This raises several fundamental theoretical questions about economic growth, its path through time, and the key causal factors that influence growth. One body of ideas approaches growth from a strictly Keynesian perspective. If the economy's productive capacity increases, then aggregate demand necessarily must increase if additional capacity is to be used. Very early after the end of World War II, two economists, Evsey Domar, an American, and Roy F. Harrod, a Briton, showed why this is true, and also demonstrated why actual growth was unstable.

Some years later in the late 1950s, MIT economist Robert Solow challenged the instability argument by examining economic growth from a neoclassical perspective. Professor Solow, who later received the Nobel Prize in economics for his work on growth, sought to show why and how a market economy would tend over time to reach a condition of balanced growth; that is, savings and investment *ex ante* would be equal, and the rate of growth would be stable. The Solow growth model is described as "neoclassical" because of certain key assumptions (see page 538).

After the 1960s, interest among economists in theoretical ideas about growth faded, in part because both the Domar-Harrod and Solow approaches to economic growth treated technological change, population growth, and important institutional factors as exogenous to the process, although casual observation suggests otherwise. This was the situation until the late 1980s, when under the label of "endogenous growth theory," a resurgence of interest

Are Things Going to Get Better?

It has long been an article of faith among Americans that each generation does better than its predecessor. Parents, in other words, want and expect life to be better for their children than it was for themselves.

Today, however, this faith is being challenged. New York Senator Daniel Patrick Moynihan has said, "We may be the first society in history of which it can be said that the children are worse off than their parents."

How this is happening and why it is happening is probably only dimly perceived and even more dimly understood. Yet there are profound intergenerational changes taking place in our society, which are economic in nature, but carry within them the seeds of bitter political conflict. They need to be understood, especially if the latter is to be avoided.

Basically, the threat to our faith in continued progress over the generations involves three developments, each one important in itself and not directly related to the others. These developments are (1) the steady reduction of poverty among the nation's aged, (2) the steady increase in poverty among the nation's children, and (3) the shrinkage of the U.S. middle class.

One of the magnificent accomplishments of this nation over the past decade and a half is the virtual elimination of poverty among people 65 years of age and older. In 1966, for example, the percentage of the population over 65 in poverty was 28.5. By 1992 this figure had been reduced to 12.9 percent. If the value of Medicare and other "in kind" benefits are added to incomes, the poverty percentage for the elderly is estimated to be less than 4 percent!

Social Security is the basic reason for this drastic change. In real terms— that is, in dollars of constant purchasing power—Social Security benefits have increased by 79 percent. Unfortunately, weekly wages in constant dollars have dropped by 13 percent in the same period—a fact which helps account for the shrinkage of the middle class.

The story of what is happening to children in our society is different and tragic. There are now more children living in poverty than at any time since 1960. Since 1970, the poverty rate for children has jumped from 15.1 percent to 21.8 percent. Children have become by far the largest single category of people living below the poverty line.

There are two reasons for the continued increase in poverty among children in the nation. The first is the continued deterioration of the nuclear family, which has pushed millions of children into single-parent households—and also into poverty. Among families headed by females, 39.7 percent are below the poverty line; this percentage has been growing since 1970.

The second reason lies in the policies of the federal government. In recent years, there has been a sharp reduction in real terms in federal transfer programs aimed primarily at children. These include AFDC (Aid to Families with Dependent Children) and child health and nutrition programs.

Finally, we come to the shrinkage of the middle class, an idea still much in dispute. Most dramatic is the fact that young families, most of whom fall into the middle-class category, are worse off economically than were their counterparts twenty years ago. Although we hear much about the affluent lifestyle of the Yuppies among the baby boomers, the sober truth is that the vast majority are earning, relatively speaking, only about 80 percent of what people in their age bracket earned in the 1960s.

Whether or not Senator Moynihan's prophecy comes true remains to be seen. But these are trends and facts we should not ignore.

---

in economic growth emerged in the economics profession. Professors Paul Romer of the University of California, Berkeley, and Robert Lucas of the University of Chicago are two key figures in this development. In the following sections we shall deal in turn with each of these three approaches to some of the problems and theory of economic growth.

The Domar-Harrod Models[20]

The appropriate point of departure for discussion of these theories is a brief review of the full-employment equilibrium in a short-run setting. Parenthetically, it is important to remember that the basic model developed in Chapter 4 is static simply because it does not involve any change over time in the fundamental determinants of the economy's productive potential. As Keynes pointed out in *The General Theory,* the analysis takes as given "the existing skill and quantity of available labour, the existing quality and quantity of available equipment, the existing technique, the degree of competition, the tastes and habits of the consumer."[21] With capacity known and fixed, the central problem is the determination of the level of aggregate demand; in static analysis the level of aggregate demand determines the output and employment level, and shifts in the aggregate demand schedule bring about shifts in both output and employment.

There is nothing wrong with this analysis since it expresses an idea fundamental to all modern income and employment theory: namely, income paid out or created during the productive process must be returned in one form or another to the income stream if the expectations of producers are to be satisfied and equilibrium maintained. But, as both Domar and Harrod observe, the equilibrium so obtained has meaning only for a relatively short period of time because the *capacity-creating* effects of investment expenditure will

---

[20] Professor Harrod developed his ideas in a series of lectures given at the University of London in 1947. Professor Domar's model appeared in the *American Economic Review* in the same year. For details, see R. F. Harrod, *Towards a Dynamic Economics* (New York: St. Martin's Press, 1966), especially Lecture Three, pp. 63–100, and E. D. Domar, "Expansion and Employment," *American Economic Review*, March 1947, pp. 34–55. For both the intermediate and advanced student of macroeconomics, the Domar-Harrod models have been and are the basic introduction to the theoretical questions involving growth in the modern, market-based economic system.

[21] Keynes, *The General Theory*, p. 245.

cause the income level that is appropriate to the full employment of both labor and other resources to rise over time.

To facilitate our understanding of why a level of income sufficient to achieve full employment of all resources today may not be sufficient to achieve full employment of all resources tomorrow, let us discuss income, investment, and saving in the net sense, that is, after proper allowance has been made for the replacement of capital goods used up in the current production process. If the discussion is cast in net rather than gross terms, it does not change the underlying principle: Full-employment equilibrium requires that investment expenditure be equal to full-employment saving. The key difference is that now the basic statement describing the necessary condition for achieving and maintaining a full-employment income level must be modified to read that *ex ante* net investment must equal *ex ante* net saving at full employment.

But when we put the analysis in net terms and define full-employment equilibrium in terms of an equality between net saving and investment, we are faced with a serious dilemma because the analytical system no longer retains its static character. Net saving is a dynamic concept. If a society steadily saves some portion of its net income and just as steadily invests the income saved in productive capital, it follows that the stock of productive capital equipment, one of the basic determinants of both capacity and output, will change. The paradox of the situation arises from the fact that net investment is by definition an addition to the economy's stock of wealth in the form of productive capital, and thus net investment must increase the economy's productive capacity. But if productive capacity is increasing, the analysis can no longer be static.

Here we encounter a common element in the Domar-Harrod approaches to economic growth: *the dual character of investment spending.* In the standard, short-term (static) Keynesian analysis, the importance of investment lies in its role as a part of aggregate demand. Investment must be sufficient to absorb the economy's full-employment saving if a slump is to be avoided. In the context of growth theory, however, investment plays a second role. It expands capacity. But if capacity is expanded, then what is required in the Keynesian model is an increase in aggregate demand to bring the added capacity into use. If aggregate demand does not expand, then the new capacity will lie idle—an unsatisfactory situation. What the Domar-Harrod models do is explore the theoretical ramifications of the dual character of investment.

A good place to begin the analysis is with a Keynesian equilibrium at full employment: the necessary condition for equilibrium is that full-employment *net* saving equals full-employment *net* investment. In equation form we have

$$I_n = S_n. \tag{13–2}$$

Now the question is by how much will the economy's productive capacity be increased as a result of net investment in the amount of I_n? This depends on the full-employment capital-output ratio (K/Y), which is the relationship between the stock of capital (K) and the amount of output (Y) associated with that stock of capital. Basically, the K/Y ratio is a way of defining the economy's productive capacity in terms of its capital stock. Since both capital (a stock phenomenon) and output (a flow phenomenon) must be measured in terms of their money values, the capital-output ratio is, as a practical matter, the number of dollars worth of capital required on the average to get a dollars worth of output. If this ratio is, say, 3, it means that, on the average, it requires $3 worth of capital to get $1 worth of output.

The reciprocal of this ratio (Y/K) is a measure of the productivity of capital; that is, it tells us how much additional output (ΔY) is obtained for each additional unit of capital (ΔK). If the capital-output ratio (K/Y) is 3, then an additional $1 worth of capital will increase productive capacity by $0.33. The ratio of a change in capital (ΔK) to a change in productive capacity or potential output (ΔY) is properly designated as the *marginal capital-output ratio*. This ratio is of key importance in the Domar-Harrod approach to the problem of growth.

The relationship between the *average* capital-output ratio (K/Y) and the *marginal* capital-output ratio ($\Delta K/\Delta Y$) is also important. If these two ratios are equal, technological progress is said to be *neutral*. Technological change does not have to be neutral. It may, and often does, change both the average and the marginal capital-output ratios. This is especially true for the marginal ratio, because new technological developments usually make themselves felt when additions to the nation's capital stock are being made. If the ratio is reduced—that is, the same output can be obtained with less capital—capital *saving* is said to have taken place. If, however, more capital is required per unit of output, capital *deepening* will have taken place.

To develop the essential features of the Domar-Harrod growth theory as simply as possible, the assumption is generally made that the average and marginal capital-output ratios are equal. That is,

$$K/Y = \Delta K/\Delta Y .$$ (13–3)

Now we come to the crux of the matter. By how much will the economy's capacity (potential) increase as the result of net investment (I_n) in a period? By definition net investment (I_n) is the increase in the economy's stock of capital (ΔK). Professor Domar solves this by multiplying net investment (I_n) by the *reciprocal* of the marginal capital-output ratio ($\Delta K/\Delta Y$). He designates this coefficient σ and calls it the *potential social average productivity of investment*. Thus we have

$$\Delta Y_Q = I\sigma .$$ (13–4)

In this equation (ΔY_q) represents the increase in productive capacity (potential output) because of net investment. This represents the supply side of the growth problem and reflects the capacity-creating aspect of investment expenditures.

Let us assume that the economy is at a full-employment income level of $6,400 billion. Planned *(ex ante)* net savings and investment are equal at $400 billion. We assume an economy without government or international economic relationships. Now if the average and marginal capital output ratio is equal to 3, the value of the Domar σ will be 0.33. The effect of net investment in the amount of $400 billion will be to increase the economy's productive capacity by $132 billion ($400 billion × 0.33 = $132 billion).

Now we can see the consequences of the capacity-creating side of investment spending. Even though $6,400 billion was a full-employment income level at the start of the income period, it is no longer such at the end. Net investment has caused capacity to grow. It will now require a level of aggregate demand equal to $6,532 billion to maintain full employment. This underscores the fundamental necessity for output to grow if full employment is to be maintained *over time*.

This brings us to the demand side of the growth problem. If net investment increases the economy's productive capacity, it is essential that output (Y) grow through time in order that the added capacity created by the investment process is continually absorbed into use. Thus, we need to determine, first, how output (Y) can be made to expand to bring into use the new capacity and, second, the necessary *rate* at which output must expand to achieve the continued full utilization of the additional capacity. These questions can be resolved within the basic Keynesian framework of aggregate demand and aggregate supply, in which the key role played by aggregate demand is to bring capacity into use.

Since we have eliminated government expenditure and international transactions from the analysis and since consumption is a dependent variable (in that it is a function of income), investment is the key determinant of the level of aggregate demand. Thus, investment will have to increase if there is to be an upward shift in the aggregate demand curve; the shift must be great enough to bring about an overall increase in aggregate expenditure sufficient to utilize, and thus justify, the added productive capacity. This aspect of the problem is easy to understand, for the reader need only recall the multiplier analysis to realize that any given total increase in aggregate expenditure depends on the amount by which investment itself has risen as well as on the value of the multiplier. The latter, of course, is dependent on the marginal propensity to save.

If the utilization of additional capacity requires an increase in aggregate expenditure equal to the amount by which capacity has increased and if changes in investment expenditure are the ultimate source of changes in effective demand, we can express the required increase in effective demand in equation form as

$$\Delta Y_D = \Delta I \times \frac{1}{s}. \qquad (13\text{--}5)$$

This equation is simply the multiplier formula applied to an increase in investment expenditure. ΔY_D represents the overall increase in effective demand or total expenditure brought about by the given increment in investment expenditure. $1/s$ is the simple investment multiplier, since s represents the marginal propensity to save.

The equation depicting the demand side of the growth problem underscores the *dual nature of the investment process.* The capacity-creating effects and the demand-creating effects of investment expenditure are dissimilar. *All* net investment expenditure adds to the economy's capital stock and thus increases the economy's productive capacity, but only *increments* to investment expenditure, operating through the multiplier effect, raise the level of effective demand. This, in short, is the real paradox of investment; if net investment expenditure simply remains constant through time, the income level will not change—that is, equilibrium will be maintained—but the result will be idle capacity and a growing volume of unemployed labor. Investment and income must grow in each succeeding income period if net investment expenditures in any specific income period are to justify themselves.

The Required Rate of Income Growth

If the maintenance of full employment for both the economy's labor force and its stock of productive capital requires that output grow at the same rate at which productive capacity is increasing because of net investment, we can bring together the equations discussed above and compute the necessary rate at which output must grow. The basic condition is that, over time, increments of effective demand must equal increments of capacity. Symbolically, this can be stated as

$$\Delta Y_Q = \Delta Y_D . \qquad (13\text{--}6)$$

We can substitute the earlier values for ΔY_Q and ΔY_D in this defining equation. Thus,

$$I\sigma = \Delta I \times \frac{1}{s} . \qquad (13\text{--}7)$$

$I\sigma$ represents the supply side of the system, for it shows the potential increase in supply that results from current investment, whereas $\Delta I \times 1/s$ represents the demand side, since it depicts the amount by which aggregate effective demand must rise if the added capacity is to be utilized.

The above equation is further modified by multiplying both sides by s and then dividing both sides by I. The result of this is the growth equation

$$\frac{\Delta I}{I} = \sigma s . \qquad (13\text{--}8)$$

The left side of this equation shows the absolute increment in investment expenditure divided by the total volume of investment expenditure. It is expressive of the percentage rate of growth of investment. Thus, Equation (13–8) means basically that *investment expenditure must grow at an annual rate equal to the product of the marginal propensity to save* s *and the potential social average productivity of investment* σ if a state of continuous full employment is to be maintained. Since in the long run the average and marginal propensities to save are equal (pages 244–45) and it is assumed the average and marginal values of σ are equal, it is easy to demonstrate algebraically that income as well as investment must grow at a constant annual percentage rate equal to the product of s and σ.[22] Thus,

$$\frac{\Delta Y}{Y} = \sigma s \ . \tag{13–9}$$

The above equation, like Equation (13–8), indicates in a simple and direct way the necessary condition for the maintenance of full-employment output over time. It shows "that it is not sufficient, in Keynesian terms, that savings of yesterday be invested today, or, as it is so often expressed, that investment offset saving. Investment of today must always exceed savings of yesterday. . . . The economy must continuously expand."[23]

The analysis of growth pursued to this point is basically the one developed by Professor Domar in his now-classic 1947 *American Economic Review* article. The analytical system we have just described is properly described as dynamic because it goes beyond the assumption made by Keynes in *The General Theory* that capacity is fixed. It examines the consequences of an increase in the quantity of a key economic resource, namely, the economy's stock of *real* capital instruments. Domar's concern with the capacity-creating effect of net investment has a dual significance for economic analysis. First, the analysis follows an old tradition, for nearly all economists who have had something meaningful to say about economic development have accorded the accumulation of capital a priority role in this process. Second, the analysis demonstrates that economic growth is not merely a desirable phenomenon for an advanced capitalistic economy, but an absolute necessity if the economy is to avoid a growing volume of unemployment of both labor and other economic resources. The analysis, moreover, shows that, although the economy may grow at a satisfactory rate, there is no reason to expect it to do so automatically.

---

[22] This can be shown algebraically as follows:
    1. $I = sY$.   (This assumes that the saving of the period is invested.)
    2. $\Delta Y_Q = \sigma sY$. [This is from Equation (13–4).]
    3. $\Delta Y_D = \sigma sY$. (This is based on the assumption that the change in aggregate effective demand
            must equal the change in capacity.)
    4. $\dfrac{\Delta Y}{Y} = \sigma s$.
               (This follows algebraically from above.)

[23] Domar, "Expansion and Unemployment," p. 42.

Our appraisal of Domar's analysis would not be complete if we did not point out some of its important limitations. For one thing, the derivation of the required rate of growth obviously depends on the existence of known and constant values for such crucial factors as the propensity to save and the productivity of capital coefficient. In reality, it is unlikely that either of these are constant all the time. But the difficulty of deriving a required rate does not in any way invalidate the basic theme of the analysis, that there exists *some* rate of growth that will ensure a full-employment equilibrium over time.

A second limitation is Domar's use of a productivity of investment coefficient that is an average for the whole economy. The capital-output ratio, both on the average and at the margin, varies widely from industry to industry because of differences in the capital requirements for different kinds of production. This means that it will be very difficult to determine the exact impact of a given volume of investment on capacity unless we know the composition in an industrial sense of the investment. For example, a given quantity of investment expenditure in an industry characterized by a high capital-output ratio will obviously have a smaller overall impact on productive capacity than the same amount of investment expenditure in an industry with a lower capital-output ratio.

Finally, Domar's analysis fails to distinguish between a rate of growth of income that will ensure full employment of the labor force and a rate of growth of income that will ensure full utilization of the economy's stock of capital. This has been a matter of concern for some economists, who argue that the rate of growth sufficient to absorb additions to the economy's stock of capital will not necessarily provide full employment for a growing labor force.

In spite of these limitations, attention should not be detracted from the important and positive contribution that the Domar type of analysis has made to an understanding of the process of economic development in an advanced economy. Admittedly, Domar's system is overly simplified and, perhaps, overly rigid. But this is a criticism that could be justly leveled at most facets of contemporary economic theory. The real task of economic theory is to direct our attention to a few strategic relationships as a means of understanding somewhat better the vast complexities of the economy in the real world. Not many economists would deny that an enlargement of the economy's productive potential is a factor of key strategic significance in the process of economic growth.

Harrod's Approach to Economic Growth

Professor Harrod's approach to the theoretical problem of maintaining growth in an advanced system of market capitalism is similar to the Domar analysis just discussed. This similarity is why it is fashionable for economists to speak of the Domar-Harrod theory when discussing developments that extend the basic Keynesian theory of income and employment to the broader realm of economic growth. Yet there are enough fundamental differences in the two approaches to warrant a separate discussion of Harrod's basic ideas.

Harrod, like Domar, is concerned with the necessary conditions under which the equality of *ex ante* saving and investment can be maintained over time, but he treats the central element in the growth process, investment expenditure, in a different manner. In Domar's schema we look to the effect that current investment expenditure has on future productive capacity, assuming that this investment expenditure is sufficient to offset the saving of the current income level. In a sense, Domar's analysis is forward-looking because such a procedure requires us to determine how much both income and investment will have to grow in the next income period in order to absorb into use at that time the added capacity that is the consequence of investment in the present income period.

Harrod, on the other hand, constructs his analysis in terms of the response of current investment expenditure to a change in the economy's output or real income level. He seeks to determine whether the rate at which income has grown in the immediate past is high enough to induce an amount of investment expenditure sufficient to absorb the saving in the current income period.

The key analytical tool that Harrod employs in his analysis is the *accelerator,* which is defined symbolically as the ratio of a change in the capital stock ΔK to a change in the output level ΔY. Since the change in the capital stock is the same as the net investment I_n, the ratio $\Delta K/\Delta Y$, or $I_n/\Delta Y$, when defined as the accelerator, represents a behavior coefficient in the sense that it seeks to express as a coefficient the investment response of entrepreneurs to a change in the output level. The acceleration approach makes current planned or *ex ante* net investment a function of the rate of change in output. Fundamental to the notion of the acceleration coefficient, however, is the concept of the capital-output ratio conceived as a technical relationship, for if a relatively fixed relationship did not exist between output and the quantity of capital necessary for the production of that output, there would be no point in asserting that investment expenditure may be induced by changes in output.

Although the treatment of investment expenditure differs in the two analyses, both Domar and Harrod accord identical roles to the saving function. Both analyses are based on the long-run saving function, on an equality between the average and the marginal propensity to save. In both analyses saving *ex ante* and saving *ex post* are presumed to be equal; this means that saving calls the tune. Other variables such as investment, the productivity of capital coefficient, and the accelerator must adjust to the rate of saving if full employment over time is to be maintained.

The most important concept used by Harrod in his analysis is the *warranted rate of growth G_w,* which he defines precisely as ''that overall rate of advance which, if executed, will leave entrepreneurs in a state of mind in which they are prepared to carry on a similar advance.''[24] In contrast to the

---

[24] Harrod, *Towards a Dynamic Economics,* p. 82.

warranted rate of growth, Harrod also uses in his analysis the *actual* rate of growth (G), which, of course, is defined as the actual, or *ex post*, change in output during an income period.

More explicitly, the warranted rate of growth concept refers to a rate of advance for the economy as a whole that will leave entrepreneurs (in the aggregate or on the average) satisfied with the outcome of economic activity. Within the framework of equilibrium analysis, a condition of entrepreneurial satisfaction is a situation in which investment and saving *ex ante* are in equilibrium. To put it differently, this is a situation in which aggregate demand and aggregate supply are in balance. The concept of a warranted rate of growth refers to a situation in which a growing absolute volume of *ex ante* investment is in equilibrium with a growing absolute volume of full employment, *ex ante* saving.

Just as there is no inherent reason why the equilibrium level of output for the economy—the output at which aggregate demand and supply are equal— is a full-employment output, there is no inherent reason why the actual rate of growth experienced during a period should correspond with the warranted rate of growth.

So, let us examine a situation in which the actual rate of growth (G) is greater than the warranted rate of growth (G_w). A high rate of actual growth will lead, via the accelerator, to an increased level of *ex ante*, or planned, investment, which turns out to be greater than the actual, or *ex post*, amount of investment. When this happens, aggregate demand is greater than aggregate supply—a condition which leads to an expansion in output and employment.

When G is greater than G_w, the economy is in a situation in which output has grown, but aggregate demand has grown even faster. Under such circumstances the economy will experience a chronic shortage of capital, as investment *ex post* continuously falls short of investment *ex ante*. The result will be further pressure on planned, or *ex ante,* investment as entrepreneurs seek to make good the economy's capital shortage, but such a reaction only serves to drive the actual rate of growth further and further from the warranted rate. Thus, it is Harrod's contention that any movement away from the line of steady advance represented by his warranted rate of growth tends to be cumulative in its effect; departures of the actual growth rate from the warranted or equilibrium rate do not, in other words, set in motion forces tending toward a restoration of equilibrium. Equilibrium once disturbed leads to a disequilibrium that becomes progressively worse.

The alternative to the situation just described is one in which the warranted rate of growth is greater than the actual rate of growth; that is, $G_w > G$. If this is the case, investment *ex ante* in the current period falls short of investment *ex post,* and consequently, excess capacity will appear and make it impossible for the economy to continue to advance at the same rate as in the past. In other words, a situation in which G_w is greater than G indicates a tendency in the economy toward stagnation and a chronic excess of productive capacity. Under such circumstances it will be difficult enough to sustain any growth at all for a significant length of time, let alone a rate of growth that will justify itself only if net investment is continually increasing in absolute amount.

To summarize briefly Harrod's analysis, we can say that the necessary condition for an equilibrium rate of growth is that the actual rate be equal to the warranted rate. This means that, in each income period, investment, which is linked to the rate at which income has grown in the immediate past, will be equal to the planned saving of the income period. Furthermore, Harrod's analysis asserts that, if G and G_w are not equal, which is a condition of disequilibrium, the result will not be a restoration of equilibrium or a return to conditions in which G and G_w are equal but rather a greater and greater divergence between G and G_w. The growth process in Harrod's view is an inherently unstable phenomenon, as even the slightest departure from the exceedingly narrow path of an equilibrium rate of growth sets in motion forces making for either secular expansion and inflation or secular stagnation.

Concluding Observations on the Domar-Harrod Analysis of Economic Growth

Both the Domar and Harrod approaches to the broad problem of economic growth in an advanced market economy accord investment the central role in the growth process. Furthermore, both Domar and Harrod undertake their analyses of the process of growth within the income-expenditure framework. They agree that the central problem in the growth process in an advanced economy is the conditions under which planned investment will be continuously equated with a growing absolute volume of planned saving. Domar and Harrod are also in agreement with respect to the key role of saving, since their analyses are based on the assumption of constant average and marginal propensities to save and on the further assumption that actual and planned savings are always equal.

The two analyses differ mainly in the ways in which they look at the investment process. Domar's analysis looks ahead, in the sense that he stresses the effect of today's net investment on tomorrow's capacity or productive potential, and thus seeks to determine the rate at which the economy must grow if this productive capacity is to be absorbed into use in the future. He is concerned primarily with the essentially technical question of the effect of present investment on future capacity. Harrod's analysis, on the other hand, tends to look backward in the sense that he is seeking to determine if output has actually grown enough between yesterday and today to induce an amount of net investment sufficient to absorb today's full-employment saving. Although his analysis rests in a fundamental sense on a technological relationship between output and capital, Harrod's key analytical tool is the concept of the accelerator, since this is the coefficient that links current planned, or *ex ante*, investment to changes in the output level. Harrod's analysis centers primarily on the reaction of entrepreneurs to past changes in the income level and assumes that, if entrepreneurs in the aggregate are satisfied with the past rate of growth, they will act in such a way as to promote future growth in the economy at the same rate.

Both the Domar and the Harrod analyses of the growth process are subject to the same general criticism of being perhaps excessively abstract and too dependent (insofar as their conclusions with respect to the economy's ability to achieve a satisfactory rate of growth are concerned) on some rather rigid assumptions concerning the values and fixity of such critical determinants as the propensity to save and the capital coefficient. Harrod, in particular, can be criticized for placing too much stress on the phenomenon of induced investment as the crucial factor in the growth process. As a consequence, there emerges a picture of the economy tied tightly to a very narrow path of growth, with the twin disasters of either secular acceleration and inflation or secular stagnation threatening in the event of the slightest divergence from the precisely determined path of advance. This has been described as movement along a razor's edge equilibrium path of output.

Despite the shortcomings we have noted, the analyses of Domar and Harrod, by directing our attention to such strategically important ideas as the capacity-creating efforts of net investment and the phenomenon of accelerator-induced investment, succeed in providing important insights into the operation of the real-world economy. More specifically, their theories enable us to understand, first, why the economy must grow if full employment is to be maintained and, second, why the economy cannot be expected to grow automatically at a rate that will ensure full employment.

Neoclassical Growth Theory

The razor-edge character of the Domar-Harrod analyses has been attacked by a number of economists as being excessively rigid and unrealistic.[25] The basic point of contention is the assumption in the Domar-Harrod analyses of a fixed value for the average and marginal capital-output ratios, with their derivatives of the accelerator used in Harrod's theory and the productivity of capital coefficient used by Domar. It is this feature which gives the analyses their razor-edge character, as the economy is tied tightly to a narrow equilibrium path. As Harrod demonstrates, any departure from this equilibrium ($G_w = G$) leads to either a surging expansion or a plunging collapse.

What the neoclassical critics of the Domar-Harrod analyses seek to show is that the economy in a growth context is stable and that it will, if left to its

---

[25] See especially Robert M. Solow, "A Contribution to the Theory of Economic Growth," *Quarterly Journal of Economics,* February 1956, and T. W. Swan, "Economic Growth and Capital Accumulation," *Economic Record,* November 1956. The model discussed in this section of Chapter 13 is a simplified version of the one developed by Professor Swan in the latter article. Professor Solow received the Nobel Prize in economics in 1987 for his work on neoclassical growth theory.

own devices, seek out a steady-state equilibrium growth path. There is a basic similarity here to the monetarist approach to the economy's behavior, for, like the monetarists and new classical economists, the neoclassical growth theorists are challenging the Keynesian notion that the economy is inherently unstable.

This approach is called neoclassical for several reasons. It assumes that full employment is normally present as the economy grows; hence, savings are continuously absorbed by investment. A competitive economy, diminishing returns, and returns to the factors of production equal to their marginal products are also assumed. But most important for our purposes is the key assumption of the substitutability of capital for labor, and vice versa. In contrast to Domar-Harrod, the capital-output ratio and its converse, the productivity of capital σ, are variable. It is this feature of the neoclassical theory that permits the system to move toward a steady-state equilibrium path of growth.

The essentials of the neoclassical model can be demonstrated with a simple diagram, as shown in Figure 13–4. The horizontal axis in the diagram shows different values for the output-capital ratio (Domar's σ), and the vertical axis represents the rate of growth of output ($\Delta Y/Y$) and the capital stock ($\Delta K/K$). Given a positive value for the propensity to save, the rate of growth will be greater, the greater is the value of the output-capital ratio. Domar's analysis

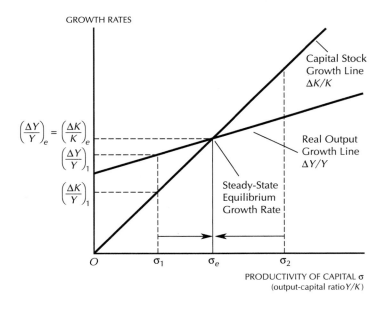

FIGURE 13–4   The Neoclassical Growth Model.   If the rate of growth of the capital stock ($\Delta K/K$) exceeds the productivity of capital (σ) or output-capital ratio (Y/K), the latter will fall. But when $\Delta K/K$ falls short of the output-capital ratio (Y/K), the latter will rise. Interaction between these ratios will bring the system into a long-term equilibrium in which the two ratios are equal.

should make this clear, for if all saving is invested (an assumption of the neoclassical analysis), then the larger the amount of saving, the greater will be the effect on productive capacity as the value of σ increases. Since full employment is assumed, it necessarily follows that the rate of growth of real output will be a positive function of σ. The real output growth line ($\Delta Y/Y$) crosses the vertical axis at a positive growth rate because some growth will take place as a result of a growing labor force and independently of the value of σ.[26]

The rate of growth of the capital stock ($\Delta K/K$) will be proportional to the output-capital ratio (Y/K, or σ), given a fixed value for the propensity to save. This can be shown quite simply. If s is the long-term propensity to save, then S (saving) will be equal to sY. But since the neoclassical model assumes that full employment is the norm and that full-employment savings are absorbed by investment, it follows that $sY = I = \Delta K$. If we divide $sY = \Delta K$ by K, we have sY/K or $s\sigma = \Delta K/K$, which shows that, given the propensity to save s, the rate of growth of the capital stock is proportional to the output-capital rate (Y/K, or σ).

Now let us examine what happens in terms of the model shown in Figure 13–4. Suppose the economy is initially at a point at which the value of the productivity of capital coefficient is σ_1. What does this show? If this is the situation, it means that output is growing faster than the capital stock, that is, $(\Delta Y/Y)_1 > (\Delta K/K)_1$. In the neoclassical world, when this happens, the productivity of capital will rise and capital will be substituted for labor. This will tend to accelerate the rate of growth of both capital and output, but, as long as the productivity of capital (σ) is increasing, the rate of increase in output will have to accelerate more than the rate of increase in the capital stock. This will continue until the two growth rates become equal—the point of intersection of the capital stock growth line and the real output growth line—and a steady-state equilibrium growth rate will prevail.

Contrast this with the Harrod analysis. If output is growing more rapidly than the capital stock, it means the economy faces a chronic shortage of capital. In Harrod's terminology, G is greater than G_w; this means an explosive upward surge in planned investment, and the system moves farther and farther away from the equilibrium growth rate of $G = G_w$. Only a full-employment ceiling can halt the upsurge.

What happens in the neoclassical model when the output-capital ratio is at a value that has the capital stock growing faster than output? This would be σ_2, to the right of σ_e in Figure 13–4. In this case, the productivity of capital will decline, labor will be substituted for capital, and this process will continue until the income-capital ratio has fallen sufficiently to bring the rate of growth of the capital stock into line with the rate of growth of output; a steady-state equilibrium will again prevail. In the Harrod analysis, however, this situation is one in which excess capacity develops ($G_w > G$) and a cumulative down-

---

[26] See Swan, ''Economic Growth and Capital Accumulation,'' for elaboration on this point.

ward movement gets underway, a collapse that will continue until the system works off its excess capacity. Without public intervention this might take a long while.

One conclusion drawn from the neoclassical growth model has significant implications for relationships between developed and less-developed nations. This finding is known as the *convergence* hypothesis. As Figure 13–4 suggests, a high rate of growth may cause a decline in the productivity of capital—this is another way of describing diminishing returns—which will lower the economy's growth rate. On the other hand, when the rate of capital growth is low, the productivity of capital can be improved by increasing capital's rate of growth, thereby raising the economy's growth rate. Since, in general, developed countries have a higher growth rate for capital than less-developed countries, it follows that over the long run the growth rates between the developed and the less-developed nations would tend to converge. Unfortunately, as we shall see in the next section when we discuss endogenous growth theory, this has not happened in the real-world international economy.

Neither the Domar-Harrod nor the neoclassical approach taken in isolation provides a wholly adequate theoretical analysis of the problems an advanced market economy confronts in attempting to attain both growth and full employment over time. Even though its underlying assumptions are more rigid than can be justified, the Domar-Harrod analysis underscores two important aspects of the economy. The first is the capacity-creating effect of net investment, and the second is the inherent instability typical of a market system. Experience tends to confirm this view more than it does the neoclassical view that the system is inherently stable. On the other hand, the neoclassical analysis helps us understand that the knife-edge equilibrium found in Domar-Harrod is probably much too extreme a view of how the system really works. Perfect substitutability of capital for labor does not exist in reality, but neither do absolutely rigid capital-output ratios in most instances. Endogenous growth theory to which we now turn deals with some of these issues.

Endogenous Growth Theory

A good starting point to sketch some of the key ideas and characteristics of emerging endogenous growth theory is the production function as initially described in Chapter 2 (page 65). This is expressed symbolically as

$$Y = f(N, K, T) . \qquad (13-10)$$

In this equation output (Y) depends on labor inputs (N), capital inputs (K), and technology (T), all of which are treated as *endogenous* in "new growth theory," as endogenous growth theory is also called. Recall that in the usual treatment of the production function in a short-term perspective, only one factor, normally labor, is deemed endogenous and variable, and the others are assumed as givens, that is, treated as exogenously determined.

Several important real-world developments in the realm of economic growth gave rise to this new surge of interest in formal growth theory.[27] One is a widening gap rather than a convergence in the growth rates of the developed and the less-developed nations. Another is the empirical fact that in developed, industrial nations, firms frequently experience increasing returns to scale, rather than diminishing returns as standard neoclassical theory suggests. Yet another centers on international trade in a way that goes beyond the theory of comparative advantage argument in favor of trade liberalization.

How can technology be treated in an endogenous fashion in the growth process? This is a critical question. The answer is to link investment spending to technological change. While analytically it may be useful in certain situations to separate technology from capital formation, reality is quite different. Technology does not exist in the abstract; it is more than scientific knowledge of the forces of the physical world. In the real economic world technology depends on investment in new capital and new machines. To be put to use, technology must be embodied in tools and machines. Further, the process is a self-reinforcing one. New knowledge of how to get things done fosters the development of new machines, and new machines, in turn, spur new advances in knowledge. The DC-3 and the 747 are both airplanes, both subject to the same laws of aerodynamics. Also, they are both capital goods. But, the 747 embodies a far more advanced technology in its power plant and its electronics than the DC-3. Consequently, the 747 is a much more efficient machine for moving people by air. Out of this continued interaction between capital formation and technological change comes increasing, rather than decreasing, returns to scale for enterprises in many sectors of the economy.

A significant part of the foregoing process takes place through the depreciation and renewal of the economy's capital stock. In national income accounting, a distinction is made between replacement investment—measured by depreciation allowances—and new (or net) investment. This distinction is necessary for accounting reasons, but it should not obscure the fact that in actuality ''replacement'' investment normally involves newer, better, and more technologically advanced capital than the tools and machines being replaced because of wear or obsolescence. As the nation's stock of capital grows, the amount of physical capital that must be replaced each year grows, so the dynamics involved in the process of replacing old capital accelerate.

In the more simplified versions of the production function discussed above, labor inputs are usually assumed to be of a given level of skill, training, and technical knowledge, something exogenously determined by society's prior investment in ''human capital'' through formal education. Here, too, reality

---

[27] See Paul Romer, ''Capital Accumulation and Long-Run Growth,'' in Robert J. Barro, ed., *Modern Business Cycle Theory* (Cambridge, Mass.: Harvard University Press, 1989), pp. 51–127; ''Symposium on New Growth Theory,'' *Journal of Economic Perspectives*, Vol. 8, Winter, 1994.

is not so simple. Workers are not static beings. On the contrary, in most instances through working they increase their skills and technical knowledge. In almost every work place or situation, there is scope for "learning by doing," for on-the-job training, that not only enhances individual worker's worth and self-esteem, but also makes the individual worker increasingly valuable to the firm. This is one reason why firms in an economic downturn are reluctant to discharge experienced workers, even though strict profit-maximization principle suggests that they should. What is involved here are additional endogenous forces that reflect interaction between inputs of one resource and technology. Technology is not a *deus ex machina*!

Although international trade is not formally included as a variable in Equation (13–10), new growth theorists recognize that trade and trade liberalization play an important role in the growth of an economy. Traditionally, economists have favored the liberalization of international trade because the law of comparative advantage says that with free trade there will be a more efficient allocation of resources between nations. This will raise the incomes of all trading partners. But trade liberalization does more than this. It can be expected to increase the rate at which new technologies are distributed. A nation open to trade will find it easier to develop new technologies, because business firms can enhance their ideas with the ideas embodied in technologies that arrive in the country through trade. Trade also broadens the markets for a country's output; this in turn may raise the return on investment in both physical and human capital—a development which spurs the rate of technological advance.

A word is in order at this point about population change. Another important empirical finding is a negative correlation between population growth and economic growth.[28] On the level of the world economy, the highest rates of output growth are in the advanced countries with the lowest rates of population growth, and the lowest rates of output growth are in the less-developed nations with the highest rates of population growth. All economically advanced nations have gone through a transition process from high to low fertility and mortality rates.[29] This process is endogenous with respect to a nation's economy, but too little is yet known about how the process works to incorporate population changes as an endogenous variable in a formal model of endogenous growth.

One major reason why there has been a resurgence of interest in growth theory among economists is that the endogenous approach offers greater scope for policy actions that can actually influence a nation's growth rate than did the earlier analyses of Domar, Harrod, and Solow. This is true, even though the research has not yet reached the stage where precise quantitative measures of the impact of policy on endogenous variables can be provided to policymakers. Nevertheless, governments can influence investment, both in physical capital and human capital, and if they do this wisely, business

---

[28] Romer, "Capital Accumulation and Long-Run Growth," p. 67, 68.

[29] Ibid.

firms will benefit from increasing returns, and society will probably enjoy a higher rate of technological advance. Recent developments in international economics, like the North American Free Trade Agreement (1993) and the approval of the Uruguay round of the General Agreement on Trade and Tariffs (GATT) in 1994, reflect positive governmental actions that aim to expand the volume of international trade and reduce barriers to trade.

Summary

1. Economic growth concerns the long-term performance of the economy, based on its ability to expand its productive capacity over time and its ability to use that productive capacity. The former is a supply-side problem, whereas the latter is an aggregate demand problem.

2. The production function is a useful concept for getting into the subject of economic growth, as it enables us to focus on the key variables that determine the economy's productive capacity over time. These include the supply of labor (N), the quantity of capital (K) and natural resources (R), and the level of technology (T).

3. Additional key concepts important in analyzing growth are productivity (output per worker-hour) and the ratio of capital to labor (K/N). Long-term historical evidence indicates that technological change, which involves using resources more efficiently, is a major factor in explaining the growth in the economy's potential for production.

4. The economy's output potential can be determined by multiplying the average output per worker per year by the labor force. This is a useful measure which most post-World War II administrations have employed in making policy decisions.

5. One post-World War II development that has had serious consequences for the U.S. economy is the productivity crisis, the slowdown in the rate of growth in U.S. productivity, which became evident in the 1970s. This was a major factor in inflation in the 1970s, since inflation is inevitable if wage increases run ahead of productivity gains.

6. The major causes of the productivity slowdown are excessive spending for military purposes during the forty years of the Cold War, a drastic slowdown in the rate of the nation's investment in public capital—its infrastructure of basic facilities—and a misdirection of private investment into office buildings and shopping malls at the expense of equipping workers with more and better machines and tools. A major program of infrastructure investment is needed, but the political climate is not favorable to this.

7. Within the income-expenditure framework, there are two major theoretical models of economic growth. These are known as the Domar and Harrod models. Both theories are concerned essentially with this basic question:

In a dynamic economy with an ever-expanding production potential, how and at what rate must aggregate demand increase in order to keep the capacity utilized and fully employ the economy's labor force?

8. Professor Domar's model focuses primarily on the capacity-creating effects of net investment. When investment (net) takes place, the economy has added capacity; in subsequent income periods the economy must grow if that capacity is to be utilized. Since, in the Keynesian income-expenditure framework, investment is the basic source of income change, Domar determines the rate at which investment must grow in order to keep the added capacity fully employed. In this sense his analysis is said to be forward-looking.

9. Professor Harrod's approach is slightly different, even though the outcome is essentially the same as in the Domar model. Both models explain theoretically why growth is an absolute necessity in a system of market capitalism, if stagnation and chronic unemployment are to be avoided. Harrod's model draws on the theory of the accelerator and poses the question of whether past growth has been sufficient to induce investment equal to full-employment savings. If not, the economy will move in either an upward or a downward direction, to either chronic inflation or chronic stagnation. Professor Harrod believes the latter is the dominant tendency.

10. Neoclassical growth theory was developed in part as an answer to the precarious knife-edge state of equilibrium found in the Harrod model. By assuming flexibility in all prices, including wages and the return on capital, plus mobility and adaptability of resources, the neoclassical model shows how the economy can settle down over time to a growth path that fully utilizes all resources.

11. Endogenous growth theory concentrates on explaining growth in terms of variables that are treated as exogenous—outside the model—in the Domar, Harrod, and neoclassical approaches. In particular, endogenous growth theory seek to bring technological change, innovation, institutions, international trade, and education into the analysis as *endogenous* not *exogenous* factors in the growth process.

14 Business Cycles and Forecasting

THIS CHAPTER EXTENDS THE theme of the last chapter—economic growth, but now we are concerned with historical patterns of growth and the tools economists use to predict future changes in the economy. Economic growth does not occur at a steady rate; it proceeds by fluctuations—ups and downs if you will.

Figure 14–1 plots the uneven nature of the economy's performance over 134 years. This chart shows the deviations of an index of general business activity from the long-term trend of the economy. The latter, of course, has been upward; as we saw in the preceding chapter, the long-term rate of growth of the U.S. economy has been around 3.5 percent per year. But this is a trend, not the reality of any given year. What Figure 14–1 reveals is that progress over time is sporadic, proceeding in a rough cyclical fashion in which a period of expansion is always followed by a period of contraction.

Historically the term "business cycle" has been used to describe the periodic ups and downs that characterize the actual movement through time of the real economy. The reason for using the word "cycle" is that economic activity over the long pull does follow a wavelike pattern with a significant amount of regularity. But there is some danger in using this word because it carries the connotation of more regularity than is the reality. For a period of time after World War II the term "business cycle" fell out of favor among economists, in part because the long postwar economic upswing gave rise to

545

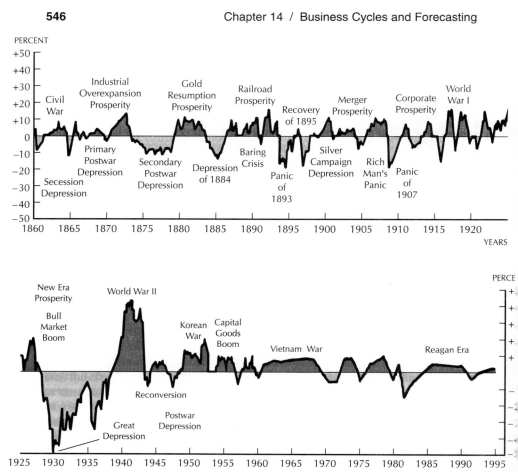

FIGURE 14–1   Business Activity in the United States, 1860–1994. Percentage Deviation from the Long-Term Trend.   This figure, based on data developed by Ameritrust, formerly the Cleveland Trust Company, charts the business cycle—the ups and downs of business activity—as far back as reliable historical records permit. The path of progress in the U.S. economy has never been smooth.

Source: Data from Ameritrust, formerly the Cleveland Trust Company.

a belief—now seen as naive—that the business cycle was a thing of the past. ''Fluctuations'' came to be the preferred term, particularly because it does not imply a regular wavelike motion as does the word ''cycles.'' As a result of the experiences of the 1970s, especially the severe downturns in 1974–75 and 1981–82, the idea of the business cycle has come back into fashion. In the final analysis, the name used is not important; our economy has not experienced a smooth growth path in the past nor is it likely to in the foreseeable future.

Our objectives in this chapter are basically three. First, we shall examine the nature of the business cycle—how it is defined, how it is measured, and what happens during the course of a typical cycle. Second, we shall take an historical look at some of the ideas economists have stressed as explanations for the cycle. Finally, we shall examine the general area of economic forecasting, including a review of the nature and effectiveness of the major forecasting techniques. Forecasting exists because the business cycle exists. If the economy always proceeded upward along a smooth trend line, then it would only be necessary to extrapolate the past in order to know what would happen in the future. Unhappily, the world is not that simple. Hence, there is a necessity for economic forecasting.

The Nature of the Business Cycle

We have, in fact, already defined the business cycle. A formal definition would be *a wavelike movement in the general level of economic activity that takes place over time.* Such a definition is broad enough to apply to the business cycle, as a general phenomenon encompassing the entire economy, or to the many individual types of economic activity that are part of a more general picture. A couple of important points need to be stressed. First, the business cycle is wavelike, but it is not regular in an exact periodic sense. Motions of the latter sort are characteristic of many physical phenomena— electric current, for example—but not of economic activity. Second, the business cycle is an economic phenomenon characteristic of *all* countries organized on market principles, which is to say organized on the basis of private property and the pursuit of private gain. Furthermore, major business cycles occur at about the same time in the leading industrial nations. Business cycle research shows, for example, that this has been true in both the nineteenth and twentieth centuries for such major industrial powers as Germany, France, Great Britain, and the United States. It is not true for the minor cycles, and it is not true that all major industrial nations have had the same number of business cycles. But in a broad, historical sense it is clear that the business cycle is an international phenomenon deeply rooted in the behavior patterns of market economies.

In the United States the most important work in defining, measuring, and understanding the business cycle has been done by the National Bureau of Economic Research, a privately funded research organization located in Cambridge, Massachusetts. In Chapter 2 it was pointed out that the National Bureau pioneered in the development of national income accounting in this country. Wesley Mitchell, a long-time leader in business cycle research, was instrumental in the creation of the National Bureau. Mitchell was the foremost advocate of the view that the cycle involves a continuing, self-generating process that is inherent in a capital-using economy organized around the exchange of money for goods and goods for money in private markets. In his classic study of fluctuations, *What Happens During Business Cycles,* Mitchell defined the cycle as follows (his definition remains the working concept of the cycle used by the National Bureau of Economic Research):

> Business cycles are a type of fluctuation found in the aggregate economic activity of nations that organize their work mainly in business enterprises: a cycle consists of expansion occurring at about the same time in many economic activities, followed by similarly general recessions, contractions, and revivals which merge into the expansion phase of the next cycle; this sequence of events is recurrent, but not periodic; in duration business cycles vary from more than one year to ten or twelve years; they are not divisible into shorter cycles of similar character with amplitudes approximating their own.[1]

Thus, the business cycle as seen by Mitchell pertains primarily to fluctuations in the overall level of economic activity, affecting most industries and activities at about the same time. It is a recurrent process, but not regular in either the magnitude of the fluctuations or the frequency with which they occur.

Measuring the Business Cycle

There are various possible ways in which the business cycle can be measured, but the one most widely used is the method developed by the National Bureau of Economic Research. This method is also used by the U.S. Department of Commerce, which, in its monthly periodical *Survey of Current Business,* publishes the most comprehensive volume of data from any source on what is happening to the economy in a cyclical sense. For its purposes the National Bureau measures the business cycle from trough to peak to trough, although it is just as possible to measure it from peak to trough to peak.

Figure 14–2 shows a simplified, idealized cycle in which real GDP moves from point A (an initial trough or lower turning point) through point B (the peak or upper turning point) and back down to point C (a second trough), from whence a new cycle begins. The fluctuations take place around a trend line that incorporates the economy's long-term growth rate. Because the economy is growing, each peak and each trough normally will be at a higher level than the prior peak or trough. The word ''normally'' is used advisedly in this context, as a glance at the long-term behavior of the economy depicted in Figure 14–1 shows that it does not always happen this way, especially when the economy collapses to the extent it did during the Great Depression of the 1930s.

Figure 14–2 includes additional technical information on the nature of the business cycle. The phase from point A to B is generally called the *upswing,* a period in which output is rising faster than its long-term trend. Normally

---

[1] Wesley C. Mitchell, *What Happens During Business Cycles: A Progress Report* (New York: National Bureau of Economic Research, Studies in Business Cycles 5, 1951), p. 6.

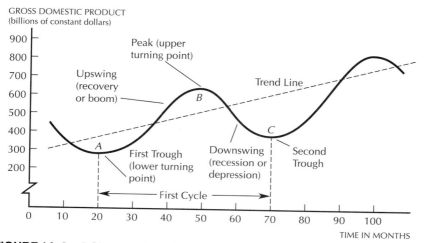

FIGURE 14–2   A Simplified Cycle Pattern. The business cycle, although never in reality as smooth as this figure indicates, does follow a regular pattern—an expansion, an upper turning point, a downswing, a trough, and, finally, a low point leading to a recovery and new upswing.

an upswing will encompass both a recovery period, which involves getting from the low of the trough to a level of output reached at the previous peak, and a period of expansion or boom, which involves output rising to levels beyond the previous peak. From point *B* to point *C* the economy is in the *downswing* of the cycle, a period which involves an actual decline of output. In the downswing the economy finds itself in either a recession or depression. Typically, the National Bureau defines a recession as any period in which *real* GDP has dropped for two successive quarters (six months). Beyond this, there is no precise definition of what constitutes a *recession* and what constitutes a *depression*. The difference between the two is a matter of judgment, depending on the depth of the fall in output (the rise in unemployment) and the length of the downswing or slump in economic activity. Most citizens have no trouble identifying the collapse of the 1930s as a depression because of its length and severity. Since World War II, however, the term ''recession'' has generally been used, because of the relative mildness of downturns except for the 1974–75 and 1981–82 slumps. The extent to which output—or any other economic variable—departs from the long-term trend is described as the *amplitude* of the cycle. It is normally measured as the average deviation (expressed as a percentage) of the series from its trend.

How frequent and how lengthy are business cycles in the United States? Although no precise answer can be given to this question because satisfactory data are lacking for the early years of the nation, reasonably good estimates are available. Table 14–1 gives business cycle data as measured by the trough to trough method from 1854 to 1991. The expansion that began in November 1982 and ended in June 1990 was the longest peacetime expansion in history.

TABLE 14–1 Duration of Business Cycle Expansions and Contractions in the United States, 1854–1991

	Business Cycle						Duration (in months) of		
		Trough		Peak		Trough	Expansion	Contraction	Full Cycle
	Dec.	1854	June	1857	Dec	1858	30	18	48
	Dec.	1858	Oct.	1860	June	1861	22	8	30
	June	1861	Apr.	1865	Dec.	1867	46	32	78
	Dec.	1867	June	1869	Dec.	1870	18	18	36
	Dec.	1870	Oct.	1873	Mar.	1879	34	65	99
	Mar.	1879	Mar.	1882	May	1885	36	38	74
	May	1885	Mar.	1887	Apr.	1888	22	13	35
	Apr.	1888	July	1890	May	1891	27	10	37
	May	1891	Jan.	1893	June	1894	20	17	37
	June	1894	Dec.	1895	June	1897	18	18	36
	June	1897	June	1899	Dec.	1900	24	18	42
	Dec.	1900	Sept.	1902	Aug.	1904	21	23	44
	Aug.	1904	May	1907	June	1908	33	13	46
	June	1908	Jan.	1910	Jan.	1912	19	24	43
	Jan.	1912	Jan.	1913	Dec.	1914	12	23	35
	Dec.	1914	Aug.	1918	Mar.	1919	44	7	51
	Mar.	1919	Jan.	1920	July	1921	10	18	28
	July	1921	May	1923	July	1924	22	14	36
	July	1924	Oct.	1926	Nov.	1927	27	13	40
	Nov.	1927	Aug.	1929	Mar.	1933	21	43	64
	Mar.	1933	May	1937	June	1938	50	13	63
	June	1938	Feb.	1945	Oct.	1945	80	8	88
	Oct.	1945	Nov.	1948	Oct.	1949	37	11	48
	Oct.	1949	July	1953	Aug.	1954	45	13	58
Post-	Aug.	1954	July	1957	Apr.	1958	35	9	44
World	Apr.	1958	May	1960	Feb.	1961	25	9	34
War II	Feb.	1961	Nov.	1969	Nov.	1970	105	12	117
Era	Nov.	1970	Nov.	1973	Mar.	1975	36	16	52
	Mar.	1975	Jan.	1980	July	1980	63	6	69
	July	1980	July	1981	Nov.	1982	12	16	28
	Nov.	1982	June	1990	Mar.	1991	91	6	97
Average, all cycles:									
31 cycles, 1854–1991							35	18	53
15 cycles, 1919–1991							44	14	58
9 cycles, 1945–1991							50	11	61

Source: *Business Conditions Digest; Survey of Current Business,* various issues (numbers rounded).

In the period covered by the data of Table 14–1 there have been 31 full cycles, averaging 53 months in length (from trough to trough). The expansion phase has averaged almost twice as long as the contraction phase. On the average, since 1854, periods of expanding economic activity have averaged 35 months, or nearly three years, whereas the downturns typically have averaged one and a half years. The data of Table 14–1 also indicate some significant changes in the cyclical pattern of the economy following World War II. Since 1945 we have had nine measurable business cycles, but the significant development has been an increase in the length of the expansion and prosperity phase of the cycle and a reduction in the average length of the downturn. After World War II expansions were 43 percent longer and contractions 39 percent shorter than the long-term average for the economy (1854–1991). In part this was the result of the unusually long upswings of the 1960s and 1980s, but not wholly since upswings for six out of the eight cycles recorded between 1954 and 1991 were longer than the historic average.

As mentioned earlier, belief that the business cycle was dead collapsed in the face of the unexpected severity of the 1974–75 and 1981–82 slumps, the worst economic downturns experienced by the economy since the 1930s. Not only was the falloff in output in these recessions more severe than any of the other post-World War II recessions, but the contraction phase in both recessions lasted 16 months, a period nearly equal to the long-term historic average for bad times. Clearly the 1974–75 and 1981–82 recessions were old-fashioned business cycles of the sort that were not supposed to happen, according to earlier optimistic observers of the post-World War II economy. But they did.

Long Waves in Economic Life

Typically the business cycle as defined and measured by the National Bureau of Economic Research lasts from three to five years. Most business cycle research has centered on this type of cycle, although from the time research into the cyclical behavior of the economy first began in the nineteenth century, there have been scholars intrigued with the idea that there are much longer economic waves at work in market economies. One of the earliest serious students of the business cycle was Clement Juglar, a French medical doctor who became so fascinated with the idea that it was possible through statistics to isolate and measure the ebb and flow of economic life that he gave up the practice of medicine and became an economist. Juglar was an early advocate of the idea that there were commercial cycles that occurred with considerable regularity. He saw that each cycle had a similar pattern, even though there was no uniformity with respect to either frequency or length. He suggested that cycles had three parts—prosperity, crisis, and liquidation—and that they always followed one another in the same order.[2] Juglar did think, however, that the average length of a cycle was nine to ten years, which is two to three times longer than the cycles recognized by contemporary theorists.

---

[2] Wesley C. Mitchell, *Business Cycles: The Problem and the Setting* (New York: National Bureau of Economic Research, 1927), p. 452.

It was a Russian economist, Nikolai D. Kondratieff, whose name became almost synonymous with the idea of long waves in economic life.[3] Kondratieff developed his theory of long waves by studying data on wholesale prices, interest rates, wage rates, and physical production for the French, British, and American economies. His studies covered the period from about 1780 to 1920, or almost a century and a half. From these studies he concluded that Western—that is, market or capitalistic—economies are subject to very long waves of a distinct cyclical character. These *Kondratieff cycles* are approximately fifty to sixty years in length with an upswing and downswing of about equal length. Furthermore, they are international in scope and appear about the same time in the major industrial states of Europe as well as the United States. Kondratieff did not offer any theoretical explanation to account for the existence of long waves, but he did suggest that they are inherent in a capitalistic economy.

Joseph A. Schumpeter, best known, perhaps, for his theory linking investment to innovation and invention (Chapter 8), developed a model of the business cycle which involved an integration of Kondratieff's long-wave theory with the ideas of Juglar and a third economist, Joseph Kitchin, who, writing in the early 1920s, developed a theory involving major and minor cycles. His minor cycle averaged 40 months in duration and his major cycle consisted of three minor cycles, which made the Kitchin major about the same length as the cycle Juglar thought he had discovered (nine to ten years). What Schumpeter did was combine the 40-month Kitchin cycle and the 10-year Juglar cycle with Kondratieff's long wave. In Schumpeter's scheme the Juglar cycle provided the link between the Kondratieff long wave and the much shorter Kitchin cycle. No special significance attaches to this, except in those rare instances when the downswings of all three cycles coincide. As Schumpeter said, "No claims are made for our three cycle scheme except that it is a useful descriptive or illustrative device. Using it, however, we in fact got *ex visu* of 1929, a 'forecast' of a serious depression embodied in the formula: coincidence of the depression phase of all three cycles."[4]

Many contemporary students of the business cycle flatly reject the notion of long waves in economic life, of either the Kondratieff variety or the shorter Juglar type. There are cycles—of this there is little doubt—but the general consensus among economists is that they average between three and five years in length, as is suggested by the data in Table 14–1. Minor cycles do exist, but most of these appear to be the result of inventory adjustments. Most economists do not believe that there is any systematic relationship such as

---

[3] Kondratieff developed his ideas about long waves in the early 1920s. He published a paper on the subject in Russian in 1925, which was subsequently translated into both German and English. The English version of his article may be found in *Readings in Business Cycle Theory* [New York: McGraw-Hill (Blakiston), 1944], pp. 20–42. Kondratieff was a Marxist economist, but he disappeared from the Soviet scene sometime in the late 1920s. It has been reported that he incurred the displeasure of Stalin, was arrested, and banished to a Soviet labor camp. His real fate remains unknown.

[4] Joseph A. Schumpeter, *Business Cycles*, Vol. I (New York: McGraw-Hill, 1938), p. 174.

Kitchin described between minor cycles and a longer cycle of perhaps ten years.

What Happens in a Typical Business Cycle

While no two business cycles are the same with respect to length, intensity, or other developments, there is a basic pattern of events that is similar in all cycles. Thanks largely to the long, painstaking research of Wesley C. Mitchell, we have a clear picture of the most important things that happen in a business cycle. To arrive at a composite picture of the cycle, Mitchell examined the behavior of more than 800 time series.[5] He never did develop a precise theory of the business cycle, although when viewed overall, his findings provide a reasonable and coherent explanation of the cyclical process.

There are two important points to note and understand with respect to Mitchell's view of the cycle. First, Mitchell, like many other economists, found the cycle to be inherent in money-using, market economies in which the quest for money profits by business enterprises is the dominant fact of economic life. Second, he found the processes at work in the typical cycle are cumulative and carry within themselves the seeds by which one phase of the cycle is transformed into the next phase. These processes are not only cumulative, but repetitive, and from this comes the fact that *all* cycles have certain common characteristics.

A convenient point of departure is a recession or depression. In the absence of deliberate policy actions by a central government (a tax cut, more spending, lowered interest rates, or any combination of these) what will bring about a recovery? In a recession prices drop (or the inflation rate lessens), labor is in ample supply because of unemployment, wages and other costs go down (or at least go up less rapidly), while money and credit become increasingly available as bank reserves grow. Profits, of course, are low or nonexistent in many cases. Profits, however, are the key to a recovery. Somewhere, in some sector of the economy, a recovery will start when the profit picture changes, usually because costs in a recession, or depression, eventually drop farther than prices. Although a recovery tends to be slow at first, once started it spreads throughout the economy and becomes cumulative in effect. Prices start rising once a recovery is well underway. Here we encounter one of Mitchell's key statistical findings, which is that as a recovery merges into an expansion or boom, the prices of finished goods and services rise more rapidly than the prices of those things which enter directly into production costs—wages for labor, rents for land and buildings, and interest on loans. There is

---

[5] Right up to the time of his death, Mitchell was still trying to find out empirically what actually happened in the cycle. His work over the years is summarized in his last book, published after his death, *What Happens During Business Cycles.* Our account of the sequence of events in a typical cycle is based largely on Mitchell's findings.

no guarantee that this pattern will hold in a recovery, but to the extent that it does, profits improve and the expansion gathers momentum. An improved profit picture not only stimulates current production, which puts people back to work, it also stimulates investment spending as pessimism in the business community gives way to optimism.

Why does prosperity not continue indefinitely? What brings an expansion to an end? Basically what happens is that the cumulative process of recovery and expansion (or boom) is subject to two fundamental stresses, both built into market systems organized around profit-seeking business enterprises. One pertains to the production process itself, and the other to the financial structure. We must keep in mind that the business cycle is a short-term phenomenon; this means that it takes place within a time period (three to five years) that does not permit large increases in productive capacity. Thus, as an expansion proceeds, the cost of doing business will begin to rise, slowly at first but at an accelerating pace as prosperity proceeds. This comes about in part because firms push up against capacity limits set by the existing stock of equipment. The cost of labor will rise, not only because prosperity pushes up standard wage rates as firms scramble for increasingly scarce labor, but also because more overtime will be paid. Furthermore, labor efficiency (worker productivity) declines as less-skilled workers are pulled into the job market and older and less efficient equipment is pressed into use, while longer hours and pressure to turn out goods at an even faster pace cause more mistakes, waste, and numerous small inefficiencies, all of which increase the costs of doing business. At some point in an upswing, prices of raw materials begin to rise faster than the selling prices for finished products—a development which puts further pressure on cost-price relationships and the profit picture.

In the meanwhile, parallel stresses are developing in the investment and money markets. Essentially what Mitchell found was that the supply of funds available for lending through the usual financial channels (the bond and mortgage markets) fails to keep pace with the demand. Neither does the supply of bank loans, which are necessarily limited by the reserves banks must hold against their expanding liabilities. Firms find that it becomes more and more difficult to negotiate new security issues, especially bonds, except on increasingly onerous terms. High levels of employment and economic activity generally soak up most of the money in circulation and leave little available for lending or to meet liquidity needs. The demand for bank loans continues to grow, not only because of expanded levels of activity, but also because of rising prices. For a time at least this demand is not responsive to higher interest rates since profit expectations remain high and firms are optimistic that they can turn borrowed money over rapidly enough to come out ahead. The growing tensions in the financial markets are a threat to continued expansion simply because sooner or later higher interest rates will cut into both actual and expected profit margins. When this happens, both current production and investment for future production will suffer.

As the foregoing pressures and tensions mount in both the real (goods) and financial (money) spheres of the economy, only one route is open to prevent disaster from overwhelming the economy. This is to continue to push up prices fast enough to keep rising costs from encroaching on profits. But this may prove to be impossible. Some prices, such as those set by law, by long-term contracts, by custom, or even by business policy, simply cannot move up rapidly. Incomes, too, may not keep pace with prices. In any event, the accumulated stresses imposed on both the production and financial sides of the economy during an expansion end sooner or later in a *crisis*. In Mitchell's view a crisis initially is a situation in which business firms attempt to liquidate some or all of the debts they have incurred during the expansion and prosperity phase of the cycle. The crisis, which marks the upper turning point of the cycle, may be mild or severe, even turning into a full-fledged monetary panic of the sort that led to the temporary closing of the banks in 1933. But once an expansion or boom slides into a crisis, the situation again becomes cumulative and spreads from the banking community to business firms to the entire community. Business firms are forced to concentrate on looking after their outstanding liabilities and husbanding their financial resources, instead of pushing sales and continuing to expand production. Thus, the volume of new orders and, with it, production and employment begin to fall—a process which is cumulative downward just as a recovery and expansion is cumulative upward. Unless checked by government intervention or some other unforeseen outside event (such as a war), the economy slides into a recession or depression, from whence, according to Mitchell, the cycle will begin all over again.

Are there limits to the amplitude of the cycle? This is a question which Mitchell never addressed directly, although his notion that each phase of the cycle carries within it the forces that lead the economy into the next phase implies the existence of limits. Nobel laureate Sir John Hicks of Oxford University developed a theory of a *constrained* cycle, in which the magnitude of fluctuations is limited by both a ceiling and a floor.[6] In Professor Hicks's analysis the cycle results from an interaction between the Keynesian multiplier and the accelerator in a fashion similar to the example developed in Chapter 7. Figure 14–3 depicts the Hicksian cycle model with the built-in floor and ceiling. The ceiling is set by the rate of growth of the full-employment labor force plus the rate of growth in its productivity. Thus, if the fully employed labor force grew at an annual average rate of 1 percent and labor productivity increased annually on the average at 2.5 percent, the ceiling at which output could grow over time would be 3.5 percent. Actual output could not exceed this figure except for a brief interval. Thus, there is an effective upper limit to cyclical fluctuations in the economy.

The floor below which output during its cyclical path cannot fall is determined differently. It results in part from the fact that the working of the accelerator over the course of the cycle is not symmetrical. The accelerator, it will be recalled, leads to more or less investment spending as a consequence

[6] J. R. Hicks, *A Contribution to the Theory of the Trade Cycle* (London: Oxford University Press, 1950), especially Chaps. 7 and 8, pp. 83–107.

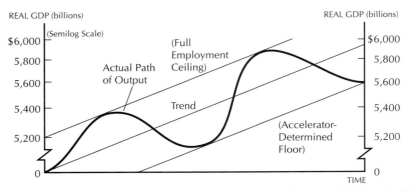

FIGURE 14–3   The Constrained Business Cycle of Sir John Hicks.   In this view of the cycle there is both a floor, which sets limits for the depth of the downswing, and a ceiling, which is set by the full-employment rate of growth of the labor force and the rate of growth of productivity. This model fits empirical experience.

of a *change in the rate* at which output is changing. During a downswing the fall in output will, of course, lead to a decline in induced investment, but there will be a limit to the amount by which total investment will fall. The reason is that all investment is not induced. Even in a severe depression some autonomous investment is likely; hence total investment will not normally fall to zero or even become negative (except for very short periods). This means, in effect, that the effective value of the accelerator may be smaller in a downswing than it is in an upswing—a fact that automatically tends to put a floor under the downswing. Furthermore, we must reckon with the Keynesian fact that, as income (that is, real output) falls, consumption does not fall as fast. Even, therefore, if gross investment fell to zero or became negative for a short period of time, consumption spending would eventually act to place a limit to the fall in output, because at some point consumption would begin to exceed output. When this happened, the floor would have been reached. The economy may experience a level of unemployment that is not acceptable politically long before the floor is reached, but this does not change the theoretical fact that a floor may exist. It merely means that positive policy actions will be taken before the floor is reached.

Causes of the Business Cycle

Although some economists have tried to understand and explain the business cycle ever since the existence of cycles in economic activity was recognized, most of this effort took place outside the mainstream of theoretical economics. The reason, of course, was the dominant position of the classical approach to economic understanding right up until the crash of 1929. Classical economics, dominated by Say's law and the belief that full employment was the normal state of affairs, simply had no place for a view of the world in which serious ups and downs in economic activity were the norm. As a consequence, most theorizing about the business cycle in the nineteenth century did not have much academic respectability; it was seen mostly as a part of an underworld of economics populated by cranks, crackpots, and assorted charlatans pushing their pet nostrums for the world's economic ills.[7] The situation did not change until the early 1900s, at which time the work of Mitchell, Schumpeter, and a few others began to have a recognized impact. Still, business cycle theorizing continued largely outside the mainstream of economic analysis until Keynes's monumental study appeared in the mid-1930s.

Even though there is no agreement today among economists on *the cause* of the business cycle, one very important thing happened because of Keynes's work: *The General Theory* brought the business cycle into the mainstream of economic analysis. Keynes did not develop a definitive theory of the business cycle.[8] But cycles are a phenomenon characteristic of the aggregate economy. Furthermore, cycles have been viewed historically as an inherent characteristic of profit-oriented, market-based economic systems. Since these viewpoints are in harmony with the content and spirit of *The General Theory,* it follows naturally that analysis of the business cycle can and should take place within the unified theoretical framework that Keynes developed.

Explanations of cycles have fallen into one of two quite broad categories, an approach we shall follow in this discussion. First, there is the *external* or *exogenous* approach. This view, characteristic of much thinking about the cycle during the nineteenth century, looks on external shocks, such as a war or a bad harvest, as the fundamental cause of the business cycle. Technically such shocks are said to be stochastic, which means random. It is true, of course, that the way in which the economy reacts to an external shock is important for understanding and explaining the cycle, but the basic cause is held to be external to the system itself. Philosophically, this approach fits in with classical thinking since the classical economists saw the economic system primarily as a self-regulating mechanism that tended (if left alone) toward an equilibrium of full employment. In their view this was its natural state.

The second stream of thought is much more in tune with modern Keynesian thinking about the nature and behavior of the economic system. It involves the belief that cycles are inherent in the economic system, that their existence is not dependent on any external forces. This clearly matches the spirit of *The*

---

[7] Karl Marx is, of course, an exception to this, as he is one of the commanding figures in the history of economic thought and a man of the nineteenth century, as well. Marx believed that the business cycle was so ingrained in the capitalistic system of ownership and production that the only possible cure was a complete change in the nature of the system. The classical economists did not accept Marx's analysis of capitalism.

[8] As we have seen, the purpose of *The General Theory* was to develop a systematic explanation of the forces which determine the level of output and employment in the mature market (i.e., capitalistic economy). Keynes did not set out to establish a theory of the business cycle, but he did believe that the theoretical framework that he developed in his classic work could also be used to explain this phenomenon. See Chapter 22, "Notes on the Trade Cycle," in *The General Theory.*

General Theory. Such *internal* or *endogenous* theories of the cycle may be wholly mechanistic, as is the case with the purely formal multiplier-accelerator model developed in Chapter 9, or they may be loose and relatively unstructured, as is a theory that revolves around the key role that Keynes accords to expectations and uncertainty. In any event, all such internal expansions of the cycle have in common a belief that profit-based, market-oriented economic systems are inherently unstable.

External Causes

One of the oldest of the external, or stochastic, attempts to explain the cycle is the *sunspot theory,* an approach developed by the English classical economist W. Stanley Jevons.[9] His investigations into fluctuations led him to suggest a cycle of approximately 10 or 11 years duration. But the main causes of such cycles were periodic upheavals in weather conditions, a development that he thought was traceable to variations in the intensity of sunspots. If there were a strong correlation between sunspots and cycles in the weather, such a theory of the business cycle might make sense for a predominantly agricultural economy, but it would not suffice to explain the business cycle in an economy in which agriculture accounts for only a small part of the output total. Subsequent research does not support the close correlation between sunspots and business cycles that Jevons thought existed, although the subject of the impact of sunspots on the earth's climate continues to fascinate scientists and laypeople alike. It remains an open question.

Money, especially gold, has sometimes been seen as the source of an exogenous shock capable of initiating a cyclical reaction in the economy. Gold discoveries in California and Alaska are examples of monetary shocks. The difficulty with this view is that such events happen only once in a great while, whereas cycles are more or less regular occurrences. Under modern conditions a monetary shock theory of the cycle simply will not do, for the money supply is no longer dependent on such chance happenings as the discovery of a new gold field at home or abroad. Thus, there is no real basis for a modern theory of the cycle based on monetary shocks.

Joseph A. Schumpeter not only studied the business cycle and its length in detail, but he also developed a theory of the cycle which should be classified with other external or exogenous explanations. Briefly, Schumpeter believed that innovation was the major external shock that would start the economy on a cyclical path. Schumpeter is at one with other theorists who see the business cycle as a continuing process, which moves through successive phases with considerable regularity. But innovation is the key originating cause in such fluctuations. He described the process in an important 1927 article:

---

[9] Jevons is perhaps best known for his role in the development of the law of diminishing marginal utility.

These booms consist in the carrying out of innovations in the industrial and commercial organism. By innovations I understand such changes of the combination of factors of production as cannot be effected by infinitesimal steps or variations of the margin. They consist primarily in changes in methods of production and transportation, or in changes in industrial organization, or in the production of a new article, or in the opening up of new markets of new sources of material. The recurring periods of prosperity of the cyclical movement are the form progress takes in capitalistic society.[10]

In this article and in his subsequent voluminous writings, Schumpeter made it clear, first, that innovations originate in regular fashion because a single individual or a relative handful of business executives see possibilities for gain not seen by the vast majority and, second, that the cycle of boom followed by collapse is the mechanism through which the benefits of any innovation get spread throughout the economy. The cycle, in other words, is the price of progress. Schumpeter's theory is classified as an external or exogenous approach because the act of innovation is an extraordinary act, not normally forthcoming through the usual, routine operation of the economy. It is in this sense that innovation is an external or exogenous cause of the cycle.

Before we look at the alternative set of explanations for the cycle—those that define it as wholly an internal affair in a market system—let us consider briefly a thoroughly modern version of the external or exogenous approach, a version that puts government in the role of the external cause. This view grows out of the neoclassical and monetarist views of the economy as being inherently stable, tending when left alone toward a full-employment equilibrium.[11] Some external shock is required to dislodge the economy from its natural, equilibrium state. When this happens, there will be public pressure for government action to restore equilibrium. But, because of lags, the government policy reaction will not only come too late, but its response is likely to be too strong in view of the fact that the forces that tend to restore equilibrium start working even before a policy decision is made. What government intervention does is exaggerate the natural corrective response of the economic system to an external shock and thus worsen rather than correct the effect of the shock. Government is seen as a cause of, not a corrective to, cyclical fluctuations. Milton Friedman is one of the leading proponents of this viewpoint, especially in the realm of monetary policy. The Federal Reserve System, he argues, usually does the wrong thing because it misreads what is happening in the economy and fails to pay enough heed to the econ-

[10] Joseph A. Schumpeter, "The Explanation of the Business Cycle," *Economica*, December 1927, p. 295.

[11] See, for example, Merton H. Miller and Charles W. Upton, *Macroeconomics: A Neoclassical Introduction* (Homewood, Ill.: Irwin, 1974). In their preface, Miller and Upton say "We believe that the course in macroeconomics should emphasize . . . that a market economy left to its own devices will settle into a full employment equilibrium. External shocks, of a variety of kinds, will dislodge it from equilibrium from time to time, but the economy's internal defenses will speedily return it to equilibrium barring new shocks or actively destabilizing policies by the government."

omy's self-correcting mechanism. For example, the Federal Reserve usually interprets rising interest rates as a sign of insufficient money rather than of excess spending. It reacts—wrongly, according to Friedman—by increasing the money supply, which only worsens the situation by leading to more spending. Government action is destabilizing rather than stabilizing.

Internal Causes

In spite of the often persuasive arguments of Professor Friedman, many economists do not accept the view that the economy is inherently stable. Cycle theories of an *internal* or *exogenous* character are more in tune with contemporary thinking about the economy's behavior than are external shock theories. Here again, however, there is no single theory, no consensus among economists on how to explain the business cycle. For simplicity in exposition we shall consider, first, some pre-Keynesian views of the internal causes of the cycle and follow that with a brief examination of the cyclical process as seen by Keynes in *The General Theory*.

Pre-Keynesian theorizing about the business cycle may be divided into two broad categories. There are, first, a group of theories usually labeled *underconsumption* theories and, second, another group generally described as *overinvestment* theories. We shall take a brief look at some of the main ideas and economic personalities associated with each of these broad categories.

Although the term ''underconsumption'' lacks a precise meaning, the underconsumptionist approach to the business cycle sees the ultimate collapse in boom conditions as caused by a failure of spending by consumers to keep pace with production, leading eventually to a glut of unsold goods. The reason why consumption fails to keep pace is not always clear; sometimes it is hoarding, sometimes an excess of saving, or sometimes simply the belief that the system does not pay out sufficient funds to buy back what is being produced. Why the latter happens is also not always clear, although it is a theme that runs through the underconsumptionist literature. The roots of the underconsumptionist viewpoint trace back to Thomas Malthus, one of the early classical economists. In one of the many letters he exchanged with David Ricardo, Malthus pointed out the possibility for demand to be deficient if a society attempts to save at a pace in excess of the willingness to invest (to employ modern terminology), but his arguments made no impression on Ricardo and other classical economists. Say's law won out over what Keynes called ''plain sense.''[12]

Prior to Keynes, the most complete development of the underconsumption approach to business cycles came from John A. Hobson, a British economist writing near the end of the nineteenth century. Hobson took issue with Say's law and asserted that the business cycle resulted from a combination of ov-

---

[12] See Keynes's essay on Malthus entitled ''Thomas Malthus: The First of the Cambridge Economists,'' in John Maynard Keynes, *Essays in Biography* (New York: Norton, 1951), p. 117.

ersaving and underconsumption. He did not deny the fundamental premise that production (that is, supply) creates the means to make payments or buy back what is produced, but he did argue that many persons produced more (that is, got more income) than they needed to consume, so their production did not translate into an equal amount of effective demand. Consequently, demand could be insufficient in the aggregate. The remedy was in less saving, an end that could be attained by some redistribution of income and wealth. Hobson recognized that redistribution could go too far and thereby impair saving and ultimately economic progress, but progress was also hurt by the periodic failures of demand to keep pace with the growth in productive power because income was too unequal. Thus, society had to thread its way toward a more equal distribution of income, but not one so equal as to threaten all saving and the progress it had made possible.

In a way the overinvestment theories are a mirror image of the underconsumptionist approach to the cycle. Like the latter, prosperity collapses because of an excess of production—a glut of goods. But in this case the goods in excess supply are capital goods, not consumer goods. Basically what happens is that an upswing in activity is set in motion by a rising tide of spending for new capital goods, a surge that eventually saturates the economy with more new capital goods than it can profitably employ. When this happens, the investment boom collapses and drags down the rest of the economy.

What causes the overinvestment boom? No specific answer exists for this question, although the practice in the theoretical literature is to lump the causes of the investment boom into two broad categories—monetary and nonmonetary. Frederick A. Hayek, an Austrian-born economist and Nobel laureate, is the best-known exponent of the monetary overinvestment theory of the business cycle. At the root of the problem is the willingness of the banking and financial system to create new bank credit and make this credit available to business enterprises on favorable terms. It is, in other words, an expansion of money and credit that gets the investment boom rolling. For investment to take place, however, there must be real savings, which involve a diversion of resources from consumer to investment goods output. In Hayek's scheme the necessary savings are *forced,* not voluntary. This is what eventually causes the investment boom to collapse. Savings are forced by the process of rising prices brought about by the bidding of producers of investment goods for increasingly scarce resources as the boom accelerates. The boom can continue as long as investment spending is fed by expanding bank credit and forced saving. But ultimately this leads to maladjustments in the structure of production; there are too many new capital goods in relation to the real ability of consumers to buy. Forced savings mean that consumers are being priced out of the market by higher prices; this process must sooner or later lead to a glut of both investment and consumer goods. The inevitable collapse is hastened by growing stringency in the financial markets as the banking system exhausts its excess reserves and interest rates begin to rise. Thus, firms find it more and more difficult to secure the credit needed to keep the investment boom rolling on favorable terms. What the crisis and downturn do, in Hayek's view, is force the economy back into a more normal situation, in which the structure of production—that is, the relationship between investment and consumption goods output—is adjusted to the level at which voluntary savings are forthcoming. Recession or depression is the price the economy pays for the excesses of an investment boom generated initially by easy money conditions.

Nonmonetary overinvestment theories of the business cycle suggest a similar sequence of events—too much investment, too little consumption demand, and an eventual turning point or collapse when the investment goods produced during the boom begin turning out increased quantities of consumer goods and services. The basic difference is that much less stress is placed on money and credit as the ultimate causal factors in the investment boom. What is common to all such theories is a belief that the cycle is caused by overproduction that results from overinvestment. Money of necessity plays a role, for no expansion is possible without more money, but the nonmonetary theorists view the money and financial system primarily as a part of the response mechanism rather than as a fundamental causative factor. Leading exponents of a nonmonetary overinvestment approach to the cycle have been a Russian economist Michael Tugan-Baranowsky; a German, Arthur Spiethoff; and a Swedish engineer who became an economist, Gustav Cassel. The key studies of these and other overinvestment theorists appeared before publication of Keynes's *The General Theory*.

The General Theory

Keynes did not set out to develop a theory of the business cycle (in *The General Theory*), but he did think about the phenomenon and draw on the theoretical apparatus that he developed in his classic work to suggest why cycles existed in a market economy. Most of the ideas discussed previously can be fitted into the sequence of events that Keynes envisioned. We shall conclude the discussion of the causes of the business cycle with a brief summary of Keynes's views on the phenomenon.

In his "Notes on the Trade Cycle" (Chapter 22 in *The General Theory*) Keynes says that the essential character of the trade cycle—the regularity and the duration of the economy's ups and downs which justify the notion of a cycle—is due mainly to "the way in which the marginal efficiency of capital fluctuates."[13] This, of course, puts investment at the heart of the matter, for the marginal efficiency of capital is the key to what happens to investment spending. Keynes approaches the question of the cycle by asking what happens in the later stages of a typical boom. As with most business cycle theorists, Keynes sees the boom carried forward mainly by investment spending,

---

[13] Keynes, *The General Theory*, p. 313.

given the essentially passive role of consumption spending. But investment spending, Keynes reminds us, depends not only on the existing scarcity and cost of capital goods, but on expectations about the future yield of newly produced capital goods. However, "the basis for such expectations is very precarious. Being based upon shifting and unreliable evidence they are subject to sudden and violent change."[14] The future and its uncertainty is a theme to which Keynes returns again and again in *The General Theory*. And here we have the basic reason for the sudden and unpredictable collapse of the marginal efficiency of capital, an event which marks the onset of the crisis and the downward plunge of the economy. In the latter stages of any investment boom, expectations of future yields must be optimistic enough to offset the growing abundance of capital, rising supply price for new capital, and increases in interest rates. At some point, however, expectations may collapse; the longer the boom goes on, the more fragile and uncertain becomes the basis on which expectations for future yields rest. Thus, as Keynes says, the "predominant explanation of the crisis is, not primarily a rise in the rate of interest, but a sudden collapse in the marginal efficiency of capital."[15] All else flows from this fundamental fact.

Following the collapse of the marginal efficiency of capital, there will be a sharp increase in liquidity preference, a consequence of the dismay and uncertainty about the future that the crisis precipitates. For a time interest rates will be high, but even after the immediate crisis passes, the marginal efficiency of capital remains so low that there is no practical way in which interest rates can be reduced enough to bring investment spending out of the slump. For a period the slump will be intractable. Unless there is outside intervention—government action, for example—some time must elapse before a recovery can begin. But there cannot be a general recovery from the slump until a revival in the marginal efficiency of capital. Recovery will not happen until the economy rids itself of surplus inventories of all goods carried over from the crisis and ensuing slump and until normal forces of growth begin to make the stock of fixed capital assets (equipment and buildings) *relatively* less abundant.

Keynes distinguishes his analysis from earlier overinvestment theories of the cycle by pointing out that in his opinion the term "overinvestment" should be used only to describe a state of affairs in which every kind of capital good is so abundant that no new investment in any kind of capital could earn more than its replacement cost—a condition in which capital ceased to have any true scarcity value. This, of course, is not the situation described in the previous paragraph, for a collapse in the marginal efficiency of capital means a collapse in the expected returns based on uncertain and flimsy knowledge about the future. Such expectations may or may not reflect the scarcity of capital in a more enduring and fundamental sense. It is the relative scarcity

---

[14] Ibid., p. 315.

[15] Ibid.

The Political Business Cycle

In 1944, Michael Kalecki, a distinguished Polish economist who fled to England during World War II, published a remarkable article entitled "The Political Aspects of Full Employment."* The gist of Kalecki's argument was that attempts to ensure full employment by large-scale government spending during a slump would sooner or later encounter strong opposition from the business community. Such opposition would arise in part because of straightforward hostility by business to deficit spending as a matter of principle and in part because of the fear that a prolonged period of full employment would strengthen the economic position of the wage earner vis-à-vis the property owner and business executive. But the general public will not tolerate a prolonged slump with high unemployment; consequently, political pressure mounts until the government acts to bring the economy out of the slump by cutting taxes, increasing public spending, or both. In any event, the policy measures taken to counter the slump involve deficit spending, which sooner or later arouses the opposition of the business community and forces the government to return to a more orthodox policy of reducing deficits. A new slump follows.

Events in the postwar era did not develop in either England or the United States quite as Kalecki foresaw, even though *stop* (putting on the fiscal and monetary brakes) and *go* (stepping on the fiscal and monetary accelerator) policies have been present in both countries. What did develop in the United States were political practices in which the administration in power sought to the extent possible to ensure that a slump, if one was to come, came early in its term in office and that prosperity was on hand when it came time for re-election. Richard Nixon was one of the most successful practitioners of the art of the "presidential political business cycle," as he was able to use both monetary and fiscal policy to stimulate the economy before the 1972 presidential election. Nixon won a landslide victory that year.

*_The Political Quarterly_, October–December 1943, pp. 322–331.

of capital in a subjective sense that governs the marginal efficiency and thus determines the pace of investment. This is the true meaning of Keynes's theory, which sees wide swings in the marginal efficiency of capital as the key to understanding the business cycle.

Economic Forecasting

Economic forecasting is an attempt to determine what will happen in the economy over the near term, which is to say what will happen in the next quarter or the next year. Most forecasting does not extend further into the future. Forecasting involves, in other words, an attempt to estimate changes in the major aggregate economic variables—output, employment, and the price level, for example—in the period immediately ahead. Forecasting requires a knowledge and understanding of what has happened in the recent past, what is happening now in the economy, and the *why* of such happenings. The latter implies a need for economic theory, for we cannot understand and interpret the observed performance of the economy without a theoretical frame of reference. Forecasting is both an art and a science, although probably more of an art, because of the uncertainty that surrounds the economic future. Thus, we touch once again on a key theme that threads its way through the Keynesian view of the economic universe.

Forecasting is necessary because the economy moves forward in an irregular fashion—in the kind of cyclical or wavelike movements that have been the subject of this chapter. If the economy's path through time were regular, then forecasting would not be necessary. We should merely have to extrapolate past trends to know what tomorrow would bring. Unfortunately, the economic world does not always work this way. Yet people want to know what is going to happen next week, next month, or next year. Thus, forecasting meets an important human need. Furthermore, accurate forecasting is essential if economic stabilization is to work. We know from the available evidence that the economy is inherently unstable, but we also believe that this instability can be minimized by a judicious use of the policy tools that are the legacy of contemporary macroeconomic theory. But unless we can forecast with reasonable accuracy the forthcoming ups and downs of the economic system, our knowledge of how to apply economic theory to improve the economy's performance will not do us much good.

This brings us to a more specific question: What do we expect from economic forecasting? Basically, forecasting should accomplish two things. First, it should tell us when the economy is approaching a turning point, which is to say that forecasting ought to send out some kind of a signal that a major change in the economic weather is coming. It should, in other words, tell us that a downturn or an upturn is in sight. Ideally, forecasts ought to tell us exactly when a turning point can be expected, but this is beyond the current capabilities of the art. Second, a forecast should have something to say about the magnitude of a forthcoming change. For example, if the economic signals say a recession is coming, they ought to give some indication of the severity or depth of the recession.

There are some knotty problems involved in the foregoing matters that are worth pointing out, although we shall not explore them in depth. For example, if policy action taken on the basis of a specific forecast is incorrect, the forecast is called into question. What does this do to the belief in the accuracy of subsequent forecasts? Another and different problem may arise if business firms and private individuals react to a forecast in ways that bring about the conditions being forecast. For example, the forecast of a downturn in economic activity may lead business firms to trim costs in anticipation of hard times by laying off some workers or persuade consumers to save more and spend less. Such actions could make future conditions worse than they might have been in the absence of a forecast. There are no ready answers to these problems although most economic forecasting is probably not yet accurate enough for these possibilities to affect seriously the economy's performance.

Methods of Forecasting

There is no *one* technique widely recognized among economists as *the method* for forecasting. The techniques actually used range from the subjective judgment of a single competent individual to the use of elaborate econometric models involving large numbers of sophisticated equations. We shall review some of the more widely used techniques, although no claim is made that our list is exhaustive.

Extrapolation

The technique that is both the simplest and the most widely used by the nonspecialist is to project into the future what is happening currently or has happened in the recent past. Possibly a simple extrapolation of the present into the future should not be designated as a technique, but this method is probably used, consciously or unconsciously, more than most people realize. Keynes believed that this was largely the way in which business executives form their expectations about the future, since he argued there was no scientific basis whatsoever they could employ for the calculation of future values. What they do, he argued, is assume, even though past experience shows this to be risky, that the present is a serviceable guide to the future. In addition, the individual business executive seeks support for a judgment by falling back on the judgments of other business executives.[16] Unfortunately, such forecasts are based on a flimsy foundation, subject to sudden and violent change. This technique may work for a while because of the cumulative character of most expansions and contractions, but it cannot, except by chance, forecast turning points in the cycle or provide evidence on the magnitude of the cyclical swing.

The Consensus Approach

Another commonly used forecasting technique is the consensus method. This method is widely employed in the press, especially by business and financial publications. It is labeled consensus because it involves getting opinions from a large number of observers about what is likely to happen to the economy in the months or year ahead. A consensus outlook is then constructed based

---

[16] John Maynard Keynes, ''The General Theory of Employment,'' *The Quarterly Journal of Economics,* February 1937, p. 214.

on these opinions. This technique is most often employed at the start of a new year. General-circulation newspapers tend to develop their forecasts by surveying leaders in business, labor, government, and education, whereas the business and financial press is more likely to direct its probing at professional economists in business and the universities. *Business Week* magazine normally publishes a major article on the economic outlook for the next 12 months at the end of the year. Its analysis typically pulls together the opinions of a broad sample of academic and business economists and compares their outlook with forecasts turned out by the best-known econometric models. Table 14–2 contains average forecast values for *real* GDP growth, the inflation rate, and the unemployment rate by individual economists and econometric models for *Business Week* magazine compared with actual values for these variables over 18 years (1972 to 1989). The number of individual economists participating in the magazine's survey varied from a low of 24 in 1975 to more than 40 in 1988. The number of econometric models used in these forecasts varied from 7 to 14. The *Business Week* forecasts showed that the forecasts by individual economists were slightly more accurate in predicting inflation and unemployment, but that the econometric models had the edge in estimating the rate of growth for *real* GDP.

The Use of Indicators

In recent years the most important forecasting tools developed are the indexes of *leading, coincident,* and *lagging* indicators. These terms refer to statistical series that either lead, coincide, or lag behind the general cyclical movement of economic activity. For forecasting purposes, the index of leading indicators is most important, because it is designed to tell us that either a downturn or an upswing in economic activity is in the offing.

The National Bureau of Economic Research in cooperation with the federal government has been primarily responsible for development of this particular forecasting technique. For more than two decades, Geoffrey H. Moore and Julius Shiskin conducted an intensive study of the behavior of several hundred time series for economic variables; they sought to discover those series which would enable economists to forecast changes in economic activity. Out of these studies they narrowed the analysis to 88 indicators, of which 36 were placed in the leading category, 25 were put in the coincident group, 11 were

TABLE 14–2   Economic Forecasts: 1972–1989 (in percent)

	Real GNP/GDP	Inflation Rate	Unemployment Rate
Estimates of economists	2.85%	5.70%	7.01%
Estimates of econometric models	2.97	5.78	7.14
Actual	3.00	6.37	6.83

Sources: Business Week and Economic Report of the President, appropriate years.

The Baby Boomers Make Forecasting Easy

Economic forecasting is a difficult and chancy art. Yet there is one area where this is less so, namely the area involving *demographics,* a fancy word for population studies.

We can learn a bit about what the future is going to be like by taking a serious look at population and population trends. The reason is simple: Population means people and most all the people who will shape the economy's future dimensions are already born. So the trends are there.

The table below shows percentage changes in the total population and the population in specific age groups for each of the last four decades. These figures provide important information about our economic and social future.

Population and the Baby Boomers

Period	Total Population Growth	Population Growth by Age Groups				
		16–19	20–24	25–44	45–64	Over 65
1955–1964	17.7%	47.8%	22.5%	−0.1%	16.5%	28.8%
1965–1974	11.4	31.4	43.0	12.9	13.5	21.7
1975–1984	10.5	−8.7	14.6	35.2	2.3	26.4
1985–1994	10.3	−8.3	15.2	15.0	14.2	18.9

Perhaps the most obvious finding in the above data is the slowdown in the rate of growth of the nation's population. This drop has been dramatic, from a 17.7 percent increase in the 1955–1964 decade to a 10.3 percent increase between 1985 and 1994. The practical meaning of this is that as a nation, we are, on the average, getting older.

When we look, however, at what is happening, and will happen, to population groups in the different age brackets, the situation becomes quite different. The fact that has dominated the population picture—and the economy—ever since World War II is the baby boom. It will continue to dominate our population and economic picture well into the next century.

The baby boom population is like an enormous lump making its way through the age group statistics as members of the "boomer" class grow older. This movement is dramatized in the table by the arrows that trace its path from the 16–19 age group through the 20–24 and 25–44 age groups. It is within these groups that most baby boomers now find themselves. "Boomers" born in 1945 began to enter the 45–64 age bracket in 1990.

If we look ahead and project the arrows into the next two decades, we can see why there are fears about Social Security. From 1955 through 1994 the growth in the over-65 population did not present any problems. But it will be a far different matter when the baby boomers begin to retire around 2010.

In the 1990s the baby boomers will be moving into the 45–64 age bracket, the middle years in which careers come to full fruition and families are raised. After those come the retirement years. These population statistics show that a truly dramatic rise in the proportion of the over-65 population is inevitable early in the next century. The numbers are already there. We should start thinking about the implications now.

TABLE 14–3   Composite Indexes and the Composition of Each Series

Composite Leading Index (11 series)
1. Average weekly hours of production or nonsupervisory workers, manufacturing
2. Average weekly initial claims for unemployment insurance
3. Mfrs.' new orders in 1982 dollars, consumer goods and materials industries (bil. dol.)
4. Vendor performance—slower deliveries diffusion index (percent)
5. Contracts and orders for plant and equipment in 1982 dollars (bil. dol.)
6. New private housing units authorized by local building permits (index: 1967 = 100)
7. Change in mfrs.' unfilled orders in 1982 dollars, durable goods (bil. dol.)
8. Change in sensitive materials prices, smoothed (percent)
9. Stock prices, 500 common stocks (index: 1941–43 = 10)
10. Money supply M2 in 1982 dollars (bil. dol.)
11. Index of consumer expectations (index: 1st Q 1966 = 100)

Composite Coincident Index (4 series)
1. Employees on nonagricultural payrolls (thous.)
2. Personal income less transfer payments in 1982 dollars (ann. rate, bil. dol.)
3. Industrial production (index: 1977 = 100)
4. Manufacturing and trade sales in 1982 dollars (mil. dol.)

Composite Lagging Index (7 series)
1. Average duration of unemployment (weeks)
2. Ratio, manufacturing and trade inventories to sales in 1982 dollars (ratio)
3. Change in index of labor cost per unit of output, mfg. (ann. rate, percent)
4. Average prime rate charged by banks (percent)
5. Commercial and industrial loans outstanding in 1982 dollars (mil. dol.)
6. Ratio, consumer installment credit outstanding to personal income (percent)
7. Change in consumer price index for services, smoothed (ann. rate, percent)

Source: Survey of Current Business, October, 1994.

classified as lagging, and 16 were not classified with respect to timing. The list was further refined and shortened; this led ultimately to the development of a composite index for each of these three categories—leading, coincident, and lagging. These composite indexes are published monthly by the U.S. Department of Commerce in the *Survey of Current Business*. Table 14–3 lists the economic time series included in each of these three composite indexes, and Figure 14–4 shows their behavior for the period 1950 to 1989. This chart shows clearly that the downturn in the composite index for leading indicators foreshadowed a recession, although there is a wide variation in the 1950-to-1989 period in the number of months by which the downturn in this index led the overall downturn in economic activity. The average forecast lead time for the last seven recessions was 9.6 months, although the actual lead time ranged from a maximum of 23 to a minimum of 3 months. If the index of leading indicators turns down for three consecutive months, trouble may lie ahead. This is the current thinking of the Department of Commerce.

More recently several indicators have been developed to provide an indication of turning points in the inflation rate. In its November 1986 *Economic Review*, the Kansas City Federal Reserve Bank examined five such indicators, all developed by private economists.[17] To date no branch of the federal gov-

[17] *Economic Review*, Kansas City Federal Reserve Bank, November 1986, pp. 3–20.

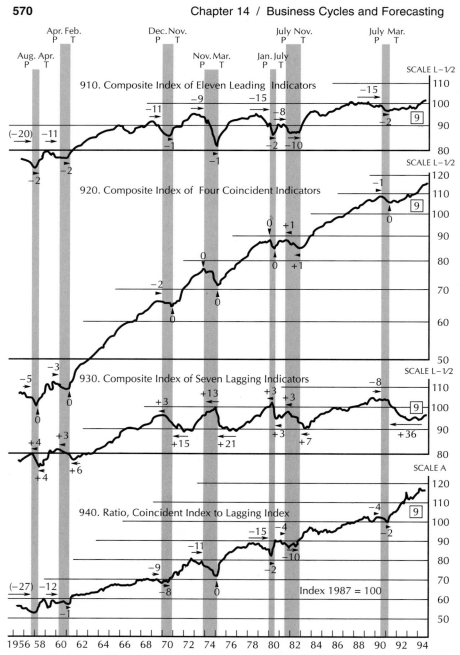

FIGURE 14–4 Major Composite Indexes: 1957–1994 (1987 = 100). A close examination of the three time series in this figure shows that the indicators are appropriately named—leading, coincident, and lagging. It is also important to note that there is no consistency in the number of months between a definite downturn or upturn in any of the indicators and the peak or trough of the business cycle.

Source: Survey of Current Business, October 1994.

ernment has developed an official set of indicators to forecast turning points in the inflation rate. Of the five measures discussed by the Kansas City Federal Reserve Bank, two were composite measures, patterned after the leading indicators for the business cycle just discussed, and the other three were simpler, involving only single variables. All the indexes, it was found, anticipated past turning points in the inflation rate rather well, but because of their newness, the bank was hesitant with respect to their ability to predict future turning points in the inflation rate.

Econometric Models

Finally some comments are in order about forecasting with econometric models of the economy. Basically, an econometric model is a mathematical representation of the economy that consists of a series of equations involving dependent (endogenous) and independent (exogenous) variables. The relationships presented in the equations are developed on the basis of a statistical investigation into the economy's past performance, using correlation analysis to determine the relationships. Judgment and skill are obviously required to determine the extent to which an empirically observed correlation between economic variables also involves a causal relationship. If an econometric model is to be used successfully in economic forecasting, then the fundamental equations that enter into the model must involve true causal relationships, not just a statistical correlation.

Econometric models developed from the fundamental structure of Keynesian economics, particularly the income-expenditure model. The procedure has been to break the major elements that enter into the aggregate demand function into their different components, to disaggregate them, and develop for each of these parts regression equations that reflect the underlying causal relationships. The result is a system of simultaneous equations that can be employed for forecasting. Since some econometric models involve sixty or more equations, an electronic computer is mandatory for their successful operation. This points up a dilemma that confronts the econometric model builder. Striving for greater authenticity, the econometrician is forced toward more disaggregation, but this increases the number of equations in the model and makes it increasingly ponderous to use. Furthermore, it may require a staff of individuals simply to keep the model up to date in the light of the fact that observed data from the past are often revised as more information becomes available. This may lead to changes in some of the basic causal relationships embodied in the equations of the model, which in turn, may force the econometrician to reconstruct some substantial portion of the model. In short, an elaborate econometric model is an expensive undertaking that requires the support of a highly trained staff. This is the basic reason why only a handful of major econometric models have been constructed in the United States. The best-known ones are those developed by the Federal Reserve Board and MIT, the Wharton School of Finance at the University of Pennsylvania, the University of Michigan, Princeton University, and the Brookings Institution. There are also two well-known models developed by private business firms: Chase Econometrics (a subsidiary of the Chase Manhattan Bank) and Data Resource Incorporated.

The Effectiveness of Forecasting

Just as there is no single technique for economic forecasting, there is no simple answer to the question of its effectiveness. There has been significant forward progress in this field since World War II, but much remains to be done to improve the accuracy and effectivenss of the art. Numerous studies in recent years have sought to answer questions about the accuracy of economic forecasts.[18]

In an analysis of the performance of econometric models in forecasting GNP and changes in GNP over the 1953 to 1964 period, Victor Zarnowitz found that forecast values for GNP were off by only about 2 percent on the average, not an excessively large error. But much larger errors were made by the econometric models in forecasting the actual change in GNP. Here the range was from 28 to 56 percent, with an average error of about 40 percent.

One important body engaged in making forecasts is the Council of Economic Advisers. Since 1962 it has included in the annual *Economic Report* forecasts of current and constant dollar value for the GNP (or GDP) as well as the inflation rate as measured by the GNP (or GDP) deflator.[19] The council employs a variety of forecasting techniques, including econometric models, to develop its projections. In general, according to Geoffrey Moore's analysis over a 13-year period, the track record of the council in forecasting change in the rate of growth of *real* GNP was good. In 10 out of the 13 forecast years, the council's forecasts of changes in the rate of growth for real GNP were in the right direction, which is to say that it correctly forecast that the rate of growth would either increase or decrease. With respect to forecasts for actual GNP (real and current dollar amounts), Moore found that the council's errors were about one-half as large as they would have been if it had

---

[18] Readers interested in this question should consult one or more of the following studies: Victor Zarnowitz, *An Appraisal of Short-Term Economic Forecasts* (New York: National Bureau of Economic Research, 1967); Geoffrey H. Moore, ''Economic Forecasting—How Good a Track Record? in *The Morgan Guaranty Survey,* January 1975; and Maury N. Harris and Deborah Jamroz, ''Evaluating the Leading Indicators,'' *Monthly Review,* Federal Reserve Bank of New York. The *New England Economic Review,* published by the Federal Reserve Bank of Boston, has done a series of articles on the predictive accuracy of macroeconomic forecasting in the United States. The July–August 1988 issue of the *Review* evaluates and reviews the accuracy of forecasting over the past 35 years.

[19] For the most recent forecast (1995 to 2000) see the *Economic Report of the President,* 1995, p. 91.

been assumed that last year's change was the same as this year (used a single extrapolation, in other words).

Recent findings of the Boston Federal Reserve Bank (see the study cited in footnote 18) were that forecast accuracy has varied greatly over time. The largest errors involved underestimating the severity of the 1973–75 and 1981–82 recessions and the acceleration of inflation in 1978 and early 1979. The forecasters had greater success in predicting the recoveries that began in 1970 and in 1975, according to the bank's findings. Not unexpectedly, the accuracy of the forecasts is inversely related to the forecast's horizons, that is, how far into the future the forecast extends. The bank also found that no single forecasting organization or econometric model was the most accurate for all or even most of the macroeconomic variables.

Probably the forecasting tool that has proved to be accurate more consistently than any other is the composite index of leading indicators. According to the Harris-Jamroz study (footnote 18), this particular index has never failed to signal any of the post-World War II downturns (Figure 14–4), although on occasion when it has dropped, no recession followed. As pointed out earlier, the chief weakness of this index is not that it does not give an accurate signal of an impending change, but that there is no consistency to the length of the lag between the downturn (or upturn) in the indicator and the subsequent change in the economy's direction.

What these various findings indicate is that no wholly satisfactory technique has evolved for forecasting either the timing or the strength of major changes in the aggregate economy. All the various techniques have a role; the National Bureau concluded that there are no major differences between the accuracy of forecasts based on informal consensus models, econometric models, and leading indicators. Perhaps that is to be expected, since all techniques must depend in greater or lesser degree on some extrapolation of present or recent past conditions into the future. But since humans can learn from their experience, the future will never be exactly like the past. Forecasting is a useful art and efforts should continue to improve it. But given the uncertainties that attach to an unknown future, we can never make forecasting into a mechanical prediction in which we push a few buttons on a computer and get an accurate reading of tomorrow's economic weather.

Summary

1. "Business cycle" is a term that is used by economists to describe the fluctuations in the output, employment, and price level that characterize the time path of the economy. The term "cycle" is used because in a rough way these fluctuations have a wavelike character, even though the cycles are highly irregular in both amplitude and length.

2. The business cycle typically has four major phases. These include the peak or upper turning point, the downswing, the trough or lower turning point, and the recovery or upswing. Historic records, both statistical and written, indicate that the business cycle is at least as old as market capitalism. The National Bureau of Economic Research found that between 1854 and 1991 the United States experienced 31 cycles. A full cycle is normally measured from trough to trough.

3. Data on the business cycle also indicate that in the post-World War II period the cycle is both less frequent and less severe. The comparative mildness of cycles prior to the 1970s gave rise to a belief that the cycle had been conquered once and for all. Experience since the 1970s has shown, however, that this is not the case. Since World War II, the economy has experienced nine cycles, two of which (1974–75 and 1981–82) were exceptionally severe.

4. In addition to the normal business cycle, with an average duration of 50 months, some economists believe that there is evidence of very long waves in economic life. The best known of these economists is the Russian Nikolai D. Kondratieff, who suggested that systems of market capitalism experience a cycle of approximately fifty to sixty years in length, half of which consist of an upswing and the other half of a downswing. In the downswing phase of a Kondratieff cycle, the normal business downturn is deeper and more prolonged than is the case when the cycle is superimposed on a Kondratieff upswing.

5. There is no simple explanation of the business cycle. One of the most thorough students of this phenomenon, Wesley C. Mitchell, spent his professional life studying what happens during the cycle, but never ventured a full theoretical explanation. Theories of the cycle are sometimes divided into those which explain it in terms of the economic system's reaction to external events and those which see the cycle as inherent (or internal) to a system of market capitalism.

6. Joseph P. Schumpeter is a major business cycle theorist who explained the phenomenon in terms of shocks to the economy that came from innovations that started the economy on a cyclical path.

7. Keynes, in *The General Theory,* did not develop a theory of the cycle as such, but he did show how the instability of investment spending was a major source of the economy's cyclical behavior.

8. Economic forecasting has become an important economic activity that attempts to foresee what will happen to the economy in the near term, usually a year or less. Methods of forecasting are both informal and formal. The U.S. Department of Commerce has developed several statistical series that have proved to be useful in forecasting. The index of leading indicators is a part of this series. It is an index that tends to tell in advance when the economy will turn up or down.

9. Econometric models are the most elaborate and complex of the forecasting tools used by economists. The models are essentially mathematical representations of the economy, which involve many different economic relationships expressed in equation form and which rest on the belief that past economic behavior can readily and accurately be extrapolated into the future. Economic forecasting, irrespective of the technique used, has proved useful but is far from perfect.

15 Sixty-five Years of Macroeconomic Policy

THIS CHAPTER HAS TWO objectives. First, we shall review briefly the major macroeconomic policy instruments at the disposal of modern governments in market-based capitalist systems. The framework for this is the basic Keynesian income-expenditure approach, using the *IS-LM* model when appropriate to illustrate how policies should work. This part of the chapter can be described as a mini refresher course on the policy implications of the theoretical ideas discussed in prior chapters.

The second and more important task of the chapter is to review, analyze, and appraise the policy actions taken by the U.S. government from the economy's collapse in 1929 into the Great Depression of the 1930s, through all administrations up to the present. This will give us a concise but complete historical account of the successes and failures in the overall macroeconomic management of the U.S. economy over the past 65 years. Although it is true that one contemporary approach to macroeconomics argues that no policy action can ever succeed (see Chapter 16, "The Rebirth of Classical Economics"), every U.S. president from Franklin Roosevelt to Bill Clinton has come to power believing that his administration could influence the course of the economy. All have tried to do so, with varied levels of success, to be sure. There is no indication that this attitude will change, although the Republican Congress that came to power in the 1994 congressional elections has sought to reduce significantly the federal government's role in the overall management of the economy. We will end this chapter with a discussion and analysis of the probable long-term effects of the 1994 "Republican revolution" on the macroeconomic management of the economy.

The Principles of Economic Policy

The formation of economic policy is a difficult and subtle art and involves, as Edwin G. Nourse, first chairperson of the President's Council of Economic Advisers, has said, choice among conflicting values and judgment about what is best in a total situation.[1] To be effective, economic policy must be grounded in sound economic theory. Therefore, we need to understand the policy implications that flow out of the theoretical analysis developed in the preceding chapters.

Economic stabilization is a major social goal believed to be within the control of government in modern society. The economic power inherent in the public sector puts government in a position to promote stability, full employment, and maximum production. In the United States, the Employment Act of 1946 gave congressional sanction to the idea that the national government has a responsibility for income and employment levels in the economy. Although neither price stability nor economic growth—nor full employment per se—is mentioned in the act, the tacit assumption was often made by economists as well as the federal government that these goals, too, were a part of the intent of the act. Later, the Full Employment and Balanced Growth Act of 1978 established a 3 percent unemployment rate for workers age 20 and over and a 3 percent inflation rate as goals to be reached by 1983. But this act lacks any realistic means to attain these goals. Thus, it remains essentially a statement of pious intent, rather than a basis for effective policy action.

As we have seen, monetary and fiscal measures are the two chief instruments at the disposal of the central government for the attainment of economic stabilization. Since, in Keynesian analysis, fluctuations in income and employment are primarily matters of too much or too little spending in relation to existing supply or capacity, stabilization policy involves action to influence the economy's overall expenditure level. Both monetary and fiscal policy measures must therefore be evaluated in terms of their impact on expenditure levels, which is to say in terms of their impact on aggregate demand. To put the matter differently, the goal of policy is full employment with stable prices—a goal which governments strive to reach by pulling on the levers marked "monetary" or "fiscal" policy. Difficulty in the mid-1960s in getting full employment without pushing the price level up at too rapid a pace gave

---

[1] Edwin G. Nourse, *Economics in the Public Service* (New York: Harcourt, Brace, 1953), p. 18.

rise to a third type of policy, generally known as *incomes policy,* discussed in Chapter 12.

Monetary Policy and Its Application

As we have seen (Chapter 6), monetary policy involves changing the money supply with the expectation that such changes will influence total spending and thus output, employment, and the price level. The central bank, which in the United States means the Federal Reserve System, is the body responsible for carrying out monetary policy. From a strictly Keynesian viewpoint, monetary policy works indirectly through the impact of money on the rates of interest, whereas the monetarists hold that changes in money affect aggregate demand directly. There are, however, other matters to consider.

Monetary policy operates through two broad sets of controls. First, there are general or indirect controls, which include changes in the reserve requirement of the commercial banks, changes in the discount rate, and open market operations by the central bank, that is, the Federal Reserve System. Second, there are selective or direct controls aimed at specific types of credit, such as installment credit, mortgage credit, or credit extended for the financing of stock market transactions. Indirect controls are used to alter the overall volume of credit available to the economy; they do not seek to influence the allocation of credit (that is, money funds) among alternative uses. As discussed in Chapter 11, the primary instruments for the exercise of indirect monetary controls are open market operations, changes in the discount rate, and control over reserve requirements. The locus for these powers is the Board of Governors of the Federal Reserve System. General (or indirect) credit controls have been by far the most important policy instrument used by the Federal Reserve System. Thus, any general discussion of monetary policy must be directed primarily toward the use and effectiveness of these controls.

The foregoing is but a part of the story. In order to carry out monetary policy, the monetary authority (the Federal Reserve System in the United States) must depend on some economic variable as a policy guide, as an *indicator* that will signal the necessity for a policy change. Such a policy guide or indicator ought to tell the monetary authority something of what is going on in the economy currently. But it ought to do more than that. It should be a variable that has an impact on the goals of policy (i.e., full employment or price stability), and it should be one that changes in response to changes in policy. In practice, two such guides have been important in recent years. These are the money supply itself (or a variable closely related to the money supply, such as the volume of commercial bank reserves) and the general state of credit conditions, often represented by one or more rates of interest. To put the matter as succinctly as possible, the question is: Should the Federal Reserve as the custodian of monetary policy pay the most attention to the money supply (however defined) or interest rates as a guide to its policy decisions? The answer is neither obvious nor simple. Figure 15–1 shows the linkages involved in this question.

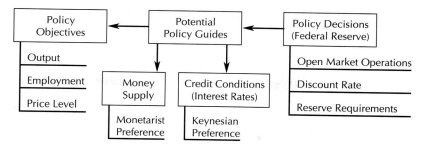

FIGURE 15–1 Policy Guides and Monetary Policy. Policy decisions by the Federal Reserve System may be targeted toward either the money supply, which is the preference of monetarists, or credit conditions and interest rates, the preference of Keynesians.

If either the money supply or interest rates are to be used as guides to monetary policy, two things are essential. First, changes in either should lead to changes in total spending (and hence output, employment, and the price level), and, second, they (money and interest rates) should be subject to control by the Federal Reserve System. The difficulty is that there is no agreement among monetary specialists, as well as economists in general, on either of these points. Take the matter of Federal Reserve control over either the money supply or interest rates. Proponents in favor of using the money supply as the basic policy guide (usually monetarists) argue that in the short term the Federal Reserve does not have good control over interest rates, primarily because credit markets are quite sensitive to other factors besides actions taken by the Federal Reserve. On the other hand, advocates of interest rates as a policy guide (generally Keynesians) say essentially the same thing about the money supply, namely, that the money supply is not under control of the Federal Reserve System to the degree required to make it a good policy indicator.

As a practical matter, the choice of a policy guide really comes down to the question of how the transmission mechanism works, which is, in effect, a question of which theory is valid—contemporary monetarism or Keynesianism. Since monetarists believe that there is a close, causal link between the money supply and the general level of economic activity, their preference is for using money as the primary policy indicator. As a matter of fact, Friedman and other monetarists fear that the use of interest rates as an indicator may actually be destabilizing rather than stabilizing. For example, if interest rates are rising because of high employment and rapid economic expansion, any attempt by the Federal Reserve System to stabilize or bring down interest rates by *adding* to the money supply would be self-defeating. More money, in their view, would fuel more spending, which would cause interest rates to go up even faster. Nonmonetarists, on the other hand, adopt what is essentially a Keynesian position, namely, the claim that the link between money and the general level of economic activity is through the interest rate (see the discussion in Chapter 12 on the Keynesian view of how the money supply may effect output, employment, and the price level, pages 472–81). Thus, the preference of Keynesians is for using interest rates as a policy guide.

Prior to the late 1970s the Federal Reserve System relied almost exclusively on credit conditions (interest rates) as a policy indicator. In October 1979, however, the Federal Reserve announced a major policy switch in its management of monetary policy. Henceforth, the agency said it would try to achieve better control of the money supply by shifting the emphasis in its day-to-day operations from controlling credit conditions through the federal funds rate (the rate charged for intrabank short-term loans, usually for one day) to the supply of bank reserves. Basically the Federal Reserve continued to focus on the money supply until mid-1982 when, in response to pressures to bring down interest rates, the money supply was allowed to increase at a relatively rapid pace. The policy of controlling the money supply was not wholly successful, as the annual rate of growth has been quite erratic most of the time. Through 1986, the growth of M1 was exceedingly rapid, but without any appreciable effect on either the price level or nominal output. The inflation rate actually declined during this time. In February 1983 the chairperson of the Federal Reserve System, Paul A. Volcker, told the Senate Banking Committee that rather than be tied specifically to the money supply as its target for policymaking, the Federal Reserve would use real GNP growth as the determinant of whether or not money was too tight or too loose. Thus ended the experiment undertaken by the Federal Reserve in the post-World War II period that came closest to the monetarist idea of concentrating wholly on the growth of the money supply as a means of controlling the economy's overall, short-term performance.

There are other concerns in the application of monetary policy. One of these is the matter of lags, which involve the length of time between a change in policy and its effect on the economy. The problem is that there is no exact statistical information on the length of such lags; what information we do have suggests, further, that their lengths may vary greatly, from a few months to nearly two years. The lack of precise information on the lengths of policy lags is another reason why monetarists such as Friedman prefer that the monetary authority adhere to a fixed rule for expansion of the money supply. Two basic types of lags are important, *inside* lags and *outside* lags. The former refers to the length of time that passes between the need for action and the actual taking of action by the Federal Reserve System. The latter pertains to the time involved between the taking of action by the Federal Reserve and the effect of that action on the goals of policy, namely, the employment or price levels.

Fiscal Policy and Its Application

Fiscal policy, as we have seen, involves *deliberate* changes in the taxes government collects and the money it spends as a means to influence the economy. Taxes and spending are the means and the government's budget is the instrument through which fiscal policy is carried out. In the definition the word "deliberate" must be stressed. Governments collect taxes and spend money for a variety of purposes, ranging from building highways to providing for the common defense. Only when they deliberately change their spending or taxes to try and affect the economy's performance is it correct to speak of fiscal policy. In the United States, the locus of fiscal policy is in the administration in power (the president) and the Congress. Usually, the president initiates fiscal policy—a tax or spending change—but nothing can happen until such changes are approved by the Congress.

The budget of the federal government is the primary instrument for the implementation of fiscal policy. The mechanics of this are relatively simple. If the federal government *at full employment* spends more for goods and services G_f than it receives in net taxes T_f, then it will be operating at a deficit; that is to say it will be putting more into the income stream via its expenditures than it is pulling out through net taxes.[2] Consequently, the overall effect of the federal budget will be expansionary. On the other hand, a surplus would have a contractive economic effect, since it entails an excess of net taxes T_f over spending for goods and services G_f, which in turn means that the federal government is pulling more out of the income flow than it is putting in. The overall expansionary or contractive effect of the federal budget depends, of course, on the absence of offsetting changes in the private sector, such as a fall in private investment when a federal deficit emerges. This was the basic way that Walter Heller, chairperson of the Council of Economic Advisers under President Kennedy, developed for looking at the budget (see pages 326–30). This is the full-(now high-)employment approach to the federal budget. What this concept does is estimate the surplus or deficit that would emerge if the economy were operating at a full-(or high-)employment level. Essentially, the argument is that this concept of the budget offers a better guide to the real economic impact of the federal government's fiscal behavior than does the *actual* deficit or surplus in any given year.

The rationale for the full-(or high-)budget concept is that the true inflationary or deflationary potential of the federal budget is apparent only when the economy is at full employment. The reasoning behind this is quite simple. If the economy is at full employment, and if, too, there is a deficit ($G_f > T_f$), then the government's fiscal activities (tax and expenditure policies) are clearly inflationary. The reverse is, of course, the case if there is a surplus ($T_f > G_f$). On the other hand, the situation is not clear-cut with respect to the real effects of either a current surplus or deficit when the economy is not at full employment. To illustrate, suppose the federal government runs a deficit. But if this deficit happened because of a recession and the resulting falloff in taxes, it would mean that the deficit was induced by changing economic conditions rather than designed deliberately to affect economic conditions. For example, in 1981, a year when the economy was struggling to recover from the brief but sharp 1981 recession, the federal government's actual deficit was $58.8 billion (see Table 9–8, page 330). The full-(or high-)employ-

---

[2] The subscript f is used to denote spending and taxes at the federal level.

ment budget for that year was a positive $21.6 billion, which indicates that the *real* impact of the budget was deflationary, a fact that helped account for the deeper recession that hit the economy in 1982.

Even if fiscal policy is a powerful instrument for economic stabilization, it, like monetary policy, is subject to difficulties and limitations. First, fiscal policy measures that involve changes in public expenditures may conflict with the long-term nature of many governmental expenditure programs. It is not possible continually to adjust expenditures for basic social goods and services to meet the shifting exigencies of economic stabilization. About 90 percent of total federal spending consists of either transfer payments, many of which are entitlements, or military outlays. Neither of these categories are easily adjusted for the sake of economic stabilization. Second, the political process through which changes in expenditures and taxes are effected is so long, drawn out, and fraught with so many uncertainties that it is nearly impossible in a democratic society to obtain the necessary speed and flexibility that fiscal policy requires if it is to be successful as an instrument for economic stabilization. This is probably true in spite of the passage of the Budget Reform Act in 1974.[3] This act gave the Congress a better understanding of the economic consequences of the budget, but it has not speeded up the political process significantly. The exception to this view, perhaps, is tax reduction, as the Congress has shown it can act with a fair amount of speed when tax cuts are involved. It took about two months for the Congress to pass the Ford administration's tax reduction proposals in 1975, but a somewhat longer period before it acted on the Carter administration requests in 1977. The Reagan tax cut package of 1981 took longer; the act did not become law until August 1981. The longer period was due to the fact that it represented the largest and most controversial tax reduction act in our history. Our limited experience to date suggests two to three months appears to be the minimum time for congressional action involving a tax reduction. This should be contrasted with the possibility that the Federal Reserve can literally act within a week if necessary.

Theoretical Limits to Fiscal and Monetary Policies

Recall that in Chapter 6 (pages 205–7), it was pointed out that the workings of fiscal or monetary policy or some combination of the two can be demonstrated by shifts in either the *IS* or *LM* curve. To complete the theoretical backdrop for our subsequent historical discussion of policy actions in the

---

[3] The 1974 Budget Act provided, first, that the entire Congress adopt in May of each year spending and revenue targets. This is done by a concurrent resolution. Later in September, just prior to the beginning of the new fiscal year on October 1, a second concurrent resolution is adopted, which either affirms or revises these targets. This second resolution becomes binding. The reform act also established committees on the budget in both houses of the Congress, which have the responsibility for developing a comprehensive budget policy each year. To help in doing this, the 1974 legislation also established the Congressional Budget Office (CBO), a body roughly designed to serve the Congress in the same way that the Council of Economic Advisers serves the president.

period from the Great Depression through the Clinton administration, an explanation of the practical limits of either policy approach is in order. Knowledge of these limits is important for understanding the circumstances under which one policy may be more effective than the other.

In the post-World War II literature of macroeconomics these possible limits on the effectiveness of either fiscal or monetary policy have come to be known as the Keynesian range (or case) and the classical range (or case). The *IS-LM* model offers an ideal vehicle for dramatizing these two alternatives. Figure 15–2 illustrates these extremes of viewpoint. In the figure, IS_1 intersects the *LM* curve in the range in which the latter is perfectly elastic with respect to the rate of interest (the Keynesian range), and IS_2 intersects the *LM* curve in the range in which this curve becomes perfectly inelastic with respect to the rate of interest (the classical range).

If the *IS* curve intersects the *LM* curve in the range in which the latter is perfectly elastic with respect to the rate of interest, certain significant policy implications follow. Such a situation might arise because the economy is in a deep depression, with both income and the rate of interest at relatively low levels. In this situation monetary policy involving an increase in the money supply will be completely ineffective. An increase in the money supply shifts the *LM* curve to the right, but this will, *ceteris paribus,* raise the income level only if the rate of interest lies above the critical level at which the *LM* curve is perfectly elastic. The point of intersection of IS_1 and the *LM* curve typifies a situation in which the demand for liquidity is so great that any increase in the money supply simply is added to existing idle balances. The increase, in

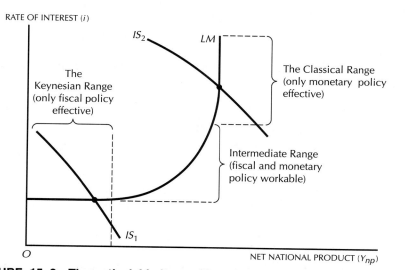

FIGURE 15–2 Theoretical Limits to Fiscal and Monetary Policies. The shape of the *LM* curve illustrates possible limits to the use of fiscal and monetary policy. In the flat range of the curve monetary policy is wholly ineffective, whereas in the vertical range of the curve fiscal policy is wholly ineffective.

other words, drops into the *liquidity trap;* consequently no change in the rate of interest, investment expenditure, or the income level will ensue. Under these circumstances it might be said that "money doesn't matter." A rise in the income level must wait on a higher position of the *IS* curve, which would require an upward shift in the aggregate demand curve. The obvious implication of this analysis is that fiscal rather than monetary policy measures are needed.

A situation quite the opposite of the one just described prevails if the *IS* curve intersects the *LM* curve at a point at which the latter is perfectly inelastic with respect to the rate of interest. This is shown in Figure 15–3 by the intersection of IS_2 and the *LM* curve in the inelastic range of the latter. This is a classic case of a situation in which the only effective means to increase income is through monetary policy. Hence, we might say that "only money matters." If the money supply is increased, the interest rate will fall, and the income level will rise as investment expenditure responds to a lower rate of interest. If the intersection of the *IS* and *LM* curves in the range in which the latter is perfectly interest inelastic implies the desirability of monetary policy, it is equally true that intersection in this range implies the complete unworkability of fiscal policy. Fiscal policy measures that induce an upward shift in the aggregate demand curve without any corresponding change in the money supply are bound to be self-defeating. The only consequence of fiscal action is an increase in the rate of interest. An upward shift in the aggregate demand curve, if we assume no change in the money supply, merely drives interest rates higher because of the rising transactions demand induced by the original shift in the aggregate demand curve. The net result ultimately is no change in the income level, but equilibrium of saving and investment at a higher rate of interest.

As a practical matter, it is the area that lies between the extreme Keynesian and classical positions that is important for policy in the real world. In terms of the diagram, this is the area in which *both* fiscal and monetary policies are workable in the sense that they can affect the level of real output—net national product (Y_{np}) in the diagram. The closer the economy lies to the classical position, the greater is the relative effectiveness of monetary policy, whereas the closer it is to the Keynesian range, fiscal policy becomes relatively more effective. Again, when we speak of the economy being close to either of these extremes, it is not meant literally. We do not have any machines that can tell us the exact state of our economic health or where we stand at any particular time. Policymakers, in the final analysis, exercise their own judgment on these matters and decide the proper mix of fiscal and monetary actions to reach desired ends. As stated at the beginning of this chapter, the formulation of economic policy is a difficult and subtle art, involving choice among conflicting values and judgment about what is best in a total situation. The reader should not forget that our discussion and analysis pertain to what takes place within the confines of a graphic model of the economy, and thus the conclusions offered with respect to the effectiveness of both monetary and fiscal policies should not be thought of as providing definitive answers to the complex problems of policy that exist in the real economic world. At best they represent insights into the workings of the economy, suggesting only the broadest sort of guidelines to actual policy formulation.

Stabilization Policy in Historical Perspective

In this section, we will survey the major policy actions taken at the macro-economic level from the onset of the Great Depression in 1929 to the Clinton administration. We will get a sense of the major economic and political developments that required policy action and of the political and economic climates in which these decisions were made. The chapter concludes with observations on the present state of stabilization policy, paying particular attention to the probable impact of the "Republican revolution" in the 1994 congressional elections on future policy.

The Great Depression and World War II

The stock market crash of October 29, 1929—a day that lives in history as "Black Tuesday"—ushered in the most devastating economic collapse that the U.S. economy has ever known. From 1929 through the depths of the depression in 1933, real output and retail prices both plunged by 29 percent, and unemployment soared from 3.2 percent of the labor force in 1929 to a depression high of 24.9 percent in 1933. It was not until 1940 that real output (GNP) almost regained the 1929 level, while unemployment had only dropped to 14.6 percent of the labor force by that year.[4]

What Caused the Great Depression and Why Did It Last So Long?

Economists are still arguing over these questions and, no doubt, will continue to argue over them for years to come. One reason for this is the sheer complexity of what happened during the decade of the 1930s, and another is that the depression was worldwide, affecting every industrialized capitalist nation in greater or lesser degree.

Monetarists, led by Milton Friedman, focus on the mismanagement of interest rates and the money supply by the Federal Reserve System. Not only did the Fed fail to slow down the unhealthy, speculative stock market boom before it burst, but from 1929 through 1930, it also allowed the nominal money supply to fall by 26.7 percent. Further, the Fed raised the discount rate in 1930 and failed to take significant measures to halt the massive run

---

[4] Jonathan Hughes, *American Economic History* (Glenville, Ill.: Scott, Foresman, 1990), pp. 467, 469.

on banks that led to thousands of bank failures. In the monetarist view, the depression was not only caused by the ineptness of the Federal Reserve, but was also prolonged unnecessarily by the agency's incompetence.

There is some validity in the monetarist view, especially because of the Fed's failure to prevent the near collapse of the banking system in 1930. One of the key functions of the Federal Reserve System is to act as a lender of last resort, which requires it to pump money into the banking system in times of crisis. It fulfilled this role admirably in the 1987 stock market crash, but not between 1929 and 1933. But mismanagement of the money supply is only part of the story.

One major factor in both the severity of the 1929 crash and the prolongation of the depression was the great increase in inequality in the distribution of both wealth and income during the 1920s. According to Robert Lampman of the University of Wisconsin, the top 1 percent of households held 32 percent of the nation's wealth in 1922 and increased their share to 38 percent by 1929. The top 1 percent also increased their share of personal income from 12 percent in 1922 to 14.5 percent by 1929. In the latter year, 54.4 percent of personal income went to the top fifth of the households. By 1929, Lampman finds, the top 1 percent of the households accounted for 80 percent of the nation's personal savings![5]

The worsening distribution of income and wealth during the Roaring Twenties must be counted as a major cause of the crash and depression that followed. The savings of the very wealthy were a major source of money that fed the stock market boom. How much of the money flowing into the stock market in the 1920s found its way into real capital investment remains unknown. But there is no doubt that the enormous loss of personal wealth from the stock market crash had a devastating effect on real investment spending. The estimated loss in stock values between 1929 and 1933 in current dollars is $85 billion, equal to 82 percent of the nation's 1929 GNP (in current dollars).[6] Investment measured in 1982 dollars fell from $139.2 billion in 1929 to $22.7 billion in 1933, a cataclysmic 84 percent drop. Net investment was a negative $63.8 billion (in 1982 prices) in 1933.[7] No country could experience such a drastic drop in real investment spending without falling into a deep depression. *Ex post* values for the downward GNP multiplier and the marginal propensity to consume out of GNP ($\Delta C/\Delta GNP$) were 1.8 and 43.9 respectively.[8] These *ex post* calculations show that the economy behaved as the Keynesian analysis suggests. A positive value for the marginal propensity to consume out of GNP meant that consumption would not fall as fast as GNP, and this eventually brought a halt to the collapse.

---

[5] Quoted in Hughes, *American Economic History*, p. 444.

[6] Ibid., p. 461.

[7] *Economic Report of the President*, 1991, pp. 288, 305.

[8] Ibid. In 1929 the *ex post* propensity to consume out of disposable income (*C/Y*) was 96.9, but by 1933 it had risen to 103.6.

There is another important way in which the increased concentration of income and wealth at the top during the 1920s helped bring on the Great Depression. The 1920s were years in which mass production of consumer durables really took off in the U.S. economy; in just eight years, from 1921 through 1929, manufacturing output nearly doubled, a faster pace of growth than the economy experienced even in the years of the "Age of Keynes" after World War II. This was also the decade in which installment (or credit) buying on a mass scale was introduced into the economy. By 1929, 75 to 80 percent of automobiles, radios, phonographs, furniture, and other household appliances were being purchased on installment credit.[9] Mass production became a part of the U.S. way of life in the 1920s. But mass production requires consumers with sufficient purchasing power to buy the goods that pour off the assembly lines. As the decade wore on, this became increasingly difficult to achieve. With one-fifth of the households receiving over 54 percent of disposable income, consumption expenditures would inevitably weaken even though total income continued to rise. Moreover, by the end of the 1920s, consumers were being forced to cut back on some consumption spending in order to maintain payments on their installment debt for autos and household durables. The stage was set for a major implosion in consumer spending once the stock market crash shattered confidence across the economy. From 1929 to 1933, consumer spending in current dollars dropped by 40 percent, in constant 1982 dollars by 20 percent![10]

Other real factors that played a role in bringing on the crash and Great Depression include a farm depression throughout the 1920s; the exhaustion of a housing boom in 1927, two years before the stock market crash; and a rise in *real* interest rates to unprecedented levels in the late 1920s, another factor that helped put the squeeze on consumption spending. *Real* interest rates rose not primarily because of action by the Federal Reserve, but because prices—both wholesale and retail—dropped continuously during the 1920s. Net farm income dropped by nearly 112 percent from 1920 through 1929, even though farm income was nearly 6 percent higher in 1929 than in 1920. The housing boom, which began in 1920, peaked in 1927, not because of rising costs—they remained stable—but because of demand exhaustion, a consequence of the lopsided distribution of income and wealth.

What Ended the Great Depression?

The near collapse of the economy by 1932 brought about the end to the Hoover administration and the beginning of Franklin D. Roosevelt's administration and his New Deal. Historically, the New Deal belongs within Roosevelt's first two terms, 1933 to 1940. Within these eight years, three distinct periods can be marked off. These are the First New Deal from 1933 through

---

[9] Hughes, *American Economic History*, p. 446.

[10] *Economic Report of the President*, 1991, pp. 286, 288.

1935, a period of ad hoc experimentation and reform, during which important parts of Roosevelt's program were declared unconstitutional by the U.S. Supreme Court; the Second New Deal from 1936 through 1938, which completed the administration's reforms, all of which survived the constitutional test; and, lastly, the years 1939 and 1940, when Roosevelt's attention and interest turned increasingly to the war in Europe, which started on September 1, 1939 with Nazi Germany's invasion of Poland.[11]

From the perspective of macroeconomics, two questions are important: (1) Did New Deal policy actions contribute to recovery and ending the Great Depression? and (2) Did John Maynard Keynes and *The General Theory* have an important influence on Roosevelt's economic views and the programs of the New Deal? The answer to both these questions is essentially no. The New Deal brought about some major structural reforms in the U.S. economy, but its fiscal and monetary policies did not end the depression. It is true that job programs like the CCC, the WPA, and the PWA (see footnote 11) helped bring the private unemployment rate down from 25.2 percent in 1933 to 14.3 percent in 1937. Further, *real* GNP was slightly above the 1929 level by 1937, but this first period of recovery was aborted in 1938 when the Roosevelt administration, in a misguided move, tried to reduce the deficit and balance the federal budget. The economy fell back into depression, with the unemployment rate's rising to 19.1 percent. Studies show that even though the federal government ran deficits every year from 1931 through 1940, these deficits barely offset other declines in spending and the perverse taxing policies at the state and local level.[12]

The question about Keynes requires two comments. First, it is true that Keynes and Roosevelt met prior to the publication of *The General Theory*, but apparently there was no meeting of the minds. Roosevelt reportedly thought that Keynes was some kind of abstruse mathematician, while Keynes quipped that he had thought the President had a better grasp of economics than he revealed during the meeting. Second, Keynes's masterwork did not appear until 1936, and it was not until the end of the 1930s that economic faculties in leading universities like Harvard, Princeton, and Yale really began to understand the essentials of his analysis.

If the New Deal did not end the depression, what did? The answer is straightforward and simple: World War II. From an economic perspective, the war was a massive ''laboratory experiment'' proving that under the proper

---

[11] The major legislative reforms during the First New Deal were the National Industrial Recovery Act (NIRA), declared unconstitutional; the 1933 Agricultural Adjustment Act (AAA), also declared unconstitutional; and the Labor Relations Act (the Wagner Act) and the Social Security Act, both of which survived the constitutional test. The New Deal put people back to work through the Civilian Conservation Corps (CCC), the Works Progress Administration (WPA), and the Public Works Administration (PWA). During the Second New Deal, a new AAA was passed, as was the Fair Labor Standards Act (FLSA), and the Rural Electrification Agency (REA) began operations. For full details on New Deal reforms and legislation, see Hughes, *American Economic History*, Chapter 25, ''The Great Depression and the New Deal,'' pp. 465–492.

[12] Hughes, *American Economic History*, pp. 478, 486.

circumstances, government spending for goods and services financed primarily by borrowing through the banking system and the Federal Reserve could bring the economy to full employment. From a level of −$3.9 billion in 1940, the federal deficit climbed to −$53.9 billion (54.7 percent of federal spending) in 1945, the year the war ended. Unemployment dropped from 14.6 percent in 1940 to a low of 1.2 percent in 1944, the peak year of the war effort. Of course, World War II represented a special set of circumstances, not readily duplicated in peacetime. Yet the evidence is clear that the analysis developed in *The General Theory* works. Out of this experiment came the Employment Act of 1946, with the responsibility it imposed on the federal government to " . . . promote maximum employment, production, and purchasing power."

The Truman-Eisenhower Years

In the 15 years from the end of World War II to the election of John F. Kennedy as president in 1960, the economy experienced four measurable recessions, although these years are generally viewed in retrospect as ones of prosperity and rising real income for most Americans. The latter is true to a degree, although not to the extent that recent nostalgia for the less turbulent 1950s has made it seem. In spite of the Employment Act, which was passed in 1946, and in spite, too, of World War II as a successful example of the application of Keynesian ideas, little effort was made during the Truman-Eisenhower years to apply the lessons of the Keynesian "revolution" to the peacetime management of the economy. Four recessions—mild though they may have been in comparison to the Great Depression—attest to this.

In the spring of 1948 Congress passed a substantial reduction in the personal income tax over President Truman's veto. The tax cut was not aimed at the economy, but turned out fortuitously to be the right thing to do. President Truman believed at the time that inflation was a much more serious threat than recession. He went so far as to ask for a substantial tax increase in his 1949 budget, even though by then the economy had definitely turned down. In June 1950—a year and a half into President Truman's second term—the Korean War broke out. After prices began to rise sharply in 1951 because of the war, the Truman administration drew on the World War II experience and instituted price controls.[13] Aside from this action, no major fiscal initiatives were undertaken by President Truman during the Korean War.

The Eisenhower administration, which took office in January 1953, was even more committed to a balanced budget philosophy than its predecessor. In his 1960 *Economic Report*, President Eisenhower said that the appropriate budget policy is one that " . . . not merely balances expenditure with reve-

---

[13] In 1950, consumer prices rose by 1.3 percent, but in 1951 they jumped by 7.9 percent. After controls were instituted, the rate of increase fell back to 1.9 percent in 1952. *Economic Report of the President*, 1991, p. 356.

nues, but achieves a significant surplus for debt retirement.[14] Further, Eisenhower had a persistent fear of inflation, which he saw as being caused by budget deficits. There is no evidence that the Eisenhower administration understood—or wanted to understand—how Keynesian ideas might be used for effective economic management.

While it is clear that neither the Truman nor the Eisenhower administration had an understanding of Keynesian principles or a willingness to pursue vigorous countercyclical policies, an important question remains: how is it that none of the four recessions in this 15-year period turned into a major, post-World War II depression? There are two reasons for this. The first involves the effectiveness of the economy's built-in stabilizers, discussed in Chapter 9 (pages 331–35). As one observer comments, the " . . . built-in fiscal stabilizers have made a substantial contribution to the stability of the postwar economy. They have pushed the federal budget strongly toward a deficit when it was needed in each of the postwar recessions, thus helping to slow the economic decline."[15] The second reason was the continued strength of the postwar demand for consumer goods, especially consumer durables, a carryover from the wartime shortages. The enormous buildup of liquid assets by consumers because of saving during World War II helped finance consumer spending through the 1950s.

The Kennedy Era

When the Kennedy administration came to power in early 1961, the entire intellectual climate as well as the character of economic policymaking changed drastically. Essentially there were two fundamental changes. First, the Kennedy administration intended to pursue a policy of aggressive economic management. President Kennedy, after all, had campaigned on the promise to "get the country moving again," and he was determined to carry out this campaign pledge. Second, the new president was a bright man, willing, even eager, to learn what modern macroeconomics had to say about the economy. John Kennedy was not knowledgeable about Keynesian economics when he assumed office, but he was a quick learner. Since the period 1961 to 1965 represents a time when the prestige of economics and economic policy attained a post-World War II high, what happened in this period is worth close analysis.

In January 1961 the major economic problem that confronted President Kennedy and his Council of Economic Advisers (CEA)[16] was the stagnant state of the economy, still floundering in the fourth recession since the end of the war. During the preceding Eisenhower years, unemployment averaged

---

[14] *Economic Report of the President*, 1960, p. 54.

[15] Wilford Lewis, Jr., *Federal Fiscal Policy in the Postwar Recessions* (Washington, D.C.: The Brookings Institution, 1962), p. 15.

[16] Members of the original Kennedy Council at that time were Professor Walter W. Heller, chairperson; Professor Kermit Gordon; and Professor James Tobin.

4.9 percent of the labor force, a figure judged excessive by the 4 percent minimum that the Kennedy council regarded as the desirable objective of stabilization policy. Just how the new administration planned to resolve this persistent problem of a sluggish economy and excessive unemployment did not become fully apparent until a year later when the first *Economic Report* of the administration appeared.

In its first full report, the Kennedy CEA stated that since mid-1955 the rate of growth of actual output was significantly below the economy's potential. The consequence of this lag in economic growth below potential was a gap of $40 billion between the actual output in 1961 and the value of the goods and services that could have been produced if there had been full employment in 1961.[17] Figure 15–3 reproduces the CEA's charts from the historic 1962 report, showing the gap between *actual* and *potential* GNP and unemployment rates (as a percentage of the civilian labor force) for 1953 through 1963.

The CEA got its measure of potential output by the simple technique of projecting a trend for the actual GNP in mid-1955 forward at an annual average rate of growth from 3¼ to 3½ percent. Mid-1955 was used as the base year for those calculations because, with unemployment down to 4 percent of the labor force, actual output was equal to potential output. In determining the growth rate to be used to measure the trend of potential output, the CEA took into account the rate of growth in the potential labor force, the annual average rate of growth in labor productivity for the entire labor force, and the downward trend in hours worked per year.

This concept of an output, or performance, gap emerged in the early 1960s as one of the key tools used by the CEA for analysis of the economy's performance. To explain the serious performance gap which characterized the U.S. economy from mid-1955 onward, the CEA developed a theory of fiscal stagnation. The council argued that the failure of the economy to expand at a rate sufficient to provide full employment was *not* due primarily to a deficiency of either private consumption or investment demand, but to the restrictive impact of the federal tax structure on the overall level of demand. This was a major shift in macroeconomic thinking. Until then, the standard Keynesian view was that a less than full employment situation was caused by excessive *private* saving relative to investment opportunities.

The major analytical tool utilized by the Council of Economic Advisers to demonstrate the restrictive effect of the federal tax structure on the economy was the concept of the full-employment surplus. Earlier in this chapter we defined the full-employment budget. The full-employment surplus is a variant of this concept. In the 1962 *Economic Report* the CEA used it to mean the budgetary surplus of the federal government that would be generated by a given budget program under conditions of full employment (a 4 percent unemployment rate). Figure 15–4 is from the 1962 CEA report and illustrates this concept. In the diagram the ratio of actual GNP to potential GNP is shown

---

[17] *Economic Report of the President,* 1962, p. 51.

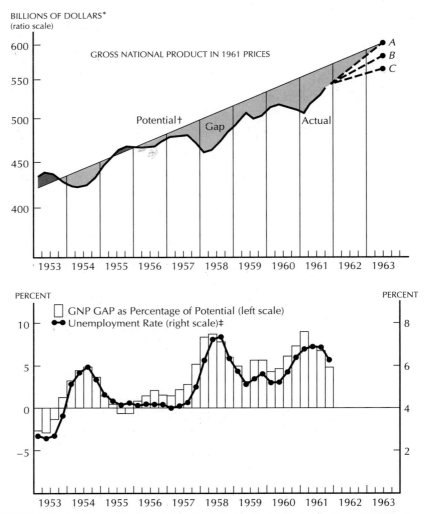

FIGURE 15–3   Gross National Product (Actual and Potential) and Unemployment Rate: 1953–1963. This figure from the 1962 *Economic Report* documents the growing gap between actual and potential output that the Kennedy administration used as a basis for the need for policy actions to bring down unemployment to a 4 percent level.

*Seasonally adjusted annual rates.

†3½ percent trend line through middle of 1955.

‡Unemployment as a percentage of civilian labor force; seasonally adjusted.

Note: A, B, and *C* represent GNP in the middle of 1963 assuming unemployment rates of 4, 5, and 6 percent, respectively.

Source: Economic Report of the President, 1962.

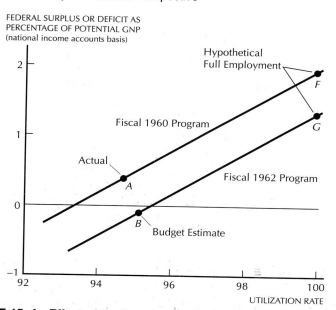

FEDERAL SURPLUS OR DEFICIT AS
PERCENTAGE OF POTENTIAL GNP
(national income accounts basis)

FIGURE 15–4 Effect of the Level of Economic Activity on the Federal Surplus or Deficit. This figure from the 1962 *Economic Report* shows the impact of federal government spending and taxation on the surplus or deficit for two different fiscal years, 1960 and 1962. Both years indicate that a sizable surplus will exist at the economy's hypothetical full-employment level; this implies a substantial fiscal drag in both years.

Source: Economic Report of the President, 1962.

on the horizontal axis. This axis is labeled the "Utilization Rate"; the 100 percent point represents full employment. It will be recalled that potential GNP is based on projecting a trend that embodies a 4 percent unemployment rate. Thus, when the ratio of actual to potential GNP equals 100, the economy must be operating at full employment. On the vertical axis, the federal surplus or deficit is measured as a percentage of the potential GNP.

Two curves are shown in the diagram, one of which reflects the tax and expenditure program of the federal government for the fiscal year 1960, and the other for the fiscal year 1962. Both of these curves slope upward to the right; this indicates that the surplus or deficit associated with any given budget program will depend on the level of economic activity prevailing in the economy. By a "given budget program" is meant a particular pattern and level of expenditures combined with a particular structure of tax rates. With fixed expenditures and a given rate structure for the tax system, a deficit will decline or a surplus will increase as the economy's utilization rate increases—or as the economy approaches full employment. The height and steepness of the curve depend on the character of the budget program that exists at any given time—namely, the level of expenditures, tax rates, and the degree of progression present in the system.

Discretionary fixed policy—action that deliberately changes the level of government expenditures or tax rates—has the effect of shifting the curve up or down. For example, a reduction in tax rates would lower the curve and thus either increase a deficit or reduce a surplus associated with a specific level of economic activity—the utilization rate shown on the horizontal axis. The effects of built-in stabilizers, on the other hand, are reflected in a movement along the curve as the level of economic activity changes. A rise in the income level will automatically generate a surplus sooner or later, as long as there is no change in expenditures. It should be noted, too, that if tax rates and expenditure programs remain constant, the full-employment surplus will rise over time. The reason for this is that over time the full-employment potential GNP grows, simply because a growing labor force which is fully employed and whose productivity is improving inevitably means a larger output. As long as tax rates are unchanged, the absolute volume of tax revenues yielded by a full-employment economy must increase over time. This being the case and with expenditures unchanged, the budgetary surplus should grow.

The economic significance of a full-employment budget surplus lies in the fact that the actual achievement of full employment requires that gross investment expenditures (including the net foreign investment in an open economy) must be large enough to offset the total private saving plus the net surplus of the public sector, which the economic system generates at full employment. In equation form, $I = S + T - G$, in which the variables represent full-employment, *ex ante* (or planned) values. The actual situation between 1955 and the early 1960s, according to the analysis of the Council of Economic Advisers, was a tendency for full-employment saving (including government saving or the full-employment surplus) to run ahead of gross investment, including net foreign investment. In symbolic terms, $S + T - G > I$.

The Remedy for Fiscal Stagnation. The solution proposed by the Kennedy administration for fiscal stagnation was a massive reduction in both personal and corporate income taxes. President Kennedy in a 1963 special message on tax reform requested that the tax rates on personal income be reduced from a range of 20 to 91 percent to a range of 14 to 65 percent and that the rate on corporate income be reduced from 95 to 45 percent. The Congress did not act on President Kennedy's request, but, following his assassination, essentially the same proposals were presented to the Congress in January 1964. Speedy action was forthcoming, and the Revenue Act of 1964 was signed into law on February 16, 1964. In its 1965 *Annual Report*, the CEA estimated that the total tax reductions taking effect in 1964 and 1965 would be $11 billion for individuals and $3 billion for corporations.[18]

---

[18] *Economic Report of the President,* 1965, p. 65. The Excise Tax Reduction Act of 1965 called for a reduction in excise taxes totaling $4.6 billion over several stages through 1969. The $13 billion total was equal to 2.0 percent of the 1964 GNP. In contrast the Reagan planned tax cuts for 1981, 1982, and 1983 averaged 1.6 percent of the GNP in each of these years.

It was expected that the tax cuts would operate to stimulate both consumption and investment spending and thus bring output closer to the full-employment potential. The reduction in the personal income tax would add directly to the personal disposable income of consumers, and, since most of this added income would be spent, the multiplier would come into play and generate a cumulative expansion in consumption. Investment spending would rise both because the after-tax profit on new facilities would be increased and because more internal funds would be available to firms for investment purposes.

In its 1963 *Annual Report,* the CEA presented a textbooklike explanation of the multiplier effects that could be expected to flow from the reduction in the rate of the personal income tax. After taking into account all the various leakages at work in the economic system, the council concluded that each additional dollar of GNP generated initially by the tax cut would generate an additional $0.50 of consumption expenditures. In other words, the marginal propensity to consume out of the GNP is 0.50, which yields a multiplier of 2 to be applied against the initial increase in consumption spending stimulated by the increase in disposable income.[19] The ultimate expansionary effect was expected to be even greater because of the stimulus to investment resulting both from the initial reduction in the corporate rate and from the expansion in consumption generated by the cut in personal income tax rates.

The Effectiveness of the 1964 Tax Cut. While there are no absolutely conclusive tests that can be employed to determine the effectiveness of the 1964 tax cut, the available evidence is strong that the tax cuts did, in fact, achieve the results expected. In the first place, the gap between actual and potential output, which reached a peak of $50 billion at an annual rate in the first quarter of 1961, was reduced to an annual rate of $10 billion in the last quarter of 1965. The unemployment rate declined to 4.1 percent by the end of 1965; in September 1966, the rate stood at 3.8 percent of the civilian labor force. These changes largely took place before the Vietnam military buildup began to have much effect on the economy.

Additional evidence for the effectiveness of the tax cut is to be found in the performance of the GNP. In 1964, the GNP (in current prices) increased by $42.9 billion, in contrast to an increase of $32.3 billion (in current prices) in 1963. The CEA stated in its 1966 *Annual Report* that statistical analysis of the impact of the tax cut indicated that it was responsible for nearly $10 billion of the gain in the annual increase of the GNP. The increase continued in 1965. With respect to the entire expansion, the CEA estimated that, by the end of 1965, the contribution of the tax cut reached $30 billion.[20]

The third piece of evidence that can be cited in support of the effectiveness of the tax cut is the fact that, from the close of 1964 to the close of 1965, federal revenues increased by $9.6 billion, in spite of the fact that in this same

[19] *Economic Report of the President,* 1963, pp. 45–51.

[20] *Economic Report of the President,* 1966, p. 34.

period tax reductions effected by both the Revenue Act of 1964 and the Excise Tax Reduction Act of 1965 totaled about \$16 billion.[21] This experience bears out the claim of the CEA that a tax reduction, if it succeeds in stimulating economic growth, would lead to an increase rather than a decrease in revenues. It was this aspect of the 1964 tax cut that led supply-siders to claim later that the Kennedy-Johnson tax cut provided support for their argument that a tax cut will produce more revenue. In any event, it is apparent that, if the level of government expenditures had remained constant during this period, the federal government would have experienced a substantial surplus by the end of 1965. Actually, total expenditures (including transfers) of the federal government rose from \$118.8 billion in 1964 (on a national income accounts basis) to \$124.6 billion in 1965—an increase of \$5.8 billion, which was less than the increase in revenue of \$9.6 billion in the same period. The federal government achieved a small surplus of \$1.3 billion in 1965.[22]

Vietnam and Its Aftermath

From 1966 to the early 1970s the economic effects of the Vietnam War and its inflationary aftermath dominated the economy and economic policy. By the end of 1966 the unemployment level fell below 4 percent, the target figure the Council of Economic Advisers established in the early 1960s as representing full employment. During 1969 unemployment was 3.5 percent, the lowest figure in the entire post-World War II years except for the Korean War years. Also in 1966 the GNP gap disappeared, not to reappear until the 1970 recession. With reduction of the unemployment rate below the target level and the disappearance of the GNP gap, inflation quickly became the number one aggregate—and domestic—economic problem.

During the Vietnam period economic policy was directed almost totally toward the control of inflation.[23] The major policy moves included imposition of a 10 percent surcharge on corporate and individual income taxes in 1968, the 1969 game plan of the Nixon administration for inflation control, and the experiment with an incomes policy which began in mid-1971. The latter was discussed in detail in Chapter 12. Here we shall discuss the 1968 surcharge and the policies pursued to control inflation by the Nixon administration during its pre-incomes policy phase.

[21] *Economic Report of the President,* 1967, p. 271.

[22] Monetary policy played a much less dramatic role than did fiscal policy in the Kennedy era. Nevertheless, the Federal Reserve stepped up the rate of growth in the money supply (M1) in 1963 and 1964; this is the basis of the claim of some monetarists that the increase in the money supply rather than the 1964 tax cut was responsible for improved economic conditions in the Kennedy era. This is an issue which will probably never be settled. The figures on government receipts and revenues are from the 1995 *Economic Report of the President.* They reflect the most recent and most accurate national income and product accounts data. There have been several revisions of the data since 1962.

[23] The major economic stimulus from the war came from 1966 through 1968 in the form of rising military expenditures, but the inflationary aftermath lasted through 1973. Thus, economically, the Vietnam War period runs from 1966 through 1973.

By mid-1966 it was evident to most economists that the heating up of the economy consequent to the escalation in Vietnam required the application of a restrictive fiscal policy, although it was not until two years later that the Johnson administration and a reluctant Congress enacted a tax increase.[24] The Revenue and Expenditure Control Act of 1968, signed into law at the end of June, provided for a 10 percent surcharge on personal and corporate income taxes, retroactive to January 1, 1968, for corporate income taxes and to April 1, 1968, for personal income taxes. Through subsequent action by the Congress, the surcharge on personal income was extended at a 10 percent rate through 1969, dropped to a 5 percent rate in the first half of 1970, and allowed to expire on June 30, 1970. The same provisions applied to the corporate income tax.

The 1968 surcharge was a fiscal policy counterpart to the tax reductions of 1964, as it was expected its impact on disposable income and corporate profits would dampen spending and thus contribute to bringing inflationary pressures under control. Was the 1968 tax increase as successful in holding down aggregate demand as its predecessor tax cut apparently had been in stimulating aggregate demand? The answer is by no means clear-cut. Consumer prices rose at an annual average rate of 4.7 percent in 1968, 6.2 percent in 1969, and 5.6 percent in 1970. It was not until the economy went into the 1969–70 recession that a slowdown in the inflation rate became evident. This happened in 1971, when the annual rate of price increase dropped to 3.3 percent. Since the surcharge was allowed to expire in mid-1970, we really do not know what might have happened if the tax had remained in effect. Furthermore, as critics of the surcharge maintain—especially some proponents of the permanent income hypothesis—consumers were well aware of the temporary nature of the tax. Consequently, they adjusted to it by reducing their saving rather than their spending when the tax increase cut into their disposable incomes. Personal saving as a percentage of disposable income declined from 8.1 in 1967 to 7.1 in 1968 and to 6.5 in 1969 and then climbed back to 8.0 in 1970, the year in which the surcharge was lifted. But 1970 was also a recession year, marked by a good deal of consumer caution and uncertainty, so the evidence on the saving ratio is not definitive.

A highly comprehensive study of the effectiveness of the 1968 surcharge was completed in 1971 by the late Arthur Okun, a former chairperson of the Council of Economic Advisers.[25] Professor Okun used four different econometric models to test the hypothesis that the surcharge was expected to curb

---

[24] In 1966 the purchase of goods and services by the federal government for military purposes jumped by $11.0 billion, an increase that took place in a fully employed economy. No new taxes were imposed to finance this vast and sudden increase in federal outlays; this caused the federal government's deficit to rise to $13.2 billion on a national income accounts basis the following year. It would be difficult to find a more perfect example of irresponsible government action that inevitably would have serious inflationary consequences.

[25] Arthur M. Okun, ''The Personal Tax Surcharge and Consumer Demand, 1968–70,'' *Brookings Papers on Economic Activity,* No. 1, 1971.

consumer demand and then compared the results obtained with the estimated actual impact on consumption. He found that, with the exception of the demand for automobiles, the surcharge was effective during the 1968–70 period in curbing consumer demand for other durables, as well as nondurables and services. Automobile demand, for reasons that are not entirely clear, displayed great strength during this period, as did business investment (including residential construction) in spite of the surcharge on corporate income. Professor Okun's general conclusion is that, overall, consumer demand responded about as expected to the reduction in disposable income, but the expansionary and inflationary forces let loose by the Vietnam War were much greater than recognized at the time. As he says,

> The medicine of the personal tax surcharge did lower the patient's fever. To be sure, the patient was more feverish than the doctors recognized and consequently their antifever prescription was inadequate. But don't blame the medicine; it did most of what it should have been reasonably expected to do. In short, the evidence of the surcharge period provides further confirmation of the general efficacy and continued desirability of flexible changes in personal income tax rates—upward or downward, permanent or temporary.[26]

The most damaging weakness of the surcharge was its application approximately two years too late, a failing of the political system rather than economic diagnosis.

The first priority of the Nixon administration when it assumed power at the beginning of 1969 was to bring inflation under control. This, it was thought, could be done by a gradualist approach, which would try and slow down the economy sufficiently to dampen the inflationary psychology that the Nixon economists believed three years of rising prices had engendered. In 1969 the administration was confident that this could be done without bringing on a recession or too much unemployment. Under the leadership of Professor Paul McCracken of the University of Michigan, the Nixon CEA put together a combination of fiscal and monetary restraints designed to accomplish this, a package that came to be known as the administration's "game plan." In 1969 the rate of growth of federal expenditures for goods and services slowed sharply, from 6.9 percent in 1968 to 1.3 percent in 1969, as did the rate of growth in the money supply, from 7.7 percent in 1968 to 3.3 percent in 1969. The percentages are for M1. We shall return to the subject of monetary policy shortly.

What were the results? Since there is a normal lag of 6 to 12 months before the initiation of an economic policy and ultimate results, 1970 was the decisive test year for the effectiveness of the 1969 game plan. By the end of the year, it was apparent that gradualism had not done the job of stopping inflation. It has already been pointed out that consumer prices rose by 5.6

---

[26] Ibid.

percent in 1970, as compared with 6.2 percent in 1969 and 4.7 percent in 1968. Yet unemployment rose from the 3.5 percent level of 1969 to a rate of 6 percent by December 1970. The failure of the gradualist approach was abetted by the Nixon administration's strongly voiced unwillingness at the start of 1969 to give any consideration to an incomes policy. Furthermore, the administration was openly hostile to the income tax surcharge and made no move to ask the Congress to extend it beyond the planned expiration date of June 30, 1970. During the first half of 1971 the Nixon administration largely marked time in terms of economic policy, uncertain about how to cope with the growing problem of both unemployment and inflation. Finally in mid-August President Nixon made his bombshell announcement that his administration had embarked on an experiment with a comprehensive incomes policy, a wage-price freeze—an approach the administration had scornfully rejected in early 1969. The results of this phase of the Nixon administration economic policies were discussed in Chapter 12 (pages 496–97).

In the meanwhile, what role did monetary policy play in the Vietnam period? In general, the acceleration in the rate of growth in the money supply that began in the Kennedy era continued, but with two important exceptions—1966 and 1969. In late 1965 and early 1966, the Federal Reserve System, worried about the growing inflationary pressures because of Vietnam, slammed on the monetary brakes. The discount rate was raised and growth in the money supply curtailed (in 1966, overall, the rate of monetary growth dropped to 2.4 percent, compared to 4.7 percent in 1965). The result was a severe credit squeeze, generally known as the *credit crunch* of 1966. Particularly hard hit was the housing industry, because the rise in open market interest rates exceeded the rates that financial intermediaries such as savings and loan associations, mutual savings banks, and life insurance companies were able to pay. Consequently, the flow of savings to these intermediaries dropped, and this in turn dried up the flow of money into home mortgages.[27] Thus, the construction of new houses slumped badly (new housing starts were off by more than 307,000 in 1966). In many respects 1969 was a repeat of 1966. As part of the Nixon game plan the money supply was tightened; the rate of growth of M1 dropped to 3.3 percent in 1969 as compared to 7.7 percent in the prior year. And again, as in 1966, housing was hurt as the flow of savings to financial intermediaries began to dry up. The crunch was not as severe as earlier, however, because the Federal Reserve moved to a less-restrictive stance early in 1970. Experience in 1966 and in 1969 demonstrates dramatically the uneven impact of monetary policy.

In the view of one knowledgeable observer, 1966 was a year of crucial significance in the development of post-World War II monetary policy. That year, according to Sherman J. Maisel, former member of the Board of Gov-

---

[27] This process is called *disintermediation*. The reason is that the financial institutions just mentioned operate essentially as channels for the transfer of funds from savers to borrowers. Hence, they are serving as intermediaries. When the process slows down or stops, we have disintermediation.

ernors of the Federal Reserve System, marked the end of the "age of innocence" for the system.[28] What he meant was that henceforth the system had to abandon the simplistic view of former chairperson William McChesney Martin that its main task in an inflationary era was to restrict the money supply; rather, it had to be equally mindful of how its credit and monetary policies would affect the different sectors of the economy, a lesson driven home by the severe and adverse effect that monetary restriction during 1966 had on the flow of funds into the housing market.

After 1966, in short, the Federal Reserve recognized that the effective use of monetary policy required that the board take into account the actual workings of financial markets in terms of traditional channels of lending and borrowing as well as the total quantity of money and commercial bank reserves available to the economy.

The 1970s

There is no clear line of demarcation that indicates precisely when the Vietnam War ceased to be the dominating factor in policymaking for the economy. In a sense, because of the pressure on the price level during the 1970s and the severe recession of 1981–82 that was necessary to reduce the inflation rate, we are still feeling the effects of that historic national misadventure. But for practical policymaking, the failure of the 1969 Nixon game plan and the shift to an incomes policy in mid-1971 represent a rough turning point. From then onward, the fiscal and monetary policies of the ill-fated Nixon administration were geared toward bringing down the unemployment rate, particularly with a presidential election in the offing.

In 1970, 1971, and 1972 fiscal and monetary policies became expansive. To illustrate, the deficit on the full-employment budget rose from $3.4 billion in 1970 to $9.6 billion in 1971 and $11.4 billion in 1972—a $16.3-billion swing in three years.[29] This resulted from a combination of tax cuts and rising expenditures. Equally expansive was monetary policy, as the money supply (M1) increased by 5.1 percent in 1970, 6.5 percent in 1971, and a phenomenal 9.2 percent in 1972, a higher rate of growth than any year since 1948. The administration was confident that the system of wage and price controls instituted in mid-1971 would contain any added inflationary pressures resulting from the fiscal and monetary stimuli.

What were the results of the switch from a policy of restraint (1969) to all-out expansion (1971 to 1972)? They were mixed—an outcome that reflects the fact that it is becoming increasingly difficult to deal adequately with either inflation or unemployment in our economy by fiscal and monetary means.

---

[28] Sherman J. Maisel, *Managing the Dollar* (New York: Norton, 1973), p. 63.

[29] In a news conference early in 1971 President Nixon said "I am a Keynesian," a remark widely interpreted as indicating the willingness of his administration to use fiscal measures to stimulate the economy. This view was strengthened by his endorsement of the concept of the full-employment budget in his 1971 Economic Message to the Congress. These figures are from Table 9–8 (page 329).

The unemployment rate continued to rise through 1971 and reached a rate of 5.9 percent for the year. In 1972 it came down slightly to 5.6 percent, but the decline was far less than expected in view of the strong fiscal and monetary stimuli applied to the economy. The stubborn resistance of unemployment to improvement by the application of the usual Keynesian remedies turned out to be one of the more persistent and difficult problems of the 1970s. Some economists argue it is rooted in the structure of the labor force, since some groups—minorities and teenagers especially—benefit only in a marginal way from higher levels of aggregate demand. With respect to the price level, there was improvement in both 1971 and 1972; this appeared to indicate that controls were working. In 1971 the inflation rate dropped to 4.4 percent, and it fell further in 1972 to 3.2 percent, a low for the 1970s. There is evidence, however, (see Chapter 12) that these gains were nothing more than a lagged consequence of the 1969–70 recession.

When Gerald Ford became president in late summer 1974, he inherited fiscal and monetary policies that had once again turned restrictive. The new president, if anything, was even more concerned than his predecessor with an inflation that was accelerating rapidly. In the first half of the year consumer prices rose at an annual rate slightly in excess of 10 percent. Americans began to hear more and more about a new economic menace—double-digit inflation. Even though the Arab oil embargo in late 1973 and poor crops were in part responsible for the acceleration in the inflation rate, the Ford administration continued to pursue policies that were strongly restrictive. This took place in spite of the fact that the crucial business cycle indicators of the Department of Commerce were pointing downward (see Chapter 14). In 1974 the money supply (M1) grew at an annual rate of 4.4 percent, down from the 5.5 percent growth rate in 1973 and well below the record rate of expansion in 1972. Fiscal policy, too, continued to be restrictive—a fact reflected in the swing of the full-employment budget from a deficit of $9.0 billion in 1973 to a surplus of $6.0 billion in 1974. Overall this was a swing in a restrictive direction of $10.6 billion. Inflation plus the combination of highly restrictive fiscal and monetary policies led to the second most severe economic slump since the Great Depression of the 1930s. Real gross national product declined in both 1974 and 1975, and the unemployment rate rose to a post-World War II high of 8.9 percent in May 1976.

Recovery began in the spring of 1975, coincident with the passage of a tax cut bill proposed by the Ford administration, a package which overall contained cuts on the order of $15 billion. Since then events moved along a path that is becoming distressingly familiar, even though there was a change in administrations at the start of 1977. Real output expanded after the turnaround came in the third quarter of 1975, but not rapidly enough to bring down the unemployment rate to even the Ford administration's suggested target of 5.5 percent for full employment. Two years after the recovery got underway (May 1977), unemployment was still at the excessively high figure of 6.9 percent of the labor force. Inflation was down from the double-digit range, which alarmed so many people in 1974, but the situation was not satisfactory. In the first four months of 1977 consumer prices rose at an annual rate of nearly 10 percent—a development that the Carter administration attributed to bad weather in the early part of the year.

In many ways the Carter administration policies were not much different from those of the predecessor Ford administration, in spite of the rhetoric of the 1976 campaign. The high unemployment from the 1974–75 recession lingered on through 1976 and made unemployment the major policy focus for the administration during its first two years in office. In 1977 the unemployment rate was 7.1 percent, down only slightly from the 1976 rate of 7.6 percent. This led the new administration to propose a two-year program of tax reductions in the amount of $31 billion, including a one-time $50 rebate on the 1976 taxes. Although the idea of a tax rebate was dropped in April 1977, when it became apparent that there had been a larger than expected boost in consumer spending in the early part of the year, the administration proposed additional personal tax reductions during 1978. In his January 1978 *Economic Report*, President Carter asked for a tax reduction of $25 billion, to take effect in October. In May this request was scaled back to $20 billion, not to take effect until January 1979; these scaled-back reductions were eventually incorporated into the Revenue Act of 1978.[30] The postponement of the tax cut in combination with a slower rate of growth in federal spending than anticipated by the administration helped reduce the full-employment deficit in the latter part of the year—a development welcomed by the administration because the inflation rate had started back up during the year.

During the last two years of the Carter administration the focus of policy shifted from stimulating the economy to lower unemployment to instituting restrictive measures to hold back the acceleration in inflation. During 1979 consumer prices rose at an annual average rate of 11.3 percent; in 1980 the rate accelerated to 13.5 percent. As already pointed out, the Federal Reserve made a major policy shift in October 1979; from then on it targeted the money supply rather than interest rates and sought to curtail sharply the growth in the money supply. From October through June of 1980 the growth of M1 (currency plus demand deposits) was practically halted. The seriousness of the inflation threat caused the administration to take even more drastic measures to control the growth of money and credit. In March 1980 the President, using the authority of the Credit Control Act of 1969, authorized the Federal Reserve to institute certain direct controls on consumer credit and some of the lending activities of larger banks.

Two consequences followed from the actions of both the Federal Reserve and the Carter administration. First, there was a sharp curtailment in the first half of 1980 in the expansion of both money and credit. Consumer credit outstanding dropped by $9.8 billion in the second quarter of 1980.[31] Second, the restrictive measures taken in late 1979 and the spring of 1980 plunged

---

[30] *Economic Report of the President*, 1979, p. 93.

[31] *Economic Report of the President*, 1981, p. 310.

the economy into one of the sharpest but shortest recessions on record. During the second quarter of 1980, *real* gross national product dropped at an annual rate of 9.9 percent.[32] The unexpected sharpness of the downturn led the Federal Reserve to ease up on the money supply, and in July the direct controls were ended as the president revoked the authority of the Federal Reserve to institute these controls. Once again, however, the potency of monetary policy to push the economy into recession had been demonstrated. As in prior recessions, there was a deceleration in the inflation rate. The upturn that began in the second half of 1980 continued until the second quarter of 1981, when the restrictive effects of the Reagan administration's fiscal and monetary policies began to be felt.

The Reagan Revolution

Ronald Reagan's economic advisers came from the new classical and supply-side school (Chapter 16). As a result, his economic program differed drastically from the Keynesian and, to some extent, monetarist policies used by other administrations. Reagan's economic advisers asserted that the tax burden on individuals was so high in this country that incentives to work and save were being badly hurt. Consequently, a reduction in taxes would unleash an explosion of work and saving great enough that federal tax revenues ultimately would increase. Not surprisingly, a significant element in the Reagan strategy was a major reduction in personal and business taxes. Initially the president asked that the tax rates on personal income be reduced by 10 percent across the board for three years, beginning July 1, 1981. This was basically the Kemp-Roth approach to tax reduction. For a number of years Representative Jack Kemp and Senator William Roth jointly introduced legislation in the Congress calling for a 30 percent reduction in federal taxes, spread over a three-year period.

As finally approved by the Congress in the Economic Recovery Tax Act of 1981, personal income tax rates were reduced by 5 percent in the first year, effective October 1, 1981, and by 10 percent in 1982 and again in 1983, effective July 1 in each year. The legislation also lowered the top rate on earned income from 70 to 50 percent, and, beginning in 1985, tax brackets were indexed to prevent bracket creep, higher taxes caused by inflation alone. With respect to business taxes, the act established a new system of accelerated depreciation, called the *accelerated cost recovery system* (ACRS), and increased the investment tax credit for certain types of investments. The Reagan tax package, irrespective of its intended supply-side effects, also was designed to bring about a major redistribution of the tax burden in favor of business and upper-income groups. The reason was that Reagan's policy aimed to stimulate investment specifically; putting more money in the hands of business and upper-income groups was thought to be the most effective way to

---

[32] Ibid., p. 235.

achieve this. They would invest in new capital, the capital would create jobs, and the tax cut's benefits would trickle down to the rest of the taxpayers in the form of more jobs and a growing economy.

The Reagan administration sought strong support from the Federal Reserve System as the overall program was implemented. The administration asked the Federal Reserve to cut the rate of growth of the money supply in half by 1986—a proposal that reflected the president's firm commitment to the monetarist position. Reagan also sought to cut the costs government imposes on business, primarily by lessening or eliminating government regulations. The belief that federal regulatory activity had become excessively burdensome for business was also an article of faith of the Reagan administration. Thus, the administration pushed for deregulation over a wide range of economic activities, including the commercial banks and the savings and loan thrifts.

A Critique of the Reagan Revolution

When the president signed the Economic Recovery Tax Act of 1981 into law in August 1981, he was extremely optimistic and predicted that the act would bring about stable prices, rising employment, economic growth, and a substantial reduction in the size and influence of the federal government in the economy. With the exception of a sharp decline in the inflation rate, none of these lofty goals of the Reagan administration was attained during the administration's first six years. Our analysis of the Reagan revolution focuses on the 1981 through 1986 period primarily because these were the years targeted by the administration for achieving the goals embodied in the 1981 legislation. There were no significant economic policy measures undertaken in the last two years (1987 and 1988) of the Reagan administration.[33]

Table 15–1 contains the necessary data to review the budgetary goals and results for the Reagan administration over the period 1981 through 1986. All the data in the table were taken from the president's original plan, *A Program for Economic Recovery*. These data are on a fiscal year rather than an annual basis. The (C) pertains to the last budget for which the Carter administration was primarily responsible (the fiscal year which ended September 30, 1981), whereas the five years labeled (R) are the budgets for which the Reagan administration was responsible. The first eight lines in the table show the planned revenue changes, how they were to be obtained, and the expected impact on the federal budget deficit or surplus. The next three lines show actual results through 1986.

Lines 1 and 2 in the table are crucial, for they show the planned increase in military spending and the planned reduction in taxes over this six-year period. The sum of these two, shown in line 3, represents the amount of revenue needed either to finance the military buildup or to offset the revenue

---

[33] The Tax Reform Act of 1986, which cut both corporate and individual income tax rates while closing in whole or in part a number of loopholes in both taxes, was a bipartisan measure, supported by the Democratic leadership in both houses of the Congress, as well as the Republican administration.

TABLE 15–1 The Reagan Economic Revolution in Review, Budget Details, 1981–1986*

Item	(C) 1981	(R) 1982	(R) 1983	(R) 1984	(R) 1985	(R) 1986	Total
1. Additional military spending	1.3	7.2	20.7	27.0	50.2	63.1	169.5
2. Tax reduction	8.9	53.9	100.0	148.1	185.7	221.7	718.3
3. Total of 1 + 2	10.2	61.1	120.7	175.1	235.9	284.8	887.8
4. Targeted budget reductions	4.4	41.4	79.7	104.4	117.6	123.8	471.3
5. Difference of 3 − 4	5.8	19.7	41.0	70.7	118.3	161.0	416.5
6. Expected revenue gains from economic growth	—	48.3	57.1	58.9	75.3	87.2	326.8
7. Estimated federal receipts after new tax policy	600.2	650.5	710.2	772.1	850.9	942.0	4,525.9
8. Targeted budget deficit (−) or surplus (+)	−54.9	−45.0	−22.9	+0.5	+6.9	+29.9	−85.5
9. Actual revenue receipts	599.3	617.8	600.6	666.5	734.1	769.1	3,987.4
10. Shortfall	0.9	32.7	109.6	105.6	116.8	172.9	538.5
11. Actual budget deficit (−) or surplus (+)	−79.0	−128.0	−207.8	−185.4	−212.3	−221.2	1,033.7

*All numbers in lines 1 through 8 are taken from the President's *A Program for Economic Recovery,* February 18, 1981, and are in billions of dollars. The actual results in lines 9 through 11 are from *Current Economic Indicators,* January 1995, p. 32.

lost through tax reduction. The total needed was $887.8 billion. One way to achieve this was by reductions in the nonmilitary parts of the budget. The reductions originally targeted in the economic recovery program are shown in line 4. The difference between lines 3 and 4 represents, therefore, the amount of revenue needed to offset revenue lost through the tax reduction and revenue needed because of larger military outlays (line 5). This was $416.5 billion. This difference is of *key* importance because it yields a quantitative measure of the task faced by supply-side economics. The basic rationale for the 5-10-10 tax cut was that it would improve incentives to such an extent that production would rise dramatically and with it the revenue of the federal government. The increases in tax revenues projected from the workings of supply-side economics contained in the economic recovery document are shown in line 6. These gains were predicated on annual average rates of growth in real GNP of 1.1 percent in 1981, 4.2 percent in 1982, 5.0 percent in 1983, 4.5 percent in 1984, and 4.2 percent in 1985 and 1986.[34] The amounts of added revenue to be gained from the supply-side effects (line 6) did not match fully the needs for more revenue (line 5), but if the plan had worked out as intended, the differences would not have been overwhelming. Unfortunately, this did not happen; one reason was that the entire program rested on projected rates of growth in real GNP that were wholly unrealistic.[35] Actual rates of growth varied widely from the projected rates, from a negative 2.2 percent in the recession year of 1982 to a vigorous 6.2 percent in the recovery year of 1984. For the six-year period of 1981 through 1986, actual growth averaged 2.6 percent as compared to the projected average of 3.9 percent.

The failure of supply-side economics to deliver on the promised growth meant that during the first six years of the Reagan administration, budgetary projections fell far short of expectations. Actual results are reflected in lines 9 through 11 of Table 15–1. Line 9 shows the actual receipts after the tax changes went into effect, and line 10 shows the budget shortfall because receipts did not measure up to expectations (line 7). There was a cumulative shortfall of $538.5 billion in this period, which accounts in large part for the expansionist thrust of the fiscal side of the recovery program. Because of this shortfall, targeted budget deficits (−) or surpluses (+) as shown in line 8 failed to materialize. Rather, the result was large budget deficits through fiscal 1986 (line 11). The cumulative deficit for this period was $1,033.7 billion—more than a trillion dollars—whereas the projected cumulative deficit was only $85.5 billion.

Other goals for the Reagan administration were not realized. As already noted, the rate of growth for real GNP failed to reach the projected goals. In only two out of the six years covered by the economic plan—1981 and 1984—did growth exceed the planned target. The vigor of the post-1982 expansion was not great enough to reach the administration's goals for unemployment. Instead of coming down to 5.6 percent by 1986, the rate averaged 8.1 percent throughout the period, a higher rate than existed when the Reagan administration took office in early 1981.

The picture for government spending and taxes in relation to the GNP as well as the rate of growth in the money supply is mixed. The tax cut of 1981 did bring the ratio of federal taxes to the GNP largely into line with projected

---

[34] *A Program for Economic Recovery* (Washington, D.C.: The White House, February 18, 1981), p. 25.

[35] The arithmetic of the Reagan program is such that added revenue expected from the supply-side effect worked out at about 45 cents for every dollar of tax income lost through the tax cuts (the total shown in line 6 divided by the total shown in line 2). There were critics in 1981 who argued that the administration numbers just did not add up, that no administration could simultaneously cut taxes, increase military outlays, and balance the federal budget. But in the euphoria that gripped the administration and the country in 1981, few were listening. Former Budget Director David Stockman has admitted in his memoirs, however, that this was the case. George Bush in his campaign for the GOP presidential nomination in 1980—and before he became Reagan's vice president—described these ideas as "voodoo economics."

goals. By 1986 federal tax receipts had fallen to 19.6 percent of the GNP, which was equal to the projected goal. The story with federal expenditures is drastically different. In spite of tax cuts and attempts to pare back the federal budget, the administration failed wholly in reaching its goal of bringing down federal expenditures to 19.0 percent of the GNP. Instead, this ratio actually rose, from 23.0 percent in 1981 to 24.5 in 1986. This ratio was the highest of the post-World War II period.[36] Given the frequently expressed objective of the Reagan revolution to scale back the size of the federal government, these results must be counted as a major failure of the administration. Growing military spending in combination with the sharp increase in interest costs and the intractability of much social spending are the major reasons for this outcome.

Finally, there are the results with respect to monetary growth. In *A Program for Economic Recovery* the objective was specific: reduce the rate of growth of the money supply (M1) to one-half the 1980 level of 6.8 percent by 1986. But the actual results with respect to monetary growth were the exact opposite of those planned. From 1981 onward, the rate of growth of M1 rose steadily and reached 16.8 percent in 1986. This was nearly triple the 1981 rate! Money growth reflects in part the reversal of policy by the Federal Reserve System in mid-1982, when it began to expand the money supply in an effort to bring down interest rates to counter the severe impact of the 1981–82 recession. Beyond this, the experience of the period casts severe doubt on one of the basic tenets of monetarism, namely, the close and direct relationship between the money supply and the price level. In a period in which monetary growth was extremely rapid, the inflation rate was falling. This is exactly the opposite of what monetarism predicts.

While the evidence to date indicates that the administration's 1981 tax cuts did not have the intended supply-side effects, there are other results whose long-term consequences may affect the economy's macroeconomic performance. These involve the redistribution and poverty rate effects resulting from the combined impact of the income tax cuts and the reductions in transfer spending for social and welfare purposes. In 1980 transfers to persons accounted for 40.3 percent of all federal spending, but by 1988 this percentage had dropped to 38.4 percent. In the same period, interest on the federal debt as a percent of federal spending rose from 8.6 to 13.2 percent. Overall, these changes tend to make the distribution of income less equal, because on balance transfers to people are directed more toward low-income than high-income persons and families, whereas the persons and families receiving interest on the federal debt are mostly in the upper-income ranges. As the *Wall Street Journal* said early on about the impact of President Reagan's tax and budget cuts, "The rich are getting richer and the poor are getting poorer."[37]

---

[36] GNP, not GDP, data are used to compute these ratios because the Reagan targets were expressed in terms of GNP. GDP had not yet come into regular use in the United States as the chief measure of output at the time.

[37] *Wall Street Journal,* December 6, 1982, "The Outlook" column.

TABLE 15–2   Distribution of Money Income to Families by Fifths for Selected Years: 1970–1992 (in percent)

Year	Lowest Fifth	Second Fifth	Share of Income Going to Middle Fifth	Fourth Fifth	Highest Fifth
1970	5.5	12.2	17.6	23.8	40.9
1975	5.5	11.8	17.6	24.1	41.1
1980	5.2	11.5	17.5	24.3	41.5
1985	4.7	10.9	16.8	24.1	43.5
1990	4.6	10.8	16.6	23.8	44.3
1992	4.4	10.5	16.5	24.0	44.6

Source: U.S. Bureau of the Census, *Current Population Reports,* Series P-60, No. 184.

Recent data confirm this view. Table 15–2 shows the distribution of money income to families and unattached individuals for selected years since 1970. The table shows that share of total income going to each 20 percent (or fifth) of families, from the lowest to the highest fifth. The figures in Table 15–2 show that income inequality has been growing in the U.S. economy since 1970, but that the degree of inequality accelerated after 1980. For example, the relative share of total income going to the lower three-fifths of families dropped by 3.3 percent between 1970 and 1980, but by 8.2 percent from 1980 through 1992. Between 1970 and 1980, the top fifth of families increased their relative share of income by 1.5 percent, but in the decade of the 1980s their relative share jumped by 6.7 percent. It is true that the trend toward greater inequality began well before the Reagan administration took office, but the latter's policies on taxes and social spending strengthened the trend toward greater income inequality.

Data on poverty reinforce the foregoing. In 1959 the percentage of Americans living below the federally calculated poverty level was 22.4. By 1965, just before the impact of President Johnson's War on Poverty legislation began to be felt, the rate had fallen to 17.3 percent. The poverty index continued to decline, reaching 11.1 percent in 1973. This was the lowest point for the index since it was first compiled. The index rose to 13.0 percent in 1980, because of the recession that year, and rose again to 15.3 percent in 1983, because of the 1982 recession. The index came down slightly in the latter half of the 1980s, and then rose again to 14.2 in the 1990–91 recession.[38]

We conclude this critique of the Reagan revolution with three observations. First, the increase in the poverty population and the trend toward greater inequality in income distribution may have serious adverse effects on the economy's long-term performance. It will be recalled from the discussion in Chapter 7 that the overall distribution of income is an important factor in

[38] Committee on Ways and Means, U.S. House of Representatives, *1993 Green Book* (Washington, D.C.: U.S. Government Printing Office, 1993), p. 1313.

Jobs and Presidential Politics

Jobs! With the possible exception of prices, no topic in economics is of greater concern to the public than the availability of jobs. Jobs, too, are usually the number one domestic concern of any administration in power in Washington.

Few administrations understood this better than the Reagan administration, which continually pointed with pride to the new jobs created during Mr. Reagan's two terms in office. Reaganomics is given credit for these results, but as is often the case with any administration, the perception of reality and reality itself are two different things. A look at historical fact with respect to job creation may be surprising, not only for the record of the Reagan administration, but for others as well.

The table following shows the growth in jobs, the labor force, and unemployment rates for nine post-World War II administrations, from John F. Kennedy's through Bill Clinton's first two years. The figures are instructive.

The Presidential Scorecard

| Administration | Years | New Jobs (in millions) | Percent Increase | | Unemployment Rate |
			Jobs	Labor Force	
Kennedy	1961–64	3.5	5.4	5.0	5.8
Johnson	1965–68	6.0	9.5	7.7	3.9
Nixon	1969–73	9.1	12.0	13.6	5.0
Ford	1974–76	3.7	4.3	7.5	7.3
Carter	1977–80	10.6	11.9	11.2	6.5
Reagan (I)	1981–84	5.7	5.7	6.2	8.6
Reagan (II)	1985–88	9.7	9.4	7.1	6.5
Bush	1989–92	2.6	2.3	4.4	6.2
Clinton	1993–94	5.0	4.6	3.2	6.5

Source Economic Report of the President, 1995.

A word of caution is in order. Job creation is a highly complex matter, about which much less is understood than commonly supposed. The forces that influence what happens to unemployment during any particular administration are by no means wholly under the control of that administration. Thus, care is needed in the interpretation of data such as that contained in the table.

Having offered the foregoing caveat, it is fair to make some judgments, especially since all administrations take credit for the good things that happen when they are in power and deny responsibility for the bad. So how do these nine administrations compare?

The best record, both in terms of the absolute number of new jobs and the percentage increase in employment belongs to the much-maligned Carter administration. One should note, too, that the percentage increase in the labor force was the greatest during the four years of this administration, a time when the baby-boomers were entering the labor force in increasing numbers.

Second place in the job-creation sweepstakes goes to Reagan (II), followed by the Nixon administration. Fourth and fifth places go to Johnson and Reagan (I), and then come Clinton, Ford, and Kennedy. The Bush administration is last.

determining the position and shape of the consumption function. A significant tilt in the direction of greater inequality might lower the consumption function and thereby make it more difficult on both a short- and long-term basis to generate sufficient investment spending to attain full employment. Actually this did not happen. During the Reagan years (1981 through 1988) consumption as a percentage of the GNP averaged nearly two percentage points higher than in prior decades as a consequence of the go-go consumption ethic of the era.[39] A second observation concerns the validity of supply-side economics. The 1981 tax cuts did not have the intended supply-side effects. There was no noticeable gain in productivity, the savings rate actually declined rather than increased after 1981, and the recovery out of the 1981–82 recession resulted primarily from demand-side factors. The latter included massive budget deficits and the expansion in military spending as well as heavy borrowing by consumers and business.[40] Finally, the results of not only the Reagan revolution, but also of actions in the Nixon, Ford, and Carter administrations demonstrate that monetary policy, when stringently applied, can reduce the inflation rate, but the cost is high in terms of unemployment and lost output.

The Bush and Clinton Administrations

The Bush administration took office in January 1989 with no major fiscal or monetary policy changes contemplated. In the 1988 campaign, the most important economic issue was candidate Bush's "read my lips" promise of no new taxes. In the first *Economic Report* his administration sent to the Congress (February 6, 1990), President Bush stressed his strong commitment to both the Gramm-Rudman-Hollings (GRH) deficit reduction law and the tax rates developed in both the Economic Recovery Tax Act of 1981 and the Tax Reform Act of 1986.[41] Undoubtedly the president felt confident in making such a commitment because at the end of the 1988 fiscal year—which came a few days before the elections—the actual deficit was only $11.1 billion larger than the revised GRH target. Further, as Table 15–3 shows, between fiscal 1986 (when GRH went into effect) and fiscal 1987, the deficit declined; this strengthened the administration's belief that economic growth would eventually eliminate the budget deficit.

The administration's confidence that the GRH target for the elimination of the deficit on schedule would be met led the president to propose a "fundamental new rule" for fiscal policy.[42] This new rule would require that after fiscal 1993 (when the GRH target of a balanced budget would be reached)

---

[39] *Economic Report of the President*, 1995, p. 274.

[40] See the concluding section of this chapter for comment on the revival of the faith of supply-side economics in tax cuts as a stimulus to the economy in the wake of the "Republican revolution" in the 1994 congressional elections.

[41] *Economic Report of the President*, 1990, pp. 4, 5.

[42] Ibid., p. 66.

TABLE 15–3   Gramm-Rudman-Hollings Targets and Actual Deficits: Fiscal Years 1986–1993 (in billions of dollars)

Fiscal Year	GRH Targets	Actual Deficit
1986	$171.9	$221.2
1987	144.0	149.8
1988	144.0	155.2
1989	136.0	152.5
1990	100.0	221.4
1991	64.0	269.5
1992	28.0	290.4
1993	0.0	254.7

Sources: *Economic Report of the President,* 1994, p. 359; Congressional Budget Office, *The Economic and Budget Outlook: An Update,* July 1990, pp. 32 ff.

the federal government maintain a balanced non-Social Security budget. The surpluses being generated by the Social Security system would be channeled into the reduction of the federal debt through a proposed Social Security and Debt Reduction Fund. Reducing the national debt, it was argued, would free up substantial funds for private capital formation and thereby stimulate economic growth.

This scenario never materialized. After fiscal 1988, the federal deficit exploded. As Table 15–3 shows, the deficit for fiscal 1990 jumped to $221.4 billion, and in the summer of 1990 there was widespread speculation in the press that the deficit in fiscal 1991 might even reach $300 billion. Under GRH if the projected deficit exceeded the target by $10 billion or more, automatic across-the-board cutbacks (a process known as *sequestration*) went into effect.[43] The primary cause of the sharp jump in the deficit in fiscal 1990 was the accelerating cost of the federal bailout for an estimated 700 or more insolvent savings and loan banks across the nation. In 1989 the Congress established the Resolution Trust Corporation (RTC) to (1) take over and sell the assets of the failed thrifts and (2) pay for deposit insurance losses that exceed the reserves of the Federal Savings and Loan Deposit Insurance Corporation (FSLDIC). The Congressional Budget Office estimated that the funds appropriated for the RTC were insufficient to pay for the S & L bailout, the full costs of which are estimated ultimately to exceed $500 billion.[44]

Facing across-the-board cutbacks under GRH and the threat of an actual shutdown of the federal government, the Bush administration and the Congress agreed in November 1990 to a deficit reduction plan involving spending cuts and tax increases. The GRH law was dropped, replaced by the Budget Reconciliation Act, which proposed reducing the deficit by $500 billion over five years. To get the package, President Bush dropped his no-new-taxes

---

[43] Congressional Budget Office, *The Economic and Budget Outlook: An Update,* July 1990, p. 56.

[44] Ibid., p. ix.

pledge—an action that many observers believe was a major factor in his defeat in 1992—and the Democrats in the Congress yielded on spending cuts for Medicare, Medicaid, other social programs, and farm price supports.

What was not known at that moment was the depth and length of the recession that began in July or the full effect of the war against Iraq, the buildup for which had already begun, although the actual ground invasion did not start until January 1991. Both developments contributed significantly to the increase in budget deficits that continued through fiscal 1992. Although the recession officially ended in March 1991, unemployment continued to rise through June 1992, when it reached a peak of 7.7 percent.[45] Because of the Gulf War, military spending jumped by $16.8 billion in fiscal year 1991—a development that further unbalanced the budget, but one that also contributed to the shallowness of the recession.[46]

After the victory in Desert Storm, President Bush failed to capitalize on the enormous boost in his popularity. As far as domestic policy was concerned, the administration was content to drift through the rest of 1991 and 1992, apparently unaware of the depth of public concern over the lingering recession and the level of unemployment. Failure to confront this also contributed to Bush's loss in 1992.[47]

Before turning to a discussion of the economic programs of the Clinton administration, a final comment on GRH—the effort to balance the budget by legislative fiat—is in order. It is clear that this effort failed miserably. The lesson should be plain: neither a legislative act nor a constitutional amendment can guarantee a balanced federal budget. No matter what the law or the constitution says there is no end to presidential and congressional ingenuity in finding a way around such pronouncements. There is no inherent obstacle to bringing the government's budget into balance when that is desirable. What is lacking is the political will to achieve this.

Although Bill Clinton received only a plurality of the popular vote in the three-way presidential contest with President George Bush and independent candidate Ross Perot, he launched an ambitious economic program on taking office in January 1993. Drawn largely from the president's campaign document, *Putting People First*, the key elements in the plan included (1) an $11 billion stimulus to speed up the sluggish economic recovery and create more jobs; (2) a four-year plan to invest $20 billion annually in the country's infrastructure; (3) tax changes, including a middle-class tax cut, higher rates for upper-income taxpayers, and aiding the working poor by increasing the earned income tax credit; (4) deficit reduction for its own sake, but also as a

---

[45] *Economic Report of the President*, 1994, p. 315.

[46] Ibid., p. 365.

[47] As noted earlier, the 1990–91 recession ended in March 1991, but the business cycle dating committee did not establish the end of the recession until after the 1992 presidential election, a fact that undoubtedly also hurt the Bush campaign. The reason for the delay was uncertainty about what was actually happening in the economy, particularly because unemployment continued to rise well into 1992.

way to lower interest rates which, in turn, would stimulate private investment; (5) expanding the United States' trade by bringing Mexico into an expanded North American Free Trade Agreement (NAFTA) and completing the Uruguay round of the General Agreement on Trade and Tariffs (GATT); and (6) reforming the country's health care system to include universal coverage and containment of increases in medical costs.[48]

Soon after taking office, President Clinton discovered that the economy was growing faster than he thought was the case during the campaign, so the stimulus idea was dropped. The new president also found out that the deficit situation was worse than expected, so deficit reduction became the first priority for his administration. This forced postponement of the promised middle-class tax cut and the planned program for public investment through a "Rebuild America Fund," as outlined in the 1992 campaign document. Health care reform, put off until 1994, was defeated in that year, but during 1993 NAFTA was approved. In 1994 GATT was passed by a "lame-duck" session of the Congress in December.

From March through October in 1993, the administration's energies were directed almost entirely toward passage of a budget bill for fiscal year 1994. The battle over the Clinton bill was extremely bitter, as Republicans in the Congress were completely united in their opposition to the president's budget. The vote in the Senate on the Omnibus Senate Reconciliation Act of 1993 (the budget bill) split 50 for and 50 against, with Vice President Gore providing the one-vote margin by which the bill passed. In the House, the bill also passed by a single vote, even though Democrats had a clear majority of members.

Essentially through a combination of spending cuts and tax increases, the 1993 budget bill sought to reduce the projected federal budget by fiscal year 1998—a five-year projection—from $333.2 billion to $187.4 billion, a reduction of $145.8 billion.[49] The spending cuts projected by the administration's budget touched nearly every part of the budget, including decreases in military outlays, reductions in the federal work force, delay in cost of living adjustments for federal employees, cuts in Medicare and agriculture and veterans' programs, and interest savings by shortening the maturity structure of the national debt. Tax increases included raising the rate on the federal income tax for the top 1.2 percent of taxpayers, applying the 2.9 percent payroll tax for Medicare to *all* earnings rather than to only the first $135,000, raising the taxable portion of Social Security benefits for the top 13 percent of recipients, and increasing the federal gasoline tax by 4.3 cents per gallon.[50]

The primary rationale offered by the administration for a shift in policy to deficit reduction rather than tax cuts for the middle class (aside from the

---

[48] Governor Bill Clinton and Senator Al Gore, *Putting People First* (New York: Times Books, 1992), pp. 3–32.

[49] *Economic Report of the President,* 1994, p. 32.

[50] Ibid., pp. 33, 34.

already mentioned fact that the deficit problem was bigger than anticipated) was that deficit reduction would cause long-term interest rates to fall, and this, in turn, would stimulate private investment.[51] Long-term interest rates (as measured by the rate for triple A corporate bonds) did fall through most of 1993, but this was also a continuation of a downward trend that began in late 1990. Gross private domestic investment rose sharply in 1993 (in current dollars it was up by 11.9 percent over 1992), but this, too, was a continuation of a trend that began in early 1992.[52] There is really no way to determine the extent to which these developments were simply a part of the recovery that got underway in 1991, and the extent to which deficit reductions contained in the administration's 1993 budget bill played a role. The latter, since they were for the fiscal year that began on October 1, 1993 (fiscal year 1994), were not felt for the most part until 1994, a year in which the expansion strengthened. In 1993, the economy grew at an annual rate of 3.1 percent, but in 1994, the annual rate of growth was 4.1 percent.[53]

It is probable that since the recovery from the 1990–91 recession got off to a sluggish start, budget developments in 1993 and 1994 helped to speed it up. On the downside, the Federal Reserve, worried as always about inflation, raised interest rates six times during 1994 and again in early 1995. At the close of 1994, many economists foresaw a slowdown in the expansion during 1995. From a political standpoint, the crucial question for the Clinton administration was whether the expansion would continue through the 1996 presidential election. With respect to the federal deficit, it dropped from $255.1 billion in fiscal 1993 to $203.2 in fiscal 1994, and was expected to decline further to $192.5 billion in fiscal 1995.[54]

The "Republican Revolution" and the Future of Macroeconomic Policy

In November 1994, the Republicans captured control of both houses of the Congress. The new Republican leadership in both the Senate and the House of Representatives is strongly committed to a smaller and leaner federal government, far less committed to social spending and macroeconomic management than the Democratic party. Some among the leadership, notably Speaker of the House Newt Gingrich, have spoken fondly of rolling back much of the social legislation passed during and since Franklin Roosevelt's New Deal. Coupled with the new leadership's hostility and disdain for an activist government is a strong attachment to private markets as the primary instrument for the organization of nearly all economic activity.

---

[51] Ibid., p. 35.

[52] *Current Economic Indicators*, May 1995, p. 1.

[53] Ibid., p. 3.

[54] Ibid., p. 32.

Because of the drastic change in economic philosophy that will dominate the Congress at least through 1996, the nation will be involved in a rough but real "laboratory test" of some of the tenets of neoclassical economics (see Chapter 16). The most important of these are, first, that government intervention into private markets should be minimal and, second, that governmental efforts to stabilize the economy are counterproductive. It is a basic article of faith of neoclassical economics that systems of market capitalism are inherently stable, and, if allowed to function with a minimum of outside intervention, they will gravitate "naturally" to a condition of full employment and maximum equilibrium growth.

The emasculation of fiscal policy as a policy instrument for macroeconomic management will continue. Aside from the fact that the Republican majority in the Congress is unlikely to approve any budgetary measures that involve macroeconomic management, the deficit and debt situation of the national government will continue to block practically any fiscal policy action aimed at controlling the economy.

If fiscal policy for all practical purposes becomes null and void, that leaves monetary policy as the only remaining instrument of macroeconomic policy. A significant lesson from nearly seven decades of macroeconomic history is that it is relatively easy to push the economy into a recession by putting on the monetary brakes, but it is not easy to get the economy out of a downturn by stepping on the monetary accelerator. The latter has been likened to "pushing on a string," not an easy way to move an object.

The deficit situation is likely to get worse rather than better, in spite of the progress the Clinton administration made in its early years in bringing about a reduction in the size of the deficit. There are two reasons for this. First—and even before the new Republican majority was installed in the Congress—the president, the Republican leadership, and some Democrats were starting to outbid one another in pledging tax cuts for the vast middle class. A "bidding war" broke out in 1981 with the Reagan tax cuts, which were a major reason for the deficit's explosion during the rest of the 1980s. It is economically irresponsible to propose tax cuts at a time when the economy is growing at a rate of 3 to 4 percent a year. This was a triumph of politics over sound economics, a story repeated too often in our nation's recent economic history. Second—and in spite of pledges for spending cuts equal to the tax cuts—Republican leaders in the House invented an updated version of supply-side economics to justify tax cuts without worrying too much about offsetting spending cuts. This was what they called "dynamic" rather than "static" budget accounting, the essence of which is the belief that the positive economic activity stimulated by the tax cuts would generate enough new revenue for the federal government to offset the cuts. This may prove to be the latest installment of "voodoo economics."

Finally, there is the balanced budget amendment. The amendment was defeated by one vote in the Senate in 1995, but its supporters will undoubtedly bring it back. Deficits, proponents of this measure argue, need not worry us unduly, for they will be eliminated once the amendment is ratified by 38 states and is in place. This is mostly empty rhetoric, used by some politicians to convince voters that they are taking meaningful action to reduce the deficit and control deficit spending. There was nothing in the proposed balanced budget amendment in the form of specific machinery to bring about a balanced budget. The Congressional Budget Office estimated that by 2004, the earliest year a balanced budget amendment could take effect, the federal deficit might reach $365 billion, 3.3 percent of the nation's GDP.[55] Balancing a budget this large in a short period would require massive spending cuts, tax increases, or both—measures so drastic that a major economic collapse could not be avoided. What is more likely to happen, if such an amendment is ever adopted, is the growth of a complex variety of misleading, and even unscrupulous, techniques and devices to take more and more legitimate activities of the federal government "off budget," which is to say, to account for them in devious ways that show they are not a part of the government's "normal budget." Dishonesty in budgeting will become the norm, not the exception, as is now the case.

Some General Observations on Macroeconomic Policy

Our review of the nation's overall experience with macroeconomic policy since the onset of the Great Depression indicates that several broad observations are in order. First, it seems clear that we have the economic knowledge necessary to manage the economy in a manner that will prevent another major depression on the order of the 1930s. None of the nine recorded recessions since 1945 has been allowed to develop into a long and damaging depression. That is a plus. What is now more uncertain, as the comments in the previous section indicate, is whether we shall continue to make use of that knowledge. The coming clash over economic policy and the macroeconomic theory that undergirds policy will rekindle academic and public debate over Keynes's argument that a philosophical fault line divides contemporary macroeconomics. This division, it will be recalled, is between those who believe systems of market capitalism are inherently stable and those who believe they are inherently unstable, always tending toward booms and busts.

What we do not have is the knowledge or skill to fine-tune the economy. "Fine-tuning" is a term that came into vogue after the success of the Kennedy tax cut. It meant the continuous use of fine adjustments in fiscal and monetary policies to keep the economy moving on a full-employment path of economic growth without excessive inflation. The experiences of the last decade have disabused most economists, not to mention the public, of the notion that

---

[55] Congressional Budget Office, *Reducing the Deficit: Spending and Revenue Options* (Washington, D.C.: U.S. Government Printing Office, 1994), p. 3.

through fine-tuning the business cycle has been banished from our economic life. As we have already indicated, the business cycle is far from dead.

Second, it should be quite plain from the experience since 1965 that inflation cannot be ended or even brought under control through fiscal and monetary policies, at least not without costs in terms of unemployment that are largely unacceptable to our society. Putting on the fiscal and monetary brakes pushes the economy into a recession much faster than it brings down the inflation rate. That is the sad lesson of the Nixon, Ford, Carter, and Reagan administrations. We shall never know, of course, *if* the prompt imposition of a tax increase in 1966 might have held the Vietnam inflation in check. What we do know is that once inflation gets started and persists, then inflationary expectations become built into the economy—expectations which tend to be cumulative in their effects.

Third—and this is a corollary of the above—the social ineffectiveness of restrictive monetary and fiscal policies stems from wage and price rigidities rooted in the structure of the economy—the power of trade unions and the giant corporations. This makes for a situation in which prices and wages, as well as other costs, are readily flexible upward, but not flexible downward. Under such conditions, the results that we have been discussing are almost inevitable when the money supply is tightened excessively or taxes are increased. Oligopolistic firms and strong trade unions tend to react to a falloff in demand by raising prices and wages. Worse yet, the impact of restrictive monetary and fiscal measures may add directly to inflationary pressures because higher interest rates become a part of the cost structure and higher taxes may lead workers to bargain for higher money wages to maintain take-home pay. The foregoing would not work in a highly competitive economic environment, such as Keynes assumed, but it surely works when there is a substantial amount of economic power in the hands of both firms and workers.

Fourth, experience since Vietnam casts doubt on our ability as a society to submit to the social discipline necessary to make fiscal and monetary policies work *in both directions*. This is aside from the necessity of creating conditions under which we can dampen the economy without plunging it into a recession. Admittedly this is more a political than an economic problem; yet it is one which economists cannot ignore. The realities of our political life suggest that policy is one-directional—expansionary in the form of tax cuts. Worse yet, it seems we as a society are unwilling to finance through taxes what we demand out of the national govenment. In 38 of the last 50 fiscal years (76 percent of the time) the federal government has run a deficit. Since 1965 there was only one year in which the federal budget was in balance or registered a surplus. This is not to suggest a return to an outmoded fiscal philosophy that says the budget must be balanced annually, but serious questions are raised about the efficacy of modern fiscal and monetary policies *if* the norm has become one of deficits in good years and bad. Federal red ink is not the sole cause of inflation as many conservative thinkers believe, but when conditions are relatively prosperous and employment high (as has been the case over much of the post-World War II era), deficits contribute to inflation.

Finally, we need to realize and keep in perspective just how far we have come in our understanding of the economy as compared to where we were in the early 1930s. Then there was no real understanding of what could and should be done in the face of the collapse that began in 1929 and quickly spread to most of the world. This was so in spite of the impressive body of theoretical analysis which had been developing over the prior century—classical economics. We have not yet found the exact key to our most vexing problem—full employment without inflation—but in modern macroeconomic analysis we have some of the necessary theoretical tools to do the job. The one major tool we still lack is an incomes policy, which is necessary to complement fiscal and monetary policy if contemporary market capitalism is to work at its most efficient level. However, our existing policy instruments, imperfect as they may be, are being used to prevent our having to face another bout with mass unemployment 1930s-style while we struggle to cure an equally damaging social evil—chronic inflation.

Summary

1. Monetary and fiscal policies are the two major policy instruments utilized by contemporary systems of market capitalism. Monetary policy focuses on the money supply and interest rates and uses either as a policy guide. If the monetary authorities (i.e., the Board of Governors of the Federal Reserve System) are oriented toward monetarism, they will focus on the money supply. If not, their focus will be on interest rates.

2. Fiscal policy operates primarily through the budget of the federal government and uses changes in taxes or changes in expenditures to achieve the desired budgetary effects. A budgetary surplus has a restrictive effect on the economy, whereas a deficit is expansionary. The full-(or high-)employment budget emerged in the post-World War II period as the primary tool for the implementation of fiscal policy.

3. There are important theoretical limits to the application of both fiscal and monetary policies. Monetary policy becomes ineffective in theory when the demand for money becomes totally elastic—the flat range in the *LM* curve—whereas fiscal policy becomes ineffective when no more money is available for transactions purposes—the vertical portion of the *LM* curve.

4. The stock market crash of October 1929 ushered in the longest and most severe depression in U.S. history. The depression years gave rise to the New Deal of the Roosevelt administration, which involved a number of fundamental reforms in the economy, but did not involve the application of fiscal and monetary policies on a large enough scale to end the depression. Keynes and Keynesian economics did not have a major influence on policy during the Roosevelt New Deal years. What finally ended the depression was World War II, an unplanned "experiment" in the application of Keynesian policies.

5. In the Truman-Eisenhower years (1945 to 1960) no conscious efforts were made to apply the principles of modern macroeconomics to the overall management of the economy. In general, this period, especially the Eisenhower era, was dominated by fears of inflation; consequently, budgetary policy tended to be restrictive. As a result, there were several recessions during the period, unemployment was relatively high, and growth was sluggish.

6. The Kennedy-Johnson era (1961 to 1968) represents the first time that an administration actively embraced contemporary macroeconomics and sought to use it for the effective management of the economy. The Kennedy administration developed the rationale for what became the 1964 tax cut entirely on the basis of the Keynesian income-expenditure approach to the economy. Evidence indicates that the tax cut was successful. The Johnson administration failed to follow through by applying the same principles to the economy in 1966, when the buildup in military expenditures called for a tax increase.

7. During the Nixon, Ford, and Carter presidencies (1969 to 1980) inflation was the primary concern most of the time. All three administrations sought to control inflation by restrictive monetary and fiscal policies, but with results which were generally less than satisfactory. Restrictive policies produced recessions which brought down the inflation rate, but the change was not permanent, as each recovery saw a new surge in inflation. The result was a decade of stagflation, excessive unemployment and excessive inflation at the same time.

8. The Reagan administration introduced the most far-reaching change in policy of any of the post-World War II administrations. It abandoned the view characteristic of the economy from the 1960s onward to the effect that overall management was necessary and that fiscal and monetary policies were the instruments for this management. Rather, it adopted a major tax cut on the basis of supply-side economic principles in the expectation that this would stimulate production. At the same time the administration embraced monetarism and opted for a restrictive monetary stance. The net result was a serious recession and then a sharp drop in inflation, followed by a recovery in early 1983.

9. In its first two years in office the Bush administration did not offer any major new initiatives in macroeconomic policy. The growing deficit in the federal budget forced it, however, to abandon its no-tax-increase stance and agree to a package of tax increases and spending cuts in the fall of 1990.

10. President Clinton in his first year in office offered an ambitious program involving a fiscal stimulus and planned tax reductions, but the deficit and debt situation forced his administration to shift course and concentrate on bringing down the federal deficit. Progress was achieved in this direction through a combination of tax increases and reductions in federal spending. The deficit dropped further in 1994.

PART V Alternative Perspectives on Macroeconomic Theory and Policy

16 The Rebirth of Classical Economics

I N THIS CHAPTER WE EXAMINE the most recent and most important challenge to mainstream Keynesian macroeconomics—the new classical economics. Although monetarism attacks the fundamental relationships and policy implications of the Keynesian income-expenditure analysis, it accepts the basic role played by aggregate demand in determining output, employment, and the price level in the short run. The new classical economics rejects in a fundamental way the Keynesian approach and philosophy and instead turns to the pre-Keynesian classical school for its intellectual framework and inspiration.

The New Classical Economics: A Challenge to Keynes

As pointed out in Chapter 11 (pages 427–31), it was the alleged failure of policies based on the Keynesian income-expenditure model of the economy to control inflation from the mid-1960s onward that stimulated the growth of contemporary monetarism. The same policy failures have also given rise to the more fundamental challenge to the structure and premises of contempo-

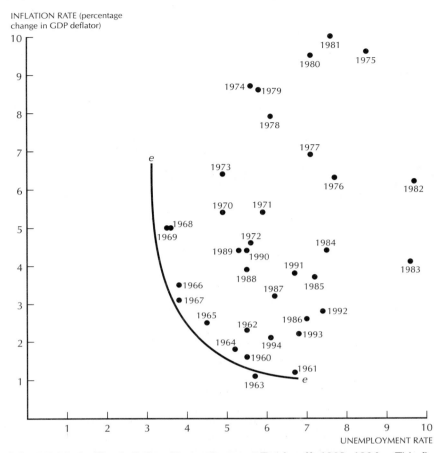

FIGURE 16–1   The Inflation-Unemployment Trade-off, 1960–1994.   This figure shows how data from the 1960s yield a scatter diagram that clearly fits the Phillips curve relationship, but beginning in the 1970s the trade-off between inflation and unemployment at acceptable rates disappeared; this opened the way to the new classical economics' criticisms of the Keynesian model.

Source: Economic Report of the President, 1991, pp. 291, 330; 1995, pp. 321, 345.

rary macroeconomic theory known as the *new classical economics*.[1] Specifically, this new school of thought built on the groundwork laid out by Milton Friedman and the monetarists. More than any other single event, it was the collapse of the Phillips curve relationship in the early 1970s that triggered this development. As we saw in Chapter 12 (pages 484–90), the Phillips curve shows an inverse relationship between the inflation rate and the unemployment rate. Figure 16–1 shows the scatter diagram relating inflation

[1] James Tobin, *Asset Accumulation and Economic Activity* (Chicago: University of Chicago Press, 1980), p. 20.

(measured by the annual rate of change in the GNP or GDP deflator) and unemployment for the period 1960 through 1990, introduced originally in Figure 12–8. The solid-line curve labeled *ee*, which covers the years 1960 through 1969, illustrates the basic hypothesis embodied in the curve. This is that there exists a short-term trade-off between the unemployment rate and the inflation rate; a decrease in one leads to an increase in the other and vice versa. What was so important about the early data (1960 through 1969) was that they suggested the possibility that by the judicious use of monetary and fiscal policies, society could achieve a low level of unemployment (say 4 percent) at an acceptable inflation rate (say 3 percent or less). Through fine tuning both price stability and full employment could be achieved. Unfortunately, this was not to be. As the data in Figure 16–1 show, after 1970 the possibility for any trade-off between inflation and unemployment at rates for either variable that were socially and economically acceptable appeared to vanish. Thus, critics of the income-expenditure approach to macroeconomics argued that policies based on such an analysis were simply not workable. The foregoing has become the generally accepted wisdom about the Phillips curve. But, as we saw in Chapter 12 (pages 492–95), Paul Omerod developed an alternative analysis involving shifts in the curve, which challenges Friedman's acceleration thesis. At this point a review of Omerod's interpretation of the Phillips curve will be helpful by adding additional perspective to the circumstances that led to the emergence of the new classical economics.

Although the new classical economics did not begin to have an impact on macroeconomics and the economic profession until the mid-1970s or later, its roots trace back to a 1961 article by Professor John F. Muth of Indiana University. In this article Professor Muth developed what has become the core idea in the new classical economics, the *theory of rational expectations*.[2] Initially, the theory was used to explain behavior in financial markets, but subsequently it was applied to macroeconomic theory. The leader in this later development was Professor Robert Lucas of the University of Chicago. In addition to Professor Lucas, important contributions to the new classical economics have been made by Professors Thomas Sargent and Neil Wallace of the University of Minnesota, Robert Barro of Harvard University, and Bennett McCallum of Carnegie-Mellon University.

The new classical economics rests on two basic theoretical propositions. The first we just mentioned, namely, the *theory of rational expectations*, originally developed by John Muth. The second is the *theory of continuous market clearing*, a fundamental premise of classical economics as it existed before Keynes. Rational expectations is the new element, but it is the older idea of market clearing, which, according to Nobel laureate James Tobin, gives the new classical school such far-reaching implications.[3] First, we shall examine

---

[2] John F. Muth, ''Rational Expectations and the Theory of Price Movements,'' *Econometrica*, Vol. 29, No. 3 (July 1961), pp. 315–335.

[3] Tobin, *Asset Accumulation and Economic Activity*, p. 22.

each of these theories separately; second, we shall examine their implications when brought together; and, finally, we shall analyze and evaluate the criticisms levied against the new classical economics.

The Theory of Rational Expectations

The logical point of departure for an analysis of this theory is to examine the role that expectations play in economics. Expectations are important, for three principal reasons. First, expectations have to do with views about future values for economic variables—prices, output, employment, and others. Second, these views exert an influence, often a strong influence, on what happens today. For example, our expectations about the future inflation rate will undoubtedly influence our current buying decisions. Some people may decide to buy now if they expect future prices to be higher, whereas others may decide that they should save more. Third, expectations have a crucial relationship to one of the fundamental ideas employed in economic analysis, namely, the concept of an equilibrium. *All* schedules used in economic analysis represent *ex ante* or expected (anticipated) values for the variables concerned. This is true at both the micro and macro levels of economic analysis. What equilibrium means, therefore, is a state or condition in which actual *(ex post)* and expected *(ex ante)* values coincide. To put it differently, in equilibrium, events turn out as people plan.

How are expectations formed? This is one of the most difficult problems in economics and one for which economists have not found a satisfactory solution. Before we examine in detail the answer to this question offered by the new classical economics, a brief review of two alternative approaches is in order.

One approach is known as the "method of adaptive expectations." It is the approach that has been incorporated into most of the large econometric models employed to forecast the economic future. Simply put, the term "adaptive expectations" means that expectations are determined primarily by recent experience, so that events of the recent past are given a greater weight than events more distant in time. In a technical or statistical sense, adaptive expectations can be measured by constructing a weighted average of past changes in some variable—the consumer price index, for example—in which the most recent data carry the greatest weight. What is involved in this method is the extrapolation of recent trends into the future, always a procedure fraught with some risk. The reason, of course, is that expectations formed in this way are tied to past behavior, but such behavior can change. This is a point of key importance made by the rational expectations theorists.

Another way to determine expectations is simply to ask people, that is to say, to attempt to measure them directly by a survey technique. This particular method has been extensively developed and pursued by the Survey Research Center at the University of Michigan. One of its most important efforts in this direction is the Index of Consumer Sentiment, designed to measure the consumer's confidence as it affects future spending plans. This index is shown in Figure 16–2.

The rational expectations hypothesis takes an entirely different approach. Whereas the foregoing methods for measuring expectations are empirically oriented, as they are derived either from recent experience (adaptive) or direct questioning (surveys), the rational expectations approach is based on what is, perhaps, the most fundamental premise of classical economics, that of individual rationality. What does this mean? Rationality in the context of classical economics means maximizing, or optimizing, behavior, that is, obtaining the best or most favorable results in a given situation. In making their economic decisions, people always try to achieve the maximum results, whether their objective is profit, income, or simply satisfaction from consumption. Maximizing must take place of course, within the limits of the individual or the business firm's income and the prevailing technology.

The roots of this principle trace back to the philosophy of *utilitarianism,* a doctrine espoused by Jeremy Bentham (1748–1832). The object of humankind, Bentham said, should be to secure the greatest happiness for the greatest number, or in economic terms, to maximize utility for the largest number of individuals. This is what a rational individual will do when confronted with the choice between "pleasure and pain," to use Bentham's words, and this

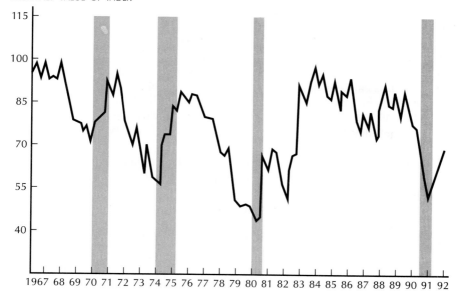

MONTHLY VALUE OF INDEX

1967 68 69 70 71 72 73 74 75 76 77 78 79 80 81 82 83 84 85 86 87 88 89 90 91 92

FIGURE 16–2   Index of Consumer Sentiment: 1978–1992.*   This index, which reflects consumer confidence with respect to future spending plans, shows a relatively close correlation with the state of the economy; it drops in times of recession and improves when the economy gets better.

*Shaded areas indicate recession periods as designated by the National Bureau of Economic Research, Inc.

Source: Survey Research Center, University of Michigan.

is what society ought to do. Thus, Bentham's *principle of utility* provides the philosophical foundation for the classical idea that an individual acts rationally when she or he maximizes advantages in a situation and minimizes disadvantages. More specifically, the consumer maximizes utility, that is, satisfaction from consuming goods and services; the business executive maximizes profit; and the worker maximizes his or her real wage, which is an offset to the disutility involved in work.

In forming their expectations, people, or *economic agents* as rational expectations theorists call them, use all available and relevant information and they use this information efficiently. This sounds both simple and obvious, but it is neither so simple nor so obvious as it may appear. In using all available and relevant information, people reflect on past errors and adjust their information accordingly. Any errors that remain in their expectations are thus of a random nature and hence unpredictable.

There is a second point which is even more fundamental, especially for the policy implications of the hypothesis. This is that, in forming expectations, people have knowledge of the relevant economic model that policymakers use in making their decisions. In its most pure form, this means that economic agents are completely aware of the structure of the economy (that is, they know the form of each equation in the econometric model which mirrors the economy) and they use this knowledge in forming their expectations.[4] In a less esoteric vein, it means simply that people learn from experience how economic variables are related to one another. For example, if the government indicates that it is going to increase the money supply in an effort to stimulate the economy, people who form their expectations rationally will expect wages and prices to go up. Why? Because they have learned from observing such action in the past that an increase in the money supply is followed by an increase in wages and prices. Consequently, they will act in response to their expectations, namely, raise prices and wages to the extent possible since this is what the relevant economic model tells them will happen if the money supply is increased.

The rational expectations theorists go even further than this. Not only will people (economic agents) learn how economic variables behave in relation to one another, they will also learn how policymakers (the Federal Reserve, for example) react to changing economic variables. Thus, economic agents can learn to anticipate policy. If, for example, it has been the practice of the Fed to react to an economic slowdown by increasing the money supply, people will learn from this experience. Hence, when the economy slows down, they will expect the monetary authorities to increase the rate of growth of money, and, consequently, they will expect a higher rate of inflation.[5]

---

[4] Michael Bleaney, *The Rise and Fall of Keynesian Economics* (New York: St. Martin's Press, 1985), p. 143.

[5] For an excellent discussion of the theory of rational expectations, see G. K. Shaw, *Rational Expectations: An Elementary Exposition* (New York: St. Martin's Press, 1984), especially pp. 47–58.

The Theory of Continuous Market Clearing

Now we come to the second crucial proposition of the new classical economics. The theory of continuous market clearing combines the older Walrasian general equilibrium theory with the more recent theory of efficient markets. The former was developed in the latter half of the nineteenth century by Leon Walras (1834–1910), a French-born economist whose academic career was spent in Switzerland at the University of Lausanne. The latter theory emerged from Professor Muth's seminal article in which he first formulated the concept of rational expectations. Efficient market theory has been concerned primarily with prices and equilibrium in financial and commodity markets—markets often described as *auction markets*.

What Walras did was to develop a basic mathematical model to show how, in an economy characterized by competitive markets, a general equilibrium will be established in which all prices will be equilibrium prices and these prices will be determined *simultaneously*. The prices so established are equilibrium prices in that in every market, quantity demanded and quantity supplied are in balance; there is, in other words, neither excess demand nor excess supply in any market, including the market for labor. In mathematical terms, the Walrasian system of general equilibrium involves solving a set of simultaneous equations in which there are the same number of prices as supply and demand functions (that is, schedules) to determine these prices. To explain how equilibrium is brought about, Walras posited the existence of a fictional *auctioneer* who cries out the price of the goods being traded and continues to do so until an equilibrium—that is, a market clearing—price is established for every good traded in the market. This process by which a general equilibrium was established Walras described as *tatonnement*, a French word which literally means groping. To put it differently, the process is one of trial and error, in which eventually all trading takes place at equilibrium prices. From a macroeconomic point of view, the general equilibrium envisioned by Walras is one in which there are no unsold quantities of goods and services left in the market, including the supply of labor services. Thus, the general equilibrium model necessarily involves full employment.

In a general way, the efficient market theory is a refinement of Walrasian general equilibrium theory in that it tells us something more about the nature of equilibrium prices in a Walrasian world. A market is efficient when the prices established in that market reflect *all* the available information about the good or service being traded. An efficient market not only processes all relevant information, but it does so quickly, almost instantaneously. This is why in the stock market, for example, one is rarely able to beat the market, that is, to profit from knowing something that no one else knows. Financial markets are presumed to be highly efficient in this sense. They quickly process all available information about the security traded, and this information finds its way into the price of the security. A significant amount of evidence has been accumulated to show that financial markets, such as the long-term bond market, are efficient in the sense that we have been using the term.[6] Tests of the hypothesis have generally shown that it is *not* possible to explain changes in yields in these markets on the basis of information available prior to the change in price (that is, yield). Thus, such changes have to be accounted for by new information. What is not evident, however, is that the efficient market theory can be applied more broadly, that is to say, to the market for goods and services generally, including labor. This, however, is one of the key assumptions of the new classical economics.

The Policy Implications of the New Classical Economics

Now we come to the fundamental policy conclusion of the new classical economics. It is that, basically, no policy action by the government can be successful if expectations are formed rationally. The reason is that people, economic agents, anticipate the policy's outcome, alter their behavior accordingly, and thus undermine the policy's intended effect.

To understand how rational expectations theorists reached this important conclusion, it is necessary to review the relationship shown in the short-term aggregate supply curve developed in Chapter 4 (pages 132–38). In this analysis, it will be recalled, movements along the short-run aggregate supply curve (the Keynesian-classical curve) took place because people suffered from a money illusion. To illustrate, if the price level rises unexpectedly, people increase the amount of labor they are willing to supply and the output they are willing to produce above the natural rates of employment and output. Conversely, when the price level falls unexpectedly, people respond by reducing their labor supply and by producing less. Production falls below the output determined by the natural rate of unemployment. However, if people form their expectations rationally, and if, too, they correctly anticipate the effects of monetary policy on the price level, they will not suffer from a money illusion. The first conclusion is that the supply of labor and the output level will be consistent with output and employment as determined by the natural rate of employment. The second conclusion—the really revolutionary conclusion of the new classical economics—is that if the object of macroeconomic policy is to influence the level of output (and employment), it will work *only* if it is unanticipated.

The new classical theorists make an argument that some economists find especially appealing, namely, that unless the government tries to fool people by causing them to mistake *general* price and wage movements for changes in *relative* prices and *real* wages, government policies cannot succeed. We

---

[6] William Poole, "Rational Expectations in the Macro Model," *Brookings Papers on Economic Activity,* 1976:2, p. 467. Such studies obviously could not take into account the massive scandals involving insider trading that devastated Wall Street in 1986 and 1987. At the very least, the fact that such trading was present and widespread over a long period of time raises some serious doubts about the whole hypothesis of efficient markets. Thus, an imporant underpinning for the entire rational expectations hypothesis is weakened.

must be careful not to overstate what is being claimed. The theory of rational expectations, and its application through the new classical economics, applies primarily to the macroeconomic policy actions of the government. It does not apply to other policies, such as the enforcement of the antitrust laws, establishment of minimum wages, regulation of public utilities, and all other traditional actions of government, most of which affect economic activity at the microeconomic level. Further, the rational expectations and new classical economics views on policy actions have been formulated almost entirely in terms of prices (relative and general), and not in terms of output or employment. This reflects the deep roots of this school in classical economics, which sees macroeconomic movement as confined entirely to the price level.

In sum, the new classical theory concludes that the government should not attempt any activist countercyclical measures to control output or employment. It believes that any countercyclical measures that are attempted will not have their desired effect unless they create unforeseen expectational errors. However, if the government is successful in creating such errors, policy actions will lead to more, not less, instability in output. This is because, as we shall see in the next section, the new classical theorists view expectational errors as the main source of variations in output, employment, and the price level over the course of the business cycle. Thus, any macroeconomic policy that attempts to fine tune the economy will not only fail, but will bring about the very thing it seeks to correct—fluctuations in output and employment. This is the fundamental and devastating policy conclusion that is drawn from the theory of rational expectations.

The policy ineffectiveness proposition is the first and most significant implication to be drawn from the new classical economics. It is not the only one, however. A second one does not concern policy directly. It is in the nature of a warning to policymakers who use econometric models to predict policy outcomes. The rational expectations hypothesis holds that people adjust their behavior in response to any policy that is announced. Therefore, if an econometric model is to reflect accurately the effect of any policy, it should be able to account for this type of change in behavior. In other words, the parameters of the model should shift to reflect the policy effects that people expect. Unfortunately, the large econometric models, which are used for policy forecasting and which contain sometimes hundreds of structural and behavioral equations, are not able to measure how people may react to an announced policy change. The Lucas critique maintains that if econometric models do not contain a rational expectations mechanism, the predictions of the models are likely to be wrong.[7] Thus, policymakers cannot rely on the big econometric models to inform them of the impact of policy.

A third implication of the new classical economics concerns the unemployment costs of reducing inflation; this implication, as we shall see later,

---

[7] Robert E. Lucas, Jr., ''Economic Policy Evaluation: A Critique,'' in Robert E. Lucas, Jr., *Studies in Business Cycle Theory* (Cambridge, Mass.: MIT Press, 1981).

was particularly relevant to the policy actions of the Reagan administration in the early 1980s. As we have seen, the core idea in the new classical economics is that an anticipated policy will have no effect on real output and employment. This means that an anti-inflationary policy will be more effective, have a smaller cost in terms of lost output and more unemployment, if the policy is anticipated, and if, too, the policy is *credible*. The latter means that the announced policy is one that people believe will be carried out. In a practical context this means if a policy to reduce inflation through monetary restraint is announced and if the policymakers are believed—are credible— then the public's inflationary expectations will be quickly adjusted downward. Inflation can be reduced at a minimal cost in unemployment.

Expectations in Keynes and in the New Classical Economics

Before we turn to the thinking of the new classical economists with respect to the business cycle, comment is in order on two fundamental differences between Keynesian theory and the new classical economics with respect to expectations. What these two schools have in common is that both accord expectations an extremely important role in explaining how the economy works. But they differ significantly with respect to (1) the aspect of the economy's performance most affected by expectations and (2) the process by which expectations get formed. Let us examine these differences. In the new classical economics, as we have just demonstrated, the strategic role played by expectations is to negate the possibility of *any* effective policy action by a central government.

In the Keynesian analysis, however, they play an entirely different role. The orientation of expectations is not toward public policy, but toward investment spending in the private sector of the economy. Investment outlays are volatile because estimates of the future yield of new capital assets (the marginal efficiency of capital) rest on expectations rooted in uncertainty. Uncertainty exists because we cannot know the future. This leads to a profound philosophical difference with respect to the basic nature of the economic system. The new classical economic theorists, like the monetarists, attribute instability in the economy to misguided policy actions by the central government. Keynesians, on the other hand, argue that instability is rooted in the fundamental nature of a market economy, primarily because decisions about a key determinant of output—investment—rest on expectations that are extremely volatile. As Keynes explained, the source of this volatility is "... the extreme precariousness of the basis of the knowledge on which our estimates of prospective yield have to be made."[8]

The second point concerns the process by which expectations are formed. As we have seen, in the new classical economics, expectation formation is wholly a rational matter, in which people marshall all available information

---

[8] John Maynard Keynes, *The General Theory*, p. 149.

in order to make the best possible judgment about the future. People not only make the best use of all available information to guide their economic behavior, but they do not repeat past mistakes. Keynes's view of how expectations are formed is entirely different. He worked out his most complete explanation of this process in a 1937 article in the *Quarterly Journal of Economics*.[9] Ostensibly, the article was a response to four reviews of *The General Theory*, but a significant portion of the article was devoted to explaining the kind of uncertainty that shapes the expectations governing investment decisions. The knowledge that lies behind the investment decision, Keynes said, is "uncertain" knowledge. By this he meant that there was no scientific basis whatsoever for any "calculable probability" with respect to the influence of the economic variables that will determine the profitability of a capital asset whose life extends into the future. "We simply do not know."[10]

Even though this is, in Keynes's judgment, the true state of economic affairs, people must act, investment decisions have to be made. How, then, in the face of the kind of uncertainty that cannot be reduced to a probability calculation, are expectations formed? Keynes's answer is that we form our expectations by acting on one or more of the following principles:

1. We assume that the present is a much more serviceable guide to the future than any examination of past experience would justify.

2. We assume that the existing state of affairs as reflected in current prices and output represents a correct summing up of future prospects.

3. Not trusting our individual judgment, we fall back on the average judgment of the majority.[11]

The problem is, Keynes went on to say, that expectations formed in this way rest on a flimsy foundation, subject to ". . . sudden and violent changes. . . . New fears and hopes will, without warning, take charge of human conduct." At all times, he continued, vague fears and vague hopes ". . . lie but a little way below the surface."[12]

It is clear that the new classical economists and the Keynesians are at polar opposites when it comes to expectations. Which school is right? Unfortunately, we really do not know, because there has not been sufficient empirical research on the complex question of how people form their expectations. Well-designed attitude surveys that chart some expectations (Figure 16–2) exist, but these do not reveal the process by which consumers and others form their views about the future. Empirical research in this important area ought to be high on the macroeconomic agenda.

[9] Keynes, "The General Theory," *Quarterly Journal of Economics,* Vol. 51, February 1937.

[10] Ibid.

[11] Ibid.

[12] Ibid.

The New Classical Economics and the Business Cycle

Although both the theory of rational expectations and the theory of continuous market clearing are key elements in the new classical economics, the latter is especially crucial. Why? Because its real meaning is that if, in effect, markets, including the labor market, do continuously clear, then full employment is always the norm. In the classical analysis the natural rate of employment—and the corresponding natural rate of unemployment—is the level at which the quantity of labor demanded and supplied are in balance at an equilibrium *real* wage (Figure 3–1). The natural rate hypothesis originated with Milton Friedman.[13] Friedman and the monetarists do not argue, however, that the actual unemployment rate cannot differ from the natural unemployment rate for substantial periods of real calender time. But with the assumption of the new classical economists that at each point in time markets clear and agents act in their own self interest, the logical conclusion is that, at most, any deviation of the actual unemployment rate from the natural rate is extremely short-lived.[14] Therefore, with continuous market clearing there is no room for any systematic policy action designed to influence the actual unemployment rate.

This theoretical conclusion confronts a formidable challenge, because it must be reconciled with the fact of the business cycle—those ups and downs in economic life which characterize the economy's behavior over real, calendar time. It is a formidable challenge because the new classical economics must not only explain the reality of the business cycle, but it must do so in a manner that is consistent with its fundamental tenets, namely, the theory of rational expectations and the theory of continuous market clearing. Two approaches to understanding the business cycle developed within the new classical framework. The first is the *nominal business cycle model,* originated by Robert E. Lucas in the early 1980s. It relies on unforeseen price level changes resulting from unexpected changes in money growth for an explanation of the business cycle.[15] The second approach rejects the notion that money changes influence output and employment and holds that real factors alone account for business fluctuations. This is the *real business cycle approach,* which we consider subsequently.

In standard classical microeconomic theory the supply curve for a seller of either goods and services or labor slopes upward; this shows that, in general, sellers (that is, producers) will offer more of their product or service as the price goes up. The reverse holds true when the price goes down. The immediate concern of any seller is with the price in comparison to other prices

---

[13] Milton Friedman, ''The Role of Monetary Policy,'' *American Economic Review,* March 1968, pp. 1–17.

[14] Robert E. Lucas and Thomas J. Sargent, ''After Keynesian Macroeconomics,'' in *After the Phillips Curve: Persistence of High Inflation and High Unemployment* (Boston: Federal Reserve Bank of Boston, 1978), p. 58.

[15] Ibid., p. 85.

of the particular good or service being sold, what economic theory identifies as a *relative* price. Any seller also has some concern about prices in general, that is the price level, but as far as the individual, optimizing decision of a particular seller is concerned, what counts initially is relative price rather than prices in general. This point is crucial to an understanding of how the new classical economists explain the reality of the business cycle.

Before proceeding further, a word is in order about the meaning of the business cycle in this context. Presumably there is a long-term trend path that the economy would follow for real output if that output were always in balance with the economy's productive potential. The latter is determined by the long-term growth of resources, especially labor and capital, and changing technology. But as we saw in Chapter 1, the actual path of real output is seldom smooth, but departs over time in both directions from the trend of potential output. These departures in both directions from the trend are not smooth, but there is enough regularity to them to warrant the name ''business cycle.''

With these comments as a backdrop, we can examine *nominal business cycle theory.*[16] We shall begin with a period of unexpected higher prices and nominal (money) wages, brought about by an unforeseen increase in the money supply. In this approach to the business cycle such *monetary surprises* are typically thought of as the starting point for a cycle. Since suppliers (including workers) have good knowledge of their own prices (including money wages), but limited knowledge of the general level of prices and wages, they will initially interpret the unexpected price and wage increases as a *relative* change, meaning that the demand for their good (or labor) has increased. Given, then, the nature of the classical supply curve, including the supply curve for labor, output will be expanded and more labor will be offered on the market. This response is shown in part A of Figure 16–3, which shows in idealized fashion the swing of output over time around the basic, underlying trend line for real GNP. What happens in this phase is an information lag, a period in which sellers are generally unaware that prices (and wages) in general are rising. This means that there has not in fact been any change in the relative price for the good or service being supplied. If every seller, including workers, understood from the start that all prices (and wages) were going up together, they would not respond because nothing had really changed. For the supplier of a good or service, relative prices would be unchanged, and for the supplier of labor, the *real* wage would be unchanged. As Robert Lucas points out, ''This scenario . . . depends crucially on the confusion on the part of agents between relative and general price movements.''[17] Furthermore, it is argued that the kind of response described above applies to investment

---

[16] Robert E. Lucas, Jr., is responsible for the seminal research in nominal business cycles. Robert Barro and Thomas J. Sargent also have made important research contributions within a similar framework.

[17] Robert E. Lucas, Jr., ''Understanding Business Cycles,'' in Karl Brunner and Allan Meltzer, eds., *Stabilization of the Domestic and International Economy* (Amsterdam: North-Holland, 1977), p. 22.

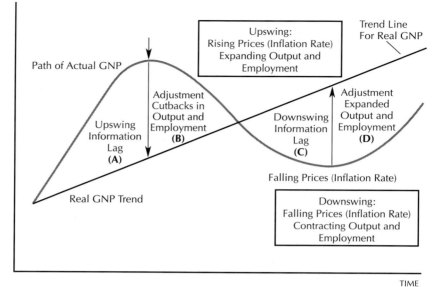

FIGURE 16–3 The New Classical Economics and the Business Cycle. During the upswing in a business cycle, information lags will lead business executives and workers to interpret rising prices and money wages as *relative* changes in their prices and wages and thus to supply more output and work than is really justified. A glut of both goods and labor results and leads to a recession or depression. In a downswing the opposite happens.

goods, as well as good and services in general. Thus, proponents of nominal business cycle theory argue that the investment boom which is often characteristic of the upswing phase of the business cycle can be explained in the same way. By the time it is recognized that general rather than relative price changes are taking place, it is too late; more capacity has been added than is necessary to meet actual demand.

Consider now what happens. In the downturn phase of the cycle, part B in Figure 16–3, adjustments are being made as producers begin to see that they were mistaken, that what they took to be a change in *relative* prices in their favor turns out not to be the case. Over time the information about what is really happening to prices (and wages) in general permeates through the economy and leads to cutbacks in production and in labor supplied. The presumption is that economic agents, now that they have the correct information, try to adjust back to their original positions on their supply curves— points where they were before prices in general started to rise. What happens after this is suggested in part C, Figure 16–3. Now prices (and wages) are falling,[18] but once again this change is perceived initially as a change in

---

[18] It would be more correct to speak of the inflation rate as falling rather than wages and prices, for rarely since World War II have prices and wages actually declined. But the principle is the same.

relative prices (and wages), rather than a general movement. Consequently, suppliers reduce their output, labor is withdrawn from the market, and actual output falls below the trend line for real GNP. We have a recession or a depression. This process will continue until producers once again are aware that relative prices (wages) are not changing, but only prices (wages) in general. Then the reduction in output will end, as will the withdrawal of labor from the market, and a recovery will begin as suppliers seek to return to their original positions.

Thus, through nominal business cycle theory, the new classical economics is able to explain the business cycle, which is conceded to exist, without having to abandon the basic tenets of classical equilibrium analysis: all behavior is rational and markets clear continuously in a Walrasian sense. The nominal business cycle begins with a monetary surprise and is perpetuated by misinformed economic agents, who are, presumably, acting rationally all the time. This is especially crucial for explaining the problem of unemployment. Since the supply of labor is a function of the real wage, any withdrawal of labor from the market must be voluntary. Workers misread the fall in money wages as a decline in real wages because they do not perceive that prices are also falling. Consequently, they withdraw from the labor market. Since they are not immediately aware of what is happening in other labor markets—particularly that wages in *all* markets have fallen—they continue their labor market search. But this withdrawal and search for another job is perceived as a voluntary act, which results primarily from an information failure.

The nominal business cycle model depends on a relationship between unexpected price changes, stemming from unforeseen changes in the money supply, and changes in real output. To put it differently, only monetary surprises are thought to have a positive correlation with output and employment changes. Conversely, monetary changes that are anticipated are necessarily neutral with respect to real variables in the economy. In early research, Lucas, Barro, and Sargent thought they had found confirmation for the view that monetary surprises caused changes in output and employment.[19] Later research showed, however, that by changing the way in which the econometric model was specified, money was not neutral. This meant that money changes, even when anticipated, would affect output and employment.[20]

Real Business Cycles

A more recent area of new classical economics research into business cycles concerns the explanation of business fluctuations that have their origin in real

[19] Robert Barro, "Unanticipated Money Growth and Unemployment in the United States," *American Economic Review*, Vol. 67, March 1977, pp. 101–115.

[20] Frederic Mishkin, "Does Anticipated Money Matter? An Empirical Investigation," *Journal of Political Economy*, Vol. 90, February 1982, pp. 22–51.

phenomena.[21] Real business cycle theorists argue that fluctuations result from random supply shocks involving changes in technology, capital, or the labor force or from random demand shocks such as changes in government spending or in consumer tastes and preferences. These supply and demand shocks alter the Walrasian general equilibrium and thus cause changes in real GDP.

Typical of the shocks that real business cycle theorists analyze is a technological change that improves productivity. This would involve an upward shift in the production function, which would give people (economic agents) new opportunities to work, produce, and consume. Being rational, they would respond positively to these opportunities, so that output, including investment, and employment would grow. On the other hand, if the economy is subjected to a random supply shock that depresses productivity, such as the oil price shocks of the 1970s or war in the Persian Gulf in 1991, rational economic agents would respond with less work. Output and employment would fall. No matter which direction a shock takes, real business cycle theorists argue that people act in accordance with the basic principles of neoclassical microeconomics. They make rational choices either to expand or to reduce work, output, and consumption when productivity rises or falls. Further, there are no market failures; that is to say, all markets continue to clear in standard Walrasian fashion and are always in equilibrium. Actually, what we observe as the economy's cyclical behavior is the collective by-product of rational decision making by the individual economic agents.

The nub of real business cycle theory is that the economy is subject to random supply and demand shocks that *permanently* alter its growth path. Thus, what appears statistically as a business cycle, with an expansion followed by a contraction followed again by an expansion, is really the economy following a random and unpredictable path.[22] Of particular significance is the belief of real business cycle theorists that, on balance, random shocks add permanently to the nation's real GDP. Thus, the long-term trend line of the latter is upward, even though growth comes in an erratic fashion. If this view is combined with the belief in the random nature of the shocks that move the economy, it follows that fiscal and monetary policies have no role to play in affecting the real economic variables of output and employment. This is in

---

[21] For further reading on real business cycles see the Fall 1986 issue of the *Quarterly Review* of the Federal Reserve Bank of Minnesota, which provides a brief debate between Edward Prescott, a leading real business cycle theorist, and Lawrence Summers, an important critic. See also Charles I. Plosser, "Understanding Real Business Cycles," *Journal of Economic Perspectives,* Vol. 3, No. 3 (Summer 1989), pp. 51–77; N. Gregory Mankiw, "Real Business Cycles: A New Keynesian Perspective," *Journal of Economic Perspectives,* Vol. 3, No. 3 (Summer 1989), pp. 17–90; and Mark Rush, "Real Business Cycles," *Economic Review,* the Federal Reserve Bank of Kansas City, February 1987, pp. 20–32.

[22] The technical term for this is a "random walk." A random walk is a walk that has no particular objective, but one in which its immediate future direction is determined by its current direction. In economics, in a random walk the value of a variable in the immediate future is best determined by its value in the current period. Statistical techniques exist to show that one-time random changes in the GDP add permanently to the level of the GDP. See Rush, "Real Business Cycles," p. 26.

accord with the general view of the new classical economics on the ineffectiveness of public policy.

Some Critical Observations

The new classical economics has a strong appeal, especially because, by linking expectations to traditional classical ideas about rational behavior, it seems to provide the bridge between micro- and macroeconomics that economists have sought for so long. A more realistic bridge is found in the Keynesian theory of the price level, and the aggregate supply curve developed from his theory (Chapter 12, pages 472–81). As a theory capable of explaining the real-world behavior of complex market economies, the new classical economics has serious limitations. Critics point to three major weaknesses in the theory.

The most fundamental weakness, perhaps, is the assumption that markets clear continuously. In reality this is nothing more than a restatement of the old classical view that markets are purely competitive, that prices (and wages) are flexible, that information is complete, and that the movement in the market is always toward an equilibrium of price and planned quantities. We must remember, however, that the market-clearing assumption is, as Professor Tobin says, "just that, an assumption. It is not justified by any new direct evidence that a Walrasian auctioneer process generates the prices observed from day to day or month to month or year to year."[23] Furthermore, as Professor Tobin has also said:

> We must therefore remind ourselves how severe a draft on credulity is the literal application of the market-clearing area. The Walrasian Auctioneer is a great myth; I emphasize both words. She must collect all the demand and supply schedules for the m commodities and n agents. She must solve the simultaneous equations, announce the market-clearing prices, and see that the scheduled transactions are consummated at those prices. For continuous market clearing the whole process must be repeated every quarter or day or second.[24]

Reality, of course, is vastly different. The majority of markets in the real world do not have the characteristics of auction markets, that is, markets in which prices are set by the interaction of many buyers and sellers, no one of whom has any control over the outcome. Participants in auction markets are known as price takers, simply because as either buyers or sellers they have no choice but to respond to the prices established in the market. Most markets in the real world, according to the late Arthur Okun, a former chairperson of

---

[23] James Tobin, "Are New Classical Models Plausible Enough to Guide Policy?" *Journal of Money, Credit, and Banking,* November 1980, p. 788.

[24] Tobin, *Asset Accumulation and Economic Activity,* p. 34. See also Bleaney, *The Rise and Fall of Keynesian Economics,* p. 154. The new classical economists do not refute Keynesian theory by empirical evidence, according to Professor Bleaney. They just dismiss it by assumption.

the Council of Economic Advisers, are ones in which sellers (or suppliers) of both commodities and labor are price makers, which is to say that they *do* have some control over the process by which prices and wages are determined.[25] Prices and wages are not necessarily set to clear the markets in the short run. For goods and services, customer-supplier relations are a major factor in the establishment of prices, a factor which leads to stability and durability, rather than volatility in price as in the auction model. The same is true for wages, because in labor markets the stability of employer-worker relations over the long term is usually of primary importance. The practical impact of price making rather than price taking as a characteristic of markets is to insulate prices and wages to a significant degree from shifts in demand; this leads to adjustments in output and employment when there are such shifts. This is quite in contrast to the views of the new classical economists, who hold that relative price adjustments occur practically instantaneously in response to changes or disturbances in demand and supply in particular markets.

Why is it, one may ask, that the classical economists insist on a view that is so much at odds with reality? In the older classical economics, the Walrasian general equilibrium solution was in practical terms seen as a long-run outcome, not a condition present at every moment of time. The answer seems to lie, in part, in a very strong feeling among the new classical economists that macroeconomics must be rooted in the optimizing individual behavior which is characteristic of microeconomics. Keynesian theoretical propositions, such as the consumption function, have been criticized for not having such a link. The view also has a strong appeal because the Walrasian general equilibrium outcome is one in which there is an optimal allocation of resources and a maximum production of the goods and services wanted by people in the economy. Since no satisfactory alternative model exists for dealing with fundamental issues of resource use and output composition, the Walrasian general equilibrium model holds great appeal, even though it simply is not possible to describe the real world in terms of continuous clearing in competitive markets. Mathematical models are useful because they can help to discover relationships among variables, but they can never yield results other than those which are embodied in their initial assumptions. As other critics have said, the rational expectations hypothesis is nothing more than a ''mathematical method of incorporating expectations into economic models. It is no more and no less. It is especially not . . . a proof that people behave rationally.''[26]

A second critical thrust centers on the other half of the new classical economics, namely, the theory of rational expectations. There are, it is said, serious deficiencies in this hypothesis, especially in the matter of how expectations are actually formed in the real-world economy. One major deficiency

---

[25] Arthur Okun, *Prices & Quantities: A Macroeconomic Analysis* (Washington, D.C.: Brookings Institution, 1981), p. 138.

[26] David C. Colander and Robert S. Guthrie, ''Great Expectations: What the Dickens Do 'Rational Expectations' Mean?'' *Journal of Post Keynesian Economics,* Winter 1980–81, p. 232.

in the rational expectations approach is that it requires that people know much more about how the economy works and the significance of all the data generated than reasonably can be expected. Given the fact that there is so much fundamental disagreement among professional economists about how the economy works, how can it be expected that the public at large have the necessary knowledge to engage in the kind of rational expectation formation envisioned by the new classical economics? There is no answer to this question other, perhaps, than to fall back on the argument that eventually people do learn enough about the way the economy works to avoid being fooled when policy decisions are made. The difficulty is, however, that economic relationships, even though they may be well-established on the basis of historical data, can and do change, sometimes in unpredictable ways. This, of course, changes the nature of the relevant economic models that the policymakers use.

It is also argued by critics of the rational expectations hypothesis that the notion that people use all information efficiently by incorporating it into their expectations ignores the fact that information is not a free good. On the contrary, the gathering and the processing of the kind of information necessary to understand what is going on in the economy and to interpret what decision makers are doing is a costly process. It is possible that the benefits to be derived from doing this may not, in many instances, outweigh the costs involved. Often the best way people have to deal with the complexities and uncertainties of the economy is to fall back on relatively simple rule-of-thumb behavior that takes into account what has happened recently. Decision making in the securities market may be truly rational in the sense in which the new classical economists employ the term. Decision makers here are highly organized, centrally located, and deal with a commodity which is basically homogeneous, all of which makes for a quick and comprehensive flow of information to all participants in the market. But these characteristics are not typical of most other markets in the economy, including labor markets.

More fundamental, perhaps, is the criticism leveled against the rational expectations hypothesis by the late George Katona, long associated with the Institute for Social Research at the University of Michigan. The formulation of expectations, Katona argued, is a psychological process, rooted in habits derived from repeated and rewarded past experiences.[27] In order to understand in a meaningful way how expectations are actually formed, economists must consider the theories and findings of psychologists, not begin with an unsubstantiated assumption about the way human beings behave, namely, the rationality postulate of the classical economics. Our behavior is rooted in the past and generally expectations are derived from the experiences of the past. But conditions change and humans are capable of learning as well as changing their attitudes and beliefs, including their expectations about the future. When something new enters the picture, people may change both their behavior and

---

[27] George Katona, ''How Expectations Are Really Formed,'' *Challenge,* November–December 1980, p. 32.

A Farewell to Armchair Economics

The key idea in neoclassical economics is the belief that humans are rational. In this context, "rational" means maximizing behavior—that humans are cool, detached calculating machines, always trying to maximize their pleasure (gain) or minimize their pain (cost). It is an old idea, going back to the eighteenth century utilitarian philosophy of Jeremy Bentham.

The trouble with this view, according to Herbert A. Simon, 1978 winner of the Nobel Prize in economics, is that human behavior is only rational if you study it in the context of the environment in which the behavior takes place, in the light of the goals that an individual is seeking to achieve, and in relation to the means by which the goals can be achieved. Neoclassical economics, Simon argues, departs from this because it ignores goals, assumes uniformly consistent behavior no matter what the circumstances, and believes that behavior is objectively rational.

Simon is the Richard King Mellon University Professor at Carnegie-Mellon University, where he specializes in economics, psychology, and computer science. Recently he and some colleagues published a book entitled *Scientific Discovery,* the main objective of which was to provide a theory of the processes by which scientists make new discoveries. The basic question he and his colleagues asked was whether in scientific discovery, theory is the driving force or whether facts or data lead and theories follow.

After examining many of the major scientific discoveries from the early seventeenth century on, Professor Simon and his colleagues concluded that most successful science is done by "looking at the world, getting puzzled by it, and the developing or testing of a theory."*

Unfortunately much economics, especially neoclassical economics, does not work this way. "That direction of movement is not impossible in economics," according to Professor Simon, ". . . But there is a lot of resistance among economists to going out and looking at the world until you have a theory about it. Economists tend to start with some global theoretical assumptions . . . and then they reason from them. If the world doesn't fit the assumptions, or you have a hard time with the regression results, so much the worse for the world."

What does this mean for economics? Professor Simon believes that the core of human economic activity involves decision making and problem solving. But to understand this, economists must take a lesson from psychology. As the psychologists do, they will have to get evidence on what information people actually have, what calculations they actually make on the basis of that information, and how they actually go about making decisions. The rationality postulate simply assumes away most of what must be discovered if economists are to understand decision making in the real world.

It is unfortunate, Professor Simon asserts, that "virtually no economic students get training in methods of observation that would lead the researcher to find out how the consumer actually makes choices, or to go inside a business firm to see how decisions are actually made there."

The problem may not be so difficult to solve as some think. Contrary, perhaps, to the conventional wisdom that getting accurate information about consumer or business behavior would require surveying thousands of people or hundreds of firms, Professor Simon argues that this is not necessarily the case. He says, "... If you studied about a dozen firms, you have a pretty good feeling of the range of behavior you are likely to encounter in firms. ..."

*Based on an interview with Professor Simon in the November–December 1986 issue of *Challenge*. All quotations are from this interview.

---

their expectations. One cannot simply assume, however, that expectations are always modified sufficiently to take into account new elements in any situation. The rational expectations approach makes such an assumption. As a practical matter, the only way to resolve this difficulty is by empirical research, which means going out and asking about expectations. Nobel laureate Herbert A. Simon of Carnegie-Mellon University has also said that economists will have to learn from the psychologists. "They will have to get evidence on what information people actually have, what calculations they actually make on that information, and how they go about making their decisions." They must, Professor Simon said, examine real-world, complex situations and abandon their practice of armchair theorizing.[28]

Finally, critics of the theory of rational expectations argue that, even if valid, it has limited applicability because it can deal only with situations in which the economic events that enter into the formation of expectations involve situations of risk and not uncertainty. Risk applies to a situation in which events, such as the presumed regularities of the business cycle, repeat themselves with enough certainty that a probability calculus can be applied to determine the likelihood of any particular event occurring. This limitation of the rational expectations hypothesis is readily granted by its advocates. "In situations of risk, the hypothesis of rational behavior on the part of agents will have usable content, so that behavior may be explainable in terms of economic theory.... In cases of uncertainty, economic reasoning will be of no value."[29] What this means is that the rational expectations theorists have constructed an abstract world in which events repeat themselves—the world of neoclassical general equilibrium economics. Risk is an appropriate concept for such a world, and in it economic agents can form their expectations on the basis of appropriate probability calculations. The real world, according to the critics, is one of *nonrepetitive* events occurring in *historical* time. Uncertainty, not risk, is the appropriate concept to be applied to such a world.[30]

---

[28] Herbert A. Simon, "The Failure of Armchair Economics," interview in *Challenge*, November–December 1986, pp. 13–25.

[29] Lucas, "Understanding Business Cycles," p. 15.

[30] Leonard Forman, "Rational Expectations and the Real World," *Challenge*, November–December 1980, p. 36

Uncertainty pervades economic life, because the economy exists in historical, real time. When we deal with real, historical time, we are dealing not only with the past and present, but also with the future, and the future is uncertain. Major economic events, such as investment spending, are tied to an uncertain and unknowable future, not to hypothetical events that tend to be repetitive. The problem, as Keynes pointed out many years ago, is that when we are dealing with uncertainty, such as the yield of a new factory over its lifetime, "... there is *no scientific basis* on which to form any capable probability whatever. We simply do not know."[31] Thus, we have to fall back on such flimsy and uncertain foundations as recent and present conditions and majority opinion as guides to the future.

The final criticism of the new classical economics centers on its explanation of the business cycle. Two things should be said about this explanation of the cycle. First, it strains the imagination to believe that long periods of unemployment, such as the economy experienced in the 1930s and even at times in the post-World War II period, can be explained by a persistent failure to understand not only what is happening in other markets, but also what is happening in the economy overall. As Arthur Okun has said, the "... theory is weak, however, in explaining why any demand disturbances ... should be so poorly perceived for so long that they create pronounced cycles in real activity."[32] The response of the new classical economics to this is basically that a long time may be needed for the economy to adjust to and reverse any output changes that result from misinformation, even though producers and workers may realize quickly what is happening in other markets and to the economy overall. Second, the new classical economics is criticized for failing to provide any direct empirical evidence that sellers of both goods and labor do not have any relevant and timely information about other prices that bear on their own decisions. "Any theory that attributes decision-making errors by private agents to missing information implies that there exists, in principle, some set of correct, timely information that would eliminate these errors. That information needs to be identified specifically."[33] This has not been done.

In concluding this discussion of rational expectations and the market-clearing postulate, two points need to be made. Granted that the logic and mathematical completeness of the new classical economics have a strong appeal to many economists, empirical evidence, which after all is the ultimate test of any theory, does not support the argument of the new classical school that *all* macro policy measures are ineffective. To verify this, look again at Figure 1–3. Output (and employment) have been much more stable in the post-World War II period than they were before the war. This has been the period of active stabilization policy, and the overall results have been more beneficial than detrimental. Even more devastating to the new classical economics from

---

[31] Keynes, "The General Theory of Employment," p. 213.

[32] Okun, *Prices & Quantities,* p. 172.

[33] Okun, "Rational-Expectations with Misperceptions as a Theory of the Business Cycle," p. 820.

an *empirical* perspective is the fact that the Reagan administration in the United States and the Thatcher government in Great Britain came into office with faith in the basic argument that if policy was credible, inflation could be reduced at a minimum cost in terms of unemployment. David A. Stockman, first director of the Office of Management and Budget in the Reagan administration and chief architect of the Reagan program for economic recovery, said in his book, *The Triumph of Politics: Why the Reagan Revolution Failed:*

> But I had acquired some amateur knowledge of rational expectations theory and the mechanics of financial markets. This permitted me to sidestep the precipice of recession with a *fiscal expectations* theory of rapid and dramatic financial market recuperation resulting from the new administration's policies.[34]

Events did not unfold as Stockman thought they would. Tight money, as is usually the case, reduced aggregate demand, and the economy dropped into the worst recession (1981–82) since the Great Depression. As another critic said, "... the new classical monetary theory also had the misfortune to run into a very severe empirical test almost as soon as it had first achieved academic popularity. After the recession of 1980–82, the more extreme forms of the policy irrelevance propositions simply could not be sustained."[35]

Even economists normally sympathetic to the new classical economic school regarded the events of the early 1980s as a defeat for this approach. Milton Friedman said that "... experience clearly contradicts the more extreme rational expectations models predicting extremely rapid adjustments to changes in monetary growth."[36] Martin Feldstein, chairperson of President Reagan's Council of Economic Advisers for two years, declared that "... the sharp recession provided no support for the extreme version of the ... rational expectations view that a clearly articulated policy of monetary contraction can reduce inflation without slowing economic activity or increasing unemployment."[37] If the commitments in the United States and Great Britain in the early 1980s to bring inflation down were not credible, then, as Canadian economist John N. Smithin pointed out, "... it is hard to imagine any policy pronouncements which would be, and the distinction between anticipated and unanticipated policy becomes meaningless for any practical purpose."[38]

The second point is that what gave the most credence to the resurgence of classical ideas was the alleged failure of standard Keynesian macroeconomic policies to cope with the dominant problem of the 1970s—the simultaneous

---

[34] David A. Stockman, *The Triumph of Politics: Why the Reagan Revolution Failed* (New York: Harper & Row, 1986), p. 72.

[35] Smithin, *Macroeconomics after Thatcher and Reagan,* p. 52.

[36] Milton Friedman, "The Case for Overhauling the Federal Reserve," *Challenge,* July–August 1985, p. 5.

[37] Martin Feldstein, "Monetarism: Open-Eyed Pragmatism," *The Economist,* May 18, 1985, p. 18.

[38] Smithin, *Macroeconomics after Thatcher and Reagan,* p. 53.

existence of excess inflation and excess unemployment. In part this rests on a misreading of the experience of the 1970s—an experience that Keynes's much-neglected theory of the price level can explain (pages 472–81). It also stems from the fact that we have not yet developed successful policies for attaining full or high employment over time with stable prices. But the answer to this dilemma is not to abandon the basic income-expenditure model in favor of reinvented classical theories found wanting in the past. Rather, we should expand and improve the model by bringing into it elements that can account for the observed fact of rising prices and wages along with slack markets and excess capacity. This was one of the primary objectives of the analysis of aggregate supply developed in Chapter 12.

Supply-Side Economics

It is worthwhile to explore a footnote to the new classical movement of the 1970s and 1980s. While its effects on macroeconomic theory and policy have not been as widespread or long-lasting as those of the new classical school, *supply-side economics* was far better known to the general public. This is most likely because it provided the basic theoretical rationale for the Reagan administration's 1981 Program for Economic Recovery.

Briefly, the supply-side economists based their argument on the classical idea of an upward-sloping supply curve. A supply curve relates price and quantity in a positive way. For example, higher wage rates lead to a higher quantity of labor supplied in the market, and higher interest rates lead to a higher quantity of savings supplied in the market. The supply-side economists argued that if the government imposes high marginal tax rates on workers, savers, or anyone who is involved in productive activities, the result is a reduction in the quantity of labor, savings, investment, and, ultimately, output.

The tax rate acts as a wedge between the returns that individuals would receive in the market without taxes and the incomes that they actually receive. Thus, high marginal tax rates reduce the incentives that people have to save more, invest more, work more, and in general be more productive. Jude Wanniski, a former editorial writer for the *Wall Street Journal*, put it this way: "The concept of marginality is crucial to an understanding of economic behavior. . . . Very few people *think* on the margin, but everyone *acts* on the margin." Production comes about, according to Wanniski, "because people are willing to work, and people work for only one reason—to maximize their welfare."[39] Here is where marginal tax rates enter the picture. Taxes are a disincentive to produce. Taxes on capital discourage investment and taxes on people discourage work. This is the essential message of supply-side economics.

---

[39] Jude Wanniski, *The Way the World Works* (New York: Basic Books, 1978), p. 42.

Although most of the supply-side revolution has lost its momentum, its legacy remains. It is currently turning up in the debate over static and dynamic budgeting models. The current budget policy of the U.S. government is to assume fairly static behavior of individuals in response to economic policies. The basic working assumption, according to Laura D'Andrea Tyson, former chairperson of President Clinton's Council of Economic Advisers, is that "behavioral responses to changes in government policy are not large enough to effect either the level of total economic output or its growth rate."[40] Under such assumptions, for example, a cut in the capital gains tax rate of 50 percent will reduce the revenues that the government can expect to receive from the capital gains tax by about 50 percent.

Opponents of static budgetary assumptions claim that this static method vastly underestimates the effects on economic activity of changes in government policy that come as a result of changes in people's behavior. Under dynamic budgeting, or "scoring" as it is also called, these opponents believe that the capital gains tax cut would lead people to respond by selling assets. The result of these sales might be an actual increase in government tax revenues.[41]

While few economists would disagree with the basic idea of taking into account microeconomic behavior in crafting budget policy, at least in the near future it seems that the federal government will continue to use a basically static approach. This is due to the often fundamental disagreements among economists over both the magnitudes and sometimes even the direction of the effects of government policies on microeconomic behaviors.

Summary

1. The new classical economics is the most recent challenge to the Keynesian-oriented income-expenditure approach to macroeconomics. It arose in part because of the alleged policy failures of Keynesian economics during the 1970s, a period when the economy experienced simultaneously too much inflation and too much unemployment. It rests on two basic propositions, namely, the theory of rational expectations and the theory of continuous market clearing.

2. The theory of rational expectations argues that all economic agents form expectations rationally by taking into account all relevant information, including how policy will affect the economy. The consequence of this is that, unless a policy action is not foreseen, the results of any policy will be antic-

---

[40] Laura D'Andrea Tyson, "Dynamic Scoring: Not Ready for Prime Time," *Wall Street Journal*, January 12, 1995, p. 1.

[41] "A Primer: What Congress Will Face in Debate over Taxes and Revenues," *Wall Street Journal*, December 27, 1994, p. 2.

ipated and therefore the policy will be ineffective. Because the rational expectations theorists believe that the economy is inherently stable and because of the way in which they believe expectations are formed, they do not believe *any* policy action by the government can affect output, employment, or the price level.

3. The theory of continuous market clearing involves the principles of Walrasian general equilibrium theory, which show how equilibrium can be established simultaneously in all markets if competition is present. This theory includes equilibrium in the labor market, which means that full employment is the normal state of affairs.

4. The new classical economics recognizes the existence of the business cycle, but explains it in terms of misinformation on the part of producers and wage earners who fail to perceive what is happening in specific markets and thus temporarily supply more goods and labor than needed. Critics argue that this is insufficient to explain the depth and duration of most cycles.

5. Supply-side economics consists of two basic propositions: (1) faith under contemporary conditions in Say's law of markets and (2) a belief that incentives to work, invest, and save are badly impaired by taxes being too high. The basic policy recommendation of supply-side economics is to cut taxes sharply. Supply-side economics formed a part of the conceptual base of the Reagan administration's Program for Economic Recovery.

17 The New Keynesian Macroeconomics

BY THE LATE 1970s rational expectations had become the dominant view about how expectations are formed. In its most straightforward statement, the rational expectations assumption is powerful. It says that people learn from their mistakes when they are forming expectations about the future, and so any errors that they make will, over time, be random. With the wide acceptance of this assumption about how expectations are formed, it appeared as if the new classical approach would dominate macroeconomic theory for years to come.

But this did not happen. In the late 1970s and 1980s a new perspective in macroeconomics, built on the assumption of rational expectations but with a wholly different conclusion, emerged. The new Keynesian economists, as this perspective is known, find that long-term unemployment and output below full employment are intrinsic to the system of market capitalism and that macroeconomic policies aimed at stimulating aggregate demand are often appropriate. Thus, using standard microeconomics, new Keynesian economists reach conclusions much like those reached by Keynes. Hence the name.

The basic difference between new Keynesians and new classical economists is not over how expectations are formed. It is over the assumption of continuous market clearing. For the new Keynesians, the major task is to explain in systematic, microeconomic terms why aggregate models might display the failures perceived by Keynes. Two issues dominate their work: sticky prices and sticky wages. First, why in the face of a recession do producers not simply lower their prices in order to sell their surplus goods? Second, why do workers fail to offer their labor at lower wages and remain unemployed? The new Keynesians have developed a set of microfoundations that show why prices and wages tend to remain stable in the face of changes in demand and have, therefore, thrust adjustment onto output and employment instead.

New Keynesian Economics and the Aggregate Supply Curve

The principle underlying the theory and policy conclusions of the new Keynesians centers on the nature and behavior of the Keynesian-classical supply curve (pages 132–38). New Keynesians agree with the new classical economists on the theory of rational expectations. But for new Keynesians it is the assumption of continuous market clearing, and not rational expectations, that leads them to the conclusion that macroeconomic policy can be effective.[1]

To understand this, recall the argument that the self-adjusting mechanism returns the economy to full employment when actual prices are consistent with the prices that workers and businesses expect. In the new classical model this means that market forces cause the changes in prices and nominal wages that eliminate involuntary unemployment. Any deviation from full employment is quickly eliminated in the new classical scheme because markets continuously clear. In a world of rational expectations and continuous market clearing, macroeconomic policy is effective only when it is unanticipated. An unanticipated policy causes expectational errors, which may lead real output and employment to depart from their natural levels. These effects are quickly eliminated as expectational errors are corrected by appropriate price and nominal wage adjustments.

When the assumption of continuous market clearing is replaced by the assumption of wage and price rigidity, the policy ineffectiveness proposition is nullified; macroeconomic policy is then a possibility.[2] Figure 17–1 shows a Keynesian-classical aggregate supply and aggregate demand model. Assume that a supply shock has moved the aggregate supply curve from AS_1 to

---

[1] For details see Stanley Fischer, "Long-Term Contracting, Sticky Prices, and Monetary Policy," *Journal of Monetary Economics,* Vol. 3 (1977), and Thomas J. Sargent and Neil Wallace, "Rational Expectations and the Theory of Economic Policy," *Journal of Monetary Economics,* Vol. 2 (1976).

[2] See John B. Taylor, "An Appeal for Rationality in the Policy Activism Debate," a paper prepared for the conference, *The Monetary and Fiscal Policy Debate: Lessons from Two Decades,* The Federal Reserve Bank of Saint Louis, October 12–13, 1984, Saint Louis, MO.

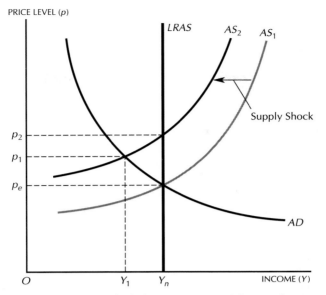

FIGURE 17–1   Macroeconomic Adjustment to an Adverse Aggregate Supply Shock.   An adverse aggregate supply shock causes increases in price and money wage expectations and creates an expectational error (expected prices and money wages are greater than actual prices and money wages). This leads to a leftward shift of the aggregate supply curve from AS_1 to AS_2 and a reduction in output from Y_n to Y_1. When expectations are adjusted, money wages and prices are bid downward as the aggregate supply curve shifts back to its original position.

AS_2 and thus resulted in a higher price level (from p_e to p_1) and a level of real output (Y_1) that is less than the natural rate of output (Y_n). The aggregate supply shock that raises the price level causes people to expect higher prices in the future. In the model, people expect the price level to be p_2, the price level that is consistent with the natural level of output, but instead the actual price level is p_1. Hence, expected prices are greater than actual prices and the level of output falls.

The natural rate hypothesis tells us that this economy will adjust to this shock through lower prices and nominal wages and that it will eventually return to the level of output that is consistent with the natural rate of unemployment (Y_n) and price level p_e. The new classical economists assume this adjustment takes place rapidly as people eliminate their expectational errors and correct their price and nominal wage expectations. This is what brings the aggregate supply curve back to its original position. Therefore, the new classical economists deny the possibility of persistent involuntary unemployment. The new Keynesians argue, however, that rigidities in nominal wages and prices slow the adjustment process. Therefore, the phenomenon of long-term involuntary unemployment is clearly possible.

The Micro Foundations of New Keynesian Economics[3]

The new Keynesian approach seeks to uncover the institutions and microeconomic imperfections in the economy leading to the price and wage rigidity that would explain involuntary unemployment. These institutions and microeconomic imperfections, which come in many forms, have been the subject of intense research in the 1980s. John B. Taylor of Stanford University and a member of President Bush's Council of Economic Advisers, has studied how labor contracts create nominal wage rigidities and make the economy resistent to anti-inflation policies. N. Gregory Mankiw of Harvard University has investigated how imperfectly competitive firms resist cutting prices even when doing so would increase profits. Lawrence Summers, also of Harvard University, Joseph E. Stiglitz of Stanford University and the chairperson of President Clinton's Council of Economic Advisers, Charles L. Schultze of the Brookings Institution and chairperson of the Council of Economic Advisers under President Carter, Steven Salop of Georgetown University, and Guillermo Calvo of Columbia University have examined under the rubric the *efficiency wage hypothesis* why firms may find it economically rational to pay wages higher than those that would clear the market. In the same vein, George A. Akerlof and Janet Yellen of the University of California at Berkeley and Alan Blinder of Princeton University and currently a member of the Board of Governors of the Federal Reserve System have studied sociological models that might underlie efficiency wages. In the next section we shall examine these institutions and micro structures in detail and show how they can result in long-term unemployment even in an economy in which it is assumed that expectations are developed rationally.

A Contract-Based New Keynesian Model[4]

One source of wage and price rigidities is long-term contracts. On the wage side, union contracts often fix, or at least guide, wages for periods of several years. The standard UAW (United Auto Workers) contract, for example, sets wage guidelines for up to 36 months. Generally speaking, such contracts do not permit the month-to-month, or even day-to-day, fluctuations envisaged by the new classical economists. Furthermore, contracts set in the unionized sector of the economy affect the nonunion labor market as well. Research on wage imitation began with the work of Arthur M. Ross and John T. Dunlop

---

[3] For a detailed review of the literature on new Keynesian economics see Robert J. Gordon, "What is New-Keynesian Economics?" *Journal of Economic Literature,* Vol. 28, No. 3 (September 1990), pp. 1115–1171.

[4] Three early sources of such models are found in Fischer, "Long-Term Contracting, Sticky Prices, and Monetary Policy"; Edmund S. Phelps and John B. Taylor, "Stabilizing Powers of Monetary Policy Under Rational Expectations," *Journal of Political Economy,* Vol. 85, No. 1 (February 1977), pp. 163–190; and John B. Taylor, "Estimation and Control of a Macroeconomic Model with Rational Expectations," *Econometrica,* Vol. 47, No. 5 (September 1979), pp. 659–680.

of Harvard University in the 1940s and 1950s. Professor Ross held that inside and outside of the union sector, considerations of equity could override supply and demand conditions in the labor market and determine the nominal wage.[5] For example, if machinists in a unionized shop receive a 10 percent nominal wage increase, other machinists in both union and nonunion firms will expect their negotiators to bargain for a 10 percent increase. Professor Dunlop argued that firms which sold their products in the same markets or which depended on similar sources for labor would, over time, establish linkages between the wages paid their laborers.[6] These linkages, which Dunlop called *wage contours,* were set with reference to key wages in an industry. If, for example, U.S. Steel (the predecessor to USX) established an agreement with its steelworkers, steelworkers for other firms would use that agreement as a pattern in their negotiations. Daniel J. B. Mitchell, of the University of California at Los Angeles, reviews the modern literature on wage imitation in his book, *Unions, Wages, and Inflation,* and finds a body of research that confirms wage imitation behavior in contract negotiations both inside and outside of the unionized sector of the economy.[7]

On the price side, contracts also limit the flexibility envisioned in the new classical model. Many firms establish contracts with the suppliers of their inputs to establish reliable sources of supply and to plan more effectively. These contracts, among other things, establish both the quantity of the inputs that will be provided and the prices paid for them. Prices are also fixed by contracts between manufacturers and their retail outlets. The auto industry is a good example of this. The wholesale price on a new car is not established by the dealer, but is set by the manufacturer. These prices are given to the dealer and remain relatively fixed in the short run.[8]

Before explaining how contracts figure in the new Keynesian model, there are two assumptions that need to be noted about labor contracts. Rational expectations theory requires that labor contracts be negotiated with an eye on the future. Specifically, wage negotiations take into account future nominal wages in other industries and the future price level. This assumption simply implies that negotiators use information currently available about the economy and macroeconomic policy (perhaps the union's econometric model) in an efficient way to forecast the price level that is expected to prevail over the term of the new contract.[9] Generally, contracts set wages in nominal terms, so workers will demand nominal wages that produce the real wage they want.

[5] Arthur M. Ross, *Trade Union Wage Policy* (Berkeley: University of California Press, 1948).

[6] John T. Dunlop, ''The Task of Contemporary Wage Theory,'' in John T. Dunlop ed., *The Theory of Wage Determination* (New York: St. Martin's Press, 1957).

[7] Daniel J. B. Mitchell, *Unions, Wages, and Inflation* (Washington, D.C.: Brookings Institution, 1980), pp. 163–207.

[8] Certainly there is some variability in price due to rebates and the bargaining allowances that are provided to dealers.

[9] John B. Taylor, ''The Role of Expectations in the Choice of Monetary Policy,'' in *Monetary Policy Issues in the 1980s* (Kansas City: Federal Reserve Bank of Kansas City, 1982), pp. 47–76.

The second assumption is that labor contracts usually cover a three-year period and that negotiations are staggered through time. This is, in fact, an accurate description of the situation as it applies to the U.S. economy. Chrysler workers, for example, may negotiate a contract four months after Ford workers.[10]

If we begin with these assumptions instead of the standard market clearing assumption of the new classical school, we get very different theoretical results. Start with a situation in which the economy is at its natural level of output. Assume also this happy circumstance has persisted long enough so that all contracts embody the expectation that actual prices equal expected prices. If the economy suffers an adverse aggregate supply shock, like the one shown in Figure 17–1, then it enters a period of stagflation with real output's falling to Y_1 and the price level's rising to p_1. In the new Keynesian model, however, contracts block the self-adjusting mechanism because prices and nominal wages cannot be bid downward.[11] The labor market and many product markets do not clear. In fact, the labor market may behave in a perverse way when contract negotiations are staggered. Those workers still unemployed are receiving lower than expected real wages because of increases in the price level, so they may pressure their representatives to bargain for higher, not lower, nominal wages. They do this in order to catch up both to the real wage they expect and to any real wage gains other workers may be getting. Furthermore, if negotiators continue to expect higher prices in the future (that is until they correct their expectational errors), these expectations will be reflected in higher nominal wage demands. This is to a large extent what happened in the 1970s, as oil price shocks accelerated inflation on their way through the economy.

With many nominal wages and prices fixed by contract, labor and product markets cannot make the adjustment back to the natural rate of output and employment until contracts are negotiated that include reduction in money wages. But, since contracts cover three-year periods and negotiations are staggered, this may take a long time. It is important to recognize that this adjustment failure results from a failure of prices and nominal wages to change, even though price expectations are rational. As Professor Taylor argues,

> The forward-looking aspects of wage and price decisions do not eliminate the problem of slow or gradual adjustment when conditions change. Because wage decisions have a finite duration, actions taken in the past have implications for today. . . . The persistence generated by past wage decisions can be quite drawn out if wage contracting is nonsynchronized or staggered and wages are set taking expectations of other wages into account.[12]

---

[10] John B. Taylor, "Staggered Wage Setting in a Macro Model," *American Economic Review*, Vol. 69, No. 2 (May 1979), pp. 108–113.

[11] Review the section "Output and Prices: Some Empirical Findings," pages 482–84, for empirical confirmation of this view.

[12] Taylor, "The Role of Expectations in the Choice of Monetary Policy," p. 57.

Therefore, an equilibrium output level that is below that natural rate can persist even after expectational errors have been eliminated.

Another implication of New Keynesian work on contracts is that disinflationary policies may be much more costly than new classical models imply. Recall from Chapter 16 that the new classical economics school argues that if expectations are rational and markets clear continuously, a credible disinflationary policy will result in lower inflation but at small social cost in terms of unemployment. Staggered wage setting, however, creates persistent inflationary wage increases throughout the economy once such increases begin. As Lester Thurow, economist and Dean of the Sloan School of Management at MIT, says:

> American wages are now set in a context of overlapping three-year indexed contracts. In such a system it becomes very difficult to phase down wage gains unless the industry is on the brink of extinction. Suppose that this year the Machinists' union is negotiating a new three-year contract. Last year the Auto Workers negotiated a three-year contract for a 10% raise per year. In many plants machinists work right next to auto workers. No leader of the machinists can settle for less than 10% per year and still remain in office. And in two years' time the auto leaders will be similarly imprisoned by what the machinists negotiate today.[13]

Once inflationary wage increases begin and if they persist, they will make a disinflation policy costly even if bargainers embrace rational expectations behavior and the disinflationary policy is credible.

Sticky Prices: Markup Pricing and Menu Costs

We have discussed how labor contracts and contracts between suppliers and producers can create rigidities that prevent the economy from making price and wage adjustments. But beyond these there are other forms of microeconomic behavior that can lead to price rigidity. The perfectly competitive firm, on which market-clearing models are based, is the exception rather than the rule in the U.S. economy. In the contemporary economy, firms match more closely the description given by models of oligopoly, monopoly, and other industry structures in which firms have some discretionary power over their prices. One characteristic of the pricing process by firms in noncompetitive markets is the *markup rule*. Prices are set administratively by adding a profit margin to the cost of producing a unit of output. This is how automobile manufacturers set the wholesale prices for their cars. The markup is the basis in part for the distribution of dividends to the firm's stockholders, and also for internally generated investment funds.[14] The markup equation takes the form

$$p = m + ac \tag{17-1}$$

---

[13] Lester Thurow, "Thurow's Third Way," *The Economist,* January 23–29, 1982, p. 32.

[14] For a full discussion of markup pricing behavior, see Alfred S. Eichner, *The Megacorp and Oligopoly* (Armonk, N.Y.: M. E. Sharpe, 1976).

where p = the price,

m = the markup, the firm's profit margin per unit of output,

ac = the average cost per unit of output.

When average costs increase, the firm will attempt to protect its profit margin by increasing its price (p). However, when average costs fall, oligopolistic firms will be slow to reduce their prices, so the margin increases. Hence, use of markup pricing by firms suggests that prices will be sticky downward but flexible upward. This is consistent with the actual behavior of prices in much of the U.S. economy since the Great Depression and, notably, since World War II.[15] From the perspective of the firm, markup pricing has two distinct advantages. First, it enables the firm to count on a relatively steady stream of investment funds for use in the future. Second, outsiders will perceive the process as being fair, since firms raise their prices only when they have experienced an increase in costs.[16]

To the extent that prices are administered through a markup strategy, another source of rigidity results beyond those stemming from formal contracts between producers and suppliers. Wages account for about 75 to 80 percent of total costs. If, as argued earlier, wages are sticky in the short run because of contractual arrangements, then the markup equation will produce a matching stickiness in prices.[17]

Another approach to price rigidity, one not involving contracts, comes from the concept of *menu costs*. The term "menu costs" comes from the cost a restaurant incurs in reprinting menus when it changes prices. The concept is much broader than this. It refers to *all* the costs involved when a business chooses to change its prices. Beyond the process of repricing all the goods or services involved, there are costs associated with notifying salespeople and their accounts, printing new catalogs and price lists, notifying the sales outlets that are supplied by the firm, and potentially losing some good will of customers if prices are substantially different from what they expect. While each of these taken separately represents a small cost for the firm, taken together menu costs may be large enough to outweigh the additional profits that the firm might achieve by lowering its prices and selling more output. Professor Mankiw has shown that when small menu costs create price rigidities, they lead to large social costs in terms of lost output and high unemployment.[18]

In order to discuss the price rigidities that result from small menu costs,

[15] Gardner C. Means is generally credited as having discovered the phenomenon of administered prices. See Warren J. Samuels and Steven G. Medema, *Gardner C. Means: Institutionalist and Post Keynesian* (Armonk, N. Y.: M. E. Sharpe, 1990), pp. 55–95.

[16] G. K. Shaw, *Keynesian Economics* (London: Edward Elgar, 1988), pp. 115–116.

[17] See John M. Blair, *Economic Concentration: Structure, Behavior, and Public Policy,* (New York: Harcourt Brace Jovanovich, 1972), pp. 405–497. Blair's study is one of the most comprehensive analyses of administered price behavior ever completed in the United States. The late Dr. Blair was for many years chief economist for the Antimonopoly Subcommittee of the U.S. Senate.

[18] Gregory Mankiw, "Small Menu Costs and Large Business Cycles: A Macroeconomic Model of Monopoly," *The Quarterly Journal of Economics,* Vol. 100, No. 2 (May 1985), pp. 529–537.

we must recall from microeconomics that the imperfectly competitive firm faces a downward-sloping demand curve; hence to sell more output, the firm must reduce its price. (The competitive firm, by contrast, faces a horizontal demand curve and can sell all it can produce at the going price.) Furthermore, we will assume that firms price their output above marginal cost. This assumption is consistent with reality.[19] How does the imperfectly competitive firm respond to a reduction in the demand for its product? There are, in fact, two possible ways for the firm to respond. It can reduce its price and continue to produce the same quantity of output, or it can hold its price constant and allow the quantity demanded of its output to fall. Just how the firm responds depends on the effect of a price change on its profits. If reducing the price leads to an increase in profits, then the firm will do so unless menu costs are larger than the marginal increase in profits. Often, however, the increase in profits due to reducing prices is small, so the firm chooses not to reduce them. As small menu costs lead businesses throughout the economy to reduce output and employment rather than to adjust prices, a small price adjustment problem snowballs into a large decline in output and employment. Mankiw's contribution, then, is to show that even though menu costs are small, they can create significant price rigidity in the economy, which leads to a substantial loss in social welfare, even when individual business firms act rationally.[20]

Efficiency Wage Theories of Involuntary Unemployment

Another area of new Keynesian research has focused on theories that deal with the phenomenon of long-term, involuntary unemployment. A central question that any theory of involuntary unemployment must answer is: Why do businesses and unemployed workers not simply bid wages down to the point where firms are willing to hire those who are willing to work? If this were done, businesses would experience increased profits and unemployed workers would find jobs. Lower wages are, of course, the cure for involuntary unemployment offered by the classical model. If the classical proposition were valid, we should find that labor markets adjust to changes in supply and demand, so that workers who want work can get it with relative ease. We should observe that wage adjustments make spells of unemployment short in their duration.

Empirical evidence, however, makes it overwhelmingly apparent that the duration of unemployment can be lengthy in the economy. This happens even

---

[19] Robert E. Hall shows that for a large portion of firms in the United States, price exceeds marginal cost, see his "The Relation Between Price and Marginal Cost in U.S. Industry," *The Journal of Political Economy*, Vol. 96, No. 5 (October 1988).

[20] Mankiw also shows that although prices may be downwardly rigid, they are not upwardly rigid. He shows that in terms of social welfare, "Private incentives produce too much price adjustment following an expansion in aggregate demand and too little price adjustment following a contraction in aggregate demand." Mankiw, "Small Menu Costs and Large Business Cycles," p. 536.

when the economy is growing at a brisk pace. Estimates of the duration of unemployment for individuals have been calculated by George A. Akerlof and Brian G. M. Main for the period 1959 to 1978[21] and by Hal Sider for the period 1968 to 1982.[22] These estimates show that laid-off workers undergo, on average, six to eight months of unemployment even when the economy is expanding. In fact, research using the growth in real GDP to predict the duration of unemployment finds that no statistically significant relationship exists between the duration of unemployment and the economy's growth.[23] This means, contrary to the classical view, that workers can be willing and able to work, but nevertheless find themselves searching for work for very long periods.[24]

So we return to the question: Why do workers and employers not bid nominal wages down when there is involuntary unemployment? Finding the answer to this question is essential for explaining why involuntary unemployment is a persistent feature of the market economy. Beyond the contractual rigidities discussed earlier in this chapter, the new Keynesians have developed a set of ideas that can be grouped together under the heading *efficiency wage theories*. Broadly speaking, these theories argue that firms may choose to pay a wage rate that is above the market-clearing rate because they believe that such a practice will, in a variety of ways, increase productivity and profits.

Microeconomics tells us that if a firm raises the wages of its workers, one of the outcomes will be a reduction in the firm's profits because of the increase in labor costs. But this may not be the case. Consider what might happen if the increase in wages causes workers to be more productive. If the increase in productivity more than offsets the increase in wages, then higher wages will produce lower production costs and higher profits. The positive effect of the real wage on productivity might lead business firms to pay *efficiency wages*—real wages above equilibrium wages—in order to realize higher profits. But what effect would this have on the labor market? We can see the effect in Figure 17–2.

If firms choose to pay an efficiency wage (W_1) that is higher than the market-clearing wage (W_e), then the effect is a disequilibrium in the labor market where the quantity supplied of labor (N_s) exceeds the quantity demanded (N_d). Those workers who are employed receive the efficiency wage, and those who are unemployed remain so until they can replace a worker who quits or is fired or until the demand for labor increases. In this model

[21] George A. Akerlof and Brian G. M. Main, "An Experience-Weighted Measure of Employment and Unemployment Durations," *American Economic Review*, Vol. 71, No. 5 (December 1981), Table 4, pp. 1003–1011.

[22] Hal Sider, "Unemployment Duration and Incidence: 1968–82," *American Economic Review*, Vol. 75, No. 3 (June 1985), Table 3, pp. 461–472.

[23] The results of such an analysis show an R^2 of .01 and the coefficient on the rate of growth in real GNP not statistically different from zero.

[24] Kim B. Clark and Lawrence H. Summers, "Labor Market Dynamics and Unemployment: A Reconsideration," *Brookings Papers on Economic Activity*, Vol. 1 (1979), pp. 13–72.

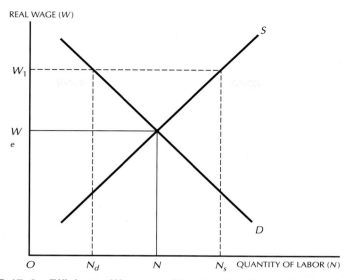

REAL WAGE (*W*)

FIGURE 17–2   Efficiency Wages and Involuntary Unemployment. If firms find that paying wages that are above their market clearing level (W_e) leads to increased productivity, they may pay an efficiency wage (W_1). This results in involuntary unemployment equal to $N_s - N_d$. This unemployment is involuntary because the unemployed workers cannot gain employment by bidding down the efficiency wage.

the unemployed worker cannot gain employment by offering to work for a lower wage, because employers do not wish to lose the extra productivity that paying the disequilibrium efficiency wage gives them. In this sense then, workers are involuntarily unemployed. As Robert H. DeFina, economist with the Philadelphia Federal Reserve Bank, argues:

> Unemployed individuals, whether they have quit, been fired, or entered the labor force for the first time, might try to get jobs by bidding down the wages of current workers. But in contrast to the simple competitive market situation, firms will not accept those offers. Firms have already weighed the benefits and costs of lower wages and decided that keeping wages high yields them their greatest profit.[25]

Explanations for Efficiency Wages

Efficiency wage theory can explain long-term unemployment, but how do we explain efficiency wages? New Keynesians identify four major explanations for efficiency wages.[26]

---

[25] Robert H. DeFina, "Explaining Long-Term Unemployment: A New Piece to an Old Puzzle," *Economic Review,* Federal Reserve Bank of Philadelphia, May–June 1987, p. 19.

[26] For a survey of efficiency wage models, see Janet L. Yellen, "Efficiency Wage Models of Unemployment," *American Economic Review,* Vol. 74, No. 2, pp. 200–205.

First, higher than equilibrium wages may reduce shirking on the job. Carl Shapiro of Princeton University and Joseph Stiglitz of Stanford University produced a formal shirking model that recognizes the threat of unemployment, given a high efficiency wage, as a device for labor discipline.[27] Their approach recognizes that workers control just how diligently they apply themselves to their work. The actual performances of workers can vary across a wide spectrum. At one end of the spectrum they may work hard and try to produce high-quality products, but at the other they may shirk. Here shirking includes taking unnecessary sick leave, extra-long coffee breaks, and generally goofing off. But there are costs and benefits involved in shirking. The cost of shirking is the risk that workers will get caught and lose their jobs and their wages. The benefits of shirking include the additional utility that is gained when workers are able to take more leisure.

The key idea in the Shapiro-Stiglitz version of efficiency wages is that employees may work more diligently if they receive a wage that is above the equilibrium real wage. Assume, first, that firms pay the equilibrium wage and hire all the labor that they need. In this scenario, when markets clear and there is no involuntary unemployment, the cost to workers of shirking is low. If caught, they can easily reenter the labor market and find other jobs. Now assume, instead, that firms decide to pay a wage rate that is above equilibrium—an efficiency wage. Now the cost of shirking has gone up. If workers are caught shirking, they lose the efficiency wage and may get only the market-clearing wage when and if they find new jobs.

It is time now to look back at the labor market and consider what happens when firms pay efficiency wages (Figure 17–2). The efficiency wage creates a disequilibrium in the labor market, resulting in a pool of involuntarily unemployed workers. According to Shapiro and Stiglitz these unemployed workers cannot become employed by offering to work at a lower wage. If workers are hired at a lower wage, they have an incentive to shirk on the job. Firms know this. Moreover, workers have no effective way to promise not to shirk if hired. Thus firms will not hire at the lower wage. Workers who lose jobs with firms that pay an efficiency wage must join the pool of unemployed and wait for openings to occur.

A second version of the efficiency wage view holds that firms will pay efficiency wages in order to minimize turnover costs.[28] *Turnover costs* arise when workers change jobs or pursue new job opportunities. Turnover costs come in many forms. Workers will be less productive if they are searching for new job opportunities while on the job. There are also costs associated with training new employees, and these trainees will initially have lower productivity than the more experienced workers they replace. Finally, there

---

[27] Carl Shapiro and Joseph E. Stiglitz, ''Equilibrium Unemployment as a Worker Discipline Device,'' *American Economic Review,* Vol. 74, No. 3, pp. 433–444.

[28] The formal model of labor turnover costs and efficiency wages can be found in Steven Salop, ''A Model of the Natural Rate of Unemployment,'' *American Economic Review,* Vol. 69, No. 2 (March 1979), pp. 117–125.

are the costs of actually conducting a search for new workers. These costs can be substantial. In 1982, Daniel Mitchell and Larry Kimbell, both of the University of California at Los Angeles, estimated that for a group of firms in Los Angeles the turnover costs were $3,600 for production workers, $2,300 for clerical workers, and $10,400 for professional and managerial workers.[29]

There are two reasons why a wage above the equilibrium level will reduce turnover costs. First, efficiency wages create a pool of unemployed workers. Workers find themselves in this pool if they leave their jobs, and the existence of a sizable pool of involuntarily unemployed workers makes leaving a job risky. Second, high efficiency wages also give workers an attractive incentive to stay on the job. The higher the wage is relative to the wage that a worker expects from another employer, the less likely it is that the worker will quit. Consequently, the turnover approach shows that firms can reduce "quits" and the costs associated with them by paying efficiency wages. From the perspective of macroeconomic theory, however, efficiency wages may lead to a waste of resources as workers become unemployed.

A third version of efficiency wage theory views above-market wages as a screening device.[30] In the *adverse selection model,* as this approach is called, business firms must hire from a heterogeneous pool of laborers. These laborers have differing skills, work habits, innate abilities, and other qualities not apparent on the surface. This approach assumes that good workers will be attracted into the pool of applicants only if the wage that is offered is higher than the market wage. By this logic it makes sense that firms will turn away laborers who offer to work for less. In the words of Professor Janet Yellen, ". . . each firm pays an efficiency wage and optimally turns away applicants offering to work for less than that wage. The willingness of an individual to work for less than the going wage places an upper bound on his ability, raising the firm's estimate that he is a lemon."[31]

Finally, Professor George Akerlof offers a novel approach to efficiency wage theory by drawing on sociological research. Akerlof views efficiency wages as a partial gift exchange between workers and employers.[32] Within a firm, workers possess a large degree of control over just how productive they are. If the workers feel they are being treated fairly, they can raise their work norms and be more productive, but if they feel they are being treated unfairly, they can respond in the opposite manner.

---

[29] Daniel J. B. Mitchell and Larry J. Kimbell, "Labor Market Contracts and Inflation," in Martin Neil Baily, ed., *Workers, Jobs and Inflation,* (Washington, D.C.: Brookings Institution, 1982), pp. 199–238, cited in Charles L. Schultze, "Microeconomic Efficiency and Nominal Wage Stickiness," *American Economic Review,* Vol. 75, No. 1 (March 1985), pp. 1–15.

[30] See Joseph E. Stiglitz, "Prices and Queues as Screening Devices in Competitive Markets," IMSSS Technical Report No. 212, Stanford University, August 1976, and Andrew Weiss, "Job Queues and Layoffs in Labor Markets with Flexible Wages," *Journal of Political Economy,* Vol. 88 (June 1980), pp. 526–538.

[31] Yellen, "Efficiency Wage Models of Unemployment," p. 203.

[32] George A. Akerlof, "Labor Contracts as Partial Gift Exchange," *Quarterly Journal of Economics,* Vol. 97, November 1982, pp. 543–569.

The wages a firm pays—both relative to other firms and in the wage structure within the firm—matter a great deal in determining how fairly workers feel they are being treated. Knowing this, an employer may raise wages above the market-clearing level as a gift to the workers. In return, the workers provide the employer with a gift by raising their norms of productivity above the minimum that is required. In this model, firms will pay wages above market-clearing levels because, though initially costly, it is an optimal strategy. It raises productivity and actually lowers the cost of a unit of output for the firm.[33] Professor Robert DeFina points out that sociological theory supports the efficiency wage argument even if there is no link between efficiency wages and labor force turnover:

> Firms might be able to pay lower wages and still retain their employees, but those employees might be less productive. Employees who feel cheated, for instance, will not "go the extra yard" for the firm, and might spend valuable time griping to co-workers. By generally increasing wages to levels considered fair or by raising certain worker's wages to maintain internal pay relationships that are deemed equitable, firms might enjoy a more satisfied and more productive workforce.[34]

These four arguments present the theoretical case for the existence of efficiency wages. Now the important question is this: are the efficiency wage theories supported by the evidence? If the evidence is there, then we have an important explanation for real wage rigidity, one in which wages are above equilibrium and create involuntary unemployment.

The Empirical Evidence for Efficiency Wages

Significant empirical support for efficiency wage theory comes from the case studies in sociology and psychology reviewed by Professor Akerlof.[35] In these studies the productivity of the subjects was positively related to how fairly they felt they were being treated. In one study by sociologist J. Stacy Adams, students were hired to do proofreading and were divided arbitrarily into two groups.[36] One group was told that they were qualified and the other told that they were not. Both groups, however, received the same wage. This last feature was intended to make the "unqualified" group feel overpaid. As a result there was far greater accuracy among the "unqualified" and "overpaid" group and a greater output per hour than was the case for the group that was "qualified." Professor Akerlof reviewed a group of similar studies and concluded that: "Not all of these studies reproduce the result that 'overpaid'

---

[33] George A. Akerlof, "Gift Exchange and Efficiency Wage Theory: Four Views," *American Economic Review,* Vol. 74, No. 2 (May 1984), pp. 79–83, and George A. Akerlof and Janet L. Yellen, "Fairness and Unemployment," *American Economic Review,* Vol. 78, No. 2, pp. 44–49.

[34] DeFina, "Explaining Long-Term Unemployment," p. 20.

[35] Akerlof, "Gift Exchange and Efficiency Wage Theory," p. 82.

[36] J. Stacy Adams, "Inequity in Social Exchange," in L. Berkowitz, ed., *Advances in Experimental Social Psychology,* Vol. 2, (New York: Academic Press, 1965), pp. 267–299.

workers will produce more, but, as might be expected, the evidence appears strongest for the withdrawal of services by workers who are led to believe they are underpaid."[37]

Beyond the experimental literature there is interesting direct evidence of the productivity-enhancing nature of efficiency wages. In 1914 the Ford Motor Company raised the wages of its production workers to $5 per day although the other auto manufacturers were paying only $2 to $3 per day. Jeremy Bulow of Stanford University and Lawrence Summers of Harvard University cite an engineering study of the effects of this wage change, in which the authors note that, "The workingmen are absolutely docile, and it is safe to say that since the last day of 1913, every single day has seen major reductions in Ford shops' labor costs."[38]

There have also been formal statistical tests of several of the predictions of efficiency wage theory. One prediction is that different firms will value the benefits of paying efficiency wages differently. The result will be a dispersion of wage rates for workers of similar skills and training across industries. For example, some firms may be able to minimize shirking if their workers can be supervised closely or if they find it efficient to pay piece rates for production. These firms are likely to pay market wages whereas firms that find supervision and piece rate expensive and inefficient often choose to pay efficiency wages. When one group of firms pays the market wage and another group pays efficiency wages, a *dual labor market* can arise. Dual labor markets, which are made up of a primary and a secondary labor market, have been researched by Peter Doeringer of Harvard University and Michael Piore of MIT.[39] In primary labor markets, as in automobile manufacturing, jobs are characterized by low quit rates, good working conditions, formal and informal on-the-job training, and high wages. In secondary labor markets, high turnover, poor working conditions, low skills, and low wages are the rule. Fastfood establishments fall into this category. Typically, the primary sector can be characterized as a payer of efficiency wages whereas the secondary sector pays market wages. In addition to the findings of Doeringer and Piore of a dual labor market in the U.S. economy, a body of statistical studies have found that similar workers receive substantially different rates of pay, depending on their industry affiliation, and that interindustry wage differentials can last for decades.[40]

---

[37] Akerlof, "Gift Exchange and Efficiency Wage Theory," p. 82.

[38] Jeremy I. Bulow and Lawrence H. Summers, "A Theory of Dual Labor Markets With Application to Industrial Policy, Discrimination and Keynesian Unemployment," *Journal of Labor Economics,* August 1986, p. 378.

[39] Peter B. Doeringer and Michael J. Piore, *Internal Labor Markets and Manpower Analysis,* (Lexington, Mass.: Heath Lexington Books, 1971).

[40] For example, see William T. Dickens and Lawrence F. Katz, "Inter-Industry Wage Differences and Industry Characteristics," in Kevin Lang and Jonathan Leonard, eds., *Unemployment and the Structure of Labor Markets* (London: Basil Blackwell, 1987), pp. 48–89, and Alan B. Krueger and Lawrence H. Summers, "Efficiency Wages and the Inter-Industry Wage Structure," *Econometrica,* Vol. 56 (March 1988), pp. 259–293.

A second prediction of efficiency wage theory is that wages are related to the job and the industry and not to the specific characteristics of the worker. Hence, when a worker moves from one job to another, efficiency wage theory predicts that the change in the wage should approximate the interindustry wage differential. For example, if a worker leaves a job in the secondary labor market for a job in the primary labor market, the increase in wages should be roughly the same as the interindustry wage differential. Lawrence F. Katz of Harvard University finds that this prediction is accurate. In other words, the impact of changing industries has about the same impact on an individual's wage as the difference in average wages between the industries.[41]

Work by Steven G. Allen of North Carolina State University finds that larger wage differentials between industries correlate with lower absenteeism among workers (when statistically controlled for other factors that might influence absenteeism). This finding can be interpreted as support for the shirking model. Since supervisors cannot be certain of the reason that a worker is absent, workers may be absent for good reason or they may be shirking.[42]

A study by Alan B. Krueger of Princeton University and Lawrence Summers supports another prediction of efficiency wage theory by finding that higher than equilibrium wages lead to lower turnover rates and longer job tenure, as well as higher productivity (also corrected for other possible causes).[43] Krueger and Summers also find that ". . . workers in better paying occupations and industries are more likely to report that their work is 'meaningful' to them and that they think about their work during their leisure time more than workers in low paying occupations and industries. These findings suggest that wage premiums are successful in eliciting better performance from workers."[44]

The empirical support for the new Keynesian efficiency wage arguments is strong,[45] but the new Keynesians have not stopped with the theory and evidence for these real rigidities. The theory explored to this point has been oriented toward the supply side of the economy and has explained how the economy might fail to adjust automatically from recessions. There has also been work among the new Keynesians concerning demand-side failures. One approach views insufficient aggregate spending as a market failure—a macroeconomic externality. Another demand-side approach, credit rationing the-

[41] Lawrence F. Katz, "Some Recent Developments in Labor Economics and Their Implications for Macroeconomics," *Journal of Money, Credit and Banking,* Vol. 20, No. 3 (August 1988), p. 515.

[42] Steven G. Allen, "Trade Unions, Absenteeism, and Exit Voice," *Industrial and Labor Relations Review,* Vol. 37, No. 3 (April 1984), pp. 331–345.

[43] Alan B. Krueger and Lawrence H. Summers, "Efficiency Wages and the Wage Structure," Discussion Paper No. 1247, Harvard Institute of Economic Research, June 1986.

[44] Ibid., p. 24.

[45] Lawrence F. Katz, "Efficiency Wage Theories: A Partial Evaluation," *National Bureau of Economic Research Working Paper,* No. 1906, April 1986, provides a survey of the empirical literature on efficiency wage theories.

ory, focuses on the failure of the economy to generate sufficient quantities of investment to bring the economy to full employment. It is to this work that we now turn.

Interdependence and Macroeconomic Externalities

An externality is a cost or benefit that does not accrue to the parties involved in an economic activity. For example, if you smoke a cigar in a crowded room, the people around you who are choking from the smoke are suffering a negative externality.

Many macroeconomists argue that because the money individuals spend and the income they receive are interdependent, an externality can arise from individual decisions to spend less. For example, if individuals decide to save more, the overall level of income in the economy falls because of their reduced spending. In this case, a group of individual decisions has the external effect of lowering national income. It follows also that if the economy is in a recession, saving to build up a cushion of protection is individually rational. However, this creates a macroeconomic externality because the individual acts of self-protection prevent the spending that is necessary for an expansion.

Another area in which interdependence can lead to poor macroeconomic performance is with respect to ''wait and see'' outcomes. Suppose that we have an economy that is characterized by imperfect competition. Each firm in the economy has control over its price, but the amount of profit any individual firm earns depends on what other firms do with respect to their prices. In this sense firms are interdependent. If, for example, demand falls, firms can reduce their prices and maintain their levels of production, although incurring menu costs, or they can hold prices steady and adjust output levels. With a reduction in demand each firm in the market must make a decision. If it reduces its price and other firms in the market do likewise, each firm will gain an increase in its profits that might be wiped out by menu costs. If it holds its price steady and reduces its output, and other firms do the same, it will lose some profit but will not pay the menu costs. Notice that there are two possible outcomes, one in which none of the firms reduce their prices and simply adjust output and another in which all firms reduce their prices and output is unchanged. Many new Keynesians argue that it is likely that an individual firm will respond to a reduction in nominal demand by reducing output, holding prices steady, and waiting to see the responses of other firms in the market. Over time, if other firms respond by reducing prices, the firm will follow along. In this case we have a price adjustment externality. When the firm finds it individually rational to maintain its price, sticky prices result and the economy fails to approach equilibrium at full employment.

Credit Rationing and Aggregate Demand[46]

It is the view of Keynes that recessions stem in large part from the failure of investment outlays to be sufficient to bring aggregate spending to a level that is consistent with full-employment output. Early Keynesians argued, in part, that the interest rate failed to fall sufficiently in recessions to bring about enough investment. This argument embodies the idea of the liquidity trap, covered in Chapter 6 (pages 184–85). They also argued that the investment demand schedule has a low elasticity, so investment spending is not responsive to the interest rate. Rather than placing so much attention on the interest rate as a key variable in determining the quantity of investment, the credit rationing approach analyzes the banker's decision to extend credit to borrowers.[47]

One of the key responsibilities of a bank is to assess the likelihood that any loan it makes will be paid back. Such an assessment depends on the quality of the borrower and on general economic conditions, factors on which there is likely to be a high degree of uncertainty. The lender does not have perfect information about the investment that his loan will finance. If it is a high-quality project, it is likely that the loan will be repaid. If it is not, the bank is likely to lose money. The bank's assessment of the quality of borrowers, in combination with its assessment of economic conditions, determines just how much credit is extended. If bankers expect the economy to expand, they will be eager to extend credit, because an economic expansion generally will increase the profitability of borrowers' investment projects and, simultaneously, the likelihood that loans will be repaid.

On the other hand, if bankers expect economic growth to slow or the economy to move into a recession, they will make fewer loans or they will reduce the size of each loan they make. Bankers know the default rate will increase during hard times. This adds up to *credit rationing,* which means that firms may be willing and able to pay equilibrium interest rates but they may not be able to get as much credit as they desire. Credit rationing is a constraint on investment, and it also may be a constraint on the ability of some firms that require additional working capital to continue their operations. Credit rationing may reduce investment and lead to lower levels of economic activity. Thus, the expectation of poor economic conditions may become a self-fulfilling prophecy for bankers.

---

[46] For a more technical discussion of credit rationing, see Olivier Blanchard and Stanley Fischer, *Lectures on Macroeconomics,* (Cambridge, Mass.: MIT Press, 1989), pp. 478–488.

[47] The material in this section draws on the work of Joseph E. Stiglitz and Andrew Weiss. For a technical treatment of the material see their article, "Credit Rationing in Markets with Imperfect Information," *American Economic Review,* Vol. 71, No. 3 (June 1981), pp. 393–410. See also Bruce Greenwald, Joseph E. Stiglitz, and Andrew Weiss, "Informational Imperfections in the Capital Market and Macroeconomic Fluctuations," *American Economic Review,* Vol. 74, No. 2 (May 1984), pp. 194–199.

Why do not banks simply increase their interest rates to compensate for the increase in perceived risk? There are two reasons for not doing so, according to credit rationing theory. First, banks may prefer to ration credit because higher interest rates give borrowers an incentive to take on riskier projects. Borrowers may feel pressed to take on riskier projects in the hope of achieving high-enough returns to pay the higher interest rates. Thus, an increase in the interest rate may increase the risk of bankruptcy for the borrower and so reduce the expected return on the loan for the bank. Second, if a bank raises the rate of interest, the more conservative potential borrowers in the market may choose not to borrow, because they fear that higher interest rates would push them closer to bankruptcy.

From the bank's perspective, then, the pool of borrowers is increasingly dominated by more risky firms, especially those that will willingly borrow at higher rates because they do not plan to repay the loan anyway. Hence, instead of meeting the loan demands of its borrowers at higher interest rates, banks will ration credit when economic conditions appear to be deteriorating. In this sense there can be an excess demand for credit that is not eliminated by adjustments in the rate of interest. If banks had perfect foresight about economic conditions and the profitability of the investment projects of their customers, they would be able to vary their interest rates as a means of compensating for risk. Like everyone else, though, bankers do not have perfect foresight. The absence of perfect information means that often they will adjust the quantity of loans rather than interest rates. As with the other new Keynesian theories discussed, credit rationing theory implies that quantity (in this case the quantity of loans) adjustments may be made rather than adjustments in nominal (price) variables, such as the interest rate.

Let us now turn to some of the policy implications of the new Keynesian theory. The most general one is that even with the rational expectations assumption wage and price rigidities ensure that activist policy measures are both possible and worthwhile.

The Policy Implications of the New Keynesian Economics

As just indicated, the principal policy implication of the new Keynesian economics is that macroeconomic policy can have an impact on output and employment *even* if people adhere to rational expectations rules and the policy is anticipated. Refer back to Figure 17–1 once again. New Keynesian macroeconomic theory argues that once the economy arrives at p_1 and Y_1—for whatever reason—it may stay there for a long time because wages and prices fail to adjust downward. This is the case even if people correctly anticipate the price level. The market imperfections and other practices like markup pricing discussed in this chapter rule out a rapid downward adjustment of wages and prices.

If the new Keynesians are right, the self-adjusting mechanism works only over a long period of time. Hence, expansionary monetary and fiscal policies are appropriate as means of shifting the aggregate demand curve rightward and thus moving the economy back to a high-employment level of output. This brings us to a major and profound policy conclusion of the new Keynesian model, one that flatly contradicts the new classical argument that only *unanticipated* policies can have impacts on real output and employment. J. Peter Neary of University College, Dublin, and Joseph E. Stiglitz argue that from the new Keynesian perspective, fully anticipated policy measures will have a *greater* impact than unanticipated policy.[48] Assume that the economy is at p_1 and Y_1 in Figure 17–1 and that the government announces an expansionary monetary policy that aims to increase real output from Y_1 to Y_n in a future period. If we assume that the public fully anticipates the future effects of this policy, current savings will be reduced because laborers expect the demand for labor to increase in the future and thus future employment and the real wage to increase. This will increase the value of the multiplier, and as a result the anticipated policy will be more rather than less effective.

　　Results of this kind have led new Keynesians to argue for policies that can be easily anticipated. Many of their policy proposals have taken the form of activist policy rules. Activist rules are such that they adjust a policy variable in response to economic conditions, but in a preset and regular way. Many new Keynesians believe that if such rules were used by policymakers, they would soon become a part of the model that people use to assess the effects of policy. Furthermore, once the rules were incorporated into the models people used to form their expectations, people could anticipate policy more easily. For example, one such activist rule, proposed by John B. Taylor, calls for an increase in the growth of the money supply whenever real GNP growth falls below its long-run growth trend, but no accommodating money growth during inflations.[49] With this rule in place, people would learn over time to anticipate expansionary policy in the future when the economy began to slow, but not to expect an accommodating policy toward inflation. The activist rule exploits the notion that people behave according to rational expectations theory to make a more powerful argument for activist policy.

Summary

1. New Keynesian economics is a macroeconomic perspective that emerged in the late 1970s and 1980s. It accepted the new classical economics' thesis of rational expectations, but challenged the view that markets clear

---

[48] J. P. Neary and Joseph E. Stiglitz, "Towards a Reconstruction of Keynesian Economics: Expectations and Constrained Equilibria," *Quarterly Journal of Economics,* Vol. 98, Supplement, pp. 199–228.

[49] John B. Taylor, "Stabilization, Accommodation and Monetary Rules," *American Economic Review,* Vol. 70, No. 2 (May 1981), pp. 145–149.

continuously. New Keynesian economists argue that wages and prices are sticky; they move upward easily but do not move downward.

2. If markets do not clear continuously and quickly, then the economic system will not normally be at full or high employment. Therefore, policy actions to get the economy to full employment are justified, even though expectations are formed rationally.

3. Extensive empirical research by new Keynesian economists has uncovered a variety of reasons why firms are willing to pay wages higher than market-clearing equilibrium levels, and why, too, business firms strongly resist any downward adjustment in their prices.

4. A major reason for rigidity, or stickiness, in money wages is found in the widespread existence of labor contracts in the economy. Most labor-management contracts are written for a three-year period; this means that wage rates cannot be changed in response to short-term changes in product and labor markets.

5. Among the major reasons for inflexibility in prices are the practice of markup pricing and the phenomenon of menu costs. Markup pricing involves adding a fixed percentage, a markup, to costs, which are determined primarily by wage costs. Menu costs mean that there are important costs involved whenever firms change prices and which may offset or exceed any gain from reducing prices to win more sales. Firms also may wait and see what rivals will do before they change prices. These practices make for rigid prices.

6. The existence of efficiency wages may also be a source of involuntary unemployment. Efficiency wages are wages above the market-clearing level, which some firms are willing to pay because they lead to a more productive work force. This is rational behavior by the firm because it may lead to higher profits, even though it results in higher social costs since some workers remain voluntarily unemployed. Efficiency wages also minimize on-the-job shirking by workers and reduce turnover costs. They are used, too, as a screening device to attract higher-caliber workers to a firm. The empirical evidence supporting the existence of efficiency wages is strong.

7. Demand-side failures are called ''macroeconomic externalities'' by the new Keynesian economists. Two important sources of demand-side failure are attempts by individuals to increase their saving, which have the external effect of lower aggregate demand, and the tendency of oligopolistic firms to follow a ''wait and see'' policy when demand falls. This lead them to hold prices steady and reduce output, which also causes a decline in aggregate demand.

8. At the macroeconomic level the phenomenon of credit rationing may depress aggregate demand, particularly in times when banks fear difficult economic times lie ahead. Credit rationing means that banks rely more on discretion and personal judgment than on interest rates in determining which firms get loans. Credit rationing is another way in which output (the supply of credit) rather than prices (interest rates) adjusts to changing economic conditions.

9. Two major policy implications flow from the new Keynesian economics. The first is that even if expectations are formed rationally and a policy change is anticipated, discretionary fiscal or monetary policy actions are justified. This is because of the long adjustment lags, which are caused by sticky wages and prices and can be shortened by policy actions. The second implication is that policy actions may be strengthened, not nullified as the new classical economists maintain, when they are fully anticipated. This is because the policy actions reinforce actions already being taken privately in accordance with the new classical view of matters. Thus, new Keynesians argue for policies that can be easily anticipated and suggest that there should be activist policy rules.

18 Post Keynesian Economics

As WE HAVE SEEN, the new classical economics discussed in Chapter 16 rejects the Keynesian relationships found in the income-expenditure model developed in Part II of this text. It also represents a return to the belief of earlier classical economists in the *inherent* stability of a market economy and its self-correcting tendencies. In contrast, the new Keynesians reject the new classical view on the futility of all policy prescriptions, at least for the short run, but they do draw on the new classical doctrine of rational expectations to explain how individual economic agents (consumers and businesses) form their expectations. This is part of their efforts to build an acceptable microeconomic foundation for Keynesian economics, a foundation that views wage and price stickiness as the norm, not the exception.

The *Post Keynesians,* the final macroeconomic perspective we shall examine, differ in significant ways from all the analyses we have just reviewed. They reject attempts to revive classical economics and apply it to the macroeconomy as both unworkable and unrealistic. They also have been sharply critical of the early post-World War II interpretations of Keynes, what has been called the *neoclassical synthesis.* They regard this and other efforts to build rigid, mathematical models of the Keynesian system as an attempt to push the ideas of Keynes into a classical mold and thus strip the Keynesian revolution of all significance. The point of departure for the Post Keynesians is what they regard as the neglect by post-World War II interpretations of

Keynes of important elements in his thinking, elements present in *The General Theory,* but largely passed over. They go beyond this, because they also seek to develop new theoretical insights into the workings of contemporary systems of market capitalism, economies far removed in time and structure from the simple competitive models that characterize the classical counterrevolutions. Their insights and theories are Keynesian in origin and inspiration, but involve much more than an attempt to update *The General Theory.*

Fundamental Concerns of the Post Keynesians

The Post Keynesian economists are a diverse group, more so, perhaps, than the monetarists, the new classical economists, or the supply-siders. In one major subgroup we find economists like Robert Clower of the University of South Carolina, and Axel Leijonhufvud, of the University of California, Los Angeles, who have challenged the Walrasian system of general equilibrium, which is one of the two key elements in the new classical economics.[1] A second group, largely but not wholly centered at Cambridge University in England, has concentrated on the dynamics of full-employment growth and paid special attention to the linkages between income distribution and growth. Among the economists in this subgroup we find Geoffrey Harcourt, Roy Harrod, the late Nicholas Kaldor, the late Joan Robinson, and Jan Kregel, as well as the late Alfred Eichner of Rutgers University. Finally, there is a third group whose interests are directed toward the workings of the real-world market economy, not an idealized vision of market systems such as is found in the new classical economics. The real-world market economy operates in *historic* time, is characterized by a high degree of uncertainty, and is one in which both financial institutions and the power of organized groups play a crucial role. Economists who fit into this subcategory include, among others, Paul Davidson of the University of Tennessee; Hyman Minsky of the Jerome Levy Institute, the late Sidney Weintraub of the University of Pennsylvania, and John Kenneth Galbraith of Harvard University.

Rejection of Walrasian General Equilibrium Theory

Perhaps the most fundamental proposition common to all Post Keynesian economists, irrespective of the particular subgroup to which they belong, is

---

[1] Strictly speaking, Professors Clower and Leijonhufvud are more properly associated with the new Keynesian than with the Post Keynesian school. They are included here, however, because Clower's important article "The Keynesian Counterrevolution: A Theoretical Appraisal," in F. H. Hahn and F. Brechling, eds., *The Theory of Interest Rates* (London: Macmillan & Co., 1965), and Leijonhufvud's seminal study, *On Keynesian Economics and the Economics of Keynes* (New York: Oxford University Press, 1968) offered important theoretical insights into themes that are of major significance in the Post Keynesian view. This is particularly the case with respect to Post Keynesian rejection of Walrasian general equilibrium and the argument that post-World War II equilibrium models of Keynesian economics neglect important elements in *The General Theory.*

a rejection of the Walrasian theory of general equilibrium as the micro foundation for macroeconomic theory. Walrasian general equilibrium theory is the basis for the belief that, when competition is present, a market system is inherently self-correcting and will automatically lead to the full utilization of labor and all other resources.

Post Keynesians find the Walrasian theory incompatible with Keynesian economics. To see how, we begin with a brief review of the key ideas in Walrasian general equilibrium theory. In the Walrasian model, planned demand represents the goods and services that people want to obtain through exchange in order to satisfy their wants. Planned supply, on the other hand, represents the goods and services, including labor services, that people bring to the marketplace to exchange for those things they want. In this context all supply, following Say's law, represents the demand for something. The quantitites of goods and services demanded cannot be determined, however, in the absence of prices. To put it differently, the quantity of demand or supply for anything depends on the price that must be paid for it when it is acquired or the price received for it when it is given up. This principle applies to labor as well as to goods and services. Prices must be known, and when prices are known, the demand and supply functions (that is, schedules) are established for all goods and services (including labor) traded in the marketplace.

Now the famous Walrasian auctioneer enters the picture.[2] A demand or a supply schedule always represents the planned (or *ex ante*) purchases or sales of any good or service at an array of all possible prices. The role of the auctioneer is to continue to call out prices until *planned* demand and supply are in balance in *every single market.* The auctioneer, in other words, supplies the basic information that makes it possible for all participants in the market to act and in acting to be on their demand or supply schedules. Only when the participants have information about prices in every other market can they act.

In the Walrasian system it is crucial to understand that *no* trading or exchange can take place until planned demand and planned supply match in every market. The job of the auctioneer is to continue to call out new sets of prices for everything being traded until prices are found that will *clear* all markets simultaneously. This is what Walras called *tatonnement,* a process of groping toward a general equilibrium solution for the whole economy.

Now we come to a crucial point in Walrasian theory, crucial both to the theory itself and to the Clower and Leijonhufvud criticisms of that theory. In a Walrasian general equilibrium situation, there can be no *false trading.* False trading is the exchange of goods and services at other than equilibrium prices. The miracle that the Walrasian auctioneer works is to have everyone in the

---

[2] Walras invented the idea of the auctioneer to explain in nonmathematical language what he was attempting to demonstrate by mathematics. At that time few economists understood mathematics. Walras was originally trained as an engineer, hence his interest in explaining the economy in mathematical terms.

market hold off making any exchange until equilibrium prices are known for everything being traded. Then all trade takes place instantaneously.

Here is the entry point for the Clower-Leijonhufvud criticism.[3] Walrasian general equilibrium theory is an idealized picture, far removed from real-world markets and exchange. In the real world, false trading takes place all the time. As a practical matter, it is nearly impossible to determine whether any price in any particular market is an equilibrium price; nevertheless, prices exist and exchange takes place. What is the consequence of this? If false trading takes place, then there is exchange at other than equilibrium prices. But if this happens, then *effective* demand may depart from planned demand (Professor Clower calls planned demand *notional* demand). This opens up the possibility for disequilibrium states because insufficient information is being conveyed to all participants in the market. Why this is so can be readily illustrated through a simple supply and demand diagram representing the labor market, as shown in Figure 18–1. Before we see how this works, however, we need to understand another principle, one that Professor Clower terms *Say's principle*. This is the idea that a buyer always plans to finance

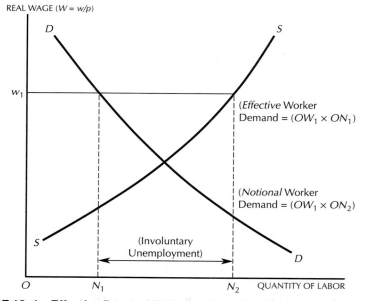

FIGURE 18–1 Effective Demand Failure in the Labor Market. If ON_2 workers were employed, they would spend on the basis of the income they received from this amount of employment ($ON_2 \times OW_1$), but since there is no way workers can convey this information to employers *in advance* of employment, employers will offer only ON_1 amounts of employment. An informational failure keeps the economy from full employment.

---

[3] See Clower, ''The Keynesian Counterrevolution,'' pp. 103–125.

purchases from the sale of goods or services. As far as workers are concerned, this means that it is the wages obtained through the sale of a year's labor service that will finance their purchases of goods and services. In Walrasian terms, the workers' planned (notional) demand for goods and services is dependent on the incomes they expect to receive from the sale of their labor services. The latter are their planned sales and are derived from the supply schedule for labor.

In Figure 18–1 the wage is W_1. At this wage, which is not an equilibrium wage, firms will use only ON_1 units of labor. This will be their effective demand for labor if we assume that an exchange actually takes place at the wage W_1. In the Walrasian system, of course, no exchange would take place at this wage since it would amount to false trading. Workers, given the wage W_1, will supply labor in the amount of ON_2. This is their planned (or notional) supply. Now, in a Walrasian world, they plan to spend on the basis of their planned supply of work, since this supply represents their demand for goods and services if we assume that their planned supply of work is translated into realized employment. Here comes the rub. The workers' planned (notional) demand for goods and services depends on their expectation that they will have a realized income based on their planned (notional) supply of labor. In the figure this is equal to $(OW_1 \times ON_2)$. Because in the real world there is no Walrasian auctioneer, workers have *no way* to convey to prospective employers the information that, if ON_2 workers are hired, they will spend this income and it will justify employers hiring at this level. Instead, employers, confronted with the wage W_1, will only hire ON_1 workers, whose total income—and hence effective demand—will be equal to $(OW_1 \times ON_1)$. Thus, we have a clear case of *effective demand failure*. There is involuntary unemployment—the distance N_1N_2 in the figure—because it is the realized current income of the workers derived from actual employment $(OW_1 \times ON_1)$ that governs the amount of employment firms can offer. Unemployment emerges and may persist, perhaps for a long time.

The Economy and Historic Time

One of the crucial weaknesses of Walrasian general equilibrium theory is its inability to deal with real, historic time. Models based on Walrasian theory are static and timeless. This follows from the basic nature of equilibrium. Equilibrium, as Nobel laureate and British economist Sir John Hicks has pointed out, is by definition a state in which the relevant variables are not changing; hence, time is not involved in equilibrium analysis.[4]

The absence of time in classical economics and in the Walrasian general equilibrium model leads to a second major proposition concerning which there is basic agreement among Post Keynesian economists. This is that the

---

[4] Sir John R. Hicks, ''Some Questions of Time in Economics,'' in Anthony M. Tang, ed., *Evolution, Welfare, and Time in Economics* (Lexington, Mass.: D. C. Heath, 1976), p. 140.

economy is seen as an ongoing process that exists in *real*, historic time. This is a simple idea, yet it has far-reaching ramifications for economics and economic theorizing. When we say that the economy and economic processes exist in real, historic time, we are saying that they exist in a world in which the past is known and irrevocable, but the future is unknown. The economy, in other words, moves continuously from a known past through the present to an unknown future. Furthermore, the process is irreversible—a view basically different from what exists in equilibrium analysis, wherein a system when disturbed returns to its original state. The knowledge observers can have about the future is, at best, no more than the knowledge of probabilities; they may surmise, guess, or speculate what might happen, but they can never know for sure what will happen. This is especially relevant for the investment decision, since such decisions are entirely future oriented.

Because the economy has an historic past, the economic process cannot be understood without knowledge of this history. To put it somewhat differently, the economic process is both evolutionary and cultural; that is to say we cannot detach the economy and economic behavior from the historic and cultural environment in which it takes place. To an extent, then, *economic principles are necessarily limited by time, place, and culture*—a fact that some may find disturbing because it limits the possibility of developing a general theory of the economic process that could be applied to any society at any time, irrespective of its technology or institutions. In sum, evolutionary change is the normal state of affairs, not movement toward a state of rest at some fixed level of economic activity.

Uncertainty and Expectations

The real world of historic time is dominated by uncertainty, the third key proposition that unites Post Keynesian economists. Uncertainty exists simply because we cannot know the future, no matter how good our knowledge of the past may be. In *The General Theory,* uncertainty emerges as, perhaps, the key element in economic life. It follows from the basic fact of uncertainty that expectations play a critical role in the economic process. What we do economically and how we do it are strongly influenced by our expectations concerning the future. What distinguishes the Post Keynesians in this respect is their belief that the foundations for expectations are uncertain and volatile. As we saw in Chapter 16, the new classical economists also strongly emphasize the role expectations play in the determination of economic activity, but they argue that their foundations are built on carefully analyzed statistical certainty.

To underscore this difference and to emphasize as strongly as possible how uncertainty and expectations enter into Post Keynesian economic thinking, it is instructive to review explicitly how Keynes viewed the matter. The problem with the classical economists, according to Keynes, was that they assumed a certainty of knowledge when such certainty was simply not possible. The classical economists held that ''facts and expectations were assumed to be given in a definite and calculable form; and risks, of which, though admitted, not much notice was taken, were supposed to be capable of an exact actuarial computation. The calculus of probability . . . was supposed to be capable of reducing uncertainty to the same calculable status as that of certainty itself."[5]

Unfortunately, Keynes maintained, most of the time human beings have only the vaguest idea of any but the most direct consequences of their acts. Moreover, the consequences with which we may be most concerned are often remote in time. This is especially true for one of the most important acts with which economics is concerned, namely, the accumulation of wealth—that is, investment. As Keynes went on to say, "the whole object of the accumulation of wealth is to produce results, or potential results, at a comparatively distant, and sometimes *indefinitely* distant, date."[6] Unfortunately, the knowledge on which decisions involving the accumulation of wealth (investment) must be based is highly uncertain. Keynes explained what he meant by "uncertain" knowledge as follows:

> By "uncertain" knowledge let me explain. I do not mean merely to distinguish what is known for certain from what is only probable. The game of roulette is not subject, in this sense, to uncertainty; nor is the prospect of a Victory bond being drawn. Or again the expectation of life is only slightly uncertain. Even the weather is only moderately uncertain. The sense in which I am using the term is that in which the prospect of a European war is uncertain, or the price of copper and the rate of interest twenty years hence, or the obsolescence of a new invention, or the position of private wealth holders in the social system in 1970. *About these matters there is no scientific basis on which to form any calculable probability whatever. We simply do not know.*[7]

Yet decisions must be made, and they must be made on the basis of expectations held about future outcomes for which, as Keynes said, there are no scientific grounds for calculable probability. What, then, do we do? As we saw in Chapter 16 (pages 632–33) when discussing the differences between expectations formation in the new classical economics and in Keynes, people form their expectations by falling back on assumptions that (1) the present is a "more serviceable guide to the future than past experience has shown it to have been," (2) existing market conditions are a sound guide to future market conditions, and (3) average or majority opinion is better than our own as a guide to the future. The practical meaning of this is that expectations formed in this fashion rest on a flimsy foundation, subject to "sudden and violent changes. . . . All these pretty, polite techniques, made for a well-panelled board room and a nicely regulated market, are liable to collapse."[8]

There are two critical points at which uncertainty and the volatility of

---

[5] John Maynard Keynes, "The General Theory of Employment," *The Quarterly Journal of Economics,* February 1937, p. 213.

[6] Ibid.

[7] Ibid., (italics added).

[8] Ibid., p. 215.

expectations based on uncertainty enter into the economic process. They enter, first, into the decisions that households, firms, and financial institutions make concerning their portfolio decisions, that is, decisions on the kind of assets they wish to hold. Second, they enter the formation of views held by business firms and lending institutions about the prospective yield for new capital assets. Liquidity and investment decisions—decisions which are key factors in explaining the ups and downs of the market economy—rest on expectations that are intimately bound up with an uncertain and unknowable future. The inescapable and practical conclusion to be drawn from this fact is that instability is *endemic* to the economic system; it is *not* something imposed on it by random events external to how the system functions.

In contrast to the Post Keynesian view with respect to the pervasive influence of uncertainty and the manner in which expectations are formed, the new classical economics, in effect, deals with uncertainty as if it were the same as predictable risk. As Paul Davidson has said, these economists "assume that the uncertainty of the future can be adequately represented by probability statements about an economic world which, without being absolutely determinate, is at least statistically predictable."[9] What this means, according to Professor Davidson, is that the new classical economists are simply replacing the certainty about the future which was built into traditional classical economics with the concept of "a known probability distribution." Instead of perfect foreknowledge, economic actors now possess actuarial knowledge; this means that they can calculate actuarial costs and benefits and thus act in the same manner as if they had perfect foreknowledge. Human behavior, therefore, fits into the general equilibrium mold, since it is not only rational in the sense in which this term was explained in Chapter 16, but all expectations are eventually realized; this is also an essential outcome in the Walrasian general equilibrium model.

Finally, there is an even more fundamental point that flows out of Keynes's ideas about uncertainty. Professor G. L. S. Shackle says that in *The General Theory* Keynes challenged the central tenet of traditional economics, which is that people pursue their interests by applying reason to their circumstances. This, of course, is the meaning of rational behavior in the classical sense. But, according to Professor Shackle, reason cannot achieve practical results unless information is complete. Only if this is the case can it be assumed that maximizing behavior is an accurate representation of the way human beings actually behave. This, perhaps, is one of the most disturbing of all the implications that flow from the Keynesian view of uncertainty, striking as it does at the central organizing principle for nearly the entire corpus of contemporary economic theory. We are not, says Professor Shackle, the "assured masters of known circumstance via reason, but the prisoners of time."[10] It would not

---

[9] Paul Davidson, "Post Keynesian Economics: Solving the Crisis in Economic Theory," in *The Crisis in Economic Theory,* Special Issue, *The Public Interest,* 1980, p. 160.

[10] G. L. S. Shackle, "Keynes and Today's Establishment in Economic Theory: A View," *Journal of Economic Literature,* June 1973, pp. 516–519.

be correct to argue that at this stage the Post Keynesians have arrived at a more suitable approach to human behavior than is found in the classical thinking. This is not the case. They do take a different approach, however. They do not start with the *a priori* assumption as in classical economics that human behavior in the economic sphere is of necessity rational; that is, it involves maximizing.[11] In the face of uncertainty of the kind described by Keynes, the Post Keynesians argue that human behavior is largely shaped or determined by the social, cultural, and economic institutions through which people act. Thus, to understand human behavior we must begin by understanding the dominant institutions of a society.

Institutions and the Economy

Post Keynesian economists stress institutions—especially economic and political institutions—for two major reasons. First, this follows from their rejection of neoclassical general equilibrium theory. In the latter theory, as Professor Davidson has pointed out, there are no institutions of any significance, save the institution of the market itself. Given markets, price flexibility, and atomistic competition—all essential ingredients in the Walrasian view of the economic universe—other institutions have no theoretical significance. They do not affect the outcome of events, which, as we have seen, is a general equilibrium situation in which all resources are fully utilized. Second, if this is not a true view of the world, then institutions count. In the view of Post Keynesians, human behavior is shaped by and filtered through institutions; the effect is often to give behavior a collective rather than an individualistic character. This contrasts sharply with the neoclassical view in which human behavior is always individualistic and free of institutional influences. Consequently, if we want to understand what happens in the economy, we must understand the institutions that shape and influence human behavior.

What are the institutions that are of major concern to the Post Keynesian economists? They are found in two major areas of economic life. First, there are those that revolve around money and finance, including the institution of money itself. They are crucial to the functioning of capitalistic, market economies. Second, there are institutions that reflect the importance that organized groups play in the life of the economy. The modern large corporation and the trade union belong in this category.

---

[11] This is a major point of difference between the new Keynesians and the Post Keynesians. The former do not challenge classical maximizing behavior. This is where they start. As Robert J. Gordon points out in a comprehensive summation of the new Keynesian economics, "Most new-Keynesian models combine rational expectations with maximizing behavior at the level of the individual agent. Any attempt to build a model based upon irrational behavior or submaximizing behavior is viewed as *cheating.* . . . So the *game* is to tease a failure of macro markets to clear from a starting point of rational expectations and the maximization of profits and individual welfare at the micro level." Robert J. Gordon, "What is New-Keynesian Economics?" *Journal of Economic Literature,* Vol. 28 (September 1990), p. 1137 (italics added). Professor Gordon does not specify precisely what he means by cheating, but the tenor of his remarks is critical of the maximization hypothesis and the unwillingness of theorists, especially micro theorists, to submit this tenet to empirical scrutiny.

The Institution of Money. Of all the institutions that color the Post Keynesian view of the economy, none is more central than money. Why is money so important to the Post Keynesians? Why is it seen as *the* central institution in the economy? These are the questions of key importance for understanding the Post Keynesian preoccupation with money. As pointed out earlier in Chapters 5 and 11, one of Keynes's major criticisms of classical economics was that it was a theory which applied only to a *real exchange economy,* Keynes's description of an economy in which money, while an instrument of great convenience, is "transitory and neutral in its effect."[12] Money is merely a link between transactions and is not supposed either to affect the essential nature of transactions, which always involve real things (hence the term "real exchange economy"), or to modify the motives and decisions of the parties involved in any transactions. But Keynes saw the matter in a fundamentally different way. Money, in his view, is *not* neutral; its role is not limited to merely facilitating the exchange of real things. Keynes anticipated that *The General Theory* would not only offer an explanation for the determination of output and employment, but that it would also constitute a "monetary theory of production." This is a key point, because the standard, post-World War II interpretation of Keynes (the neoclassical synthesis) has been criticized for holding that money does not matter.[13] Such a viewpoint, according to the Post Keynesian perspective, runs counter to the real spirit of *The General Theory.*

By a monetary theory of production, Keynes meant an economy in which money "plays a part of its own and affects motives and decisions and is, in short, one of the operative factors in the situation, so that the course of events cannot be predicted, either in the long period or in the short, without a knowledge of the behavior of money between the first state and the last. And it is this which we ought to mean when we speak of a *Monetary Economy.*"[14] In short, money is *not* neutral, it is not a mere convenience, something that facilitates an underlying, *real* process of exchange. Rather, it dominates the economic process. Making money is seen as the end objective of economic activity, and production is a means to this end, rather than the other way around as in the classical analysis.

Several significant corollary ideas flow from the foregoing. In a pecuniary society, money becomes the *ultimate* consumer good, the thing that is valued above all else. This is so because it opens the door to power, to wealth, to attention, to status and prestige, to all the things that humans value along with and often to a greater extent than consumption. Production is, of course, crucial, but it is seen in a different perspective than it is seen in classical economics. In a monetary economy, money flows to people who control those things that command a price, that have value in the marketplace. Marketplace

---

[12] John Maynard Keynes, "On the Theory of a Monetary Economy," *Nebraska Journal of Economics and Business,* Autumn 1963, p. 7.

[13] The argument was that money did not matter in a policy sense because of the interest inelasticity of the investment demand schedule and, perhaps, the interest elasticity of the demand for money.

[14] Keynes, "On the Theory of a Monetary Economy," p. 9.

value can originate in productive activity—in classical analysis this appears to be the only source of value—but it can also result from the activities of persons skilled in the arts of manipulation (what Keynes described as a speculative in contrast to an enterprise type of activity) or from the acquisition of sufficient power to control the terms on which an exchange takes place. Keynes was especially critical of highly organized financial markets like the New York Stock Exchange, believing that they fostered speculation much more than enterprise.

Money is crucially important, too, because it provides the necessary link between the present and the future, a future which, as we have seen, is shrouded in uncertainty and hence unknowable. What the possession of money does, according to Keynes, is "lull our disquietude" about the future. The desire to hold money as a form of wealth is a barometer of "the degree of our distrust of our own calculations and conventions concerning the future."[15] This involves the role that money plays as a source of liquidity. In the standard *IS-LM* model of the economy (Chapter 6), the distinction is made between the real sphere—the *IS* curve—and the monetary sphere—the *LM* curve. In the Post Keynesian view, the *IS-LM* model, while useful, fails to capture the essential properties of money that make the economic system inherently unstable. What may happen, according to Keynes, is that, periodically, fear and uncertainty about the future create such a strong demand for the safety found in money—a demand for liquidity—that collapse in the real sector of the economy is brought about. The problem lies in the institutional peculiarities of money. It is not like other commodities. It does not obey the normal laws of the market, increasing in supply when the demand for it goes up—as when there is a scramble for liquidity—or by having other things substituted for it when its price (the rate of interest) goes up. The demand for money, because of its peculiar ability to calm our fears with respect to an uncertain future, is the systemic flaw in the system. "Unemployment develops," according to Keynes, "because people want the moon; —men cannot be employed when the object of desire (i.e., money) is something which cannot be produced and the demand for which cannot be readily choked off."[16]

One more aspect of a monetary economy needs to be stressed. In all modern economies, as Professor Davidson points out, "contracts denominated in money terms are a ubiquitous human institution. . . . "[17] This means that when production takes place, future dates are specified for both delivery and payment. Production, of course, takes time, and during this time labor must be paid and materials used in production must be purchased. Both these activities require money or finance. This is not the case in the world of Walrasian

---

[15] Keynes, "The General Theory of Employment," p. 216.

[16] Keynes, *The General Theory*, p. 235.

[17] Paul Davidson, *Post Keynesian Macroeconomic Theory: A Foundation for Successful Economic Policies for the Twenty-First Century* (Cambridge: Edward Elgar, 1994), p. 17.

general equilibrium, for there it is assumed that all goods are traded simultaneously and that all payments are made at the instant trade takes place. In the actual economic world, producers incur obligations to make payments to labor and to suppliers while production is taking place. Unless they were able to do this, efficient production planning would not be possible in the world of real, historic time. The expectation is that the sale of output will supply the necessary proceeds to cover all the costs incurred in production. Meanwhile it is crucial that entrepreneurs have the necessary liquidity—that is, money on hand—or access to necessary finance through borrowing to sustain the production process until such time as the product is finished and sold. Then, but not until then, obligations that are incurred in order for production to take place can be liquidated. For any of this to happen, including production itself, there must be an array of money and finance-creating institutions.

Trade Unions, Large Corporations, and Other Institutions. Professor Davidson's emphasis on the practice of *forward contracting* in today's market economy leads us to consider the second major area in which institutions play a critical role—the domain of organized groups. Of all the types of forward contracting taking place in the economy, none is more widespread than the money wage contract. Money wages are crucial because the relationship between them and the productivity of labor largely determines prices for newly produced goods and services. Unlike the classical economists, the Post Keynesians believe that the level of money wages is strongly influenced by trade unions, particularly in the central core of the economy where production is concentrated in large corporate enterprise. Wages are, to a degree, an exogenous rather than an endogenous variable, although since the 1980s the power of trade unions in the U.S. economy has been drastically weakened. And what about prices? Here again the Post Keynesians view the economy from a different perspective. In the economy's central core where large, oligopolistic firms are dominant, prices are administered; the basic technique is a markup over labor costs per unit produced. Thus, trade unions and large corporations are institutions crucial to the determination of both individual prices for much of the nation's output, and for prices in general.

Other corollaries follow from the foregoing. The distribution of income and power is a central concern of most Post Keynesians. This stems in part directly from *The General Theory,* since Keynes held that the inequitable distribution of income and wealth along with the failure to provide for full employment were the outstanding faults of the economy. It also stems from the fact that the Post Keynesians recognize that a dominant characteristic of the society in which we actually live—not the hypothetical world of Walrasian general equilibrium—is the ongoing struggle of people to gain greater control over their own lives. In the economic context this means control over their incomes, which involves, as Professor Galbraith has phrased it, an escape from ''the impersonal tyranny of the market.'' How is this to be done? Unless one possesses unique personal characteristics that offer a degree of monopoly power—artists and athletes come to mind—the alternative is either organization or recourse to the power of the state; the end in either instance is to bend market forces in one's favor. In the modern economy the trade unions and large corporations reflect the thrust toward organizations as a way to modify the forces that determine incomes.

More than personal control over one's income is at stake. Both inflation and economic growth are linked in the minds of the Post Keynesians to administered wage and price behavior. This follows because the struggle to exercise control over the money wage engenders a competitive struggle among organized groups, each seeking to obtain both control and a larger share of the national output for members of the group. This can lead to what one observer terms "competitive inflation," a situation in which groups (organized or not) compete with one another to raise the prices of the goods and services they sell (including labor services) in order to raise their real incomes.[18] (Even Keynes in *The General Theory* recognized that the struggle about money wages primarily affected the *distribution* of the aggregate real wages among different labor groups, not the average wage per worker). The Post Keynesians have expanded on this idea and made the drive to get control of one's income a major factor in the economy's endemic potential for inflation. Economic growth is affected because of its linkage to investment, which in turn, is linked to the pricing behavior of the large corporation. If internal funds are required for investment expenditure, as is the practice in reality, then by raising prices through a higher markup, the corporation can increase the flow of internal savings for investment purposes.

Minsky's Financial Instability Hypothesis

Professor Hyman Minsky, formerly of Washington University and now of the Jerome Levy Institute, has developed a theoretical model characteristic of Post Keynesian work.[19] This involves a "financial instability" explanation for the systematic instability of contemporary market capitalism. We shall conclude this chapter on the Post Keynesians with an analysis of the salient features of the Minsky model. (A review of the section on "The Financing of Investment," pages 292–300, will be useful prior to reading this section on Minsky's theory.)

Professor Minsky's point of departure is the basic argument of Keynes in *The General Theory* that the economy is characterized by both persistent unemployment and persistent instability. The latter is systemic, not the result of random, external shocks. It is this perspective of *The General Theory* that was lost when the neoclassical synthesis emerged as a major school of mac-

[18] W. David Slawson, *The New Inflation: The Collapse of Free Markets* (Princeton, N.J.: Princeton University Press, 1981), p. 13.

[19] Hyman P. Minsky, *Stabilizing an Unstable Economy* (New Haven, Conn.: Yale University Press, 1986).

roeconomics in the post-World War II era. As we have seen, the neoclassical synthesis forced the Keynesian revolution back into a classical mold by demonstrating that, in the absence of rigidities in either wages and prices (or both), the system is ultimately self-correcting, and, given sufficient time, it will reach a full-employment equilibrium. The existence of wage and price rigidities may justify the use of fiscal and monetary policies to attain full employment for the pragmatic reason that it may take longer than is politically feasible for the self-correcting features of the system to bring about a full-employment equilibrium. Thus, the neoclassical synthesis denies that the Keynesian revolution was a revolution in theory. Keynes, it has been said, may have won the policy war, but he did not win the theoretical war.

The foregoing viewpoint is rejected by Minsky, both because experience since the mid-1960s flatly contradicts the neoclassical interpretation of the economy's macroeconomic behavior and because it ignores elements in *The General Theory* that are necessary for understanding how the economy really works. Not only have we had five recessions since the 1960s (1969–70, 1974–75, 1980, 1981–82, and 1990–91), as well as excessive inflation, but we have had a series of financial crises, each one of which threatened to degenerate into a full-blown debt-deflation process with catastrophic results for the economy.[20] Only the timely intervention by the Federal Reserve System as lender of last resort prevented this from happening. Professor Minsky's model is designed to explain why the economy behaved this way.

What is fundamentally wrong with the neoclassical synthesis is that it ignores the importance that Keynes attributed in *The General Theory* to financial factors in explaining how market capitalism works. In Keynes's theory, fluctuations in investment spending are the primary cause of economic instability—a viewpoint common to most post-World War II interpretations of Keynes. There is, in other words, no serious disagreement with the basically Keynesian view that the investment decision is the key to the level of aggregate demand. What is wrong with the standard interpretations of Keynes, according to Professor Minsky, is that the crucial elements that account for the chronic instability of investment spending are neglected. These are the disequilibrating forces at work in the economy's financial markets. Such forces affect primarily the valuation—that is, the present value or demand price—of capital assets relative to the cost (or supply price) for newly produced capital. As in *The General Theory,* it is the ratio of these two variables which is the key to the level of investment activity. In *The General Theory* Keynes saw money and the demand for liquidity as the primary sources of financial instability, the major elements around which financial forces operate.

---

[20] See Irving Fisher, "The Debt-Deflation Theory of Great Depressions," *Econometrica,* 1933:1, pp. 337–357. The debt-deflation process is brought on by the economy getting into a state of over-indebtedness in the sense that payment commitments for debt exceed the ability of firms and individuals to meet their obligations. This leads to debt liquidation through distress selling, the contraction of the money supply as bank loans are paid off or defaulted, falling prices and falling profits, bankruptcies, and ultimately reductions in output and employment. The whole process tends to be cumulative once it gets started.

Today the economy is far more complex because the financial system embraces many more types of financial instruments than originally envisioned by Keynes. It is the complexity and sophistication of the financial system that must be taken into account if we are to gain an understanding of how investment decisions are actually made in the real world of market capitalism.

The basic problem with standard economic theory is that it starts from what Minsky terms a "village fair" perspective.[21] This means that economic analysis originates with the idea of barter, as implied by Say's law, and then proceeds to elaborate on the basic process of exchange by adding production, capital goods, and money and financial assets to the process. In this way it can be shown how a decentralized market mechanism may lead to coherent—that is, nonchaotic—results. What is wrong with the village fair paradigm is that it cannot explain why there are periodic disruptions to the process, why, in other words, we have the business cycle.

It is Professor Minsky's contention that the proper starting point for understanding the economy's behavior is what he describes as a "Wall Street" perspective. From this perspective the economic world is not one dominated by the exchange of goods for goods, as in the village fair paradigm, but one dominated by commitments to obtain cash today and pay cash in the future. It is a world in which the distinction between making goods and making money has great relevance. Of crucial importance in this paper world are cash flows. Cash flows are a legacy of past contracts in which money is obtained (by issuing debt) in exchange for a commitment to make money payments in the future by repayment of debt. In this view, investment decisions are bound up with deals that involve commitments to pay cash in the future in exchange for getting cash today. In the world of Wall Street the investment process flows from money to real investment to money, not from investment to money to consumption, as in the classical view. To put the matter differently, the cash flows that are the bedrock of the Wall Street perspective have two primary dimensions. First, cash obtained today is exchanged for the expectation of getting cash in the future. This is what happens when investment takes place. Second, the cash obtained today is also exchanged for a *promise* to pay cash in the future. This is what happens when borrowing to finance investment takes place.

If cash flows are at the center of a Wall Street perspective on the economy, how does the real economy of production and exchange fit into the picture? The viability of the paper world of Wall Street rests on the cash flows that business firms, households, and governments receive through the income-generating process. Income in the form of profits, wages and salaries, and taxes generate the cash flows that sustain the commitments to repay debt contracted in the past. The real economy of production and employment must sustain the paper economy that is dominant in a Wall Street view of the world. The basic problem of market capitalism is that periodically the real world of

[21] Minsky, *Stabilizing an Unstable Economy*, p. 103.

production and employment goes sour because of what happens in the paper world of money and finance. Unlike the classical world, in which money is a mere convenience that has no effect on the real exchange economy, in the paper world of Wall Street, developments that center around debt, finance, and cash flows are the tail that frequently wags the dog of output and employment.

Essential Elements in How Market Capitalism Works

Now that we have examined Minsky's Wall Street perspective, we are in a position to examine key elements that explain how the economy behaves over time and why it is subject to periodic breakdowns. The key to this process is a knowledge of how the liability structures of firms, banks, and other financial institutions evolve *over time* and the manner in which these affect investment spending, the key to fluctuations in the private economy.

In a capitalist economy every economic unit has a portfolio, that is, a set of the tangible and financial assets owned and the financial liabilities owed. Every unit also must make portfolio decisions, decisions that have two facets. First, there is a decision about the kind of assets to be held or acquired and, second, there is the decision about how ownership or control of these assets is to be financed. In the world of money and finance, the latter decision is described as how one's *position* in assets is to be financed. The assets and liabilities in the portfolio of an economic unit may also be viewed as annuities in that they set up a series of cash receipts and cash payments which are expected and which must be met over some fixed or variable future time period. In the modern capitalist economy there is an enormous variety of both assets and liabilities that yield future income or incur future payment obligations.

In its essentials, a capitalist economy works through the process of acquiring tangible assets—that is, real investments—which are expected over time to yield a cash flow. This cash flow results from the sale of the final goods and services that are to be produced in the future with the aid of the capital. This cash flow, as we saw in the analysis of the investment decision in Chapter 8 (pages 266–71), must be large enough to cover the actual supply price of the new item of capital plus the costs involved in financing it. This brings us to a second point. Assets are acquired by the creation of financial liabilities. The latter may take a variety of forms, including shares and the many different forms of debt. Unless an economic unit (business firms and households) finances its investment outlays wholly from internal sources— retained earnings, in other words—what buys real capital for the unit in a system of market capitalism is a stream of commitments the unit makes for future payments. It is expected that ordinarily these payments will be met from the income-producing operations of the economic unit, that is, wages and salaries in the case of households and gross sales or profits in the case of business firms. Money and other highly liquid assets that are near-monies play a peculiar role in this situation. As Professor Minsky points out, the possession of money (or liquidity) acts as a kind of insurance against the economy's malperformance, that is, against a possible economic downturn that would make it difficult for economic units to continue to meet their payment obligations from the cash flows generated by income-producing operations. Then the possession of money can keep the economic unit afloat, at least temporarily. Money is a cushion against adversity.

The portfolio decisions that lie at the heart of the capitalist economic process are significantly affected by two sets of institutions that are of strategic importance. There are, first, the pricing institutions, especially those which affect investment. Second, there are the financial institutions through which borrowing and lending take place and which control the terms on which positions in assets are financed.

In the realm of pricing, a capitalist economy is characterized by two sets of *relative* prices: one relating to the production and distribution of current output and the other to capital assets. Classical economics focused its attention almost exclusively on the former set of prices, but it is the latter set that is crucial to the investment decision and an understanding of the basic instability of the system. Both sets of prices have a role to play in the investment decision, however. The demand price for newly produced capital goods is the discounted present value of the expected income stream for newly acquired capital assets. This depends on long-term expectations, which, as we have seen, are rooted in uncertainty. Prices for current output enter into the investment decision because they relate to the supply price for newly produced capital assets. Prices for goods and services currently being produced, including capital assets, are based on demand conditions in the short term. The interplay between these two sets of prices with vastly different time horizons is a major determinant in the investment decision. The other is financing conditions.

Financial institutions, such as banks, are organizations that take a position in (that is, acquire) financial assets by emitting their own liabilities. Thus, when a bank creates a new demand deposit by making a loan, it, in effect, acquires a financial asset, namely, a note from the borrower to pay off the loan, in exchange for creating a liability in the form of a demand deposit. The liabilities of financial institutions usually involve a commitment to pay cash on demand, as is the case with the demand deposit. Financial institutions differ from ordinary business firms in that the latter take positions in real capital assets, for which they issue liabilities—that is, debt—whereas the financial institutions take positions in financial rather than real assets.

Because positions are financed, for both business firms and financial institutions, by issuing liabilities within the banking system, the process involves not only the creation of demand deposit money, but the almost continuous innovation with respect to new types of instruments that increase the amount of financing available. A second point is that, whenever liabilities are issued to finance positions in assets, both financial and real, future cash payment commitments are created. Every business firm and every financial institution engage in speculation when they make such commitments. As Professor Minsky says, "The firm in accepting a liability structure in order to hold assets is betting that the ruling situation at future dates will be such that the cash payment commitments can be met; it is estimating that the odds in an uncertain future are favorable."[22] Decisions made in this manner rest on some margin of safety, some estimate of just how much of the firm's future income can be safely committed to meeting the cash payment commitments that grow out of the liability side of the firm's balance sheet. This margin of safety lies in the excess of the firm's receipts and holdings of liquid assets over its payment commitments. Whenever the margin of safety erodes, the firm is in financial trouble. Such erosion may come about from a collapse of its current receipts because of a downturn in economic activity or from going too deeply in debt—creating new liabilities—in order to finance additional assets.

The Sequence of Events

To pull together all the foregoing elements and show how a financial crisis develops, we should begin at a point in the business cycle when the economy is doing reasonably well. What we want to show is how a boom develops and how the boom carries within itself the seeds for its own destruction. From a Keynesian perspective, an expansion will get underway whenever conditions are favorable to a high level of investment spending. This requires that the demand price for capital goods (D_k) exceed the supply price (S_k) or that the marginal efficiency of capital (r) exceed the rate of interest (i). If an expansion is underway, it may also be assumed that the liability structures that a firm has inherited from the past are not yet a problem; that is to say the margins of safety are for the time being adequate. Given this setting, what will take place as good times continue and an expansion turns into a boom? According to Professor Minsky's financial instability hypothesis, events can be expected to unfold in roughly the following sequence.

1. Investment and Profits. A high and growing volume of investment spending is the key to the gross profits of business firms. Gross profits play two roles in the boom. First, they provide the cash flows to meet current commitments for the repayment of debt, and second, through the dividends paid to stockholders, they help determine the valuation of the firms and their assets in the stock market. Shareholders in boom conditions enjoy capital gains on their holdings—a development which affects favorably the prospects for further investment. High profits, in other words, reverberate back through the stock market and boost the demand price for more new capital.

2. Unfolding of a Boom. As the boom continues, it becomes apparent to the managers of firms and financial institutions that existing debts and their pay-

---

[22] Hyman Minsky, *John Maynard Keynes* (New York: Columbia University Press, 1975), p. 87.

ment commitments are being easily managed. This means that borrowing to acquire new assets turns out to have been worthwhile. Business and financial units that were heavily in debt prosper—a sign to managers that their existing margins of safety are, perhaps, too conservative. This leads to further leveraging, or an increase in the ratio of total debt to total assets. This, of course, increases the commitment to make payments in the future. The capital gains being experienced by shareholders as prosperity continues reinforce this process, sometimes at a feverish pitch. In his discussion of how a boom unfolds and its effect on the asset and liability structure of firms, Professor Minsky distinguishes between *hedge* and *speculative* finance. Hedge finance takes place when the cash flows from current operations are large enough to meet the payment obligations on the existing debt structure. It is the safest position for the firm. Speculative finance, on the other hand, takes place when the cash flows from current operations are not large enough to meet current payment commitments, even though overall the present value of expected receipts is greater than the present value of the firm's payment commitments. In the long run, in other words, the asset-liability position of the firm is sound, but in the short run the firm may have difficulties. Firms that engage in speculative finance find it necessary continually to refinance debt, that is, borrow anew, to obtain the funds necessary to meet current payment obligations. Speculative finance does not cause trouble as long as the economy is expanding, but any units that engage in speculative finance are increasingly vulnerable as the boom lengthens. They are vulnerable because they may find that they must pay higher interest rates for their refinancing operations (something which raises the magnitude of their payment obligations) and because any shortfall in cash receipts relative to payment commitments can cause rapid changes in what the financial community regards as acceptable margins of safety. The latter are highly subjective.

3. The End of a Boom. Why does the boom end? This is the crucial question. The essence of Professor Minsky's thesis is that, as a boom continues, firms and financial institutions increasingly create for themselves financial structures that are vulnerable to any rise in interest rates or to any slowdown in the pace of economic activity. Excessive leveraging leads to an increase in the commitments to make future payments, an increase not necessarily matched by the ability of firms in the economy to meet these commitments from their current operations. The process is wholly endogenous and results from the normal functioning of financial markets. A financial crisis may explode quite suddenly as interest rates rise, sources for new loans dry up, or expectations about the continued profitability of additional investment collapse. Margins of safety with respect to the liability structure of firms that seemed perfectly secure during the boom are quickly and dramatically reduced. Runs on banks and other financial institutions take place as firms and financial institutions scramble for additional liquidity so that they can secure cash to meet their commitments. Borrowing to finance new investment will cease and firms will use whatever internal funds they are able to obtain for meeting existing payment commitments. In this way the investment boom comes to an end, and there is a downturn in the level of economic activity and rising unemployment.

4. Avoidance of Depression. The final question that Professor Minsky addresses is: Why, in the post-World War II era, does the endogenous financial crisis generated by boom conditions *not* degenerate into a full-blown debt-inflation crisis and depression on the scale of the 1929 debacle? He argues that the most significant economic event since World War II is something that has not happened, namely, a deep and long-lasting depression. There are two basic reasons why it has not. First, the Federal Reserve in its role of lender of last resort can feed money into the financial system and prevent a full-blown debt-deflation process from developing. Unfortunately, such intervention in recent years was not accompanied by any serious financial reforms, so that a legacy of liquidity fueled a new round of inflation once the crisis was past. As Professor Minsky has said, a big depression has been avoided by "floating off untenable debt structure through inflation. Stagflation is a substitute for a big depression." The second reason is big government and the many built-in stabilizers that lead to massive government deficits as production and factor incomes fall. This puts a floor under the economy and keeps it from tumbling into a deep and long-lasting depression on the scale of the 1930s. The price, however, has been continued fragility in the nation's financial structure and vulnerability to inflation.

Some Conclusions

Two broad conclusions emerge from Professor Minsky's financial instability hypothesis. The first is that our system of market capitalism is inherently and inescapably flawed because the forces that periodically generate financial and output crises are rooted in the system's structure. This does not mean, according to Minsky, that capitalism should be rejected. But it does underscore the importance of institutions for shaping the economy's behavior. If we want to modify that behavior in a fundamental way, we shall have to change the institutions. It also shows that the economy must be managed, that the neoclassical view of a self-regulating system is an illusion.

The theory also points toward some specific policy changes. In Minsky's view, as was the case with Keynes earlier, investment is the source of the instability. But Minsky goes beyond Keynes and argues that the periodic need to bail out threatened financial structures by Federal Reserve action is one of the major causes of inflation. Both instability and inflation might be lessened if the economy were more oriented toward the production of consumer goods through techniques less capital-intensive than those now in use. Policy, in other words, should be directed toward growth through consumption rather than through investment, the practice since the 1970s. Any such policy switch should be accompanied by policies that would simplify financial structures, although this may be difficult to achieve.

Summary

1. "Post Keynesian economics" is the name applied to the beliefs of a diverse group of economists who look to Keynes's *The General Theory* for inspiration, but reject efforts to push the ideas of Keynes into a classical mold, as the neoclassical synthesis has done. They are concerned with developing a macroeconomic theory appropriate to contemporary market capitalism with its strong tendencies toward concentration of economic power in a relatively small number of giant corporations.

2. The Post Keynesians reject Walrasian general equilibrium theory as an explanation of how the market economy works in reality. One specific reason for this is that Walrasian theory is not able to deal with an economy that exists in real, historic time. Emphasis on economic activity as a *process* that exists in real, historic time is a key characteristic of the Post Keynesians.

3. The Post Keynesian viewpoint also stresses uncertainty and expectations formed on the basis of uncertain knowledge. Uncertain knowledge of a kind that cannot be reduced to calculable probabilities is a fundamental feature in the economic world in which we actually live, not the ideal world of general equilibrium theory. Expectations, particularly expectations that govern the creation of new wealth, are highly volatile because they rest on expectations that themselves are volatile and uncertain.

4. In the Post Keynesian view, the roots of inflation are found in the behavior patterns shaped by key institutions. Key institutions shaping the economy are those revolving around money and finance, including money itself, and trade unions and large corporations which have a pervasive influence on the process by which money wages and prices are determined.

5. There does not exist a single model that can be said to be the dominant Post Keynesian model. A comprehensive effort in this direction is the financial instability hypothesis, developed by Hyman Minsky. Minsky's model seeks to explain the *systemic* instability of market capitalism because of the dominant role that financing and financial institutions play in accounting for investment behavior, the major source of fluctuations in output and employment.

6. Minsky's model is dominated by a Wall Street perspective, by which he means that the paper world of money and finance, in which the basic objective is to make money by lending and borrowing, dominates the *real* world of actual investment in structures and equipment. Because the paper world of money and finance frequently overextends itself—the process is seen as endogenous to a system of market capitalism—booms followed by busts are a frequent occurrence.

7. Since the end of World War II, two factors have kept recessions from turning into major depressions on the scale of the collapse in the 1930s. The first is the role that the Federal Reserve System plays as a lender of last resort to bail out large banks and other firms when necessary to prevent the kind of collapse that could trigger a general debt-deflation process through the entire economy. The second is the sheer size of the federal government, whose large deficits in a downturn provide a substantial floor for the economic system.

A Glossary of
Macroeconomic Terms

Accelerator is the ratio of a change in the capital stock to a change in the level of output.

Activist Rules are rules whereby policy makers adjust their policy tools in response to economic conditions in a regular and predictable manner.

Adaptive Expectations are expectations that are based on past experience with less weight placed on events that occurred in the more distant past. See also rational expectations.

Administered Prices are prices set independently of market forces by firms possessing some degree of economic power.

Aggregate Demand is the total flow of money expenditures in the economic system during a given time.

Aggregate Demand Curve (Keynesian) consists of the total expenditures forthcoming from households, government, business, and the foreign sector at each possible level of real GDP.

Aggregate Demand Curve (Classical) consists of the total expenditures on real GDP forthcoming from households, government, business, and the foreign sector at each possible price level.

Aggregate Supply is the total output produced by the economic system in a given period of time.

Aggregate Supply Curve (Keynesian) consists of the total supply of goods and services forthcoming from all firms in the economy at every level of expected expenditures for real GDP.

Aggregate Supply Curve (Classical) consists of the total supply of goods and services forthcoming at each possible price level.

Appreciation of the Currency is an increase in the value of the currency relative to the values of foreign currencies.

Automatic (Built-in) Stabilizers involve government fiscal policies that automatically tend to generate a budget surplus during expansionary periods and a deficit during contractionary periods.

Balanced Budget Multiplier measures the increase in output resulting from an increase in government spending matched by an increase in taxes.

Bretton Woods System is the name given to the system of fixed exchange rates set up after World War II. It was dismantled by President Nixon in 1971.

Business Cycle is the periodic swings in economic output over time.

Capital (Physical) consists of manufactured goods that are used to produce goods and services in conjunction with labor. Machines, tools, and buildings are forms of capital.

Capital (Money) consists of the funds used by business firms to purchase physical capital.

Capital Account in the balance of payments measures the inflow and outflow of financial capital for a country.

Capital Consumption Allowance is a monetary measure of the quantity of capital that is used up during a production period.

Capital Deepening consists of a change in capital stock leading to an increase in the ratio of capital to labor.

Capital Inflows are international transactions that, on balance, involve foreign lending to the domestic economy.

Capital Outflows are international transactions that, on balance, involve lending to foreign countries.

Capital-Output Ratio is the ratio of a nation's capital stock to its total production.

Capitalism is an economic system in which the means of production are privately owned and the allocation of resources is performed by a system of markets.

Central Bank is the bank that in one way or another exercises overall control of the banking system. In the United States, the Federal Reserve is the nation's central bank.

Commercial Banks are banks that accept demand deposits in addition to their other services.

Consumer Price Index (CPD) measures the average price of a specified market-basket of goods and services purchased by consumers.

Consumption is the using up, by consumers and government, of goods and services in the satisfaction of human wants.

Consumption Function is the curve showing total consumer expenditures forthcoming at various levels of disposable income.

Continuous Market Clearing is a condition in which all trade occurs in equilibrium.

Cost-Push Inflation is the inflation that occurs when producers, workers, or both succeed in raising their money wages or prices above those that would occur in a purely competitive economy.

Current Account in the balance of payments records exports and imports of merchandise and services, as well as international transfer payments, for a country.

Demand for Money is a demand for the purchasing power that money possesses.

Demand-Pull Inflation is the inflation caused by excess of demand (spending) relative to the available supply of goods and services.

Depreciation is the part of the country's stock of capital that wears out each year.

Devaluation of the Currency is a reduction in the value of a country's currency relative to foreign currencies.

Discount Rate is the interest rate paid by banks on money borrowed from the Federal Reserve.

Disinvestment is a net reduction in the economy's stock of capital.

Disposable Income is personal income less personal income taxes and payroll taxes.

Durable Goods are consumer goods that provide a continuing flow of useful services to their owner. Examples include automobiles and major appliances.

Econometric Models are mathematical models that describe the economy through a series of equations representing dependent (endogenous) and independent (exogenous) variables.

Economic Equilibrium is a situation in which there is no tendency for variables to change.

Economic Forecasting involves using economic analysis to predict future economic activity.

Economic Growth is the long-term expansion of the output of goods and services caused by an expansion of the economy's productive capacity.

Economic Indicators are variables that fluctuate with the economic system. There are leading, lagging, and coincident economic indicators. Leading indicators, like new orders for durable goods and the money supply, are sometimes used in forecasting.

Economic Model is a simplified representation of all or part of the economy that lends itself to analysis and testing.

Efficiency Wage Theory is the notion that firms choose to pay a real wage that is above the market clearing wage because they believe that this will result in increased productivity and profits.

Employment Act of 1946 is one of the most important pieces of economic legislation in U.S. history. It committed the federal government to "promote maximum employment, production, and purchasing power." The act also established the Council of Economic Advisors to report to the President on the economy.

Endogenous Money Supply is that portion of the money supply which is a positive function of the interest rate.

Equilibrium Income Level is the level of income in the economy at which aggregate demand and aggregate supply are in balance.

Equilibrium Price Level is the price level that equates the aggregate quantity demanded with the aggregate quantity supplied in the classical or Keynesian-classical aggregate supply and aggregate demand models.

Ex Ante means intended or planned.

Ex Post means actual or existing.

Excess Reserves are the amount of reserves in banks in excess of those required by the Federal Reserve System.

Exchange Rate measures the value of one national currency in terms of another national currency.

Exogenous Money Supply is that portion of the money supply which is independent of the rate of interest.

Federal-Funds Rate is the interest rate charged when banks loan other banks their excess reserves.

Federal Reserve Notes are non-interest-bearing debt of Federal Reserve banks, used as common currency.

Federal Reserve System consists of the system of the 12 Federal Reserve Banks that constitute the central bank for the U.S. economy.

Fiscal Policy involves deliberate changes in government spending, transfer payments, or taxes, designed to increase or decrease aggregate demand.

Foreign-Exchange Market is an international market, linked today by telecommunications and computer technology, in which currencies are bought and sold.

Frictional Unemployment is unemployment that occurs because workers are changing jobs or have left the labor force temporarily.

Gold Standard is a monetary system in which the value of currency is based on gold and convertible to it on demand.

Gross Investment is total investment spending for real capital in the economy, including replacement of worn-out capital.

Gross Domestic Product is the value in current prices of all final goods and services produced by the economic system during a calendar year. *Real* GDP is output measured in constant prices.

Human Wealth is investment vested in the individual, including expenditures to develop skills, education, and knowledge.

Hysteresis means that the current value of an economic variable is affected significantly by the history of that value.

Identity Equation is an equation stating an equality that is true by definition.

Implicit GDP Deflator is an index measuring the price of all the goods and services included in the GDP.

Income is the flow of output of an economy over a time period. Income also means the flow of receipts to households during a time period.

Income Elasticity of Money Demand is the ratio of the percentage change in the quantity of money demanded to a 1 percent change in income.

Incomes Policy is concerned with a rate for the growth in money incomes that does not create intolerable inflationary pressures as the economy approaches full employment.

Inflation is a sustained increase in the general price level.

Information Lag is a period during which producers and workers suffer money illusion.

Interest is the price paid for the use of loanable funds. The rate of interest is the price paid per time period.

Interest Elasticity of Money Demand is the ratio of the percentage change in the quantity of money demanded to a 1 percent change in the interest rate.

International Monetary System is the system of institutions, practices, and policies that facilitates international exchange.

Investment to the economist, is the purchase of capital goods produced during the year. Financial transfers, such as the purchase of stocks or bonds or the purchase of a factory produced in an earlier year, are not considered investment.

Labor is human energy used in the production of goods or services.

Labor Force is the stock of worker-hours available to an economy during a given period of time. The Department of Commerce defines the labor force as the number of adults who either hold jobs or are actively seeking jobs.

Laffer Curve is a curve that relates tax rates to total tax revenues. The hypothesized shape of the Laffer curve shows that, if tax rates are set above their optimal rate, a cut in taxes will yield an increase in total tax revenues.

Lag is the length of time between the implementation of a policy action and its eventual effect on output and employment.

Land is all natural things used in the production of useful goods or services. It is also called natural resources, and includes land, minerals, water, or any other material things that are used in production and are not manufactured.

Legal Reserve Requirement is the percentage of a bank's deposits that the Federal Reserve System requires that the bank hold as either cash or deposits with the Federal Reserve System.

Liquidity Preference is the theory that people prefer to hold assets in the form of money because it is more readily converted into anything else with economic value than any other type asset. Hence, money is liquid.

Lucas Critique asserts that if econometric models do not include a rational-expectations mechanism, the predictions from those models are likely to be wrong.

Margin Requirements are the required cash down payments on purchases of securities; margin requirements are controlled by the Federal Reserve.

Marginal Propensity to Consume is the proportion of any given increment of income that is spent for consumption purposes.

Marginal Propensity to Save is the proportion of any given increment of income that is saved. The marginal propensity to save equals (1—the marginal propensity to consume).

Menu Costs are the costs associated with changing the prices of goods or services.

Monetarists are economists who view the money supply as the single most important determinant of both the price level and the general level of economic activity.

Money Multiplier is the ratio of a change in deposit money to a change in the monetary base.

Monetary Base is the sum of currency held by the public and reserves held by the banks.

Monetary Policy is a change in the money supply, usually undertaken with the intent of influencing output, employment, the price level, the rate of economic growth, or the balance of international payments.

Monetization of Debt is the creation of more money through increasing debt.

Money is anything that performs the functions of money. Money can only be defined in terms of its functions.

Money Functions include service as a medium of exchange, a standard of value, a standard of deferred payments, and a store of value.

Money Illusion is the error that people may make when their nominal incomes increase but they believe their real incomes have increased.

Money Supply consists of currency, demand deposits, and other forms of assets currently in use as money. The Federal Reserve system uses four different definitions of money for the economy.

Money Wage is the value of a wage in money terms. The *real wage* is what the money wage buys.

Mundell-Fleming Condition refers to a situation in which the central bank loses control of the domestic money supply when it attempts to influence exchange rates.

Multiplier Effect is the principle that in response to a change in the aggregate demand schedule, the total change in output will be greater than the amount by which the aggregate demand schedule has shifted.

National Income is what the Department of Commerce defines as the aggregate earnings of persons arising from the production of goods and services in an economy during a calendar year.

Natural Rate Hypothesis is a situation in which expected inflation equals actual inflation and the actual unemployment rate equals the natural rate of unemployment.

Natural Rate of Unemployment is the rate of unemployment at which the rate of inflation is stable.

Near-monies are financial instruments with some of the attributes of money. Near-monies include savings deposits, U.S. Treasury Bills, and the cash value of personally held life insurance policies.

Net Exports is the difference between a country's exports and imports.

Net Investment is the amount by which the economy's total stock of wealth has increased in the current income period. It is gross investment less the amount of replacement investment.

Net National Product (NNP) is the net output of final goods and services produced by the economy during the calendar year. It is gross national product less capital used up in production.

New Classical Economics is the theoretical perspective that holds that if economic agents develop rational expectations and if markets clear continuously, the economy will operate at its natural rate of output. Furthermore, the new classical school holds that the only monetary or fiscal policy that can affect real output and employment is one that surprises economic agents.

New Keynesian Economics is a school that accepts the assumption of rational expectations, but does not accept the assumption of continuous market clearing. Consequently, full employment is not the norm and policy actions can be successful.

Nominal Shocks are changes that are not expected in nominal variables, such as the money supply and the price level.

Open-Market Operations involve the buying and selling of securities by the Federal Reserve as a means of affecting the reserves of commercial banks. This procedure in turn affects the money supply of the economy.

Personal Income is the current money income actually received from all sources by persons and households during a calendar year. It includes government transfers and interest income.

Phillips Curve is a curve that shows the relationship between the rate of unemployment and the rate of inflation.

Post-Keynesian Economics is a school that argues that interpretations of Keynes after World War II ignored the stress he placed on the role of money in market capitalism, the importance of historical time, and the significance of uncertainty.

Potential GDP is the economy's capacity to produce goods and services. It is limited by the stock of capital goods, the available labor force, and the level of technology.

Precautionary Motive for Holding Money is the desire to hold money in case of unexpected events.

Price Deflators are indexes of the price level used to convert variables in current prices to variables in constant prices.

Price Index is a statistical device for comparing the amounts by which prices have changed during a given period of time. A specific year is chosen as the base year and prices in all other years are measured as a percentage of the prices in this base year.

Producer Price Index measures changes in the wholesale prices of most commodities.

Productivity is output produced per unit of labor resources employed.

Progressive Tax System is a tax system in which tax rates increase as the tax base, usually income, increases.

Proportional Tax System is a tax system in which tax rates remain constant in proportion to increases in the tax base.

Public Sector is that part of the economy in which decisions of a collective nature predominate; it is the realm of government.

Quantity Theory of Money is the theory that asserts there is a direct correlation between the money in circulation and the price level.

Rational Expectations are expectations formed by using relevant information in an efficient way to predict the course of economic variables. A key characteristic of rational expectations is that they are formed in such a way that, over time, any forecast errors are corrected. See also *adaptive expectations.*

Real Business Cycle Theory is the belief that fluctuations in economic activity are the result of random shocks due to changes in technology, capital stock, or tastes and preferences of consumers.

Real Exchange Economy is the view that money forms a neutral link between transactions. Money has no role to play apart from its medium-of-exchange function.

Real Income is the purchasing power of money income.

Real Shocks are changes in real factors such as technology, capital stock, or labor force.

Real Wage is the purchasing power of a money wage.

Recession is a downturn in economic activity, usually signified by two consecutive quarters of negative growth in real GDP. Decreased investment, falling incomes, falling consumption, and increased unemployment are characteristic of this phase.

Regressive Tax System is a tax system in which the tax rate declines as the tax base increases. Often taxes, such as sales taxes, are regressive in practice but not in design.

Relative Price is the price of one commodity compared to the price of another commodity.

Required Reserves are the cash reserves that commercial banks are required by law to hold. Required reserves put an upper limit on the amount of credit banks can extend.

Reserves are cash in a bank's vault or deposits with the central bank to meet the cash demands of customers or to meet the reserve requirements of the Federal Reserve.

Risk is the calculable probability that an event will occur.

Special Drawing Rights (SDRs) are issued by the International Monetary Fund; they are often called "paper gold" and serve as international currency.

Sherman Act was the first antitrust legislation in the United States (1890); it outlawed restraint of trade and the monopolization of commerce.

Social Security is the social welfare program in the United States in which employees receive old-age retirement benefits or disability income depending on their previous earnings. The system is financed by payroll taxes paid by employers and employees.

Socialism is an economic system in which the society or social system owns the major means of production. Some form of planning is required to perform the allocation process.

Speculative Finance involves borrowing to finance the acquisition of assets with the expectation that the assets will generate sufficient cash flows to meet payment obligations in the future.

Speculative Motive for Holding Money is the desire to hold money balances in anticipation of future capital gains.

Stagflation is a condition where the price level and unemployment rate are increasing together.

Structural Unemployment is the displacement of workers as a result of technological change in production processes or a shift in demand toward new products and services.

Tax Wedge is the gap between what people get for working and what they are allowed to keep.

Technological Change is the growth in the skill and efficiency with which resources are used in the production of goods and services.

Technology is the stock of knowledge and skills necessary to use resources in production.

Terms of Trade is the ratio at which the output of one country exchanges for the output of another country.

Tight Money refers to monetary policy with a restrictive impact on economic activity. It is usually associated with high interest rates.

Transactions Motive for Holding Money is the desire to hold money balances for exchange purposes.

Transfer Payments are disbursements by the government for which it receives no products or services in return at the time. Items such as social security payments, unemployment compensation, and certain business subsidies are included because they channel tax revenues back to households and businesses without directly absorbing resources.

Unemployment is a situation in which workers are involuntarily out of work.

Unemployment Compensation is a government stabilization program that provides payments to the unemployed.

Unemployment Rate is the percent of the civilian labor force that is out of work as measured by the U.S. Bureau of Labor Statistics.

Unintended Investment involves unforeseen inventory accumulation in the economic system. This is the means by which actual saving and actual investment are brought into equality in the economy.

Velocity of Money measures the rate at which a unit of money turns over during a specific period. The income velocity of money is obtained by dividing the GDP by the money supply.

Wage is the price paid for units of labor service supplied in the market per unit of time.

Wage Imitation is the phenomenon in which nonunion workers receive wage increases that are similar to increases received by union workers.

Wage-Price Guideposts is a policy that permits money wages to increase at a rate no higher than the average rate of growth in productivity.

Warranted Rate of Growth is the rate of growth in the economy with which business is satisfied.

Wealth is the stock of material things possessing value in an economy, measured at a single instant of time.

Welfare State involves the government's assumption of responsibility for systems of old-age pensions, unemployment compensation, medical care, and income provision for families unable to participate in the market economy.

Index